EXTENDING JUSTICE

Extending Justice

STRATEGIES TO INCREASE INCLUSION AND REDUCE BIAS

The Honorable Bernice B. Donald
Professor Sarah E. Redfield

EDITORS

Carolina Academic Press
Durham, North Carolina

Copyright © 2023
Carolina Academic Press, LLC
All Rights Reserved

LIBRARY OF CONGRESS CATALOGING-IN-PUBLICATION DATA

Names: Donald, Bernice Bouie, 1951- editor. | Redfield, Sarah E., editor.
Title: Extending justice : strategies to increase inclusion and reduce bias / edited by Bernice B. Donald, Sarah E. Redfield.
Description: Durham, North Carolina : Carolina Academic Press, LLC, [2022]
Identifiers: LCCN 2022023217 (print) | LCCN 2022023218 (ebook) | ISBN 9781531024697 (paperback) | ISBN 9781531024703 (ebook)
Subjects: LCSH: Justice, Administration of--United States--Psychological aspects. | Discrimination in justice administration--United States. | Prejudices--United States.
Classification: LCC KF384 .E98 2022 (print) | LCC KF384 (ebook) | DDC 347.73--dc23/eng/20220729
LC record available at https://lccn.loc.gov/2022023217
LC ebook record available at https://lccn.loc.gov/2022023218

Carolina Academic Press
700 Kent Street
Durham, North Carolina 27701
(919) 489-7486
www.cap-press.com

Printed in the United States of America
2023 Printing

I dedicate this book to current and future generations of young lawyers who I hope will dedicate themselves to the work of ensuring justice, equality, and inclusion for all people and thereby complete the arc of justice!

—Judge Donald

I join Judge Donald in her dedication to our current and future lawyers and leaders. I also dedicate this book to my granddaughter, Harriet R. M. Redfield, in hopes that Hattie's life and choices will be unharmed by bias and enhanced by inclusion and equity.

—Professor Redfield

We dedicate this book to all of the family of authors of Enhancing Justice: Reducing Bias *and* Extending Justice: Strategies to Increase Inclusion and Reduce Bias. *Our lives are enriched by the opportunity to work with these thought leaders. We are honored by their participation and support and applaud their work here and beyond.*

Contents

Acknowledgments	xxiii
One · Diverse Voices: A Critical Conversation about Bias	
The Honorable Bernice B. Donald, Professor Justin D. Levinson, Professor Sarah E. Redfield	3
About the Panelists	23
Two · The Evolving Science on Implicit Bias: An Update for the Court Community	
Jennifer K. Elek, Andrea L. Miller	25
Acknowledgments	26
Preface	26
1. Understanding Implicit Bias	28
A. Key Terms	28
B. Implicit Bias: The Basics	29
C. Is it implicit bias?	31
D. What is known about the origins of implicit biases?	31
i. Ingroup favoritism: We favor the familiar.	31
ii. Social learning: We are taught, but also "catch," biases from others.	32
iii. Cultural knowledge: Our beliefs are shaped by our environment.	32
E. What is known about the pervasiveness and impact of implicit biases?	32

F. What types of situations are likely to bring out implicit biases? ... 33
   i. Situational incentives encourage speed over fairness and accuracy. ... 33
   ii. Clear criteria for making a good decision are absent. ... 34
   iii. Decisions are made in a distracting or otherwise stressful environment. ... 34
2. The Role of Implicit Bias in Understanding Inequality ... 35
   A. Systemic Inequality ... 35
   B. Cultural Inequality ... 35
   C. Institutional Inequality ... 35
   D. Organizational Inequality ... 36
   E. Interpersonal Inequality ... 36
   F. Bringing It All Together ... 37
3. The State of the Science on Bias Interventions ... 38
   A. General Interventions to Reduce Prejudice and Discrimination ... 38
      i. Intergroup Contact ... 38
      ii. Structure versus Discretion ... 39
   B. Implicit Bias Interventions ... 40
      i. Interventions that attempt to change associations in memory ... 40
      ii. Interventions that affect the expression of implicit bias ... 42
         a. Bypassing interventions ... 42
         b. Disruption interventions: Harnessing intrinsic motivation ... 43
         c. Disruption interventions: Harnessing interpersonal motives ... 43
         d. Disruption interventions: Forming new decision-making habits ... 43
      iii. Key Takeaways ... 44
4. Implications for Courts and Their Communities ... 45
   A. Lead by example—and know where you're headed. ... 45
   B. Educate not just to raise awareness, but to build capacity for change. ... 47
   C. Gather information to understand what is really happening in your court and community. ... 48
   D. Experiment: Design interventions based on the evidence and evaluate interventions for efficacy. ... 49
Conclusion ... 50
So, You'd Like to Know More ... 51
Appendix ... 52
   Executive Order on Advancing Racial Equity and Support for Underserved Communities Through the Federal Government ... 52
About the Authors ... 52
   Endnotes ... 53

Three · An Essay: Understanding the Threat of Right-Wing Extremism

Dr. Peter Simi — **69**

1. Background	70
2. We've got the names wrong and that impedes our understanding and response.	71
3. We believe their labels, which are not the reality.	71
4. January 6th: The "new" problem that isn't so new.	72
5. Combatting Misconceptions and Misperceptions	74
So, You'd Like to Know More	75
About the Author	76
Endnotes	76

Four · Implicit/Unconscious Bias in the Courtroom

The Honorable Mark W. Bennett (Ret.) — **77**

Introduction	78
1. The Admissibility of Expert Witnesses Testimony about Implicit/Unconscious Bias	78
2. *Batson* Challenges and Implicit/Unconscious Bias	81
3. Implicit Bias Jury Instructions and Implicit Bias Venire Videos	86
Conclusion	92
So, You'd Like to Know More	92
About the Author	93
Endnotes	93

Five · Algorithmic Bias in the Courtroom

Andrew Grosso, Antony Haynes — **101**

Introduction	102
1. Artificial Intelligence: An Overview	103
2. Predictive Algorithms and Risk Assessments: Warnings and Risks	105
A. Danger! Beware GIGO (Garbage In, Garbage Out)	105
B. Bad Programming → Bad Modeling → Error	106
C. Finding the Track Record: Are the Results Trustworthy? For Whom Does the Algorithm Fail?	107
3. Case Studies in Due Process: Computer Generated Risk Assessment	109
4. Statistical Fairness and Legal Fairness	111
5. Predictive Policing: The Minority Report Revisited	112
6. Facial Recognition Technology	114

7. Judicial Analytics and Robot Judges	116
8. Algorithmic Accountability in the Courts	117
Conclusion	118
So, You'd Like to Know More	118
About the Authors	119
Endnotes	119

Six · Should Justice Really Be Blind? Can We Really Stay Silent? Implicit Bias in the Courtroom

Jack Fiander — 125

1. A Personal Introduction	126
2. The Price of Implicit Bias	127
3. The Language of the Nation of Laws	127
4. What Can We Do?	129
A. An Example of Judicial Discretion to Limit Bias	129
B. An Example of the Use of Common Law to Limit Bias	130
C. An Example of Judicial Policy and Intervention to Limit Bias	131
5. Call to Action	132
So, You'd Like to Know More	133
About the Author	133
Appendix	134
Endnotes	137

Seven · Roundtable Conversation: Prosecutors' Reflections on Implicit Bias — 139

Roundtable Participants	139
Calvin David Biggers, Jr.	139
Justin Bingham	140
The Honorable John T. Fowlkes, Jr.	140
Kim Parker	141
The Conversation	141

Eight · The Empathetic Prosecutor: Reducing Bias When Working with Victims, Survivors, and Witnesses

Linda Ford, Kristine Hamann, Tyear Middleton, Audrey Moore, Luis Morales, Sophia Roach, The Honorable Sherry Thompson Taylor — 159

Introduction	161
1. What Is Bias?	162

A. Types of Bias	162
B. Impact of Bias in the Criminal Justice System	164
2. Initiatives for Interrupting and Reducing the Impact of Bias in the Prosecutor's Office	165
A. Training	165
i. Training Topics	165
ii. Who Should Be Trained?	167
iii. Who Should Conduct the Training?	168
iv. When to Train	169
v. How to Train	169
vi. Invite the Community to the Office	170
B. Focusing on the Witness—Science-Based Interviewing	170
C. Officewide Procedural Justice	171
i. Guidelines for Interactions with Witnesses, Survivors, or Victims	171
ii. Make the Office Inviting and Appropriate	171
D. Hiring	172
E. Data Collection	172
F. Accountability	172
3. Initiatives for Interrupting and Reducing the Impact of Implicit Bias Outside the Prosecutor Office	173
A. Meet Community Members	173
B. Training in Schools and the Community	173
C. Internships and Mentoring	174
D. Community Outreach and Satellite Offices	174
E. Training of Law Enforcement	175
Conclusion	176
So, You'd Like To Know More	176
About the Authors	177
Appendix	178
General Law-Related References	178
Literature Exploring Bias	179
Endnotes	180

Nine · Narrative, Culture, and Individuation: A Criminal Defense Lawyer's Race-Conscious Approach to Reduce Implicit Bias for Latinxs

Walter I. Gonçalves, Jr.   **183**

Introduction	185
1. Race Consciousness and the Client-Centered Approach	185

2. Strategies to Mitigate the Impact of Implicit Bias	187
A. Recognizing Implicit Bias Within Oneself and the Office	187
B. Interviewing and Consulting with Clients Through Client-Centered Advocacy	189
C. Pretrial Motion Practice	190
D. Voir Dire	191
E. Client Testimony	192
F. Use of Expert Testimony	193
G. Narrative	193
H. Jury Instructions	194
I. Sentencing Advocacy	195
3. Strategies to Mitigate the Impact of Racial Bias for Latinx Clients	195
A. Implicit Bias and Its Impact on Latinxs	195
B. Negative Racial Bias from Historic and Contemporary Media Depictions	196
C. Individuation and Client Narratives to Counter Stereotypes and Schemas	198
D. The Use of Culture to Mitigate Implicit Bias and Negative Racial Stereotyping	201
E. Use of Checklists for Latinxs	203
F. Documentation and Summaries of Implicit Bias Research	204
Conclusion	204
So, You'd Like to Know More	205
About the Author	205
Endnotes	205

Ten · Pain, Power, and Courage: An Interview on the Role of Judges in Addressing Bias

The Honorable Bernice B. Donald, The Honorable Steven C. González, Professor Sarah E. Redfield	**215**
Appendix	228

Eleven · Judicial Education on Implicit Bias: Instilling a Lifelong Pursuit of Fairness

The Honorable Reba Ann Page, The Honorable Benes Z. Aldana	**231**
Introduction	232
1. The Urgency of Equal Justice for All	233

2. Lingering Legacies: Explicit Bias and the Evolution of Implicit Bias
   in the Judiciary 234
   A. The Difficulties of Assessing the Persistent Influence of Bias 234
   B. Echoes of Yesteryear: Today's Challenges of Implicit Bias in
      Race, National Origin/Ethnicity, and Gender 235
3. Views from the Bench 237
   A. Conversations Regarding Implicit Bias with Jurists and Their
      Recommendations 237
      i. Judge Reggie B. Walton 238
      ii. Justice Robert J. Torres, Jr. 238
      iii. Judge Veronica A. Galván 239
      iv. Judge Kristin L. Rosi 239
   B. Compiled Responses and Recommendations for Combatting
      Implicit Bias and Judicial Education 240
      i. Responses to Question 2: Speaking both professionally and
         personally, what do you find most effective in combatting
         implicit biases? 240
      ii. Responses to Question 3: With the goal of addressing implicit
         bias in the judiciary, what measures do you recommend for
         judicial education? 241
   C. Responses to The National Judicial College's Surveys of Judges
      on Implicit Bias 242
      i. July 2020 One-Question Survey 243
      ii. July 2021 One-Question Survey 244
4. *You've Got to Be Carefully Taught*: Means and Methods of Judicial
   Education in Overcoming Implicit Bias 244
   A. Sources of Judicial Education on Implicit Bias 245
      i. The American Bar Association 245
      ii. The National Center for State Courts 246
      iii. The Innovative Response of the Iowa Judicial Branch to
         Implicit Bias 247
   B. The National Judicial College's Efforts at Overcoming Implicit Bias ... 248
      i. The NJC's Work Generally Speaking 248
      ii. The NJC's Work on Implicit Bias in Particular 249
5. Measuring, Managing, and Responding to Questions of Judicial
   Ethics and Implicit Bias 249
Conclusion: A Path Forward in Overcoming Implicit Bias 251
So, You'd Like to Know More 252
About the Authors 252
   Endnotes 253

Twelve · The Past, Present, and Future Trajectory of Implicit Bias Education for the Judiciary

Tyler N. Livingston, Shawn C. Marsh, The Honorable John H. Larsen   **257**

Introductory Note	258
1. The General Trajectory of Implicit Bias as a Topic in Judicial Education	260
2. Past: Initial Promise and Adoption	261
A. Research: The IAT Uncovers the Implicit Social Mind	261
B. Education: Legal Scholars Embrace Self-Insight	262
3. Present: Controversy and Criticism	264
A. Research: Thrust into the Popular Culture and Associated Attention	264
B. Education: Disparate Methods and Varied Success	266
C. A Note on Positionality: Effects of Judicial Attitudes on Judicial Decision-Making	267
4. Future: Preserving the Best and Improving the Rest	268
A. Research: Future Directions More Apparent Under Pressure	269
B. Education: Recent Insights Fuel Future Innovation	270
Conclusion	272
So, You'd Like to Know More	273
About the Authors	273
Endnotes	273

Thirteen · Leveraging and Interrupting Implicit Biases Concerning Women Trial Lawyers

Cynthia Eva Hujar Orr   **279**

Introduction	280
1. Defining the Context: Implicit or Unconscious Bias	281
A. Confirmation Bias and Ingroups	282
B. Male Lawyers as the Apex Ingroup	283
2. A Possible Solution: Bringing the Research on Women and Ingroups Together	285
A. Forming Ingroups to Neutralize Our Biases	285
B. Enhancing Affinity	286
Conclusion	287
So, You'd Like to Know More	287
About the Author	288
Endnotes	288

Fourteen · Confronting Implicit Bias in the Nonprofit Sector: A Personal Perspective

Angelic Young	**293**

Introduction	295
1. Industry Profile	296
2. Focus on Diversity, Equity, and Inclusion (DEI) Initiatives	298
A. Representation, Voice, and Agency in Nonprofit Organizations	300
B. The Dangers of Performative Allyship	301
C. The Importance of Agency and Accountability in Nonprofits	302
D. Exclusionary Language	305
E. Identity as a Liability	306
F. White (or Male) Fragility as a Crutch	307
3. Leadership and Organizational Action	310
A. *Fit* as Bias, Bias Disguised as Protectionism	310
B. Burden-Shifting	312
C. Mission Formulation for Nonprofits to Achieve DEI	313
4. Developing an Action Plan	314
A. Everyday Actions Leaders Can Take to Foster Inclusive Decision-Making in the Workplace	315
B. Everyday Actions Leaders Can Take Foster Inclusive Language in the Workplace	316
C. Everyday Actions Leaders Can Take to Foster Inclusive Culture	317
D. Track Your Progress	318
Conclusion	319
So, You'd Like to Know More	320
About the Author	321
Endnotes	321

Fifteen · Gender and Evaluation

Dr. Virginia Valian	**325**

Introduction	327
1. Men's and women's achievements are recognized and evaluated differently.	327
A. Three Small Local Phenomena	327
B. A Large-Scale Phenomenon	328
C. Laboratory Experiments and Audit Studies	330
D. Putting the Data Together	331
2. The way our minds take shortcuts (schemas) explains the differences.	332

A. Schemas	332
B. Generality of Schemas	333
C. How Schemas Work	335
3. Schemas can mesh or clash and can do so within or outside of awareness.	336
A. Accumulation of Advantage	336
B. Flawed Decision-Making	338
C. Moral Licensing	338
4. How can we achieve change such that evaluations will be more equitable?	340
A. The Individual Level: Education	340
B. The Individual Level: Intervention and Prevention	340
C. The Institutional Level: Policies and Procedures	341
Conclusion	342
So, You'd Like to Know More	342
About the Author	343
Endnotes	343

Sixteen · "Ducks Pick Ducks": The Military's Institutionalized Unconscious Bias Challenge

Lieutenant Colonel Susan E. Upward, USMC   **347**

Introduction	348
1. Defining the Problem	349
A. The Gender Divide	349
B. The Racial Divide	352
C. 2020: The Tipping Point	354
2. 2021 and Beyond: "Getting After" the Problem	356
A. Judge advocates should take the lead.	357
B. Make diversity AND inclusion the goal.	359
C. Training must be mandatory and meaningful.	361
D. Leaders must buy-in and tie-in.	363
E. Learn from others.	365
F. Use the military's professional reading lists.	367
G. Re-value physical fitness as a valuation metric.	368
3. The System Is Blinking Red…and Pink, Black, Brown, Yellow	370
Conclusion	372
So, You'd Like To Know More	372
About the Author	373
Endnotes	373

Seventeen · Addressing Underrepresentation in the Legal Profession
Tannera Gibson, Terrence Reed   **385**

Introduction	387
1. Calls to Increase Diversity and Inclusion	387
A. Shockingly Low Numbers	388
B. Responding to the Numbers et al.	388
C. Setting the Stage for Change, Recognizing Implicit Bias	390
D. Practical Reasons to Increase Diversity	391
2. Acknowledging Bias and Promising DEI Practices	392
3. Best Practices for Diverse Recruiting	393
A. Be intentional and deliberate with the hiring pipeline.	393
B. Collaborate with predominately minority law schools.	394
C. Collaborate with minority and female bar associations and participate in minority job fairs.	394
4. Best Practices for Increasing Diverse Hires	395
A. Use objective hiring standards—and stick with them.	396
B. Use blind resume reviews.	396
C. Use a standardized interview process.	396
D. Use job-related problem-solving tests.	397
E. Engage a diverse interview panel.	398
F. Separate and then aggregate evaluators' scoring.	399
G. Re-evaluate predictors of future job success.	400
5. Best Practices for Retaining and Developing Diverse Attorneys	402
A. Make the organizational culture more inclusive and equitable.	403
i. Understand diversity, equity, and inclusion.	403
ii. Lead from the top.	404
iii. Align the culture.	405
B. Use specific implementation strategies.	405
i. Offer customized employee training to address identified bias.	405
ii. Have minority leaders in the organization.	406
iii. Offer an anonymous complaint channel.	406
iv. Intentionally build diverse business units.	406
v. Provide for meaningful mentor and sponsor opportunities.	407
vi. Support employee network and affinity groups.	408
vii. Rid your organization of microaggressions and use microaffirmations.	409
viii. Overcoming Implicit Bias in the Employee Evaluation Process	411
6. Avoiding Reverse Discrimination Liability When Implementing Initiatives to Increase Diversity, Equity, and Inclusion	412

Conclusion	413
So, You'd Like to Know More	413
About the Authors	414
Endnotes	414

Eighteen · From Rosie the Riveter to Health Equity: The Kaiser Permanente EID Journey

Mark Zemelman, Dr. Ronald L. Copeland, Professor Sarah E. Redfield	**423**
Participants	424
Dr. Ronald Copeland	424
Mark Zemelman	424
Sarah E. Redfield	424
About the Authors	443

Nineteen · Confronting the Hurricane

The Honorable Kevin S. Burke	**445**
Introduction	446
1. Recognizing There Is Bias	447
2. Progress in Reducing Bias	449
3. The Dimensions of the Problem Facing Courts	449
4. Significant Forces Impeding Effective Action to Combat Bias	452
5. Preparing for Hurricane Bias: The Parable of Two Wolves	455
6. Dealing with Hurricane Bias with Procedural Fairness	457
7. Is There a Storm in the Courthouses?	459
Conclusion	461
So, You'd Like to Know More	462
About the Author	462
Endnotes	462

Twenty · Roundtable Conversation: Reflections on Implicit Bias, Silence, and Invisibility

Patty Ferguson-Bohnee, Mary Smith, Sarah E. Redfield	**467**
So, You'd Like to Know More	482
So, You'd Like to Do More	483
About the Panelists	483
Appendix	484

Twenty-One · Children and the Law: Bias and the Juvenile Justice System

The Honorable Rhonda Hunter	**487**

Introduction	488
1. Historical Context	489
2. The Supreme Court Speaks to Juvenile Due Process et al.	491
A. *In Re Gault* (1967), Juvenile Due Process Rights	491
B. *Kent v. United States* (1966), Juveniles' Rights Before Transfer to Adult Court	492
C. *Roper v. Simmons* (2005) and *Graham v. Florida* (2010), Life Without Parole and Death Sentence for Minor as Cruel and Unusual Punishment	493
3. Collateral Consequences and Adultification of Youth of Color	494
4. The Impact of Discretionary Decision-Making	496
5. Promising Approaches for Addressing Implicit Bias in Decision-Making	497
Conclusion	499
So, You'd Like to Know More	500
About the Author	500
Endnotes	501

Twenty-Two · Implicit Bias and People with Mental Disabilities: Taking Stock of the Criminal Justice System

Elizabeth Kelley, Nick Dubin	**505**

Introduction	506
1. Types of Prejudices Against Persons with Disabilities	508
A. Ableism	508
B. Essentialism	511
C. Sanism	512
D. Intersectionality	513
2. Interventions or Strategies for Participants in the Criminal Justice System	515
A. Training	515
B. Using Bias-Free Language	515
C. Re-examining Barriers and Assumptions	516
3. Participant-Relevant Approaches to Implicit Bias	517
A. Judges	517

B. Prosecutors	518
C. Criminal Defense Lawyers	520
D. Jail and Prison Officials	522
E. Police and Other Law Enforcement	523
Conclusion	523
So, You'd Like to Know More	524
About the Authors	524
Endnotes	525

Twenty-Three · Educational Disparity, the Great Unequalizer: How Racial and Learning Disability Biases Thwart Equity in Education

The Honorable Julian Mann, III, The Honorable Stacey Bice Bawtinhimer — **529**

Introduction	531
1. Historical Perspective on Race, Disability, and Educational Disparities	532
A. Race and education disparities became deeply rooted during slavery and the Jim Crow era.	532
B. The separate but equal doctrine was eliminated, but education disparities persist.	533
2. Current Civil Rights Legislation Concerning Educating Students with Disabilities	534
3. Perpsective from the School to Prison Pipeline	535
A. Comparative Reading Scores	536
B. Disproportionate Graduation Rates	537
C. Disproportionality in Students with Disabilities	537
4. Literacy Skills & Lifelong Achievement	538
A. The Need for Early Literacy Skills Foundation	538
B. Dyslexia and Problems with Early Identification	539
C. Considering Dyslexia in the Context of the IDEA Mandate	541
5. Implicit Bias and the Disconnect Between Educational Aspirations and Achievement	543
A. Expectations	544
B. The So-Called Uncaring Parent	544
C. Stereotype Threat	544
D. Race	545
6. The Detrimental Impact of Teacher Bias and Racial Disparity in Public School Teachers	545
A. Teachers don't know what they don't know.	545
B. Communication must be improved between teacher and students.	546

C. The eligibility process must be objective.	546
Conclusions and Recommendations	547
A. Identify dyslexia early and use proven teaching methods.	547
B. Remove subjective race-based eligibility decisions.	548
C. Support school funding reform.	548
Postscript: The irony is we know how to teach kids to read.	548
About the Authors	549
So, You'd Like to Know More	549
Endnotes	550

Twenty-Four · The Logic of Poverty: Rethinking Approaches to Socioeconomic Bias in Judicial Decision-Making

The Honorable Jennie D. Latta — 559

Introduction	560
1. Social Class, Socioeconomic Status, Socioeconomic Bias—What's the Difference?	562
A. Social Class	562
B. Socioeconomic Status	562
C. Socioeconomic Bias	565
2. Supreme Court Approaches to Constitutional Questions Concerning the Poor	565
A. The District Court's Opinion — *In re Kras*	566
B. The Supreme Court's Decision — *United States v. Kras*	568
C. The Court's Analysis of Poverty	571
D. The Rest of the Story on *In Forma Pauperis* Bankruptcy	572
3. The Potential for Implicit Socioeconomic Bias in Judicial Decision-Making	572
4. Judicial Empathy and Judicial Diversity as Protections Against Socioeconomic Bias in Judicial Decision-Making	574
So, You'd Like to Know More	577
About the Author	577
Endnotes	577

Twenty-Five · Sexual Orientation and Gender Identity (SOGI)

Meghan DuPuis Maurus — 583

1. It's critical to learn the terminology.	584
A. Gender Identity	586
B. Sexual Orientation	587
C. A Note on Pronouns	588

2. Even where laws protect LGBTQI+ persons, society has not always caught up.	589
3. Legal systems can fail to protect (or disproportionately impact) LGBTQI+ persons.	590
A. Employment	590
B. Criminal Law and Prisons	591
C. Identification Laws	592
4. There are best practices when working with LGBTQI+ individuals.	593
A. Eight General Strategies	593
B. Best Practices Specific to the Legal Profession	595
i. In Your Workplace, with Your Coworkers	595
ii. With Clients	595
Conclusion	597
So, You'd Like to Know More	597
About the Author	598
Appendix: Terminology Continued—Terms that Can Express	
Gender Identity	598
Intersex Identities	600
Terms that Can Express Gender Expression (but not limited to)	601
Sexual Orientation	601
One Other Important Term	602
Endnotes	602

Twenty-Six · Law Enforcement and Implicit Bias
Chief Anthony Holloway, Major Patrice Hubbard, Major Markus Hughes, Supervisor Jo-Anne Swensson   605

Introduction	606
1. Why Do We Train Biased-Based Policing?	608
A. Procedural Justice	608
B. Manifestation of Implicit Bias	611
2. Who Receives Biased-Based Policing Training?	611
3. Best Practices for Implementing Biased-Based Policing Training	613
A. Training	613
B. Park, Walk and Talk	615
C. Community Partnerships	616
Conclusion	617
So, You'd Like to Know More	618
About the Authors	618
Endnotes	619

Index   621

Acknowledgments

For their thoughtful and generous contributions to this book, we thank the Judge's Administrative Paralegal, Amy Duenes, and the Judge's clerks and former clerks: Michael Brody, Briaunna Buckner, the Honorable Charmiane Claxton, Pablo Julian Davis, Malik Gerdes, Matthew Langley, Angel Lasley, Chase Teeples, Naira Umarov, and LaFonda Willis. We also express our special gratitude to Kristin Alatorre, Aubony Burns, Edward Cohen, Barbara Creel, the Honorable Ronald J. Hedges, Dr. Victoria (Tori) Knoche, the Honorable Jennie Latta, Kelli Murray, and Dr. Stewart Smith. We also thank the extraordinary people at Carolina Academic Press for their excellent work, for their vision in publishing this book, and for their commitment to its ideals.

EXTENDING JUSTICE

ONE

Diverse Voices

A Critical Conversation about Bias

The Honorable Bernice B. Donald, U.S. Court of Appeals, Sixth Circuit
Professor Justin D. Levinson, University of Hawaiʻi
Professor Sarah E. Redfield, University of New Hampshire

A Note from the Editors: Rather than write an introductory chapter, we decided to take a step back and reflect on our work since the first book, *Enhancing Justice: Reducing Bias*. We invited Professor Levinson to interview us and to discuss his research and perspective. Justin is a law professor and empirical scholar at the University of Hawaiʻi. He researches, writes, and teaches about implicit bias. He and his colleagues, Drs. Danielle Young and Laurie Rudman, contributed the *Social Science Overview* to our first book. We've been together with him in this work from our beginning interest; and he is among our most committed and greatly respected colleagues. We found his questions and comments thought- and action-provoking—so much so that we're motivated to continue this kind of conversation, hopefully with interested readers joining us.

Professor Levinson: Thank you so much for inviting me to be a part of this exciting conversation. I'd like to ask the two of you a couple of questions that should provide a helpful framework for our discussion. The first book, *Enhancing Justice: Reducing Bias* (which I'll call *Enhancing Justice*, as compared to the second book, *Extending Justice: Strategies to Increase Inclusion and Reduce Bias*) was published in 2017 and very well received. And then there was a moment in time when the two of you decided that you needed to do a second in the series. What was that moment like, and why did it happen?

Judge Donald: The first book, as you observed, was a wonderful work. We had many authors and many voices. We had many lawyers and judges, and many social scientists, who all brought their perspectives to the understanding of implicit bias. Justin, you were one of the chapter authors, and you know, as do I, that one of the best aspects of that work was its diversity in thought and practice. We were focused initially on awareness and helping to put the emerging science into context for our colleagues. In introducing this topic to people, we wanted to make sure that it was accessible and well-grounded in the research.

As we talked to people about the topics in *Enhancing Justice* and got more deeply into it, we saw that as people were reading and absorbing the science, awareness intensified. But there was an immediate follow-up question: *What do we do to lessen the negative manifestations of implicit bias?* Admittedly, *Enhancing Justice* was short on tools to interrupt or to mitigate bias. I suppose you could say that inferentially some tools were there, but they were not set out in as concrete a format as we wanted. We wanted people to be able to read a section of the book and immediately be able to actualize some of the concepts in that section. So, that's the first and most significant motivator for *Extending Justice.*

A second factor that motivated us was an interest in having more diverse voices. Because we recognize that implicit bias is not something that is reposed in one book, or, for that matter, in one occupation or one sector, we wanted to expand our range of author perspectives.

A third factor is pretty self-evident. The world has changed immensely, and we felt writing and teaching in this field was ever more critical in terms of both implicit and explicit biases and their relationship with each other. We needed to reach wider and different audiences.

Professor Redfield: I'd add only a few points to what Judge Donald has said. First, in terms of diversity of voices, we know from the research that perhaps the most commonly recommended strategy for interrupting implicit bias is to seek meaningful diverse contact. Trying to practice what we preach, we pushed ourselves to find and elevate more voices, some who worked on the previous book and others who were new to us or even new to writing for this kind of publication. Related to this, in the years between books, we ourselves became more aware of how broad the concept of *implicit* was in practice. It's not just about race and ethnicity. It's about many other groups, it's about status, and it's about the way we make decisions—confirmation bias, blank spot bias, groupthink.

Second, in terms of how the world has changed: we know that attention to the topic of *implicit bias* has grown exponentially in the media, in statutes and rules, in policy, and in practice. While the term has entered the national vocabulary, it is often used imprecisely. If we are going to achieve and sustain equal justice under law or the goals of DEI (Diversity, Equity, and Inclusion), it's important to have resources that are precise, that offer an educated and grounded perspective. We're hoping this book will also be valuable in that sense.

Judge Donald: Consistent with what Professor Redfield has said, given the wider palette of voices and perspectives, we expect that *Extending Justice* will reach wider audiences beyond the legal system. As you know, *Enhancing Justice* was supported by three segments of the American Bar Association—Criminal Justice, Judicial, and Litigation—and was intended to be a bench book kind of reference. It served that purpose and was also widely read beyond that circle. But here we see a broader perspective in the chapters on implicit bias as it relates to health care, business, employment, disability, artificial intelligence, education, and socioeconomic bias, to name a few. We also have chapters from a wider range of group perspectives. We have the view of educators, and of judges, prosecutors, public defenders, and other attorneys; we also have those talking about Gender, Sexual Orientation and Gender Identity, Native Americans, Latinx, and nonprofits and the military, again, to name a few. Here we expect *Extending Justice* to be of interest to the general populace who are living their everyday lives trying to be their best selves and trying to bring their whole selves to their work in as much of a bias-free way they possibly can.

Professor Levinson: Can we focus in a little bit on this moment in history? Leading up to the present day, we had the legal intellectual conversation, the social science academic conversation, and the courtroom conversation around implicit bias, all developing over the years from the early 2000s to the present day. During the first decade or so of that time, I personally thought about the idea of explicit bias as being something that was socially disfavored; indeed the days of explicit bias being openly expressed seemed limited. Yet, during that time, historical racial disparities in criminal justice, housing, healthcare, and education all continued to be perpetuated, and it seemed so clear that work on implicit bias needed to be elevated. The moment really created this intense need for discourse and empirical research around understanding implicit bias in legal settings. Reflecting on the past few years, do you feel like the presence, or perhaps I should say the visibility, of explicit bias has changed? And how do you see that affecting the way we talk about explicit and implicit bias together?

Professor Redfield: Right to the point! We have to recognize that both explicit and implicit bias are now common and visible. I agree with your timeline perspective on this. It was just at the point that *Enhancing Justice* went to print that we started to see the change you are suggesting. We started to see it become far more acceptable to be explicitly biased in speech and in actions. It was no longer as necessary for people to have code for their biases. In some ways, this has made writing the second book harder, but in other ways, it opened some avenues for discussion. For example, one of the chapters we have in *Extending Justice* is an essay by Pete Simi, who is a professor in the Department of Sociology at Chapman University and an expert on extremist groups and violence. His work is very powerful and very thought provoking. As I think you are suggesting, Justin, in 2004 or even 2017, we were not thinking about reaching out to Pete to be part of this kind of book. Today, not including his work was unthinkable. Still, at the same time, there are many who are genuinely committed to fairness and inclusion, whose articulated and consciously held views are not explicitly biased, and we also want to continue to speak to them about ways we can address our unintentional biases to achieve a more equitable society.

Judge Donald: I would agree with you both. I was one of those individuals who felt that we as a country, evolving against the backdrop of complex and painful history, were moving slowly but steadily in the right direction. We were moving toward a more pluralistic society where "different" was not a negative. We recognized that diverse groups brought strengths and positives that provided a net positive value to every aspect of society; and not just to the conversation but to the evolution and the work of DEI in the fabric of America. I also agree that there seems to be regression to a point where explicit bias has gained prominence.

Professor Levinson: What do you see happening when explicit bias has that kind of prominence?

Judge Donald: It seems to me that we start to look at conduct of our fellow citizens with less care or precision. We become numb, or we excuse conduct because law and public policy extol equality, diversity, and inclusion. We like to believe that the past is the past!

I grew up as an African American woman in the South. I started my life's journey in the segregated South. All my life I have been one of those people who believes that people, broadly speaking, are basically good. Of course, I know that even good people at times can do things that are bad, things that are concerning, harmful, or even hateful, as you and Sarah have observed. I've never really been comfortable neatly categorizing all those actions in a particular bucket, good or bad. I didn't always have a neat label for my own life experiences. Today, where there is so much tension and division, we run the risk of being too quick to characterize behavior as "good" or "bad," to assign it or misassign it as racism, prejudice, or some other *ism when there may be other motivations, perhaps motivations that are implicit and that could change if called into consciousness and light. I think absent real education, this tendency to just label or assign actions to a particular group may be mischaracterizations that are likely to multiply. So I do think it's important to have this kind of education, this kind of material, this kind of exposure to a wide range of ideas.

Professor Levinson: It sounds as though you are talking about social and cultural differences that are meaningful in the way we understand people's actions, differences that are driven by implicit as opposed to explicit bias?

Judge Donald: I suppose I am. We have to understand that sometimes our implicit biases are not always aligned with our articulation of who we are and how we project our core values. It's not just one racial group against another. For example, socioeconomic bias is also a critical area—and we have a great chapter in *Extending*

Justice on that very topic written by the bankruptcy judge for the Western District of Tennessee, Jennie Latta.

Professor Levinson: The two of you appear to be quite focused on a very broad understanding of the role of group membership and identity and the complexity around those things across American law and society.

When you think about writing a book with this breadth in mind, how do you go about organizing your approach? I had a similar challenge when Robert Smith and I formulated our edited volume, *Implicit Racial Bias Across the Law*. We set the chapters up topic by topic and recruited people who were experts to reflect upon those areas. This book seems to be structured similarly, in a very zoomed in way, where the authors seek to unpack these concepts within their areas of expertise. But one of the risks of doing that is that it doesn't allow us—and I think there's no book that can—to explore the interconnectedness between what makes each of the authors' experiences and expertise come together as one, which essentially is the interconnectedness of life itself. What do you think?

Professor Redfield: I'm intrigued by the philosophical bent our conversation is taking, and I'm thinking about the different groups represented among the authors for *Extending Justice*. There are a lot of varied topics, as you suggest, and there is also a lot of commonality. Setting out the order of chapters was a challenge. Putting like next to like would seem the way to go, but there was a lot of crossover to consider as well. For example, the two chapters focused most on women are the one by Virginia Valian on *Gender and Evaluation* and the one by Cynthia Orr on *Leveraging and Interrupting Implicit Bias Concerning Women Trial Lawyers*. Dr. Valian's work also shares focus with the DEI and employment chapters and Attorney Orr's shares focus with the court chapters—which is where I lodged them. Of course, I'm putting this interview as Chapter 1! More seriously, we hope everyone reads everything, and the order won't be that concerning.

Professor Levinson: Thank you. I'd love to push a little bit more on the topic of the complexity and interconnectedness of bias in our society, even within the topics of the chapters themselves. For example, the chapter on the military is certainly a new topic for *Extending Justice*. When people serve in the military, they're in a space that is governed by a culturally unique set of rules and expectations. My current neighbors are in the military, for example. They go to the base during the day, and when they aren't deployed, they come back to the neighborhood at night. The expectations, choices, and interactions they have in our neighborhood—including those related to implicit bias—are likely not the same as the ones they had on base just moments before. So in my view, each of these topics, all of the chapters in the book, are part of a bigger conversation that hopefully helps to capture the complexity, interconnectedness, and continuing challenges around dealing with implicit bias in daily life and the law. How did you think about those bigger challenges with this book? Is there any way to succeed in both going into the kind of detail that this book does and also retaining that anchor I heard you talking about, which is really about humans striving to be good on a fundamental level?

Professor Redfield: This very conversation is a way to do that; so is another conversation that's in the book, one which I had with Judge Donald and the Chief Justice of the Washington State Supreme Court, Steve González. We are calling that chapter *Pain, Power, and Courage: An Interview on the Role of Judges in Addressing Bias*. If I were to characterize the tone of their interview, I'd say it's about who they are as humans and how they use their humanity to work always toward equal justice under law. There are also chapters like Angelic Young's *Confronting Implicit Bias in the Nonprofit Sector*, which she titled *A Personal Perspective*. Even though I've mentioned these two chapters, the humanity and commitment to humanity of every author showed through. For just one other example, I'm thinking of the chapter by Kristine Hamann and her colleagues, aptly titled the *Empathetic Prosecutor*, discussing implicit bias as it may impact victims, survivors, and witnesses in the legal system.

In an entirely different way, I'd say that the very existence of this book is a kind of commentary on all of our interconnectedness. For *Enhancing Justice*, we had an in-person authors meeting and committed to peer review, both of which turned out to be significant aspects of that book. Because of Covid and the difficulties in people's lives and schedules, these opportunities were reduced. While that was a substantive loss, I know that it was a human reality that we needed to be patient with each other as we tried to work and live in depressive times. That said, it's my hope that once it is published *Extending Justice* will be used to help people connect or re-connect across disciplines and distance.

Professor Levinson: Do you believe that each of the authors succeeded in reflecting a commitment to humanity even as they wrote in their own specialized areas, and even without the expected cross-chapter collaborations?

Professor Redfield: Yes, I do. I'd say every one of the authors holds true to that commitment in their own work and was motivated by that to contribute the significant time and effort (and I'd also say patience) to write here.

Judge Donald: It's a difficult thing to cover everything. Still, while we recognized the need for areas of focus, we also understood the need to get away from a siloed approach. Some of our authors talk about intersectionality specifically, and many wrote on broad topics. As Sarah said, we're hoping that in reading the various perspectives, people can see the interconnections and can take the information from the book to build out their own diverse networks. Even though we may not always use the term *intersectionality*, we anticipate readers seeing intersectionality as they go through the book. When you're reading about implicit bias in African Americans, you can see me in that. But also, when you're reading about evaluations of women, or women litigators, you can see me in that as well. We expect readers to make this kind of connection and draw on those experiences and project from what I'd call a multidimensional perspective.

Professor Redfield: One thing that was somewhat different for us in this book and different from your first book—you notice I said first as if there's going to be a second, Justin—was how intently we were focused on visibility and audibility of diverse voices. As I said earlier, while we were focused on subject matter, we also concerned ourselves with whose voice would speak to that subject matter, what diversity of thought and experience we could bring to bear in those choices. It turned out to be a learning experience for me as I watched people talk from their own voice and place as well as from their subject-matter expertise. I think if there's any one characteristic of the book that will help do what you asked in your prior question—keep us connected to the humanity of this work—I think it will be this authenticity. Because we do really hear it.

Judge Donald: I don't know that there's any group that is homogenous from an etiological or an experiential perspective. I hope one of the takeaways from reading these different chapters and making these cross connections, is that we recognize that people are complex, that we're not one dimensional.

Professor Levinson: Earlier you mentioned the causes of bias and acknowledged how complex an issue causation can be. You even mentioned that we may not all agree on the story of bias and why it's here and how it's here. I did want to ask you about your thoughts on the role of the media. Right outside my office, at this very moment, there is an episode of Magnum PI being filmed in our law school's moot courtroom. I haven't seen the script, and I don't know what this episode is about, but when I saw the set, I couldn't help but wonder what messages the episode is going to send viewers about courts, juries, and the legal system, especially when it comes to race and group membership.

When you think about the way media and the entertainment industry has addressed bias, both implicit and explicit, over the years, do you see the media and entertainment industry as causes of implicit bias? Or do you see them as possible solutions?

Judge Donald: As to the questions of whether media plays a positive or negative role and whether it can be a part of a solution, I think the answer to each is yes. We are influenced very heavily and broadly by media. Media can create and perpetuate biases and stereotypes. It can also mold and help people see and replace stereotypes with different, even positive, stereotypes.

When we think about early media, when you look at the role of women, it was usually women being objectified. When African Americans were in the media, they were in servile, entertaining, or marginalized roles. Today, on the positive side, you will see women in many different roles including roles of authority. But there's still a lot of objectification in media with respect to women. We recognize that this is entertainment, but the more people see an individual in a particular role, the more they absorb that message and the more they are likely to embed that stereotype and rely on it in situations where it may or may not be appropriate. The same is true with African Americans.

One of the things that Sarah and I use in our teaching is a real-life example from the press in the aftermath of Hurricane Katrina. There are two images of people in a survival mode in the wake of the hurricane. There is what appears to be an African American male in the flood waters with a bag of food and soda, with the caption describing a young man *looting*. Juxtaposed against that is an image of what appears to be two White individuals also carrying bags in the flood water. For this picture, the caption portrays the conduct as the innocent *finding* of bread and soda from a local grocery store.

We also use a piece from a community in Iowa where, in the same time period, White and Black men were arrested for burglary. The three young White male suspects were depicted using what looks like their high school yearbook photos, in suits and ties. In the corresponding photo of the African American men, they are wearing T-shirts in what looks like mug shots. One connoted innocence and the other criminality. Whether the press intended these messages or not, they have the effect of projecting and reinforcing stereotypes of criminality for people of color.

Recently we've added a discussion of the image from the Kyle Rittenhouse case where the defendant is pictured sitting comfortably next to the judge, or perhaps I should say the judge is pictured sitting comfortably next to the defendant, promoting the message subliminally, *the presumption of innocence.*

Professor Levinson: It sounds as though the images you describe work to perpetuate stereotypes, rather counter them.

Judge Donald: Yes, I think media does a lot in the way of reinforcing or creating stereotypes by the way they depict people in the news. Every time I get ready to look at the 6:00 o'clock news, if there is a breaking news photo, I cringe at what I'm likely going to see. If we say somebody looks like a criminal, what we're really saying is they look like the image that we've seen projected and reinforced time and time again, most likely a person of color.

At the same time, I think if media takes a responsible position in popular culture, entertainment, sports, and other things, we can start to address some of the power of those stereotypes and create alternative narratives that allow people to see individuals of all races and cultures and sexual orientations as *people* in all of their complexity and different roles. That can be the beginning of needed change to mitigate the negative stereotypes that we've seen previously.

Professor Levinson: Sounds optimistic, and I am an optimist by nature. But I feel like we have enough reason to be skeptical that the media will step up to that kind of challenge to undo some of the harms. What will it take for that kind of reckoning to occur?

Judge Donald: Justin, I share your skepticism. And that's why I use the word "can." They have the power to do it, but I don't know that they have the will to do it because the current narrative really meets their needs—it sells and it's easy.

Professor Levinson: I agree.

Professor Redfield: I agree as well. I'm thinking here of my discussion with Patty Ferguson-Bohnee and Mary Smith about how they saw change occur in terms of re-naming of sports teams and mascots to eliminate the negative portrayals of Native Americans. It took corporate intervention against those images to bring about change.

It's in this context that one of the things that we sometimes suggest when we're talking to people about ways to interrupt bias, one of the strategies we sometimes offer, is that they hold a *media contest* for a couple of weeks. The idea is to be watchful for the kind of reporting and imaging we have just been talking about and share it around and call attention to it so it doesn't just slip into our brains implicitly. Because we suggest this media-watch, many people call us and write to us with what I would describe as egregious examples like the ones that the Judge has just mentioned. At the same time, while the widespread ways that this happens are still clearly dominant in our society, there is some increased effort to call attention to it. I think this is what the Judge was just talking about when she mentioned the image of Rittenhouse sitting close to the Judge in his trial as they're looking (together) at evidence. The picture is not just out there being absorbed. We are consciously focusing on the idea that this judge and this defendant are close and comfortable together, they are clearly not afraid of each other. Still, I am probably with you on this one in terms of skepticism.

Judge Donald: On the photo of Kyle Rittenhouse, I applaud the media for showing that one. Defense counsel across the country are saying that they could only hope to be treated with that kind of dignity, care, and respect. And we wouldn't have known about that aspect of the proceeding had it not been for that image. I would have probably assumed that the conduct of one judge and one defendant was pretty much like all others. So, in this case, the power of media got information out there that let us see that these biases, positive and negative, are everywhere, and that they manifest themselves in real ways that can have very powerful effects.

Professor Levinson: One of the things you mentioned that this book really takes on is the development of concrete tools that people can use to actualize the battle against implicit bias. How much progress can we expect if people take advantage of all those tools in the context of all the biases we've just been talking about?

Professor Redfield: We asked every author to offer specific strategies for bias interruption, and virtually every chapter has done so. Some could easily serve as playbooks, for example, the chapter by Terrence Reed and Tannera Gibson on *Addressing Underrepresentation in the Legal Profession* or the chapter by Mark Zemelman and Dr. Ronald Copeland that maps out the work at Kaiser Permanente, *From Rosie the Riveter to Health Equity: The Kaiser Permanente EID Journey*—just to single out a few. The NCSC chapter updating the state court work on implicit bias is also a tremendous resource reflecting years of work on the science of implicit bias and translating that science into practice.

Answering your question more directly, I think we can expect incremental progress. Over the years since your book, Justin, and since the *Enhancing Justice* book, I think we can each say that we have seen that change has happened. We see it in our day-to-day lives and in the experiences that people share with us. Is that change scientifically or even specifically measured to our satisfaction? In some cases, yes. I'm thinking here particularly of the work done by the women in the STEM fields who have measured and reported real change in real numbers at their universities. In other cases, the accounting is not so careful. Still, it's hard to ignore. Many courts have certainly changed their procedures; I'm thinking about how jury instructions have changed, as one clear example. Looking at all of this, I think there has been progress and that we can and should expect more.

Justin, at the time of your first book, we were using the word *debias*. But fairly early on we stopped using that word and started using a more realistic label by saying that the work was to *interrupt* implicitly biased connections and decisions. I don't have a doubt at all that that is happening among people of good faith and decision-makers who are trying to be fair as we speak today and as we will write and talk in years to come.

Professor Levinson: Do you think that at least some actors in the legal system were initially too optimistic about the ways we could respond to implicit bias?

Professor Redfield: Yes, I suppose so. But, of course, implicit bias awareness and training was never going to be a silver bullet. It's important to recognize that really significant changes have been initiated since Tony Greenwald and Mahzarin Banaji's work promoting ways to measure implicit bias in the mid-1990s. It's also important to remember that it's not a cure for society's ills. Last year there was a piece in the national media critical of implicit bias training. The gist of it was that a police department had participated in such training and then one of their officers had used excessive force against a Black protestor. From this, the reporter concluded that implicit bias training is a failure. We can't look at the impact of this work with this kind of simplistic thinking. We have to watch for change, for the ripples from that change, and for the long view.

Judge Donald: It's my hope that we're going to play a real role in the criticality of implicit bias training. And I am encouraged. Even with the knowledge that progress is very incremental, I do see change that heartens me. Every time I get a call from a judicial organization, and they want to have a program, or they want to talk about training on implicit bias, I'm encouraged by their awareness of the need and their desire for change. Now it's true that oftentimes when I get there the demographic in the room is not as diverse as I would have hoped. But at least I'm getting the calls.

Training for the judiciary is critical. We generally think of implicit bias with respect to criminal matters and guilty pleas, but civil matters are affected also. Civil matters often get decided by a single judge on summary judgment or other dispositive motions. I remind judges that when we are in isolation deciding summary judgment motions, and we're applying the plausibility standard, it's not an objective standard. We are exercising our discretion, and, as we do, each one of us views the matter through our own lens. We need to understand that the potential impact of implicit bias is heightened in those situations. Hopefully even just causing judges to slow down to consider this will lessen the tendency toward a decision that might be implicitly biased. Even if it is at a glacial pace. There's a lot of work to do, and there's no segment or quadrant of society that doesn't need to get started and keep moving. There's that adage, "a journey of a thousand miles begins with the first step." We must take these first steps!

Professor Levinson: I'd love to ask you a follow-up, Judge Donald. You've talked about hearing from external experts and about courts' desires for more training, and we've actually seen quite a bit of progress in the specificity of solutions being offered, such as some of your own work or Professor Jerry Kang's published suggestions for trial judges. When you reflect on the federal bench at the time of your first book and compare it to the federal bench at the time of this book, how much progress have we made in terms of understanding and addressing both implicit and explicit bias?

Judge Donald: I'm going to be very candid with you. I think we have made some progress on the awareness front. But I think there is still a lot of denial—because we're federal judges, we have life tenure. We were put in these places because we are smart, neutral, and fair. And I really do believe that there is a desire to be fair. At the same time, I believe that there are a lot of factors that potentially allow bias to creep in. The slow rate of change is frustrating. I'd say that the federal judiciary has probably not been as robust in their response as the state bench. That said, I do see progress. For example, Jeremy Fogel, who used to lead the Federal Judicial Center and who's now at the Berkeley Judicial Institute, put implicit bias training into some of the new judges training. That is still occurring under the current director.

Professor Levinson: Thanks for that. It makes me wonder about—and I'm always cautious about—low hanging fruit. Because when you pick low hanging fruit, sometimes it creates a relief of sorts that can obscure longer term goals. But I do think it's worth asking you because this particular book doesn't have a specific chapter focused only on judges. Right?

Judge Donald: Right, though some chapters are written by judges. Judges Bennett and Burke, who wrote chapters in the first book are back for an encore; and, as we mentioned earlier, bankruptcy judge Jennie Latta joined us to write an insightful chapter on the *Logic of Poverty*. Dallas judge Rhonda Hunter, National Judicial College leaders judges Benes Aldana and Reba Ann Page, and administrative law judges Julian Mann and Stacey Bawtinhimer also joined this effort. The perspectives of these jurists, of course, offer valuable insight; there are also several other chapters that talk about judges and courts. In addition, Dr. Shawn Marsh returned with his colleagues Dr. Tyler Livingston and California PUC Commissioner John Larsen to write a chapter on judicial education on these topics.

Professor Levinson: With regard to federal judges and federal courts, is there low hanging fruit in terms of practices that federal judges can embrace to really take on implicit biases in the system? Judge Bennett, who's written a chapter in *Extending Justice* as he did in the first book, has been a leader in writing about this and attempting to address implicit bias in his own courtroom.

For example, I'm thinking about voir dire. In the federal system, unlike in many states, federal judges do most of their own voir dire and rarely if ever do we see jurors being engaged in meaningful discussions of implicit biases. Federal courts bring people in from the public to serve on juries, and sometimes, if we are lucky, they are asked about their explicit biases. But we know that given the decades of research on implicit bias this can be problematic. When people self-report, they may honestly believe that they can be fair and impartial. But that self-report may not be accurate; and they absolutely may harbor harmful implicit biases. If we don't probe those biases, if we don't create awareness around them, then we really run the risk of leaving in place a major barrier to a fair trial. We risk leaving in place unchecked, unexamined, and powerful biases that courts have essentially blessed by ignoring them. And furthermore, we fail to provide the impetus, the laboratory, for the juror to engage in self-reflection before serving such a crucial societal function. Is this something federal judges can do something about?

Judge Donald: That's an important question. When I was in the trial court, I allowed lawyers to do voir dire. There was a situation where we were trying a drug case. The prosecutor and I had done our own comprehensive voir dire. The defense attorney stepped to the well of the court and asked the venire the following question: "How many of you know what a drug dealer looks like?" She asked them to raise their hands. They all raised their hands. Now, in truth, none of us know what a drug dealer looks like. But I surmise that based on images from popular media, the venire made an association with a certain type of individual and a drug dealer and this is what these potential jurors were reflecting. Left unchecked, how do you ensure that a defendant is able to get a fair trial when the very fact finders say "I know what a drug dealer looks like, and they look just like you?" Judges must be aware of the power and pervasiveness of stereotypes and the role they play in the civil administrative and criminal legal systems.

As judges, we are in a constant battle with the economies of time and all of the duties that we have to discharge. Do we prioritize economy over fundamental fairness? We would never explicitly do that. But I have to ask myself if that's the effect or consequence of what we're doing if we don't prioritize exploring implicit bias with potential jurors.

Professor Levinson: Are there other examples?

Judge Donald: I mentioned motions and sentencing before. Our presentence reports typically include a description that supplies information on race or ethnicity and some socioeconomic indicators. I have to wonder if this primes us for certain stereotypes, which could be avoided by what Jerry Kang calls dimming or cloaking. There's a similar issue when we exclude evidence and tell the jury to disregard it. We know that when that jury hears this information, they don't unhear it because we say so, sometimes by the very act of saying disregard, we actually cause greater emphasis to be placed on that information. I don't know what we can do to correct these things other than to call attention to them. There are some areas where judges can affect immediate change by giving close attention: when we apply the rules; how we interpret the rules; whether we do in limine hearings on the front end so we get issues out of the way before the jury is impaneled; whether or not we strip out racial information from the presentence report; and whether we accord respect to every person in the courtroom. These are all examples of low hanging fruit that we can address immediately.

Professor Levinson: You didn't mention jury diversity in this list of low hanging fruit. The research suggests that diverse juries make more accurate decisions. Yet, researchers have also found that the diversity of juries in federal courts often does not reflect the diversity of the surrounding community. Are there things such as blinding names, identities, and addresses of jurors that could help secure and maintain diverse jury pools?

Judge Donald: How we create the jury roster can have a great effect on diversity, equity, inclusion, and fairness. Many areas use property taxes. A lot of people who are recent immigrants or people who are people of color or poor people are not going to be property owners, so you're already selecting out a huge number of diverse people.

Also, we have to keep in mind that the federal districts are going to be much broader than those in a state court. For example, in west Tennessee, where I presided, the jury venire, or the jury call, would include ten or twelve counties, rural areas as well as inner city areas; and the further out you go, the less diverse the jury becomes.

Professor Levinson: What's your thinking about the impact of peremptory challenges on this question?

Judge Donald: I'm not going to say that peremptory challenges is a low hanging fruit issue. But I think we can question and be more firm in how we interpret and apply *Batson*. I recently saw that a judge recognized a lack of diversity, but then said there was nothing the judge could do. In these United States, there should never be a situation where we feel that there is nothing that we can do once we recognize that there is an issue that fundamentally impacts the quality of justice.

Professor Levinson: I agree that helplessness in the face of likely bias implicates justice and should never be ignored. As to *Batson,* the idea that *Batson* and implicit bias are intertwined is something that's regularly appeared in the legal literature for such a long time now. So to me it does feel like if that's still low hanging fruit, then almost nothing has been picked, at least in federal courts.

Professor Redfield: I'd note here that you and several of our authors are the ones who have been talking and writing about this. In *Extending Justice*, I'd note particularly Judge Bennett's chapter on implicit bias in the courtroom and my interview on the role of judges in addressing bias with Judge Donald and Washington Supreme Court Chief Justice Steve González. I think it's also important to recognize progress has been made as a result of this work. We are seeing change around the difficulties *Batson* has caused in terms of seating a diverse jury, at least in state courts. Washington, for example, has adopted a specific rule focused on this point, and other states are following suit.

Professor Levinson: Sarah, when you received back the drafts for these many exciting chapters, even though this is something you've been working on for well over a decade, were there things in these chapters that raised your eyebrows, things you had never thought about?

Professor Redfield: That's a great question. And the answer is yes, very, very much so. I'd have to say that I learned something significant from every draft. But I'm reflecting here particularly back to my answer at the beginning of our conversations about our effort to hear from different voices. One chapter that was hugely powerful for me is the one on mental disability. We invited our colleague Elizabeth Kelley, who is a criminal defense lawyer specializing in representing people with mental disabilities, to write the chapter; she introduced us to her co-author Nick Dubin, who is an individual on the autism spectrum and who describes himself as having lived experience in the criminal justice system. We know that bias against individuals with disabilities is prevalent, but this chapter really focused my attention on ableism, sanism, and intersectionality, and it reminded me just how much we do prejudge a book by its cover. The SOGI chapter (Sexual Orientation and Gender Identity) by Meghan Maurus had a similar effect. The other area where our authors really pushed my thinking was the work of our Native American colleagues: Yakama tribal attorney Jack Fiander's chapter, *Should Justice Really Be Blind? Can We Really Stay Silent? Implicit Bias in the Courtroom,* and the *Roundtable Conversation: Reflections on Implicit Bias, Silence, and Invisibility,* which is the interview I did with Patty Ferguson-Bohnee, Pointe-au-Chien, and Mary Smith, Cherokee. These authors call for further action to change the way we see and hear Indigenous populations; it's a call which I might not have understood previously, but which I intend to answer now.

There were also areas where the authors brought such a depth of experience and expertise that I had to acknowledge how relatively little I knew. Here, again, to name just a few, I'm thinking of Judge Latta's chapter, *The Logic of Poverty: Rethinking Approaches to Socioeconomic Bias in Judicial Decision Making* and the chapter on the military, *"Ducks Pick Ducks"—The Military's Institutionalized Unconscious Bias Challenge,* by our colleague from the Criminal Justice Section Task Force on Women in the Profession, Lieutenant Colonel Susan Upward, USMC. Here too I'd put the chapter by Terrence Reed and Tannera Gibson, *Addressing Underrepresentation in the Legal Profession*, and the one by Mark Zemelman and Dr. Ron Copeland, the General Counsel of Vice President and Chief Equity, Inclusion and Diversity Officer for Kaiser Permanente, *Rosie the Riveter to Health Equity: The Kaiser Permanente EID Journey.* These last two are both terrific playbooks for DEI strategies. And the chapter by Andrew Grosso and Antony Haynes, *Algorithmic Bias in the Courtroom,* certainly opened a new avenue for my thinking. Well, I'll leave my list there. I'm proving my first point; every chapter had its depth and power for me.

Professor Levinson: Beginning in the earlier years of my work on implicit bias, I have had the wonderful opportunity to converse with scholars who have been writing about racial justice issues for decades. One scholar who has mentored me is Charles Lawrence III, who as you know wrote a tremendously influential article on unconscious racism in the 1980s, along with so many other groundbreaking pieces. When he and I would talk about my early research on implicit bias, he always expressed support, but also conveyed a deep worry about the framing of responsibility in some of the then-emerging scholarship on implicit bias. I'm not going to summarize it as eloquently as he did, but one of his concerns was that if implicit bias was framed as *it's not your fault* by scholars—or even received that way by readers—then the work risks shifting the responsibility for America's racism away from a culpable society. As a result, I've always been motivated to pursue implicit bias work in a way that tries to add to the idea that America must deal with its race and racism problems and that implicit bias research is one tool to do that. That is, in no way is our work intended to replace the work of critical race theorists and others who talk about America's history of racism. I worry, though, particularly with the evolution of diversity, equity, and inclusion trainings in a corporate marketplace with so much demand, that many trainers are sending the *it's not your fault* message as they conduct their "gigs"—although I realize that might not be the right word.

Professor Redfield: Maybe it is just gigs for some. I understand your concern. I think the reason we see trainers in their gigs talking about *no blame* is that it is a method to get people to hear the training out. If I am made to come to training, and I come in expecting to be called a racist or a sexist or some other kind of *ist, it's going to be very hard for me to hear what's being said and to take it in and reflect on it. On the other hand, if we talk about the idea that it is a neurological fact that as human beings we are going to respond implicitly, that can lead to a conversation with people who otherwise just couldn't hear you. Along these lines, I think it can also be helpful to engage people on topics besides affinity biases. For example, the Judge and I always talk about confirmation bias, where we as decision-makers actively seek out and give more weight to evidence or information that confirms our hypothesis than we do for evidence that does not.

Professor Levinson: I still worry though that some trainers go into their paid gigs and tell people that implicit bias is not your fault because we all have it, and then they leave it at that. And I worry about trainings conducted by people who don't fully understand a lot of the things we have been talking about because they have expertise in things like, well, like doing trainings. To me, the more important question around implicit bias is not whether it's something we're aware of or not but, rather, if it has become automatic, how did that happen, and what does that mean about us. So I do think that's something worth talking about.

Judge Donald: I do, too. We need to be concerned that when we talk about implicit bias as something we all have we are not skewing the conversation so that folks think they have no responsibility to effect change. Something I was reading lately analogized this to a leaky roof: What if you bought a house that had a leaky roof? You didn't cause it. You bought it. So once you move in, do you just stay there and let the rain come in because you didn't cause the leak, or do you do something? I think that right now we have in our society a leaky roof. And we all bear some responsibility for fixing it. We can't just stay there and allow ourselves to be rained on. In talking about and training on implicit bias interruption, we should never excuse or relieve people of the obligation to do something to move us toward a less biased society. We can't stop at awareness but must move to action.

I often tell people about an experience I had when I first became a judge. The clerk assigned me an all-African American court staff. The first person to enter the courtroom was a young, White male. He looked around, and he saw no one that looked like him. He came up and asked for a continuance, which I granted. He came back with an African American defense attorney. I didn't know this young man, and he didn't know me. But I have to suspect that his actions were the result of him believing that he couldn't get justice in a place where no one looked like him, where it was likely no one would understand him. This is a story about diversity, and I add to it that I stepped in to make a change and diversify the courtroom staff. When I told that story in Toledo, Ohio an African American woman stood up and said, "That's all well and good; but why do we always to have to be the ones to accommodate? Why do we have to always be the ones to make people comfortable?"

Professor Redfield: I think about this in a slightly different way. I became interested in implicit bias out of a sense of frustration, even depression, about what I saw as a lack of progress diversifying our profession. As you know, my teaching and scholarship were primarily in the area of education law. As part of that, I did a lot of work considering the education pipeline, what I describe as the pipeline from preschool to the professions. Within this, I developed a pretty deep understanding of the representational diversity data for law and medical schools and for the education system that leads up to those. I saw report after report, call to action after call to action, but really precious little change on the numbers of diverse attorneys, certainly precious little for a profession that thinks of itself as powerful. I was often invited to speak on my research, but after a while, I started saying that I didn't think we meant it when we said we wanted a more diverse profession. You can imagine I received fewer speaking invitations, but there were also times that the person who followed after me said, "I agree with Sarah." At around that point, our colleague Charna Sherman encouraged me to be on a newly forming committee for the Litigation Section of the ABA on implicit bias. Judge Donald was part of that formative effort as well. This gave me a new perspective.

The point that you mentioned earlier, Justin, that it was possible for us to legitimately hold and articulate egalitarian views and still be implicitly moved to make decisions that resulted in disproportionalities like the numbers in the profession, was helpful to me. I wasn't so quick to blame our colleagues. While I don't see implicit bias as an excuse, I began to see it as an explanation. And given that explanation, I think we then have to move forward and act for change.

Professor Levinson: And how can we best do this?

Judge Donald: That's the critical question, isn't it? I think we need to be mindful that there is a sense out there of a responsibility placed on one party but not on all parties. And I think we need to be making the case that when it comes to the corrosive effect of bias on our society, all of us have an obligation and a role to play in addressing it.

Professor Redfield: I agree with what you are both saying about making sure we don't void people's sense of responsibility. We need to name explicit bias for what it is, intentional and *explicit*. We should not even not suggest it is without blame; in fact, the contrary. With implicit bias, we see awareness discussed in many trainings, but then as soon as people start to feel okay about it, the training is over. We need to insist on the next step. We don't typically see this second action-oriented, responsibility piece. It's much harder to define and to teach. It tends to get lost in what you called the gigs.

I also think there's another troubling aspect to it. The research on moral licensing seems particularly concerning here. This is something Virginia Valian writes about in her chapter on *Gender and Evaluation*. If I understand it correctly, it goes like this: We implicitly tell ourselves, *I did a really good job, and I didn't have dessert for three days, and I walked an extra 5,000 steps, so I'll have dessert*. Or, in our terms, *I did a really good job, I went to implicit bias training, and just yesterday I made a decision that was clearly not biased when I hired Harper*, so *today it's okay if I fall into my stereotypes and make biased decisions*. Note that this is implicit. It's not that I consciously think through all of these points, I just help myself to the cake, so to speak.

Professor Levinson: And how best to avoid this?

Professor Redfield: Of course we don't know the exact answer. In the talking and training that Judge Donald and I do, we offer some specific strategies. But in very broad-brush terms, I think of it as making the issues—the likelihood of falling into stereotypes or confirmation biases or the like—making those salient. This is the language from Sam Sommers early jury research, and it's also what I think Professor Rachlinski was saying in *Enhancing Justice* when he reported his research that judges are implicitly biased like the rest of us, but they can catch themselves and avoid biased decisions.

Professor Levinson: I'm thinking about what Judge Donald was saying earlier—she didn't say it quite like this—that we haven't picked the low hanging fruit yet, even though it's been there for a long time. Prosecutors are still doing the same thing within their prosecutorial discretion. Not all, but many prosecutors still are not reflecting on the risks that implicit biases pose to their own discretion. And defense attorneys aren't often reflecting either. This makes me wonder if the idea of *it's not your fault*, despite having that disarming effect that we talk about, Sarah, whether it really just sends this message that this is not something you need to worry about when you are doing your job. Is there a way to change the frame for judges and prosecutors and defense attorneys and even in the civil context? Is there a way to change the frame where parties in the legal system will be more motivated to take the necessary risks to undo some of these harms and at least pick the low hanging fruit?

Judge Donald: It seems like we have to talk about motivation, be that internal or external. When office leaders use their power to create an atmosphere that focuses on bias-free decision-making, that's going to have a role. I think the conversation that several of our colleagues had with Judge Fowlkes in the *Roundtable Conversation: Prosecutors' Reflections on Implicit Bias* reflects this. So does the work of Kristine Hamann and her colleagues concerning *Empathetic Prosecutors*; and, on the other side, the work of defenders like Walter Gonçalves that he describes in his chapter *Criminal Defense Lawyer's Race-Conscious Approach To Reducing Implicit Bias for Latinx*.

But we also know that it's not enough. I am thinking right now about the progressive prosecutor in Missouri who had so much difficulty effectuating the release of Kevin Strickland, who was wrongfully convicted and spent 43 years in prison on unsubstantiated eyewitness testimony that was later recanted. To me this illustrates that prosecutors have a role in educating the executive and legislative branches, as well as making charging decisions that are fair and impartial. I think the heads of offices have to look at the actions of their line prosecutors and call out bias when they see it.

When I was on the trial court, I found that in certain types of cases, different decisions were made regarding the prosecution of African Americans and their White counterparts. When I recognized that, I called it out. Another Judge, who happens to be African American, has also called out such policies. In other words, judges were motivating change. While we can't interfere with prosecutorial discretion, we can't interfere with charging decisions or plea bargains, we can ask tough questions when we see differences that are influenced by bias.

Professor Levinson: There is a lot to consider in your answer. I truly hope we can pursue this in another conversation. But now I want to switch gears a bit, to come back to the two of you and your role in addressing implicit bias in the legal system. This has been a major project, two volumes, many authors, so many exciting topics. What's on tap? What else are you working on? What's next?

Professor Redfield: I am going on vacation from editing for a very, very long time. Seriously, this book was the hardest writing project I've ever taken on. It was complicated by the number of authors. And it was even more complicated by the various personal and professional places our authors found themselves in the shadow of Covid and racial crisis. We ended up with fifty authors. We also lost some along the way. As a result, *Extending Justice* has been literally years in the making. As schedules and participants changed, I found myself apologizing to some authors who had long since submitted their chapters while coaxing others to make extraordinary effort to finish expeditiously. I hope I haven't alienated anyone permanently and that they all feel a sense of accomplishment at this point. I know we certainly do.

Judge Donald: You know, I don't know exactly how this work will continue in my life. I have an accumulated life of experiences where I have seen biases manifest themselves in ways large and small, good and bad. I can talk about it from my own lived experiences, from those of my family, from my life as a judge on four different courts over four decades. I believe that over the course of my career there have been decisions that I have made, where, if I knew then what I know now, I may have made different decisions. My cousin used to always say to me, *when you know better, you have to do better*. And when we learn, and we can actually recognize it in our own actions and decisions, then I think we have to make different decisions.

Professor Redfield: Well, as usual, the Judge has put me to shame for saying that I've had enough.

Judge Donald: You only said you wouldn't be editing another book soon.

Professor Redfield: That's right. Like you, I have my own lived experiences in the professoriate and since where I have seen biases manifest themselves. Like you, once I started doing this work, I often said to myself, *if only I'd known then what I know now.* These experiences and reflections propel me to want to engage with others so that they can know now. Speaking more generally, I have no doubt that I and all the people who've worked on this book feel the way the Judge does. I've mentioned several already in this conversation, but I'd be remiss if I didn't specifically recognize here the longstanding and very important work of the NCSC, which is included, in part, in Jennifer Elek's and Andrea Miller's chapter on *Evolving Science*. I think of the work of Chief Holloway and the St. Petersburg police in the same way—important, thoughtful work, that has been ongoing for years. In short, I think we are all committed to taking what we know and using it for good, and we are not likely to stop.

Justin, I hope you'll comment on this question and talk a bit about the work you see for yourself going forward. Even though the change is incremental, it is a ripple of change. And I think it's clear to both the Judge and me that achieving some level of bias interruption has been the case as a result of your book and from *Enhancing Justice,* and it will be the case from this book. As researchers, teachers, authors—as human beings, we are never going to be able to put this down.

Professor Levinson: Yes. I agree with that, Sarah. As far as where I'm heading: My work on implicit bias is now in a place where I find myself trying to be helpful in a way that responds to where judges are—as Judge Donald framed it—they are curious, still educating themselves, but have mostly not picked any fruit on their own. My work has evolved to trying to come up with very specific legal inquiries that can be pinpointed in time and quality. I'm trying to unravel empirically the ways in which a law or practice or rule manifests in biased ways. From this I hope that judges and lawyers can see the inequality in the very thing that is in front of them at that moment. To put it another way, I've been trying to create the realism of the implicit biased moment to force judges to see that their decision at that moment is either to allow known bias to continue under their watch or to make an alternative choice. This involves creating studies zoomed in on very discrete, clear moments in a case and then examining implicit bias in those. For example, I will soon be publishing a study that looks specifically at "future dangerousness" inquiries in criminal law (with co-authors G. Ben Cohen and Koichi Hioki). The study examines whether "future dangerousness" tests—which are either codified by statute or permitted by judges—act to specifically introduce implicit bias into the trial process. And our research results confirm that they do just that.

I don't know whether this approach will ultimately be helpful. I have to say that I sometimes reflect on my work and wonder whether it was worth it in the sense that the changes that I hoped to see seem quite small at this point in time—especially with this resurgence of explicit bias and society's current use of the term *implicit bias* imprecisely. I have spent a lot of time approaching this topic as objectively as possible because I want and need the social science to speak when I do a study. But when you think about the role of courts and social science and implicit bias knowledge, it's often an uphill battle. My work is getting cited by courts now, but it's mostly dissents. So…

Professor Redfield: Yes. But we all know that powerful majorities come later on from those dissents.

Professor Levinson: So we're still waiting for that.

Judge Donald: This has been an interesting conversation. Justin, it's always a pleasure to talk to you. And, Sarah, your stamina in this work and your continued interest in confronting hard questions is commendable! Thank you for being sure we took this chance to reflect and for your expert guidance as we pull things together and approach the finish line for book two. We owe you a debt of gratitude and a special thanks. We're in partnership, but your leadership and vision, your energy, and your intellect have been the driving force in the second book just as it was in the first.

Professor Levinson: It has been such a pleasure talking with you both about this exciting book! You two deserve a big audience for every conversation. So I'll try to start a YouTube channel or something.

Professor Redfield: Thank you so much. All kidding aside, Justin, we should have this kind of talk again, even when we're not on a deadline. It was powerful to have even a beginning of this kind of conversation with you. The Judge and I don't often reflect in such a philosophical way on what we're doing, and we should. I hope others will be inspired to join in.

About the Panelists

The Honorable Bernice B. Donald is a judge on the U.S. Court of Appeals for the Sixth Circuit. Prior to being appointed to the U.S. Court of Appeals by President Barack Obama in 2011, she served on the U.S. District Court for over fifteen years. She was the first African American woman to serve on the U.S. District Court for the Western District of Tennessee, the first African American woman to serve on the U.S. Bankruptcy Court, and the first African American female judge in Tennessee. She received her J.D. from the University of Memphis School of Law, her LL.M. from Duke University School of Law, and an honorary Doctors in Law from Suffolk University.

Judge Donald is a member of the prestigious American Law Institute. She is active in the American Bar Association (ABA), having held leadership positions in the Judicial Division and the Sections of: Litigation, Antitrust, Labor and Employment Law, Criminal Justice, and Civil Rights and Social Justice. Judge Donald served as Chair of the ABA Criminal Justice Section, focusing on issues concerning implicit bias, children of incarcerated parents, mass incarceration, and the collateral consequences of incarceration. Judge Donald also served as Chair of the Center for Human Rights and chaired a committee which published an implicit bias resource book for judges and practitioners titled, *Enhancing Justice: Reducing Bias*. Having previously served as Secretary of the ABA, Judge Donald served in the ABA House of Delegates until August 2018. She has been faculty at the National Judicial College, the Federal Judicial Center, and the Judge Advocate General's Legal Center & School. She served as Jurist in Residence at American University, Washington University, University of Cincinnati School of Law, and the University of Georgia School of Law. In addition, she has served as faculty for international programs in more than twenty countries.

Justin D. Levinson is a Professor of Law at the University of Hawaiʻi at Manoa. He is a leader in the field of implicit bias and the law and an expert in psychological decision-making in the legal system. His scholarship, which regularly employs experimental social science methodology, has appeared in the NYU Law Review, Yale Law Journal Forum, UCLA Law Review, and Duke Law Journal, among others, and has been cited by the United States Supreme Court. Professor Levinson served as lead editor of *Implicit Racial Bias Across the Law*, a volume that was published by Cambridge University Press in 2012 (co-edited by Robert J. Smith). Professor Levinson earned his B.A. from the University of Michigan, his J.D. from the University of California, Los Angeles, and his LL.M. from Harvard Law School.

Sarah E. Redfield is a Professor of Law at the University of New Hampshire and a member of the Maine Bar. Her research and scholarship have focused on diversity, equity, and inclusion (DEI) in the legal profession and along the education pipeline. Her current work concentrates on implicit bias and on strategies to interrupt that bias and reduce the negative consequences of its manifestations in legal, medical, education, and workplace environments. Professor Redfield is a nationally respected author, presenter, and trainer. She was the editor and chapter author of the ABA book on implicit bias, *Enhancing Justice: Reducing Bias*. With Judge Donald, Professor Redfield is Co-Chair of the Criminal Justice Section Implicit Bias Initiative and a member of the CJS Women's Task Force.

Professor Redfield earned her B.A. degree from Mount Holyoke College, her J.D. degree from Northeastern University School of Law, and her LL.M. from Harvard Law School. Professor Redfield is the proud mother of two young adults, Alex Redfield and Althea Rose Redfield, and the ecstatic grandmother of Harriet Redfield.

TWO

The Evolving Science on Implicit Bias
An Update for the Court Community

Jennifer K. Elek, Principal Court Research Associate, National Center for State Courts

Andrea L. Miller, Senior Court Research Associate, National Center for State Courts

A Note from the Editors: The National Center for State Courts (NCSC) has been a true leader in work concerning implicit bias, and we truly appreciate their generosity in sharing this update with us. It's really a terrific manual for anyone who wants to understand implicit bias terminology, scientific basis, research, and implications for our system of justice. The interventions and key takeaways suggested here are well researched and clearly presented. We can move a long way to limiting the negative manifestations of implicit bias by following these suggestions.

We also note there that many other Chapters refer to and rely on the definitions and other discussion offered by NCSC.

CHAPTER CONTENTS

Acknowledgments

Preface

1. Understanding Implicit Bias
   A. Key terms
   B. Implicit Bias: The Basics
   C. Is It Implicit Bias?
   D. What is known about the origins of implicit biases?
   E. What is known about the pervasiveness and impact of implicit biases?
   F. What types of situations are likely to bring out implicit biases?

2. The Role of Implicit Bias in Understanding Inequality
    A. Systemic Inequality
    B. Cultural Inequality
    C. Institutional Inequality
    D. Organizational Inequality
    E. Interpersonal Inequality
    F. Bringing It All Together
3. The State of the Science on Bias Interventions
    A. General Interventions to Reduce Prejudice and Discrimination
    B. Implicit Bias Interventions
4. Implications for Courts and Their Communities
    A. Lead by example—and know where you're headed.
    B. Educate not just to raise awareness, but to build capacity for change.
    C. Gather information to understand what is really happening in your court and community.
    D. Experiment: Design interventions based on the evidence and evaluate interventions for efficacy.

Conclusion

Appendix: Executive Order on Advancing Racial Equity and Support for Underserved Communities Through the Federal Government

Acknowledgments

With permission from the authors and the State Justice Institute, this chapter is adapted from a 2021 National Center for State Courts publication of the same name (the complete original report is available at www.ncsc.org/ibeducation), developed with support from the State Justice Institute under grant number SJI-17-T0130. The points of view expressed are those of the authors and do not necessarily represent the official position or policies of the State Justice Institute.

Preface

An independent and impartial judiciary is a cornerstone of government in the United States. Judicial officers are duty-bound to uphold these ideals of fairness. The American Bar Association has promulgated a model Code of Judicial Conduct to provide guidance on these matters, which most states have adopted in some form.[1] Specific ethics rules address issues of fairness, such as Rule 2.2, which explicitly instructs judges to "perform all duties of judicial office fairly and impartially." Rule 2.3 (A) calls for judges to perform these duties "without bias or prejudice." Rule 2.3 (B) reads: "A judge shall not, in the performance of judicial duties, by words or conduct manifest bias or prejudice, or engage in harassment, including but not limited to bias, prejudice, or harassment based upon race, sex, gender, religion, national origin, ethnicity, disability, age, sexual orientation, marital status, socioeconomic status, or political affiliation, and shall not permit staff, court officials, or others subject to the judge's direction and control to do so." Judges are also required to hold attorneys in proceedings accountable for conduct that does not meet this ethical standard.

Moreover, the judiciary is regarded by the public as a legitimate authority largely because of the perception of independence and impartiality. That perception is under threat. There is a growing distrust of government and one another in the United States, and this distrust makes problem-solving in the public interest harder.[2]

In 2020, civic life was fundamentally altered by the global Covid-19 pandemic, its impact on the economy, and a cultural awakening to systemic racism. This further challenged traditional assumptions about fairness in criminal justice and healthcare systems, employment, housing, and other social institutions, buoyed by a steady stream of inequities laid bare by and exacerbated during the public health crisis.[3] During this turbulent year, public trust in government declined across the globe.[4] At a time when citizens and governments are called upon to cooperate and mobilize coordinated responses to a variety of global challenges, an erosion of trust risks devastating consequences.[5] As public trust declines, the ability of the judiciary to skillfully and effectively demonstrate the ideals of fairness and impartiality under law becomes ever more critical.

In recognition of the need for leadership during such times, on July 30, 2020, the Conference of Chief Justices (CCJ) and the Conference of State Court Administrators (COSCA) passed a resolution "in support of racial equality and justice for all."[6] This resolution came in the wake of dozens of official statements by state courts in response to the deaths of Breonna Taylor, Ahmaud Arbery, and George Floyd.[7] The resolution urged those organizations "to continue and to intensify efforts to combat racial prejudice within the justice system, both explicit and implicit, and to recommit to examine what systemic change is needed to make equality under the law an enduring reality for all". It acknowledged that "current events have underscored the persistence in our society of institutional and structural racism resulting in policies and practices that disproportionately impact persons of color." The resolution further noted that "courts in many states, with the encouragement, support, and guidance of CCJ and COSCA, have initiated efforts... to identify and address unconscious bias, and facilitate the uncomfortable conversations that arise from the recognition of such bias."

The National Center for State Courts published a new report in March 2021 to update previous work on implicit bias and assist the state courts in responding to this national call to action.[8] The present chapter is adapted from that report. This chapter provides court practitioners with current definitions of terms commonly used in scholarly and public discourse on implicit bias; summarizes what is currently known from implicit social cognition research in the psychological and brain sciences, including bias intervention strategies generally found to be effective and ineffective; and identifies some implications of this knowledge for state court leaders and other court practitioners who seek to better understand and address the reproduction and perpetuation of systemic biases through this lens.

1. Understanding Implicit Bias

A. Key Terms

Reflecting how ubiquitous the term *implicit bias* has become, many who use this language in public discourse today do not define it. Among those who define the term, many rely on imprecise definitions that are difficult to understand or that vary from one another. To communicate clearly about the state of the science of implicit bias, it is useful to first define several key terms as understood by scientists today.

- ***Bias***: The influence of factors that are not meant to be considered on a final decision or result.[9] Bias can occur either when relevant information does not influence the decision or when irrelevant information influences the decision. The particular situation or legal context surrounding a decision determines which factors are considered relevant or irrelevant.
- ***Conscious:*** Mental processes involving both awareness and volition.[10]
- ***Unconscious:*** Mental processes that lack either full awareness or full volition.[11]
- ***Explicit bias***: A bias that is measured using an explicit, or direct, measure.[12] ***Explicit measures*** require participants to self-report their responses. They rely on the assumption that individuals are aware of their responses and are willing to express them.[13]
- ***Implicit bias***: A bias that is measured using an implicit, or indirect, measure.[14] ***Implicit measures*** capture participants' responses in ways that do not rely on individuals' awareness or willingness to respond, such as by

measuring reaction time to different groups of stimuli.[15] The scientific field of study that uses these implicit or indirect measures in research on attitudes, stereotypes, and self-esteem is classified as **implicit social cognition.**[16]

In contrast to current prevailing scientific definitions, the term *implicit bias* is rarely used in public discourse to refer to a specific measurement of bias. Instead, *implicit bias* and *unconscious bias* are often used synonymously to refer to an attitude, stereotype, or prejudice that a person is unaware of possessing but which may operate automatically to influence thinking or behavior. (Similarly, the term *explicit bias* is sometimes used to refer to a biased attitude, stereotype, or prejudice that a person is consciously aware of.) This can create confusion because researchers have concluded that there is "no evidence that people are unaware of the mental contents underlying their implicit biases."[17] In fact, when asked, people are able to predict the pattern of their implicit biases "to a high degree of accuracy."[18]

Although people appear to be generally aware of their personal beliefs and cultural stereotypes (referred to as *content awareness*), they may not be aware of or fully understand how they developed this knowledge (referred to as *source awareness*), or how and to what extent that knowledge influences their everyday thinking and behavior (referred to as *impact awareness*).[19] Researchers are still working to fully test relevant hypotheses and to develop a precise scientific understanding of the differences between biases documented using indirect versus direct measures.

In the meantime, the public (including the media and educators) continues to find *implicit bias* and *unconscious bias* useful terms.[20] They serve as shorthand labels for the notion, widely supported by research evidence, that social discrimination is like a virus: It can be easily and rapidly "caught" by a person from the social environment. This infection triggers an immune response: It influences the person's thinking and behavior in that environment to reinforce existing patterns of social discrimination, often in ways the person does not fully appreciate or understand. For consistency with public understanding and clarity in this report, the term *implicit bias* will be used hereafter to refer to this shorthand label, rather than the more restrictive technical definition focused on its scientific measurement.

B. Implicit Bias: The Basics

We each accumulate a unique set of experiences in our lives that shape our perspectives about the world around us. But we are limited in the information available to us about our world. Science tells us that what we experience is not what objectively exists, but what we are able to interpret based on the information we collect through our bodily senses. We do not have direct access to information about what others are feeling or thinking, but we use our observations about their facial expressions, tone of voice, choice of words, mannerisms, and other behavioral information to deduce what we can about them—and decide whether and how to interact with them. So when the human brain processes information, it is making predictions about, or a best guess at, what is going on in our external reality so we can decide how to act within it.[21] These predictions are far from perfect, but they help us survive.

In addition to the subjective point of view that we cultivate through our experiences, our cognitive capacity to observe, think, and act is a finite resource. But research in the psychological and brain sciences paints a picture of a cognitive system with astonishing efficiencies built in. As we interact with the world, our mental machinery is designed to quickly search for patterns (e.g., certain types of small, spherical objects are *apples*) and make associations (e.g., *apples* are red, sweet, juicy, and edible). Our brains do this between groups of people (e.g., older adults) and characteristics (e.g., slow, frail) as well. These associations occur, to some degree, automatically. Unlike *controlled* mental processes, which require at least some intention, effort, or conscious awareness to be enacted, *automatic* associations are formed without apparent mental effort; we may not be consciously aware of or intend to make these associations.[22] This automaticity in the human mind frees up our limited cognitive resources to perform other tasks. Because of this, we are generally not always fully aware of all the activity our minds are undertaking to help us detect, process, and act on information.

Although automatic associations make navigating the world possible, they are sometimes incorrect or even harmful. The problem is that when the brain automatically associates certain characteristics with specific groups, the association is not accurate for all members of the group. Following the above examples, not all apples are red; not all older adults are slow. Kang (2009) describes the problem this presents for the justice system:

> Though our shorthand schemas of people may be helpful in some situations, they also can lead to discriminatory behaviors if we are not careful. Given the critical importance of exercising fairness and equality in the court system, lawyers, judges, jurors, and staff should be particularly concerned about identifying such possibilities. Do we, for instance, associate aggressiveness with Black men, such that we see them as more likely to have started the fight than to have responded in self-defense?[23]

Our minds are constantly classifying incoming information into categories that have meaning to us. These categories may be meaningful because they are categories that society has defined for us or that we have learned from others over time. Embedded in the architecture of our daily lives, many of these associations can be, or have become, invisible to us. We may not endorse these associations, but they can nevertheless contaminate our choices and leak out through our behavior to impact others in ways that we do not intend.

C. Is it implicit bias?

Automaticity and control occur on a continuum. There are many forms of bias that may not fit neatly into a category of purely automatic or purely controlled. For example, *microaggressions* are brief, everyday exchanges that send denigrating messages to certain individuals because of their membership in certain groups.[24] Microaggressions can be subtle, as they include verbal speech, non-verbal cues, and outward behaviors, but they can do substantial harm to their targets.[25] Because microaggressions are defined by how they are *experienced by the receiver*, as opposed to being defined by the *intentions of the actor;* they vary widely in the extent to which they involve any intent or knowledge on the part of the actor that he or she may be manifesting a bias. In other words, an individual can engage in a microaggression with full knowledge and intent to harm the receiver, or with a complete lack of awareness of the harm being done, or with some level of intent and knowledge that falls between these two extremes. Depending on these factors, a microaggression may or may not be an instance of *implicit bias.*

D. What is known about the origins of implicit biases?

Researchers believe that implicit biases have a few common origins, including the following.

i. Ingroup favoritism: We favor the familiar.

People tend to demonstrate preferences for their *ingroup*, or members of the groups to which they belong.[26] Favoritism can benefit, for example, the decision-maker's family members and friends, those who share the same political or religious ideology, or fans of the same sports teams. Although we tend to favor those who we think share our values, favoritism can result from any perceived similarity between the decision-maker and the person being judged—even when the similarity is superficial or coincidental. Why?

Scientists believe this occurs because we tend to like things that are familiar, and nothing is more familiar to us than ourselves.[27] People demonstrate consistent and strongly positive attitudes toward themselves, and this positive attitude can transfer easily to other things, people, and groups when they bear a resemblance to those attributes.[28] For example, when choosing between products, people tend to prefer brands that resemble their own names.[29] Similarly, ingroup favoritism is often observed even among strangers in artificial research settings, based on seemingly random similarities (e.g., the person being judged was randomly assigned a code number that matched the decision-maker's birthdate, or was assigned to wear the same color shirt as the decision-maker in the research study).[30] Bottom line: People categorize others very easily and quickly to determine how to interact with them—that is, whether they are "in" or "out."

ii. Social learning: We are taught, but also "catch," biases from others.

Implicit biases can develop and strengthen over time with the accumulation of personal experience. Personal experiences include not only direct learning experiences between ourselves and the object, person, or group (i.e., classical conditioning), but also by observing the behavior of parents, friends, bosses, coworkers, and other influential people in our lives (i.e., social learning).[31] For example, children observing the behavior of adults interacting with one another will: a) indicate a preference for the adult who received positive treatment from the main speaker, relative to the adult who received negative treatment; b) choose to share resources (i.e., a teddy bear) with adults who received the positive treatment; c) systematically imitate the adults who received positive treatment and shun those who received negative treatment from the main speaker; and d) generalize these approach-avoid preferences to similar-looking others, illustrating the rapid and unintentional intergenerational transmission of social group bias.[32] Implicit biases in children are positively correlated with the implicit biases of their parents; however, consistent with social learning theory, this is found only among children who have a positive attachment relationship with their parents.[33] Implicit biases can develop relatively quickly through such experiences and have been found in children as young as 5 years old.[34]

iii. Cultural knowledge: Our beliefs are shaped by our environment.

Cultural preferences and expectations, including stereotypes, are communicated in a variety of ways. They are embedded in a society's laws; upheld by government leaders; highlighted in the news; and reproduced in entertainment media such as movies, television, and video games. Society is structured around these cultural beliefs and values, which are baked into the formal and informal rules, social scripts, language, and symbols that people encounter, follow, or use every day. As a result, people develop a shared understanding of the social norms and stereotypes that are pervasive in their culture, and this cultural knowledge can foster the development of automatic associations.[35] Even if the attitudes we personally endorse differ or change over time, the implicit biases that arise from cultural knowledge can be resistant to change if those cultural stereotypes continue to be reproduced and reinforced throughout our social environment.[36] And so long as representations of cultural stereotypes persist in our environment, people will have implicit biases reflecting those communicated preferences.

E. What is known about the pervasiveness and impact of implicit biases?

Implicit biases can influence a number of judgments and actions in professional settings, where they have significant impacts on people's lives.[37] In the legal domain, for example, researchers have demonstrated correlations between judges' implicit biases and their sentencing decisions,[38] as well as between labor arbitrators' implicit biases and their decisions in real arbitration cases.[39] Police officers' implicit biases correspond to their decisions to shoot criminal suspects of different races.[40] In medicine, researchers have found correlations between medical providers' implicit biases toward their patients and the quality of care that patients receive,[41] as well as between nurses' implicit biases and their likelihood of remaining in their jobs.[42] Employers' implicit biases correspond to their hiring decisions.[43]

In addition to professional decision-making, implicit associations correspond to a variety of behaviors outside of the laboratory that affect people's experiences, behaviors, and life outcomes. For example, implicit biases have been linked to self-reported racially hostile behavior, such as the use of verbal slurs and physical harm against people of color.[44] Voters' implicit attitudes about electoral candidates have been shown to predict election outcomes.[45] Scores on implicit measures can distinguish between adolescents who are likely to engage in suicide ideation or suicide attempts and those who are not,[46] and between sex offenders who commit crimes against children and those who commit crimes against adults.[47] Implicit associations have also been shown to correspond to substance use among those with addictions to drugs or alcohol.[48]

Finally, there is a large body of research demonstrating other less-than-intentional biases and disparities in professional decision-making. These studies do not use implicit measures of bias, but they use experimental methods to identify disparities in decision-making that participants most likely are either not fully aware of or do not fully intend. For example, trial court judges in one research study decided a series of hypothetical cases; the facts of the cases were identical for all participants, except the social categories (e.g., gender, race) of the litigants involved.[49] Although most judges in the sample stated that they were confident in their abilities to make case decisions free from gendered and racial biases, these litigant characteristics had significant effects on case outcomes. A wide variety of social and cognitive decision-making biases have been demonstrated using similar methods in other studies of judges,[50] as well as in studies of professionals in other fields.[51]

F. What types of situations are likely to bring out implicit biases?

Implicit biases are more likely to be expressed in people's decisions and behaviors under certain conditions. Although a comprehensive review of situational triggers of implicit biases is beyond the scope of this chapter, a few common examples follow.

i. Situational incentives encourage speed over fairness and accuracy.

The performance that organizational leaders pay attention to and reward has an influence on what employees prioritize in their work. Some organizations do not provide employees with any meaningful feedback on their performance. In absence of feedback, people are less likely to remain vigilant for possible biases in their decision-making processes over time.[52]

Many organizations provide some performance feedback to employees, but this is limited to what can be easily measured. What is easily measured (e.g., productivity) may not be what matters most to the organization or the community it serves (e.g., quality). For example, organizations that emphasize efficiency measures over quality measures are motivating their employees to work faster, potentially at the expense of at least some degree of accuracy and fairness. People can process information faster, and produce more decisions, when they rely more on automatic associations and stereotypes. In these instances, the decision-maker develops inferences and expectations about the person or people being judged earlier on in the information-gathering process. However, those expectations bias the decision-maker's attention and memory in favor of stereotype-confirming evidence.[53] Moreover, biased expectations can influence how the decision-maker interacts with the person or people being judged, creating a self-fulfilling prophecy. That is, the decision-maker may then act in ways that elicit from others the very behaviors that would confirm his or her own biased expectations.[54]

ii. Clear criteria for making a good decision are absent.

Decision-making environments vary in the extent to which they provide structure and clarity for the person making the decision. When the basis for judgment is somewhat vague (e.g., situations that call for discretion; cases that involve the application of new, unfamiliar laws; decisions for which there is not a clear decision-making process laid out in advance), biased judgments are more likely. Without more explicit, concrete criteria for decision-making, individuals tend to disambiguate the situation using whatever information is most easily accessible—including stereotypes.[55]

iii. Decisions are made in a distracting or otherwise stressful environment.

Making decisions under cognitive load can increase the risk of biased outcomes. Cognitive load includes conditions such as being tired (e.g., long hours, fatigue), stressed (e.g., heavy, backlogged, or very diverse caseloads; loud construction noise; threats to physical safety; popular or political pressure about a particular decision; emergency or crisis situations), or otherwise distracted (e.g., interruptions, multitasking).[56] Specifically, situations that involve time pressure, that force a decision-maker to form complex judgments relatively quickly, or in which the decision-maker is distracted and cannot fully attend to incoming information all limit the ability to fully process case information.[57] Decision-makers who are working under cognitive load are more likely to apply stereotypes—recalling facts in ways biased by stereotypes and making more stereotypic judgments—than decision-makers whose cognitive capacities are not similarly constrained.

2. The Role of Implicit Bias in Understanding Inequality

Implicit biases are measured at the level of the individual person, so implicit bias education and interventions often focus on the individual. However, this phenomenon exists in a rich social and historical context. Implicit associations are both formed and expressed within that context, so taking context into account is crucial for the development of interventions. This section describes the different levels of inequality within which implicit biases operate.

A. Systemic Inequality

Bias and inequality generally operate in ways that permeate multiple facets of society in multiple ways, and they tend to reinforce and re-create themselves over time.[58] The concept of systemic inequality captures this dynamic. *Systemic inequality* is the combination of a diverse array of discriminatory and inequitable practices in society, including the unjustly gained economic and political power of some groups over others, ongoing resource inequalities, ideologies and attitudes that regard some groups as superior to others, and the set of institutions that preserve the advantages of some groups over others.[59]

B. Cultural Inequality

Within a society, certain social groups have the power to define the culture's value system.[60] *Cultural inequality* is the inequality that is "built into our literature, art, music, language, morals, customs, beliefs, and ideology" to such an extent that it defines "a generally agreed-upon way of life."[61] Dominant culture dictates what is regarded as "good, bad, just, natural, desirable, and possible,"[62] while being presumed to be neutral and inclusive.[63] For example, the people who appear in movies, television shows, and advertisements in the United States are disproportionately slim, White, able-bodied people with Eurocentric facial features. The fact that this is the agreed-upon standard of beauty in our culture is an example of cultural inequality.[64] Another example of cultural inequality is that Black men are over-represented as violent criminals in works of fiction, such as movies and television shows.

C. Institutional Inequality

Institutional inequality refers to the network of institutional structures, policies and practices that create advantages and benefits for some groups over others.[65] Institutions can be defined broadly to include any collective body that influences social norms and the allocation of resources to individuals and social groups. Institutions can include the justice system, schools, media, banks, business, health care, governmental bodies, family units, religious organizations, and civic groups.[66] Institutional inequality can be intentional or unintentional; it often occurs as a result of decisions that are neutral on their face but have disparate impact with regard to race, gender, and other categories. Whether institutional inequality occurs in subtle ways or as a result of overt practices that limit the rights, mobility, or access of certain groups, the actions that lead to the disparity are sanctioned by the institution.[67] One example of institutional inequality in criminal justice is the use of different punishments for crack and powder cocaine, which are chemically similar but disproportionately used by different racial groups. This policy appears race-neutral on its face, but it results in African Americans receiving more severe punishments than White Americans for, effectively, the same drug use behavior.

D. Organizational Inequality

Organizational inequality exists when the practices, rules and policies of formal organizations (such as corporations or government agencies) result in different outcomes for different groups.[68] Like institutional inequality, organizational inequality can occur as a result of intentional decisions designed to produce different outcomes for different groups or as a result of policies and practices that appear neutral on their face.[69] For example, a retail corporation might have a policy that requires newly promoted supervisors to relocate to a new branch. Because women bear a disproportionate amount of housekeeping and caregiving duties and experience significant wage inequality compared to men, they are less likely to be able to relocate their families for their jobs. This policy appears gender-neutral on its face, but it results in greater promotion potential for men than for women, and it exacerbates the gender wage gap.

E. Interpersonal Inequality

Interpersonal inequality exists when inequality manifests at the individual, person-to-person level. The term "bias" gets used in ways that conflate what are actually different psychological processes: stereotypes, prejudice, and discrimination. Any of these three processes can exist on a continuum from highly automatic (generally measured with implicit measures) to highly controlled (generally measured with explicit measures).

- *Stereotypes* are beliefs and opinions about the characteristics, attributes, and behaviors of members of a group (e.g., "soccer moms are energetic").[70] In other words, stereotyping is cognitive in nature. When one engages in the act of stereotyping, one assumes that because an individual belongs to a particular social group, the individual must share the characteristics of the group. When an individual automatically associates a particular trait with a particular social group in long-term memory (largely outside of conscious awareness), we can measure this association with an implicit measure, and we refer to this association as an implicit stereotype.

- ***Prejudice*** is the emotion, attitude, or evaluation that a person feels about members of a particular social group (e.g., "I don't like soccer moms").[71] In other words, prejudice is affective, or emotional, in nature. When an individual automatically associates a particular attitude or evaluation with a particular social group in long-term memory (largely outside of conscious awareness), we can measure this association with an implicit measure, and we refer to this association as implicit prejudice.

- ***Discrimination*** consists of treating people differently from others, based on their membership in a particular social group (e.g., "soccer moms cannot attend my party").[72] In other words, whereas stereotyping is *cognitive* and prejudice is *affective*, discrimination is *behavioral* in nature. This differential treatment can range from fully intentional, controlled behavior, to fully automatic, unconscious behavior. It can occur as a result of stereotypes about the other group, prejudicial attitudes about the other group, or both.

F. Bringing It All Together

The different levels of inequality, from systemic inequality at the societal level to interpersonal inequality at the individual level, are closely intertwined. Although we conceptualize these levels separately for the purpose of defining them, the boundaries between these levels are not always clear-cut. Furthermore, many forms of bias operate across multiple levels. For example, microaggressions, described above, can take the form of verbal speech by an individual person (e.g., telling an Asian American who was born and raised in the U.S. that they speak English so well), or they can take the form of environmental conditions created by an organization (e.g., adorning the walls of a courthouse with portraits of influential figures from history who are exclusively White men).[73]

Although court professionals are often taught to think about implicit bias as an individual, interpersonal phenomenon, implicit bias exists in the broader context of inequality and discrimination at multiple levels in society. Implicit associations form as a result of repeated exposure to certain stereotypes and attitudes about different social groups. In other words, implicit biases at the individual level are shaped by the history and culture of the society in which the person lives and the experiences and social interactions that the person has as a result of that culture and history. For example, most White Americans hold automatic associations in memory between the concept of Black men and the concept of violent crime. The widespread existence of this automatic association is not a coincidence; it stems from the fact that Americans grow up in a society characterized by racial inequality at systemic, cultural, institutional and organizational levels, and in which popular media disproportionately depict Black men as violent criminals.

Thus, although implicit bias is typically measured at the level of the individual person, it is important to consider how it both results from and reinforces different forms of inequality at multiple levels of society. The field of implicit social cognition addresses how biases can arise in individual information processing, decision-making, and behavior in ways that reproduce and reinforce, and are reinforced by, dynamics that are historical, cultural, institutional, and interpersonal in nature. A comprehensive and successful approach to implicit bias intervention must be one that takes into account the importance of this broader social context and addresses the full array of forces that contribute to observed inequities.

3. The State of the Science on Bias Interventions

Psychologists have made significant strides over the last 10 years toward understanding which intervention strategies are effective in reducing the expression of biases. The section that follows summarizes what was learned from recent implicit social cognition research and from consideration of relevant ideas drawn from the broader research literature on prejudice and discrimination.

A. General Interventions to Reduce Prejudice and Discrimination

Over the course of several decades, psychology research has produced evidence to clearly support the effectiveness of some general interventions in reducing prejudice or discrimination at the interpersonal level. These interventions are not necessarily targeted at *implicit* bias, but they offer important insights regarding the factors that are likely to make an implicit bias intervention more successful.

i. Intergroup Contact

Intergroup contact is one of the most thoroughly researched prejudice interventions in social psychology. Originally articulated as a research hypothesis in 1954,[74] the contact hypothesis received support over several decades and hundreds of research studies.[75] The findings show that when members of different social groups interact with each other, reductions in prejudice and discrimination follow.[76]

In this regard, researchers have also shown that not all intergroup contact is equally effective in reducing explicit prejudice. Contact situations that include all four of the following features have the greatest impact: 1) the groups are working toward a common goal, 2) the groups have equal status within the contact situation, 3) the situation allows individuals to get to know each other on an individual basis, and 4) the contact situation receives institutional support or support from the relevant authority figures.[77] Contact situations that include two or three of these factors also tend to reduce prejudice, but to a lesser degree. Research suggests that intergroup contact is effective because it increases a person's knowledge of the outgroup, decreases the level of anxiety that a person feels about interacting with members of the outgroup, and increases a person's empathy for members of the outgroup.

One specific intervention aimed at providing meaningful intergroup contact that has received significant attention from researchers in psychology is the "Jigsaw Classroom." It has primarily been studied in educational settings but it can be implemented in any situation involving collaborative group work. In a Jigsaw Classroom set-up, students are divided into groups to complete a project, and each student is responsible for a particular portion of the final product.[78] In the first phase of the project, students work independently on their own portion of the project. In the second phase, students gather together with each of the students from the *other* groups who are assigned to the same portion of the project (these are called "expert groups"). Finally, in the third stage, students report their progress back to their own group, sharing their new-found expertise. The group then works together to finish the final product.

The Jigsaw Classroom is a particular type of intergroup contact that emphasizes some of the factors that are known to make intergroup contact more effective. Specifically, it puts students in a situation where they are working toward a common goal. It also puts each student on equal footing with the others, allowing each individual to serve as an "expert" in a particular portion of the project and requiring students to be interdependent on one another.[79] Research suggests that, in addition to providing some educational benefits, the Jigsaw Classroom increases individuals' evaluations of outgroup members and decreases the extent to which individuals engage in the stereotyping of outgroup members.[80]

Researchers have begun to examine the effects of intergroup contact on *implicit* bias, but this area of research is relatively young. Findings suggest that intergroup contact may also be effective for reducing implicit prejudice.[81] For example, one recent study showed that among non-Black physicians, the extent of interracial contact over several years in medical school predicted lower anti-Black prejudice (measured both explicitly and implicitly), while the number of hours spent in diversity training did not.[82] In contrast to explicit prejudice, which is influenced by the *quality* of intergroup contact, implicit prejudice seems to be influenced only by the *quantity* of intergroup contact.[83]

ii. Structure versus Discretion

A second major area of research on bias interventions has focused on the context in which individuals are acting and making decisions. A substantial body of research in social cognition shows that individual decision-making discretion makes room for bias and prejudice to manifest as discrimination and inequality.[84] Specifically, when individuals make decisions under conditions of limited structure, ambiguous decision-making procedures, or subjective criteria, they are more likely to make decisions that manifest their biases.[85] These effects can include changing the relative weights of the decision criteria (depending on the social group membership of the people targeted by the decision),[86] applying available options differently to members of different groups,[87] holding members of different groups to different standards,[88] or changing the decision-making procedures from one decision to the next.[89]

The major implication of this research for bias interventions is that one way to reduce group disparities in decision-making is to limit individual discretion as much as possible.[90] Embedding structure in the decision-making process, specifying decision-making procedures as clearly as possible, and relying more extensively on criteria that can be measured objectively may limit the extent to which an individual's biases can leak out into the final decision outcome.[91]

B. Implicit Bias Interventions

In addition to these more general bias interventions, researchers have developed several interventions aimed specifically at *implicit* bias. Implicit bias interventions tend to fall into one of two categories, which this section will discuss in turn. The first category includes interventions that attempt to retrain the underlying implicit association in memory. The interventions in this group tend to be impractical for most purposes outside of the laboratory, and they have demonstrated limited success. The second category includes interventions that leave the underlying association in memory intact but attempt to interrupt its outward expression (in other words, limit the extent to which the implicit association can leak out into the individual's decisions or behavior). The interventions in this group vary in the extent to which they are practical to implement outside the lab, and they show more promise in their effectiveness.

i. Interventions that attempt to change associations in memory

Some implicit bias interventions attempt to retrain the brain by changing the implicit association that exists in the individual's long-term memory. For example, if an individual automatically associates members of a particular racial group (e.g., Black) with a negative evaluation (e.g., bad, lazy) in memory, the intervention would attempt to re-write this automatic association as a relationship between the racial group and an opposing, positive evaluation (e.g., good, hardworking). From this body of research on *change* interventions, three main lessons have been learned.

- ***Lesson #1:*** *Some change strategies may slightly reduce the strength of negative implicit associations.*

Researchers have examined several different approaches to re-writing the automatic associations in long-term memory. It is possible to reduce the strength of a negative implicit association, but the effectiveness of this strategy is inconsistent.

For example, evaluative conditioning is a procedure that involves repeated exposure to a new idea that runs counter to the person's automatic association. It teaches people to automatically link concepts together in memory that were not linked together previously. For example, one study placed participants in front of a computer screen and showed them a series of images of Black faces paired with positive words, as well as White faces paired with negative words.[92] The idea is that prior to the study, many participants had a pre-existing automatic association between Black faces and negative evaluations (and, conversely, White faces and positive evaluations). Having these participants repeatedly view images presenting the opposite idea might lead their pre-existing associations to weaken, or, with enough exposure, become negated. In some, but not all, studies, researchers have found that participants' negative implicit associations with the social group in question decreased in strength after an evaluative conditioning activity.[93]

Other methods for re-writing a negative automatic association in memory include exposing research participants to positive, counter-stereotypical exemplars (i.e., example members of the social group in question),[94] asking participants to imagine the perspective of members of the other group (imagined perspective-taking),[95] or inducing a positive emotion while participants consider members of the other group (emotion induction).[96]

Meta-analyses (i.e., research studies that measure the effects of many research studies combined) of these intervention strategies have generally found that evaluative conditioning and counter-stereotypical exemplars are sometimes effective in reducing the strength of implicit racial biases to a small degree; in contrast, imagined perspective-taking, emotion induction, and other strategies are generally not effective.[97]

- **Lesson #2:** *Reductions in implicit bias resulting from change interventions typically don't last long.*

Even when researchers successfully reduce the strength of a person's negative implicit associations in memory, these changes typically do not last long enough to have an effect outside the lab. Over the past few years, researchers have devoted more attention to measuring how long changes in implicit associations last after a single experimental intervention. Unfortunately, meta-analyses reveal that most reductions in negative implicit associations following these discrete interventions do not last longer than one or two days.[98] There are a few notable exceptions to this time limit, but in each of these exceptions, the intervention itself took place over the course of weeks or months, rather than in a single experimental session.[99]

- **Lesson #3:** *With change interventions, reductions in implicit bias typically don't alter downstream behavior.*

Even when researchers are able to reduce the strength of a person's negative implicit associations in memory, this change typically does not affect downstream thoughts or behaviors. In order for implicit bias interventions to have a meaningful effect outside the lab, they must cause changes in the individual's decisions about, or behaviors toward, members of the social group in question. Unfortunately, meta-analyses of implicit bias intervention studies find that very few studies measure the impact of changes in implicit associations on downstream behaviors; those that do measure the impact of interventions after a delay tend to find no effects.[100] Recent research suggests that because implicit bias is intertwined with the culture and environment within which individuals are acting, the stability of our social environments makes it unlikely that small reductions in implicit associations in memory will manifest as noticeable reductions in prejudice and discrimination.[101]

ii. Interventions that affect the expression of implicit bias

Another broad class of implicit bias interventions are ones that attempt to bypass or disrupt the expression of the implicit association. Unlike the first type of strategy discussed above, this class of *expression* interventions leaves the underlying implicit association in memory intact. Instead of re-writing the association, the goal is to limit the extent to which it can leak out in decisions and behaviors. For example, bypassing interventions may teach people how to prevent implicit associations from getting activated in the first place; disruption interventions may teach people how to override their automatic gut reactions or decisions with a more egalitarian response. Researchers have examined several different interventions that address the expression of implicit bias.[102] Generally, this class of interventions shows more promise than interventions that try to retrain the brain.

a. Bypassing interventions

One well-known bypassing intervention is commonly referred to as a *blinding* procedure. Blinding procedures are structural practices that block the transmission of information that would trigger decision-makers' implicit biases. This is the principle behind now-commonplace practices such as blind auditions, blind peer-review, and double-blind clinical studies.[103] Blinding procedures are already used at other decision points in the justice system process. For example, as part of the National Research Council's recommended best practices for conducting eyewitness identification lineups, the administering police officer should not know the identity of the suspect in the lineup.[104] Jurisdictions are already experimenting with race-blinding procedures as a technique to reduce disparate treatment in prosecutorial charging decisions.[105] Blinding procedures can be helpful, but it can sometimes be difficult or impractical to blind for all factors that may activate implicit bias.

b. Disruption interventions: Harnessing intrinsic motivation

One approach to disrupting the influence of implicit associations involves activating the individual's egalitarian goals. Researchers have shown, for example, that people who are *intrinsically* motivated to avoid prejudiced responding are more successful at overriding their implicit biases in favor of more egalitarian responses.[106] An intrinsic motivation, as opposed to an extrinsic motivation, is one that comes from within the person, as part of his or her personality or sense of self. Reminding these individuals of their intrinsic motivation to promote equality in the moment can help them override their implicit associations. However, this strategy is risky and can backfire. If the intervention produces an *extrinsic* motivation to promote equality (i.e., a motivation that is guided by the chance to earn external rewards, such as social approval, prestige, or financial/material gains), it can result in greater implicit bias.[107]

c. Disruption interventions: Harnessing interpersonal motives

A second approach to teaching people strategies for overriding their automatic associations involves interpersonal motives. Research suggests that people adapt their thoughts and behaviors in subtle ways to fit into the context they are in. In the domain of implicit bias, this can mean that the mere presence of people who belong to other social groups or who support egalitarian norms can result in less implicit bias and more egalitarian behavior.[108] For example, participants in one study either interacted with a Black experimenter or a White experimenter before completing a measure of implicit racial prejudice; those who interacted with the Black experimenter exhibited lower implicit bias.[109] Similar effects have been shown in research studies that did not measure implicit associations directly. A study of jury decision-making, for example, found that juries composed of White and Black jurors engaged in higher-quality deliberations and made more egalitarian verdict decisions than juries composed of only White members.[110] Importantly, these effects were not limited to the Black jurors; White jurors engaged in better decision-making when they were in the presence of Black jurors.

d. Disruption interventions: Forming new decision-making habits

A third approach to teaching people to override their automatic associations involves breaking the "habit" of a person's automatic response. Treating implicit bias like a bad habit that can be broken involves the same kinds of strategies a person would use to break any other bad habit (such as smoking or biting one's fingernails).[111] There are two types of strategies that researchers have found to be effective in breaking the habit of automatic biases. First, researchers have developed long-term educational experiences (often weeks or months long) that teach people to become aware of situations when they are most vulnerable to implicit biases, replace their automatic responses with a more egalitarian response, and practice the new egalitarian response until it becomes habit. Several versions of this approach have demonstrated effectiveness, often resulting in behavioral changes months or years after the intervention has ended.[112]

The second type of habit-breaking intervention involves getting individuals to establish a behavioral plan for deciding or responding in a future situation in which they may be prone to bias. *Implementation intentions* have shown promise in this context. An implementation intention is an "if-then" statement that lays out contingencies between a situation and a response (e.g., "If situation X is encountered, then I will initiate egalitarian response Y").[113] Researchers have found that participants who commit to an implementation intention in advance (for example, a plan to think "good" after seeing a Black face) are more likely to be able to override their automatic responses in favor of a more egalitarian response.[114] Reasons why this strategy is effective include that it increases the individual's commitment to the response,[115] makes the response more accessible in the individual's mind,[116] makes the response more automatic and less effortful,[117] and helps shield the individual from the intrusion of unwanted thoughts.[118]

iii. Key Takeaways

Meta-analyses of these intervention strategies suggest they show promise as tools for reducing the influence of implicit associations on decisions and behavior.[119] Interventions that prevent the activation of implicit associations, leverage individuals' intrinsic egalitarian motivations, create diverse decision-making contexts with shared norms of equality, and help people break the habit of their automatic, biased responses have been shown to reduce disparities in subsequent decisions and behaviors, even when they are not meant to change the underlying implicit association in memory.

Although psychological research on bias interventions is still in a state of rapid change and advancement, it points to three key takeaways that have practical implications for courts and their communities.

- *Key Takeaway #1: General interventions that attempt to reduce prejudice and discrimination through positive, meaningful intergroup contact and by structuring discretionary decisions are still some of the most effective strategies for courts.* Intergroup contact has been widely studied as a bias reduction strategy for over half a century. Engagement activities that include the following features have the greatest impact: 1) different groups are working toward a common goal, 2) the groups have equal status in the activity, 3) the activity allows individuals to get to know each other on an individual basis, and 4) the activity receives institutional support or support from the relevant authority figures. In addition, researchers and practitioners have long known that greater structure in decision-making processes can limit opportunities for bias to infect decision outcomes.

- *Key Takeaway #2: Implicit bias interventions that attempt to <u>change</u> implicit associations in memory are not consistently effective.* Although some *change* interventions, such as evaluative conditioning and counter-stereotypical exemplars, can reduce the strength of implicit associations in some contexts, they are difficult to implement outside the lab, have inconsistent effects that do not last longer than a few days, and tend not to change subsequent decisions and behaviors.
- *Key Takeaway #3: Implicit bias interventions that <u>bypass or disrupt</u> biased responding show more promise.* Specifically, there is evidence to support *expression* interventions that prevent the activation of implicit associations, leverage individuals' intrinsic egalitarian motivations, create diverse decision-making contexts with shared norms of equality, and give people tools to break the habit of their automatic, biased responses.

4. Implications for Courts and Their Communities

What is known from the evolving science on implicit bias has implications for the state courts and their communities, where court leaders and other practitioners seek to better understand and address the reproduction and perpetuation of systemic biases through this lens. Four interrelated implications are discussed below.

A. Lead by example—and know where you're headed.

The science of implicit bias highlights the influence of the social environment on our thinking, decisions, and behavior. The court is a specific type of social environment, with a unique institutional culture, formal rules, and informal social norms that create expectations about appropriate behavior. Interpersonal influences, such as the conduct of leadership, play an important role in constructing that social environment.[120] Attitudes, preferences, and behavior may be readily learned or "caught" by observing the conduct of respected authorities and peers. And, as previously noted, strategies (such as intergroup contact) may be more effective at reducing prejudice and discrimination when implemented under certain conditions. One of those conditions is clear institutional support or support from relevant authority figures.[121]

Court leaders can influence the social environment of the court in a variety of ways. In the wake of the killing of George Floyd, one of the most common ways organizational leaders across the country responded was by issuing a public statement to demonstrate social accountability. Dozens of state court leaders also issued public statements, reaffirming commitments to identifying and addressing systemic injustices.[122] Over the years, the Conference of Chief Justices and the Conference of State Court Administrators have passed numerous policy resolutions on issues pertaining to equal justice.[123] States have established leadership teams and task forces charged with overseeing such activities.[124] Some states have created centralized Diversity, Equity, and Inclusion (DE&I) offices to, for example, create DE&I goals and implementation plans, coordinate activities and programs, establish metrics for measuring progress, and monitor DE&I goals.[125] Such leadership efforts can be valuable first steps for establishing a court culture that supports DE&I initiatives and produces concrete reforms that materially improve the lives of court users who have not historically been equally served.

Ultimately, judicial leadership must determine the goals of institutional efforts to address systemic and implicit biases. Terms such as diversity, inclusion, equality, and equity are often used interchangeably, but these terms represent different goals that implicate different strategies.

- *Diversity* refers to the presence of individuals who represent a variety of groups or perspectives. It captures the quantitative representation of different groups, but it does not capture how much each group is heard or how much influence each group has.[126]
- *Inclusion* refers to the meaningful involvement of people from different groups, or the extent to which diverse perspectives are incorporated into systems, processes, and decisions.[127] In contrast to diversity, which reflects the *quantity* of representation, inclusion reflects the *quality* of representation.
- *Equality* refers to the equal treatment of different individuals or groups; it occurs when people receive the same treatment or distribution of resources, regardless of their needs or starting positions.[128] An equality mindset assumes that everyone will benefit from the same supports to meet their needs.[129]
- *Equity* refers to the state that exists when we cannot predict outcomes based on a person's group membership, and outcomes for all groups are improved. Equity often involves the differential treatment of different individuals, based on their needs and starting positions, with the goal that everyone will arrive at the same outcome.[130]

Keeping in mind these different end goal states, court leaders will need to articulate objectives using appropriate terminology. Depending on the nature of the problem and the stated needs of the people who are most affected by the problem, the court might strive to achieve diversity, inclusion, equality, or equity. In recent years, members of the public, justice partners, and stakeholders are increasingly pushing to achieve equity.[131]

B. Educate not just to raise awareness, but to build capacity for change.

As succinctly noted by Ivuoma Onyeador and colleagues, "No one-size-fits-all solution addresses organizational diversity. Although implicit bias trainings can help address diversity, equity, and inclusion, they are not sufficient. Organizations must also change structures and improve climate."[132] On their own, implicit bias educational sessions can realistically achieve only so much. They can add value when used to raise awareness and educate staff about bias and inequality, and train staff on specific individual and organizational strategies to be implemented in pursuit of organizational goals.

Much ink has been spilled over the efficacy of corporate diversity training efforts in recent years. As these trainings have proliferated, researchers have studied various programs for evidence of effectiveness. Historically, quality field research on diversity training has been relatively scarce. Research on educational interventions can be challenging to conduct for a variety of reasons, limiting conclusions researchers can draw about them collectively (e.g., substantial differences in program design, including program goals, featured content, methods, trainers used, type of audience, and more, make comparisons difficult; barriers in data collection, such as the inability to locate participants for follow-up evaluations, can preclude meaningful evaluations; other intervening factors can complicate interpretation of results). The evidence to date suggests that most corporate diversity training programs, including various implicit bias programs, are generally ineffective at reducing bias and inconsistent at changing behavior.[133] Part of this is because diversity training is often offered as a single, standalone training session or workshop. Experts suggest the efficacy of diversity trainings can be improved by incorporating training into a broader comprehensive strategy aimed at building capacity for change.[134] Specific recommendations include: tailoring training programs to match institutional goals, linking content to desired outcomes; preparing trainers to manage participant discomfort as part of the learning process, rather than trying to avoid discomfort; training attendees on how to use a limited number of concrete strategies for managing bias (i.e., 2–3 specific strategies) that are most relevant to their work; and, importantly, developing a plan for evaluating the efficacy of the training.[135]

Although it is unlikely that an implicit bias educational program will change attendees' implicit biases, it may offer other benefits.[136] For example, as a result of participation, people may become more aware of, concerned about, and motivated to address discrimination, become more sensitive to the biases of others and more likely to label biases as wrong, and have more confidence in their ability to effectively engage in equity-promoting behaviors. Studies of one educational curriculum designed by academic researchers at the University of Wisconsin-Madison have found that participants, when contacted several weeks after completing a version of the course, expressed greater concern about discrimination and reported feeling more comfortable discussing the issues. Two years after their seminars, those who completed the program were better able to identify biased behavior in others or were more likely to publicly object to others' expressions of bias. Such changes may be valuable to those seeking to motivate and engage professional staff in DE&I efforts to advance specific organizational goals.

C. Gather information to understand what is really happening in your court and community.

Disparities in the justice system vary by jurisdiction and decision point. Because of meaningful variations in the social environment (such as the composition of local communities, local history and politics, and other factors), it is important to collect data that can shed light on the specific types, direction, and magnitude of disparities—and their root causes—in a particular jurisdiction.[137]

Understanding the nature of the problem is crucial for determining which types of interventions are needed and which are likely to be successful. The more the court can use data to inform its strategy, the better positioned it will be to channel resources toward the interventions with the biggest impact. The following are some broad questions court personnel might consider when defining the problem:

- What is the specific disparity or hardship we are trying to address?
- Do we have enough information about the size and scope of the problem, or do we need more information?
- What kinds of data are needed (e.g., case processing or case outcome data, employment data, anonymous surveys of the affected populations, town halls or targeted listening sessions with the affected populations)?
- At which points in the justice process does this disparity or hardship emerge? Which components of the problem are under the direct control of the court, which components could the courts influence through its role as a convener of important social institutions, and which components are outside the control of the court?
- Who are the people most affected by this disparity or hardship?
- What do the people in this group say they need?

After considering these questions, the court should determine whether the problem is one of internal organizational culture, public outreach and communication, individual decision-making, or policy. Often, more than one of these domains will be in play simultaneously. Depending on the nature of the problem, an implicit bias intervention may or may not offer the best possible solution.

Examining data is an essential step in uncovering disparities and bias, but many courts face challenges when seeking to document disparities in the justice system. This typically involves the lack of quality data and the fragmented nature of data systems. Common reported barriers to court collection of race and ethnicity data, for example, include the lack of staff time, limitations in technology systems, confusion about race and ethnicity categories, and concerns about data being misused or misinterpreted.[138] However, courts have undertaken significant efforts in this area.

Court leaders in some states have conducted or commissioned disparity analyses using administrative data. For example, the late Massachusetts Supreme Court Chief Justice Ralph Gants recently commissioned a report from researchers at Harvard Law School focused on documenting racial disparities in the state criminal court process using administrative data from multiple state agencies and survey data from the U.S. Census Bureau.[139] Other states have commissioned other types of reviews. For example, the New York State Courts recently charged an independent commission with comprehensively examining and documenting institutional racism in the state court system to inform and guide current improvement efforts.[140] This commission adopted a multimethod approach involving document reviews of institutional policies, programs, and practices and historical reports on issues of racial bias; reviews of employment statistics; engagement with various court and community stakeholders through numerous interviews and solicitation of written submissions; in-person court observations; and more to generate recommendations for improvement. Finally, scientists have started using the audit method to conduct large scale field experiments to document discrimination. This method has been widely used to provide the bulk of the evidence of discrimination in housing, employment, healthcare, education, and the delivery of other public services.[141] This may be another useful method to consider.

It is important to note that bias can also influence how data are interpreted and how decisions are made based on those interpretations. Some justice system leaders have sought to address this challenge by engaging diverse perspectives, including the voices of directly impacted communities, in collaborative efforts to determine what information to collect, identify disparities and understand their root causes, brainstorm potential solutions, decide how best to address problems, and decide how to allocate resources to the most promising strategies.

D. Experiment: Design interventions based on the evidence and evaluate interventions for efficacy.

Once the court identifies specific disparities that may benefit from a bias intervention, interventions should be customized to address the problem at the targeted decision point. The custom intervention should be pilot tested and evaluated to determine its effectiveness.

Depending on the nature of the problem, one or more implicit bias intervention strategies may be appropriate. Approaches may include the following.

- Redesign the decision-making environment to **remove or minimize situational triggers** of implicit biases and create conditions for success.
- **Structure decision-making processes** to bypass or disrupt the expression of implicit biases, such as by establishing clear decision-making criteria before evidence is presented and a decision is made or incorporating blinding procedures to redact biasing information.
- Cultivate opportunities for staff to **engage in positive, meaningful intergroup contact**. In addition to the discrimination-reduction benefits of these activities, under certain conditions, the sharing of diverse perspectives can produce other performance-enhancing benefits in the form of greater creativity, more innovation, and better decisions.[142] Intergroup contact may be increased, for example, by:
    - being intentional about the composition of program committees, task forces, and other decision-making bodies;
    - fostering workforce diversity by improving recruitment, hiring, retention, and promotion processes; and
    - building staff communication skills to navigate crucial conversations and prepare them to conduct community outreach and engagement work.[143]
- Equip individuals with the tools for improved decision-making, such as by training them to develop **new decision-making habits** by using specific, tested techniques such as implementation intentions.[144]

Conclusion

The science on implicit bias is still evolving, and researchers and practitioners continue to assess its implications for broader efforts aimed at reducing prejudice and discrimination and improving equality, equity, diversity, and inclusion. As observed by neuroscientist and psychologist Lisa Feldman Barrett:[145]

> And now we get to the toughest issue of all: what it means to control your behavior and therefore be responsible for your actions. The law (like much of psychology) usually considers responsibility in two parts: actions caused by you, where you have more responsibility, and actions caused by the situation, where you have less.

[But] the concepts in your head are not purely a matter of personal choice. [...] They are forged by the social reality you live in. [...] You learn from the environment like any other animal. Nevertheless, all animals shape their own environment. So as a human being, you have the ability to shape your environment to modify your conceptual system, which means that you are ultimately responsible for the concepts that you accept and reject.

In the meantime, courts leaders forge ahead, continuing to make the best decisions they can with the knowledge we have today. On June 9, 2020, days after the death of George Floyd, Connecticut Chief Justice Richard A. Robinson wrote:[146]

> The existing imperfections in our justice systems have profound and lasting effects on all of us, but it is more severe on those of us who are the most vulnerable. There is a need for real and immediate improvement. America can—and must—do a better job of providing "equal justice under law," the very words that are engraved on the front of the United States Supreme Court Building in Washington, D.C. [...]
>
> Many of you have heard me talk about race, implicit bias and my own life experiences facing these issues. Many of you have attended Judicial Branch training and programs that were designed to help us deal with these issues in our own lives and in order to fulfill the mission of the Branch to serve the interests of justice and the public by resolving matters brought before it in a fair, timely, efficient and open manner.
>
> I am proud of the work that we have started, but there is so much more to do. I know that I am asking a lot of you. I know that you are tired, you are weary and maybe even rightfully disillusioned, but this is a battle for the nation's soul. We must double and even triple our efforts to provide equal justice for all those whom we serve. We have but two choices: to keep working hard and succeed; or to quit and fail. As for me, the latter is not an option.

So, You'd Like to Know More

- National Center for State Courts' Racial Justice webpage: https://www.ncsc.org/information-and-resources/racial-justice.

Appendix

Executive Order on Advancing Racial Equity and Support for Underserved Communities Through the Federal Government

On January 20, 2021, President Joseph Biden signed an executive order establishing that the Federal Government should pursue a comprehensive approach to advancing equity for all, "including people of color and others who have been historically underserved, marginalized, and adversely affected by persistent poverty and inequality." In the executive order, the President acknowledged that "[b]ecause advancing equity requires a systematic approach to embedding fairness in decision-making processes, executive departments and agencies […] must recognize and work to redress inequities in their policies and programs that serve as barriers to equal opportunity." The executive order continued, calling on all federal agencies to "assess whether, and to what extent, its programs and policies perpetuate systemic barriers to opportunities and benefits for people of color and other underserved groups. Such assessments will better equip agencies to develop policies and programs that deliver resources and benefits equitably for all."[147]

About the Authors

Jennifer K. Elek, Ph.D., is a Principal Court Research Associate at the National Center for State Courts (NCSC). Since joining NCSC in 2010, she has directed numerous international, national, and state research and policy projects on a variety of court topics such as the use of evidence-based practices in pretrial, sentencing, and community corrections; decision-making and fairness in the courts; and judicial education and professional development. Dr. Elek also provides support to the Blueprint for Racial Justice national initiative to improve racial equity in the justice system.

Andrea L. Miller, Ph.D., J.D., is a Senior Court Research Associate at the National Center for State Courts and a Clinical Assistant Professor of Psychology at the University of Illinois Urbana-Champaign. She sits on the Illinois Supreme Court Committee on Equality and is a licensed attorney in Minnesota. She holds a Ph.D. in social psychology from the University of Minnesota and a J.D. from the University of Minnesota Law School. Dr. Miller's research focuses on the social-psychological foundations of prejudice, discrimination, and inequity, particularly as they operate in the courts and under the law.

Endnotes

1. American Bar Association (2020). *ABA Model Code of Judicial Conduct.* Chicago: Authors. Available at https://www.americanbar.org/groups/professional_responsibility/publications/model_code_of_judicial_conduct/. For information about the jurisdictional adoption of a revised model code of judicial conduct, see https://www.americanbar.org/groups/professional_responsibility/resources/judicial_ethics_regulation/map/.

2. Rainie, L., & Perrin, A. (July 22, 2019). Key findings about Americans' declining trust in government and each other. Available at https://www.pewresearch.org/fact-tank/2019/07/22/key-findings-about-americans-declining-trust-in-government-and-each-other/.

3. Engel, L., Abaroa-Ellison, J., Jemison, E., & Cumberbatch, K. (November, 2020). Racial disparities and Covid-19. Washington, D.C.: Council on Criminal Justice.

4. Edelman (2021). 2021 Edelman Trust Barometer. Available at https://www.edelman.com/trust/2021-trust-barometer

5. For example, Americans who had less trust in social institutions were less willing to get vaccinated during the global Covid-19 pandemic. The Covid States Project (September 2020). The state of the nation: A 50-state Covid-19 survey. Report #13: Public trust in institutions and vaccine acceptance. Available at https://covidstates.org/.

6. Conference of Chief Justices and Conference of State Court Administrators (July 30, 2020). *Resolution 1: In support of racial equality and justice for all.* Available at: https://www.ncsc.org/_data/assets/pdf_file/0029/42869/07302020-Racial-Equality-and-Justice-for-All.pdf

7. National Center for State Courts, *State court statements on racial justice.* Available at: https://www.ncsc.org/newsroom/state-court-statements-on-racial-justice.

8. Elek, J. and Miller, A. (2021, March). *The Evolving Science on Implicit Bias: An Updated Resource for the Court Community.* Williamsburg, VA: National Center for State Courts. Available at www.ncsc.org/ibeducation.

9. Evans, J. (2008). Dual-processing accounts of reasoning, judgment, and social cognition. *Annual Review of Psychology, 59,* 225–278. Available at https://www.annualreviews.org/doi/10.1146/annurev.psych.59.103006.093629.

10. Evans, J. (2008). Dual-processing accounts of reasoning, judgment, and social cognition. *Annual Review of Psychology, 59,* 225–278. Available at https://www.annualreviews.org/doi/10.1146/annurev.psych.59.103006.093629.

11. Evans, J. (2008). Dual-processing accounts of reasoning, judgment, and social cognition. *Annual Review of Psychology, 59,* 225–278. Available at https://www.annualreviews.org/doi/10.1146/annurev.psych.59.103006.093629.

12. Greenwald, A., & Lai, C. (2020). Implicit social cognition. *Annual Review of Psychology, 71,* 419–445. Available at https://www.annualreviews.org/doi/10.1146/annurev-psych-010419-050837.

13. Olson, M. & Zabel, K. (2016). Measures of prejudice. In Nelson, T. (Ed.), *Handbook of Prejudice, Stereotyping, and Discrimination* (2nd ed.). Oxfordshire: Taylor & Francis Group.

14. Greenwald, A., & Lai, C. (2020). Implicit social cognition. *Annual Review of Psychology, 71,* 419–445. Available at https://www.annualreviews.org/doi/10.1146/annurev-psych-010419-050837.

15. Olson, M. & Zabel, K. (2016). Measures of prejudice. In Nelson, T. (Ed.), *Handbook of Prejudice, Stereotyping, and Discrimination* (2nd ed.). Oxfordshire: Taylor & Francis Group.

16. Greenwald, A., & Banaji, M. (1995). Implicit social cognition: Attitudes, self-esteem, and stereotypes. *Psychological Review, 102,* 4–27. In this seminal publication, the authors proposed the term and explained that the "signature of implicit social cognition is that traces of past experience affect some performance, even though the influential earlier experience is not remembered in the usual sense—that is, it is unavailable to self-report or introspection" (p. 4).

17. Gawronski, B. (2019). Six lessons for a cogent science of implicit bias and its criticism. Perspectives on *Psychological Science, 14,* 574–595.

18. Hahn, A., Judd, C., Hirsh, H., & Blair, I. (2014). Awareness of implicit attitudes. *Journal of Experimental Psychology: General (143),* 1369–1392.

19. Gawronski, B. (2019). Six lessons for a cogent science of implicit bias and its criticism. Perspectives on *Psychological Science, 14,* 574–595.

20. E.g., Benson, T., & Fiarman, S. (2020). *Unconscious bias in schools: A developmental approach to exploring race and racism.* Cambridge, MA: Harvard Education Press.

21. E.g., see Barrett, L. F. (2017). *How emotions are made: The secret life of the brain.* Boston: Houghton Mifflin Harcourt.

22. Correll, J., Judd, C.M., Park, B., & Wittenbrink, B. (2010). Measuring Prejudice, stereotypes, and discrimination. In The SAGE Handbook of Prejudice, Stereotyping, and Discrimination. Thousand Oaks: SAGE Publications. Devine, P. G., & Sharp, L. B. (2009). Automaticity and control in stereotyping and prejudice. In T. D. Nelson (Ed.), Handbook of prejudice, stereotyping, and discrimination (p. 61–87). Psychology Press.

23. Kang, J. (2009). *Implicit bias: A primer for courts.* Williamsburg, VA: National Center for State Courts.

24. Sue, D., Bucceri, J., Lin, A., Nadal, K., & Torino, G. (2007). Racial microaggressions and the Asian American experience. *Cultural Diversity and Ethnic Minority Psychology, 13,* 72–81. Sue, D., Capodilupo, C., & Holder, A. (2008). Racial microaggressions in the life experience of Black Americans. Professional Psychology: *Research and Practice, 39,* 329–336.

25. Blume, A., Lovato, L., Thyken, B., & Denny, N. (2012). The relationship of microaggressions with alcohol use and anxiety among ethnic minority college students in a Historically White Institution. *Cultural Diversity and Black Minority Psychology, 18,* 45–54. Harwood, S., Huntt, M., Mendenhall, R., & Lewis, J. (2012). Racial microaggressions in the residence halls: Experiences of students of color at a Predominantly White University. *Journal of Diversity in Higher Education, 5,* 159–173. Huynh, V. (2012). Ethnic microaggressions and the depressive and somatic symptoms of Latino and Asian American Adolescents. *Journal of Youth and Adolescence, 41,* 831–846. Nadal, K., Wong, Y., Griffin, K., Davidoff, K., & Sriken, J. (2014). The adverse impact of racial microaggressions on college students' self-esteem. *Journal of College Student Development, 55,* 461–474. Sue, D., Capodilupo, C., & Holder, A. (2008). Racial microaggressions in the life experience of Black Americans. Professional Psychology: *Research and Practice, 39,* 329–336. Torres, L., Driscoll, M., & Burrow, A. (2010). Racial microaggressions and psychological functioning among highly achieving African-American: A mixed-methods approach. *Journal of Social and Clinical Psychology, 29,* 1074–1099.

26. Azevedo, R. T., Macaluso, E., Avanti, A., Santangelo, V., Cazzato, V., & Aglioti, S. M. (2013). Their pain is not our pain: brain and autonomic correlates of empathic resonance with the pain of same and different race individuals. *Human brain mapping, 34*(12), 3168–3181.

27. E.g., Tajfel, H. (1982). Social psychology of intergroup relations. *Annual Review of Psychology, 33,* 1–39. Turner, J.C., Brown, R.J., & Tajfel, H, (1979). Social comparison and group interest in ingroup favouratism. *European Journal of Social Psychology, 9,* 187–204. Tajfel, H., Billig, M., Bundy, R., & Flament, C. (1971). Social categorization and intergroup behavior. *European Journal of Social Psychology, 1,* 149–177. Zajonc, R. (2001). Mere exposure: a gateway to the subliminal. *Current Directions in Psychological Science, 10,* 224–228. Zajonc, R. (1968). Attitudinal effects of mere exposure. *Journal of Personality and Social Psychology, 9,* 1–27.

28. For a review, see Banaji, M. R., & Heiphetz, L. (2010). Attitudes. In: S. T. Fiske, D. T. Gilbert, & G. Lindzey (Eds.), Handbook of social psychology (pp. 348–388). New York: John Wiley & Sons.

29. Brendl, C. M., Chattopadhyay, A., Pelham, B. W., & Carvallo, M. (2005). Name letter branding: Valence transfers when product specific needs are active. *Journal of Consumer Research, 32*(3), 405–415.

30. E.g., see Billig, M. & Tajfel, H. (1973). Social categorization and similarity in intergroup behaviour. *European Journal of Social Psychology, 3,* 27–52. Molenberghs, P. (2013). The neuroscience of in-group bias. *Neuroscience & Biobehavioral Reviews, 37,* 1530–1536.

31. Olson, M. A., & Fazio, R. H. (2001). Implicit attitude formation through classical conditioning. *Psychological Science, 12*(5), 413–417. Greenwald, A. G., & Banaji, M. R. (1995). Implicit social cognition: attitudes, self-esteem, and stereotypes. *Psychological review, 102*(1), 4.

32. Skinner, A., Meltzoff, A., & Olson, K. (2017) "Catching" social group bias: Exposure to biased nonverbal signals creates social biases in preschool children. *Psychological Science, 28,* 216–224. Skinner, A., Olson, K., & Meltzoff, A. (2020). Acquiring group bias: Observing other people's nonverbal signals can create social group biases. *Journal of Personality and Social Psychology: Interpersonal Relations and Group Processes, 119,* 824–838. Skinner, A., & Meltzoff, A. (2017). How societal prejudices seep into the minds of our children. UNESCO *IBE In Focus: Education & the Future,* 98–101.

33. Bandura, A. (1997). *Self-efficacy: The exercise of control.* Macmillan. Sinclair, S., Dunn, E., & Lowery, B. (2005). The relationship between parental racial attitudes and children's implicit prejudice. *Journal of Experimental Social Psychology, 41*(3), 283–289.

34. Williams, A., & Steele, J. R. (2019). Examining children's implicit racial attitudes using exemplar and category-based measures. *Child development, 90*(3), e322–e338. See also Mandalaywala, T., Ranger-Murdoch, G., Amodio, D., & Rhodes, M. (2018). The nature and consequences of essentialist beliefs about race in early childhood. *Child Development, 90,* e437–e453.

35. Devine, P. G. (1989). Stereotypes and prejudice: Their automatic and controlled components. *Journal of personality and social psychology, 56*(1), 5. Fazio, R. H., Jackson, J. R., Dunton, B. C., & Williams, C. J. (1995). Variability in automatic activation as an unobtrusive measure of racial attitudes: A bona fide pipeline?. *Journal of personality and social psychology, 69*(6), 1013. Karpinski, A., & Hilton, J. L. (2001). Attitudes and the implicit association test. *Journal of personality and social psychology, 81*(5), 774. Nosek, B. A., Hawkins, C. B., & Frazier, R. S. (2011). Implicit social cognition: From measures to mechanisms. *Trends in cognitive sciences, 15*(4), 152–159.

36. Payne, B., Vuletich, H., & Brown-Iannuzzi, J. (2019). Historical roots of implicit bias in slavery. *Proceedings of the National Academy of Sciences, USA, 116,* 11693–11698. Payne, B., Vuletich, H., & Lundberg, K. (2017). The bias of crowds: How implicit bias

bridges personal and systemic prejudice. *Psychological Inquiry, 28,* 233–248. Vuletich, H., & Payne, B. (2019). Stability and change in implicit bias. *Psychological Science, 30,* 854–862.

37. Greenwald, A. G., Banaji, M. R., & Nosek, B. A. (2015). Statistically small effects of the Implicit Association Test can have societally large effects. *Journal of Personality and Social Psychology, 108(4),* 553–561.

38. Rachlinski, J., Johnson, S., Wistrich, A., & Guthrie, C. (2009). Does Unconscious Racial Bias Affect Trial Judges? *Notre Dame Law Review, 84,* 1195–1246.

39. Girvan, E., Deason, G., & Borgida, E. (2015). The generalizability of gender bias: Testing the effects of contextual, explicit, and implicit sexism on labor arbitration decisions. *Law and Human Behavior, 39(5),* 525–537.

40. Correll, J., Park, B., Judd, C., Wittenbrink, B., Sadler, M. S., & Keesee, T. (2007). Across the thin blue line: Police officers and racial bias in the decision to shoot. *Journal of Personality and Social Psychology, 92,* 1006–1023. Plant, E. A., & Peruche, B. M. (2005). The consequences of race for police officers' responses to criminal suspects. *Psychological Science, 16,* 180–183.

41. Green, A. R., Carney, D. R., Pallin, D. J., Ngo, L. H., Raymond, K. L., Iezzoni, L., & Banaji, M. (2007). Implicit bias among physicians and its prediction of thrombolysis decisions for black and white patients. *Journal of General Internal Medicine, 22,* 1231–1238. Onyeador, I., Wittlin, N., Burke, S., Dovidio, J., Perry, S., Hardeman, R., Dyrbye, L., Herrin, J., Phelan, S., & van Ryn, M., (2020). The value of interracial contact for reducing anti-Black bias among non-Black physicians: A cognitive habits and growth evaluation (CHANGE) study report. *Psychological Science, 31(1),* 18–30. Ashford, R.D., Brown, A.M., & Curtis, B. (2019). The language of substance use and recovery: novel use of the Go/No-Go Association Task to measure implicit bias. *Health Communication, 34(11),* 1296–1302. Liang, J., Wolsiefer, K., Zestcott, C., Chase, D., & Stone, J. (2019). Implicit bias toward cervical cancer: Provider and training differences. *Gynecologic Oncology, 153(1),* 80–86. FitzGerald, C. & Hurst, S. (2017). Implicit bias in healthcare professionals: A systematic review. *BMC Medical Ethics, 18(19).* Schwartz, M., Chambliss, H., Brownell, K., Blair, S., & Billington, C. (2003). Weight bias among health professionals specializing in obesity. *Obesity Research, 11(9),* 1033–1039. Tomiyama, A., Finch, L., Belsky, A., Buss, J., Finley, C., Schwartz, M. & Daubenmier, J. (2015). Weight bias in 2001 versus 2013: Contradictory attitudes among obesity researchers and health professionals. *Obesity, 23(1),* 46–53.

42. von Hippel, W, Brener, L., & von Hippel, C. (2008). Implicit prejudice toward injecting drug users predicts intentions to change jobs among drug and alcohol nurses. *Psychological Science, 19,* 7–11.

43. Rooth, D. (2007). *Implicit discrimination in hiring: Real world evidence* (IZA Discussion Paper No. 2764). Bonn, Germany: Forschungsinstitut zur Zukunft der Arbeit (Institute for the Study of Labor). Rudman, L. A., & Glick, P. (2001). Prescriptive gender stereotypes and backlash toward agentic women. *Journal of Social Issues, 57,* 743–762. McDonnall, M.C., Cmar, J.L., Antonelli, K. & Markoski, K.M. (2019). Professionals' implicit attitudes about the competence of people who are blind. *Journal of Visual Impairment and Blindness, 113(4),* 341–354.

44. Rudman, L. A., & Ashmore, R. D. (2007). Discrimination and the Implicit Association Test. *Group Processes and Intergroup Relations, 10,* 359–372.

45. Arcuri, L., Castelli, L., Galdi, S., Zogmaister, C., & Amadori, A. (2008). Predicting the vote: Implicit attitudes as predictors of the future behavior of decided and undecided voters. *Political Psychology, 29,* 369–387.

46. Nock, M. K., & Banaji, M. R. (2007). Prediction of suicide ideation and attempts among adolescents using a brief performance-based test. *Journal of Clinical and Consulting Psychology, 75,* 707–715.

47. Gray, N. S., Brown, A. S., MacCulloch, M. J., Smith, J., & Snowden, R. J. (2005). An implicit test of the associations between children and sex in pedophiles. *Journal of Abnormal Psychology, 114*, 304–308.

48. Palfai, T. P., & Ostafin, B. D. (2003). Alcohol-related motivational tendencies in hazardous drinkers: Assessing implicit response tendencies using the modified-IAT. *Behaviour Research and Therapy, 41*, 1149–1162. Wiers, R. W., Houben, K., & de Kraker, J. (2007). Implicit cocaine associations in active cocaine users and controls. *Addictive Behaviors, 32*, 1284–1289. Wiers, R. W., Van Woerden, N., Smulders, F. T. Y., & De Jong, P. J. (2002). Implicit and explicit alcohol related cognitions in heavy and light drinkers. *Journal of Abnormal Psychology, 111*, 648–658. Thush, C., & Wiers, R. W. (2007). Explicit and implicit alcohol-related cognitions and the prediction of future drinking in adolescents. *Addictive Behaviors, 32*, 1367–1383. Thush, C., Wiers, R. W., Ames, S. L., Grenard, J. L., Sussman, S., & Stacy, A. W. (2007). Apples and oranges? Comparing indirect measures of alcohol-related cognition predicting alcohol use in at-risk adolescents. *Psychology of Addictive Behaviors, 21*, 587–591.

49. Miller, A. (2019). Expertise fails to attenuate gendered biases in judicial decision-making. *Social Psychological and Personality Science, 10(2)*, 227–234.

50. Guthrie, C., Rachlinski, J., & Wistrich, A. (2001). Inside the Judicial Mind. *Cornell Law Review, 86*, 777–830. Guthrie, C., Rachlinski, J., & Wistrich, A. (2007). Blinking on the bench: how judges decide cases. *Cornell Law Review, 93*, 1–44. Guthrie, C., Rachlinski, J., & Wistrich, A. (2009). The "Hidden Judiciary": An Empirical Examination of Executive Branch Justice. *Duke Law Journal, 58*, 1477–1530. Lassiter, G., Diamond, S., Schmidt, H., & Elek, J. (2007). Evaluating videotaped confessions: Expertise provides no defense against the camera-perspective effect. *Psychological Science, 18(3)*, 224–226. Rachlinski, J., Guthrie, C., & Wistrich, A. (2007). Heuristics and Biases in Bankruptcy Judges. *Journal of Institutional and Theoretical Economics, 163*, 167–186. Rachlinski, J., Guthrie, C., & Wistrich, A. (2011). Probable Cause, Probability, and Hindsight. *Journal of Empirical Legal Studies, 8*, 72–98. Rachlinski, J., Wistrich, A., & Guthrie, C. (2015). Can Judges Make Reliable Numeric Judgments? Distorted Damages and Skewed Sentences. *Indiana Law Journal, 90*, 695–739. Robbennolt, J. (2002). Punitive damage decision-making: The decisions of citizens and trial court judges. *Law and Human Behavior, 26*, 315–341. Wistrich, A., Guthrie, C., & Rachlinski, J. (2005). Can Judges Ignore Inadmissible Information? The Difficulty of Deliberately Disregarding. *University of Pennsylvania Law Review, 153*, 1251–1345.

51. Ayres, I. (2001). *Pervasive prejudice? Unconventional evidence of race and gender discrimination.* Chicago: University of Chicago Press. Bertrand, M., & Mullainathan, S. (2004). Are Emily and Greg more employable than Lakisha and Jamal? *American Economic Review, 94*, 991–1013. Pager, D. (2003). The mark of a criminal record. *American Journal of Sociology, 108*, 937–975. Riach, P. A., & Rich, J. (2002). Field experiments of discrimination in the market place. *Economic Journal, 112*, F480–F518.

52. Neuberg, S., & Fiske, S. (1987). Motivational influences on impression formation: Outcome dependency, accuracy-driven attention, and individuating processes. *Journal of Personality and Social Psychology, 53*, 431–444. Tetlock, P. (1983). Accountability and complexity of thought. *Journal of Personality and Social Psychology, 45*, 74–83.

53. Bodenhausen, G., & Wyer, R. (1985). Effects of stereotypes in decision-making and information processing strategies. *Journal of Personality and Social Psychology, 46*, 267–282. Darley, J., & Gross, P. (1983). A hypothesis-confirming bias in labeling effects. *Journal of Personality and Social Psychology, 44*, 20–33.

54. e.g., Word, C., Zanna, M., & Cooper, J. (1973). The nonverbal mediation of self-fulfilling prophecies in interracial interaction. *Journal of Experimental Social Psychology, 10*, 102–120.

55. e.g., Dovidio, J., & Gaertner, S. (2000). Aversive racism and selection decisions: 1989 and 1999. *Psychological Science, 11*, 319–323. Johnson, J. Whitestone, E., Jackson, L, & Gatto, L. (1995). Justice is still not colorblind: Differential racial effects of exposure to inadmissible evidence. *Personality and Social Psychology Bulletin, 21*, 893–898.

56. Eells, T., & Showalter, C. (1994). Work-related stress in American trial judges. *Bulletin of the American Academy of Psychiatry & the Law, 22*, 71–83. Hartley, L., & Adams, R. (1974). Effect of noise on the Stroop test. *Journal of Experimental Psychology, 102*, 62–66. Keinan, G. (1987). Decision-making under stress: Scanning of alternatives under controllable and uncontrollable threats. *Journal of Personality and Social Psychology, 52*, 639–644.

57. E.g., see Bodenhausen, G., & Lichtenstein, M., (1987). Social stereotypes and information-processing strategies: The impact of task complexity. *Journal of Personality and Social Psychology, 52*, 871–880. Gilbert, D., & Hixon, J. (1991). The trouble of thinking: Activation and application of stereotypic beliefs. *Journal of Personality and Social Psychology, 60*, 509–517. Sherman, J., Lee, A., Bessenoff, G., & Frost, L. (1998). Stereotype efficiency reconsidered: Encoding flexibility under cognitive load. *Journal of Personality and Social Psychology, 75*, 589–606. van Knippenberg, A., Dijksterhuis, A., & Vermeulen, D. (1999). Judgment and memory of a criminal act: The effects of stereotypes and cognitive load. *European Journal of Social Psychology, 29*, 191–201.

58. Jones, J. (1972). Prejudice and Racism. New York: McGraw-Hill.

59. Feagin, J. R. 2001. *Racist America: Roots, Current Realities, and Future Reparations.* New York: Routledge.

60. Jones, J. M. (1997). *Prejudice and racism* (2nd ed.). New York, NY: McGraw-Hill.

61. Benokraitis, N. V., & Feagin, J. R. (1995). *Modern sexism: Blatant, subtle, and covert discrimination.* Pearson College Division.

62. Charlton, J. I. (1998). Nothing About Us Without Us: Disability Oppression and Empowerment, Berkeley, CA: University of California Press (p. 51).

63. Schmidt, S.L. (2005). More than men in white sheets: Seven Concepts critical to the teaching of racism as systemic inequality. *Equity and Excellence in Education, 38,* 110–122.

64. Kite, M. & Whitley, B. (2016). *The Psychology of Prejudice and Discrimination* (3rd ed.). New York, NY: Routledge.

65. Wijeyesinghe, C. L., Griffin, P. and Love, B. (1997). Racism curriculum design. In *Teaching for diversity and social justice: A sourcebook* (Eds. Adams, M., Bell, L. A., &Griffin), pp. 82–109. New York: Routledge. Feagin, J. R. 2001. *Racist America: Roots, Current Realities, and Future Reparations.* New York: Routledge. Carmichael, S. [now Ture, K.] & Hamilton, C.V. (1967). Black Power: The Politics of Liberation in America. New York: Vintage Books.

66. Schmidt, S.L. (2005). More than men in white sheets: Seven Concepts critical to the teaching of racism as systemic inequality. *Equity and Excellence in Education, 38,* 110–122.

67. Jones, J. M. (1997). *Prejudice and racism* (2nd ed.). New York, NY: McGraw-Hill.

68. Benokraitis, N. V., & Feagin, J. R. (1995). *Modern sexism: Blatant, subtle, and covert discrimination.* Pearson College Division.

69. Kite, M. & Whitley, B. (2016). *The Psychology of Prejudice and Discrimination* (3rd ed.). New York, NY: Routledge.

70. Kite, M. & Whitley, B. (2016). *The Psychology of Prejudice and Discrimination* (3rd ed.). New York, NY: Routledge.

71. Kite, M. & Whitley, B. (2016). *The Psychology of Prejudice and Discrimination* (3rd ed.). New York, NY: Routledge.

72. Kite, M. & Whitley, B. (2016). *The Psychology of Prejudice and Discrimination* (3rd ed.). New York, NY: Routledge.

73. Kite, M. & Whitley, B. (2016). *The Psychology of Prejudice and Discrimination* (3rd ed.). New York, NY: Routledge.

74. Allport, G. (1954). *The Nature of Prejudice.* Boston: Addison-Wesley.

75. Pettigrew, T. F., & Tropp, L. R. (2006). A meta-analytic test of intergroup contact theory. *Journal of Personality and Social Psychology, 90(5),* 751–783. Pettigrew. T. & Tropp, L. (2005). Allports' intergroup contact hypothesis: Its history and influence. *In* Dovido, J.F., Glick, P., & Rudman, L., (Eds.), *Reflecting on the nature of prejudice: Fifty years after Allport.* Malden, MA: Blackwell (pp. 262–277). Pettigrew, T. F., & Tropp, L. R. (2011). Essays in social psychology. When groups meet: The dynamics of intergroup contact. Psychology Press. Tropp, L. & Prenovost, M. (2008). The role of intergroup contact in predicting children's interethnic attitudes: Evidence from meta-analytic and field studies. *In* Levy, S. & Killen, M. (Eds.), *Intergroup Attitudes and Relations in Childhood Through Adulthood.* New York: Oxford University Press, pp. 236–248.

76. Pettigrew, T. F., & Tropp, L. R. (2006). A meta-analytic test of intergroup contact theory. *Journal of Personality and Social Psychology, 90(5),* 751–783. Research also suggests that the causal relationship flows in both directions: intergroup contact reduces prejudice, and prejudice reduces intergroup contact. Binder, J., Zagefka, H., Brown, R., Funke, F., Kessler, T., Mummendey, A., Maquil, A., Demoulin, S., & Leyens, J.-P. (2009). Does contact reduce prejudice or does prejudice reduce contact? A longitudinal test of the contact hypothesis among majority and minority groups in three European countries. *Journal of Personality and Social Psychology, 96(4),* 843–856. See also Mousa, S. (2020). Building social cohesion between Christians and Muslims through soccer in post-ISIS Iraq. *Science, 369,* 866–870. Paluck, E., Green, S., & Green, D. (2019). The contact hypothesis reevaluated. *Behavioral Public Policy, 3,* 129–158.

77. Pettigrew, T. F., & Tropp, L. R. (2006). A meta-analytic test of intergroup contact theory. *Journal of Personality and Social Psychology, 90(5),* 751–783.

78. Aronson, E. (2000). The jigsaw classroom. Retrieved from: http://www.jigsaw.org/. Aronson, E. & Patnoe, S. (1997). *The Jigsaw Classroom: Building Cooperation in the Classroom.* London: Longman. Kite, M. & Whitley, B. (2016). *The Psychology of Prejudice and Discrimination* (3rd ed.). New York, NY: Routledge.

79. Aronson, E. & Bridgeman, D. (1979). Jigsaw groups and the desegregated classroom: In pursuit of common goals. *Personality and Social Psychology Bulletin, 5(4),* 438–446.

80. Aronson, E. & Bridgeman, D. (1979). Jigsaw groups and the desegregated classroom: In pursuit of common goals. *Personality and Social Psychology Bulletin, 5(4),* 438–446. Aronson, E. (2002). Building empathy, compassion, and achievement in the jigsaw classroom. *In* J. Aronson (Ed.), *Improving academic achievement* (pp. 209–225). New York, NY: Academic Press. Walker, A. & Crogran, M. (1998). Academic performance, prejudice, and the jigsaw classroom: New pieces to the puzzle. *Community and Applied Social Psychology, 8,* 381–393.

81. Aberson, C. L., Porter, M. K., & Gaffney, A. M. (2008). Friendships predict Hispanic student's implicit attitudes toward Whites relative to African Americans. *Hispanic Journal of Behavioral Sciences, 30,* 544–556. Dasgupta, N. & Rivera, L. M. (2008). When social context matters: The influence of long-term contact and short-term exposure to admired group members on implicit attitudes and behavioral intentions. *Social Cognition, 26,* 112–123.

82. Onyeador, I., Wittlin, N., Burke, S., Dovidio, J., Perry, S., Hardeman, R., Dyrbye, L., Herrin, J., Phelan, S., & van Ryn, M., (2020). The value of interracial contact for reducing anti-Black bias among non-Black physicians: A cognitive habits and growth evaluation (CHANGE) study report. *Psychological Science, 31(1),* 18–30.

83. Tam, T., Hewstone, M., Harwood, J., Voci, A., & Kenworthy, J. (2006). Intergroup contact and grandparent-grandchild communication: The effects of self-disclosure on implicit and explicit biases against older people. *Group Processes and Intergroup Relations, 9,* 413–429. Turner, R. N. Hewstone, M., & Voci, A. (2007). Reducing explicit and implicit outgroup prejudice via direct and extended contact: The mediating role of self-disclosure and intergroup anxiety. *Journal of Personality and Social Psychology, 93,* 369–388.

84. Heilman, M. & Haynes, M. (2008). Subjectivity in the appraisal process: A facilitator of gender bias in work settings. *In* E. Borgida & S. Fiske (Eds.), *Beyond Common Sense: Psychological Science in the Courtroom* (pp. 127–155). Oxford: Blackwell Publishing.

85. Heilman, M. & Haynes, M. (2008). Subjectivity in the appraisal process: A facilitator of gender bias in work settings. *In* E. Borgida & S. Fiske (Eds.), *Beyond Common Sense: Psychological Science in the Courtroom* (pp. 127–155). Oxford: Blackwell Publishing. Nieva, V. & Gutek, B. (1980). Sex effects on evaluation. Academy of *Management Review, 5(2),* 267–276.

86. Foschi, M., Lai, L., & Sigerson, S. (1994). Gender and double standards in the assessment of job applicants. *Social Psychology Quarterly, 57,* 326–339. Heilman, M., Wallen, A., Fuchs, D., & Tamkins, M. (2004). Penalties for success: Reactions to women who succeed at male gender-typed tasks. *Journal of Applied Psychology, 89(3),* 416–427. Phelan, J., Moss-Racusin, C., & Rudman, L. (2008). Competent yet out in the cold: Shifting criteria for hiring reflect backlash toward agentic women. *Psychology of Women Quarterly, 32,* 406–413.

87. Bobbitt-Zeher, D. (2011). Gender discrimination at work: Connecting gender stereotypes, institutional policies, and gender composition of workplace. *Gender and Society, 25(6),* 764–786.

88. Biernat, M. (2003). Toward a broader view of social stereotyping. *American Psychologist, 58,* 1019–1027. Biernat, M. (2012). Stereotypes and shifting standards: Forming, communicating, and translating person impressions. In P. Devine & A. Plant (Eds.), Advances in Experimental Social Psychology, vol. 45 (p. 1–59). San Diego: Elsevier. Biernat, M., Crandall, C. S., Young, L. V., Kobrynowicz, D., & Halpin, S. M. (1998). All that you can be: Stereotyping of self and others in a military context. *Journal of Personality and Social Psychology, 75,* 301–317. Biernat, M., Fuegen, K., & Kobrynowicz, D. (2010). Shifting standards and the inference of incompetence: Effects of formal and informal evaluation tools. *Personality and Social Psychology Bulletin, 36(7),* 855–868. Biernat, M, & Manis, M. (1994). Shifting standards and stereotype-based judgments. *Journal of Personality and Social Psychology, 66,* 5–20. Biernat, M., Manis, M., & Nelson, T. E. (1991). Stereotypes and standards of judgment. *Journal of Personality and Social Psychology, 60,* 485–499. Biernat, M., Tocci, M. J., & Williams, J. C. (2011). The language of performance evaluations: Gender-based shifts in content and consistency of judgment. *Social Psychological and Personality Science, 3,* 186–192. Biernat, M. & Vescio, T. K. (2002). She swings, she hits, she's great, she's benched: Implications of gender-based shifting standards for judgment and behavior. *Personality and Social Psychology Bulletin, 28,* 66–77.

89. Biernat, M., Fuegen, K., & Kobrynowicz, D. (2010). Shifting standards and the inference of incompetence: Effects of formal and informal evaluation tools. *Personality and Social Psychology Bulletin, 36(7),* 855–868. Bobbitt-Zeher, D. (2011). Gender discrimination at work: Connecting gender stereotypes, institutional policies, and gender composition of workplace. *Gender and Society, 25(6),* 764–786.

90. Heilman, M. & Haynes, M. (2008). Subjectivity in the appraisal process: A facilitator of gender bias in work settings. *In* E. Borgida & S. Fiske (Eds.), *Beyond Common Sense: Psychological Science in the Courtroom* (pp. 127–155). Oxford: Blackwell Publishing. Heilman,

M. (2012). Gender stereotypes and workplace bias. *Research in Organizational Behavior, 32,* 113–135.

91. *E.g.,* Baltes, B. B., Bauer, C. B., & Frensch, P. A. (2007). Does a structured free recall intervention reduce the effect of stereotypes on performance ratings and by what cognitive mechanism? *Journal of Applied Psychology, 92(1),* 151–164. Bauer, C.C. & Baltes, B.B. (2002). Reducing the effects of gender stereotypes on performance evaluations. *Sex Roles, 47,* 465–476.

92. Olson, M. A., & Fazio, R. H. (2006). Reducing automatically-activated racial prejudice through implicit evaluative conditioning. *Personality and Social Psychology Bulletin, 32,* 421–433.

93. See Kawakami, K. Phills, C. E., Steele, J. R., & Dovidio, J. F. (2007). (Close) distance makes the heart grow fonder: Improving implicit racial attitudes and interracial interactions through approach behaviors. *Journal of Personality and Social Psychology, 92,* 957–971. Wennekers, A. M., Holland, R. W., Wigboldus, D. H. J., & van Knippenberg, A. (2011). First see, the nod: The role of temporal contiguity in embodied evaluative conditioning of social attitudes. *Social Psychological and Personality Science, 3,* 455–461. Kawakami, K., Dovidio, J. F.,Moll, J., Hermsen, S., & Russin, A. (2000). Just say no (to stereotyping): Effects of training in the negation of stereotypic associations on stereotype activation. *Journal of Personality and Social Psychology, 78,* 871–888. Gawronski, B. Deutsch, R., Mbirkou, S., Seibt, B., & Strack, F. (2008). When "just say no" is not enough: Affirmation versus negation training and the reduction of automatic stereotype activation. *Journal of Experimental Social Psychology, 44,* 370–377.

94. E.g., Columb, C. & Plant, A. (2016). The Obama Effect Six Years Later: The Effect of Exposure to Obama on Implicit Anti-Black Evaluative Bias and Implicit Racial Stereotyping. *Social Cognition, 34(6),* 523–543. Murrar, S. & Brauer, M. (2018). Entertainment-education effectively reduces prejudice. *Group Processes and Intergroup Relations, 21(7),* 1053–1077. *But see* Lybarger, J. & Monteith, M. (2011). The effect of Obama saliency on individual-level racial bias: Silver bullet or smokescreen? *Journal of Experimental Social Psychology, 47,* 647–652. Schmidt, K. & Axt, J. (2016). Implicit and Explicit Attitudes Toward African Americans and Barack Obama Did Not Substantively Change During Obama's Presidency. *Social Cognition, 34(6),* 559–588. Schmidt, K. & Nosek, B. (2010). Implicit (and explicit) racial attitudes barely changed during Barack Obama's presidential campaign and early presidency. *Journal of Experimental Social Psychology, 46,* 308–314.

95. Galinsky, A. D., & Moskowitz, G. B. (2000). Perspective-taking: Decreasing stereotype expression, stereotype accessibility, and in-group favoritism. *Journal of Personality and Social Psychology, 78(4),* 708–724. Todd, A. R., Bodenhausen, G. V., Richeson, J. A., & Galinsky, A. D. (2011). Perspective taking combats automatic expressions of racial bias. *Journal of Personality and Social Psychology, 100(6),* 1027–1042. Lai, C. K., Marini, M., Lehr, S. A., Cerruti, C., Shin, J.-E. L., Joy-Gaba, J. A., Ho, A. K., Teachman, B. A., Wojcik, S. P., Koleva, S. P., Frazier, R. S., Heiphetz, L., Chen, E. E., Turner, R. N., Haidt, J., Kesebir, S., Hawkins, C. B., Schaefer, H. S., Rubichi, S.,... Nosek, B. A. (2014). Reducing implicit racial preferences: I. A comparative investigation of 17 interventions. *Journal of Experimental Psychology: General, 143(4),* 1765–1785. Edwards, D.J., McEnteggart, C., Barnes-Holmes, Y., Lowe, R., Evans, N., Vilardaga, R. (2017). The impact of mindfulness and perspective-taking on implicit associations toward the elderly: A relational frame theory account. *Mindfulness, 8,* 1615–1622.

96. Lai, C. K., Marini, M., Lehr, S. A., Cerruti, C., Shin, J.-E. L., Joy-Gaba, J. A., Ho, A. K., Teachman, B. A., Wojcik, S. P., Koleva, S. P., Frazier, R. S., Heiphetz, L., Chen, E. E., Turner, R. N., Haidt, J., Kesebir, S., Hawkins, C. B., Schaefer, H. S., Rubichi, S.,... Nosek, B. A. (2014).

Reducing implicit racial preferences: I. A comparative investigation of 17 interventions. *Journal of Experimental Psychology: General, 143(4),* 1765–1785.

97. FitzGerald, C., Martin, A., Berner, D., & Hurst, S. (2019). Interventions designed to reduce implicit prejudices and implicit stereotypes in real world contexts: a systematic review. *BMC Psychology, 7,* 29. Forscher, P. S., Lai, C. K., Axt, J. R., Ebersole, C. R., Herman, M., Devine, P. G., & Nosek, B. A. (2019). A meta-analysis of procedures to change implicit measures. *Journal of Personality and Social Psychology, 117(3),* 522–559. Lai, C. K., Marini, M., Lehr, S. A., Cerruti, C., Shin, J.-E. L., Joy-Gaba, J. A., Ho, A. K., Teachman, B. A., Wojcik, S. P., Koleva, S. P., Frazier, R. S., Heiphetz, L., Chen, E. E., Turner, R. N., Haidt, J., Kesebir, S., Hawkins, C. B., Schaefer, H. S., Rubichi, S.,... Nosek, B. A. (2014). Reducing implicit racial preferences: I. A comparative investigation of 17 interventions. *Journal of Experimental Psychology: General, 143(4),* 1765–1785. Calanchini, J., Lai, C. K., & Klauer, K. C. (2020). Reducing implicit racial preferences: III. A process-level examination of changes in implicit preferences. *Journal of Personality and Social Psychology.* Advance online publication. https://doi.org/10.1037/pspi0000339

98. Lai, C. K., Skinner, A. L., Cooley, E., Murrar, S., Brauer, M., Devos, T., Calanchini, J., Xiao, Y. J., Pedram, C., Marshburn, C. K., Simon, S., Blanchar, J. C., Joy-Gaba, J. A., Conway, J., Redford, L., Klein, R. A., Roussos, G., Schellhaas, F. M. H., Burns, M.,... Nosek, B. A. (2016). Reducing implicit racial preferences: II. Intervention effectiveness across time. *Journal of Experimental Psychology: General, 145(8),* 1001–1016. Greenwald, A. & Lai, C. (2020). Implicit social cognition. *Annual Review of Psychology, 71,* 419–445. Lai, C., Hoffman, K., & Nosek, B. (2013). Reducing implicit prejudice. *Social and Personality Psychology Compass, 7(5),* 315–330.

99. McNulty, J.K., Olson, M.A., Jones, R.E., & Acosta, L.M. (2017). Automatic associations between one's partner and one's affect as the proximal mechanism of change in relationship satisfaction: Evidence from evaluative conditioning. *Psychological Science, 28(8),* 1031–40 (participants took part in 13 training sessions over 6 weeks). Shook, N.J. & Fazio, R.H. (2008). Interracial roommate relationships: an experimental field test of the contact hypothesis. *Psychological Science, 19(7),* 717–23 (participants lived with a roommate of another race for a full semester). Dasgupta, N. & Asgari, S. (2004). Seeing is believing: Exposure to counterstereotypic women leaders and its effect on the malleability of automatic gender stereotyping. *Journal of Experimental Social Psychology, 40,* 642–658 (participants had ongoing contact with female instructors over the course of an academic year).

100. Forscher, P. S., Lai, C. K., Axt, J. R., Ebersole, C. R., Herman, M., Devine, P. G., & Nosek, B. A. (2019). A meta-analysis of procedures to change implicit measures. *Journal of Personality and Social Psychology, 117(3),* 522–559. Vuletich, H. & Payne, K. (2019). Stability and change in implicit bias. *Psychological Science, 30,* 854–862.

101. Vuletich, H. & Payne, K. (2019). Stability and change in implicit bias. *Psychological Science, 30,* 854–862.

102. Lai, C., Hoffman, K., & Nosek, B. (2013). Reducing implicit prejudice. *Social and Personality Psychology Compass, 7(5),* 315–330. Lai, C. K., Marini, M., Lehr, S. A., Cerruti, C., Shin, J.-E. L., Joy-Gaba, J. A., Ho, A. K., Teachman, B. A., Wojcik, S. P., Koleva, S. P., Frazier, R. S., Heiphetz, L., Chen, E. E., Turner, R. N., Haidt, J., Kesebir, S., Hawkins, C. B., Schaefer, H. S., Rubichi, S.,... Nosek, B. A. (2014). Reducing implicit racial preferences: I. A comparative investigation of 17 interventions. *Journal of Experimental Psychology: General, 143(4),* 1765–1785.

103. E.g., see Goldin, C., & Rouse, C. (2000). Orchestrating impartiality: The impact of "blind" auditions on female musicians. *American Economic Review, 90,* 715–741. Psaty, B., &

Prentice, R. (2010). Minimizing bias in randomized trials: The importance of blinding. *Journal of the American Medical Association, 304,* 793–794. Snodgrass, R. (2006). Single- versus double-blind reviewing: An analysis of the literature. *ACM SIGMOD Record, 35*(3), 8–21.

104. National Research Council. (2014). *Identifying the culprit: Assessing eyewitness identification.* Washington, DC: National Academies Press. See also Dysart, J. E., Lawson, V. Z., & Rainey, A. (2012). Blind lineup administration as a prophylactic against the post-identification feedback effect. *Law and Human Behavior, 36,* 312–319. Garrett, B. L. (2014). Eyewitness identifications and police practices: A Virginia case study. *Virginia Journal of Criminal Law, 2,* 2013–2026. Wells, G. L. (1988). *Eyewitness identification: A system handbook.* Toronto, Ontario, Canada: Carswell Legal.

105. Queally, J. (2019, June 12). *San Francisco D.A. unveils program aimed at removing implicit bias from prosecutions.* Available at https://www.latimes.com/local/lanow/la-me-san-francisco-da-prosecutions-implicit-bias-software-20190612-story.html. Stanford Computational Policy Lab (2021). Blind charging: mitigating bias in charging decisions with automated race redaction. Available at https://policylab.stanford.edu/projects/blind-charging.html. Chohlas-Wood, A., Nudell, J., Yao, K., Lin, Z., Nyarko, J., & Goel, S. (2021). Blind justice: Algorithmically masking race in charging decisions. Association for the Advancement of Artificial Intelligence. See also Sah, S., Robertson, C., & Baughman, S. (2015). Blinding prosecutors to defendants' race: A policy proposal to reduce unconscious bias in the criminal justice system. *Behavioral Science & Policy, 1,* 69–76.

106. Allen, T. J., Sherman, J.W., & Klauer, K. C. (2010). Social context and the self-regulation of implicit bias. *Group Processes and Intergroup Relations, 13,* 137–150. Legault, L., Green-Demers, I., & Eadie, A. L. (2009). When internalization leads to automatization: The role of self-determination in automatic stereotype suppression and implicit prejudice regulation. *Motivation and Emotion, 33,* 10–24. Maddux, W. W., Barden, J., Brewer, M. B., & Petty, R. E. (2005). Saying no to negativity: The effects of context and motivation to control prejudice on automatic evaluative responses. *Journal of Experimental Social Psychology, 41,* 19–35. Moskowitz, G. B., Gollwitzer, P. M., Wasel, W., & Schaal, B. (1999). Preconscious control of stereotype activation through chronic egalitarian goals. *Journal of Personality and Social Psychology, 77,* 167–184. Legault, L., Gutsell, J. N., & Inzlicht, M. (2011). Ironic effects of antiprejudice messages: How motivational interventions can reduce (but also increase) prejudice. *Psychological Science, 22,* 1472–1477.

107. Legault, L., Gutsell, J. N., & Inzlicht, M. (2011). Ironic effects of antiprejudice messages: How motivational interventions can reduce (but also increase) prejudice. *Psychological Science, 22,* 1472–1477.

108. Castelli, L., & Tomelleri, S. (2008). Contextual effects on prejudiced attitudes: When the presence of others leads to more egalitarian responses. *Journal of Experimental Social Psychology, 44,* 679–686. Richeson, J. A., & Ambady, N. (2001). Who's in charge? Effects of situational roles on automatic gender bias. *Sex Roles, 44,* 493–512. Richeson, J. A. & Ambady, N. (2003). Effects of situational power on automatic racial prejudice. *Journal of Experimental Social Psychology, 39,* 177–183. Sechrist, G. B., & Stangor, C. (2001). Perceived consensus influences intergroup behavior and stereotype accessibility. *Journal of Personality and Social Psychology, 80,* 645–654. Sinclair, S., Lowery, B. S., Hardin, C. D., & Colangelo, A. (2005). Social tuning of automatic racial attitudes: The role of affiliative motivation. *Journal of Personality and Social Psychology, 89,* 583–592. Williams, J. (2018). Accountability as debiasing strategy: Testing the effect of racial diversity in employment committees. *Iowa Law Review, 103(4),* 1593–1638.

109. Lowery, B. S., Hardin, C. D., & Sinclair, S. (2001). Social influences on automatic racial prejudice. *Journal of Personality and Social Psychology, 81,* 842–855.

110. Sommers, S. (2006). On Racial Diversity and Group Decision-Making: Identifying Multiple Effects of Racial Composition on Jury Deliberations. *Journal of Personality and Social Psychology, 90(4),* 597–612.

111. Devine, P. G., & Monteith, M. J. (1999). Automaticity and control in stereotyping. In S. Chaiken & Y. Trope (Eds.), Dual-process theories in social psychology (p. 339–360). The Guilford Press. Monteith, M. J., Parker, L. R., & Burns, M. D. (2016). The self-regulation of prejudice. In T. D. Nelson (Ed.), Handbook of prejudice, stereotyping, and discrimination (p. 409–432). Psychology Press.

112. Carnes, M., Devine, P.G., Baier Manwell, L., Byars-Winston, A., Fine, E., Ford, C.E., Forscher, P., Isaac, C., Kaatz, A., Magua, W., Palta, M., & Sheridan, J. (2015). The effect of an intervention to break the gender bias habit for faculty at one institution: A cluster randomized, controlled trial. *Academic Medicine, 90,* 221–230. Devine, P.G., Forscher, P.S., Cox, W.T.L., Kaatz, A., Sheridan, J., & Carnes, M. (2017). A gender bias habit-breaking intervention led to increased hiring of female faculty in STEMM departments. *Journal of Experimental Social Psychology, 73,* 211–215. Forscher, P., Mitamura, C., Dix, E., Cox, W., & Devine, P. (2017). Breaking the prejudice habit: Mechanisms, timecourse, and longevity. *Journal of Experimental Psychology, 72,* 133–146.

113. Monteith, M. J., Parker, L. R., & Burns, M. D. (2016). The self-regulation of prejudice. In T. D. Nelson (Ed.), Handbook of prejudice, stereotyping, and discrimination (p. 409–432). Psychology Press.

114. Mendoza, S. A., Gollwitzer, P. M., & Amodio, D. M. (2010). Reducing the expression of implicit stereotypes: Reflexive control through implementation intentions. *Personality and Social Psychology Bulletin, 36,* 512–523. Stewart, B. D., & Payne, B. K. (2008). Bringing automatic stereotyping under control: Implementation intentions as efficient means of thought control. *Personality and Social Psychology Bulletin, 34,* 1332–1345. Webb, T. L., Sheeran, P., & Pepper, J. (2012). Gaining control over responses to implicit attitude tests: Implementation intentions engender fast responses on attitude-incongruent trials. *British Journal of Social Psychology, 51,* 13–32. Rees, H., Rivers, A., Sherman, J. (2019). Implementation intentions reduce implicit stereotype activation and application. *Personality and Social Psychology Bulletin, 45(1),* 37–53.

115. Monteith, M. J., Parker, L. R., & Burns, M. D. (2016). The self-regulation of prejudice. In T. D. Nelson (Ed.), Handbook of prejudice, stereotyping, and discrimination (p. 409–432). Psychology Press.

116. Aarts, H., Dijksterhuis, A., & Midden, C. (1999). To plan or not to plan? Goal achievement or interrupting the performance of mundane behaviors. *European Journal of Social Psychology, 29,* 971–979.

117. Bayer, U. C., Achtziger, A., Gollwitzer, P. M., & Moskowitz, G. (2009). Responding to subliminal cues: Do if–then plans facilitate action preparation and initiation without conscious intent? *Social Cognition, 27,* 183–201. Gollwitzer, P. M., & Brandstätter, v. (1997). Implementation intentions and effective goal pursuit. *Journal of Personality and Social Psychology, 73,* 186–199. Martijn, C., Alberts, H., Sheeran, P., Peters, G. Y., Mikolajczak, J., & de vries, N. K. (2008). Blocked goals, persistent action: Implementation intentions engender tenacious goal striving. *Journal of Experimental Social Psychology, 44,* 1137–1143.

118. Achtziger, A., Gollwitzer, P. M., & Sheeran, P. (2008). Implementation intentions and shielding goal striving from unwanted thoughts and feelings. *Personality and Social Psychology Bulletin, 34,* 381–393.

119. Calanchini, J., Lai, C. K., & Klauer, K. C. (2020). Reducing implicit racial preferences: III. A process-level examination of changes in implicit preferences. *Journal of Personality and Social Psychology.* Advance online publication. https://doi.org/10.1037/pspi0000339. Lai, C. K., Marini, M., Lehr, S. A., Cerruti, C., Shin, J.-E. L., Joy-Gaba, J. A., Ho, A. K., Teachman, B. A., Wojcik, S. P., Koleva, S. P., Frazier, R. S., Heiphetz, L., Chen, E. E., Turner, R. N., Haidt, J., Kesebir, S., Hawkins, C. B., Schaefer, H. S., Rubichi, S.,... Nosek, B. A. (2014). Reducing implicit racial preferences: I. A comparative investigation of 17 interventions. *Journal of Experimental Psychology: General, 143(4),* 1765–1785.

120. Trevino, L., den Nieuwenboer, N., & Kish-Gephart, J. (2014). (Un)ethical behavior in organizations. *Annual Review of Psychology, 65,* 635–660.

121. Pettigrew, T. F., & Tropp, L. R. (2006). A meta-analytic test of intergroup contact theory. *Journal of Personality and Social Psychology, 90(5),* 751–783.

122. National Center for State Courts, *State court statements on racial justice.* Available at: https://www.ncsc.org/newsroom/state-court-statements-on-racial-justice.

123. For information about recent activities, see https://www.ncsc.org/information-and-resources/racial-justice/principles-and-policy

124. See the National Consortium on Racial and Ethnic Fairness in the Courts' website at https://www.national-consortium.org/state-efforts and the National Center for State Courts website at https://www.ncsc.org/information-and-resources/racial-justice.

125. See https://www.ncsc.org/information-and-resources/racial-justice

126. Roberson, Q. (2006). Disentangling the Meanings of Diversity and Inclusion in Organizations. *Group and Organization Management, 31,* 212–236.

127. Roberson, Q. (2006). Disentangling the Meanings of Diversity and Inclusion in Organizations. *Group and Organization Management, 31,* 212–236.

128. Espinoza, O. (2007). Solving the equity–equality conceptual dilemma: a new model for analysis of the educational process. *Educational Research, 49,* 343–36. Morgan, W. & Sawyer, J. (1967). Bargaining, expectations, and the preference for equality over equity. *Journal of Personality and Social Psychology, 6,* 139–149.

129. Shriver Center on Poverty Law, https://www.povertylaw.org/

130. Cook, K. & Hegtvedt, K. (1983). Distributive justice, equity, and equality. *Annual Review of Sociology, 9,* 217–241. Espinoza, O. (2007). Solving the equity–equality conceptual dilemma: a new model for analysis of the educational process. *Educational Research, 49,* 343–36. Morgan, W. & Sawyer, J. (1967). Bargaining, expectations, and the preference for equality over equity. *Journal of Personality and Social Psychology, 6,* 139–149.

131. *E.g.,* National Center for State Courts, *State court statements on racial justice*, available at: https://www.ncsc.org/newsroom/state-court-statements-on-racial-justice. JustLead Washington, *Washington Race Equity & Justice Initiative Organizational Race Equity Toolkit*, https://justleadwa.org/learn/rejitoolkit/.

132. Onyeador, I., Hudson, S., & Lewis, N. (2021). Moving beyond implicit bias training: policy insights for increasing organizational diversity. *Policy Insights from the Behavioral and Brain Sciences, 8,* 19–26.

133. Dobbin, F., & Kalev, A. (2016). Why diversity programs fail—and what works better. *Harvard Business Review, 94,* 7. Available at https://hbr.org/2016/07/why-diversity-programs-fail. Greenwald, A. & Lai, C. (2020). Implicit social cognition. *Annual Review of Psychology, 71,* 419–445. Onyeador, I., Wittlin, N., Burke, S., Dovidio, J., Perry, S., Hardeman, R., Dyrbye, L., Herrin, J., Phelan, S., & van Ryn, M., (2020). The value of interracial contact for

reducing anti-Black bias among non-Black physicians: A cognitive habits and growth evaluation (CHANGE) study report. *Psychological Science, 31(1),* 18–30.

134. Dobbin, F., & Kalev, A. (2016). Why diversity programs fail—and what works better. *Harvard Business Review, 94,* 7. Available at https://hbr.org/2016/07/why-diversity-programs-fail. Carter, E., Onyeador, I., & Lewis, N. (2020). Developing & delivering effective anti-bias training: Challenges & recommendations. *Behavioral Science & Policy, 6,* 57–70.

135. Carter, E., Onyeador, I., & Lewis, N. (2020). Developing & delivering effective anti-bias training: Challenges & recommendations. *Behavioral Science & Policy, 6,* 57–70.

136. E.g., Carnes, M., Devine, P. G., Manwell, L. B., Byars-Winston, A., Fine, E., Ford, C. E., . . . & Palta, M. (2015). Effect of an intervention to break the gender bias habit for faculty at one institution: a cluster randomized, controlled trial. *Academic Medicine: Journal of the Association of American Medical Colleges, 90*(2), 221. Devine, P. G., Forscher, P. S., Austin, A. J., & Cox, W. T. (2012). Long-term reduction in implicit race bias: A prejudice habit-breaking intervention. *Journal of Experimental Social Psychology, 48*(6), 1267–1278. Devine, P., Forscher, P., Cox, W., Kaatz, A., Sheridan, J., & Carnes, M. (2017). A gender bias habit-breaking intervention led to increased hiring of female faculty in STEMM departments. *Journal of Experimental Social Psychology, 73,* 211–215. Forscher, P. S., Mitamura, C., Dix, E. L., Cox, W. T., & Devine, P. G. (2017). Breaking the prejudice habit: Mechanisms, timecourse, and longevity. *Journal of experimental social psychology, 72,* 133–146. Moss-Racusin, Pietri, E., Hennes, E., Dovidio, J., Brescoll, V., Roussos, G., & Handelsman, J. (2018). Reducing STEM gender bias with VIDS (video interventions for diversity in STEM). *Journal of Experimental Psychology: Applied, 24,* 236–260.

137. E.g., see Livingston, R. (2020). *How to promote racial equity in the workplace: a five-step plan.* Harvard Business Review. Available at https://hbr.org/2020/09/how-to-promote-racial-equity-in-the-workplace.

138. National Center for State Courts (2021, February 8). *Court Statistics Project data governance special topic: Collecting race & ethnicity data.* Available at https://www.ncsc.org/__data/assets/pdf_file/0016/60343/Race_special_topic_v2.pdf.

139. E.g., Bishop, E., Hopkins, B., Obiofuma, C., & Owusu, F. (2020). *Racial disparities in the Massachusetts criminal system.* Available at https://hls.harvard.edu/content/uploads/2020/11/Massachusetts-Racial-Disparity-Report-FINAL.pdf-:~:text=Racial%20Disparities%20in%20the%20Massachusetts%20Criminal%20System%20.,Hopkins%2C%20Chijindu%20Obiofuma%2C%20Felix%20Owusu%20.%20September%202020.

140. Equal Justice in the Courts Task Force (2020, October 1). *Report from the Special Adviser on Equal Justice in the New York State Courts.* Available at http://www.nycourts.gov/whatsnew/pdf/SpecialAdviserEqualJusticeReport.pdf.

141. Gaddis, S. M. (2021, March 23). Invited panelist on the prevalence and pervasiveness of implicit bias. *National Academy of Sciences Virtual Workshop on the Science of Implicit Bias: Implications for Law and Policy.* See https://www.nationalacademies.org/event/01-12-2021/the-science-of-implicit-bias-implications-for-law-and-policy-a-workshop. Gaddis, S.M. (2018). *Audit studies: Behind the scenes with theory, method, and nuance.* Cham, Switzerland: Springer International.

142. E.g., see van Knippenberg, D., Nishii, L., & Dwertmann, D. (2020). Synergy from diversity: Managing team diversity to enhance performance. *Behavioral Science & Policy, 6,* 75–92.

143. For more information about the types of engagement and the characteristics of effective community engagement activities, see Advancing Pretrial Policy and Research (2020). *Strengthening and sustaining public engagement.* Available at https://cdn.filestackcontent.com/security=policy:eyJleHBpcnkiOjQwODAxNDY0MDAsImNhbGwiOlsicmVhZCIsImNvbnZlcnQiXX0=,signature:bf9d04ed62530c164d6fed395e4f74c04e606b95f4b72448ff976857a1e3a5f5/NO0eDBcfQKB66K4pnC0t. See also the National Center for State Courts' Community Engagement and the State Courts Initiative at https://www.ncsc.org/information-and-resources/racial-justice/community-engagement-initiative.

144. An implementation intention is an "if-then" statement that lays out contingencies between a situation and a response (e.g., "If situation X is encountered, then I will initiate egalitarian response Y"). Researchers have found that participants who commit to an implementation intention in advance (for example, a plan to think "good" after seeing a Black face) are more likely to be able to override their automatic responses in favor of a more egalitarian response. Reasons why this strategy is effective include that it increases the individual's commitment to the response, makes the response more accessible in the individual's mind, makes the response more automatic and less effortful, and helps shield the individual from the intrusion of unwanted thoughts. Mendoza, S. A., Gollwitzer, P. M., & Amodio, D. M. (2010). Reducing the expression of implicit stereotypes: Reflexive control through implementation intentions. *Personality and Social Psychology Bulletin, 36,* 512–523. Monteith, M. J., Parker, L. R., & Burns, M. D. (2016). The self-regulation of prejudice. In T. D. Nelson (Ed.), Handbook of prejudice, stereotyping, and discrimination (p. 409–432). Psychology Press.

145. Barrett, L. F. (2017). *How emotions are made: the secret life of the brain* at 248–9. Boston: Houghton Mifflin Harcourt.

146. Robinson, R. (2020, June 9). Current events letter. Available at https://jud.ct.gov/Homepdfs/Currenteventsletter.pdf.

147. Biden, J. (2021, January 20). *Executive order on advancing racial equity and support for underserved communities through the federal government.* Available at https://www.whitehouse.gov/briefing-room/presidential-actions/2021/01/20/executive-order-advancing-racial-equity-and-support-for-underserved-communities-through-the-federal-government/.

THREE

An Essay: Understanding the Threat of Right-Wing Extremism

Dr. Peter Simi, Chapman University

A Note from the Editors: Over the time we were working on this book, the reality of explicit bias and beyond dominated the news. We are committed to the idea that people of good faith may reach biased decisions without their awareness (implicit or unintentional bias) and recognize that those decision-makers want to interrupt that bias to achieve a more just and equitable society. Most of this book is written about and for them. But we cannot ignore the reality that others have no such interest or intention. We invited Professor Simi, a leading expert in the social psychology of extremist groups, to write for us about white supremacism in its various guises. His essay is a clear call for us to not fall into stereotypes, but to be vigilant and clear in paying attention to this threat—battling hate by studying hate.[1]

CHAPTER HIGHLIGHTS

- The way we categorize and label extremist groups impedes our ability to understand them and to respond effectively.
- White supremacist extremism is not a membership-based movement. While organizations are important, what we are really dealing with is a broad world view focused on ideas and emotions.
- White supremacist violence is the only form of terrorism in our country's history that has been state-sanctioned. This problem has existed for too long unnamed, unacknowledged, and without systematic efforts in place to combat it.

CHAPTER CONTENTS

1. Background
2. We've got the names wrong and that impedes our understanding and response.
3. We believe their labels, which are not the reality.
4. January 6th: The "new" problem that isn't so new.
5. Combatting Misconceptions and Misperceptions

1. Background

The 2008 presidential election of Barack Obama, our country's first Black president, will forever be a milestone in the movement toward a multicultural democracy consistent with the ideals enshrined in the Declaration of Independence, ideals that for too long we have failed to attain. The potential for change represented by that election helped catalyze what history professor Carol Anderson refers to as "white rage," a backlash with historical precedent dating back to at least the Reconstruction Era following the U.S. Civil War.[2] In the days following Obama's election, for those who were monitoring the issue, it was a bleak time in terms of a looming threat of white supremacist terror. Anti-immigrant and anti-Muslim fervor had been building and a new movement, "Birtherism," emerged challenging the citizenship and, thus, the legitimacy of Obama's presidency. Gun sales spiked as conspiratorial rumors about "Obama coming for our guns" spread across the country. Within this context of fear and paranoia, a second wave of the militia movement emerged that remains present on the current landscape. In 2009, the Department of Homeland Security issued a brief report that warned about a resurgence of far-right extremism on the horizon, but the agency quickly retracted the report after critics blasted it for profiling conservatives and veterans.[3] The opportunity for a sustained discussion about white supremacist terrorism was lost and attention diverted to other issues.

It is hard to imagine that just a few years ago, the threat of white supremacist terrorism generated little more than blank stares (especially from White Americans). In the aftermath of Charlottesville, Pittsburgh, El Paso and too many other sites of white supremacist terror attacks—along with the January 6th insurrection— many of those blank stares have been replaced with nods of understanding. Too be sure, a sizeable portion of the country remains entrenched in either denial or sympathy toward white supremacist terror. But the sea change is undeniable in the public discourse, including the recent acknowledgements by the Federal Bureau of Investigation and Department of Homeland Security that white supremacist extremism represents the top national security threat in the United States.

The essay below provides an effort to understand different facets of white supremacist terror including our general failure to acknowledge the seriousness of this particular threat.

2. We've got the names wrong and that impedes our understanding and response.

Part of the confusion related to right-wing extremism is our penchant for a dizzying array of labels, false distinctions, and false equivalencies. For the purpose of this essay, I refer to right-wing extremism as a broad constellation of individuals, informal groups, and formal organizations that hold some combination of the following beliefs: ultranationalism and racism (including xenophobic and anti-immigrant attitudes); misogyny and homophobia; and anti-government views (primarily focused on anti-federal government although some elements reject all forms of government). Observers often describe three types of right-wing extremists: white supremacist extremists; anti-government/militia extremists; and single-issue extremists (anti-immigrant, anti-gay etc.). The federal government recently adopted a categorization system that delineates between racially-motivated and anti-government extremists, where the former includes both white supremacists and "Black Nationalists," and the latter includes both militia groups and left-wing anarchist type groups. (The fact that white supremacists and Black Nationalists have virtually nothing in common is apparently lost on the federal government.) While helpful, in some respects these categories and buckets oversimplify a reality that is far more convoluted where substantial overlap exists among these types.

3. We believe their labels, which are not the reality.

Another mistake is our tendency to accept the self-definitions offered by right-wing extremists when instead we should see them as part of a front stage marketing effort rather than an accurate description. If they were to be believed, there really are no white supremacists. For example, many groups like the Oath Keepers claim a "race neutral" ideology. This is a disavowal strategy that is common across right-wing extremist groups, including those most observers would widely recognize as white supremacist (e.g., KKK factions). A similar example is the way representatives of the militia movement's second wave claimed they were responding to federal overreach during Obama's administration; but it is curious that the second wave did not emerge during the George W. Bush administration following the passage of the 2001 Patriot Act, which some observers have described as one of the greatest threats to civil liberties in recent history.[4]

Regardless of their self-ascribed labels, groups like the Oath Keepers and Three Percenters, in my experience, have a range of beliefs consistent with those found among groups more commonly defined as white supremacist.[5] There is also cross-fertilization among individuals associated with militia and white supremacist groups with some individuals going back and forth and other individuals simultaneously affiliated with both types of groups. The high degree of overlap can render clear delineations artificial and misleading.

To be clear, the idea that militias are race neutral is an illusion. Militias routinely oppose immigration and, in some cases, conduct armed patrols at the southern U.S. border. Rarely have militia groups sent armed patrols to the northern border to monitor the flood of "illegals" from Canada. Militias also generally oppose Muslims as an existential threat to western civilization and more specifically (although inaccurate) as the primary source of terrorism. Militias' selective opposition to immigration and rejection of Muslims can only be described as xenophobic and racist. In other cases, militias often hold views about the "New World Order" that quickly bleed into old tropes regarding the "International Jew." Their views on citizenship suggest "natural or sovereign citizenship" only applies to those who gained full rights prior to the 14th Amendment—a not so thinly veiled credo that would deny Blacks equal protection under the law.

4. January 6th: The "new" problem that isn't so new.

On January 6th, 2021, tens of thousands of Trump supporters gathered in Washington, DC to protest the November presidential election where Joe Biden defeated Donald Trump. The Trump supporters described a "stolen election." Former Homeland Security cybersecurity chief, Christopher Krebs described it as the most secure election in U.S. history.[6] The Capitol insurrection represented a broad constellation of far-right extremists. The January 6th mob included hardcore white supremacists, with well-known public figures who were live streaming the events; assorted individuals with the Confederate flag; a "Camp Auschwitz" t-shirt; a noose hung outside the Capitol as part of a staged gallows to execute known "traitors"; and a substantial presence of the anti-Semitic Qanon movement. And, of course, there were large numbers of generic "MAGA" supporters, some of whom are now, more than ever before, associated with the most extreme strands of the far-right. In fact, as we speak, the radicalization of MAGA supporters is being hailed on various neo-Nazi Telegram channels. (Telegram is a semi-encrypted communication platform that has become popular among white supremacists in recent years.)

We should not see January 6th as either new or an aberration. When people say, "as Americans, we don't do this," I appreciate the sentiment, but the sentiment is wrong. As Americans, we *do* do this, and we have a long history of doing this. Pretending otherwise does not help address the problem. Violent far-right extremism (like we saw at the Capitol) has been allowed to fester for decades as these networks built a massive infrastructure in online and offline spaces where highly emotive propaganda is created and widely shared. For too long, the United States has denied and minimized this problem.

On April 19, 1995, 168 Americans lost their lives when a fertilizer bomb demolished the Murrah Federal Building in Oklahoma City, OK. The three individuals convicted in connection with the attack were all military veterans and, the primary culprit, Timothy McVeigh, was deeply inspired by neo-Nazi leader William Pierce's novel *The Turner Diaries*. Just over a year later, another military veteran and far-right terrorist, Eric Rudolph, targeted the 1996 Summer Olympics in Atlanta, GA, killing two and injuring over 100. Prior to his arrest, Rudolph executed three other bombings targeting two healthcare clinics where abortions were performed and a gay nightclub. Based on our research, McVeigh's and Rudolph's military background was not uncommon among domestic right-wing terrorists operating at that time. My colleagues and I found that among the far-right extremists arrested on federal terrorism-related charges during the 1980s and 1990s, approximately one-third had military experience.[7]

Dozens of other terror plots, both those that were foiled and those that were executed, followed the Olympic Park bombing over the next several years. During this time there were multiple federal indictments involving militia groups many of which expressed various hallmarks of white supremacy. In 1998, long before ISIS made news for their beheadings, James Byrd Jr., an African American was beheaded by white supremacists in Jasper, TX. A year later, 1999 became known as "the summer of hate" where multiple white supremacist shooting rampages terrorized communities across the country. During this time, our most lethal "school shooting" also occurred. Often mislabeled and disconnected from domestic terrorism, Columbine's primary planner, Eric Harris, was obsessed with Adolf Hitler and Timothy McVeigh and designed Columbine to be a bombing attack followed by sniper shots aimed at those who managed to survive the explosives. Harris's goal was to achieve a larger body count than McVeigh.[8] What is most shocking and saddening, however, is that even with this high level of targeted violence in what was clearly a wave of terrorism, many Americans failed to connect the dots. Had the perpetrators been people of color or Muslim, you can be sure the response would have been dramatically different. Instead, America remained comfortable with its concerted or intentional ignorance about the longstanding threat from terrorists inside our own borders.

The 1990s terror wave was preceded by another terror wave during the 1980s when underground paramilitary cells like the Silent Brotherhood, armed encampments with military grade weapons like the Covenant, the Sword, and the Arm of the Lord, and roving racist skinhead gangs attacked and murdered people across the country. The 1980s followed decades of KKK and other white supremacist inspired violence that included church bombings, political assassinations, and lynchings. This may sound like "ancient history" to some, but, as Attorney General Merrick Garland stated in his confirmation hearing, there is a straight line that connects the founding of the Ku Klux Klan during the Reconstruction Era to the 1995 Oklahoma City bombing to what happened in our nation's capital on January 6th, 2021.[9] This straight line, if nothing else, tells us this problem is anything but new.

5. Combatting Misconceptions and Misperceptions

Some people looked at the images of January 6th and commented, "they don't look like extremists or terrorists." That, of course, begs the question, "what do extremists or terrorists look like?" The answer is obvious: extremism and terrorism are not about what you look like; extremism and terrorism are about a person's beliefs, feelings, and actions. If you think, feel, and act like an extremist then you are an extremist, and it should not matter whether you look like someone's "next door neighbor" or co-worker. When extremists and even terrorists wrap themselves in the U.S. flag and/or hold positions within law enforcement and the military, that does not make them any less of an extremist or terrorist.

I do not want to oversimplify because there are some complicated issues here in terms of defining extremism and terrorism, but as we struggle with those issues, we should be cognizant of our perceptual biases that may lead to highly distorted interpretations regarding what extremism and terrorism look like. We typically imagine white supremacists in terms of hooded Klansmen or shaved headed neo-Nazi skinheads. Such people exist but do not represent the entire spectrum of the problem. More often, white supremacy is practiced by ordinary looking White Americans (and oddly enough not always White). Sometimes they wear black robes and carry gavels; sometimes they hold Ph.D. degrees and teach our young people; and, yes, sometimes they wear blue uniforms with silver badges and are granted the authority to take another's life when they deem such force is necessary.

There is a longstanding tendency to gauge a problem like white supremacy by focusing on how many groups and members exist across the country. Those numbers are important but can be very misleading. White supremacist extremism is not a membership-based movement and while organizations are important, what we are really dealing with is a broad worldview focused on ideas and emotions. The worldview spreads by shaping and promoting narratives about race, religion, gender and the like to ensure American society remains polarized. The goal is an America divided by race and politics where white domination is framed as necessary to avoid social collapse which will inevitably result in untold "white victimization." And this goal is furthered every time a racist joke is told, a hateful meme is reposted, and, of course, every time a law enforcement officer misuses their authority, lethal or otherwise in a racist manner. In these ways and others, white supremacy wins.

If white supremacy is a virus, it is not a foreign agent attacking us from abroad. This is a virus of our own making. It is institutionalized, embedded in our culture, and etched so very deeply in our collective psyche that we are often unaware of our own collaboration with this system. And white supremacist violence is the only form of terrorism in our country's history that has been state-sanctioned. This problem has existed for too long unnamed, unacknowledged, and without systematic efforts in place to combat it. That time should end.

So, You'd Like to Know More

- Pete Simi, Kathleen Blee, Matthew DeMichele & Steven Windisch, Addicted to Hate: Identity Residual among Former White Supremacists, 82 Am. Sociological Rev. 1167 (2017).
- Pete Simi & Robert Futrell, American Swastika: Inside the White Power Movement's Hidden Spaces of Hate (2nd ed. 2015).
- Carol Anderson, White Rage: The Unspoken Truth of Our Racial Divide (2016).
- Kathleen M. Blee, Inside Organized Racism: Women in the Hate Movement (2002).
- Seyward Darby, Sisters in Hate: American Women on the Frontlines of White Nationalism (2020).
- Elizabeth Hinton. America on Fire: The Untold History of Police Violence and Black Rebellion Since the 1960s (2021).
- David Cunningham, Klansville, U.S.A.: The Rise and Fall of the Civil Rights-Era Ku Klux Klan (2012).

About the Author

Pete Simi is an Associate Professor in the Department of Sociology at Chapman University. He has studied extremist groups and violence for more than 20 years, conducting interviews and observations with a range of violent gangs and political extremists. Dr. Simi is a member of the NCITE at the University of Nebraska, Omaha, which is the newest university-based research center funded by the Department of Homeland Security committed to the scientific study of the causes and consequences of terrorism in the United States and around the world. Simi is also co-author of an award-winning book manuscript, *American Swastika: Inside the White Power Movement's Hidden Spaces of Hate,* and frequently serves as an expert legal consultant on criminal cases related to political extremism. Professor Simi earned his B.A. from Washington State University and his Masters and Ph.D. from the University of Nevada at Las Vegas.

Endnotes

1. *Battling Hate by Studying Hate*, Chapman University, February 26, 2020, https://blogs.chapman.edu/wilkinson/2020/02/26/11933/; *see also* Stephanie House, *NPR's 'Here and Now' Interviews Chapman Professor Pete Simi on His Research Into Racist Hate*, Chapman University Newsroom (Aug. 20, 2019), https://news.chapman.edu/2019/08/20/nprs-here-and-now-interviews-chapman-professor-pete-simi-on-his-research-into-racist-hate/.

2. Carol Anderson, White Rage: The Unspoken Truth of Our Racial Divide (2016).

3. Daryl Johnson, Right-Wing Resurgence: How a Domestic Terror Threat is Being Ignored (2012).

4. *See* Timothy Lynch, *Threats to Civil Liberties*, CATO Institute (2004).

5. *See, e.g.,* Shane Bauer, *I Went Undercover With a Border Militia. Here's What I Saw.* Mother Jones (2016), https://www.motherjones.com/politics/2016/10/undercover-border-militia-immigration-bauer/.

6. *See* Zack Budryk, *Krebs Doubles Down After Threat: '2020 Election Was Most Secure in US History',* The Hill (Dec. 2, 2020).

7. Pete Simi, Bryan Bubolz & Ann Hardman, *Military Experience, Identity Discrepancies, and Far Right Terrorism: An Exploratory Analysis*, 36 Studies of Conflict & Terrorism 654 (2013).

8. *See* Dave Cullen, Columbine (2009).

9. *See* Merrick Garland Confirmation Hearing, Senate Judiciary Hearing, February 22–23, 2021; Jake Lahut, *Domestic Terrorism Is 'More Dangerous' Post-Jan. 6, Biden AG Pick Says*, Insider (Feb 22, 2021), https://www.businessinsider.com/domestic-terror-more-dangerous-after-jan-6-merrick-garland-says-2021-2.

FOUR

Implicit/Unconscious Bias in the Courtroom

The Honorable Mark W. Bennett (Ret.)

A Note from the Editors: Our colleague Judge Bennett was an author for the first *Enhancing Justice* book, and we are grateful that he has joined us again here. Judge Bennett's work in this area is deep and expansive; it is highly-respected by us and by the entire community of learners and teachers who try to apply and extend his wisdom. His groundbreaking research and thinking, together with the honesty with which he writes and discusses these topics, has influenced a generation of scholars and jurists. We recognize and applaud Judge Bennett's real ability to bring about social change; his impact is enduring. Here, he continues and expands on his work on the threat that implicit biases pose to the viability of our judicial system. This remains a vital and timely topic.

CHAPTER HIGHLIGHTS[1]

- Implicit bias threatens the viability of our judicial system.
- Courts have been reluctant to admit expert testimony about implicit bias.
- In light of *Batson*'s failure to secure diverse juries, courts and legislatures are initiating their own improvements.
- Implicit bias education and instructions for jurors are increasingly common.

CHAPTER CONTENTS

Introduction

1. The Admissibility of Expert Witnesses Testimony about Implicit/Unconscious Bias
2. *Batson* Challenges and Implicit/Unconscious Bias
3. Implicit Bias Jury Instructions and Implicit Bias Venire Videos

Conclusion

Introduction

"Implicit biases threaten the very foundation of our criminal justice system."[2] So wrote my friend and nationally recognized judicial expert on implicit bias, United States Court of Appeals Sixth Circuit Judge, Bernice Bouie Donald. She was writing in a federal criminal case, and I know first-hand she would agree with me that the same statement is true of our civil justice system. I have selected three areas of implicit bias in the courts to discuss. The first is the propriety of admitting expert witness testimony on implicit bias in jury trials. The second issue is the increasing recognition that U. S. Supreme Court's 1986 decision in *Batson*[3] has utterly failed to achieve its goal of eliminating explicit bias in the use of preemptory challenges and has failed altogether to address implicit bias in jury selection. I include some suggestions for reform of *Batson*. The third issue examines what courts are doing about instructions on implicit bias. Here, I include juror information as well as examining the Western District of Washington's cutting-edge implicit bias juror training venire video. This third issue is near and dear to my heart because I was the first trial judge in the nation to develop and use an implicit bias jury instruction.[4]

1. The Admissibility of Expert Witnesses Testimony about Implicit/Unconscious Bias

The increasing use of expert witnesses on implicit bias reveals no clear consensus on their admissibility.[5] A recent law review article, exceptionally critical of admitting implicit bias expert testimony, noted that as a result of emerging experts on both sides of the implicit bias movement "[a] cottage industry was born."[6] Other articles are more supportive and suggest a path for admitting implicit bias expert testimony in employment discrimination litigation.[7] However, the research for this article, as indicated below, does indicate the recent trend is to not allow expert testimony on implicit bias, even though the opinions doing so are often not well-reasoned and perhaps demonstrate an implicit bias against implicit bias.

In *Samaha v. Washington State Dep't of Transp.*, an early case denying defendant's motion to exclude the implicit bias expert testimony of Dr. Anthony G. Greenwald, one of the three inventors of the Implicit Association Test (IAT), the federal judge, applying the gatekeeper function of *Daubert*,[8] rejected the defense position that his testimony was "neither relevant nor helpful to the jury because the testimony does not explain how specific conduct is consistent with any bias or stereotyping based on any identified stereotype."[9] The judge also rejected the defense argument "that Dr. Greenwald neither applies the principles of implicit bias to the case nor opines to any degree whether implicit bias played any role in any employment decision made by the Defendants."[10] Mr. Samaha, "on the other hand, argues that Dr. Greenwald's testimony is relevant and helpful to the jury because it will provide a framework for the jury to understand the presence of implicit bias in the employment setting in addition to counteracting the jury's own potential bias."[11] The judge, citing *Price Waterhouse*,[12] held that: "Testimony that educates a jury on the concepts of implicit bias and stereotypes is relevant to the issue of whether an employer intentionally discriminated against an employee."[13]

In *Maciel v. Thomas J. Hastings Properties, Inc.*, a housing discrimination case, the court ruled that plaintiff's expert on implicit bias may "testify regarding the housing market and about explicit and implicit bias in general, but may not testify regarding explicit or implicit bias in this case or the appropriateness of fair housing training, or lack thereof, in this case."[14]

In *Salami v. Von Maur, Inc.*, an Iowa state trial court judge admitted the testimony of Salami's implicit bias and social framework analysis expert, Dr. Phillip Goff, in an employment discrimination case, over the objection of the defense.[15] In resisting the motion to exclude Dr. Goff's testimony, the plaintiff argued:

> Dr. Goff's conclusions are based on a simple examination of the factors that have long been known to make it more likely for implicit bias to occur and those that make it less likely that implicit bias will occur. It should be noted that the focus of Dr. Goff's proposed testimony is not whether Plaintiff herself was discriminated against. Social science has no way of knowing that. What scientists do know, based on decades of peer-reviewed research, is what factors in an organization and in a decision-making process tend to make it more likely that discrimination will occur. These are essentially "risk factors." Although this knowledge is not within the common experience of most jurors, it is knowledge that responsible employers should have.[16]

The Iowa Court of Appeals noted that:

At trial, Goff testified regarding a "social framework analysis" of racial discrimination. He discussed six elements that he asserted provide a context for understanding ways in which racial bias may have influenced the decisionmaking related to the discipline and termination of Salami, one of which was aversive racism or implicit bias. To the question, "If you were to create a study and in one condition you wanted to kind of stack the deck, facilitate bias in that situation, would it include the six elements we talked about today?", Goff responded, "Absolutely." On cross-examination, Goff testified he "wasn't tasked with figuring out whether or not Sara Whitlock fits a caricature of a bigot. I was tasked with figuring out whether or not the kind of situations that we tend to study as social psychologists were present or absent in this particular case."[17]

The Iowa Court of Appeals also noted that:

> The district court found Dr. Goff was qualified to testify in the area of social psychology; he specialized in identity and social justice issues, particularly race and gender; and was not going to render an opinion or ultimate opinion on the question... whether or not there was, in fact, discrimination against this particular plaintiff, but [would] be allowed to testify regarding the concept of implicit racial bias and how the presence of certain factors may lead to discriminatory decision-making, even by well-meaning individuals.[18]

Other courts have ruled that implicit bias expert testimony is inadmissible. In *Karlo v. Pittsburg Glass Works, L.L.C.*, the trial court excluded the testimony of Dr. Greenwald.[19] The court found that Dr. Greenwald's testimony did not satisfy the requirements of Federal Rule of Evidence 702, because his opinions were not based on sufficient facts or data, his methods were unreliable, and that his opinions did not "fit" the case.[20] On appeal, the case was reversed on other grounds but the Third Circuit added:

> The District Court concluded that Dr. Greenwald's testimony lacks fit to this case because his population-wide statistics have only speculative application to PGW and its decision-makers. The District Court also observed that disparate-impact claims do not inquire into the employer's state of mind. We agree. Plaintiffs are not required to prove that any particular psychological mechanism caused the disparity in question; they are only required to demonstrate that the disparity itself is "sufficiently substantial that [it] raise[s] such an inference of causation." *Watson*, 487 U.S. at 995, 108 S. Ct. 2777. That is not to say, however, that implicit-bias testimony is never admissible. Courts may, in their discretion, determine that such testimony elucidates the kind of headwind disparate-impact liability is meant

to redress. We are simply unable here to conclude that the District Court abused its discretion in excluding this evidence.[21]

In *White v. BNSF Ry. Co.*, the Ninth Circuit Court of Appeals affirmed the exclusion of White's implicit bias expert.[22] The court found that the expert's report "was not based on a significant review of the facts of the case" and that "White never explained how testimony regarding implicit bias would be helpful to the jury in a disparate treatment case requiring evidence of intentional discrimination."[23]

2. *Batson* Challenges and Implicit/Unconscious Bias

Batson v. Kentucky[24] was the United States Supreme Court's 1986 attempt to limit racial discrimination in jury selection by preventing the prosecution in criminal cases from using peremptory challenges to strike potential Black jurors based on their race. The United States Supreme Court has extended *Batson's* reach to defense counsel in criminal cases;[25] all counsel in civil cases;[26] a defendant of any race in a criminal case;[27] strikes based on ethnicity;[28] and strikes based on gender.[29]

In *Batson*, Justice Powell's opinion penned the now-familiar three part framework: the first stage requires the challenging party to present a prima facie showing of discrimination; in the second stage, the burden of producing a race neutral explanation for the strike shifts to the party exercising the peremptory strike; and in the third stage, the judge must decide if the moving party has carried its burden of proving purposeful discrimination by demonstrating the race neutral reason for the strike was pretextual.[30] Justice Marshall's now famous prescient concurring opinion predicted: "The decision today will not end the racial discrimination that peremptories inject into the jury-selection process. That goal can be accomplished only by eliminating peremptory challenges entirely."[31] Justice Marshall understood that unconscious bias may be afoot in exercising peremptory challenges when he wrote:

> Nor is outright prevarication by prosecutors the only danger here. "[I]t is even possible that an attorney may lie to himself in an effort to convince himself that his motives are legal." A prosecutor's own conscious or unconscious racism may lead him easily to the conclusion that a prospective black juror is "sullen," or "distant," a characterization that would not have come to his mind if a white juror had acted identically. A judge's own conscious or unconscious racism may lead him to accept such an explanation as well supported.[32]

Batson is now widely regarded as a complete failure.[33] Not that long after *Batson* was decided a scholar noted: "The Batson doctrine has been rendered so ineffective a tool against racism or sexism that one jurist has been led to note that Batson and its progeny have proven to be less an obstacle to discrimination than a roadmap to it."[34] The scholar also observed that any "savvy litigator can succeed with the most blatant discriminatory purpose by a simple manipulation of the neutral explanation coupled with a dose of disingenuousness."[35] More recently, the authors of an extensive empirical study of 269 published and unpublished federal decisions from 2000–2009 concluded that Batson was "as ineffective as a lone chopstick."[36] Similarly, another scholar concluded:

> What is left of Batson is an infinitely cumbersome procedural obstacle course, created by the Court, which now plagues every voir dire in the land, civil and criminal. Through it all, the peremptory challenge is alive and well for those who know how to use it. Only the most overtly discriminatory or impolitic lawyer can be caught in Batson's toothless bite and, even then, the wound will be only superficial.[37]

Indeed, "in the thirty-plus years since it was decided by the Court, the doctrine has been subject to unrelenting criticism for its inability to stop discriminatory preemptory challenges."[38] As Chief Justice Robinson of the Connecticut Supreme Court recently wrote, Batson "has been roundly criticized as ineffectual in addressing the discriminatory use of peremptory challenges during jury selection, largely because it fails to address the effect of implicit bias...."[39] Quoting an article of mine that is now more than a decade old, Chief Justice Robinson noted that I referred to Batson's standards for ferreting out explicit and implicit biases as "a shameful sham."[40] In a recent concurring opinion Justice Humes of the Court of Appeal in California noted the "even if the Batson framework helps root out intentional discrimination in jury selection, it plainly fails to protect against—and likely facilitates—implicit bias."[41]

Other courts, too, have been critical of Batson's ability to root out both intentional and unconscious bias in jury selection. As far back as 1981, Justice Nix of the Pennsylvania Supreme Court urged the court to adopt a test to "prohibit the use of peremptory challenges based on group membership" because it is an indicator of unconscious bias.[42] In 2016, Chief Judge Van Amburg observed that: "Missouri courts cannot ignore, however, the growing body of evidence that racial bias, whether purposeful or unconscious, impacts jury selection to the detriment of citizens of color and the integrity of our justice system."[43] Chief Judge Van Amburg continued with: "Implicit bias, precisely because it is a subconscious phenomenon, does not lend itself to credibility determination by trial judges. Consequently, Batson and its proof framework does not, and cannot, address implicit bias injury selection."[44] Foreshadowing what was to come in the State of Washington, Chief Judge Van Amburg noted: "We are not the only jurists grappling with the limitations of Batson in the face of voluminous research confirming the perpetuity of racial bias despite three decades of *Batson* challenges. Our colleagues in Washington offer a thorough examination and discussion in *State v. Saintcalle*."[45]

In *Saintcalle*, the Washington Supreme Court concluded that "twenty-six years after *Batson*, a growing body of evidence shows that racial discrimination remains rampant in jury selection."[46] The Court noted that this was due, in part, because *Batson* only involves "purposeful discrimination," and "racism is often unintentional, institutional, or unconscious."[47] Justice González, concurring in *Saintcalle*, boldly called for the abolition of peremptory challenges because they are often exercised based "largely or entirely on racial stereotypes or generalizations."[48] Justice González noted that: "Many jurists and scholars have called for the elimination of peremptory challenges but no jurisdiction in the United States has been willing to be the first to take that necessary step."[49] Citing the Washington State Minority and Justice Task Force, Justice González observed that even after *Batson*, many lawyers, judges and court personnel in the State of Washington have witnessed the use of peremptory challenges to systematically excluded minorities from juries.[50]

The lack of relief *Batson* has provided to parties asserting a challenge to discriminatory jury selection is breathtaking. A 2020 comprehensive report from the Berkeley Law Death Penalty Clinic observed that: "Racial discrimination is an ever present feature of jury selection in California."[51] This report evaluated nearly 700 cases decided by the California Courts of Appeal from 2006 through 2018, which involved objections to prosecutors' peremptory challenges. The report found that "[i]n nearly 72% of these cases, district attorneys used their strikes to remove Black jurors. They struck Latinx jurors in about 28% of the cases, Asian-American jurors in less than 3.5% of the cases and White jurors in only 0.5% of the cases."[52]

California Supreme Court Justice Liu recently observed in a powerful dissent: "It has been more than 30 years since this court has found Batson error involving the peremptory strike of a black juror."[53] And it's not just California. In commenting about *Batson* challenges in North Carolina, researchers noted: "North Carolina's highest court has never once in those thirty years found a substantive Batson violation."[54] The Washington Supreme Court noted that in "over 40 cases since *Batson*, Washington appellate courts have *never* reversed a conviction based on a trial court's denial of a *Batson* challenge."[55]

It is against this backdrop of the understanding of *Batson's* failures that the State of Washington took a remarkably bold step in April of 2018 when the Washington Supreme Court exercised its rulemaking authority to adopt General Rule 37 ("the Rule") with the "purpose of this rule" to "eliminate the unfair exclusion of potential jurors based on race or ethnicity."[56] The Rule has several important features briefly summarized here: (1) The Rule specifically allows the court to raise an objection to a peremptory challenge on its own.[57] (2) The Rule establishes and defines an "objective observer" standard for evaluating peremptory challenges: "an objective observer is aware that implicit, institutional, and unconscious biases, in addition to purposeful discrimination, have resulted in unfair exclusion of potential jurors in Washington State."[58] (3) The Rule list five "circumstances" the court should consider in evaluating a challenge to a peremptory challenge, including whether the proffered reason "might be disproportionately associated with a race or ethnicity," and if the party that exercised a peremptory challenge has used them in this case or in prior cases "disproportionately against a given race or ethnicity."[59] (4) Perhaps the most unique innovation—the Rule lists commonly alleged non-discriminatory reasons offered to rebut a *Batson* challenge that are now "presumptively invalid." These presumptively invalid reasons include prior contact with law enforcement, a belief that law enforcement engages in racial profiling or being distrustful of law enforcement, having a close relationship with individuals "who have been stopped, arrested, or convicted of a crime," residing in a "high-crime" neighborhood, having a child out of wedlock, "receiving state benefits," and "not being a native English speaker."[60]

On September 30, 2020, California Governor Gavin Newsom signed into law AB-3070, modeled after Washington's General Rule 37.[61] The California law is effective for criminal juries selected on or after January 1, 2022 and civil juries selected on or after January 1, 2026.[62] The purpose of this legislation, according to the language in the bill, was to express "the intent of the Legislature to was to put into place an effective procedure for eliminating the unfair exclusion of potential jurors based on race, ethnicity, gender, gender identity, sexual orientation, national origin, or religious affiliation, or perceived membership in any of these groups, through the exercise of preemptory challenges."[63] Judge McMurdie, of the Arizona Court of Appeals very recently found "merit in Washington's "objective observer" test" because it "protects the integrity of the jury-selection process from both purposeful and unconscious discrimination."[64]

In light of the longstanding criticism by legal scholars, judges, and empirical studies that *Batson* has been a failure in reducing both explicit and implicit bias in jury selection, local, state, and national bar groups, and the development of committees for every level of courts were encouraged to study potential improvements to modify or replace *Batson* with innovative approaches that would make *Batson's* hope for increasing persons of color on juries a reality. This is precisely what Chief Judge Van Amberg was referring to when he wrote in a concurring opinion that: "Simply put, we cannot pretend that *Batson* adequately addresses racial bias in jury selection. In my view, we must prioritize the guaranty of a fair trial in the State of Missouri by acknowledging the reality of unconscious bias in our courtrooms and joining the national conversation seeking alternatives to *Batson*."[65] It was also recently suggest by the Supreme Court of Vermont when Justice Carroll wrote: "because we consider implicit bias a potential threat to the judicial system, we invite counsel in this case to propose strategies to combat any negative effect that implicit bias might have on the criminal justice system to all existing and relevant agencies or commissions."[66]

Improving on *Batson's* failed attempt to increase the number of persons of color on juries is important for several critical reasons. Empirical studies have demonstrated that having diverse juries reduces inaccuracies in jury deliberations; motivates jurors to deliberate longer; motivates White jurors to contribute more to fact based and less biased discussions and to be more amenable to discussions of racism than in a nondiverse jury.[67] Even before juror deliberations, Whites in diverse groups compared to all-White groups "were significantly less likely to vote guilty than Whites in all-White groups" when the defendant was Black.[68] This demonstrated that the effects of diversity occur not solely through the exchange of information in deliberations, but also as a result of making race salient in the court process.[69]

A recent comprehensive report entitled *Whitewashing the Jury Box, How California Perpetuates the Discriminatory Exclusion of Black and Latinx Jurors*, notes that: "Researchers have demonstrated that implicit bias against African-Americans affects jury selection, specifically influencing the exercise of preemptory challenges."[70] A leading cognitive psychologist on race, jury selection, and peremptory challenges based on race has noted:

> The discretionary nature of peremptories renders them susceptible to the nonconscious influence of race; peremptories also remain the easiest route by which attorneys can intentionally manipulate jury racial composition. Eliminating or reducing in number peremptory challenges would therefore seem likely to decrease the influence of race on jury selection and increase jury representativeness, a conclusion supported by Baldus et al.'s (2001) mathematical modeling of over 300 murder trials in Philadelphia.[71]

The authors note that a complication of eliminating or reducing peremptory challenges is that "attorneys might still be able to use challenges for cause to influence jury racial composition."[72] However, the authors also note that that if peremptory challenges were eliminated or reduced, many scholars have suggested that this should be "accompanied by expanded voir dire of individual jurors and loosening of standards for granting challenges for cause."[73]

The Canadian Supreme Court recently affirmed as constitutional the statutory abolishment of peremptory challenges.[74] The Canadian Bar Association lauded the ruling noting that peremptory challenges are "an invitation to discrimination," and "that England, the birthplace of peremptory challenges, abolished them in 1988."[75]

Finally, empirical studies of actual jury trials in criminal cases support the views that: (1) race diversity in the jury pools have a significant effect on the probability of conviction; (2) conviction rates for White and Black defendants are similar when there are some Blacks in the jury pool but that Black defendants are much more likely to be convicted in the absence of such representation; (3) both Black and White defendants are less likely to be convicted when the jury pool contains more members of their own race; (4) that Black defendants are disadvantaged compared to White defendants when the jury pools contain a small percentage of Blacks; and (5) attorneys, especially prosecutors use peremptory challenges strategically to increase conviction rates.[76]

3. Implicit Bias Jury Instructions and Implicit Bias Venire Videos

More and more jurisdictions have drafted implicit bias jury instructions, and the Western District of Washington has created an Unconscious Bias Juror Video that appear to be reaching desired outcomes.

I not only was the first trial judge in the nation to develop an implicit bias jury instruction, I used it in hundreds of civil and criminal jury trials in federal trial courts spanning from the Middle District of Florida (civil) to the District of the Northern Mariana Islands in Saipan (civil and criminal), including in both districts in Iowa (civil and criminal), Arizona (civil), and North Dakota (civil and criminal) before I retired as a United States District Judge in 2019. In addition to discussing the use of pattern jury instructions for implicit bias, this third section examines the 2017 cutting-edge implicit bias educational video developed by the federal court in the Western District of Washington for use with jury venires.

In 2010, I mentioned in a law review article the initial jury instruction I had developed and was using in both civil and criminal jury trials.[77] That instruction was:

> As we discussed in jury selection, growing scientific research indicates each one of us has "implicit biases," or hidden feelings, perceptions, fears and stereotypes in our subconscious. These hidden thoughts often impact how we remember what we see and hear and how we make important decisions. While it is difficult to control one's subconscious thoughts, being aware of these hidden biases can help counteract them. As a result, I ask you to recognize that all of us may be affected by implicit biases in the decisions that we make. Because you are making very important decisions in this case, I strongly encourage you to critically evaluate the evidence and resist any urge to reach a verdict influenced by stereotypes, generalizations, or implicit biases.[78]

This instruction morphed into two instructions. But, unlike virtually all other state or federal trial judges, I gave each juror a complete set of final instructions before opening statements for their use throughout the trial.[79] The very first jury instruction titled "Introduction," included, *inter alia*, the following: "In making your decision, you are the sole judges of the facts. You must not decide this case based on personal likes or dislikes, generalizations, gut feelings, prejudices, sympathies, stereotypes, or biases."[80]

The second implicit bias instruction came near the end of the instructions in an instruction titled: "Conduct of Jurors During Trial" and included the following language:

> Do not decide the case based on "implicit biases." As we discussed during jury selection, everyone, including me, has feelings, assumptions, perceptions, fears, and stereotypes—that is, "implicit biases"—that we may not be aware of. These hidden thoughts can impact what we see and hear, how we remember what we see and hear, and how we make important decisions. Because you are making very important decisions in this case, I strongly encourage you to evaluate the evidence carefully and to resist jumping to conclusions based on personal likes or dislikes, generalizations, gut feelings, prejudices, sympathies, stereotypes, or biases. The law demands that you return a just verdict, based solely on the evidence and the instructions that I give you. Our system of justice is counting on you to render a fair decision based on the evidence, not on biases.[81]

Many courts now give a variety of implicit bias jury instructions.[82] For example, the federal court in the Western District of Washington through its creation of a bench-bar-academic committee has developed several implicit bias jury instructions including an "instruction that can be given before jury selection if the parties are going to ask questions during *voir dire* regarding bias, including unconscious bias."[83] That instruction states:

> PRELIMINARY INSTRUCTIONS TO BE GIVEN BEFORE OPENING STATEMENTS
>
> DUTY OF JURY
>
> Jurors: You now are the jury in this case, and I want to take a few minutes to tell you something about your duties as jurors and to give you some preliminary instructions. At the end of the trial I will give you more detailed [written] instructions that will control your deliberations. When you deliberate, it will be your duty to weigh and to evaluate all the evidence received in the case and, in that process, to decide the facts. To the facts as you find them, you will apply the law as I give it to you, whether you agree with the law or not. You must decide the case solely on the evidence and the law before you and must not be influenced by any personal likes or dislikes, opinions, prejudices, sympathy, or biases, including unconscious bias. Unconscious biases are stereotypes, attitudes, or preferences that people may consciously

reject but may be expressed without conscious awareness, control, or intention. Like conscious bias, unconscious bias, too, can affect how we evaluate information and make decisions. In addition, please do not take anything I may say or do during the trial as indicating what I think of the evidence or what your verdict should be—that is entirely up to you.[84]

California was one of the first states to adopt a model implicit bias instruction. It provides as follows:

> 113. Bias
>
> Each one of us has biases about or certain perceptions or stereotypes of other people. We may be aware of some of our biases, though we may not share them with others. We may not be fully aware of some of our other biases.
>
> Our biases often affect how we act, favorably or unfavorably, toward someone. Bias can affect our thoughts, how we remember, what we see and hear, whom we believe or disbelieve, and how we make important decisions. As jurors you are being asked to make very important decisions in this case. You must not let bias, prejudice, or public opinion influence your decision. You must not be biased in favor of or against parties or witnesses because of their disability, gender, gender identity, gender expression, race, religion, ethnicity, sexual orientation, age, national origin, [or] socioeconomic status[, or [insert any other impermissible form of bias]].
>
> Your verdict must be based solely on the evidence presented. You must carefully evaluate the evidence and resist any urge to reach a verdict that is influenced by bias for or against any party or witness.[85]

Illinois has adopted the following pattern civil jury instruction on implicit bias:

> We all have feelings, assumptions, perceptions, fears, and stereotypes about others. Some biases we are aware of and others we might not be fully aware of, which is why they are called "implicit biases" or "unconscious biases."
>
> Our biases often affect how we act, favorably or unfavorably, toward someone. Bias can affect our thoughts, how we remember, what we see and hear, whom we believe or disbelieve, and how we make important decisions.
>
> As jurors you are being asked to make very important decisions in this case. You must resist jumping to conclusions based on personal likes or dislikes. You must not let bias, prejudice, or public opinion influence your decision. You must not be biased in favor of or against any party or witness because of his or her disability, gender, race, religion, ethnicity, sexual orientation, age, national origin, [or] socioeconomic status[, or [insert any other impermissible form of bias]].

> Your verdict must be based solely on the evidence presented. You must carefully evaluate the evidence and resist, and help each other to resist, any urge to reach a verdict that is influenced by bias for or against any party or witness.[86]

Illinois Instruction, No. 108 titled, Implicit Bias, Notes on Use and Comment, were approved May 2018 and the Notes on Use were revised in May of 2019.[87] The Notes on Use state *inter alia*: "This instruction shall be given at the start of trial and again before the jury begins its deliberations."[88] The Notes on Use also state:

> Jurors, in their role as impartial decision-makers, need to be aware of their own implicit biases so that these biases do not affect their view of the case. Ideally, jurors would have already seen a short video about implicit bias when they were waiting in the Jury Assembly Room, as is done in some jurisdictions, but even if they are not shown such a video, they should still be given this instruction.[89]

The Comment section notes that the American Bar Association has focused on implicit bias as part of its mission to improving the courts and legal profession.[90] Lastly, the Comment section observes that "Illinois case law does not require an implicit bias instruction…."[91]

In *State v. Plain*,[92] the Iowa trial court declined to give the following implicit bias jury instruction because the trial judge believed it lacked the authority to give the instruction:[93]

> Reach your verdict without discrimination. In reaching your verdict, you must not consider the defendant's race, color, religious beliefs, national origin, or sex. You are not to return a verdict for or against the defendant unless you would return the same verdict without regard to his race, color, religious belief, national origin, or sex.[94]

The Iowa Supreme Court held that the trial court erred in declining to give the instruction because it was a correct statement of "antidiscrimination principles" and "would have been permitted under Iowa Law" but that the error was harmless.[95] The court concluded:

> While there is general agreement that courts should address the problem of implicit bias in the courtroom, courts have broad discretion about how to do so. One of the ways courts have addressed implicit bias is by giving jury instructions similar to the one proposed by Plain in this case. We strongly encourage district courts to be proactive about addressing implicit bias; however, we do not mandate a singular method of doing so. As we conclude Plain was not prejudiced by the denial of the requested instruction in this case, we affirm on this issue.[96]

There were several special concurrences by Iowa Supreme Court Justices well worth reading. Justice Appel thoroughly discusses an overview of implicit bias, the science behind it, the actions of the American Bar Association and the National Center for State Courts, judicial acceptance of implicit bias, and jury instructions to remedy implicit bias, before concluding: "For me, in light of the large body of science demonstrating implicit bias, the time for an implicit-bias instruction in Iowa courtrooms is now."[97] Justice Waterman also specially concurs:

> We have required all Iowa judges to undergo implicit-bias training and testing. But I would not require courts to give an implicit-bias jury instruction without further research and study. For now, like the majority, I leave it to the trial judge's discretion whether to instruct separately on implicit bias.[98]

Other appellate courts have reached the same conclusion that trial judges have discretion to instruct on implicit bias but are not required to do so.[99]

A major innovation in presenting information about implicit bias to jurors is the Western District of Washington's Unconscious Bias Juror Video, which is posted on the court's website with the tag line: "The video and jury instructions on this page were created by a committee of judges and attorneys and will be presented to jurors in every case with the intent of highlighting and combating the problems presented by unconscious bias."[100] The video is approximately eleven minutes in length.[101] A very recent law review article does a superb job of summarizing the video as follows:

> The video opens with the Honorable Judge John C. Coughenour reminding the court's goal of finding jurors "who will decide cases without prejudice or bias." Then, without much context, Judge Coughenour goes on to say that "it has been proven that most biases happen at an unconscious level," and that "researchers have found that unconscious bias is part of how we all think and process information."
>
> Next, the video transitions to Attorney Jeffery Robinson who discusses the fact that "biases can be both positive and negative." Robinson gives a variety of examples of unconscious biases and explains the harmful effects they can have by preventing a person from receiving a fair trial. Yet again, it is pointed out that "unconscious bias is something we all have simply because we are human." The jurors watching the video are repeatedly reminded that the process is "deep in our brains" and that they are "automatic preferences." Attorney Robinson then tells the jury to "consciously think about it," warning about the discrepancies between initial impressions and "what we really know to be fair."
>
> Attorney Robinson then discusses examples of unconscious bias in an attempt to present to the jurors a first-hand experience of somehow realizing their unconscious bias. As an example, the video uses possible inferences the jurors may have had about Judge Coughenour versus a "biker." Again, it is reiterated that "through

unconscious bias, our minds make quick decisions that we are not aware of." Next, the video uses the visual test by psychologist John Ridley Stroop regarding processing colors and the words associated with them.

Finally, the video ends with Attorney Annette Hayes discussing how unconscious bias affects day-to-day decision-making and reiterating that we are "not always aware" biases are working. Again, the jurors are told generalized statements to "check" their unconscious bias without giving context to the decisions that they have to make at hand and how to consider the video during jury deliberations.[102]

The American Society of Trial Consultants ("ASTC") is currently undertaking an extensive empirical study of the Western District of Washington's Unconscious Bias Juror Video. The study is described on the ASTC website as follows:

The study will be conducted in three phases. Phase 1 will collect jury-eligible participants' opinions of and reactions to the Video in order to understand how jurors will perceive the Video. Phase 1 will also guide the focus of the experimental design in Phase 2. Phase 2 will examine the impact of the Video on mock jurors' verdicts. Phase 3 will gather attorneys' opinions about the Video.[103]

Phase 1 of the study, conducted in 2019, involved collecting data from 133 jury-eligible respondents. When asked if they had ever heard of implicit or unconscious bias, 58% answered "yes" and 42% answered "no." Of the respondents who both had heard of the term and indicated they understood it, when asked: "How do you feel about this statement? Everyone holds some sort of implicit or unconscious bias," 43% strongly agreed, 49% somewhat agreed, 6% somewhat disagreed, and 2% strongly disagreed. When asked: "to what extent do you think implicit or unconscious bias impacts the way juries make decisions during criminal and civil trials," 28% (criminal) and 23% (civil) answered "a great deal," 47% (criminal) and 49% (civil) answered "Somewhat," 24% (criminal) and 27% (civil) answered "A little bit," and 1% for each criminal and civil answered "Not at all." When asked if "implicit or unconscious bias is a very serious problem in today's society," 32% "Strongly agreed," 53% "Somewhat agreed," 13% "Somewhat disagreed," and 2% "Strongly disagreed."

After viewing the Western District of Washington's Unconscious Bias Juror Video, the respondents in the study had a dramatic increase in their perception of how well they now understood the term implicit or unconscious bias and could explain it to others. When asked: "If you were on trial as a defendant accused of a crime, would you want the jurors in your case to see the video?" 97% answered "Yes," and 3% answered "No." In response to the question: "If you were suing someone in a civil case would you want the jurors in your case to see this video?" 90% answered "Yes" and 10% answered "No." Similar responses were given when asked if they were being sued in a civil case. When asked "When watching the video did you feel as if the video was accusing you of being racist, sexist, or ageist?," 90% answered "No," and 10% answered "Yes."[104]

The author suggests that the combination of implicit bias jury instructions and a Western District of Washington type Unconscious Bias Juror Video is the most effective method of both properly educating jurors about implicit bias and accomplishing efficiency, especially for busy courts.[105] The author also notes favorably my approach: "Judges can also get involved as Judge Bennett did by personalizing implicit bias lessons by showing it is something they experience as well."[106] Continuing with this theme: "Having the judge admit to them [the potential jurors] that they too have implicit biases could help the jurors realize that this is something that they really have to take a second to think about."[107]

Of course, not every trial judge agrees. A recent federal district court denied a Hispanic defendant's request in a criminal case to show the Western District of Washington video.[108] The court concluded that the Ninth Circuit jury instruction on implicit bias was "more than sufficient to prevent jurors from deciding Covarrubias's guilt or innocence based in any part on his race or national origin."[109]

Conclusion

This Chapter addressed three critical issues about implicit bias in the courtroom. The first is the admissibility of expert testimony to assist jurors in understanding how implicit bias may affect the decisions made in the case or impact their decision-making. The trend definitely leans towards exclusion of the experts. The second issue is the failure of the United States Supreme Court's decision in *Batson* to remedy both explicit and implicit bias in jury selection. It discusses several approaches to accomplish what *Batson* has failed to accomplish. The third issue is the emerging trend of implicit bias jury instructions and the new cutting-edge Western District of Washington's Unconscious Bias Juror Video. It concluded that a combination of both the video and a jury instruction is the best approach to address implicit bias in juries.

So, You'd Like to Know More

- Thomas Ward Frampton, For Cause: Rethinking Racial Exclusion and the American Jury, 118 Mich. L. Rev. 785 (2020).
- Frank Harty and Haley Hermanson, Implicit Bias Evidence: A Compendium of Cases and Admissibility Model, 68 Drake L. Rev. 1 (2020).

About the Author

Mark W. Bennett retired on March 2, 2019, after serving as a United States District Judge in the Northern District of Iowa for twenty-four years and as a United States Magistrate Judge in the Southern District of Iowa for an additional two and one-half years to become the first Director of the Drake University Law School's Institute for Justice Reform & Innovation. Judge Bennett earned his B.A. from Gustavus Adolphus College and his J.D. from Drake University Law School.

Endnotes

1. For purposes of this Chapter the terms *implicit bias* and *unconscious bias* are used interchangeably.

2. United States v. Robinson, 872 F.3d 760, 785 (6th Cir. 2017) (Donald, J., concurring in part, and dissenting in part).

3. Batson v. Kentucky, 476 U.S. 79 (1986).

4. Mark W. Bennett, *Unraveling the Gordian Knot of Implicit Bias in Jury Selection: The Problems of Judge-Dominated Voir Dire, the Failed Promise of Batson, and Proposed Solutions*, 4 HARV. L. & POL'Y REV. 149 (2010).

5. *See* Frank Harty & Haley Hermanson, *Implicit Bias Evidence: A Compendium of Cases and Admissibility Model*, 68 DRAKE L. REV. 1, 13 (2020) (discussing the admissibility of implicit bias experts in employment discrimination litigationand concluding that, "Courts have not yet reached consensus on whether this testimony should be admissible.") (Written by two excellent employment defense lawyers at Iowa's largest law firm, their anti-implicit bias perspective comes through on virtually every page of the article, e.g., "implicit bias science is being used to circumvent the fundamental substantive and procedural safeguards upon which the U.S. legal system is built." *Id.* at 2; "Though the concept of implicit bias is not new, its admission as evidence of discrimination threatens to punish mere thoughts and does not promote inclusive workforces." *Id.* at 40.)

6. *Id.* at 7

7. Annika L. Jones, Comment, *Implicit Bias As Social-Framework Evidence In Employment Discrimination*, 165 U. PA. L. REV. 1221 (2017); Anthony Kakoyannis, *Assessing the Viability of Implicit Bias Evidence in Discrimination Cases: An Analysis of the Most Significant Federal Cases*, 69 FLA. L. REV. 1181 (2017).

8. Daubert v. Merrell Dow Pharm., Inc., 509 U.S. 579 (1993).

9. Samaha v. Washington State Dep't of Transp., No. CV-10-175-RMP, 2012 WL 11091843 at *3 (E.D. Wash. Jan. 3, 2012).

10. *Id.*

11. *Id.*

12. Price Waterhouse v. Hopkins, 490 U.S. 228, 250–51 (1989).

13. *Samaha*, 2012 WL 11091843 at *4. The court summarized Dr. Greenwald's proposed testimony follows:

Dr. Greenwald's findings include the following, as outlined in his declaration: (1) seventy percent of Americans "hold implicit prejudiced views" based on race, color, national origin and ethnicity; (2) implicit bias is prevalent in the employment context; (3) job performance evaluations conducted by personnel using subjective criterion permit implicit biases to affect the outcome; (4) "significant majorities of Americans prefer lighter skin tone over darker and European–American relative to Arab ethnicity"; (5) awareness of potential or actual implicit biases helps diminish the effect of these biases; and (6) members of a decision-maker's ingroup those people who share common demographic characteristics are more likely than those in the outgroup to receive more favorable treatment. ECF No. 40-1 at 8–10. Dr. Greenwald's findings are based on his "own research as well as on [his] knowledge of published works of others who have conducted research relevant to the conditions of this case." ECF No. 40-1 at 5. Dr. Greenwald reviewed only Plaintiff's complaint to acquaint himself with the alleged circumstances in this matter and was not asked by Plaintiff to review any other case materials. ECF No. 40-1 at 5." *Samaha*, 2012 WL 11091843 at *1.

14. Maciel v. Thomas J. Hastings Properties, Inc., No. 10-12167-JCB, 2012 WL 13047595 at *7 (D. Mass. Nov. 30, 2012).

15. Salami v. Von Maur, Inc., No. 12-0639, 2013 WL 3864537 at *2 (Iowa Ct. App. July 24, 2013).

16. *Id.*

17. *Salami*, 2013 WL 3864537 at *3. (footnote omitted). As quoted in the opinion, the The six elements were:

(1) The "psychology of rumor"—perceptions and attributions for behavior are more likely to be consistent with group stereotypes when information is conveyed second or third-hand.

(2) "Aversive racism," which he explained as: "the vast majority of folks in the United States would like to see ourselves as nonracist. Many of us also feel uncomfortable when crossing racial lines.... And that discomfort leads us to avoid certain situations, maybe just avoid the whole point of contact altogether."

(3) A "colorblind" ideology or approach to organizations is likely to produce "increased reliance on stereotyping and increased racial bias" in decision-making.

(4) Two different organizational factors, accountability and subjective versus objective criteria—are not optimal. When decision-makers are not held accountable to meet diversity goals, stigmatized group members tend not to receive rewards. And second, when decision-makers are encouraged to use subjective, as opposed to objective criteria, this tends to increase the degree of racial bias in decision-making processes.

(5) Customer service is a "stereotype relevant domain," that is, a situation where negative stereotypes would more likely occur: for example, black women would more likely be stereotyped as being loud, abrasive, sassy, angry, and rude. So "bias assimilation" would make it more likely that "someone might be willing to accept a stereotype of someone even though they never observed that person act in that manner."

(6) "Contemporary prejudice and the perils thereof." "[I]f you don't do anything to address contemporary forms of bias," racial bias is likely to "creep in" to organization and will affect how people affiliate and evaluate one another. *Salami*, 2013 WL 3864537 at *10 n.1.

18. *Salami*, 2013 WL 3864537 at *3.

19. Karlo v. Pittsburg Glass Works, L.L.C., No. 2:10-cv-1283, 2015 WL 4232600 at *1 (W.D. Pa. July 13, 2015), *vacated on other grounds*, 849 F.3d 61 (3d Cir. 2017).

20. *Karlo,* 2015 WL 4232600 at *7–8.

21. *Karlo,* 849 F.3d at 84–85.

22. White v. BNSF Ry. Co., 726 F. App'x 603, 604 (9th Cir. 2018).

23. *Id. See also* Jones v. Nat'l Council of Young Men's Christian Associations of the United States of Am., 34 F. Supp. 3d 896, 898–901 (N.D. Ill. 2014) (excluding the proposed testimony about implicit bias by Dr. Greenwald).

24. *Batson,* 476 U.S. 79 (1986).

25. Georgia v. McCollum, 505 U.S. 42 (1992).

26. Edmonson v. Leesville Concrete Co., 500 U.S. 614 (1991).

27. Powers v. Ohio, 499 U.S. 400 (1991).

28. Hernandez v. New York, 500 U.S. 352 (1991).

29. J.E.B. v. Alabama ex rel. T.B., 511 U.S. 127 (1994).

30. *Batson,* 476 U.S. at 94–98.

31. *Id.* at 102–103.

32. *Id.* at 106.

33. Jonathan Abel, *Batson's Appellate Appeal and Trial Tribulations,* 118 COLUMBIA L. REV. 713, 713 (2018).

34. Leonard L. Cavise, *The Batson Doctrine: The Supreme Court's Utter Failure to Meet the Challenge of Discrimination in Jury Selection,* 1999 WIS. L. REV. 501, 545 (1999).

35. *Id.*

36. Jeffrey Bellin & Junichi P. Semitsu, *Widening Batson's Net to Ensnare More Than the Unapologetically Bigoted or Painfully Unimaginative Attorney,* 96 CORNELL L. REV. 1075, 1093 (2011).

37. Leonard L. Cavise, *The Batson Doctrine: The Supreme Court's Utter Failure to Meet the Challenge of Discrimination in Jury Selection,* 1999 WIS. L. REV. 501 (1999).

38. Jonathan Abel, *Batson's Appellate Appeal and Trial Tribulations,* 118 COLUMBIA L. REV. 713, 713 (2018).

39. State v. Holmes, 221 A.3d 407, 411 (Conn. 2019).

40. *Id.* at 431, citing Mark W. Bennett, *Unraveling the Gordian Knot of Implicit Bias in Jury Selection: The Problems of Judge-Dominated Voir Dire, the Failed Promise of Batson, and Proposed Solutions,* 4 HARV. L. & POL'Y REV. 149, 165 (2010).

41. People v. Bryant, 253 Cal. Rptr. 3d 289, 308 (Ct. App. 2019) (Humes, J., concurring).

42. Commonwealth v. Futch, 424 A.2d 1231, 1235–36 (Pa. 1981) (Nix, J., concurring).

43. State v. Rashad, 484 S.W.3d 849, 860 (Mo. Ct. App. 2016) (Van Amburg, C.J., concurring).

44. *Id.*

45. *Id.*

46. State v. Saintcalle, 309 P.3d 326, 329 (2013).

47. *Id.*

48. *Id.* at 349 (González, J., concurring).

49. *Id.* at 350 (González, J., concurring).

50. *Id.* at 356–57 (González, J., concurring).

51. Elisabeth Semel, et al., WHITEWASHING THE JURY BOX IV (2020).

52. *Id.* at VI.

53. People v. Rhoades, 453 P.3d 89, 139 (2019) (Liu, J., dissenting from denial of rehearing) (Jan. 29, 2020).

54. Daniel R. Pollitt & Brittany P. Warren, *Thirty Years of Disappointment: North Carolina's Remarkable Appellate Batson Record*, 94 N.C. L. REV. 1957, 1959 (2016).

55. Saintcalle, 309 P.3d at 335.

56. WASH. CT. GEN. R. 37(a). For a history of the extensive background and study that preceded the adoption of this rule, *see* Annie Sloan, Note, *"What To Do About Batson?": Using A Court Rule To Address Implicit Bias In Jury Selection*, 108 CAL. L. REV. 233 (2020). *See also* Taryn Luna, *California lawmakers Approve Bills to Address Racism in Criminal Charges and Jury Selection*, L.A. TIMES (Aug. 31, 2020), https://www.latimes.com/california/story/2020-08-31/california-lawmakers-approve-bills-to-limit-racism-in-criminal-charges-and-jury-selection.

57. WASH. CT. GEN. 37(c).

58. The Rule to includes that "an objective observer is aware that implicit, institutional, and unconscious biases, in addition to purposeful discrimination, have resulted in unfair exclusion of potential jurors in Washington State." WASH. CT. GEN. R. 37(e) & (f).

59. The five reasons include whether the proffered reason "might be disproportionately associated with a race or ethnicity," and whether the party that exercised a peremptory challenge has used them in this case or in prior cases "disproportionately against a given race or ethnicity." WASH. CT. GEN. R. 37(g).

60. WASH. CT. GEN. R. 37(h)(i)-(vii).

61. *A.B. 3070*, OPENSTATES https://openstates.org/ca/bills/20192020/AB3070/.

62. *Id.*

63. CAL. ASSEMB. BILL NO. 3070 (Sept. 30, 2020), available at https://leginfo.legislature.ca.gov/faces/billTextClient.xhtml?bill_id=201920200AB3070

64. State v. Porter, 460 P.3d 1276, 1291 (Ariz. Ct. App. 2020) (McMurdie, J., dissenting).

65. State v. Rashad, 484 S.W.3d 849, 862 (Mo. Ct. App. 2016) (Van Amburg, C.J., concurring).

66. State v. Jones, 206 A.3d 153,158 n. 4 (VT 2019) (Citing the following articles in this footnote including one of mine: M. Bennett & V. Plaut, *Looking Criminal and the Presumption of Dangerousness: Afrocentric Facial Features, Skin Tone, and Criminal Justice*, 51 U.C. DAVIS L. REV. 745 (2018); J. Levinson, *Forgotten Racial Equality: Implicit Bias, Decisionmaking, and Misremembering*, 57 DUKE L.J. 345 (2007); J. Levinson et al., *Guilty by Implicit Racial Bias: The Guilty/Not Guilty Implicit Association Test*, 8 OHIO ST. J. CRIM. L. 187 (2010); J. Rachlinski et al., *Does Unconscious Racial Bias Affect Trial Judges?*, 84 NOTRE DAME L. REV. 1195 (2009).

67. Linda Peter-Hagene, *Jurors' Cognitive Depletion and Performance During Jury Deliberations as a Function of Jury Diversity and Defendants Race*, 43 L. & HUM. BEHAV. 232, 232 (2019); Samuel R. Sommers, *On Racial Diversity and Group Decision-Making: Identifying Multiple Effects of Racial Composition on Jury Deliberations*, 90 J. PERSONALITY & SOC. PSYCHOL. 597, 606 (2006).

68. *Id.* (Sommers) at 603.

69. *Id.*

70. ELISABETH SEMEL, ET AL., WHITEWASHING THE JURY BOX IV (2020) (citing Samuel R. Sommers & Michael I. Norton, Race-Based Judgments, *Race-Neutral Justifications: Experimental Examination of Peremptory Use and the Batson Challenge Procedure*, 31 L. & HUMAN BEHAV. 261 (2007)).

71. Samuel R. Sommers & Michael I. Norton, *Race and Jury Selection, Psychological Perspectives on the Peremptory Challenge Debate*, 63 AMERICAN PSYCHOLOGIST 527, 534 (2008).

72. *Id.* at 535.

73. *Id.*

74. Her Majesty the Queen v. Pardeep Singh Chouhan, 2021 S.C.C. 26 (Can. Oct 7, 2020). The Canadian Department of Justice described the legislation as follows:

Prior to the Act, section 634 of the *Criminal Code* set out the rules governing peremptory challenges. Peremptory challenges are a set number of challenges given to both Crown and defence counsel during jury selection. These challenges may be used at their discretion to exclude a potential juror from the panel without providing a reason. In some cases, this has led to their discriminatory use to ensure a jury of a particular composition, an issue that was recently litigated before the Yukon Court of Appeal in *R v Cornell* (2017). The number of peremptory challenges allowed generally varies from 4 to 20 depending on the seriousness of the crime, the number of jurors, and whether there are co-accused.

Discrimination in the jury selection process in Canada has been well documented. Retired Supreme Court Justice Frank Iacobucci discussed how peremptory challenges could be used in a discriminatory manner. The Report recommended further consideration of this issue with a view to possible *Criminal Code* amendments to prevent the discriminatory use of peremptory challenges. Senator Murray Sinclair also documented the discriminatory use of peremptory challenges and recommended that they be abolished. Similar calls for reform have been made by legal experts and advocacy groups, such as the Aboriginal Legal Services of Toronto.

The Act abolishes peremptory challenges. This approach is consistent with other common law countries laws, such as England, Scotland and Northern Ireland. Abolishing peremptory challenges addresses the concern that this aspect of the jury selection process may be used to discriminate unfairly against potential jurors and will strengthen public confidence in the jury selection process. The amendments signal that discrimination of any kind has no meaningful role in promoting fairness and impartiality in the criminal justice process.

Legislative Background: An Act to amend the Criminal Code, the Youth Criminal Justice Act and other Acts and to make consequential amendments to other Acts, as enacted (Bill C-75 in the 42nd Parliament), CAN. DEPT. JUSTICE, https://www.justice.gc.ca/eng/rp-pr/csj-sjc/jsp-sjp/c75/p3.html (last visited Jul. 29. 2021).

75. The Canadian Bar Association, https://www.cba-alberta.org/Publications-Resources/Resources/Law-Matters/Law-Matters-Spring-2018/A-Good-Step-Towards-Diverse,-Impartial-Canadian-J.

76. Frances X. Flanagan, *Race, Gender and Juries: Evidence from North Carolina*, 61 J. L. AND ECONOMICS, 189 (2018); Shamena Anwar, et al., *The Impact of Jury Race in Criminal Trials*, 127 Q. J. Econ. 1017 (2012).

77. Mark W. Bennett, *Unraveling the Gordian Knot of Implicit Bias in Jury Selection: The Problems of Judge-Dominated Voir Dire, the Failed Promise of Batson, and Proposed Solutions*, 4 HARV. L. & POL'Y REV. 149, 171 n. 85 (2010).

78. *Id.*

79. Mark W. Bennett, *Reinvigorating and Enhancing Jury Trials Through an Overdue Juror Bill of Rights: A Federal Trial Judge's View*, 48 ARIZ. ST. L.J. 481, 505–09 (2016).

80. *See, e.g.*, United States v. Lopez, No. CR 15-4051-MWB (N.D. Iowa May 26, 2016) (jury instructions).

81. *Id.*

82. Anona Su, *A Proposal to Properly Address Implicit Bias in the Jury*, 31 Hastings Women's L.J. 79, 89 (2020) ("Some courts have developed specific jury instructions on implicit bias.").

83. Criminal Jury Instructions, https://www.wawd.uscourts.gov/sites/wawd/files/CriminalJuryInstructions-ImplicitBias.pdf.

84. *Id.*

85. *See* Cal. Judicial Council, Cal. Civ. Jury Instructions (CACI) 113 (2020).

86. Illinois Pattern Jury Instructions, 1.08 Implicit Bias (2019), available at https://www.illinoiscourts.gov/Resources/8deb3cf2-50a9-4c86-be15-d0f575b56a7b/1.08.pdf.

87. *Id.*

88. *Id.*

89. *Id.*

90. *Id.*

91. *Id.*

92. State v. Plain, 898 N.W.2d 801, 816–17 (Iowa 2017).

93. *Id.* at 817. ("Here, the district court declined to give the requested implicit-bias instruction because it knew of no authority approving or requiring the instruction and because the instruction was not included in the Iowa State Bar Association's model instructions.") *Id.* at 817.

94. *Id.* at 816.

95. *Id.* at 817.

96. *Id.*

97. *Id* at 830–836 (Appel, J., concurring specially joined by C.J. Cady and Wiggins, J.).

98. *Id* at 836–841 (Waterman, J., concurring specially joined by Mansfield and Zager, JJ.).

99. *See, e.g.*, United States v. Graham, 680 F. App'x 489, 491–93 (8th Cir. 2017) (affirming, on an abuse of discretion review, a district court's refusal to grant a specific implicit bias instruction in addition to a boilerplate fairness instruction); *see also* State v. Nesbitt, 417 P.3d 1058, 1068 (Kan. 2018) (holding defendant was not entitled to a race-switching jury instruction to probe for implicit biases when both defendant and the victim were members of the same race).

100. Both the video and the jury instructions the District uses may be found here: https://www.wawd.uscourts.gov/jury/unconscious-bias.

101. *Id.*

102. Anona Su, *A Proposal to Properly Address Implicit Bias in the Jury*, 31 Hastings Women's L.J. 79, 92–93 (2020).

103. *ASTC Implicit Bias Research Project*, ASTC, https://www.astcweb.org/page-1857948 (last visited Jul. 29, 2021).

104. All of the data discussed about the ASTC Phase 1 empirical study was presented at its 2019 Annual meeting in St. Louis, Missouri. The authors of the study are Andrea Krebel, Ph.D, Patty Kuehn, M.A., J.D., & Gent Silberkleit, M.A. Permission to share this data was given to the author of this Chapter by the President of the ASTC, Leslie Ellis, Ph.D. Dr. Ellis is the Director of the Northeast Division of DecisionQuest in Washington D.C.

105. Anona Su, A Proposal to Properly Address Implicit Bias in the Jury, 31 Hastings Women's L.J. 79, 99 (2020)

106. *Id.* at 98.
107. *Id.* at 99.
108. United States v. Covarrubias, No. 3:18-CR-00099-LRH-CLB, 2020 WL 1170216 at *1 (D. Nev. Mar. 11, 2020).
109. *Id.*

FIVE

Algorithmic Bias in the Courtroom

Andrew Grosso, Andrew Grosso & Associates, Washington, D.C.

Antony Haynes, Associate Dean for Strategic Initiatives; Director of Cybersecurity and Privacy Law, Albany Law School

A Note from the Editors: The irony of algorithmic bias is that we want to use AI in order to avoid our own human biases, implicit and explicit. While there is something very appealing in the idea that a machine did it, the reality is that our existing biases are transferred as we build those machines. As our authors put it, we need to beware of GIGO (Garbage In, Garbage Out). With algorithms, as with other areas of practice, even very small implicit biases can produce significant differences in the final results. In courts and related aspects of the criminal justice system, the costs of error are hugely high, and the ability of lawyers and judges to understand the issues, critical. In this Chapter, Attorney Grosso and Associate Dean Haynes display their extraordinary expertise and their ability to synthesize a technical and complex area and make it an understandable and usable roadmap for addressing AI concerns. We appreciate their work and generosity.

CHAPTER HIGHLIGHTS

- Fundamental issues with automated decision systems are that they appear to users as a "black box," and then they exploit the human tendency to give greater weight to an automated black box because it appears scientific.

- There is an old saying in the computer profession, "Garbage in, garbage out" (GIGO), which highlights the data-sensitive nature of computer algorithms. The GIGO problem can be subtle but widespread. Human beings—not some hypothetical flawless and impartial entities—are responsible for coding algorithmic inputs.

- The fundamental problem with these crime prediction systems is that they are based upon a false premise. They do not predict crime.
- Facial recognition is not without its problems, societal and technological as well as legal.

CHAPTER CONTENTS

Introduction

1. Artificial Intelligence: An Overview
2. Predictive Algorithms and Risk Assessments: Warnings and Risks
    A. Danger! Beware GIGO (Garbage In, Garbage Out)!
    B. Bad Programming → Bad Modeling → Error
    C. Finding the Track Record: Are the Results Trustworthy? For Whom Does the Algorithm Fail?
3. Case Studies in Due Process: Computer Generated Risk Assessment
4. Statistical Fairness and Legal Fairness
5. Predictive Policing: The Minority Report Revisited
6. Facial Recognition Technology
7. Judicial Analytics and Robot Judges
8. Algorithmic Accountability in the Courts

Conclusion

Introduction

Law is not immune to the march of technology. In yesteryears, lawyers mastered computer assisted research. Today, they encounter automated decision systems (ADS), predictive policing, facial recognition technology (FRT), and more. Lawyers and judges routinely rely on data and statistics to make legal arguments and reach judicial decisions; and the courtroom has come to depend upon statistical evidence. Predictive algorithms, often applying artificial intelligence (AI)/machine learning (ML), are part of an array of automated tools confronting the legal practitioner. Yet, what is the exact nature of these technologies, what types of biases do they possess, and how do they affect the legal practice—for good and ill—in and out of the courtroom? This Chapter breaks out and examines these questions in several subtopics:

(i) technology overview, (ii) courtroom limitations, (iii) statistical fairness, (iv) recidivism risk analysis, (v) predictive policing, (vi) facial recognition, (vii) judicial analytics, and (viii) algorithmic accountability. Ultimately, legal practitioners and court systems cannot abdicate their responsibility to evaluate the usefulness and fairness of AI tools and to make legal and ethical arguments about biases and errors that exist in automated decision systems.

1. Artificial Intelligence: An Overview

AI is an automated mechanism for making decisions and reaching conclusions based upon previous programming, current data, and ongoing machine learning. It is called "AI" because it seeks to mimic human intelligence as applied to solving specific problems and to other goals. The field began in the 1940s, stalled in the 1960s, recovered in the 1990s, and is now progressing at an accelerating pace. Today, systems based on AI are being used for evaluating—and generating—evidence for use in court and other judicial proceedings. In criminal justice, AI systems are being used to identify perpetrators of crimes and to determine the risks of recidivism and danger to the community for bond and sentencing purposes. Thus, the attorney who encounters or uses these systems must be aware, at some basic level, how they work, and how they are being treated by police, prosecutors, and courts.

Let us start with the simplest AI system, or what is known as an "expert system." Given data that it may already have in its memory (that which is already available to it or which you may provide it when you ask your question), it will give you an answer (hopefully one that is "right" or reasonably close to being right). It seems that this is a smart computer. Actually, it is dumb—very dumb. All it does is follow rules.

What is happening inside this computer is that someone loaded its memory with "data," and that someone, or another person—some days, months or years before—wrote a computer program telling it what to do with that data. The computer *has no intelligence* in the matter. Change the data so that it is inaccurate, and the answer that the computer gives to you will be inaccurate. Modify the program in a way that no longer reflects the real world, and the answer the computer gives will be incorrect. The problem is that without knowing, in advance, the accuracy and sufficiency of your data and your program, you cannot know whether the answer provided can or should be relied upon. In the criminal justice system this can be a real problem.

Today we have more advanced computer systems: these are known as machine learning (ML) systems. They actually teach themselves. And some do so in a manner that makes it impossible for their users and designers to know how they process information and reach their conclusions. Let us briefly look at two types of machine learning systems.

The first is pretty straight forward. It teaches itself: each time it is asked a question, runs its program, and reaches a result, it compares the conclusions that it reaches with real world facts. (These are facts that are sometimes provided by the user or programmer, and sometimes accessed by the system itself directly from electronic sources to which it is has access, such as the Internet or cable.) In this manner, it learns: seeking to obtain better results for the next time, it—on its own—adjusts either its code, the data stored in its memory, or both. The system is now different from what it was before the last time it was used. After numerous uses, or "runs," the system may be significantly different than when it began its first run.

An important attribute of this system is that it can be "opened-up" for examination, so to speak: its modified programming code and internal data can be studied after each run, enabling an understanding of how the computer is reaching its conclusions. Nonetheless, it has disadvantages. First, significant effort must be expended to get the functionality of the initial versions of the programming code (and the database) "close enough" to how real world works so that the early steps that enable the system to teach itself don't start down the paths of wrong directions. Concerns are that these systems are not very malleable (code is code—and thus brittle not bendable); and that the system can bump against resource limits. This later limitation is due to the fact that a computer program deals with lines of code, which take up computer resources; and the computer must maintain a continuously-updating database, which similarly consumes resources.

A second machine learning system is what is known as a "neural network." Today this is cutting edge technology. It is called a neural network because its design mimics the neurons and neural pathways in an organic brain. As the system learns, the connections between and among its subroutines (i.e., the system's "neurons") are modified after, and even *during*, each run—in contrast to modifying its programming code or changing its database. And, like a human brain, it *self*-modifies: it modifies its computing structure on its own, without input from a user or programmer, and even with limited input from the outside world. Such systems have demonstrated their definitive superiority over other forms of machine learning.

When it comes to the law, neural networks have problems: (1) since they are changing their network connections, as opposed to changing lines of code or a database, it is difficult to identify the new structure and the changes that were made; (2) since the network is constantly changing, it is difficult to go back to learn how the system functioned at any previous point in time; and (3) since the system is constantly changing, it is difficult to take a "snap shot" of what the system looks like on any occasion when an operation is being run.

All of these are concerns for the rules of evidence, due process, and judicial procedure.

2. Predictive Algorithms and Risk Assessments: Warnings and Risks

Why must practitioners be concerned?

Picture this. You are a defense attorney, and your client is facing prison. The prosecution (or probation office) presents to the court a report generated by an automated and artificially intelligent system. It says that if released on probation, or given a lenient sentence, your client is likely to commit another crime promptly upon entering society. And the crime will be violent. And the report assigns numbers to these probable outcomes: 40%, 80%, 99%....

You disagree. But..., how do you rebut a computer?

Remember these three key phrases: data, programming, track record. Keeping in mind that these three can be intertwined, let's examine them one at a time.

A. Danger! Beware GIGO (Garbage In, Garbage Out)

Fundamental issues with automated decision systems are that they appear to users as a "black box," and then they exploit the human tendency to give greater weight to an automated black box because it appears scientific.[1] In addition, the apparent precision of statistical and algorithmic data can give the false impression that such evidence is more accurate and more reliable than other forms of evidence, regardless of whether any such apparent precision is valid.[2] For example, in the criminal sentencing context, researchers found that assessments of recidivism risk generated by a court-sanctioned computer algorithm were less reliable than assessments performed by untrained humans.[3] There is an old saying in the computer profession, "Garbage in, garbage out" (GIGO), which highlights the data-sensitive nature of computer algorithms.[4]

The quality of the conclusions reached by a computer is directly tied to the data fed to it, particularly training data. Take this example: As an experiment, computer scientists at the University of Washington designed a self-learning computer system for the purpose of distinguishing domesticated dogs—specifically huskies—from wild wolves. The method by which the scientists trained the system was by feeding it image after image of both dogs and wolves, initially telling the system which was which. After a sufficient amount of this data had been provided, allowing the system to construct for itself an internal program for distinguishing between the characteristics of dogs and wolves, the scientists began feeding to it just the images, without the additional information as to of which of the two animals each of the images was depicting. At this point, the scientists asked the computer system to tell them which category of animal each image depicted.

Remember: huskies and wolves resemble each other closely, much more than, say, do a pug and a wolf. The computer performed magnificently: it determined correctly 90 percent of the images as being a dog or wolf. Then the scientists examined the programming mechanism that the computer had designed to enable it to make these determinations. Wolf images are normally accompanied by an outdoor background. After all, few wolves are kept as household pets. But dogs, including huskies, *are* kept as pets, and kept indoors. Their images included indoor backgrounds. The computer system had constructed a data processing program that focused not on the animals, but on their backgrounds. The data had introduced a bias, it linked the environment in which the animal was situated when its photograph was taken with the animal itself. The scientists had given birth to an outstanding system for distinguishing between domestic settings and the great outdoors—but useless for distinguishing dogs from wolves.[5] Had such a system been disseminated for its supposed purpose, the results would have been arbitrary and without value—or worse.

The GIGO problem can be subtle but widespread. Human beings—not some hypothetical flawless and impartial entities—are responsible for coding algorithmic inputs.[6] (Indeed, one method of sabotaging AI algorithms is intentionally to inject flawed or inaccurate data into such systems.[7]) The typical scenario is one where the algorithm's data inputs reflect the biases of the humans providing those inputs—no matter how inaccurate or even morally reprehensible those biases may be. For example, search engines such as Google Search and Google Adwords have long equated non-White women (e.g., search for keywords such as "Asian girls," "Black girls," or "Latina girls") with pornography.[8]

B. Bad Programming → Bad Modeling → Error

A computer program is more than a set of equations embodied in computer code. It is a mathematical model, constructed with computer code and simulating a relevant portion of the real world.[9] Models may be complex, and if the model is inaccurate in any way, or is mismatched with other models with which it must work, the result will be inaccurate.

Assume the data fed to the computer system is both accurate and unbiased, but the code used by the computer is flawed. These kinds of errors typically develop as the device embedding the computer code is "calibrated" across a range of text subjects. For example, the pulse oximeter is an inexpensive, blood oxygen gauge used in both hospitals and private homes. However, the model the pulse oximeter uses to detect blood flow is designed to work almost exclusively through lighter skin.[10] As a result, the device reports an artificially high blood oxygen level when used through darker skin, leading to potentially life-threatening consequences for non-White users of the device.[11]

This issue of flawed models is particularly worrisome in the social sciences, such as the law, where many sociological processes (such as "crime") are not understood well enough to create valid models. Thus, any data inputs, no matter how accurate, cannot generate any useful outputs because of a lack of understanding of the underlying phenomena.

For another example of the danger of a flawed model we look to the space program. In late 1998, the National Aeronautics and Space Administration (NASA) launched the Mars Orbiter on a ten-month journey to Mars. The goal was for it to enter into orbit around the planet and conduct studies in coordination with two other space craft already exploring the planet. It reached Mars—but never made it into orbit.[12]

Throughout the journey from Earth, the spacecraft periodically executed small corrections to its trajectory. These were calculated by computer. Two sets of programmable code were used, the first developed by the Lockheed Martin Corporation, who built the craft; and the second by NASA's Jet Propulsion Laboratory (JPL),[13] which controlled the operation of the craft while in transit. Lockheed's code needed to speak with JPL's code throughout the journey. Unfortunately, although they spoke the same computer language, they used different dialects. Lockheed programmed its code using the English system of measurements: pounds, feet, yards, etc. JPL used the metric system: kilograms, meters, kilometers, etc. Yards and meters are very close to each other—but not close enough for the precise measurements needed to be made for a journey to Mars. By the time the craft was within distance of the planet to enter orbit, it was far too off-course to successfully do so. (Whether it flew past the planet or crashed into it is not known. But the $300 million plus dollar space craft disappeared.)

Noteworthy is the reality that the problem was not discovered until after disaster struck. Things seemed fine—until they weren't.

C. Finding the Track Record: Are the Results Trustworthy? For Whom Does the Algorithm Fail?

When all is said and done, there are two ultimate questions: Are the computer's results trustworthy? In other words, for whom does the algorithm fail?

Answering the question of trustworthiness is not as simple as here stated. Computer scientists have a method for determining if a system works. This is *formal verification:* the process of proving or disproving the correctness of a system with respect to a certain formal specification or property.[14] Few if any computer systems commercially available to the public (or the courts), AI or otherwise, are subjected to such a process. But there is another way.

Look at the validity of the results that the system has produced to date. Has it given correct (or reasonably correct) answers? Does the proprietary owner or user of the system encourage and utilize feedback for fine-tuning? Does such owner document previous results or permit outside users or experts to evaluate such results and the effects of incorporating feedback? In looking at the system's track record, one must examine both previous results based upon data similar to the data with which you are concerned and data that is significantly different from yours. Why is this?

You do not know how the computer is functioning. (Remember our dogs and wolves?) Making sure that the system works with similar data is obvious. But using dissimilar data is also important, to ensure that the operation of the computer's algorithmic method is robust. That is, we want to ensure that there is no particular variant of data that, while seemingly insignificant to you and to all other parties concerned, is very significant to the computer that is going to give you results and that can—without warning—give devastating incorrect output. (Remember our Mars Orbiter?) Indeed, an entire academic, mathematical discipline has developed around these phenomena—Chaos Theory.[15]

Even if an AI system had perfect inputs, modeling, and verification, there are multiple definitions of fairness, and it is impossible for an algorithm to simultaneously optimize these conflicting metrics of fairness. Algorithmic models will often have trade-offs between predictive accuracy and fairness; a model cannot be both calibrated fairly and have balanced error rates across different groups. The Constitution and other laws place limits on the use of race, gender, and other protected classes in actions undertaken by public and private actors. Yet some of these factors must be included in algorithms designed to model our society. Thus, regardless of the automated nature of AI systems, legal practitioners must advocate for one or more competing notions of fairness, and courts must render a decision on which notion of fairness will prevail.

To achieve fairness and due process, particularly in high stakes litigation, such as where a party's Constitutional rights are at stake, attorneys need to focus more on identifying and abating errors than on statistical demographic parity. Demographic parity is a measure of individual fairness; an algorithm that achieves demographic parity assigns similar outcomes to individuals who are similar. With demographic parity, the algorithm equalizes the total predicted positive rates across protected groups; thus, the distribution of positive outcomes mirrors the general population. In contrast, equalized group error rates (or equalized odds) are a measure of group fairness; an algorithm that achieves equalized error rates returns false positives and false negatives at the same rate for all groups.

3. Case Studies in Due Process: Computer Generated Risk Assessment

Here are at least three areas where criminal justice routinely employs AI: risk assessment, DNA analysis, and inmate housing. This section will focus on risk assessment. Two judicial decisions—one criminal and one civil—exemplify the difficulties posed by "predictive algorithms" for practitioners in the justice system. Both decisions turn on whether the proprietary nature of the predictive algorithm raises due process concerns that prevent its use. In the criminal case, a state court determined that the proprietary nature of a risk assessment algorithm did not bar its use at criminal sentencing, while in the civil case, a federal court determined that an algorithm's propriety nature did bar its use in the employment context.

In 2016, the case of *State v. Loomis* reached the Supreme Court for the State of Wisconsin.[16] In the court below, a trial judge made use of a computer generated "risk assessment" tool when determining the sentence to impose on a criminal defendant. The tool was known as "COMPAS,"[17] developed by Northpointe Inc. for the purpose of assisting Departments of Corrections in making post-sentencing determinations as to the eligibility of prisoners for early release. Here, during sentencing, the trial court and probation office used a "risk assessment" score generated by COMPAS to assist in the court's determination of the appropriate punishment. The information that COMPAS used was an internal database compiled by Northpointe, supplemented by answers to twenty-one questions about the defendant and his background, provided by the probation office.

The COMPAS database was a proprietary product, protected by confidentiality agreements and trade secret laws. Because of this, the defendant and his counsel were denied the opportunity to review, and contest, both the program's algorithm and its internal database, although they were allowed to review and contest the information provided by the probation office.

This procedure was challenged for lack of due process. As phrased by the Wisconsin courts, it was (in pertinent part):[18] "whether the use of a COMPAS risk assessment at sentencing 'violates a defendant's right to due process, either because the proprietary nature of COMPAS prevents defendants from challenging the COMPAS assessment's scientific validity....'" The trial court answered this question in the negative. The appellate courts affirmed.

What happened in *Loomis* is of troubling concern to practitioners. Essentially, the court used a computer as a witness, and the defendant was not allowed to cross-examine this witness. What might be repercussions from this decision? One study conducted after the *Loomis* decision came down, and published by ProPublica,[19] found that the COMPAS algorithm lacked reliability: only 20% of the defendants who it predicted would go on to commit violent crimes actually did so. Further, the risk scores were biased, giving higher risks of recidivism to Black than White defendants, whereas a follow-up analysis found that often the reverse was true. Clearly, the track record was poor, but the track record was not available to the parties at the time Mr. Loomis was sentenced. Perhaps an analysis of COMPAS' database or its algorithm might have assisted the defense and the court in evaluating the validity of the risk assessment?

The Wisconsin Supreme Court upheld the lower courts' refusal to permit disclosure of the algorithm and database for such an analysis. Among its holdings was the following: that the defendant's knowledge of the information provided by the Probation Office and used as input to the COMPAS program, and his opportunity to challenge and correct errors in, and otherwise clarify such information, satisfied any applicable due process requirements.[20] The disconnect is obvious: the defendants' information, alone, was an incomplete basis for understanding how COMPAS arrived at its risk assessment for Mr. Loomis. The Wisconsin Supreme Court also relied upon the fact that Mr. Loomis was given the opportunity to challenge the risk assessment itself. But—without an understanding as to how COMPAS reached its conclusions—this boils down to little more than a "he said she said" argument, with one party being (here) an indigent defendant and the other a computer system whose credibility is vouched for by the company that created and markets it.

Let us examine another case, this time in federal court in a civil dispute, where the holding went the other way: *Houston Fed'n of Teachers, Local 2415 v. Houston Indep. Sch. Dist.*[21] In *Houston*, a Texas School District used a private company, SAS, to evaluate teacher performances. SAS used confidential student data and proprietary algorithms to conduct these evaluations. The teachers' procedural due process challenge was based on two factors: *first*, the teachers' were denied access to the student data and to the algorithms; and, *second*, the results were not reproduceable since, once the computer program ran using one set of data, it could no longer "back track" and explain how the results from that run were achieved.

The School District moved for summary judgment. Although the Court granted the District's motion on multiple claims brought by the teachers, it denied the District's motion as to the teachers claim that their rights to procedural due process had been denied. The Court explained: "On this summary judgment record, [the] teachers have no meaningful way to ensure correct calculation of their [evaluation] scores, and as a result are unfairly subject to mistaken deprivation of constitutionally protected property interests in their jobs."[22] The Court accepted the argument that, without a means to review and challenge the method used for their evaluations, that method could not be used to judge their performance. The Court went further, explaining that "secret algorithms" cannot be used to adversely affect a government employee's livelihood, and that any need of SAS to maintain the confidentiality of their algorithms for business purposes cannot override a teacher's right to examine the way those algorithms calculate his or her evaluation.[23]

A final note on this point: the issue is not limited to American jurisprudence. An Italian Court has ruled that while the underlying algorithm code may not be needed, an explanation of how it functions must be provided.[24] Another Italian court has held that administrative procedures cannot be relegated entirely to algorithmic decision-making, as the human judgment cannot be replaced by artificial intelligence.[25] Such arguments and considerations will appear in the courts of the United States.

4. Statistical Fairness and Legal Fairness

One factor courts can use in selecting a definition of statistical fairness is the context of model use. For example, in the context of criminal justice, group fairness measures such as equalized error rates may be more appropriate than individual fairness measures such as demographic parity. In the debate over the use of the COMPAS algorithm, the vendor claimed its system was "fair" because it achieved a rough demographic parity in predicting the risk of recidivism of White and Black offenders.[26] However, critics showed the COMPAS algorithm was unfair because it failed to satisfy equalized error rates for recidivism risk prediction for White and Black offenders.[27] The algorithm was twice as likely to label a Black offender, when compared to a White offender, as being at high risk of re-offending even though the Black offender did not re-offend; and the algorithm was twice as likely to label a White offender, when compared to a Black offender, as low risk of re-offending, even though the White offender did re-offend.[28] What about COMPAS error rates?

The Due Process Clause and the Equal Protection Clause of the Fourteenth Amendment both serve to prevent the improper consideration of race and gender, with a standard of heightened scrutiny applied to the use of gender and strict scrutiny applied to the use of race. Another trade-off in seeking statistical and legal fairness in decision-making algorithms lies between fairness through awareness (FTA) and fairness through unawareness (FTU). Under the FTU principle, an algorithm is fair only when it does not contain or use variables that refer directly to a protected status such as race or gender. Under FTA, an algorithm is fair when it classifies individuals the same when they have similar characteristics relevant to performing a particular task.

At first blush, it would appear that AI algorithms that explicitly consider race, perhaps under the FTA principle, would violate these Constitutional protections (thus requiring an algorithm to follow FTU with regard to race and gender to comport). However, in one case examining the explicit use of gender in an algorithm used to support criminal sentencing decisions, a state court found that "if the inclusion of gender promotes accuracy, it serves the interests of institutions and defendants, rather than a discriminatory purpose" under the Due Process Clause.[29] Thus, the court in that case implicitly adopted statistical parity as its measure of fairness and was willing to permit the explicit consideration of gender (i.e., under a FTA principle) in order to maximize that measure.[30] While the court in that case was willing to allow the explicit consideration of gender in criminal sentencing, it may be less likely that the explicit consideration of race would comport with either the Due Process Clause or the Equal Protection Clause.

Unfortunately, simply relying on a vendor to construct an algorithm that does not explicitly consider a protected characteristic, such as race or gender, will not prevent an algorithm from implicitly considering one or more protected characteristics. As we saw with the dogs versus wolves MLS, the power of statistical algorithms, particularly of the AI variety, is their ability to find correlations between characteristics and develop internal or hidden variables that can serve as proxies for protected characteristics. In addition, input variables that superficially appear not to consider a protected characteristic may ultimately do so implicitly.

5. Predictive Policing: The Minority Report Revisited

Law enforcement employs AI in policing in several ways: predictive policing, facial recognition, social media monitoring, gang databases, and so on. This section will focus on predictive policing—"the application of computer modeling to historical crime data and metadata to predict future criminal activity."[31] This approach is an attempt to make real the fantasy of catching law breakers before a crime is committed, particularly as popularized in fiction and film.[32] Thus, as automated data collection, fueling algorithmic predictions, moves outside the courtroom and into personal space and lives. These algorithms mine historical crime and personal data for the purpose of, both, identifying locations where crimes are most likely to be committed, and *identifying persons who are likely to commit a crime, before a crime is committed.*

The fundamental problem with these crime prediction systems is that they are based upon a false premise. They do not predict crime. The AI algorithms—like PredPol, Hunchlab, ShotSpotter, and Beware—purportedly learn patterns in the occurrence of crime, but *less than half* of all crimes are reported.[33] Furthermore, these algorithms seek to predict crime by using police records; however, most police departments use *arrest records* to train these systems, not *conviction records*. Then, using these patterns, the AI algorithm will supposedly predict the geographic location of future criminal offenses; however, the system is simply predicting the location of *future arrests*, not of incidents that will result in criminal convictions. Thus, "[a]s police are then dispatched to the locations with the highest predicted rate of [*arrests*], new recorded [*arrests*] validate initial biased predictions and amplify their influence in subsequent forecasting."[34] This is the classic example of a runaway feedback loop because the AI algorithm results in further over-policing of already over-policed neighborhoods. In an analysis of thirteen jurisdictions employing predictive policing, researchers found that crime prediction software merely served to automate and exacerbate preexisting racist, corrupt, and biased policing.[35]

As with other AI systems, these crime prediction algorithms evade scrutiny by an appeal to their proprietary nature. For example, ShotSpotter blocked public access to its data as its contracts with the government granted it ownership over gunfire data and the company did not want others to profit from its data.[36] The inability of researchers and the public to validate these systems raises the risk that any resulting judicial, policing, and policy decisions will be faulty.

While primarily focused on neighborhoods, the application of these crime prediction tools has narrowed down to individual persons. The Pasco County Sheriff's Office, in the Tampa Bay region of Florida, for example, has been using automated algorithms to identify persons who deserve "special attention" from its police, including persons having no prior criminal record.[37] The Chicago, Illinois Police Department watched subjects likely to be involved in a violent crime and sent customer notification letters to subjects who remain on the watch list too long.[38] The Office of the Inspector General examined the Chicago Police surveillance program and found that it did not predict crime, worsened preexisting racial disparities, and breached citizen's civil liberties.[39]

The desire to "stop crime before it happens" has led to deploying statistical algorithms to children and to using student data to identify certain children as future criminals. In the Pasco County example, the Sheriff's Office chose to target not just adults, but also juveniles. Specific attention is paid to children, using their confidential school records.[40] The information collected includes whether the person has "antisocial" parents and siblings, received poor rearing as a child, has a history of drug use, "hang[s] around" in a public place, has low intelligence, has a poor school record, and has delinquent friends.[41] The information is processed by computer using an algorithm created by the Sheriff's Office.

Once identified as a probable future offender, and if placed within the "top five" on a list of such probable offenders, the "suspect" is made a target of aggressive police attention, *e.g.*, deputies visit the prolific offenders and the other targets as part of their daily responsibilities. The purpose of this is to "bother" the "suspect,"[42] to make him "feel the pressure,"[43] and "ultimately help us [the Sheriff's Office] as an agency to prevent future crimes from occurring."[44]

Due process and civil rights questions abound with such a program.[45] Employed in an under-privileged or minority neighborhood, the risk factors used by the system will be biased toward identifying more persons as probable future offenders than persons in a privileged neighborhood. Further, the targeted suspects have no way or means to challenge the algorithm used, or the data fed to it—indeed, the identified suspects may never be notified that a computerized "confidential informant"—an artificially intelligent non-human—is accusing him or her of being a law breaker before any law is broken.

But the concern lies not only in the (predicted) perpetrator of the offense. AI systems are being used to evaluate the claims of *victims* of crimes. In Spain, police stations are being equipped with an AI system designed to detect if a victim is being truthful. It accomplishes this by detecting and analyzing the use by a victim, during her police interview, of the most common words generally utilized by persons who lie to police officers.[46] Computer scientists (who have evaluated this system) are concerned about: its inability to place into context cultural differences of the persons interviewed, including different word-use and different reactions to authority figures; implicit biases occurring in the system due to the data fed to and relied upon the algorithm; and its reliance upon the words, phrases, and substance of police reports that are supplied to it pertaining to the specific offenses under investigation.

And, if prediction and victim-doubting are not already problematic enough, in the near future, computer systems may be used to posit what it is you are thinking, while you are thinking it, whether it is about committing a crime, skipping a work day for a baseball game, or telling your significant other that you like his cooking when in fact... You do not. Experiments are currently being conducted using neural networks to evaluate human thoughts using brain imaging scans.[47] With such technology, police, courts, and examining attorneys will have the means to determine who is telling the truth and who is not, subject to an adequate algorithm and database—and subject to the Constitutional rights of individuals to the privacy in their own thoughts.

6. Facial Recognition Technology

Facial recognition technology (FRT) uses computer-based AI systems able to detect and identify human faces. Like most AI machine learning systems, FRT depends on an algorithm and on a system trained using a generic database of human faces. First, the system recognizes that an image is that of a human face, and it then extracts this image from its background. The system may then take measurements of various points on the face, such as the distance between the eyes, the shape of the cheekbones and other distinguishable features. These points are compared to equivalent points found in a database provided to it for the purpose of finding a match.

Newer technologies are being developed that will rely on three-dimensional models, using digital photographs of people.[48]

Such systems have been in use for an extended period of time. In 2001, the City of Tampa used FRT to increase security at Raymond James Stadium during Super Bowl XXXV.[49] The Federal Bureau of Investigation uses the technology, including a program whereby it searches databases containing mugshots, fingerprints, and criminal records.[50] More recently, the Staten Island District Attorney's Office, in the City of New York, purchased FRT from a company known as Clearview AI (Clearview).[51] The Clearview software uses a database of some three billion photos, scraped from public websites including Facebook, LinkedIn, Venmo, and YouTube. Law enforcement (or other users) upload the image of a person of interest, and the software returns photographs that appear to be similar, along with links to the websites where the photograph was obtained.[52]

Facial recognition is not without its problems, societal and technological as well as legal. In a case raising societal privacy issues, the State of Vermont sued Clearview. The Court found that Vermont had an interest in avoiding "societal harm" from the mass surveillance of its citizens resulting from Clearview's scraping of photographs and other personal information from websites. In denying Clearview's motion to dismiss the complaint, the Court said: "Mass surveillance could reasonably chill citizens' freedoms of assembly and political expression."[53] Although generally available in the United States, Clearview's software has been declared to be illegal in Canada due to privacy concerns.[54]

A key technical issue is that FRT is less accurate for women (as opposed to men) and for dark-skinned people (as opposed to light-skinned people).[55] For example, in a highly publicized and embarrassing occurrence, Google software identified two persons who were African Americans as being gorillas, and included photographs of these persons in its publicly available online album captioned "Gorillas."[56] In another incident, New Jersey police obtained a warrant for the arrest of a man for shoplifting, assault, and drug dealing, only to have the case dismissed because of mistaken identity after the defendant had spent a week in jail.[57] A similar incident occurred in Detroit, Michigan, where the defendant was held for a day before his charges were dismissed for lack of evidence.[58]

FRT poses significant legal risks, particularly in law enforcement, and this has led to calls to ban the technology. The Georgetown Center on Privacy and Technology has flagged several legal risks in the use of face recognition:

- Face recognition poses a threat to privacy.
- Face recognition risks having a chilling effect on free speech.
- Searches may lead to misidentifications.
- Face recognition may have a disparate impact on communities of color.

- The failure to disclose a face recognition search may deprive a defendant of due process.[59]

In June 2020, the U.S. Technology Policy Committee (USTPC) of the Association for Computing Machinery (ACM), which is the leading global society of computing professionals, called for the immediate suspension of the use of facial recognition, explaining that, at the current time, the technology is too rife with problems to be reliable. In a formal policy statement, this group of global computing professionals said: "[T]he technology too often produces results demonstrating clear bias based on ethnic, racial, gender, and other human characteristics recognizable by computer systems [and, consequently, that] its use has often compromised fundamental human and legal rights of individuals to privacy, employment, justice and personal liberty."[60]

Given these experiences, it is hardly surprising that the technical and legal problems with FRT have led to bans on the use of facial recognition in several states[61] and to proposed federal legislation to ban use of FRT in public housing.[62]

7. Judicial Analytics and Robot Judges

Automated decision systems continue to invade all aspects of the legal system, including in the areas of judicial decision-making and judicial analytics. For example, an automated tool handles contested parking tickets for London and New York.[63] Outside of the U.S., governments from Estonia to China have begun to deploy AI to judge small claims cases and to automate recordkeeping, as part of an effort to remove the human element from judicial decision-making.[64] While a goal of AI judges is to remove human error, the previously discussed limitations and flaws of AI still impact the automated decision-making. Indeed, even when humans and algorithms work together to eliminate bias in criminal sentencing, studies show that, in such circumstances, judges used computer risk predictions to exacerbate their prior human leanings.[65] In other words, and as one researcher noted, "AI algorithms end up being a rationalization for what the judge wants to do."[66]

While the U.S. permits the use of analytics in the court system, it is illegal in France to provide statistical analysis for judicial decision-making.[67] The French law prohibits using court records to "assess, analyze, compare or predict" judicial outcomes.[68] In the U.S., various companies provide AI tools to improve litigation strategy, predict judicial decisions, select experts, understand opposing counsel, and manage clients.[69]

With regard to litigation between private parties, the spread of software automation may result in exasperating inequalities in the access to justice, as only the wealthiest clients may be able to afford the most sophisticated analytics.[70] As a simple example, currently, the U.S. court system generally restricts access to judicial opinions behind attorney-only websites, or through publicly available but for-pay sites (e.g., the PACER database of legal documents), thus making it inconvenient or expensive for citizens to access, learn, and use the law.

The use of judicial analytics extends to jury pools, potentially providing litigants personal information about jurors and facilitating the shaping of juries in ways that may breach Constitutional protections.[71] When judicial analytics interpret various legal cases databases, there is the potential for data bias, as the engineers who develop the algorithms have biases on what would be the relevant search results.[72] These data biases become compounded by the human tendency to trust blindly the "black box" of automated legal research, thereby potentially compromising the lawyer's ethical duties under Model Rule 2.1.[73]

8. Algorithmic Accountability in the Courts

At its base, an algorithm is simply a sequence of steps that transforms some set of inputs into a set of outputs. When embedded in a computer device, an algorithm becomes a computational process that serves as the mathematical logic or "brains" behind how an automated decision system (ADS) makes its decisions. The embedding of computational logic into a "black box" computer device has frequently led users of the device to fail to identify potential flaws in its functioning. AI algorithms are highly dependent upon the abstract representations, or models, they use to represent an underlying process.

Due to the technical and legal complexity associated with AI and statistical algorithms in general, the Partnership on AI[74] has established a set of ten minimal requirements before courts should adopt these tools:

1. Training datasets must measure the intended variables.
2. Bias in statistical models must be measured and mitigated.
3. Tools must not conflate multiple distinct predictions.
4. Predictions and how they are made must be easily interpretable.
5. Tools should produce confidence estimates for their predictions.
6. Users of risk assessment tools must attend trainings on the nature and limitations of the tools.
7. Policymakers must ensure that public policy goals are appropriately reflected in these tools.
8. Tool designs, architectures, and training data must be open to research, review, and criticism.

9. Tools must support data retention and reproducibility to enable meaningful contestation and challenges.
10. Jurisdictions must take responsibility for the post-deployment evaluation, monitoring, and auditing of these tools.

Adding to this is the recognition that to be accepted by society, a system of justice must not only *strive* for fairness but must also be seen *to be* fair. Thus, the tools and their biases should be transparent; they should be validated; and the communities wherein these tools are used should find their use acceptable.

In regard to both concerns, substantive objectivity and appearance, an important factor for ensuring algorithmic accountability, is a requirement for vendors to submit to an audit or external third-party review of their algorithms. Even if a vendor claims that the algorithm and its source data or code is proprietary, the outputs of such an algorithm can still be benchmarked to identify any demographic disparities. Proposed federal legislation would grant the Federal Trade Commission (FTC) authority to require covered entities to conduct bias impact assessments for high-risk automated decision systems and high-risk information systems.[75] Other proposed legislation would also use FTC authority, requiring covered entities not to "act on an unfair algorithmic eligibility determination" and to keep a five-year audit trail of algorithmic decisions.[76]

By applying these criteria to any AI algorithm, ADS, or other statistical tools, lawyers can ensure algorithmic accountability in courts.

Conclusion

A significant and legitimate rationale for adopting algorithmic tools is to promote uniformity and equality in the making of legal decisions. However, lawyers and judges must not abdicate their responsibilities to ensure the adequate implementation of notice, fairness, and the opportunity to be heard; and the entities designing and implementing these systems must insure transparency, validity, and community acceptance. In other words, fundamental due process in the use of algorithms and AI must be both the starting and ending points for the growing use of this technology.

So, You'd Like to Know More

- Cathy O'Neil, Weapons of Math Destruction (2016).
- Darrell M. West & John R. Allen, Turning Point: Policymaking in the Era of Artificial Intelligence (2020).

- Reflections on Artificial Intelligence for Humanity, Bertrand Braunschweig & Malik Ghallab, eds. 2021.

About the Authors

Andrew Grosso is a former Assistant U.S. Attorney who now practices in Washington, D.C. In addition to his law degree from the University of Notre Dame, he holds Master of Science degrees in both Physics and Computer Science from Rensselaer Polytechnic Institute. He has served on the Council for the Criminal Justice Section of the ABA, and chairs the Law Committee of the U.S. Technology Policy Council of the Association for Computing Machinery (ACM).

Antony Haynes is the Associate Dean for Strategic Initiatives; Director of Cybersecurity and Privacy Law; Associate Professor of Law at Albany Law School. He has extensive litigation experience in the intellectual property, securities, and criminal defense areas. Associate Dean Haynes holds a B.S. from the U.S. Air Force Academy, an M.S., Computer Science, from the University of Illinois at Urbana/Champaign, and a J.D. from Georgetown University.

Endnotes

1. CATHY O'NEIL, WEAPONS OF MATH DESTRUCTION 1–49 (2016).

2. There is also a distinction between accuracy and precision, both of which are important aspects when evaluating outputs of a system. Precision is an indicator of how close a system's outputs are to each other when given the same inputs (e.g., when measuring a person's height, whether the height of the person changes from measurement to measurement or is repeatable and reproducible). Since automated systems are deterministic, they always provide the same outputs for a given set of inputs. Accuracy, in contrast, is an indicator of how close a system's outputs are to the true value (e.g., if a crime prediction tool consistently labels a given subject as highly likely of committing a violent crime but then the subject never commits a violent crime, the system is precise (repeatable results) but inaccurate (results do not reflect the true value of reality)). Data biases, or GIGO, are a source of inaccuracy in ADS and AI algorithms.

3. Julia Dressel & Hany Farid, *The Accuracy, Fairness, and Limits of Predicting Recidivism*, 4 SCIENCE ADVANCES 1 (Jan. 17, 2018), https://advances.sciencemag.org/content/4/1/eaao5580 (While the 137-variable COMPAS algorithm had a predictive accuracy of 65.2%, untrained humans reviewing just 7 of the 137 inputs had an accuracy of 67%.).

4. *Work with New Electronic 'Brains' Opens Field for Army Math Experts*, HAMMOND, INDIANA TIMES, Nov. 10, 1957, at 65, https://www.newspapers.com/clip/50687334/the-times/.

5. Marco Tulio Ribeiro, Sameer Singh & Carlos Guestrin, *"Why Should I Trust You?" Explaining the Predictions of Any Classifier*, arXiv:1602.04938v1 [cs.LG] (Aug. 9, 2016).

6. *See, e.g.*, McCleskey v. Zant, 580 F. Supp. 338, 354 (N.D. Ga. 1984), *aff'd in part, rev'd in part sub nom. McCleskey v. Kemp,* 753 F.2d 877 (11th Cir. 1985), *aff'd,* 481 U.S. 279 (1987) ("As will be noted hereafter, no statistical analysis, much less a multivariate analysis, is any better than the accuracy of the database.").

7. Panagiota Kiourti et al., *TrojDRL: Trojan Attacks on Deep Reinforcement Learning Agents,* arXiv:1903.06638 [cs.CR] (Mar. 1, 2019), https://arxiv.org/pdf/1903.06638.pdf.

8. Safiya Noble, *Google Search: Hyper-Visibility as a Means of Rendering Black Women and Girls Invisible,* Invisible Culture (Oct. 29, 2013), http://ivc.lib.rochester.edu/google-search-hyper-visibility-as-a-means-of-rendering-black-women-and-girls-invisible/; Leon Yin & Aaron Sankin, *Google Ad Portal Equated "Black Girls" with Porn,* THE MARKUP (July 23, 2020), https://themarkup.org/google-the-giant/2020/07/23/google-advertising-keywords-black-girls.

9. O'NEIL, WEAPONS OF MATH DESTRUCTION at 15–31 (2016).

10. Amy Moran-Thomas, *How a Popular Medical Device Encodes Racial Bias,* BOSTON REVIEW (Aug. 5, 2020), https://bostonreview.net/science-nature-race/amy-moran-thomas-how-popular-medical-device-encodes-racial-bias.

11. *Id.*

12. NAT'L AERONAUTICS & SPACE ADM., MARS CLIMATE ORBITER MISHAP INVESTIGATION BOARD, PHASE I REPORT (Nov. 10, 1999).

13. JPL is owned by NASA and managed by the California Institute of California. *See* Jet Propulsion Laboratory, Wikipedia, https://en.wikipedia.org/wiki/Jet_Propulsion_Laboratory.

14. R. Chatila, V. Dignum, M. Fisher, F. Giannotti, K. Morik, S. Russell & K. Yeung, *Trustworthy AI* § 5, *in* REFLECTIONS ON ARTIFICIAL INTELLIGENCE FOR HUMANITY 25 (2021).

15. JAMES GLEICK, CHAOS: MAKING A NEW SCIENCE (1987).

16. State v. Loomis, 881 N.W.2d 749 (Wis. 2016).

17. COMPAS is an acronym for Correctional Offender Management Profiling for Alternative Sanctions.

18. Another due process challenge was based upon COMPAS taking gender into account for its evaluations.

19. J. Angwin, J. Larson, L. Kirchner, *Machine Bias,* PROPUBLICA, May 23, 2016.

20. *Loomis,* 881 N.W.2d at 761 ("Although Loomis cannot review and challenge how the COMPAS algorithm calculates risk, he can at least review and challenge the resulting risk scores set forth in the report attached to the PSI").

21. Hous. Fed'n of Tchrs., Loc. 2415 v. Hous. Indep. Sch. Dist., 251 F. Supp. 3d 1168 (S.D. Tex. 2017).

22. *Id.* at 1180.

23. "When a public agency adopts a policy of making high stakes employment decisions based on secret algorithms incompatible with minimum due process, the proper remedy is to overturn the policy, while leaving the trade secrets intact." *Id.* at 1179.

24. C. Casonato, *AI and Constitutionalism: The Challenges Ahead* § 5.2, *in* REFLECTIONS ON ARTIFICIAL INTELLIGENCE FOR HUMANITY 134 (2021).

25. *Id.*

26. Julia Dressel & Hany Farid, *The Accuracy, Fairness, and Limits of Predicting Recidivism,* SCIENCE ADVANCES (Jan. 17, 2018), vol. 4, no. 1, https://advances.sciencemag.org/content/4/1/eaao5580 (noting an overall accuracy of 67.0% for White offenders and of 63.8% for Black offenders).

27. Julia Angwin et al., *The Legal System Uses an Algorithm to Predict If People Might Be Future Criminals. It's Biased Against Blacks*, MOTHER JONES (May 23, 2016), http://www.motherjones.com/politics/2016/05/machine-police-future-crime-algorithm-bias/; Julie Angwin et al., *Machine Bias*, PROPUBLICA (May 23, 2016), https://www.propublica.org/article/machine-bias-risk-assessments-in-criminal-sentencing/.

28. *Id.* (while 23.5% of Whites who did not re-offend were labeled as high risk, 44.9% of Black were; and while 47.7% of Whites labeled as low risk did re-offend, 28.0% of Blacks did).

29. *Loomis*, 881 N.W.2d at 766. "We determine that COMPAS's use of gender promotes accuracy that ultimately inures to the benefit of the justice system including defendants." *Id.* at 767.

30. However, Chief Justice Roggensack stated in his concurring opinion, "Defendants have a due process right *not* to be sentenced in reliance on improper factors such as on race or gender," (emphasis added), and clarified the majority holding this way, "consideration of COMPAS is permissible; reliance on COMPAS for the sentence imposed is not permissible." *Id.* at 773 and 774.

31. Rohan George, *Predictive Policing: What Is It, How It Works, and Its Legal Implications*, THE CENTER FOR INTERNET & SOCIETY (Nov. 24, 2015), https://cis-india.org/internet-governance/blog/predictive-policing-what-is-it-how-it-works-and-it-legal-implications (citing Elizabeth E. Joh, *Policing by the Numbers: Big Data and the Fourth Amendment*, 89 WASH. L. REV. 35 (2014)).

32. The 2002 science fiction film *Minority Report*, based on the 1956 Phillip K. Dick novella by the same name, takes place in 2054, where three computer-networked psychics have eliminated all murder in Washington, D.C. The "PreCrime" law enforcement unit is tasked with arresting law-abiding citizens whom the psychics predict are likely to commit a murder in the future.

33. John Gramlich, *Most Violent and Property Crimes in the U.S. Go Unsolved*, PEW RESEARCH (Mar. 1, 2017), https://www.pewresearch.org/fact-tank/2017/03/01/most-violent-and-property-crimes-in-the-u-s-go-unsolved/ (reporting that 47% of violent crimes and 35% of property crimes were reported to police).

34. Adapted and modified from slide presentation by William Isaac & Kristian Lum, *To Predict and Serve? Predictive Policing with Biased Training Data* (Oct. 2016) (slide presentation for the Human Rights Data Analysis Group), https://static1.squarespace.com/static/55d4b562e4b091eeab6f80d9/t/580505bcd2b85773b25fce9f/1476724159820/William+Isaac.pdf.

35. Rashida Richardson et al., *Dirty Data, Bad Predictions: How Civil Rights Violations Impact Police Data Predictive Policing Systems, and Justice*, 94 N.Y.U. L. REV. 192, 193–227 (2019), https://www.nyulawreview.org/wp-content/uploads/2019/04/NYULawReview-94-Richardson-Schultz-Crawford.pdf.

36. Jason Tashea, *Should the Pubic Have Access to Data Police Acquire Through Private Companies?*, ABA JOURNAL, Dec. 1, 2016, https://www.abajournal.com/magazine/article/public_access_police_data_private_company.

37. Neil Bedi & Kathleen McGrory, *Targeted | A Times Investigation*, TAMPA BAY TIMES, Nov. 19, 2000, https://projects.tampabay.com/projects/2020/investigations/police-pasco-sheriff-targeted/school-data/.

38. Susan Crawford, *Arresting Crime Before It Happens*, WIRED, Nov. 25, 2015, https://www.wired.com/2015/11/arresting-crime-before-it-happens/.

39. *Advisory Concerning the Chicago Police Department's Predictive Risk Models*, CITY OF CHI. OFF. OF INSPECTOR GEN. (Jan. 23, 2020), https://igchicago.org/wp-content/uploads/2020/01/OIG-Advisory-Concerning-CPDs-Predictive-Risk-Models-.pdf.

40. As explained by its Intelligence-Led Policing Manual: "The Pasco Sheriff's Office has partnered with the Pasco County School Board and Department of Children and Families... to identify juveniles who are at-risk of becoming prolific offenders. The school board uses an Early Warning System, which identifies underperforming students who are at risk of failing. The system takes into account a student's grades, attendance, and behavior. Through DCF's Florida Safe Families Network (FSFN), we are able to identify juveniles who have had adverse childhood experiences (ACEs), which significantly increase their likelihood of developing into serious, violent, and chronic (SVC) offenders. Research suggests that with each additional ACE a child experiences their risk of becoming an SVC offender increases by 35 and children who have experienced four or more are at significant risk of developing into an SVC offender (Fox et al., 2015). Last, our records management system can identify predictors of criminal behavior such as arrests at an early age, arrests for certain offenses, frequently running away, and a juvenile's social network. We combine the results of these three systems to identify those juveniles who are most at-risk to fall into a life of crime...." PASCO SHERIFF'S OFFICE, INTELLIGENCE-LED POLICING MANUAL 13 (revised Jan. 2018).

41. *Id.*

42. Neil Bedi & Kathleen McGrory, *Targeted*, TAMPA BAY TIMES (Sept. 3, 2020), https://projects.tampabay.com/projects/2020/investigations/police-pasco-sheriff-targeted/intelligence-led-policing/.

43. PASCO SHERIFF'S OFFICE, INTELLIGENCE-LED POLICING MANUAL 17–18 (Rev. Jan. 2018).

44. *Id.* at 18.

45. *See generally* Hannah Bloch-Wehba, *Access to Algorithms,* 88 FORDHAM L. REV. 1265, 1283–90 (2020).

46. Veripol, *The 'Intelligent' Polygraph of the Police, Questioned by Experts in Algorithm Ethics*, THE TIMES HUB, March 9, 2021; https://thetimeshub.in/veripol-the-intelligent-polygraph-of-the-police-questioned-by-experts-in-algorithm-ethics/15185/.

47. Shilo Rea, *Beyond Bananas: CMU Scientists Harness "Mind Reading" Technology to Decode Complex Thoughts* (June 26, 2017), https://www.cmu.edu/dietrich/news/news-stories/2017/june/brain-decoding-complex-thoughts.html.

48. FACE SURVEILLANCE AND BIOMETRICS, ELECTRONIC PRIVACY INFORMATION CENTER, https://epic.org/privacy/facerecognition/.

49. Dana Canedy, *Tampa Scans the Faces in Its Crowd of Criminals*, N.Y. TIMES (July 4, 2020), at A1, https://www.nytimes.com/2001/07/04/us/tampa-scans-the-faces-in-its-crowds-for-criminals.html.

50. *Law Enforcement's Use of Facial Recognition Technology: Before the H. Comm. on Oversight and Gov't Reform* (2017) (statement of Kimberly J. Del Greco, Deputy Assistant Directory, Crim. Just. Info. Servs. Div., Fed. Bureau of Investigation).

51. George Joseph, *Staten Island DA Quietly Purchased Controversial Facial Recognition Software*, GOTHAMIST (Jan. 21, 2021), https://gothamist.com/news/staten-island-da-quietly-purchased-controversial-facial-recognition-software.

52. *Clearview AI*, WIKIPEDIA, https://en.wikipedia.org/wiki/Clearview_AI (last visited November 2, 2021).

53. State v. Clearview AI, Inc., No. 226-3-20 Cncv, 2020 Vt. Super. LEXIS 4 (Sept. 4, 2020).

54. Kashmir Hill, *Clearview AI's Facial Recognition App Called Illegal in Canada*, N.Y. TIMES (Feb. 3, 2021), https://www.nytimes.com/2021/02/03/technology/clearview-ai-illegal-canada.html.

55. Joy Buolamwini et al., *Gender Shades: Intersectional Accuracy Disparities in Commercial Gender Classification*, Conference on Fairness, Accountability and Transparency 77–91 (2018), http://proceedings.mlr.press/v81/buolamwini18a/buolamwini18a.pdf (finding commercial facial recognition technology from Microsoft and IBM had higher error rates of up to 20% on female faces, 19% on darker faces, and 34% on darker female faces).

56. Maggie Zhang, *Google Photos Tags Two African-Americans As Gorillas Through Facial Recognition Software*, FORBES, July 1, 2015, https://www.forbes.com/sites/mzhang/2015/07/01/google-photos-tags-two-african-americans-as-gorillas-through-facial-recognition-software/?sh=6588d5e1713d.

57. Asa Fitch, *Facial-Recognition Tools in Spotlight in New Jersey False-Arrest Case*, W.S.J., Dec. 29, 2020, https://www.wsj.com/articles/facial-recognition-tools-in-spotlight-in-new-jersey-false-arrest-case-11609269719.

58. *Facial Recognition Technology Cited in False Arrest Case*, CRIME & JUSTICE NEWS (Dec. 30, 2020), https://thecrimereport.org/2020/12/30/facial-recognition-technology-cited-in-false-arrest-case/.

59. James Spivack & Clare Garvie, *A Taxonomy of Legislative Approaches to Face Recognition in the United States*, in Amba Kak, *Regulating Biometrics: Global Approaches and Urgent Questions*, AI Now (Sept. 2020), at 86–95, https://ainowinstitute.org/regulatingbiometrics-spivack-garvie.pdf.

60. STATEMENT ON PRINCIPLES AND PREREQUISITES FOR THE DEVELOPMENT, EVALUATION AND USE OF UNBIASED FACIAL RECOGNITION TECHNOLOGIES, ACM U.S. TECHNOLOGY POLICY COMMITTEE (June 30, 2020), https://www.acm.org/binaries/content/assets/public-policy/ustpc-facial-recognition-tech-statement.pdf.

61. Max Read, *Why We Should Ban Facial Recognition Technology*, NY MAGAZINE: INTELLIGENCER (Jan. 30, 2020), https://nymag.com/intelligencer/2020/01/why-we-should-ban-facial-recognition-technology.html (noting California, New Hampshire, and Oregon, among other states, ban use of FRT); Amnesty International, *Ban Dangerous Facial Recognition Technology That Amplifies Racist Policing*, AMNESTY (Jan. 26, 2021), https://www.amnesty.org/en/latest/news/2021/01/ban-dangerous-facial-recognition-technology-that-amplifies-racist-policing/.

62. No Biometric Barriers to Housing Act of 2019, H.R. 4008, 116th Cong. (2019), https://www.congress.gov/bill/116th-congress/house-bill/4008/text?r=9&s=1.

63. Samuel Gibbs, *Chatbot Lawyer Overturns 160,000 Parking Tickets in London and New York*, THE GUARDIAN (June 28, 2016), https://www.theguardian.com/technology/2016/jun/28/chatbot-ai-lawyer-donotpay-parking-tickets-london-new-york.

64. Joshua Park, *Your Honor, AI*, HARV. INTERNAT'L REV. (Apr. 3, 2020), https://hir.harvard.edu/your-honor-ai/; *Robot Justice: The Rise of China's 'Internet Courts'*, VOICE OF AMERICA (Dec. 11, 2019), https://learningenglish.voanews.com/a/robot-justice-the-rise-of-china-s-internet-courts-/5201677.html.

65. Andrew Van Dam, *Algorithms Were Supposed to Make Virginia Judges Fairer, What Happened Was Far More Complicated*, WASH. POST (Nov. 19, 2019), https://www.washingtonpost.com/business/2019/11/19/algorithms-were-supposed-make-virginia-judges-more-fair-what-actually-happened-was-far-more-complicated/.

66. *Id.*

67. Jason Tashea, *France Bans Publishing Judicial Analytics and Prompts Criminal Penalty*, ABA J. (Jun. 7, 2019), https://www.abajournal.com/news/article/france-bans-and-creates-criminal-penalty-for-judicial-analytics.

68. *Id.*

69. Rachel Beithon, *5 Reasons to Leverage Litigation Data for Your Case*, THOMSON REUTERS, https://legal.thomsonreuters.com/en/insights/articles/5-reasons-to-use-litigation-analytics-on-westlaw-edge.

70. *See generally* Virginia Eubanks, AUTOMATING INEQUALITY (2019), for further discussion of the ways in which ADS and AI algorithms have worsened wealth inequity and denied the poor access to justice.

71. Andrew Guthrie Ferguson, *The Big Data Jury*, 91 NOTRE DAME L. REV. 935, 941 (2016), https://scholarship.law.nd.edu/cgi/viewcontent.cgi?article=4641&context=ndlr.

72. Daniel Faggella, *AI in Law and Legal Practice—A Comprehensive View of 35 Current Applications*, EMERJ (Mar. 14, 2020), https://emerj.com/ai-sector-overviews/ai-in-law-legal-practice-current-applications/.

73. Katherine Medianik, *Artificially Intelligent Lawyers: Updating the Model Rules of Professional Conduct in Accordance with the New Technological Era*, 39 CARDOZO L. REV. 1497, 1518 (2018) ("In terms of implementing the work of an AI lawyer to a case, when a lawyer relies solely on ROSS's outputs, independent professional judgment—as required by Model Rule 2.1—vanishes because reliance on such outputs turns into dependence on the judgments of a technological apparatus.").

74. CRIMINAL JUSTICE SYSTEM, PARTNERSHIP FOR AI, REPORT ON ALGORITHMIC RISK ASSESSMENT TOOLS IN THE U.S. (Apr. 26, 2019), https://www.partnershiponai.org/report-on-machine-learning-in-risk-assessment-tools-in-the-u-s-criminal-justice-system/.

75. Algorithmic Accountability Act of 2019, H.R. 2231, 116th Cong. (Apr. 10, 2019), https://www.congress.gov/bill/116th-congress/house-bill/2231 (FTC can require entities with more than $50 million annual revenues and who act as a data broker or control personally identifiable information of one million or more people/devices to conduct bias impact assessments for high-risk automated decision systems and high-risk information systems).

76. Algorithmic Fairness Act of 2020, S. 5052, 116th Cong. (Dec. 17, 2020), https://www.congress.gov/bill/116th-congress/senate-bill/5052/text.

SIX

Should Justice Really Be Blind? Can We Really Stay Silent?

Implicit Bias in the Courtroom

Jack Fiander, Yakama Nation member representing tribes and tribal members in Washington State

A Note from the Editors: One of our goals for this second book was to include an even greater diversity of authors and expertise than the first—diversity broadly defined in terms of topics, authors, perspectives, and expertise. We wanted to use our voices to promote hearing more voices. In this—knowing how often they are invisible or excluded—we were particularly interested in hearing from our Native American colleagues. We met Attorney Fiander through reading his work and are honored to be able to offer his insights here, and there are many. We urge our readers to consider Attorney Fiander's thinking and work in their own settings, paying special attention to the enduring importance of language to do ill or good. We intend to heed his call to action to take action in our own professional settings, even if it is unusual action, "in the interests of justice" to "avoid unjust results or bias." We invite you to join us in this work.

CHAPTER HIGHLIGHTS

- Explicit and implicit bias against Native people is long-standing, well-documented, and well-known.
- This bias is evident in court opinions and proceedings. "Such past opinions can continue to perpetuate injustice by their very existence"[1] to the detriment of Native people and us all.
- We can use the tools of our trade as lawyers and judges to directly address biased precedent and historical injustice.

CHAPTER CONTENTS

1. A Personal Introduction
2. The Price of Implicit Bias
3. The Language of the Nation of Laws
4. What Can We Do?
    A. An Example of Judicial Discretion to Limit Bias
    B. An Example of the Use of Common Law to Limit Bias
    C. An Example of Judicial Policy and Intervention to Limit Bias
5. Call to Action

Appendix: *State v. Towessnute*, 197 Wash. 2d 574, 486 P.3d 111 (2020)

1. A Personal Introduction

As a young lawyer I entered the criminal courtroom of the local rural county courthouse accompanied by my able assistant and co-counsel, whom I shall refer to as Elizabeth, to attend the arraignment of a low-income client. We were promptly asked by the presiding judge who we were "because I don't see your names on the docket." Apparently, being Yakama Indians, neither Elizabeth nor I fit the profile of normal attorneys and were presumed to be criminal defendants. Implicit bias.

Some thirty years later, I similarly arrived at court in a major metropolitan area to represent a fellow tribal member. Upon seeking to enter the bar where other counsel awaited their clients' cases to be called, I was stopped by the bailiff who informed me that "only attorneys were allowed up here." Upon providing proof of bar admission, I was allowed to cross. Upon arrival of the Clerk five minutes later, I was asked whether I was the court interpreter. Implicit bias. Fortunately, as a long time litigator my larger than normal ego is immune to indignities, but it was not always the case.

One day in 1989 the government of my tribe realized that it had grown to a size meriting the need for In-House counsel to address its many affairs. On that day I happened to be litigating a trial nearby, and a member of the Tribal Council was sent to observe me. Subsequently, I was contacted by a partner of the law firm that theretofore had represented the tribe. I acknowledged my availability, and we agreed upon a salary. At the end of our discussion he sheepishly informed me of one problem—my long hair. The Vice Chairman of the Council wanted me to get a haircut. Apparently, my appearance was not deemed "professional" enough. Our tribal culture, having been publicly suppressed and derogated for so long in favor of adopting nontribal norms has made many of my people uncomfortable with who they are. Implicit bias turned inward.[2]

Still, embedded in the culture of Yakama Indians is the need to ceremoniously prepare for important events. On the day of my interview a friend meticulously braided my hair. Upon arrival at the interview I was met by the tribal chairman, a traditional Yakama. His immediate greeting at which the remaining Council members were present was "hey, I like your hair." Problem solved. Ingroup supported.

You have my apologies. Like any lawyer making a presentation, I have digressed into anecdotes and war stories rather than sticking to the topic of remedying past injustices and restraining implicit bias from entering the courtroom.

2. The Price of Implicit Bias

As was eloquently stated by Judge Chad Schmucker and Joseph Sawyer regarding implicit bias in the first volume of this series:

> Also referred to as heuristics, mental shortcuts, cognitive blind spots, schemas, mental associations, and implicit associations, implicit biases allow the brain to operate more efficiently. But unfortunately, the increase in efficiency can come at a price with a human toll.[3]

In terms of this human toll, our present will one day be our past. As participants in the judicial system, we have an obligation to ask ourselves whether there are biases we are currently blind to that we may look back upon a hundred years from now with embarrassment. In furtherance of the goals of the American Bar Association to promote justice and the rule of law, let's examine this issue together. Certainly, each of us holds the power to descend within ourselves to examine the implicit or explicit biases we knowingly, or unwittingly, hold and attempt to construct a wall preventing them from entering the courtroom.

3. The Language of the Nation of Laws

The more difficult task we must acknowledge is that there are explicit biases—which often rise to the level of prejudices—that are enshrined in many of the published decisions of the courts of our nation. The slogan so firmly embedded in our culture that "we are a nation of laws, not of men" expresses the principle of *stare decisis* requiring courts to follow prior precedent in administering justice (notwithstanding that the maxim carries within its words its own misogyny). I often wish there were a means by which to purge such writings from our public view.

If, within the confines of the First Amendment, we can block harmful speech and prohibit its presentation to our vulnerable, and presumably susceptible, public and selves, why do we allow the harmful and often defamatory speech to remain in the reporters on the bookshelves of our public institutions?

How do we reconcile this idea of being a nation of laws with the language of decisions such as these:

- *Johnson v. M'Intosh* where tribal natives are described as "fierce savages," as "mere occupants" of the soil "incapable of transferring the absolute title to others" but subject to the "ultimate dominion" of the nations of Europe.[4]
- *Dred Scott v. Sandford*, where Americans descended from slaves are described as "subordinate" and "inferior" and found not to be citizens notwithstanding their birth in the United States.[5]
- *Elk v. Wilkins*, where Indians are described as not fit to be "let out of the state of pupilage."[6]
- *Lone Wolf v. Hitchcock*, where members of the confederated tribes of Kiowas, Comanches, and Apaches are said to be subject to the "paramount" and "plenary power" of the United States over their affairs.[7]
- *Leschi v. Washington Territory*, where, in my home state, Chief Leschi was convicted and hung for the murder of an Army officer in a battle between the Niqually Tribe and the territorial militia, notwithstanding that the death was a casualty of war and notwithstanding prior assurances by the army that the Nisqually would not be prosecuted for acts committed during the Indian War.[8] (Chief Leschi's case was later reconsidered by a specially convened History Court of Inquiry and Justice, and the Chief exonerated.[9])

Notwithstanding that some of the more visible of such decisions have been reviewed or overruled,[10] many such precedents portraying certain classes of people as less human than Euro-American immigrants remain in the official reporters and have not been withdrawn or vacated. That is, many published court decisions remain that explicitly describe my fellow tribal people (and thereby describe me) as incapable, fierce savages.

This kind of language perpetuates itself and has power. Consider, for just one example the language of the 1877 decision in *Beecher v. Wetherby*.[11] In discussing a property claim involving tribal use of land subject to a treaty with the Menomonee nation of Indians, the Court said, "It is to be presumed that in this matter the United States would be governed by such considerations of justice as would control a Christian people in their treatment of an ignorant and dependent race."[12] This language is quoted in the *Lone Wolf* decision discussed above and in numerous other cases (and cited in even more). While the more recent of these cases may interpret the treaties in question with more deference to the Indian nations, the repetition of the language in itself remains both explicitly and implicitly biased.[13] That is, the flip side of the implicit bias of maintaining such opinions rather than denouncing or vacating them is that such portrayals remain as part of the language of the law, open to readers without contradiction, seeping into the media of our society, to be absorbed as part of the culture—in other words, contributing to ongoing explicit and implicit bias against the image and self-image of my people.

4. What Can We Do?

Having dabbled a bit in trying to remedy past injustices in past cases, I now believe that, in the absence of statutory authority, calling on the court to exercise its discretion with implicit bias in mind, using court policy and rules, and invoking the common law are potentially the most effective approaches for causing the vacation and withdrawal of unjust court opinions—examples follow.

A. An Example of Judicial Discretion to Limit Bias

One of the implicit biases that judges presiding over civil cases sometimes display is favoring the expert testimony of those possessing advanced degrees and a record of extensive publications over the testimony of ordinary persons whose knowledge is based upon lived experience or oral history. In many of the diverse cultures of this nation, especially those that until recently lacked a written language, knowledge is passed on generationally by oral tradition.

In 1997, Senior United States District Judge Alan McDonald—also known as The Duke—was faced with the task of determining the intent of the parties to an Indian treaty by considering the trial testimony of three expert witnesses. The Duke concluded as follows:

> Dr. Deward Walker also testified as an expert on behalf of plaintiffs. Dr. Walker possesses a Ph.D. in anthropology, the comparative study of past and present human cultures.
>
> ...
>
> Dr. Kent Richards, a professor of history at Central Washington University, testified on behalf of state defendants.
>
> ...
>
> Mr. Yallup was taught the meaning of the Treaty by his grandparents.
>
> ...

> With all due deference to the experience and impressive credentials of Dr. Walker and Dr. Richards, the court considers Mr. Yallup the ultimate expert in this proceeding. From his early childhood, Mr. Yallup was taught the meaning of the Treaty, as understood by the Yakamas, through oral history passed down through the generations.[14]

In other words, Fed. R. Evid. 702 does not confer greater expert witness status or credibility to those possessing educational degrees. To avoid implicit bias, we should be aware that expert knowledge comes in many forms.

B. An Example of the Use of Common Law to Limit Bias

As lawyers, we are aware of the roots of the United States Constitution in the Magna Carta, the writings of Coke and Blackstone, the Federalist Papers, even the Code of Hammurabi. Given the youth of our country, we Americans tend to think that newer is better and, perhaps unfortunately, that ancient civilizations were less advanced. However, much wisdom upon which our Constitution was founded, was based upon principles of common law traceable to Latin antecedents. Upon their formation, most states in the nation enacted "reception" statutes adopting the common law. And that common law is replete with extraordinary writs designed to remedy injustices *nunc pro tunc*, or "now for then."

Hirabayashi v. United States illustrates the value of using common law writs to rectify past wrongs. Gordon Hirabayashi, an American citizen of Japanese descent, was convicted of violating the wartime curfews imposed on him. Saying that they could not "close [their] eyes to the fact, demonstrated by experience, that in time of war[,] residents having ethnic affiliations with an invading enemy may be a greater source of danger than those of a different ancestry,"[15] the Supreme Court upheld the conviction. In the 1980s, after evidence of new materials regarding the initial military report was found, Hirabayashi invoked the writ of *habeas corpus coram nobis* to overturn his unjust 1942 conviction. Interestingly, the Ninth Circuit's opening explanation of the case lays out my point about implicit bias and the need to call biased court opinions to task.

> The *Hirabayashi* and *Korematsu* decisions have never occupied an honored place in our history. In the ensuing four and a half decades, journalists and researchers have stocked library shelves with studies of the cases and surrounding events. These materials document historical judgments that the convictions were unjust. They demonstrate that there could have been no reasonable military assessment of an emergency at the time, that the orders were based upon racial stereotypes, and that the orders caused needless suffering and shame for thousands of American citizens. The legal judgments of the courts reflecting that Hirabayashi and Korematsu had been properly

convicted of violating the laws of the United States, however, remained on their records.¹⁶

The Ninth Circuit described the petitioner as seeking "a writ of error *coram nobis* to vacate his convictions and thus to make the judgments of the courts conform to the judgments of history."¹⁷

C. An Example of Judicial Policy and Intervention to Limit Bias

While the 1987 *Hirabayashi* decision by the Ninth Circuit is an iconic example of using the common law to overturn a past, biased, unjust opinion, courts have other methods available to them. I consider a leading example here to be the use by the Washington State Supreme Court of policy and intervention to correct injustices like *Hirabayashi* and *Korematsu*. In June 2020, the nine justices of the Washington State Supreme Court were "compelled by recent events to join other state supreme courts around the nation in addressing our legal community" and issued a letter to "members of the legal community" stating *inter alia* that:

> As judges, we must recognize the role we have played in devaluing black lives. This very court once held that a cemetery could lawfully deny grieving black parents the right to bury their infant. We cannot undo this wrong—but we can recognize our ability to do better in the future. We can develop a greater awareness of our own conscious and unconscious biases in order to make just decisions in individual cases, and we can administer justice and support court rules in a way that brings greater racial justice to our system as a whole.¹⁸

Essentially, the Washington Supreme Court announced to the judiciary and members of the bar over which it presides that, when circumstances warrant, the blind application of prior precedents should be viewed through a current lens. True to its commitment, one month later, the court unanimously repudiated a its century-old decision portraying members of Native American tribes as "savages" who merely "wandered about" squandering vast acreages of fertile lands.¹⁹ Three months later, the Washington Court, in a footnote, quietly yet expressly overruled *Price v. Evergreen Cemetery Company of Seattle*,²⁰ which had upheld the exclusion of those of African American descent from being buried in a "White" cemetery.²¹ The Court said:

> We take this opportunity to overrule this court's opinion in *Price v. Evergreen Cemetery Co. of Seattle*, 57 Wn.2d 352, 357 P.2d 702 (1960). We may overrule a prior case when it is both incorrect and harmful.... It is harmful for two reasons: first, because it suggests a more stringent standard than is required to survive an article II, section 19 challenge, second, and more importantly, the case is harmful because of Justice Mallery's concurrence,

which condemns civil rights and integration, "As judges, we must recognize the role we have played in devaluing black lives." Letter from the Wash. State Supreme Court to the Members of the Judiciary and the Legal Cmty. 1 (June 4, 2020) (addressing racial injustice). The Price concurrence is an example of the unfortunate role we have played. (internal citations omitted).[22]

The leadership shown by the Washington Supreme Court by its willingness to examine its prior opinions for bias has already filtered down to lower courts, freeing them to depart from blindly following precedents they know to be unjust. For example, on February 2, 2021, the Washington State Court of Appeals, an intermediate appellate tribunal, issued an opinion in an appeal by an Indian tribe of a trial court decision denying its motion to vacate an agreed order that contained a settlement with a local county that had failed to comply with its terms. The opinion of the three judge panel begins as follows: "This appeal concerns one of endless broken promises by American government authorities toward Native Americans. The breach of an agreement in this instance also encompasses a violation of a court order."[23] I anticipate more Washington courts to speak similarly under the rubric of the state's Supreme Court letter.

5. Call to Action

Our justice system only works if our citizens have faith in its ability to administer justice. As a member of that justice system I am proud to state that, of late, the courts of our nation appear to have not hesitated in removing bias from the system. Admittedly, however, many litigators are failures at improving the administration of justice and accepting our special responsibility in the preservation of society. Rather than directly and openly seeking to eliminate implicit bias from the courtroom, I myself am guilty of exploiting it. I cannot say I am ashamed of the many times I have given criminal defendants a complete makeover in order to play to implicit biases of jurors, because it often results in acquittal. There have been occasions on which I transformed for a trial into a God fearing patriotic small town country lawyer as easily as a chameleon if it served my purpose. The law professor and former prosecutor under whom I interned as a third-year law student suggested early on that, in representing the Iranian American students attending the University on student visas, I should have them remove their jewelry and watches before entering the courtroom lest they risk a prejudicial result.[24] As I near the end of my career I have abandoned such tactics and am mildly embarrassed at the lack of faith I previously had in our justice system. Addressing the concept of implicit bias and whether or how it impacts the administration of justice is frustrating. We are all products of our environment who are influenced by nature and nurture.

When our beliefs are implicit we necessarily are not consciously aware of them. As participants in the judicial system we have a responsibility to examine ourselves and decide whether justice is best served by fashioning our conduct to play to implicit biases to our advantage or by resolving to join the authors of this desk book and our judiciary in seeking its elimination. This work can be seen as a call to action for all of us. For example, I enlisted the aid of the Washington State Attorney General, who joined in the effort to vacate Alec Towessnute's unjust conviction discussed earlier.

As lawyers and members of the bar, we must recognize the harms that are caused when meritorious claims go unaddressed due to systemic inequities or the lack of financial, personal, or systemic support. And we must also recognize that this is not how a *justice* system must operate. Too often in the legal profession, we feel bound by tradition and the way things have "always" been. We must remember that even the most venerable precedent must be struck down when it is incorrect and harmful. The systemic oppression of Black or other peoples is not merely incorrect and harmful—it is shameful and deadly. It perpetuates itself if we do not interrupt and intervene.

Members of the judiciary, as controllers of the courtroom please feel free to invoke the principles of common law or the court rules meriting unusual actions "in the interests of justice" if that is necessary to avoid unjust results or bias in the courtroom.

So, You'd Like to Know More

- Walter R. Echo-Hawk, In the Courts of the Conqueror: The 10 Worst Indian Law Cases Ever Decided (2010).
- Jimm G. Good Tracks, Native American Non-Interference, 18 Social Work 30 (1973).

About the Author

Jack Fiander, a Yakama attorney and enrolled Yakama tribal member, has practiced law in Washington State for more than 35 years. He is a graduate of the University of Washington School of Law in Seattle.

Appendix

State v. Towessnute

Supreme Court of Washington

July 10, 2020, Decided; July 10, 2020, Filed

No. 13083-3

Reporter 197 Wn.2d 574 *; *State v. Towessnute*, 486 P.3d 111 (Wash. 2020) **; 2020 Wash. LEXIS 763 ***; *State v. Towessnute*, No. 13083-3, 2020 WL 9439422 (Wash. July 10, 2020)

THE STATE OF WASHINGTON, *Appellant*, v. ALEC TOWESSNUTE, *Respondent*.

Counsel: *Andrew K. Miller, Prosecuting Attorney*; and *Robert W. Ferguson, Attorney General*, for appellant.

Jack W. Fiander (of *Towtnuk Law Offices*), for respondent.

Judges: Stephens, C.J. Johnson, J., Madsen, J., Owens, J., González, J., Gordon McCloud, J., Yu, J., Montoya-Lewis, J., Whitener, J.

Opinion

[Unpublished order redesignated as opinion and ordered published by order of the Supreme Court April 26, 2021.]

En Banc

[1, 2] ¶1 "The injustice still plaguing our country has its roots in the individual and collective actions of many, and it cannot be addressed without the individual and collective actions of us all." Letter from the Wash. State Supreme Court to Members of Judiciary & Legal Cmty. (June 4, 2020), https://www.courts.wa.gov/content/publicUpload/Supreme%20Court%20News/Judiciary%20Legal%20Community%20SIGNED%20060420.pdf [https://perma.cc/QNT4-H5P7]. Injustice has many faces and forms, and some of its history lies in the past opinions of this court. Such past opinions can continue to perpetrate injustice by their very existence. Today, we address one of those historical injustices.

¶2 On May 15, 1915, the State charged Alec Towessnute, a Yakama tribal member, with multiple fishing crimes. These criminal charges stemmed from the fact that he was fishing in the usual and accustomed waters of the Yakama tribe the day before. The charging document filed in Benton County stated that Mr. Towessnute was fishing with a "gaff hook in the Yakima river … more than five miles away [*576] from any Indian Reservation." Information, No. 13083-3 (Benton County Super. Ct. Wash. May 15, 1915). On May 29, 1915, C.W. Fristoe, Benton County Prosecuting Attorney, [***2] and Francis Garrecht, United States Attorney and Attorney for Mr. Towessnute, filed a stipulation. They agreed that Mr. Towessnute was a Yakama tribal member, that he had engaged in fishing in the Yakima River without a state issued fishing license, that he used an unpermitted fishing hook, and, critically, that the fishing took place "in the usual and accustomed fishing places of the members of the confederated tribes and bands of Indians known as the Yakima Nation." Stipulation at 2, No. 13083-3 (Benton County Super. Ct. Wash. May 15, 1915). The stipulation further stated that the United States had entered into a treaty with the Yakama Nation on June 9, 1855 (ratified [**112] by the U.S. Senate on March 8, 1855) and that the area where Mr. Towessnute fished "has been used and enjoyed by said Indians during the fishing season of each and every year since said treaty was made, that said fishing place has from time immemorial been used and enjoyed by said Indians and their ancestors and known by the Indian name of 'Top-tut.'" *Id.*

¶3 Mr. Towessnute objected to the charges. Relying on the Stipulation, he explained that Benton County had no jurisdiction over the matter because he had committed no crime by exercising his treaty fishing rights. The trial [***3] court judge agreed: on June 10, 1915, Benton County Superior Court Judge Bert Linn entered a final judgment in the matter, dismissing all the charges against Mr. Towessnute.

¶4 The Benton County Prosecutor's Office, however, disagreed. The prosecutor filed a notice of appeal to this court, and it was fully briefed. This court issued the opinion that gives rise to this matter now before the court: *State v. Towessnute*, 89 Wash. 478, 154 P. 805 (1916). In that opinion, the court reversed the trial court's decision to dismiss the charges, mandated that the criminal charges be reinstated, and overruled Mr. Towessnute's objections. The record in [*577] this matter following the mandate of the Washington State Supreme Court cannot be located, so it is not clear whether Mr. Towessnute was convicted of the offenses with which he was charged—though a companion case to his did result in a conviction, which was vacated in 2015.

¶5 In 2015, the descendants of Mr. Towessnute, represented by attorney Jack Fiander and supported by the Washington State Attorney General, sought vacation of any record of conviction against Mr. Towessnute. Given that such a conviction could not be proven by the record, the trial court declined to take any action.*[1]

¶6 Mr. Fiander brought [***4] this matter to our court's attention again, in 2020, seeking remedial action to right the injustice against Mr. Towessnute and the

---

* Under Wash. Rev. Code § 9.96.060(4), "Every person convicted prior to January 1, 1975, of violating any statute or rule regarding the regulation of fishing activities, including, but not limited Wash. Rev. Code § 75.08.260, 75.12.060, 75.12.070, 75.12.160, 77.16.020, 77.16.030, 77.16.040, 77.16.060, 77.16.240 who claimed to be exercising a treaty Indian fishing right, may apply to the sentencing court for vacation of the applicant's record of the misdemeanor, gross misdemeanor, or felony conviction for the offense. If the person is deceased, a member of the person's family or an official representative of the tribe of which the person was a member may apply to the court on behalf of the deceased person."

Yakama Nation. The Washington Attorney General supports this request for the court to take action in this matter, and the court agrees that it can and should act.

¶7 The opinion in *State v. Towessnute* is an example of the racial injustice described in this court's June 4, 2020 letter, and it fundamentally misunderstood the nature of treaties and their guarantees, as well as the concept of tribal sovereignty. For example, that old opinion claimed: "The premise of Indian sovereignty we reject.... Only that title [to land] was esteemed which came from white men, and the rights of these have always been ascribed by the highest authority to lawful discovery of lands occupied, to be sure, but not owned, by any one before." *Id*.. And that old opinion rejected the arguments of Mr. Towessnute and the United States that treaties are the supreme law of the land. It also rejected the Yakama Treaty's assurance of [*578] the tribal members' right to fish in the usual and accustomed waters, in the usual and accustomed manner, as the tribe had done from time immemorial. This court [***5] characterized the Native people of this nation as "a dangerous child," who "squander[ed] vast areas of fertile land before our eyes." *Id*..

¶8 Today, we take the opportunity presented to us by the descendants of Mr. Towessnute; their counsel, Mr. Fiander, the Washington State Attorney General Robert Ferguson; and by the call to justice to which we all committed on June 4, 2020, to repudiate this case; its language; its conclusions; and its mischaracterization of the Yakama people, who continue the customs, traditions, and responsibilities that include the fishing and conservation of the salmon in the Yakima River. Under the Rules of Appellate Procedure (RAP) 1.2(c), [**113] this court may act and waive any of the RAP "to serve the ends of justice." We do so today. We cannot forget our own history, and we cannot change it. We can, however, forge a new path forward, committing to justice as we do so.

¶9 Therefore, it is hereby ordered:

¶10 That the mandate issued by this court in 1916 is recalled and any conviction existing then or now against Mr. Towessnute is vacated.

¶11 DATED at Olympia, Washington, this 10th day of July, [***6] 2020.

STEPHENS, C.J., and JOHNSON, MADSEN, OWENS, GONZÁLEZ, YU, GORDON MCCLOUD, MONTOYA-LEWIS, and WHITENER, JJ., concur.

Endnotes

1. State v. Towessnute, 197 Wash. 2d 574, 575, 486 P.3d 111, 111 (2020) (recalling order and vacating conviction State v. Towessnute, 89 Wn. 478 (1916)).

2. Stereotype threat is sometimes described as implicit bias turned inward. Being aware of a negative stereotype about one's group, one's behavior may confirm that belief. *See generally* Claude M. Steele & Joshua Aronson, *Stereotype Threat and the Intellectual Test Performance of African Americans*, 69 J. PERSONALITY & SOC. PSYCHOL. 797 (1995).

3. Chad Schmucker & Joseph Sawyer, *Decision Making, Implicit Bias, and Judges in* ENHANCING JUSTICE: REDUCING BIAS (Sarah E. Redfield ed. 2017).

4. Johnson v. M'Intosh, 21 U.S. (8 Wheat) 543, 590, 571 (1823). The Court goes on to describe this as inevitable given *the law of the land:* "If the property of the great mass of the community originates in it, it becomes the law of the land, and cannot be questioned. So, too, with respect to the concomitant principle, that the Indian inhabitants are to be considered merely as occupants, to be protected, indeed, while in peace, in the possession of their lands, but to be deemed incapable of transferring the absolute title to others." *Id.* at 591.

5. Scott v. Sandford, 60 U.S. (19 How.) 393, 404–05 (1857). The Court poses the question as, "Can a negro, whose ancestors were imported into this country, and sold as salves, become a member of the political community formed and brought into existence by the Constitution of the United States, and as such become entitled to all the rights, and privileges, and immunities, guaranteed by that instrument to the citizen?" and answers, "We think they are not, and that they are not included, and were not intended to be included, under the word 'citizens' in the Constitution, and can therefore claim none of the rights and privileges which that instrument provides for and secures to citizens of the United States. On the contrary, they were at that time considered as a subordinate and inferior class of beings, who had been subjugated by the dominant race, and, whether emancipated or not, yet remained subject to their authority, and had no rights or privileges but such as those who held the power and the Government might choose to grant them." The Court distinguishes the "slaves" from the "Indian race," which it describes as both "uncivilized" and " yet a free and independent people, associated together in nations or tribes, and governed by their own laws. *Id.* at 403–5.

6. Elk v. Wilkins, 112 U.S. 94, 106–07 (1884) (In finding in a suit by John Elk against the Omaha registrar of voting that the Indian plaintiff was not a citizen, the Court observed: "But the question whether any Indian tribes, or any members thereof, have become so far advanced in civilization, that they should be let out of the state of pupilage, and admitted to the privileges and responsibilities of citizenship, is a question to be decided by the nation whose wards they are and whose citizens they seek to become, and not by each Indian for himself.").

7. Lone Wolf v. Hitchcock, 187 U.S. 553, 566 (1903). In reviewing the precedent the Court notes: "In one of the cited cases it was clearly pointed out that Congress possessed a paramount power over the property of the Indians, by reason of its exercise of guardianship over their interests, and that such authority might be implied, even though opposed to the strict letter of a treaty with the Indians." *Id.* at 221.

8. Leschi v. Wash. Territory, 1 Wash. Terr. 13 (1857). Many at the time and since—including the hangman—maintained the Chief's innocence and a symbolic panel of retired jurists later determined him to have been combatant in a war between tribes and the United States. *See* Hans Sherrer, *Chief Leschi Exonerated of Murder—146 Years After His Execution*, http ://forejustice.org/wc/chief_leschi/chief_leschi.htm.

138 Extending Justice

9. In 2004, an Historical Court of Inquiry and Justice retried Leschi in absentia. The court was comprised of one judge representing the Nisqually Tribe and six state court judges including Washington Supreme Court Chief Justice Gerry Alexander. Chief Leschi was unanimously exonerated with the judges concluding that "regardless of who shot [Colonel] Moses, [t]he killing was a legitimate act of war, immune from prosecution." Hans Sherrer, *Chief Leschi Exonerated of Murder—146 Years After His Execution*, http://forejustice.org/wc/chief_leschi/chief_leschi.htm.

10. As discussed in this Chapter, Leschi by a special court; Hirabayashi and Korematsu by subsequent appeals, Dredd Scott by the 14th Amendment.

11. Beecher v. Wetherby, 95 U.S. 517, 525 (1877).

12. *Id.* at 525.

13. *See, e.g.,* Oneida Nation v. Vill. of Hobart, 968 F.3d 664 (7th Cir. 2020) (quoting *Beecher* though observing that the harsh rule of *Lone Wolf* and *Beecher* has been mitigated).

14. Yakama Indian Nation v. Flores, 955 F. Supp. 1229, 1236–37 (E.D. Wash. 1997).

15. Hirabayashi v. United States, 320 U.S. 81, 101 (1943); *see also* Korematsu v. United States, 323 U.S. 214 (1944), Korematsu v. United States, 584 F. Supp. 1406 (N.D. Cal. 1984) (granting writ of corum nobis); Trump v. Hawaii, 138 S. Ct. 2392 (2018) (stating in the context of an immigration decision, in regard to Korematsu: "The dissent's reference to Korematsu, however, affords this Court the opportunity to make express what is already obvious: Korematsu was gravely wrong the day it was decided, has been overruled in the court of history, and—to be clear—"has no place in law under the Constitution." 323 U. S. at 248 (Jackson, J., dissenting)." *Trump* at 2423.

16. *Hirabayashi,* 828 F.2d 591 at 593, 608.

17. As the Ninth Circuit explains, "coram nobis relief is available to challenge the validity of a conviction, even though the sentence has been fully served, "under circumstances compelling such action to achieve justice" *Id.* at 593 (citing United States v. Morgan, 346 U.S. 502 (1954) (internal citations omitted)).

18. Open Letter from the Washington State Supreme Court to the Members of the Judiciary and the Legal Community (June 4, 2020).

19. *Towessnute,* 197 Wn.2d 574, 486 P.3d 111 (2020).

20. Price v. Evergreen Cemetery Company of Seattle, 57 Wn.2d 352 (1960), *overruled by* Garfield Cty. Transp. Auth. v. State, 196 Wash. 2d 378, 390 n.1, 473 P.3d 1205 (2020).

21. *See* David Gutman, *A Black Seattle Family Couldn't Bury Their Young Son Where They Wished Because of Racism, 60 Years Later, Does An Apology Help?*, SEATTLE TIMES (Nov. 24, 2020), https://www.seattletimes.com/seattle-news/a-black-seattle-family-was-barred-from-burying-their-young-son-60-years-later-does-an-apology-help/#:~:text=In%201957%2C%20the%20Price%20family%20was%20kept%20from,Hansen%20%26%20Ramon%20Dompor%20%2F%20The%20Seattle%20Times%29.

22. Garfield Cty. Transp. Auth. v. State, 196 Wash. 2d 378, 390, n.1, 473 P.3d 1205, 1205 n.1 (2020).

23. Confederated Tribes v. Okanogan County, No. 37129-8-III (Wn. Ct. Appeals, Feb. 2, 2021) (unpublished opinion).

24. The late Professor Charles Z. Smith went on to serve as a justice of the Washington State Supreme Court.

SEVEN

Roundtable Conversation: Prosecutors' Reflections on Implicit Bias

A Note from the Editors: For this Chapter, we convened a session where leading practitioners could talk about their experiences. We were honored to have a diverse, experienced, and thoughtful panel, and equally honored to have the benefit of Judge Fowlkes' experience and wisdom in asking important questions and moderating the conversation. The questions ranged from prosecutorial discretion to hiring, to office management, to accountability, and to DEI (Diversity, Equity, and Inclusion writ large). The answers and discussion were honest, perceptive, and shrewd. The collective intellect and insight here can't be overstated.

Roundtable Participants

We invited a group of prosecutors to reflect on their experiences with implicit bias in their work. The Honorable John T. Fowlkes, Jr., himself an experienced public defender and prosecutor, as well as a Judge, served as a thoughtful and thought-provoking moderator.

Calvin David Biggers, Jr.

Mr. Biggers is a native of Tuskegee, Alabama. At the time of this panel, Mr. Biggers was an Assistant United States Attorney in the Western District of Tennessee. He previously served as Executive Assistant United States Attorney, Deputy Chief United States Attorney, re-entry and outreach coordinator, and project "safe neighborhoods" coordinator in the office. He has contributed to the formation of the Western District Federal Re-Entry Council and established a U.S.

Attorneys' Office Re-Entry program. He also oversaw violent crimes and firearms prosecution efforts from 2015–2020. Prior to coming to Western Tennessee, Mr. Biggers was a Special Assistant United States Attorney in the Northern District of Alabama, from 2008–2011. There, he prosecuted federal drug and violent crime offenses such as bank robberies, and car jackings. He also participated in the launch of the federal drug court program team in Northern Alabama. He began his career as a prosecutor as an Assistant District Attorney in Jefferson County, Alabama, handling juvenile court matters. Mr. Biggers has also been involved in many community projects, professionally and socially, volunteering his time with community groups and organizations.

Justin Bingham

Justin Bingham has served as a prosecuting attorney for the City of Spokane since 2001 and was appointed the City Prosecutor in 2014. During his career as a prosecutor, Mr. Bingham has dealt with every type of crime punishable in the Municipal Court system. He has participated in numerous specialty court models including Mental Health Court, Veterans Court, Community Court and Domestic Violence Court. Mr. Bingham is heavily involved in the criminal justice reform efforts currently taking place in Spokane. Hehas served on the Spokane Regional Law and Justice Council for many years and is a member of the local MacArthur Foundation Safety & Justice Challenge core team. Mr. Bingham has been actively engaged in criminal justice reform on both a statewide and national level. Mr. Bingham sits as a prosecutor representative on the WSBA Council on Public Defense, has served on both the Washington State Pre-Trial Reform Taskforce and the Jury Diversity Taskforce, and is the chair-elect of the American Bar Association (ABA) Criminal Justice Section. Mr. Bingham is a proud graduate of the University of Tennessee, as well as Gonzaga University School of Law. His rules for prosecutors are fairly simple: work hard, be nice to people, and seek justice.

The Honorable John T. Fowlkes, Jr.

John T. Fowlkes, Jr. is a United States District Judge of the United States District Court for the Western District of Tennessee. He began his career as an Assistant Public Defender in the Shelby County Public Defender's Office in Memphis, Tennessee. He served as an Assistant District Attorney General in the Shelby County District Attorney General's Office from 1979 to 1989. He then served as an Assistant United States Attorney in the Western District of Tennessee from 1989 to 2002. He was Chief Administrative Officer of the Shelby County Government from 2002 to 2007 and he served as judge of the Shelby County Criminal Court from 2007 to 2012. Nominated by President Barack Obama to replace Judge Bernice Bouie Donald who was elevated to the United States Court of Appeals for the Sixth Circuit, Judge Fowlkes joined the federal bench in August of 2012. Judge Fowlkes received his Bachelor of Arts Degree in 1975 from Valparaiso University. He received his Juris Doctor in 1977 from the University of Denver School of Law.

Kim Parker

Kim T. Parker has spent 40 years as a criminal justice litigator, policy maker, administrator, and manager. She has been a member of the American Bar Association Criminal Justice Council since 2011 and served as Chair of the CJS council from 2019–2020. She continues the council as Past Chair. Her contributions to the ABA Criminal Justice Section include work with the Executive Committee for the Council, Criminal Discovery Standards Task Force, Diversion Standards Task Force, and the Women in Criminal Justice Advisory Council. As a Kansas prosecutor for over 35 years, she litigated crimes of violence against women and children including sexual assault, child abuse, domestic violence and multiple high profile homicide cases. Ms. Parker served on the State of Kansas Child Death Review Board for over 10 years, and the board of the Wichita Area Sexual Assault Center from 1991 to 1994, prior to becoming the Center's president in 1995. She has also worked diligently over 10 years on sentencing, re-entry and recodification projects for the Kansas Judicial Council and the Kansas legislature.

Ms. Parker has been active in the development, implementation, and training of Best Practices for Prosecutors on national, state, and local levels. She has worked with Kansas legislators for the Kansas County and District Attorneys to improve the criminal justice system and for the Children's Advocacy Centers of Kansas to improve the government response to children who have suffered from neglect and abuse. Ms. Parker is a frequent lecturer and instructor for civic groups, academic, attorneys, medical, forensic and law enforcement professionals.

The Conversation

Judge Fowlkes: What is your definition of implicit bias as opposed to explicit bias? I would like to begin with Mr. Bingham. Have you thought about this? Any comments about it?

Mr. Bingham: Yes, Judge. Implicit bias really is, sort of, at the core of—one of the bigger issues we have to deal with. Explicit bias is a lot easier to figure out and to see because it's just that—it's explicit. It's where you can touch, and feel, and hear it. Implicit bias, in my estimation, is something more difficult, because it's sort of engrained in our system. I know that our mutual friend, Judge Bernice Donald, has been really focused on this issue because she sees it as one of the things that keeps the justice system in this sort of perpetual area of racist outcomes. So, I think that implicit bias, really, at the end of the day, is caused by the stereotypes that so many people—myself included—have. And those quick, immediate brain decisions are based upon those stereotypes that we are fed our entire lives. In my mind, it really does affect every single area that we touch, whether it is charging, or plea offers, or bail decisions. We are dealing with these things not just in one area but in multiple areas. It is more difficult to deal with because it is sort of just how we are unfortunately hardwired. Seeing that we have issues is many times more difficult than figuring out what the solutions are.

Judge Fowlkes: Ms. Parker, do you agree with that? Do you agree that all of us suffer from implicit bias?

Ms. Parker: I see implicit bias as a function of attitude and belief that we each have gathered over time. No one is immune. If we are human, we are implicitly biased. We are born of our experiences. As Justin noted, implicit bias is not that easy to see or recognize, especially in ourselves. Because it is so firmly rooted, it goes undetected. Even though implicit bias is present in our beliefs and attitudes and operates without conscious thought or understanding of the existence or nature of our bias, aversion, or preference, it affects our decisions and judgments. Unless we intentionally focus and become introspective about the attitudes and beliefs we carry, it can function in our life in a detrimental way. The challenge is to interrupt our biased inclinations so they do not operate unfairly and unjustly to harm others. Explicit bias runs out there and hits us in the face, while implicit bias hides in the creases of our brain.

In studies of sports and fitness, you may hear of the phenomenon "muscle memory." Implicit bias functions a little like muscle memory, where the ability to reproduce a particular movement—or in this case thought pattern—without conscious thought, is acquired as a result of frequent repetition of that movement. Typing is a great example of muscle memory in action.

Judge Fowlkes: Just to follow up on that. If it's like muscle memory that we have obtained over—I'm assuming years or decades—how do you break that cycle?

Ms. Parker: Exactly. That's the tough part. Can we be aware enough to even say, "Oh, I made that decision because I was making an unconscious decision based on biases and where did I get those? Why do they exist? How did I come to be in this place?" The answer to these questions lies in a combination of a lifetime of experiences, exposures, and environment: what we hear and see from other people, what we tend to rely upon, what we trust. Because these sources are often a hidden thing, we need to be aware that our brains are absorbing what is around us. We need to be watchful and to engage in a process of identifying the presence of our bias and responding to the bias in a way that pushes back. Of course, we are naturally resistant to the suggestion that we are biased, implicitly or explicitly, saying "I can't be biased, are you kidding me?" But unless we accept, and encourage others to accept, that bias is part of all of us, I think it's a tough challenge.

Judge Fowlkes: Mr. Biggers, what do you think about all that?

Mr. Biggers: Your Honor, I have to admit that I agree with both Justin and Kim in the distinction between explicit and implicit bias and, more importantly, how implicit bias is created within an individual. As Kim pointed out, we all come to life with our own different experiences that are molded not only by our own personal experiences in life but also by example and advice of those we look to for guidance to tell us how we should live life. And some of those experiences are based on our actual exposure. Kim used that term and that's important, because for individuals who have spent the bulk of their lives in a neighborhood of a city or a region of a country, there are certain things that will be foreign and will remain foreign to them until they take active steps to truly see what else, or what other opinions exist on those particular topics. When you start talking about breaking the cycle of implicit bias, you have to first be aware that bias exists. Once you do that, the next step is actively looking for a way to break the cycle. Using Kim's analogy to muscle memory, it is equally difficult—probably even more difficult to break these patterns in the way our brains respond. If you think about a runner who has bad form, or a pitcher who has bad form, they have coaches and trainers who have to teach them to break that cycle and relearn how to throw, relearn how to run with correct form. We, as humans, have to relearn how to think beyond our quick brain response and be more thoughtful when need be.

Judge Fowlkes: What if we can't? Let me give you an example. You mention sports, golf, things like that. I am a golfer. I am a terrible golfer. I have taken lessons, I have practiced, I have played for decades, and I am still bad. If you take that into the implicit bias area, where someone has tried to change and they can't, what do you do with that? We will start with Mr. Bingham. What do you do with a bad golfer like me? Or an individual who suspects they have implicit bias, but says "Well, I am what I am?"

Mr. Bingham: You know, any of us who have managed attorneys will tell you that it's almost like managing feral cats. They're going to do what they're going to do because they think they know all the answers. As part of the McArthur grant, we were provided with the opportunity to have trainers come in and talk about implicit bias. So, I have concrete examples of what happens when you sometimes have good attorneys that have issues, and they don't really know how to change. One of the best attorneys in the office—a great litigator, essentially the guy who trained me as a brand-new attorney in our office in 2001—really didn't see that he had a blind or blank spot for certain issues. We went through the discussion of implicit bias in our training—which was really quite well presented. The next morning, he came to my office and just railed at me, telling me that essentially this issue, this issue, and this issue in the training were defective, all made up. He was clear he didn't have these issues. Essentially everyone he prosecuted, he prosecuted because they were bad people, and there was nothing wrong with anything he did.

So how do you deal with someone who just is really bad at this? It takes a lot of effort on your part. At least from a manager standpoint, it means that I have to provide him more concrete examples of how he is wrong. I think a lot of it goes to some of the solutions that organizations have suggested for prosecutors' offices. Particularly important is to show them the data. It's not just anecdotal that there is implicit bias in the decisions that prosecutors make. There is data that shows very clearly that, in like cases, treatment differs where an individual is White, or of color. People are treated differently because of the color of their skin; the neighborhoods in which they live; and many times, their names. People have this weird thing about names that sound of one race or another. And you take all those other factors away but you leave those things that are identifiers, we get these weird outcomes. So, I think we have to show people that are really resistant to this, that it is a real thing. It's not something made up. It really is based in facts, and not in anecdotes.

Judge Fowlkes: I understand. Ms. Parker, have you ever come across an individual who has been confronted, as Mr. Bingham says, but their view is that "there may be this bias going on but it is terribly exaggerated, it is blown way out of proportion." Have you seen a person like that? And if so, how do you deal with them, in your experience.

Ms. Parker: Of course, I see that kind of thing frequently. When we are talking about bias and prejudice toward individuals, it is very human to be defensive. If we think someone is suggesting that we are biased, we feel attacked, and we respond by lining up all the reasons why it's not me, and why they are wrong, and so forth.

Does implicit bias training work? It is really hard to manage implicit bias or change people's minds through training courses. Training is, of course, essential because it represents an exposure to the notion of implicit bias. However, like Justin said, the collection of data and gathering statistical information is also essential to exposing implicit bias.

I also think anecdotes are a powerful way to expose implicit bias. When people tell their own stories the message is amplified and powerful. If repeated experiences build implicit bias, then I suggest increasing the time we expose ourselves to experiences that might interrupt our bias. For example, the bias of a prosecutor might be interrupted by spending a night in a jail cell. I like to promote the adage that "Prejudice rarely survives proximity." I believe that we need to be engaged and involved with diverse individuals to influence our implicit bias. Especially anyone who is different from ourselves, in mind, body, or culture. When you become close or proximate to someone, it is hard to be prejudiced. You begin to see things through a different lens and understand why they see things in a certain way, and why they do things differently than you do. I think we have to be creative and find ways to provide experiences and exposures for individuals who are resistive to the notion of implicit bias so they can come to their own conclusion.

Judge Fowlkes: I can appreciate that. Mr. Biggers, do you agree with what Ms. Parker just said that a one-on-one encounter is sometimes what is needed? I can give you an example of a friend that I had, a White person. This was decades ago, but basically he said, "well, you, John, you're ok. But it's all those other people, all those other Black people, the way they act and what they do. That's the real problem." Do you agree that contact necessarily brings about a different thought process?

Mr. Biggers: Your Honor, I have to agree with Kim on that. Again I will go back to my view that probably the most important thing after acknowledging that implicit bias is real, is exposure. In my mind, what you are describing is exposing individuals to different lifestyles, backgrounds, and life experiences that they otherwise may be unfamiliar with. Unfortunately, in the criminal system, in the criminal world, oftentimes, the people that are making the decisions—the prosecutors, the judges, sometimes the defense attorneys, and the jurors as well—are completely unfamiliar with the lifestyle and circumstances under which crime is committed. And because of that, there are certain things that can come up where our only experiences with it is what we see on television, what we read in the newspaper. It's not from our personal experiences. So, when a defendant tries to offer an explanation as to why they were in the circumstances that they were in to commit the crime or a justification or why an explanation as to why they should not be held criminally liable, those descriptions are sometimes completely foreign. I'll give an example that I'm sure most of us have heard. I've heard defendants say, "I put on someone else's pants, and the contraband in the pants was not mine." Now, if we are talking about a small amount of narcotics, I could understand that. If we're talking about loaded pistol, or something more noticeable, those are the instances that I would say I don't buy it.

But I really think—when we are looking at it overall—that the best way to deal with that from the prosecution's standpoint has to do with what you were talking about, has to do with exposure. Of course, we can't each have experiences with people from every walk of life. But we can broaden our perspective by ensuring we have a diverse attorney setup, where we can come in, have dialogue about the cases, and bounce ideas as it relates to what is an appropriate punishment and why. And what I found is when attorneys have to articulate out loud what distinguishes one case from another, oftentimes we can see that some of the things we think are based on sound logic and reasoning are really unfounded, and we can find and interrupt the implicit bias in that.

Judge Fowlkes: Mr. Biggers, why don't you follow up on that. We have been talking generally about bias, implicit and otherwise. I think it's time we go ahead and start taking our discussion toward things that happen in prosecutors' offices across the country. The way that prosecutors first come into contact, of course they talk with investigators, police officers. But basically, a decision has to be made whether to take a case or not. What I am talking about is prosecutorial discretion. Are there problems as far as discretion is concerned, vis-à-vis implicit bias? Does it impact the charging decisions and the discretion that prosecutors have? If so, has it been positive, or negative? Just talk for a moment about what has happened in your experience with the various offices that you've worked in. Mr. Biggers, can you go into that in more detail?

Mr. Biggers: Well, I can definitely say that in my years of experience I have definitely seen implicit bias impact not only whether charges are filed, but also types of charges that are actually brought in a case, and ultimately the sentence imposed. I can be honest and tell you, I did not always recognize it as implicit bias at the time. But looking back in hindsight, I definitely realize it.

Judge Fowlkes: Are you talking about yourself or others in the office?

Mr. Biggers: I'll say both. The first point I'll make is this: You're looking at the types of crimes being investigated. Socially, what do we accept as conduct worthy of criminal charges? That's an area where I think most people have a firm boundary as to what crime constitutes criminal charges. I really don't think we spend enough time thinking about how we come to that decision.

Marijuana, for example. I think socially, it is getting more acceptable, which causes law enforcement and sometimes prosecutors to not bring charges related to the marijuana offenses. By the same token, I have seen cases where insignificant marijuana amounts have been used to justify the filing of charges against individuals arrested in their particular part of town, particular neighborhood. In fact, one instance comes to mind. When I was a methamphetamine attorney in Alabama, at the time, it was typically associated with a rural community, shake and bake. And a case came in. The agent on the case was aware of the arrest and did not actually interview that defendant by himself: he was in a hotel, it was a meth case, he came in and described it to the attorney. The lead attorney on the case laid out what the appropriate punishment was, what the charge would be. Then he found out the defendant was a different race. Initially he thought it was a White defendant, but when he found out otherwise, he started backtracking and asking questions. "Well, why would this defendant be in that area, that part of town? Why would he have methamphetamine? Who was he selling it to?" These are all questions that would not have been as significant of a concern at the time he laid out how he would proceed with the prosecution, but now he was using that to beef up the

Seven · Roundtable Conversation: Prosecutors' Reflections on Implicit Bias

charges. Because of that, I think, I was curious as to how that came about, and I posed a question: what changed? He had not thought about it, so he could not say. So, we ended up with the charges that he initially articulated. But that's just an example as to how implicit bias can impact the criminal justice system from the prosecution's aspect.

Judge Fowlkes: Mr. Bingham, do you agree with some of the things that Mr. Biggers said? Bias. Has it permeated prosecutorial discretion? Decisions, investigations, things like that. Have you seen it? Any steps taken to root it out?

Mr. Bingham: You know, Judge, it does not matter if you are in Tennessee or Alabama, or Washington or Kansas. You're going to have these issues. They may just be of a different degree, based upon location. Where I live in Spokane, our population is about 90% White. It is very White, and there are very few persons of color. And so, it's interesting to have that conversation within an office, because what you will hear is: "We have this large majority of our cases against White people, so how can we be making bad charging decisions? We charge a lot more people that are White than we do that are Black, Native American, Hispanic." But the problem is, if you start looking at the actual outcomes you will see that those numbers are way off statistically. They are disproportionate with the population. You start seeing that there is this sort of implicit bias that peeks through. For example, when the Vera Institute reviewed the Manhattan D.A.'s office it found that regardless of the race of the prosecutor, there were variations in their charging when it came to a person's color. That with similar circumstances they were doing it again, and again, and again.

And we've done a lot of work in McArthur with Vera, so they provided a lot of this background information to us, saying you should look at this too. You should take a look at what you're doing on your charging. We had that conversation internally in our office, that we need to see if we are just as complicit with our implicit bias in our decision making. You cannot imagine the response that I got. It was nasty, it was visceral, it was "you're calling us all racist." But then, when you start looking at some of the cases, you think, wow, maybe there is a problem. I had one case where a guy was telling me he was taking a case to trial on a driving suspended charge, and I thought why in the world. Well, it ends up that the individual was African American, and he had been involved in our community court for a long time, he had failed out of that, and he just really annoyed this prosecutor. And I asked him afterwards, when he didn't take the case to trial, why were you that focused on this? He couldn't really articulate it, why that particular guy on that particular minor charge. And in the back of my mind, I am thinking this is implicit bias. He's going after the Black guy when he would never go after a White guy with this exact same thing. He would've just dismissed the case immediately. I think what David was talking about, how you look at things in the prism of an office is so important. Prosecutors' offices, just like defender offices, are very negligent in letting groupthink prevail. We do this again, and again, and again. We give ourselves credibility by telling everyone else that it's ok, this makes sense. When you don't have diverse voices in your office, your groupthink becomes even more toxic. So, how do you fix it? You call it out. But you have to have leadership that is willing to do the work, because, if it doesn't come from the top, you're just going to have this continue to churn within these offices. There are probably 1001 examples that we could give you of this, but many of them just go unseen.

Ms. Parker: I agree with Justin. There are likely countless examples of implicit bias against people of color that show up in the charging decisions in prosecutors' offices across the country. Implicit bias can often only be realized by collecting data. Unfortunately, a large number of prosecutors' offices have no data collection process in play and if so it is not adequate or sufficiently advanced to be helpful. The same is true with arrest data.

Judge Fowlkes: Have you ever seen implicit bias show up in arrest and charging decisions? What did it look like and what strategies were employed to interrupt it?

Ms. Parker: I have thought that an office policy around the charging review process that is 'blind' to race information could be helpful to limit the functions of implicit bias. The process would be broken into stages so that the prosecutor is blind to race and other demographics until the final stage. For example, at Stage 1 the probable cause affidavit or reports of law enforcement would be stripped of the demographics that might trigger a race bias. The charging prosecutor is to first determine if there are any facts to support that a crime was even committed. Stage 2 would require the prosecutor to ensure the legality of the law enforcement interaction with the accused; for example, the prosecutor would consider if there was an illegal search or arrest, and if there is proof beyond a reasonable doubt present in the evidence and witness testimony gathered. The final stage would allow the inclusion of the identification information and demographics collected by law enforcement. This step process is consciously interruptive to the thought process. The charging prosecutors would be provided the opportunity to check their own bias *at each stage*.

Judge Fowlkes: Mr. Biggers, do you agree with that?

Mr. Biggers: I can see how that can be beneficial. And I think regardless of the method or strategy employed, the most important thing is to get your decision-makers at those levels thinking about why they are doing what they are doing and ensuring that their decisions are not based on some bias or discriminatory reason. It's important to force them to articulate why charges should be brought. This thinking needs to go on with other individuals, not just with themselves. I think that's very important. And that group that they are articulating those points to should be a diverse group. Even if it involves offices with limited resources, even if it's just three individuals, I think it is something that should be encouraged. One point that everyone has brought out that I'd like to emphasize. Those involved need to include someone with some level of stature and experience. We all know how law enforcement can be as it relates to charges they believe should be brought, investigations that they have conducted, and arrests that they have made by the time the case arrives at the prosecutors' office. I think that group would probably have to get those tough questions on the front end, so that they can not only understand what types of cases would be accepted but also how they will be treated if they come into the office. It's important to make clear that it's not something that is just going to be passed by, but it's going to be vetted and checked to ensure that it passed the test.

Judge Fowlkes: How diverse is your office as far as intake is concerned?

Mr. Biggers: So, based on a number of factors, such as consistency of review and oversight in recent years, I would say our office could be more diverse in that area. We are working to achieve that. But I think the most important thing, as Kim pointed out, is ensuring that gatekeeper role—the person responsible for reviewing the case in the office is diverse and deals with multiple individuals, not just one person. You always get into trouble where one individual says "this is a case we want to charge," especially if it's based on something outside the law such as a news release, high priority, or notoriety. Those are things that you want to stay away from. But I definitely think that what Kim suggested, leaving some of those facts out of it, is important as it relates to identifiers, race, etc.

One other thing that's important. I'll go ahead and say it: Raising concerns about implicit bias draws a lot of ire and lack of cooperation because most people confuse it with racism. If you've actually paid attention to implicit bias training, you understand that while it has similar elements to racism, it's not the same. The other thing that's difficult and unfortunate is what most people realize—what I realized—when they do the Implicit Association Test (IAT) is that we may find that we have implicit bias toward our own groups. These are difficult issues and that's why I think it's important from a supervisory, managerial level to embrace implicit bias awareness and training and convey the importance of it to the team.

Judge Fowlkes: Mr. Bingham, how important is it to have diversity in the office, especially with the intake and review of the cases? And if you don't have diversity, how do you make up for it?

Mr. Bingham: You've essentially just described my problem, Judge. I live in an area of the country that is exceptionally White. The Pacific Northwest is not diverse.

Judge Fowlkes: Let me say this to you. Memphis, Tennessee is a heavily Black area. I mean 70% of the city is Black, and 25% are poor. Mr. Biggers has already indicated that they can do better as far as diversity is concerned. So, I hear you when you say that Spokane is White. But does it end there?

Mr. Bingham: Well, the issue is that it doesn't. In my office, we have zero persons of color on staff at this point. I have not had one person of color even apply for one of my positions in over four years. And we have tried to aggressively advertise when we have openings, which we don't have very often. Then the issue becomes, how do you diversify thought in your office if you're all sort of the same. One of the public defenders that I know, she left the city Public Defender's office to go to Seattle, she's African American. She said that it was hard even working in her own office because she said there was a continuous issue with implicit bias. Everything that David just said is spot on. We conflate implicit bias with racism, day in and day out. And people don't want to talk about that because they don't want to be labeled as a racist. I think when you talk about implicit bias we have to acknowledge that we all have it. When we have seen studies—I was talking about the Vera study in Manhattan—African American prosecutors were just as likely to show implicit bias on charging as White prosecutors.

Judge Fowlkes: Because they came through the same system, they learned the same techniques.

Mr. Bingham: They did. Kim was talking about the blind charging theory where you take out identifying information. There have been several offices that have attempted it. I believe the Philadelphia D.A.'s office is one of the largest offices to do that. What they found is that you can't just take out the race, you can't just take out the gender. You have to take out the location, you have to take out everybody's name, because even when you get the witnesses that have a particular name that may be associated with one particular race or the other, implicit bias starts rearing its ugly head. Because the brain started making those connections. It goes so deep. What David was just talking about, that it has to be continuous and it has to be from the top.

Judge Fowlkes: Well, do we go back to what I said before? It is somewhat exaggerated? Now, when the charging decision is made, Mr. Prosecutor, we had a break in somewhere in the city, somebody broke into this person's home and stole some items from it. I mean, how do you do that? How do you make a prosecutorial decision if you don't have any information about the case? You don't have the names of the victims, names of the defendants, suspects, witnesses, area of town. How can you homogenize a case to that point?

Mr. Bingham: I think that's exactly the issue that people have in charging, is that you have an ethical duty to bring cases that you believe have the basis for conviction. You can't just willy-nilly file charges. When you do blind charging, many times you just have a skeleton of a case. Are you meeting your ethical burden when you are filing that charge? But at the same time, you're trying to possibly cure an ill that is just as bad as overcharging or undercharging. In Washington, the vast majority of our cases on the non-felony side, on the misdemeanor and gross misdemeanor level, are directly filed from the cops. They file everything. We file around 10,000 cases a year in the name of the City of Spokane. My office, out of those 10,000 files maybe a 1,000 on our own. Everything else is filed by the officer. When Kim was talking about doing your due diligence, we essentially do that at the arraignment stage. We make those calls. But, you as a longtime prosecutor, Judge, articulated really well how officers, if they really want something, they push, and they push. And it makes people more willing to do things because you are afraid of that blowback that comes from law enforcement.

Judge Fowlkes: Well, I always believed in Nancy Reagan who said, "Just say no and mean it."

Mr. Bingham: It's hard, it's hard. What David was talking about with young prosecutors doing this work. They are very likely to say yes just because they fear what happens when that officer goes and talks to their boss. You end up having a cycle. We built this system. It didn't just magically show up this way. What our main focus as prosecutors has to be is acknowledging that implicit bias exists, trying to train our staffs the best we can to eliminate it or at least to mitigate it, and follow through by giving them the tools to do it. We can try to deal with our staffing issues from the beginning, try to hire a diverse workplace and workforce so we have different ideas. We can provide the statistics to show that we're not just making this up. That's where a lot of prosecutors' offices fail, being afraid to show what their work is. One of our good friends within the ABA is Melba Pearson, who is at Florida International University. She works with prosecutor performance measures and helps people see the data. It can be transformative for an office. I think that's really one of the main tools that I would say you can give to a staff to be to change the way they can deal with cases in regards to implicit bias.

Judge Fowlkes: Ms. Parker, do you agree with the things that they've said? Mr. Biggers said that that everyone is afraid to be identified as someone with implicit bias. No one wants to be called a racist. On the other hand, once you embrace this, would you agree that some people will come to the conclusion that "well, everyone has a little racism in them. Everybody has a little sexism in them." So, we live with that. Agree or disagree with that?

Ms. Parker: I think both Justin and David are brilliant men, and I think they're working hard to come up with solutions. I do think it's easier when people realize, "Well, it's not just me," when they can embrace the idea that this is part of all of us, it's a natural thing. It may be as simplistic as explaining to people that it's a function of human nature. So yes, I do agree. I think we need solutions to interrupt that bias, and creative ways to do it. You were talking about diversity in the offices, and Kansas is quite a bit like Spokane. It's always hard to get people of color to apply. Look at us right now. Most prosecution offices, most government places say you have to live in the jurisdiction. What if we were hiring people to do charging decisions or to be part of the charging team and manage the process electronically, digitally. You could hire someone from Tennessee to be a prosecutor in your Washington office to review the evidence and information and make the charging decisions. We have to be open to new ways of looking at things. Certainly, different problems can arise. But it's just like anything else. If we fail to venture out and look for solutions, we are stuck where we are. And that's not what we want to be. We can do better than that.

Judge Fowlkes: We've talked quite a bit about prosecutorial discretion. But prosecutors have their hands on the entire system. When we talk about things like setting bail, we've made decisions trying to mask race, sex, where they come from. But when you're setting bail, you have to know all those things in order to set a bail that is reasonable. I would like to know if you all agree or disagree, taking in to account that state systems are different than federal in terms of setting bail. On the federal side, you can detain people without bail if they are a danger to the community or a flight risk. I know on the state side, in Tennessee, it's very hard to detain someone without bail. Only way you can do that is murder in the first-degree charge, otherwise the bail has to be reasonable. Does implicit bias impact the decision as far as bail is concerned? I will start with Mr. Biggers.

Mr. Biggers: I think Kim and Justin have more recent experiences with this. But I will say, I have seen, even in federal court to some degree, where someone is a flight risk or a danger to the community, certain things come to play that really should not. Such as socioeconomic status. Oftentimes, individuals who have support in the courtroom, a mother, or a father, or both, or appear to have jobs and an ability to pay, may get more preferential treatment as to whether a bail is granted or not. From my experiences in court in Alabama, what was reasonable was not a blanket, across the board amount. Now, looking back, I think implicit bias played a very big role in that decision process. Because most people in our positions are at a certain socioeconomic level.

Judge Fowlkes: Have you ever witnessed implicit bias in plea negotiations/agreements? If so, what did it look like and what strategies should be employed to eliminate it?

Ms. Parker: I think the answer is the same across the board. Implicit bias shows up in all phases of the criminal legal system.

Judge Fowlkes: Mr. Biggers, anything that's happened in your office?

Mr. Biggers: The short answer is yes. They were noticed and addressed prior to completion of those actions. I learned from experience, not only to have dialogue but also to have multilayer reviews. That is when we are trying to interrupt implicit bias. All of us have been prosecutors and part of what you appreciate about the job is the general autonomy to handle your case the way you see fit. Still, it is imperative to have a multi-level oversight and review, not only on the charging decisions but more importantly when you are talking about pleas. You have to look at the plea for the recommended disposition of a case in totality. What I mean by that is that if there is a multi-defendant case, offices will handle each defendant as that day comes up for the plea. But you have to look at it collectively and comparatively, not only for those defendants but across the board for all defendants charged with similar conduct. For example, in one instance that I was aware of, a defendant was charged with a drug trafficking offense where firearms were also involved. He had a relatively small criminal history, but this is the case where we would discuss the appropriate penalties for the disposition of the case to see how other cases have been treated. Ironically enough, this defendant was from a decent background. I heard attorneys say he just made a mistake; it shouldn't happen again. There were comments I rarely heard before, especially at this juncture in the case. I had to pose the question to the group. What is the difference between this defendant and that defendant? Oftentimes confronting will reveal and encourage future discussions.

Judge Fowlkes: We've talked quite a bit about bias in our charging decisions, what happens with bail and plea agreements. Any final comments before we move on to another area?

Mr. Bingham: As to the operation of the office, when are talking about calling things out it really comes from the top. You have to have someone in charge of the office who is willing to have those conversation. If you have someone who refuses to acknowledge, you will have pretty hostile reactions. So, it comes down to leadership. These aren't fun topics to discuss with people you work with. You're telling them that their internal stereotypes are causing problems. I do believe that you have to start from the top. You have to have support from the institutional standpoint.

Judge Fowlkes: Mr. Biggers, anything on that?

Mr. Biggers: One last thing requires attention. We talk about recruitment. I encourage everyone to confront this statement: "I can't find qualified individuals in a particular group." Saying that there weren't any qualified applicants, an office I was in hired three or four people from the same group. It may just be that we have to look in different places and different ways, with a focus on job needs, not just the way we have always done it. Still, it is oftentimes hard to get an office that reflects the entire community that it serves. That is why I am a proponent of exposure. Looking at our office, for example. Everyone is in a similar socioeconomic group. So, even though we look different, when we start to talk about our ideas and what we think, we are similar. Outreach and community involvement can change this. To me, that is the way to expose employees and office personnel to a different perspective.

I found that getting office members out into a group, dealing with outreach initiatives with people from different socioeconomic backgrounds than our own, helps us see people differently.

Judge Fowlkes: Have you run across issues when you talk about community involvement. Why can't you let me handle my caseload? I am a prosecutor, and I was here before you got here, and I have civil service protection, and I will be here long after you're gone. How do you deal with a person like that?

Mr. Biggers: You hear that. That's not our role, that's not the job. But times have changed, and as time moves on, we should be better. We should look for alternative ways, as Justin and Kim have pointed out, better ways to be better public servants to our community. Your work is not just about the caseload. If we are here to allow the rise in crime numbers to continue, then we are pointless. The second scenario is probably more problematic. Individuals who say, "Listen, you can't do anything to me." Unfortunately, your Honor, they're right. The only thing you can try to do is bring in new people, good people, to get a change of culture and those individuals will become isolated on their own as a new culture becomes more prominent.

Judge Fowlkes: Ms. Parker, what do you think about that? How do you deal with people like that?

Ms. Parker: You know, Justin made a point that leadership needs to come from the top, setting a policy and example with your employees. I have not worked in an office that has civil service protection, but I understand that limits the ability of the leadership to do things as it relates to their employment. A strong leader can say, "That is fine, we need some research done, and change the individuals assignment so their influence and bias is restrained." So, taking them away from the decision-making process in the office and is literally interrupting implicit bias. I think that there can be creative solutions to employees like that and what their assignments may be. David makes a really good point. You may have the toughest individual and sometimes the right exposure may turn them around. I don't know if it's always possible.

I think most prosecutors' offices are living case to case. They don't take the time or take the moment to look at the big picture and really monitor what is going on in their offices. A lot of offices do not gather any data, let alone review the aggregate information. To me, especially when it comes to implicit bias, it's important that there is attention given to monitoring and keeping statistics.

Judge Fowlkes: Thank you for all the input. There is one last thing I want to talk about. I think we have a panel here who represent different positions in prosecuting offices, different long-term experiences. This whole thing about bias, has it reared its ugly head in the offices that you've worked in? Not involving the handling of the defendants, but the staff. Any issues, any accusations, relationships of lawyers with support

Seven · Roundtable Conversation: Prosecutors' Reflections on Implicit Bias

staff? Any accusations of being treated unfairly. If you have seen things like that, what steps were taken to remedy this? Any comments on office relations vis-à-vis bias?

Mr. Bingham: When I first started, at the time, there was one female attorney and then they got two. It was an interesting time. Most of the individuals there were retired military, and they brought a very male-dominated command structure to how they ran the office. If I were female, I would not have felt comfortable in that setting. There was also low-level racism that was thrown around. One of my supervisors would say, and I apologize to anyone who is offended, "drunker than 10,000 Indians." He used to say that again, and again, and again. One of our attorneys who was assigned to a Mental Health Court docket used to wear a Loony Tunes tie to courts, and no one noticed until one day he said "no one ever said anything about my tie." At the time, we didn't have protections. Now we have union protections with for-cause termination. But regardless no one would say anything because the people doing these things were setting this culture up. That doesn't exist now because those people have long gone away. It really comes down to people that are in charge. I had an attorney who would continually use the R-word "retarded" about defendants. I would tell him, that word has been retired, if you say it again you will be disciplined. In situations like that, do you think people would feel comfortable bringing up implicit bias? No. The world has changed so much. When David was saying how you explain this to older attorneys who have been doing this for so long that the world has changed, and you really have to change with it. We talk about finding the right solution for the defendants. I think we have to have a concept of holistic prosecution as well. That it's not just about winning or losing a case but about crime prevention. A lot of it has to come down to looking at things like bias. Yes, unfortunately I have seen and experienced first-hand bias—both explicit and implicit—in my office,

Judge Fowlkes: Ms. Parker, any experience that you have seen in your office with these types of complaints?

Ms. Parker: I have. A lot of times the person suffering from biased treatment, decisions or judgments never complains to anyone. It only comes up because a co-worker is keeping an eye out, and then brings a complaint on their behalf. Like Justin, the leadership of an office has to set an environment in the office that allows people to feel comfortable bringing a complaint. In my own experiences I have seen some of the worst bias against the LGBTQI+ community and LGBTQI+ professionals in the office. Individuals affected by bias often just take it or quit, because no one was making it a place where they would not suffer the bias. It requires dedication, leadership, and implementation of a comfortable environment for everyone.

Judge Fowlkes: Mr. Biggers, you've also been in different levels. Any experiences that you've seen in house?

Mr. Biggers: Yes. One thing that I can say is the culture of the office makes a difference. If you allow biased feelings and sentiments to permeate your office, not only is it bad for morale, but it also creates division in the office. And going back to what Kim alluded to, at that point, it comes down to inclusion. We hear about individuals and why they had to leave an office and seek another employment opportunity because of how they were treated. Our mind initially goes to explicit bias. What is often unspoken and ignored is the implicit bias. As Justin pointed out, the tie. How individuals may see it and may not comment on it but everyone is aware of it. For those individuals who are in the minority, whatever group that may be, they notice that it's real, and those are reasons that make them seek other employment. Ultimately, the office in the end suffers because they lack that perspective.

Judge Fowlkes: At this point I want to hear some comments on steps that you've taken to work on implicit bias. We worked through some issues of sexism, racism. Many times, these things are covert, but sometimes they come to life. We have training sessions available now. Have those efforts been used in your offices? Are they effective or are they too weak to deal with the depth of bias?

Mr. Biggers: I think the trainings are essential. Unfortunately, because it's a systematic problem that exits, there needs to be some more intensive programs. Our office had undergone a training but that alone is ineffective to really address implicit bias at the forefront of attorney's minds.

Judge Fowlkes: So, you've had training at least on one prior occasion, I am assuming a few years ago. I don't know if you can even measure any difference after the training? Any observations?

Mr. Biggers: I think measurable. Our roles have changed in the community. What we do internally and what we measure has to change too. Who had the most trials and convictions? We should de-emphasize who won most trials and promote other priorities consistently in the office.

Judge Fowlkes: Any last comments? Any follow up as far as efforts and whether those efforts have been successful or a total failure. Ms. Parker?

Ms. Parker: I think that training is absolutely important but training programs around implicit bias are just taking hold. Therefore, it is hard to measure their effectiveness at this point. Prosecutors are leaders in their communities—they can be vigilant not only in the office—but they also have to communicate it broadly to law enforcement and communities. It has to be a priority.

Judge Fowlkes: Have the efforts you have seen in the office been a success or a failure? I'm talking specifically now. The steps taken to address bias inside the office.

Ms. Parker: I think that it's effective. I can't say that training is not effective. I think it's most effective if you have trainers presenting to cultures and groups where they have shared lived experiences. For example, you can bring in an outside trainer that has never done prosecution, then the prosecutors are unlikely to listen. Same with the police, you have to work from the inside out because they can claim "you don't really know what it's like here," and completely dismiss what is said to them. So the attention has to be on working the training from the inside and identifying those individuals to make it more effective.

Judge Fowlkes: Closing out with Mr. Bingham. Did you hear what Ms. Parker said that training has to be inside out. If you're bringing someone from the outside, it won't be effective.

Mr. Bingham: I totally agree because that's essentially what happened in our office. We had two trainings where both of the trainers were brought in, were well-known and from large national organizations, but they were not prosecutors. We had a fairly good response to the overview of implicit bias, but they could not answer questions on what the next steps should be. And everyone came away from the final training dismayed and disheartened. I strongly agree with Kim. We have to have appropriate training by those who understand the confines in which we work as prosecutors. Not only do you have to have meaningful training but you have to do it continuously, because you will change staff continuously. Just because you do it once does not mean you're cured. This takes time and effort and commitment from individuals to check themselves. That's one of the things you have to do as you go forward, is check yourself. Take a moment, step back, assess the situation. We have to realize that some of these things take time. We try to do that quickly, but when we do that, we step into these traps that have been laid for us. And the last thing I will say on what can offices do, and Kim talked about it as well. It's data, data, data. Otherwise, it's just a bunch of anecdotal stories. But the data, when you look at it, it's hard to ignore.

Judge Fowlkes: I really appreciate it everyone. I think the discussion went well and I hope you all agree. We covered a lot of territory in a short amount of time. You all have let me benefit from your experiences. I have been around the corner a little bit too, but it is always good to talk to professionals in the area. I want to thank each of you for your time today.

EIGHT

The Empathetic Prosecutor

Reducing Bias When Working with Victims, Survivors, and Witnesses[*][†]

Linda Ford, Senior Trial Counsel, New York County District Attorney's Office (Manhattan)

Kristine Hamann, Executive Director Prosecutors' Center for Excellence (PCE)

Tyear Middleton, Chief Diversity/Equal Employment Opportunity Officer, Queens County District Attorney's Office (NY)

Audrey Moore, Equal Employment Officer and Special Counsel, New York County District Attorney's Office (Manhattan)

Luis Morales, Chief Immigrant Affairs Unit, New York County District Attorney's Office (Manhattan)

Sophia Roach, Senior Attorney, Prosecutors' Center for Excellence

Sherry Thompson Taylor, Judge, San Diego Superior Court (CA)

---

[*] Excellent assistance was provided by Brittany Appleby-Rumon, a student at Georgetown Law School.

[†] Deep gratitude and respect goes to the prosecutor advisory group who provided guidance and editorial oversight for this paper. The group included the writers listed above as well as Chief Diversity Officer Renee Gregory of the Brooklyn District Attorney's Office, Witness Aid Director Beverly Gilchrest of the New York County District Attorney's Office, Deputy Commissioner Janine Gilbert of the Department of Information Technology, and Assistant District Attorney Nigel Farinha of the Office of the Special Narcotics Prosecutor of the City of New York.

This project was supported in part by the Innovative Prosecution Solutions Grant No. 2017-YX-BX-K002, awarded by the Bureau of Justice Assistance to AEquitas. The Bureau of Justice Assistance is a component of the U.S. Department of Justice's Office of Justice Programs, which also includes the Bureau of Justice Statistics, the National Institute of Justice, the Office of Juvenile Justice and Delinquency Prevention, the Office for Victims of Crime, and the SMART Office. Points of view or opinions in this document are those of the authors and do not necessarily represent the official position or policies of the Department of Justice.

A Note from the Editors: We thank our colleague Kristine Hamann, who brought to us the excellent idea of a Chapter on implicit bias as it may relate to victims, survivors, and witnesses. Ms. Hamann agreed to serve as primary author and then enlisted and coordinated her expert colleagues as co-authors. The teamwork produced an excellent how-to Chapter for prosecutors who want to interrupt the negative manifestations of bias in their work. The Chapter's emphasis on procedural justice, community, training, and accountability is of value well beyond prosecutors' offices.

CHAPTER HIGHLIGHTS

- It is important to recognize that bias can pervade every aspect of a criminal case and influence all parties involved from the litigants to the victims, survivors, and witnesses.
- To provide the best and most equitable approach possible, training that encompasses these relationships is important.
- An approach that engages the community and diverse community members is most likely to be successful and sustainable.

CHAPTER CONTENTS

Introduction

1. What Is Bias?
   A. Types of Bias
   B. Impact of Bias in the Criminal Justice System
2. Initiatives for Interrupting and Reducing the Impact of Bias in the Prosecutor's Office
   A. Training
   B. Focusing on the Witness—Science-Based Interviewing
   C. Officewide Procedural Justice
   D. Hiring
   E. Data Collection
   F. Accountability
3. Initiatives for Interrupting and Reducing the Impact of Implicit Bias Outside the Prosecutor's Office
   A. Meet Community Members
   B. Training in Schools and the Community

    C. Internships and Mentoring
    D. Community Outreach and Satellite Offices
    E. Training of Law Enforcement
Conclusion
Appendix
    General Law-Related References
    Literature Exploring Bias

Introduction

Up until now, Francisco's mother, who is African American, had only heard rumors, news stories, and scant details from detectives about the case against the rival gang member who shot her son in the middle of a busy street. Today, when she was asked to come to court for the trial, was the first time she heard from the prosecutor. Though she deserved compassion and empathy, what she got at the courthouse was a security screening that made her feel like she had done something wrong, contempt from a busy receptionist, and a long wait for the prosecutor. This was after she and her family members had navigated downtown in traffic and shelled out $30.00 to park close enough so they would not be late. When she met the prosecutor, the murder was repeatedly referred to as a gang fight, not an attack, as if to suggest her son deserved what happened to him. By the time they got to court, she barely registered the whispers of the court personnel who certainly seemed to be doing their best to make the family feel unwelcome, even threatening expulsion after involuntary expressions of anguish occurred during the prosecutor's display of autopsy photos. Francisco's family was poor, some suffered from addiction and mental health issues, some had been previously incarcerated. This certainly was not the first or last time they had been made to feel "other-than," and they had no different expectations of the all-White court staff, judge and attorneys.

As this example demonstrates, it is important to recognize that bias can pervade every aspect of a criminal case and influence all parties involved from the litigants to the victims, survivors, and witnesses. These conscious and unconscious biases may lead to discounting a witness's credibility, undervaluing loss, and misperceiving events. While much of the focus of anti-bias efforts has been on the accused, fair and unbiased treatment from the criminal justice system should be equally available to victims, survivors, and witnesses.

This Chapter discusses the most common forms of bias that intersect with a prosecutor's evaluation of victims, survivors, and witnesses, provides practical advice for recognizing and reducing bias from decision-making, suggests communication techniques designed to cultivate trust and understanding with witnesses, and highlights prosecutor programs designed to reduce the impact of bias.

1. What Is Bias?[‡]

All people have biases that range from conscious and explicit to unconscious and implicit. Bias is driven by the cognitive processes of the brain that are designed to order information regarding sense and emotion and to assign value based on what is seen, heard, and felt.[1] This natural process of categorization is impacted by many factors including upbringing and environment.[2] It is exacerbated by printed, televised, and posted media that has become an important source of information about "others" with whom we have little actual experience. The unrelenting barrage of information from the media can perpetuate positive and negative feelings about people based on many factors including gender, race, ethnicity, religion, politics, sexuality, socio-economic status, age, and ability.[3]

The role of the prosecutor is to dispense justice without fear or favor and to act impartially. In their role as public officers, they must deal fairly with all involved in the criminal prosecution of a case. Prosecutors must examine the impact of bias in their work. The following are some of the various forms of bias that deserve attention as they most immediately impact a prosecutor's interaction with witnesses, survivors, or victims.

A. Types of Bias

All people have some form of bias, it is part of being human. It is important for prosecutors to understand their own biases and the possible biases of their witnesses. These crosscurrents of bias happen in many different and complex ways depending on the people involved.

- **Explicit Bias:** Explicit bias is, as the name suggests, obvious and outward revealing. It is the manifestation of overt racism, sexism, and other intolerances. Explicit bias is present in prosecution offices, as evidenced by the recent discovery of racist emails between two prosecutors pertaining to an Asian American defendant and racist comments about Mexicans sent out by a supervising prosecutor on a communication app.[4] In both of these instances negative racial stereotypes were the basis of "jokes."

[‡] See also Chapter 2 providing an overview and definitions.

Prosecutors need to create an office culture that does not tolerate racist comments and other forms of explicit bias.

- **Implicit Bias**: Implicit Bias is unconscious and springs from brain functions that automatically classify and categorize information.[5] It is difficult to uncover and requires self-evaluation to detect and reduce. Given its unconscious nature, implicit bias can be particularly troublesome when a prosecutor is very busy and has to make quick decisions.

- **Confirmation Bias**: Confirmation bias, often implicit, is also referred to as "tunnel vision" and exists when a person has a preconceived idea or interest in the outcome. Confirmation bias can happen when a conclusion comes from a trusted person, such as a respected detective or a well-liked witness. As evidence in criminal cases is rarely neat and straightforward, it is possible to give interpretations to the facts that are skewed by confirmation bias. This bias can lead to the superficial review of facts and the overlooking of evidence so that the desired conclusion is supported.

- **Affinity Bias**: Affinity bias, sometimes referred to as ingroup/outgroup bias, can be manifested both implicitly and explicitly. It is the feeling of kinship with others who share something in common, such as allegiance to a sports team, attendance at a college, ethnic background, political party, etc. Affinity bias can lead a prosecutor to favor or disfavor a witness based on their mutual affinity, but unrelated to the facts of the case.

The following example illustrates how affinity bias and lack of diversity can impact a prosecution: A White prosecutor who grew up in a White neighborhood, went to a White religious institution, attended a largely White school and works in a mostly White office may have only met people of color in the context of criminal prosecution. Thus, the scope of the prosecutor's experience with people of color is focused on criminal matters. The prosecutor is not interacting with people of color as neighbors, churchgoers, or students, all of whom are overwhelmingly law-abiding citizens. Failing to recognize this limited view of people of color may interfere with the prosecutor's ability to fairly assess the credibility of a witness and evaluate the strength of a case.

Prosecutors need to develop critical thinking and communication skills that target the identification and reduction of harmful biases of all kinds. They need to also understand that witnesses, survivors, or victims may develop biases, based on their life experience and the impact of systemic racism or other social inequities, which impair their trust of the prosecutor. It is the prosecutor's responsibility to forge a relationship with the witness.

B. Impact of Bias in the Criminal Justice System

An important step in creating an equitable criminal justice system is to recognize the existence of bias and its influence on every stage of a case. Some critical junctures where bias can have an impact include:

- **Assessing Credibility**: Assessing credibility of witnesses is a significant part of a prosecutor's job and can be impacted by a prosecutor's bias. A prosecutor may believe that when people lie they have trouble looking you in the eye and shift in their seat when they are lying. However, the witness's actions may be a cultural communication style, or they may be driven by concerns other than the matter being discussed. Also, the prosecutor may disagree with choices made by a witness, such as previous criminal behavior, and thereby discount the witness. There is no iron clad method of assessing credibility other than comparing a statement against known facts. Improved interview techniques discussed below can assist with an objective assessment of credibility.

- **The Uncooperative or Hostile Witness**: An uncooperative or hostile witness is difficult for a prosecutor, particularly if negative biases are at play. The prosecutor may feel frustrated or uncomfortable and therefore assume that the witness is lying or not worth the effort. However, every witness must be given a full opportunity to be heard with an open mind. Needless to say, it is still a prosecutor's duty to evaluate credibility and compare the witness's account with other undisputed facts.

- **Charging**: Prosecutors must conduct an objective assessment of an officer's arrest and evaluate the witnesses to determine appropriate charges. At this stage, prosecutors must be vigilant in assuring that charging decisions are not based on preconceived notions and biases, but on the facts of the case. This can be especially challenging if incomplete information is available at the time of the evaluation.

- **First Appearance**: First appearance or arraignment is where defendants are apprised of the charges and bail is set. This process can be fast paced and require prosecutors to make snap decisions. When there is little time to weigh all the circumstances of the case, prosecutors must be wary of biases that can influence their decisions.

- **Plea Bargaining and Sentencing**: Prosecutors must make reasoned decisions about plea bargaining and sentencing that are not swayed by biases. For example, plea offers for similar crimes should be the same whether the victim lives in a wealthy part of town or in an underserved neighborhood. Collateral consequences should also be taken into account, as they vary depending on the person.

2. Initiatives for Interrupting and Reducing the Impact of Bias in the Prosecutor's Office

Acknowledging implicit bias and defining its many variants is just the beginning. Once a prosecutor's office has completed the work of identifying existing biases, it must develop a framework for interrupting and reducing their impact, while also fostering cultural competency.[6] Prosecutors must ask and answer the question: How does race or culture impact the dynamics of criminal prosecution? To do so, a prosecutor's office should look both internally and externally. Office resources and office size will influence the type and frequency of trainings and initiatives that can be offered. However, prosecutor offices of any size can take significant steps through self-reflection, training, and community outreach.

It is encouraging to note that improving interactions between prosecutors and witnesses, survivors, or victims will result in better case outcomes, enhanced community trust, and a stronger sense of justice for the community the prosecutor serves.

Prosecutors should conduct a self-assessment of their approach to victims, survivors, and witnesses. This may reveal many areas of improvement. Several steps can be taken to reduce bias including training, improved interview techniques, development of checklists to identify relevant factors, implementation of procedural justice initiatives, data collection, accountability for prosecutor actions, and community outreach. Though limited resources may restrict the ability to accomplish all of the objectives immediately, every prosecutor office can do something meaningful.

A. Training

Many prosecutor offices have taken the laudable step of requiring implicit bias training for their staff. However, the focus may be on bias that impacts the accused rather than on witnesses, survivors, or victims. A prosecution office should assess existing training and, if needed, expand it to include witness-focused programming. The following suggestions demonstrate how a prosecutor's office can work toward that goal.[7]

i. Training Topics

Implicit bias training covers many topics and is conducted in a variety of ways.[8] This paper does not review all aspects of bias training; instead it focuses on the principles that apply to witnesses, survivors, or victims. Ultimately, anti-bias discussions should be infused in all training programs, so that they "become part of the DNA of training."[9] The following are issues and practical tips that should be included in bias training applicable to witnesses, survivors, or victims.

- **Have Empathy**: A core principle of bias training is that prosecutors should have empathy for their witnesses, survivors, or victims. The Golden Rule states "Treat others as you wish to be treated yourself." Scientific studies show that this simple tactic may hold a cure for eliminating harmful biases.[10] Following this principle, prosecutor staff should place themselves in the role of the witness and imagine how the witness feels. For example, the prosecutor should take into account that many witnesses, survivors, or victims have never been in a courthouse or met with a lawyer. They may have trauma from the event itself, they may be losing time from work or worrying about childcare, or they may be distrustful of police and prosecutors. Simply arriving at the courthouse, which is often severe and unwelcoming, will be daunting for many witnesses, survivors, or victims.

- **Refrain from Judgment**: Prosecutors should not be judgmental when meeting with witnesses. Witnesses come from all walks of life, from every race and every neighborhood. They may also have issues such as mental illness, joblessness, or substance abuse disorder. In contrast to some witnesses, prosecutors are well educated and have stable jobs with benefits. Thus, prosecutors and their witnesses may respond to circumstances very differently. Prosecutors should keep an open mind and engage in empathetic and meaningful communication. Witnesses are more likely to respond with trust and cooperation if they are treated with respect and not judged for their lifestyles or decisions. This will aid a prosecutor in obtaining the evidence needed to evaluate a case. Even if the prosecutor has a concern about the witness's statement, the prosecutor should explore this directly with empathy and lack of judgment.

- **Increase Communication**: The workings of the criminal justice system are unknown to most witnesses, survivors, or victims. Thus prosecutors, victim advocates, and paralegals need to explain criminal procedures in layperson's terms, set expectations for the courtroom, provide a timeline of events, and make decisions as to how and where to meet based on the witness's needs.

- **Meeting with the Witness:** The prosecutor can meet with the victim, survivor or witness in the office, at the individual's home, or in a neutral location.
    - **Meeting in the Office:** Prosecutors, office staff, and security guards should be trained to make witnesses, survivors, or victims feel invited and comfortable when they come to the prosecutor's office. The meeting should be in an appropriate and private space. Offices should eliminate the display of defendant photos and consider the impact of

historical photos of current and former prosecutors or other honorees that are not reflective of the diversity of the community they serve.[11]

- **Meeting at Home**: When meeting in a witness's home it is important not to be judgmental about the appearance of the home. The safety of the witness should be taken into account, as in some instances it is not safe for the witness to have a prosecutor or police officer be seen at their home.[12]

- **Be on Time:** The prosecutor should respect the witness's time and not make them wait unnecessarily. Though court schedules are unpredictable and cause many delays, the prosecutor should explain this to the witness in advance, so they are prepared. Paralegals or victim advocates may be able to meet with the witness if the prosecutor is unexpectedly unavailable.

• **Avoid Microaggressions**: Microaggressions are a subtle form of bias that manifest themselves in comments, questions, assumptions, and behaviors based on a person's appearance or identity. Verbal or nonverbal, they are the everyday indignities that members of marginalized groups endure in their routine interactions with people in all walks of life. People are often unaware that they are communicating through subtle cues, such as talking over a person, ignoring their comments, or walking away from a conversation. These small actions convey a prosecutor's lack of respect for the witness. If a prosecutor is confronted about a microaggression, they should replace defensiveness with empathy and apologize.

• **Avoid Offensive Comments**: Well-meaning people trying to make a connection with a witness or issue a "compliment" can unintentionally offend and reveal their biases. Comments that can easily offend include:

- Touching or asking to touch Black people's hair.
- Asking Black women if their hair is real.
- Telling Asian women to smile or commenting that they look upset.
- Asking non-White, Hispanic, or Asian people where they are from or commenting on how well they speak English.
- Asking LGBTQIA+ people personal sexual information.
- Commenting on one's use of a religious garment (Hijab, yarmulke).
- Commenting on women's appearance and weight.

ii. Who Should Be Trained?

Training on implicit bias and cultural competency as it impacts witnesses, survivors, or victims should be required for all prosecution staff that come into contact with them. It can be productive to bring relevant staff members together for the trainings, such as prosecutors and victim advocates.[13] The staff that should receive the training include:

- Prosecutors
- Paralegals
- Trial Assistants
- Interns
- Victim Advocates
- Office Security staff
- Receptionists
- HR staff

The office can also consider officewide training, so that leadership can convey the importance of the issue to all staff and demonstrate the office's commitment to reducing bias in prosecutorial work. Attendance by the chief prosecutor at bias training sends an important message that the training is valued.

BIAS TRAINING

The San Diego County District Attorney provides bias training to all new interns, post-bar clerks, and prosecutors. The training varies for each group and combines scientific education about the formation and disruption of bias as well as practical exercises that focus on prosecution activities at various stages in a case. The Tolerance Museum and Fair and Impartial Policing have both worked on prosecutor based anti-bias programs and videos are widely available on the internet for those who desire more information about how to detect and disrupt bias.[14]

iii. Who Should Conduct the Training?

Training can be conducted by internal and external trainers. A significant consideration for selecting a trainer is whether they can credibly deliver the desired message to the staff. Trainers can include a variety of people, alone or in combination, such as:

- Prosecutors from within the office
- Prosecutors from other offices

- Implicit bias experts from outside the office
- Victim advocates
- Victims, survivors, or witnesses who have experienced implicit bias
- Community members

iv. When to Train

Implicit bias training is relatively new to prosecutor offices and is not always warmly received. To overcome resistance and to instill a deeper understanding of the issues, an office should consider a training strategy that includes:

- **Mandatory Training**: All staff that have contact with witnesses, survivors, or victims, both legal and non-legal, should be required to attend the training.
- **On-Boarding**: The on-boarding process for all staff, legal and non-legal, should include implicit bias training.
- **Follow-Up Training**: As prosecutors progress to more serious cases, such as assaults, sex crimes, and homicides, they should receive additional training on implicit bias and cultural competence regarding their witnesses.
- **Annual Training**: The office should support annual events that address implicit bias and cultural competence.

v. How to Train

To improve engagement by the participants in the training, various interactive approaches can be taken:

- **Breakout Groups**: It is helpful to include breakout groups after training lectures. This allows the staff to discuss the points made in the training, raise questions, and examine new approaches to working with witnesses, survivors, and victims.
- **Interactive Exercises**: Trainings can also go beyond the traditional lecture format and can involve sessions that include interactive exercises and direct participation. These can place the trainee in the role of the victim or witness, which can foster empathy and a greater understanding of the communities that the office serves. Consider blind casting these roles, so as not to unintentionally reinforce biases or stereotypes.

WORKSHOP ON INTERGENERATIONAL POVERTY

In 2021, the San Diego District Attorney's Office partnered with Jodi Pfarr, the author of "Bridges out of Poverty," for a workshop on intergenerational poverty, which included interactive exercises and simulations.[15]

- **Walk in the Shoes of a Witness**: Another exercise requires prosecutors and prosecutor staff to walk into the courthouse and the office, as if for the first time. They are then asked questions such as: What is the first impression of the office? Was it clear where to go? Are staff helpful? Are there offensive materials posted in the office? How can the space be improved?

vi. Invite the Community to the Office

In addition to training on implicit bias, it is important to bring the voice of the community into the training room. A prosecutor office can regularly host panels and presentations where community members provide insight into the public's view of the intersection of public safety, prosecutors, and law enforcement. This will promote a better understanding of the witnesses, survivors, or victims with whom the prosecutors work.

COMMUNITY PANEL

In February 2021, the New York County District Attorney's Office hosted a panel on "The Complexities of the Relationship Between the Black Community and Prosecutors." The panel consisted of community members and was organized with the goal of amplifying the voice of community members, enhancing the office's relationships with the communities it serves, and promoting racial equity.[16]

B. Focusing on the Witness—Science-Based Interviewing

Science-Based Interviewing teaches interviewers to be active listeners and takes into consideration the values and perspective of those being interviewed. Using the science-based approach, interviewers plan and prepare for questioning by conducting a detailed review of the case, making distinctions between what is known (facts), what is believed to be true but not verified (information), and what is supposition based upon underlying knowledge (inference).

By analyzing the information in an objective, structured manner, the interviewer can identify premature assumptions and weed out conclusions that are unsupported by the facts. Any beliefs that are the result of implicit bias and not grounded in the facts can be identified and discarded through this process. The planning process also helps interviewers anticipate and plan for implicit biases that may be held by the interviewee. During the interview, the interviewer maintains an open, non-judgmental approach based on the principles of Motivational Interviewing and Observing Rapport-Based Interpersonal Techniques (ORBIT) to gather informationto encourage the interviewee to be an information-provider rather than question-answerer.[17]

These two approaches help to prevent the interviewer from communicating their biases to the interviewee. The witnesses or victims are then able to give their account free from two major sources of contamination: overwhelming pressure to maintain an acceptable image and narrative changes that occur when an interviewee's memory is altered in favor of an interviewer's expectations about the sequence of events.[18]

Introductory training on this approach can last one day, while more advanced interactive training can last several weeks.[19]

C. Officewide Procedural Justice

Procedural justice is based on four central principles: "treating people with dignity and respect, giving citizens 'voice' during encounters, being neutral in decision-making, and conveying trustworthy motives."[20] These principles should apply to how prosecutors interact with their witnesses, survivors, or victims.

i. Guidelines for Interactions with Witnesses, Survivors, or Victims

An office can do an assessment of how witnesses are treated and whether it comports with procedural justice. To do so, a prosecutor office can convene a procedural justice working group to develop guidelines for interacting with witnesses at various stages such as: interviews prior to charging, office visits, case updates, trial preparation, and court appearances. The working group should involve representatives from all sections of the office including attorneys, paralegals, administrative staff, receptionists, witness and victim advocates, and security personnel.

ii. Make the Office Inviting and Appropriate

Prosecutor offices and courthouses are not usually welcoming spaces; however, efforts can be made to make the space more inviting. Posting clear signage is one simple step that will help witnesses, survivors, or victims navigate through unfamiliar space. Also, prosecutor offices should be free of offensive material. Political cartoons or memes, photos of offenders or crime scenes, and other potentially upsetting items are not uncommon in a prosecutor's office. Since witnesses often come into a prosecutor's office, all employees should understand that certain photos, posters, or other materials may make some people uncomfortable or offended. The office should have a policy that outlines what can be in public view based on what might be considered offensive by members of the community.

D. Hiring

Hiring a diverse staff can help to reduce the impact of bias. Offices should create targeted recruitment programs to increase racial and ethnic diversity among prosecutors, especially in underrepresented communities impacted by the work of the office. Simply working with people who are different from oneself can provide valuable insights. The office can also develop an internal committee where all staff can regularly discuss diversity and inclusion issues.[21] Staff diversity should include not only prosecutors, but all staff, including victim advocates who often have more contact with witnesses, survivors, or victims than any other staff.[22]

E. Data Collection

One way to examine the impact of implicit bias is to collect data to determine if similarly situated witnesses, survivors, or victims are treated differently. Data collection and analysis will promote the awareness and self-evaluation essential to improving prosecutorial practices. Prosecutors should consider gathering data on the race, gender, and other status information on witnesses and defendants in order to identify whether there are discrepancies in charging decisions, plea bargains, and dispositions. If such discrepancies exist, a further analysis is needed to determine if it is driven by bias, other factors, or both. At the very least, the data may reveal areas where more training or community outreach is needed. Once new procedures are implemented, a re-analysis of the data can uncover areas for further improvement. However, it should be noted that collecting and analyzing data about potential bias is complex, detailed, and time consuming.[23]

F. Accountability

The chief prosecutor and office leadership must demonstrate by word and deed that they are committed to reducing bias. Developing the programs described in this Chapter sends a clear message to the office about the prosecutor's commitment to this issue. Leadership can also attend the trainings along with staff to show commitment to the issue and that staff at all levels can benefit from bias training.

The office's evaluation process should include a component that gauges the staff member's commitment to procedural justice, reducing bias, and community service activity. One indicator of this can be the amount of community outreach work done by the prosecutor. Unfortunately, some prosecutors have overwhelming caseloads that do not allow time for community outreach work.

There have been regrettable incidents of prosecutors behaving inappropriately in actions that range from their treatment of witnesses, survivors, or victims to comments made in public.[24] Prosecutors should be sanctioned for such behavior. The degree of the sanction will depend on the nature and gravity of the offense.

3. Initiatives for Interrupting and Reducing the Impact of Implicit Bias Outside the Prosecutor Office

Prosecutors can have an impact on reducing bias by forming partnerships outside their office. A number of excellent programs have been spearheaded by prosecutors. A few of those programs are highlighted in this section.

A. Meet Community Members

It is critical that a prosecutor's office not limit itself to classroom instruction and internal training. Countering bias requires getting out of the office and directly interacting with the people that the office serves. By engaging with the lived experiences of those in the community, prosecutors will better understand commonalities between themselves and their witnesses, survivors, or victims and will be more likely to recognize their own biases. Increased collaboration between prosecutors and their communities will also improve the public trust of the office.

B. Training in Schools and the Community

Prosecutors can establish partnerships with local schools, non-profit organizations, and other community hubs to schedule regular visits and to create programming that focuses on meeting their needs.[25]

SCHOOL PROGRAMS

The New York County District Attorney's Office has a Community Partnership Unit that develops curriculum for local schools and arranges opportunities for prosecutors to facilitate those workshops throughout the school year. The office also has a Moot Court competition at a school in lower Manhattan.[26]

SCHOOL MENTORSHIP

The San Diego District Attorney's Office has developed a weekly after-school program for 3rd through 6th graders centered on social and emotional learning, facilitated by prosecutors, investigators, and D.A. staff. This year long program pairs youth with mentors in a group setting to encourage self-confidence, emotional development, and problem-solving skills.[27]

C. Internships and Mentoring

Some prosecutors have created internships and mentorship opportunities that serve the dual goal of bringing prosecutors into the community and the community into the prosecutor's office.

INTERNS

Each summer, the New York County District Attorney's Office hosts a diverse cohort of interns who are representative of the borough as a whole. The office uses a structured interviewing process to eliminate bias and ensure fairness in the selection process. In 2018, the office expanded its programming and launched a gun control advocacy fellowship for two graduating high school students who were survivors of gun violence.[28]

D. Community Outreach and Satellite Offices

Prosecutors can designate staff to work regularly with community members to form relationships that encourage witnesses, survivors, or victims to participate in the criminal justice system.

COMMUNITY OUTREACH

The San Diego County District Attorney employs four Community Partnership Prosecutors who do outreach to a wide variety of community groups including businesses, faith-based organizations, schools, and non-profit groups to assist in meeting the needs of their various communities. The office also maintains a Community, Action, Resource, and Engagement Center open to the public. The center provides a hub for food, shelter, clothing, and job seeking services for justice-involved community members and the general public. In addition, there are regular meetings with faith advisory and youth advisory boards that serve to inform the office of community needs and ideas.[29]

Prosecutor offices of any size can convene community advisory boards, made up of respected members of the community, that can regularly meet with the prosecutor to provide advice about how they can best serve their communities and encourage witness participation.

In larger jurisdictions, prosecutors have established satellite offices in communities that are geographically isolated from the main prosecutor's office. This provides easier access for witnesses, survivors, or victims who need to meet with the prosecutor.

COMMUNITY BASED OFFICES

The New York County District Attorney's Office, which is physically located on the southern end of Manhattan, opened locations in Harlem and Washington Heights to establish a presence for communities on the northern end of Manhattan. Those offices are staffed by personnel from various units, including Community Partnerships, Domestic Violence, Immigrant Affairs, and Witness Aid Services.[30] Services are available in many languages.

E. Training of Law Enforcement

Prosecutors should collaborate with law enforcement partners to ensure that police officers and investigators receive training on the impact of bias. This is particularly important as officers are usually the first point of contact with a witness and that initial meeting can determine whether or not a witness is willing to come forward.

CULTURAL AWARENESS APP

The San Diego County District Attorney's Office created a mobile application that provides key cultural knowledge about San Diego County's various, diverse communities to help law enforcement officers respond respectfully during non-emergency situations. The Cultural Awareness Project (CAP App) was developed under the guidance of the D.A.'s Interfaith Advisory Board, which conducted focus groups with various community representatives to inform its content. The app provides information on cultural norms across 11 communities including African American youth, Mexican/Mexican American, Asian, Vietnamese, East African/Somali, East African/Somali Youth, Muslim, Samoan, Native American and more. The Board continues to provide cultural insight to law enforcement officials in non-emergency situations.[31]

Conclusion

To move towards an equitable criminal justice system, prosecutors must embark on a journey that identifies and reduces bias in their work with victims, survivors, and witnesses. Prosecutor offices of any size should engage in this self-reflection and improvement. Everything cannot be done at once, but one step forward will lead to another. The ultimate goal is for victims, survivors, witnesses, and the community to see their prosecutor as a public servant who is committed to public safety, equal protection, and justice for all. They deserve no less.

So, You'd Like To Know More

- Please see the Appendix for an excellent recommended reading list.

About the Authors

Linda Ford is a Senior Trial Counsel with the New York County District Attorney's Office (Manhattan) where she handles all aspects of homicide prosecutions from pre-arrest investigations through grand jury, trial, sentencing and post-conviction litigation. ADA Ford has developed and delivers training workshops for law enforcement, prosecutors, and judges at home and abroad. ADA Ford serves on the Editorial Board of the International Investigative Interviewing Research Group Journal.

Kristine Hamann is the Executive Director and founder of Prosecutors' Center for Excellence (PCE). PCE provides consulting and research services for prosecutors to promote best practices, spur innovations and implement solutions. From 2013 to 2016, Kristine Hamann was a Visiting Fellow at DOJ/Bureau of Justice Assistance where she worked with prosecutors in over 30 states. She chairs the NY State Best Practices Committee for prosecutors and teaches at Georgetown Law School. She was a member of the American Bar Association (ABA) Criminal Justice Council and is on the ABA Criminal Justice Journal Editorial Board. Ms. Hamann was a prosecutor in the New York County District Attorney's Office (Manhattan) where she served on the Executive Staff.

Tyear Middleton serves as the Chief Diversity/Equal Employment Opportunity Officer for the Queens County District Attorney's Office (NY). She has committed the entirety of her career to public interest work. She began her career as an Assistant District Attorney in the Kings County District Attorney's office (Brooklyn, NY). She then served as a Principal Court Attorney in Brooklyn Supreme Court, Criminal Term assisting an Acting Supreme Court Justice. She joined the New York City Police Department where, among other things, she trained police on the constitutionality of stop, question, and frisk and worked to eradicate unlawful discriminatory practices within the Department. She has worked with many bar associations to assist them in their diversity and inclusion efforts within the profession.

Audrey Moore serves as First Assistant District Attorney at the New York County District Attorney's Office (Manhattan). She is tasked with setting policy on matters handled by all of the Office's divisions in a manner consistent with the Office's core values and tenets. Ms. Moore is also the Chief Diversity Officer, charged with strengthening the office's policies relating to workforce diversity and inclusion and enhancing diversity recruitment strategies. Additionally, Ms. Moore oversees the Manhattan District Attorney's Harlem and Washington Heights Offices. Previously she served as Chief of the Special Victims Bureau, where she oversaw the management of the Child Abuse, Domestic Violence, Elder Abuse, Sex Crimes, Human Trafficking Response, and Witness Aid Services Units.

Luis Morales is the Chief of the Immigrant Affairs Unit for the New York County District Attorney's Office (Manhattan). He has served in the Appeals Bureau and Financial Frauds Bureau, following a federal clerkship and brief stint in private practice. He is also the Executive Director of the Manhattan D.A. Academy and an instructor with the Inside Criminal Justice program that brings together incarcerated students and prosecutors. Before attending law school, Luis taught English Language Arts in a New York City public middle school.

Sophia Roach was a senior gang prosecutor from the San Diego County District Attorney's Office (CA). She is a frequent instructor on elimination of bias in prosecution work and in the selection of juries. She has served as a liaison to various task forces and the San Diego Crime Laboratories. She was a member of her office's Training and Advisory Committee, an Ethics Advisor, and a veteran instructor of lawyers, law enforcement, and students at both the law school and college level. Ms. Roach served on the Board of Directors for the California District Attorneys Association, the San Diego Deputy District Attorneys Association and helped form the NDAA Women's section. She currently consults on prosecution issues and works as a Senior Attorney at Prosecutors' Center for Excellence.

Sherry Thompson Taylor is a Superior Court Judge in San Diego County. Before her appointment to the bench, she served as the Division Chief of the Insurance Fraud & Workplace Justice Division of the San Diego District Attorney's Office where she supervised 60 employees including attorneys, paralegals, investigators, and support staff. In addition to insurance fraud, the unit focused on worker's rights, wage theft, and labor tracking. Sherry's responsibilities also included managing grant applications for six grant funded units with a $12 million dollar budget. She has held several other positions in the office including Assistant Chief in the South Bay Branch, prosecutor in the Special Operations Unit handling high profile and sensitive matters and was a prosecutor in the Judge Unit which focused on gangs and drug enforcement.

Appendix

General Law-Related References

ABA, Diversity and Inclusion Center (last visited June 4, 2021).

ABA, Diversity and Inclusion 360 Commission Toolkit Introduction (2016).

ABA, Implicit Bias Toolkit (last visited June 4, 2021).

Alafair S. Burke, Improving Prosecutorial Decision Making: Some Lessons of Cognitive Science, 47 Wm. & Mary L. Rev. 1587 (2006).

Cory Collins, What is White Privilege, Really?, Learning for Justice (2018).

Rachel D. Godsil & Alexis McGill Johnson, Transforming Perception; Black Men and Boys, Executive Summary, Perception Institute (March 2013).

Wendy Gu & Priscilla Hamilton, Confronting Racial Bias Against Black and African American Victims in the Prosecution of Sexual Violence, Domestic Violence, Stalking, and Human Trafficking, AEquitas & the National Black Prosecutors Ass'n (April 2021).

William C. Hubbard & Sherrilyn Ifill, Joint Statement on Eliminating Bias in the Criminal Justice System, ABA & NAACP Legal Defense and Educational Fund, Inc. (July 2015).

Akhi Johnson, What's in a Name? A Small Step Prosecutors Can Take to Build a More Humane System, Vera Institute of Justice (July 24, 2020).

Peggy McIntosh, White Privilege: Unpacking the Invisible Knapsack, Wellesley College for Research on Women (1990).

National Museum of African American History & Culture, Being Antiracist (last visited June 4, 2021).

Keith Payne, Laura Niemi, & John M. Doris, How to Think about 'Implicit Bias,' Sci. Am. (March 27, 2018).

Praatika Prasad, Implicit Racial Biases in Prosecutorial Summations: Proposing an Integrated Response, 86 Fordham L. Rev. 667 (2018).

Prosecutors' Center for Excellence & National Black Prosecutors Association, The Conscious Prosecutor Implicit Bias Toolkit for Prosecutors (March 21, 2017).

Robert J. Smith & Justin D. Levinson, The Impact of Implicit Racial Bias on the Exercise of Prosecutorial Discretion, 35 Seattle U. L. Rev. 795 (2012).

Literature Exploring Bias

Michelle Alexander, The New Jim Crow: Mass Incarceration in The Age of Colorblindness.

Carol Anderson, White Rage: The Unspoken Truth of Our Racial Divide.

Maya Angelou, Letter to My Daughter (2009).

Eduardo Bonilla-Silva, Racism Without Racists.

Robin DiAngelo, White Fragility.

Reni Eddo-Lodge, Why I'm No Longer Talking to White People About Race.

George Fredrickson, Racism: A Short History.

Malcolm Gladwell, Blink (2005).

Malcolm Gladwell, Talking to Strangers (2019).

Kelly Lytle Hernández, City of Inmates.

Elizabeth Hinton, From the War on Poverty to the War on Crime: The Making of Mass Incarceration in America.

Stephanie E. Jones-Rogers, They Were Her Property: White Women as Slave Owners in the American South.

Ibram Kendi, How to Be An Antiracist.

Ibram Kendi, Stamped From the Beginning.

Eric Mann, Katrina's Legacy.

Toni Morrison, The Origin of Others.

Ijeoma Oluo, So You Want To Talk About Race.

Dorothy Roberts, Killing the Black Body: Race, Reproduction, and the Meaning of Liberty.

Richard Rothstein, The Color of Law.

Ousmane Sembène, God's Bits of Wood.

Andrea Smith, Conquest.

Richard Valencia, Chicano Students and the Courts.

Isabel Wilkerson, The Warmth of Other Suns.

Franklin E. Zimring, When Police Kill.

Endnotes

1. *See* Emily Kwong & Pragya Agarwal, *Understanding Unconscious Bias*, Short Wave NPR (July 15, 2020) ("Our conscious mind" cannot process all the information "coming at us" in a "very rational, logical manner. Otherwise we would be agonizing over every decision we make." Instead, the brain "sometimes take[s] cognitive shortcuts to help make those decisions easier, shortcuts that can lead to...bias").

2. *Id.* When we process information while making "rushed" decisions, "we're matching the information to pre-existing stereotypes...stereotypes...we pick up over time from the environment around us – our family, our school, our community, [and] the media".

3. *Id.*

4. *See* Debra Cassens Weiss, *After Judge Cites Prosecutors' Racist Emails, D.A. Declines to Retry Asian American Woman For Murder*, ABA JOURNAL, Oct. 5. 2020; *see also* Meagan Flynn, *A Black Defendant's Lawyer Harbored Such 'Extreme' Racist Views That A Court Has Granted His Client A New Trial*, WASH. POST (Jan. 22, 2020) (Capital defense attorney "regularly made racist comments about his own clients" including that a "Hispanic defendant 'deserved to fry.'").

5. Kirwan Institute for the Study of Race and Ethnicity, *Mythbusters: Implicit Bias Edition, Clearing Up the Confusion Surrounding Implicit Bias*, The Ohio State University (2020) ("Implicit biases are activated involuntarily and beyond our awareness or intentional control. Implicit bias is concerned with unconscious cognition that influences understanding, actions, and decisions....").

6. National Center for Cultural Competence, *Definitions of Cultural Competence*, Georgetown University Center for Child & Human Development (last visited June 9, 2021) ("Cultural

competence is defined as a set of values, behaviors, attitudes, and practices within a...organization...or among individuals...which enables them to work effectively cross culturally..... [I]t refers to the ability to honor and respect the beliefs, language, interpersonal styles and behaviors of individuals and families receiving services, as well as staff who are providing such services. Striving to achieve cultural competence is a dynamic, ongoing, developmental process that requires a long-term commitment.").

7. The Tolerance Museum and Fair and Impartial Policing have both worked on prosecutor based anti-bias programs, and videos are widely available on the internet for those who desire more information about how to detect and disrupt bias, https://fipolicing.com/resources/;https://www.museumoftolerance.com/for-professionals/programs-workshops/tools-for-tolerance-for-law-enforcement-and-criminal-justice.

8. *See* resources from Prosecutors' Center for Excellence, https://pceinc.org/wp-content/uploads/2019/11/2-20170321-The-Conscious-Prosecutor-Interactive-Implicit-Bias-Toolkit-PCE.pdf (last viewed May 22, 2021) and the ABA Diversity and Inclusion Center, https://www.americanbar.org/groups/diversity/resources/implicit-bias/.

9. Assistant District Attorney Renee Gregory, Chief Diversity Officer, Brooklyn District Attorney's Office (May 21, 2021)

10. The "consider the opposite" theory has its roots in early bias science. In the seminal article published in December of 1984, *Considering The Opposite: A Corrective Strategy For Social Judgment*, authors Charles Lord, Mark Lepper and Elizabeth Preston found that considering an opposing position, fact or viewpoint is an "effective method of retraining social judgment." Charles G. Lord, Mark R. Lepper & Elizabeth Preston, *Considering The Opposite: A Corrective Strategy For Social Judgment*, 47 J. PERSONALITY & SOCIAL PSYCHOL 1231 (1984). Newer studies, as recent as 2020, have confirmed the efficacy of this strategy.

11. *See, e.g.,* Commonwealth of Virginia v. Terrance Shipp, Jr. Case # FE-2020-8, Dec. 20, 2020 (ruling favorably on motion of defendant's counsel to remove pictures of White judges from the courtroom); *see generally* NICOLE GONZALES VAN CLEVE, CROOK COUNTY: RACISM AND INJUSTICE IN AMERICA'S LARGEST CRIMINAL COURT (2016) (describing the author's impression as a new employee at Cook County prosecutors).

12. A detailed discussion of steps prosecutors can take to protect their witnesses is beyond the scope of this Chapter; however, see *Witness Intimidation – What You Can Do to Protect Your Witness*, Prosecutors' Center for Excellence (2016), https://pceinc.org/wp-content/uploads/2019/11/20160610-Witness-Intimidation-What-You-Can-Do-To-Protect-Your-Witnesses-PCE.pdf.

13. The New York County District Attorney's Office conducts joint trainings for prosecutors and victim advocates on issues relating to victims and witnesses.

14. Interview with Deputy District Attorney Sophia Roach, San Diego District Attorney's Office (May 2021).

15. *San Diego County District Attorney*, https://www.sdcda.org/Office/diversity/community-involvement; *see also*, Molly Miron, 'Bridges Out of Poverty': Professionals Study Ways to Change Social Situations, Bemidjii Pioneer, Nov. 14, 2009, https://www.bemidjipioneer.com/236782-bridges-out-poverty-professionals-study-ways-change-social-situations.

16. Interview with First ADA Audrey Moore, New York County District Attorney's Office, (June 9, 2021).

17. D. Rosengren, *Building Motivational Interviewing Skills: A Practitioner Workbook.* (2018); Sunghwan Kim, Laurence Alison, & Paul Christiansen, *Observing Rapport-Based Interpersonal Techniques to Gather Information from Victims*, PSYCHOL. PUBLIC POLICY & LAW (2020).

18. El Dorado District Attorney Vern Pierson, President of the California District Attorneys Association, has adopted Science-Based Interviewing (also called Subject-Centered Interviewing) in his county and is a leader in advancing the methodology across California to eliminate false confessions, encourage witness cooperation, and ensure procedural justice.

19. Tailored Training Programs (TTP) has partnered with the Los AngEles Police Department, the New York City Police Department Intelligence Division, and several federal law enforcement agencies to transition cutting edge human behavior research into science-based interview and interrogation techniques. For additional information about their Science-Based Interview Training, contact Kristin Richmond at krichmond@ttp-usa.com.

20. National Initiative for Building Community Trust and Justice, https://trustandjustice.org/. *See* Center for Court Innovation and Institute for Innovation in Prosecution's free 2-part curriculum toolkit and accompanying PowerPoint presentation on Procedural Justice to improve public trust and confidence. https://www.courtinnovation.org/publications/procedural-justice-prosecutors.

21. *See* PCE Website, *Talking with Dan Clark about Race, Social-Justice and Equity in a Prosecutor's Office*, https://pceinc.org/talking-with-dan-clark-about-race-social-justice-and-equity-in-a-prosecutors-office/ (last viewed May 29, 2021).

22. The various approaches for recruiting and retaining a diverse staff is beyond the scope of this Chapter. Those wanting additional resources on this topic should be in touch with the individual chapter authors or editors Hon. Bernice Donald and Professor Redfield.

23. A full discussion of data collection on this issue is beyond the scope of this Chapter. To see more on how prosecutors have gathered data on a variety of topics, including the race of defendants and witnesses, see PCE's *Did You Know* on Prosecutor Data Dashboards, https://pceinc.org/prosecutor-data-dashboards/. (Last viewed June 9, 2021).

24. *See* Charles Maldonado, *Federal Appeals Court Affirms Denial Of Immunity For Prosecutors Who Used Fake Subpoenas*, The Lens (April 21, 2020); Jon Campbell, *Fired Louisiana Prosecutor Had 'Whites Only' Sign in Property He Owned*, The Appeal (March 26, 2020).

25. Wendy Gu & Priscilla Hamilton, *Confronting Racial Bias Against Black and African American Victims in the Prosecution of Sexual Violence, Domestic Violence, Stalking, and Human Trafficking*, AEquitas & the National Black Prosecutors Association (April 2021) (prosecutors can form and strengthen relationships with the community through organizing listening sessions in community centers and conducting written surveys).

26. Manhattan District Attorney's Office, Community Partnerships, https://www.manhattanda.org/our-work/community-partnerships/.

27. San Diego District Attorney Mid-term Report 78, https://www.sdcda.org/content/office/SDCDA%20Midterm%20Report%202021.pdf.

28. Manhattan District Attorney's Office, Internship Opportunities, https://www.manhattanda.org/careers/internship-opportunities/.

29. See San Diego County District Attorney, https://www.sdcda.org/office/Community-Partnership-Prosecutors/; *see also* https://www.sdcda.org/office/care/index.

30. Manhattan District Attorney's Office, Victim Resources, https://www.manhattanda.org/victim-resources/.

31. San Diego County District Attorney, https://www.sdcda.org/office/cultural-awareness.

NINE

Narrative, Culture, and Individuation

A Criminal Defense Lawyer's Race-Conscious Approach to Reduce Implicit Bias for Latinxs[*]

Walter I. Gonçalves, Jr., Assistant Federal Public Defender, Arizona[†]

A Note from the Editors: We first met Attorney Gonçalves through his writing and are honored to be able to share here a part of his work on reducing implicit bias. He offers us thoughtful, well-researched advice from a Latino public defender on how to limit the negative manifestations of implicit bias that he sees in his practice. He advocates a client-centered approach that uses storytelling and narrative. While written from the criminal defense perspective, many of Mr. Gonçalves bias-interruption strategies will prove generally applicable. We thank him for his work.

CHAPTER HIGHLIGHTS

- Implicit racial bias impacts bail, jury deliberations, and sentencing outcomes but lawyers can use pretrial motions, voir dire, counter-narratives, jury instructions, and experts to blunt its effect.

---

[*] Much of this chapter is available with additional citations at Walter I. Gonçalves, Jr., *Narrative, Culture, and Individuation: A Criminal Defense Lawyer's Race-Conscious Approach to Reduce Implicit Bias for Latinxs*, 18 Seattle J. Soc. Just. 333 (2020).

[†] For their thoughtful feedback, many thanks to Denise Barrett, Molly Kincaid, Jay Sagar, Edie Cunningham, Sarah Gannett, Meghan Graham, Andy Silverman, and Kenney Hegland. For their encouragement and support, thank you Jon M. Sands (Arizona Federal Public Defender) and supervisory assistant public defenders Leticia Marquez (Capital Habeas Unit, Tucson office), Victoria Brambl (trial unit Tucson), and Eric Rau (trial unit Tucson).

- Public defender offices can employ strategies to minimize the negative impact of implicit bias such as checklists, educating staff about implicit bias, and hiring diverse lawyers.
- A race-conscious approach to criminal defense practice is client-centered and requires input and involvement from the client to craft narratives focused on the individual person.
- The use of client culture in storytelling and narrative is a novel way to approach individuation and can be used in pretrial motions, the trial's theory of defense, and sentence.
- Latinxs, like African Americans, have been historically portrayed in the media in negative ways to the point where they are negatively impacted by implicit racial bias in the criminal justice context.

CHAPTER CONTENTS

1. Race Consciousness and the Client-Centered Approach
2. Strategies to Mitigate the Impact of Implicit Bias
    A. Recognizing Implicit Bias Within Oneself and the Office
    B. Interviewing and Consulting with Clients Through Client-Centered Advocacy
    C. Pretrial Motion Practice
    D. Voir Dire
    E. Client Testimony
    F. Use of Expert Testimony
    G. Narrative
    H. Jury Instructions
    I. Sentencing Advocacy
3. Strategies to Mitigate the Impact of Racial Bias for Latinx Clients
    A. Implicit Bias and Its Impact on Latinxs
    B. Historic and Contemporary Media Depictions of Latinxs Increase Negative Racial Bias
    C. Individuation and Client Narratives to Counter Stereotypes and "Schemas"
    D. The Use of Culture to Mitigate Implicit Bias and Negative Racial Stereotyping
    E. Use of Checklists for Latinxs

F. Documentation and Summaries of Implicit Bias Research

Conclusion

Introduction

When a criminal defense attorney is assigned a case and shows up at the first court appearance, more often than not the client will be a person of color. Depending on the region, the client has a greater chance of being African American, Latinx, or Native American compared to White. This is true for most federal trial courts in the United States.[1] To make matters worse, racial minorities receive longer sentences compared to similarly-situated Whites.[2] These facts are problematic because the percentage of minorities charged with crimes is greater compared to their percentage of the country's population. Due to implicit racial bias, these racial inequities coexist with, and are heightened by, the behavior of defense attorneys, prosecutors, judges, jurors, and probation and pretrial service officers. Implicit bias has real-life consequences on bail, jury deliberations, and sentencing.

A body of social science and legal literature shows that certain strategies can blunt the negative impact of implicit bias. Lawyers can use pretrial motions, voir dire, counter-narratives, jury instructions, and experts in novel ways, to open judges and jurors' minds about social issues that underlie the facts and law of the case.[3] The literature also encourages indigent defense offices to change their internal culture through hiring practices and training.[4] The line attorney may not have the power to change office policy but can apply said strategies in his or her practice. These strategies apply to any client of color, but nothing in the literature specifically addresses Latinx criminal defendants.

What follows is a framework for criminal defense lawyers to reduce implicit bias by the use of narrative, client culture, and individuation. While focused on examples of Latinx criminal defendants—the fastest growing minority nationwide and the largest subset of criminal defendants in the federal system—the client-centered and race-based strategies can apply to any minority client.[5]

1. Race Consciousness and the Client-Centered Approach

The race-conscious approach embodies client-centered representation, a model that emphasizes client autonomy and needs. Client-centered representation demands that the lawyer involve the client in decisions requiring more than just the decision to plead guilty or not guilty, accept a plea agreement, or testify or concede guilt on any count as a strategy during trial. One example of client-centered advocacy includes the decision to call a particular character witness over another for trial. Traditionally, this decision is left to the lawyer, but the client may possess insights about the habits or proclivities of the witness known only to a few people.

A race-conscious approach requires client-centered research into a client's life, in order to present him/her in the best possible light. Applying client-centered principles allows the lawyer to zero in on facts and decisions otherwise unknown. Using client-centered strategies, such as presenting important life experiences of the client, decreases bias because it humanizes the person and allows the court to see him/her as more than just a "defendant." Detailed narratives present the client as a unique human being.

Fortunately, many defense lawyers recognize that a client-centered approach is effective—the best way to fulfill ethical responsibilities to clients.[6] Some defense lawyers may acknowledge that the prevalence of racial disparities resulting from implicit racism, shows that client-centeredness without race consciousness fails standards of "zealous representation."[7] Nonetheless, the decision to incorporate race is one only the individual attorney can make depending on the attorney's knowledge, case-specific factors (judge, prosecutor, and charges), and the client's consent. There is no "one size fits all" philosophy to incorporating race.

The race-conscious defense attorney should ask clients if they are comfortable incorporating race in the defense. Some clients may not want the lawyer to mention race as a factor in motions or court proceedings; but after enough interactions with the client, the lawyer may gain insight into the client's experience with racial prejudice, especially by asking questions relevant to mitigation. Through this knowledge building comes trust. With enough trust, both lawyer and client may feel more comfortable discussing racial prejudice and its potential influence in the representation. My experience is that many clients appreciate lawyers who are sensitive to racial prejudice and willing to do something about it within the system.

Using a client-centered approach to combat the negative effects of race in client interactions, pretrial motions, sentencing memoranda, jury instructions, voir dire, and opening and closing arguments helps the individual client and the system, even if substantive arguments are unsuccessful in a particular case. For example, a trial court may rule not to include an implicit bias instruction with final jury instructions. Even so, the defense lawyer discussed matters of race supported by social science evidence and created a record for appeal. The defense lawyer educates the court, prosecutors, and other criminal justice players and also primes the court for the next trial when the attorney can request the same or similar instruction. Therefore, from a race-based approach, success means "creating a courtroom situation in which implicit race discrimination and bias are openly joined on the record instead of relegated to the background."[8] The hope is that over time judges will be more accepting of race-based arguments and open to ruling favorably for the defense.

2. Strategies to Mitigate the Impact of Implicit Bias

As the Kirwan Institute's annual review of implicit bias research explains, people form both favorable and unfavorable assessments about others based on characteristics such as race, ethnicity, age, or appearance, implicitly, without conscious thought. Researchers of implicit bias have determined that everyone possesses biases, formed from an early age through exposure to direct and indirect messages, including media and news programming. People's biases develop at an early age, and they affect how we view the world. The implicit associations we hold are not related to our declared or committed beliefs, nor do they even reflect positions we would explicitly endorse.[9] People often hold implicit biases that favor their own ingroup; however, research has shown that people can still hold implicit biases against their own ingroup.[10]

As psychologist Dr. Leslie Roose explains, the mental process for the activation of implicit biases begins in an area of the brain called the amygdala, which activates when humans feel fear, threat, anxiety, and distrust. For example, people with a fear of snakes or spiders have higher levels of amygdala activation when they view pictures of these animals, compared to other creatures.[11] For some people, seeing photos of persons with darker skin triggers this amygdala response,[12] with darker skin tone triggering more amygdala activation compared to persons with lighter skin tone.[13] Fortunately, implicit biases are malleable and can be gradually unlearned and replaced with new mental associations. It is the defense attorney's job to learn about implicit biases and their negative effects so they can help judges, jurors, and prosecutors to reduce the negative impact of those biases.

Given the neuroscience, scholars have talked about what defense lawyers can do to mitigate the effects of implicit bias among themselves, judges, and juries. No study, however, specifically analyzes the representation of Latinxs through a racial lens in criminal defense. Because strategies for raising implicit bias and mitigating its impact are universal (they apply to clients of any ethnicity), this is not surprising. But different racial, ethnic, or cultural groups have unique characteristics and contexts that set each apart.

A. Recognizing Implicit Bias Within Oneself and the Office

The experience of many public defenders is that they eventually "burn out" due to the volume and seriousness of cases. When lawyers are tired, and morale is low, clients of color may not get the same attention as White clients because implicit bias favors some clients over others. The advantage of a race-conscious approach is that it teaches lawyers to take their time and to treat each client individually.

The first step to remediating implicit bias in the criminal defense office is to recognize it. One consequence of subscribing to the myth of a "post racial" society, or employing a "colorblind" approach to practice, is that defense lawyers, untrained in implicit racism, perpetuate office cultures that allow its impact to persist.[14] Defense lawyers often become desensitized to the injustices they see every day,[15] detached, while racism, explicit and implicit, goes unrecognized.[16] While always aware of racial disparities in the system from when I started trial practice as an Assistant Pima County Public Defender in Tucson, Arizona, it was only ten years into practice as an Assistant Federal Public Defender that this reality became more alarming. The percentage of minority criminal defendants in federal court in southern Arizona is greater than in Pima County Superior Court.[17] This greater disparity concerned me because colleagues rarely discussed race issues, and did not employ tactics to make race salient in practice other than through *Batson* challenges, motions challenging cross-racial identifications, and—in rare cases—Fourth Amendment litigation. It was only at a National Trial College in Macon, Georgia in 2016, over ten years into practice, that I was first exposed to trial and pretrial strategies (mostly voir dire) to address racial bias. The training addressed implicit bias and racial stereotypes concerning African Americans.

To recognize and minimize implicit bias, lawyers must address it among themselves and promote racial diversity in the workplace. Jonathan Rapping, founder of Gideon's Promise, proposes raising self-awareness by recruitment of defenders motivated to address racial inequities, by training lawyers to understand the role their own implicit racial bias can play in driving disparate outcomes, and by building an office culture in which resistance to the pressures that drive implicit racial biases is an explicit value. This type of recruiting requires offices to reward lawyers who are motivated to learn about implicit bias and those who apply tactics to mitigate it. Promoting racial diversity in work environments is encouraged because it increases opportunities for positive interactions between racial group members of equal status. This helps to create positive associations and motivates people to make more accurate, nonstereotyped judgments. Only after building awareness can the defense lawyer begin to educate others in the system about unconscious biases.[18] Finally, attorneys should be directed to perceive their minority clients differently than their popular stereotypes. For instance, Muslims should be perceived as peaceful. This approach goes hand-in-hand with attorneys reading disclosure with the viewpoint that their client is innocent, and that "if a client is black/brown I will think 'innocent.'"[19]

Public defender offices, accustomed to taking in an overwhelming number of cases, leave no other option but for trial attorneys to triage. To avoid implicit bias, Professor Song Richardson urges public defender offices to establish systems, based on objectively measurable criteria. For example, cases could be prioritized based on factors such as the person's custody status, at random, on speedy trial date, treatment status for mental health, drug or alcohol abuse, and other factors that may help reduce the risk of an unreasonable sentence—factors that do not rely on attorneys' subjective or idiosyncratic judgments. Professor Richardson also advocates using checklists to reduce biased judgments because having predetermined criteria to guide decision-making can hinder people's unintentional tendency to change the criteria on which their decisions are based to fit their preferred course of action. Offices can also ask lawyers to document how much time they spend on cases.[20] Defenders should be able to explain any racial disparities in how they allocated their resources. This rule can reduce implicit bias because people exercise more care when they know their decisions are monitored and must be explained.[21]

B. Interviewing and Consulting with Clients Through Client-Centered Advocacy

Professor Kristin Henning proposes client-centered advocacy to reduce bias.[22] This advocacy promotes nonjudgmental, empathetic, and non-manipulative approaches at various decision points. Defenders that employ this approach appreciate their client's expressed interest in context and help clients make decisions consistent with their own culture and worldview. As lawyers genuinely seek to understand and accept their client's perspectives, they have increasingly less need to impose their own dominant, often middle class norms in the relationship.

To promote this client-centered advocacy, offices should develop written attorney practice standards, mission statements, client Bill of Rights, and statements of key principles that mirror client-centered approaches. Offices should require yearly trainings on ethical obligations to client decision-making and client-centered loyalty.

To reduce implicit bias in client interactions, Professor Henning suggests these five steps:

1. "Stereotype replacement," or being patient and not responding in frustration to a client's anger, hostility, or disengagement in the interview.

2. "Counter-stereotype imaging," which requires defenders to imagine their clients in counter-stereotypic ways.

3. "Individuation" compels defense lawyers to suspend disbelief when listening to a client's account of events. There should be a rejection of the notion that the case is a "typical" drug case or a "typical" robbery. Lawyers can develop positive narratives that counter traditional notions of "suspects" or "defendants."[23] For example, the client could be a promising student, a devoted father or mother, a reliable employee, a caretaker of siblings, an active church member, a talented musician, an artist, or an athlete.

4. "Perspective taking" involves defenders assuming the first-person perspective of their client during any communication, advocacy, counseling, or decision-making.

5. "Increased opportunities with commonly stereotyped groups" encourage defenders to see their clients or members of their communities in different ways by engaging in community service or extracurricular activities such as sports teams, tutoring at school, the local church, or recreational events.

If applied, these interventions will both increase the defender's awareness of subtle biases and discrimination in the system and revive the defender's waning sense of outrage about racial injustice.

C. Pretrial Motion Practice

Traditional and less common pretrial motions can be used strategically by defense counsel to minimize implicit bias in the courtroom. Traditional pretrial motions include motions regarding cross-racial identification, oppositions to 404(b) other-act evidence, and motions to suppress evidence. Less traditional motions include motions to dismiss the formal accusation.

In traditional pretrial motion practice, issues of race are most commonly raised in Fourth Amendment litigation. Contemporary Fourth Amendment jurisprudence requires that defense counsel present evidence that law enforcement officers intentionally used race for detention or search. In *Whren v. United States*, the Supreme Court of the United States reviewed a pretrial motion to suppress and held that, as long as facts give rise to an objectively reasonable basis for an officer to conduct a search or seizure, the fact that the officer was actually motivated by the race of the target might not be considered by a court assessing the legality of the officer's actions.[24]

The defense attorney practicing from a race-conscious approach should argue that research demonstrates that implicit bias affects how police officers evaluate facts, causing them to likely interpret ambiguous behavior as consistent with criminal involvement when the target is a person of color.[25] The likelihood of such bias being at play dilutes the possibility of finding an objectively reasonable basis for a traffic stop, detention, or search. Similarly, implicit bias affects how we later remember facts, causing us to likely misremember them in ways consistent with criminality when relating to darker-skinned persons. Defenders should argue that the influence of implicit bias "undermines the objective basis claimed by the officer, both by improperly skewing how (s)he evaluated the facts on the scene and how (s)he recollects them at the hearing on the motion to suppress."[26] If the court refuses to consider expert testimony without knowing whether the particular officer is influenced by implicit bias, defense counsel might consider requesting that the officer either be evaluated by an implicit bias expert or submit to testing designed to answer this question.[27] In motions to suppress evidence, the defense attorney can also ask the court's permission to introduce evidence of the officer's record of arrests, whether the neighborhood is actually a "high crime area," and witness accounts of the entire interaction between the officer and the defendant.[28]

Pretrial motions to dismiss based on race are uncommon. Many jurisdictions allow the filing of a motion to dismiss when the equities favor sparing the defendant the risks of moving forward. A defense attorney can move to dismiss "in the interests of justice." The broad title is an excellent vehicle to get race-related issues before the court that would otherwise not be admissible. The lawyer can file this motion when he/she represents a minority client, and the alleged victim is a White law enforcement officer, in a jurisdiction with advisory sentencing guidelines, where racial overtones are explicit, or in cases that would cause greatly disproportionate sentences.[29] As the government emphasizes the importance of "public safety," the defense attorney can counter, for instance, with a discussion of "public justice" when litigating this motion. As with other strategies relating to race, the defense attorney should weigh the pros and cons of filing such a motion in terms of appellate review, plea bargaining, or possible reactions from the specific trial judge.

Another way to raise race through pretrial motions involves motions to suppress cross-racial identifications, which has been the subject of abundant literature in psychology, law, and in many court decisions.[30] Psychological research shows that cross-racial identifications are inherently less reliable compared to same race identifications.[31] In a case with cross-racial identification, the defense attorney should call an eyewitness identification expert to testify at a motion to suppress hearing and at trial.

Last, the defense lawyer should file motions to preclude other act evidence under Federal Rule of Evidence 404(b). Judges admit 404(b) evidence over defense objections unfairly.[32] But other act evidence, if not objected on grounds of negative implicit bias repercussions, may harm minority clients.[33]

D. Voir Dire

The attorney's primary goal during voir dire is to learn as much as possible about jurors, to ask the court to strike members for cause, and to exercise peremptory strikes properly.[34] For the race-conscious lawyer, an important goal of voir dire should be to educate the jury about implicit racial bias.[35] The attorney should highlight the significance of race so those who end up on the jury will be more aware of how race may have shaped the perceptions of persons involved and how race may influence jurors' perceptions.[36]

First, attorneys can address implicit bias at jury selection by filing a motion, well before trial, requiring the entire venire to take an Implicit Association Test (IAT), the most commonly used evaluation for implicit bias. Research shows that taking the IAT and seeing the results can help address implicit bias.[37] Second, the attorney can also ask that the court explain implicit racial bias to the jury and instruct the venire on the influence it has over all of us, including the risk it poses to the jury's ability to reach a verdict based solely on appropriate considerations. The Western District of Washington shows a video to educate jurors about this, and Senior District Court Judge Mark W. Bennett in the Northern District of Iowa shows a PowerPoint presentation on implicit bias to the venire before allowing individualized attorney voir dire.[38] These practices may be worth bringing to the attention of the trial judge by attaching a copy of the PowerPoint presentation to a pretrial motion seeking permission to discuss implicit bias and racial stereotyping. An explanation from the court would likewise educate the judge and jury because it would be supported by a review of the social science literature.

As research shows, jurors are more forthcoming with lawyers than with judges; and therefore lawyers should ask for attorney-conducted voir dire.[39] The race-conscious lawyer can question and follow up in a more effective fashion than the judge by asking about the jurors' life experiences that may help to reveal already-established relevant attitudes and belief systems. The lawyer should explore jurors' beliefs about race, but also look for attitudes that make it more likely that a juror will consciously guard against the influence of implicit racial bias.[40] For example, "Describe a particularly impactful interaction that you or someone you know had with a member of another race."[41] Another useful starting point is for the attorney to share a personal story about race. If the lawyer cannot recall an experience, the attorney can share that Jesse Jackson, a well-known African American civil rights activist, admitted, "There is nothing more painful for me at this stage of my life, than to walk down the street and hear footsteps and start to think about robbery, and then look around and see somebody white, and feel relieved."[42] Stories like this will personalize the issue for the jury. The lawyer should then ask whether jurors are receptive to or critical of the concept of implicit bias.[43]

Finally, the attorney can ask the court, in a pretrial motion, to submit questionnaires with questions about race. This is appropriate in all jurisdictions but is especially necessary for jurisdictions that do not allow attorney-directed voir dire.

E. Client Testimony

Minority defendants should have their own voice. Defenders should think more liberally about whether the client should testify. Generally, criminal defendants are encouraged to let their lawyers do the talking for them, but silence undermines the system's goal of individualized consideration. Clients know about their thoughts, fears, and motivations better than anyone.

When the client has prior convictions, the defense lawyer should move the court to disallow (or at least sanitize) impeachment based on those.[44] Although an uphill battle, the motion should highlight the importance of individuation about the client's life and conduct relating to the case. This narrative, which usually only comes from the client, should take precedence over the prosecutor's ability to impeach with prior convictions.[45]

F. Use of Expert Testimony

Defense lawyers should use implicit bias experts to explain its prevalence and how it can be overcome. Experts, whose testimony will likely be given more weight than other witnesses or lawyers, can testify about the differences between explicit and implicit beliefs, explain how egalitarian-minded persons can overcome their implicit biases by motivation, and discuss the concept of "cognitive busyness" and "time pressures."[46] The latter are especially relevant where jurors may want to speed up the deliberative process.[47] The expert can explain the importance of being patient and focused, especially where there is ambiguous evidence.

G. Narrative

A person is more than just an accused. Defense lawyers should know humans harbor subconscious schemas and stereotypes that shape how we view the world.[48] A schema is a "cognitive structure that represents knowledge about a concept or type of stimulus, including its attributes, and the relations among those attributes."[49] Social psychology shows we fit items into schemas based on how closely related those items resemble the exemplars we have in our minds. For example, a lion may more readily fit our schema for mammal rather than a dolphin, even though both are mammals. We use mapping rules to determine the schema to which a person or object belongs. We then ascribe meanings based on the category we place on the items or the person. Schematic thinking, particularly in a racial context, operates automatically, nearly instantaneously, but may be incorrect.[50] For example, a Latina woman may be perceived and "schematized" as a house cleaner or housekeeper.[51] If she is an engineer, this will conflict with the original schema, reducing its effect. As the engineer example suggests, there are three strategies to create narratives to minimize implicit bias. One is to get jurors to focus on individual facts by developing a narrative that promotes the client as a devoted husband, a loving father, a committed son, or a dedicated employee, to list a few examples.[52]

A second strategy is to suppress racial stereotypes by promoting jurors' subconscious thinking about "ideals of fairness and equality."[53] This strategy is based on research that shows that reminding jurors during closing arguments of our nation's highest ideals, the role of the jury in promoting justice, and the important principles of law that protect each of us as persons against a far more powerful government may mitigate the impact of implicit bias.[54] Even if the case is based on a compelling

194 Extending Justice

story of innocence, lawyers should spend time discussing the importance of the presumption of innocence and fairness. In doing so, jurors are reminded of the need to comb through the evidence carefully and not simply because they were told to by the lawyer. They should take their time deliberating because the Constitution and our traditions call for it.[55]

A third strategy is to paint a "three-dimensional picture of the client," to mitigate and blunt the impact of racial bias. In this approach, the defense attorney paints this picture during opening statement, again during character witness testimony, and at closing argument to reduce the implicit presence of racial bias.[56] Opening and closing arguments are especially effective avenues because the lawyer speaks to jurors directly to remind them of the narratives presented by witnesses in cross-examination and during the defense case.

H. Jury Instructions

Jury instructions that address implicit bias or racial stereotypes should be requested for both the beginning of the trial and after the close of evidence. Jury instructions are a powerful tool carrying credibility from the judge.[57] They are read aloud, without interruptions, and in many jurisdictions are physically given to jurors to refer to during deliberations. Lawyers can refer to them during closing arguments. Judge Mark Bennett reads the following implicit bias instruction before opening statements:[58]

> Do not decide this case based on "implicit biases." As we discussed in jury selection, everyone, including me, has feelings, assumptions, perceptions, fears, and stereotypes, that is "implicit biases," that we may not be aware of. These hidden thoughts can affect what we see and hear, how we remember what we see and hear, and how we make important decisions. Because you are making every important decision in this case, I strongly encourage you to evaluate the evidence carefully and resist jumping to conclusions based on personal likes or dislikes, generalizations, gut feelings, prejudices, sympathies, stereotypes, or biases. The law demands that you return a just verdict, based solely on the evidence, your individual evaluation of the evidence, your reason and common sense, and these instructions. Our system of justice is counting on you to render a fair decision based on the evidence, not on biases.[59]

This instruction helps jurors reduce implicit bias by introducing them to the concept before the parties present any evidence. If jurors pay attention, they will be guarded as they see and hear evidence.

Another example of a race-based jury instruction asks jurors to "flip the script," that is switch the race of the client. For example, if the defendant is a Latino, the instruction would suggest that before reaching any final conclusion the jurors ask themselves if they would make the same decision if it were a White male/a White female. If their internal answer is no, the instruction should suggest that they reexamine their conclusions for stereotype. Other types of instructions to educate the jury about implicit bias include a self-defense instruction that people are more likely to perceive a given ambiguous action as aggressive and dangerous when performed by an African American compared to a White person,[60] and that people misread hostility in African American faces more often than White faces.[61]

I. Sentencing Advocacy

In my experience, sentencing hearings can be less stressful than jury trials. From a race-conscious perspective, sentencing hearings will mostly be about arguments on the specifics of the client's life, the circumstances of the offense, and legal objections.[62] But sentencing should also include a discussion, with all judges—conservatives and liberals—of implicit bias. While many judges may decide not to respond to arguments on implicit bias because they may find it difficult to apply to the particular case or for fear of negative appellate review,[63] this should not stop the lawyer from at the very least raising the issue to educate judges in a particular case and for future cases.

Given the goal of reducing disproportionality in sentencing, sentencing memoranda should have a section devoted to how race and ethnicity impacts sentencing decisions. The lawyer may also include statistics that show the extent to which race accounts for sentencing disparity in the criminal justice system.[64] If the data were available, counsel could compile statistics about sentencing patterns of the particular judge or the jurisdiction. During argument, the lawyer should discuss the client in a schema distinct from race (father, son, dedicated employee, coach, deacon, volunteer, good neighbor, to name a few) and appeal to the judge's role in promoting fairness in our criminal justice system.[65]

3. Strategies to Mitigate the Impact of Racial Bias for Latinx Clients

A. Implicit Bias and Its Impact on Latinxs

African Americans have been the focus of most research on implicit bias, while other racial minorities such as Latinxs and Native Americans have been understudied.[66] However, the available research shows that Latinxs are deeply affected by implicit biases.[67] In a study by Professor James Weyant, forty-one college students took longer to associate traits indicative of intelligence with Hispanic than non-Hispanic names, while they could more quickly associate traits indicative of lack of intelligence with Hispanic names.[68] In another study, 210 primary care providers (PCPs) and 190 community members from the same area completed IATs and self-reported measures of implicit and explicit bias. The PCPs showed substantial implicit (but not explicit) bias against both Latinxs and African Americans.[69] Adjustments for background characteristics showed that PCPs had slightly weaker ethnic/racial bias than community members.[70] In yet another study, an IAT measured automatic attitudes toward Latinxs vis-à-vis White immigrants. The results showed that participants more easily associated positive words with Whites and negative words with Latinxs.[71]

Negative implicit biases toward Latinxs, such as those demonstrated by this research, have real-world implications. People favor their own group at the expense of other groups in terms of their evaluations, judgments, and behavior in intergroup situations.[72] Manifestations of implicit bias include the appearance of being uncomfortable and anxious in terms of non-verbal behavior during interracial reactions: more speech errors, shorter conversations, more tense body posture, sitting further away, and less eye contact.[73] As one can imagine, criminal justice professionals not in tune with their negative implicit biases could treat Latinx defendants less favorably compared to Whites, especially in stressful, hurried situations.

B. Negative Racial Bias from Historic and Contemporary Media Depictions

Explanations for the origins of overt and unconscious racism vary. One explanation theorizes that from an early age social categories are assigned, generated, and assimilated over an extended period of learning and internalizing preferences and evaluations.[74] Mass media perpetuates these shared ideas, images, and representations of the social world, offering an array of characterizations that associate different identity groups with different possibilities for how a person is or should be in society. These representations typically reflect stereotypes of groups (e.g., African Americans as athletes and musicians, women as sexualized beings) that vary in quantity, quality, and accuracy. For the White middle class, the media is replete with positive and varied representations; for other racial and ethnic groups, it is often the opposite.[75]

The powerful role of the media in reinforcing and perpetuating negative images about Latinxs helps form and maintain implicit bias.[76] Mainstream American perceptions of Latinxs, already unfavorable, are worsened by their historic and contemporary depictions. Although Latinxs represent a population of over 54 million people that now surpasses 17 % of the United States national total, stories about Latinxs and Latinx issues are disproportionately minimal and negative.[77] Year after year, Latinxs and Latinx issues constitute less than 0.78 % of the news in studied networks, about one percent of the stories considered newsworthy by national network news programs. Even more troubling, the primary topics of coverage remain focused on Latinxs as people with problems or causing problems and on news related to immigration or crime, or a combination of both.[78] Studies of Latinx portrayals in crime reporting in Los Angeles and Orlando, for instance, have found that Latinxs are more likely to be represented as perpetrators than as victims of crime.[79] Similarly, in the coverage of ongoing trials, Latinx defendants, along with African American defendants, are more likely to be linked to prejudicial information in comparison with Caucasians.[80]

The media also broadcasts political messages about Latinxs. The Reagan administration framed unauthorized migration as a national security issue, using images of Central Americans as terrorists. President Reagan said, "Terrorists and subversives are just two days' driving time from Harlingen, Texas," and described Central American refugees as undesirables coming in "tidal waves."[81] President Trump described Mexicans as rapists and "bad hombres" during his presidential campaign in 2016 and his use of derogatory language about Latinxs and other minorities continued during his presidency.[82]

Latinx news coverage also focuses on negative aspects of immigration.[83] A study of network and cable TV news from 2008 to 2012 found that Latinxs are overrepresented as undocumented immigrants compared to figures from official reports.[84] Similarly, a 2005 study of newspaper coverage of the Minuteman[85] project—an anti-immigration campaign that has gained national attention—revealed negative characterizations of immigrants through abstract and general language.[86] As with the political speech, the metaphors used to describe migration in these stories is also troubling and included the words "tides," "floods," and "pollutants."[87]

Negative language and news articles generate negative perceptions about Latinxs among White viewers.[88] The word "alien" brings forth images of space invaders seen on television and in movies, such as the blockbuster Independence Day. Popular culture reinforces that aliens will take over the world if they are not killed, incarcerated, or subjugated. The word legitimizes the mistreatment of noncitizens, helps mask human suffering, and serves as a means of dehumanization.[89] In a step to counteract this, in 2021 President Biden requested agencies that deal with immigration, such as U.S. Customs and Border Protection, to change their official language practices. President Biden requested these agencies to change the terms "alien" and "illegal alien," to "noncitizen"; and "assimilation" to "integration."[90] Still, the comprehensive immigration statute, the Immigration and Nationality Act, still defines an "alien" as "any person not a citizen or national of the United States."[91]

The historical record of studies about Latinxs depicted in the media paints an equally disturbing picture. Before the second half of the twentieth century, the media largely ignored Latinxs.[92] When they were covered, news outlets featured Latinxs in immigration crises and as safety threats, with heavy use of the pejorative labels "Zoot Suiter," "Wetback," and "Pachuco," among others.[93] In fictional accounts, Latinx characters have been typically depicted either as criminals, unfaithful hot-blooded "Latin lovers," or as comic relief.[94] Some studies have found that the media often portrays Latinxs in a limited set of occupations, usually as law enforcement officers, and increasingly as low-skilled domestic and service workers.[95] Individually and collectively, such ubiquitous depictions in the media over a long period contributed to contemporary racial stereotypes of Latinxs. These depictions impact everyone, including criminal justice professionals who represent Latinxs in criminal court.

C. Individuation and Client Narratives to Counter Stereotypes and Schemas

Like their media portrayals, schemas and stereotypes for Latinx criminal defendants are negative, with parallels to long-established stereotypes frequently applied to African American males.[96] Research shows that Latinxs have been associated with "innate criminality," typified as "dangerous," as drug traffickers, violence-prone, "predatory," "disposed to chronic criminal offending," "ruthlessly violent," and "gang bangers."[97]

With Latinx clients, schemas such as "drug dealer" or "illegal immigrant" will trigger negative stereotypes.[98] The defense attorney representing a Latinx client should counter the schemas with narrative that uses positive details about the client's life to create a meaningful story of innocence or mitigation. In shaping a client's narrative, the defense attorney needs to be aware that narratives that might be successful for White defendants may not be so for Latinxs.[99] Highlighting a Latinx client's horrific childhood situations and the "bad" neighborhoods he or she grew up in may actually reinforce traditional views among judges, prosecutors, and jurors that Latinxs criminal defendants are violent, drug traffickers, or gangbangers.

Instead, the defense attorney must find success stories about their client to counter traditional schemas. Here a narrative consists of (1) a scene or setting, (2) an agent (or cast of characters), (3) action (the plot), (4) agency (the means or instruments of action), and (5) purpose (the motivations and goals of characters).[100]

A leading example of the compelling use of narrative is Professor Pamela Wilkins's description of the death penalty sentencing of a New York man, Alan Quinones[101] Although Quinones's attorneys applied this strategy to a death penalty sentencing, it can be applied to any phase of a criminal case that permits the use of narrative, including plea negotiation letters, or settlement conferences. As Professor Wilkins explains: The government portrayed Alan Quinones as a "Latinx drug trafficker." Evidence during the guilt phase portrayed him as a high-level drug dealer in Pennsylvania and New York who set an informant on fire after learning he snitched on him. At trial, his lawyers had to combat these deeply embedded narratives and images. The schemas ascribed to "Latinx drug traffickers" are that they are "ruthless, violent, avaricious, parasites of the underworld who prey on economically depressed communities and kill brutally without compunction." To counter these descriptions, his lawyers used metaphors and altered the setting.[102] They called the defendant a "child of God." This primed jurors with values animating the Eighth Amendment cruel and unusual punishment prohibition of the United States Constitution, such as respect for the dignity of the person. They presented him as a counter-stereotypical exemplar among drug traffickers, exempting him, to a degree, from the "Latinx drug trafficker" schema. They emphasized that rather than spending his money on jewelry or cars, he spent it as a "Secret Santa" for orphans in his neighborhood and on bribes to secure housing for his mentally ill mother. His lawyers also introduced evidence to present Mr. Quinones as respectful and friendly to women because he had several trusted female friends. This gender-based narrative countered the traditional schema of the "Latinx drug trafficker" as a womanizer and a misogynist. Mr. Quinones was presented as a "Father/Protector" and self-sacrificing, first-generation immigrant. He entered the drug trade to lift his family from poverty, saved food for his siblings, worked at a grocery store, and gave money to his mother. He remembered birthdays, gave Christmas cards, took his family out to eat, and talked about the importance of education and staying off the streets.

During closing argument, his lawyers invoked the cultural master narrative about the immigrant story and the American dream. This placed Mr. Quinones squarely within a broad American tradition that challenges that he is a foreigner and aligns him with other immigrant populations. His lawyers depicted his entry into the drug business and return to it after attempting a low-paying wage job as opportunities for his immediate family and the next generation as opposed to any selfish motive. These successful strategies, backed up with evidence, spared his life.

Lawyers should dig deep by interviewing family members, counselors, teachers, and community members to find and then present evidence that runs counter to traditional schemas. For example, the defense team should investigate if the client read books to his children, nieces, and nephews, or saved money for hospital bills. In a case of United States-Mexico drug trafficking, interviews should be conducted to discover if the client worked in agricultural fields in Mexico before being recruited by a drug cartel. The defense lawyer should be encouraged to get to know his/her client as more than just a defendant, but almost as friend or member of his/her community. Despite their worse deeds, even the cruelest-appearing clients have humanity. It is the defense attorney's job to find that humanity and present it to the court.[103] The defense attorney should focus on the client's strengths and responsibilities. For example, emphasize the client's role as "father/protector" or "provider." Female clients with children can be presented as self-sacrificing to properly provide for and take care of their children. Investigators, paralegals, and mitigation specialists can help construct not simply a list of sentencing mitigators, but a story that includes all five elements of the narrative. This story separates the client from traditional schemas.

Part of the narrative involves the defense lawyer setting the stage, or "scene and setting," for the action. Along the border between the United States and Mexico, where many Latinxs are federally prosecuted, drug cartels often recruit innocent men and women at soccer matches, taco stands, clubs, and grocery stores; these persons are selected because of their desperate economic situation.[104] With Mexicans along the United States-Mexico border, income differentials almost always play a part in the commission of crimes. The United States-Mexico border has the highest income differential compared to any other border in the world.[105] Socioeconomic evidence should be emphasized at sentencing and woven into the narrative. One example is the use of studies that show that imposing prison sentences have no deterrent impact on society.[106] Other types of studies discussing low economic standards of living in areas where clients reside helps the trial judge see a setting for the story.[107] This includes any possible economic motivations for the crime.

For clients who claim lack of knowledge of drug trafficking, the lawyer should align the narrative with others falsely accused. If the defense is lack of knowledge of drugs, the attorney should introduce evidence of actual "blind mule" (i.e., innocent courier) cases investigated by the FBI.[108]

Clients charged with illegal entry make up a large segment of federal cases and present unique opportunities for narrative. In those cases, the lawyer may change the narrative by describing the life-threatening journey across the border.[109] For Latinxs in illegal reentry cases with violent or serious prior felony convictions, the attorney should seek to neutralize the impact of prior crimes. Inevitably, the client will face the stereotype of entering the country as a "Latinx drug trafficker" if (s)he has a drug trafficking prior conviction. To combat this stereotype the defense attorney needs to study the prior conviction to elicit facts that set the client apart from traditional schemas. For instance, if the prior conviction was for theft, the lawyer could elicit mitigating circumstances such as the financial motive for the crime (i.e. providing for the family). If the client is an addict and committed the crime to fund his/her drug habit, this can also be elicited. Sometimes, it may not be worth the effort if the circumstances of the prior conviction are unfavorable, for example, if the crime was violent. The attorney should not discuss gory details otherwise unknown. But if the prior conviction is old or if there are good facts, the attorney can construct meaningful counter-narratives. An old prior conviction may be too far removed from present circumstances to relate to the sentencing at hand. The attorney needs to weigh the pros and cons of building counter schemas from facts of prior convictions.

Because many Mexicans, Central and South Americans, and Caribbean people enter the country to reunite with family,[110] opportunities abound for narratives of family reunification, sacrifice, and description of journeys to the border from far-away regions. These circumstances are fertile for storytelling. The socioeconomic reality that most immigrants face bolsters the narrative of arduous work and self-sacrifice. Most immigrants enter the workforce in the United States earning mediocre wages.[111] Many have to endure grueling living and working conditions. Some clients enter temporarily to earn money for their Mexican businesses or only enter for seasonal labor.[112] Many Latinx criminal defendants enter the United States to work at jobs many Americans do not want.[113] For many, remitting money abroad is part of their American dream.[114] investigations into these circumstances and thoughtful construction of counter-narratives can decrease the implicit biases of prosecutors, judges, and juries.

D. The Use of Culture to Mitigate Implicit Bias and Negative Racial Stereotyping

"Culture" is defined in many ways. A standard definition is that it consists of "[a] set of rules or standards shared by members of a society which, when acted on by the members, produce behavior that falls within a range of variance the members consider proper and acceptable."[115] Culture enmeshes our day-to-day lives. It dictates what we do and how we think, and it gives meaning to our lives.

Although not legally recognized, lawyers occasionally obtain favorable outcomes when applying cultural defenses.[116] A cultural defense is an affirmative defense in which a defendant is excused of a crime because s(he) complied with the dictates of his or her culture when committing the criminal act.[117] Although trial judges are reluctant to admit cultural evidence, defense attorneys should not give up. Unsuccessful attempts to admit cultural evidence can educate and prime judges for future cases.[118]

If successful, using a cultural defense can distinguish the client and can decrease bias.[119] Cultural influences can invoke positive and negative traits. A positive example of a Latin American cultural trait is family unity. A negative cultural trait is patriarchy. An example of a Latino cultural trait that has both positive and negative implications is "machismo." Positive elements include notions of pride, honor, courage, responsibility, and obligation to family. Along with positive traits, however, machismo ideals also imply sexual prowess, aggressive behavior, and the belief that men are physically and morally superior to women; the male resolves male/female conflicts through absolute dominance.[120]

The defense attorney can use machismo to reduce racial stereotypes by intertwining it with the theory of defense. Consider a drug trafficking case with a Latina client. Machismo cultural norms may help explain the client's lack of knowledge of drugs in a trafficking or importation case. Many macho boyfriends or husbands keep their girlfriends or wives out of all their dealings.[121] They only meet with friends in private or outside the home, assume charge of major decisions in the relationship, and, often, are verbally or physically abusive. In a duress scenario, machismo could help a jury understand why a Latina was targeted. Threats may have come from a family member in a drug organization.

In other duress cases, machismo can help explain domestic violence. Depending on the charge or facts, cultural explanations give meaning to evidence and places the client in a favorable light. Details of abuse individualizes, reducing negative racial undertones. This humanization also paints her as a victim of a larger patriarchal system.

Migrant families in the United States likewise feel the impact of machismo.[122] A Latina migrant woman in the United States accused of drug trafficking or alien smuggling may be afraid to call the police to report threats that led her to commit the crime due to fear of deportation.[123] The drug cartel may have targeted her due to her undocumented status. The defense lawyer must be judicious and consider the benefits and pitfalls of this strategy if the client's legal status is not part of the admissible evidence.

Many cultures have some variant of machismo.[124] The concept resonates with most jurors.[125] To educate prosecutors, judges, and jurors, the defense lawyer should move to admit expert evidence by arguing that although many are familiar with machismo, they are unaware of its full effect on the client or witness. Jurors may not understand that in some communities, women are expected not to ask certain questions, stay in the home, only tend to the children, and leave husbands to their own affairs. Although mainstream jurors generally understand these concepts and see parallels of it in their own lives, they do not understand its prevalence in Latinx households. They also do not understand how deeply patriarchy is embedded in culture.[126] The defense attorney can also attach a social science article on machismo such as the article by Professor Wilkins discussed earlier as an exhibit to a pretrial motion.

Defense lawyers can incorporate culture in myriad other ways when representing Latinxs. Assistant Federal Public Defender and trial unit supervisor in Tucson, Victoria Brambl's use of culture in defending clients is illustrative. Her lawyering philosophy is to present the defense from the client's perspective. Her defense of a Tohono O'odham man, in two cases, shows how use of culture can lead to excellent outcomes.[127] Even though the example is of a Native American man, the cultural traditions used are common to Latinxs in the southwest and could have easily been applied if the client was Latinx.[128]

The following two case summaries were obtained from an interview with Ms. Brambl: In the first case, the United States charged the client with possession of ammunition by a convicted felon. Police found two shotgun shells in the top drawer of a dresser in the client's mother's house. When the family was outside, the police found the two shotgun shells that the client's brother placed in the drawer without the client's knowledge. Ms. Brambl called family members to testify that the brother lived with his mother and shared the drawer when the client came to visit. The arrest fell on "Día de los Muertos" (the Day of the Dead/All Souls Day), an important day for Mexicans in the southwest and the Tohono O'odham. They cook a feast, place it outside, and visit the graveyard. The defense described the cultural practice, its importance, the cooked meal, and that the client visited to help his single parent who was frail and required a cane to walk. Evidence of this cultural practice, along with a narrative that the client was a dutiful son, helped a no possession defense. The case ended after two hung juries and a favorable guilty plea to six months' time-served in custody.

In a second case involving vehicular manslaughter, the same client pled guilty to the lesser of involuntary manslaughter. While driving intoxicated, he crashed, killing his first cousin and best friend. In presenting a mitigation counter-narrative, Ms. Brambl argued that the victim's mother forgave him for the accident, and that he spent lots of time with her after the death, helping take care of her as her son did before his death (the victim's mother was on kidney dialysis for many years). The client built a memorial for the victim at the accident site as was customary in his culture.[129] He worked every weekend for a year after the accident, cooking and selling burritos to raise money to build the memorial. The memorial was finished a year after the death, a culturally significant period, as the Tohono O'odham believe a deceased's spirit lingers before departing to heaven.

Incorporating the client's culture in helping family during Día de los Muertos and erecting a shrine for the deceased after one year, as culturally prescribed, not only gave the jury facts supporting the theory of defense or mitigation but also connected him to the larger community. Undoubtedly, these meaningful injections of culture mitigated racial stereotypes before the judge and jury and resulted in a favorable plea agreement and sentencing decision.

Other, more mundane, but no less important aspects of culture should be addressed when representing Latinxs. One of them is eye contact. Children from many Latin American communities are told, when they are in trouble, not to look at a parent or authority figure.[130] In my experience many Latinxs look at the floor or avoid eye contact when talking to lawyers or to judges. Before testifying in front of a jury or at any other time in court, clients should be told to make eye contact. At least, the defense lawyer should explain these ingrained habits to jurors and the court as clients may not stop the deeply inculcated behavior during proceedings.

E. Use of Checklists for Latinxs

Checklists mitigate the negative impact on Latinx clients because they force the attorney to complete all tasks for all clients.[131]

While defenders could spend less time going through the checklist for some clients, checklists decrease mistakes being made and any corner cutting. They can be an impetus for and record of quality representation. Various defender offices, including the San Francisco Public Defender's Office, have created checklists to account for dozens to hundreds of tasks that support criminal defense representation.[132] Federal defender offices have also developed outlines and checklists for the representation of illegal entry prosecutions, drug busts, and other types of offenses.[133] An office that primarily represents Latinx clients accused of importation of drugs and illegal entry can make use of this kind of checklist to combat implicit bias that permeates those specific case types. Ideally, each indigent defense office should assign a "checklist committee" to draft checklists for the most common cases. A checklist on mitigation would help to encourage lawyers to find strengths and weaknesses that can help counter stereotypes.

F. Documentation and Summaries of Implicit Bias Research

To alert prosecutors and judges of the impact of implicit bias to all minority defendants, defense lawyers should be familiar with the social science studies mentioned in this article as they relate to Latinxs and other minority clients. There has been an increase in awareness of implicit bias among the defense bar, courts, and prosecutors. But not all judges, and only a minority of prosecutors, are familiar with the social science research on implicit bias. By including the studies in sentencing memoranda, pointing them out in motions relating to voir dire, and sending the studies to judges and prosecutors, the defense lawyer raises awareness. While not all prosecutors and judges will read all or even part of the studies, this could be a starting point for discussion and knowledge building. The defense attorney should also try to summarize the findings at pretrial motion hearings, and bench and settlement conferences. Even though there is scant research on Latinxs and implicit bias, the defense lawyer, by extrapolation, can assist judges in understanding how it applies to Latinxs.[134]

Conclusion

While it is socially improper for mainstream Americans to act out on racist attitudes and behaviors, the problem of implicit bias and racial stereotyping persists for all Latinxs and other minority defendants. Without awareness and education, implicit bias and stereotyping will continue to negatively influence the behavior of criminal justice professionals and jurors. This will cause harsher outcomes for minority clients.[135] Given this reality, defense attorneys should carefully study and become familiar with racial stereotyping and implicit bias. Only in this way will they be able to educate others in the system.

The application of this new knowledge for Latinx clients can be creatively applied to fit the person, whether (s)he is Puerto-Rican, Brazilian, Mexican, or El Salvadorian. The use of narrative, client culture, and individuation can be applied to the client's specific life circumstances and background. The lack of studies and articles on Latinxs in the criminal justice system, despite their increasing presence, calls for more research. This article presents a starting point.

So, You'd Like to Know More

- Jonathan A. Rapping, Implicitly Unjust: How Defenders Can Affect Systemic Racist Assumptions, 16 N.Y.U. J. Legis. & Pub. Pol'y 999 (2013).
- L. Song Richardson & Phillip Atiba Goff, Implicit Racial Bias in Public Defender Triage, 122 Yale L.J. 2626 (2013)
- Andrea D. Lyon, Race Bias and the Importance of Consciousness for Criminal Defense Attorneys, 35 Seattle U. L. Rev. 755 (2012).
- Nicole Gonzalez Van Cleve, Crook County: Racism and Injustice in America's Largest Criminal Court (2016)
- Ediberto Román, Who Exactly is Living La Vida Loca?: The Legal and Political Consequences of Latino-Latina Ethnic and Racial Stereotypes in Film and Other Media, 4 J. Gender Race & Just. 37 (2000).

About the Author

Walter I. Gonçalves, Jr. holds a B.A. degree in International Studies from Southwestern University, and M.A. and J.D. degrees from the University of Arizona. He is a supervisory Assistant Federal Public Defender for the District of Arizona. Prior to federal practice he was an assistant Pima County public defender for ten years. In addition to trial practice Mr. Gonçalves is the author of several law review articles.

Endnotes

1. *See* U.S. Sentencing Comm'n, FY2017 Sourcebook of Federal Sentencing Statistics (2017), tbl. 4, https://www.ussc.gov/sites/default/files/pdf/research-and-publications/annual-reports-and-sourcebooks/2017/2017SB_Full.pdf. State figures are available on a state-by-state basis. *See* Bureau of Just. Stat, FAQ Detail, https://www.bjs.gov/index.cfm?ty=qa&iid=418.

2. *See* Christopher Hartney & Linh Vuong, *Created Equal: Racial and Ethnic Disparities in the US Criminal Justice System*, 3 Nat'l Council on Crime and Delinquency (2009), https://

www.nccdglobal.org/sites/default/files/publication_pdf/ created-equal.pdf [https://perma.cc/JB9E-5XE8].

3. *See generally* Jonathan A. Rapping, *Implicitly Unjust: How Defenders Can Affect Systemic Racist Assumptions*, 16 N.Y.U. J. LEGIS. & PUB. POL'Y 999, 1016–1042 (2013).

4. *See* L. Song Richardson & Phillip Atiba Goff, *Implicit Racial Bias in Public Defender Triage*, 122 YALE L.J. 2626, 2644 (2013).

5. *See* Anna Brown & Mark Hugo Lopez, *Mapping the Latinx Population, by State, County, and City*, PEW RESEARCH (2013), http://www.pewhispanic.org/2013/08/29/mapping-the-Latinx-population-by-state-county-and-city.

6. *See* Nathan M. Crystal, *The Lawyer's Duty to Disclose Material Facts in Contract or Settlement Negotiations*, 87 KY. L.J. 1055, 1092 (1999).

7. PROFESSIONAL RESPONSIBILITY CANON 7 (1983); *see also* Charles P. Cursit, *The Ethics of Advocacy*, 4 STAN. L. REV. 3 (1951).

8. *See* Robin Walker Sterling, *Raising Race*, in THE CHAMPION 26, April 2011.

9. *See* GEOFFREY BEATTIE, OUR RACIST HEART? AN EXPLORATION OF UNCONSCIOUS PREJUDICE IN EVERYDAY LIFE (2013).

10. *See* Anthony G. Greenwald & Linda Hamilton Krieger, *Implicit Bias: Scientific Foundations*, 94 CALIF. L. REV. 945, 951 (2006).

11. *See* Leslie E. Roos et al., *Can Singular Examples Change Implicit Attitudes in the Real-World?*, FRONTIERS IN PSYCHOL. (Sept. 5, 2013), https://www.frontiersin.org/articles/10.3389/fpsyg.2013.00594/full.

12. *See* Elizabeth A. Phelps et al., *Performance on Indirect Measures of Race Evaluation Predicts Amygdala Activation*, 12 J. COG. NEUROSCI. 72933 (2000).

13. *See* Mark W. Bennett & Victoria C. Plaut, *Looking Criminal and the Presumption of Dangerousness: Afrocentric Facial Features, Skin Tone, and Criminal Justice*, 51 U.C. DAVIS L. REV. 745 (2018).

14. Andrea D. Lyon, *Race Bias and the Importance of Consciousness for Criminal Defense Attorneys*, 35 SEATTLE U. L. REV. 755 (2012).

15. *Id.*

16. *See* NICOLE GONZALEZ VAN CLEVE, CROOK COUNTY: RACISM AND INJUSTICE IN AMERICA'S LARGEST CRIMINAL COURT, (2016) (describing overt racist practices in Cook County Superior Court) and L. Song Richardson, *Systemic Triage: Implicit Racial Bias in the Criminal Courtroom Crook County: Racism and Injustice in America's Largest Criminal Court by Nicole Van Cleve Stanford University Press, April 2016*, 126 Yale L.J. 862, 86971 (2017) (Professor Richardson's review of this book, examining implicit racism).

17. DAVID F. SANDERS, THE ADULT PROBATION DEPARTMENT PIMA COUNTY, ANNUAL REPORT (2015), http://www.sc.pima.gov/Portals/0/AP/AdultProbation2015AnnualReportForInternet.pdf.

18. Jonathan A. Rapping, *Implicitly Unjust: How Defenders Can Affect Systemic Racist Assumptions*, 16 N.Y.U. J. LEGIS. & PUB. POL'Y 999, 1022 (2013).

19. L. Song Richardson & Phillip Atiba Goff, *Implicit Racial Bias in Public Defender Triage*, 122 YALE L.J. 2626, 2648 (2013).

20. *Id.*

21. *See* Casey Reynolds, *Implicit Bias and the Problem of Certainty in the Criminal Standard of Proof*, 37 L & PSYCHOL. REV. 229 (2013).

22. Kristin Henning, *Race, Paternalism, and the Right to Counsel*, 54 AM. CRIM. L. REV. 649 (2017).

23. *See* George C. Chen, *Beneath the Surface: Why Diversity and Inclusion Matter for Lawyers of Color, and What Lawyers Can Do to Address Implicit Bias in the Legal Profession*, FED. LAW. 28–29 (2015) http://www.fedbar.org/Resources_1/Federal-Lawyer-Magazine/2015/June/Beneath-the-Surface.aspx?FT=.pdf.

24. Whren v. United States, 517 U.S. 806 (1996).

25. Jonathan A. Rapping, *Implicitly Unjust: How Defenders Can Affect Systemic Racist Assumptions*, 16 N.Y.U. J. LEGIS. & PUB. POL'Y 999, 1026 (2013).

26. *Id.* at 1027.

27. *Id.*

28. *See* Robin Walker Sterling, *Defense Attorney Resistance*, 99 IOWA L. REV. 2245, 2268 (2014); *see also* Commonwealth v. Warren, 475 Mass. 530, 58 N.E.3d 333 (2016) (finding that Black males in Boston are disproportionately and repeatedly targeted for FIO [field interrogation observation] encounters... a judge should, in appropriate cases, consider the [such] findings in weighing flight as a factor in the reasonable suspicion calculus).

29. Robin Walker Sterling, *Raising Race*, *in* THE CHAMPION, April 2011, at 24.

30. Manson v. Brathwaite, 432 U.S. 98 (1977); *see also* Timothy P. O'Toole & Giovanna Shay, Manson v. Braithwaite *Revisited: Towards a New Rule of Decision for Due Process Challenges to Eyewitness Identification Procedures*, 41 VAL. U. L. REV. 109, 137 (2006).

31. *See* Sheri Lynn Johnson, *Cross-Racial Identification Errors in Criminal Cases*, 69 CORNELL L. REV. 934 (1984).

32. *See* Demetria Frank, *The Proof is in the Prejudice: Implicit Racial Bias, Uncharged Act Evidence & The Colorblind Courtroom*, 32 HARV. J. RACIAL & ETHNIC JUST. 1, 55 (2016).

33. *Id.*

34. Scott v. Lawrence, 36 F.3d 871, 874 (9th Cir. 1994).

35. *See* Mark W. Bennett, *Unraveling the Gordian Knot of Implicit Bias in Jury Selection: The Problems of Judge-Dominated Voir Dire, The Failed Promise of Batson, and Proposed Solutions*, 4 HARV. L. & POL'Y REV. 169 (2010).

36. Cynthia Lee, *Making Race Salient: Trayvon Martin and Implicit Bias in A Not Yet Post-Racial Society*, 91 N.C. L. REV. 1555, 1593 (2013).

37. *See* Anna Roberts, *(Re)forming the Jury: Detection and Disinfection of Implicit Juror Bias*, 44 CONN. L. REV. 827, 873, n. 346 (2012).

38. *See Unconscious Bias Juror*, Video, D. CT. W.D. WASH, https://www.wawd.uscourts.gov/jury/unconscious-bias; Mark W. Bennett, *Unraveling the Gordian Knot of Implicit Bias in Jury Selection: The Problems of Judge-Dominated Voir Dire, The Failed Promise of Batson, and Proposed Solutions*, 4 HARV. L. & POL'Y REV. 169 (2010).

39. *See* Leonard B. Sand & Steven A. Reiss, *A Report on Seven Experiments Conducted by District Court Judges in the Second Circuit*, 60 N.Y.U. L. REV. 423, 432 (1985).

40. *See* Jonathan A. Rapping, *Implicitly Unjust: How Defenders Can Affect Systemic Racist Assumptions*, 16 N.Y.U. J. LEGIS. & PUB. POL'Y 999, 1034 (2013).

41. *See* Ira Mickenberg, *Materials for North Carolina Defender Trial School, Voir Dire and Jury Selection*, http://www.ncids.org/defender%20training/2011defendertrialschool/voirdire.pdf [https://perma.cc/WV3P-LFJZ].

42. *See* James McComas & Cynthia Strout, *Combating the Effects of Racial Stereotyping in Criminal Cases*, THE CHAMPION 2223 (August 1999).

43. *Id.* McComas and Strout recommend using the word "stereotype" as it is a less accusatory term.

44. *See* Anna Roberts, *Reclaiming the Importance of the Defendant's Testimony: Prior Conviction Impeachment and the Fight Against Implicit Stereotyping*, 83 U. CHI. L. REV. 835 (2016).

45. *Id.*

46. *See* Jonathan A. Rapping, *Implicitly Unjust: How Defenders Can Affect Systemic Racist Assumptions*, 16 N.Y.U. J. LEGIS. & PUB. POL'Y 999, 1036–37 (2013).

47. *Id.*

48. *See* Joan R. Rentsch *et al.*, *Identifying the Core Content and Structure of a Schema for Cultural Understanding, Technical Report* 1251, U.S. ARMY RESEARCH INSTITUTE FOR THE BEHAVIORAL SCIENCES (2009) https://apps.dtic.mil/dtic/tr/fulltext/u2/a501597.pdf [https://perma.cc/GN8M-NUKJ].

49. *See* Pamela A. Wilkins, *Confronting the Invisible Witness: The Use of Narrative to Neutralize Capital Jurors' Implicit Racial Biases*, 115 W. VA. L. REV. 305, 317 (2012) (citing SUSAN T. FISKE & SHELLEY E. TAYLOR, SOCIAL COGNITION 98 (2d ed. 1991)).

50. *Id.*

51. *The Impact of Media Stereotypes on Opinions and Attitudes Towards Latinos*, in THE NATIONAL HISPANIC MEDIA COALITION 4 (Sept. 2014), http://www.latinodecisions.com/blog/wp-content/uploads/2012/09/RevisedNHMC.Aug2012.pdf [https://perma.cc/6T7S-RRS7].

52. *Id.*

53. *Id.*

54. *Id.*

55. *See* Walter I. Gonçalves Jr., *Tips and Strategies for Excellent Closing Arguments*, CRIM. JUST. 48, 49 (2018).

56. *See* Robin Walker Sterling, *Defense Attorney Resistance*, 99 IOWA L. REV. 2245, 2279 (2014).

57. *See Note: Controlling Jury Damage Awards in Private Antitrust Suits*, 81 MICH. L. REV. 693, 708 (1983).

58. *See* Janet Bond Arterton, *Unconscious Bias and the Impartial Jury*, 40 CONN. L. REV. 1023, 1029 (2008).

59. *See* Jerry Kang *et al.*, *Implicit Bias in the Courtroom*, 59 UCLA L. REV. 1124, 1182–3 (2012).

60. *See* Birt L. Duncan, *Differential Social Perception and Attribution of Intergroup Violence: Testing the Lower Limits of Stereotyping of Blacks*, 34 J. PERSONALITY & SOC. PSYCHOL. 590, 595 (1976).

61. *See* Kurt Hugenberg & Galen V. Bodenhausen, *Ambiguity in Social Categorization: The Role of Prejudice and Facial Affect in Race Categorization*, 15 PSYCHOL. SCI. 342, 345 (2004).

62. FED. R. CRIM. P. 32.

63. *See* Christine Gwinn, *Judicial Discretion in Sentencing: Is Presumptive or Mandatory Reassignment on Remand the Most Ethical Directive for All Parties?*, 30 GEO. J. LEGAL ETHICS 837, 851 (2017).

64. Jerry Kang *et al.*, *Implicit Bias in the Courtroom*, 59 UCLA L. REV. 1124, 1148–52 (2012).

65. *See* Jonathan A. Rapping, *Implicitly Unjust: How Defenders Can Affect Systemic Racist Assumptions*, 16 N.Y.U. J. LEGIS. & PUB. POL'Y 999, 1041 (2013).

66. *See* Kerwin K. Charles & Jonathan Guryan, *Studying Discrimination: Fundamental Challenges and Recent Progress*, 3 ANN. REV. ECON. 479, 511 (2011).

67. *See* Jerry Kang, *Trojan Horses of Race*, 118 HARV. L. REV. 1489, 1514–15 (2005).

68. *See* James M. Weyant, *Implicit Stereotyping of Hispanics: Development and Validity of a Hispanic Version of the Implicit Association Test*, 27 HISPANIC J. BEHAV. SCI. 355, 358–62 (2005); *see generally* Judge Bennett, Chapter 4 in this volume.

69. *Id.*

70. *See* Irene V. Blair et al., *Assessment of Biases Against Latinxs and African Americans Among Primary Care Providers and Community Members*, 103 AM. J. PUB. HEALTH 92 (2013).

71. *See* Christelle Fabiola Garza & Philip Gerard Gasquoie, 35 *Implicit Race/Ethnic Prejudice in Mexican Americans*, HISPANIC J. BEHAV. SCI. 121 (2012).

72. *See* Nilanjana Dasgupta, *Implicit Ingroup Favoritism, Outgroup Favoritism, and Their Behavioral Manifestations*, 17 SOC. JUST. RES. 143 (2004).

73. *See* Denise Sekaquaptewa *et al.*, *Stereotypic Explanatory Bias: Implicit Stereotyping as a Predictor of Discrimination*, 39 J. EXP. SOC. PSYCHOL. 75 (2003); Nilanjana Dasgupta, Paper at the Annual Meeting of Society for Personality and Social Psychology, *Beyond the Black Box: the Behavioral Manifestations of Implicit Prejudice* (Savannah, GA, Feb. 2, 2002).

74. *See* Charles R. Lawrence III, *The Id, the Ego, and Equal Protection: Reckoning with Unconscious Racism*, 39 STAN. L. REV. 317, 337 (1987).

75. Peter A. Levitt et al., *"Frozen in Time": The Impact of Native American Media Representations on Identity and Self-Understanding*, 71 J. SOC. ISSUES, 39, 40 (2015).

76. Jerry Kang, *Trojan Horses of Race*, 118 HARV. L. REV. 1489, 1561 (2005).

77. *See* Federico Subervi, *et al. Latinxs in TV Network News 2008–2014: Still Mostly Invisible and Problematic*, 2, 20 (April 2015) (unpublished report, submitted to the Communication Workers of America), https://www.mediadiversityforum.lsu.edu/latinos-intv-network-news-2008-14.pdf.

78. *Id.*

79. *See* Travis L. Dixon & Daniel Linz, *Race and the Misrepresentation of Victimization on Local Television News*, 27 COMM. RES. 547 (2000); *see also* Travis L. Dixon & Cristina L. Azocar, *The Representation of Juvenile Offenders by Race on Los Angeles Area Television News*, 17 HOW. J. COMM. 143 (2000).

80. *See* Travis L. Dixon & Daniel Linz, T*elevision News, Prejudicial Pretrial Publicity, and the Depiction of Race*, 46 J. BROADCASTING & ELECTRONIC MEDIA 112 (2002).

81. *See* Yolanda Vazquez, *Constructing Crimmigration: Latinx Subordination in A "Post-Racial" World*, 76 OHIO ST. L.J. 599, 636 (2015).

82. *See* Janell Ross, *From Mexican Rapists to Bad Hombres, the Trump Campaign in Two Months*, WASH. POST (Oct. 20, 2016); Gregory Korte & Alan Gomes, *Trump Ramps Up Rhetoric on Undocumented Immigrants: "These Aren't People. These Are Animals,"* USA TODAY (May 16, 2018), https://www.usatoday.com/story/news/politics/2018/05/16/trump-immigrants-animals-mexico-democrats-sanctuary-cities/617252002/.

83. *See* Erik Bleich and A. Mauritis van der Veen, *Sure, A Lot of Newspapers' Coverage of Latinos Is Negative—But Not When It Comes to Cultural Achievements*, WASH. POST (Jan. 23, 2019), https://www.washingtonpost.com/news/monkey-cage/wp/2019/01/23/sure-a-lot-of-newspaper-coverage-of-latinos-is-negative-but-not-when-it-comes-to-cultural-achievements/.

84. *See* Travis L. Dixon & Charlotte L. Williams, *The Changing Misrepresentation of Race and Crime on Network and Cable News*, 65 J. COMM. 24 (2014).

85. *See* Justin A. McCarty, *The Volunteer Border Patrol: The Inevitable Disaster of the Minuteman Project*, 92 IOWA L. REV. 1459, 1477 (2007).

86. *See* Federico Subervi et al., *Latinxs in TV Network News 2008–2014: Still Mostly Invisible and Problematic*, page 2 (April 2015) (unpublished report, submitted to the Communication Workers of America https://www.mediadiversityforum.lsu.edu/latinos-intv-network-news-2008-14.pdf).

87. *See* Eileen Diaz McConnell, *An 'Incredible Number of Latinxs and Asians: Media Representations of Racial and Ethnic Population Change in Atlanta, Georgia*, 9 LATINX STUD. 177 (2011).

88. *See* CLARA E. RODRIGUEZ, LATIN LOOKS: IMAGES OF LATINAS AND LATINOS IN THE U.S. MEDIA (1997).

89. *See* Kevin R. Johnson, *"Aliens" and the U.S. Immigration Laws: The Social and Legal Construction of Nonpersons*, 28 U. MIAMI INTER-AM. L. REV. 263, 272 (1997) (citing Jonathan Freedland, *Aliens are Coming Home*, OBSERVER, July 7, 1996 at T7).

90. *See* Moustafa Bayoumi, *The Biden Administration Has Ended Use of the Phrase 'Illegal Alien.' It's About Time*, THE GUARDIAN (April 22, 2021)

91. INA § 101(a)(3); 8 U.S.C. § 1101(a)(3)(1994).

92. *See* CLARA E. RODRIGUEZ, LATIN LOOKS: IMAGES OF LATINAS AND LATINOS IN THE U.S. MEDIA at 2. (1997).

93. *See* FÉLIX GUTIÉRREZ, THROUGH ANGLO EYES: CHICANOS AS PORTRAYED IN THE NEW MEDIA (1978); Ralph H. Turner & Samuel J. Surace, *Zoot-Suiters and Mexicans: Symbols in Crowd Behavior*, 62 A. J. SOC. 14 (1956).

94. *See*, e.g., Ediberto Román, *Who Exactly is Living La Vida Loca?: The Legal and Political Consequences of Latino-Latina Ethnic and Racial Stereotypes in Film and Other Media*, 4 J. GENDER RACE & JUST. 37, 39 (2000); LIFE ON TELEVISION: CONTENT ANALYSIS OF U.S. TV DRAMA 3–12 (Bradley S. Greenberg ed., 2005).

95. *See* John F. Seggar & Penny Wheeler, *World of Work on Television: Ethnic and Sex Representation in TV Drama*, 17 J. BROADCASTING & ELECTRONIC MEDIA 201 (1973).

96. *See* IMAGES OF COLOR, IMAGES OF CRIME: READINGS (Coramae Richey-Mann et. al, eds., 2013).

97. *See*, e.g., Malcolm D. Holmes et. al., *Minority Threat, Crime Control, and Police Resource Allocation the Southwestern United States*, 54 CRIM. & DELINQUENCY 128 (2007); Theodore Curry & Guadalupe Corral-Camacho, *Sentencing Young Minority Males for Drug Offenses*, 10 PUNISHMENT & SOC'Y 253 (2008); STEVEN W. BENDER, GREASERS AND GRINGOS: LATINXS, LAW, AND THE AMERICAN IMAGINATION (2003).

98. *See* Dana E. Mastro & Elizabeth Behm-Morawitz, *Latinx Representation on Primetime Television*, 82 JOURNALISM & MASS COMM. Q. 110 (2005).

99. *See* Pamela A. Wilkins, *Confronting the Invisible Witness: The Use of Narrative to Neutralize Capital Jurors' Implicit Racial Biases*, 115 W. VA. L. REV. 305, 343 (2012).

100. Ty Apler et al., *Introduction to Stories Told and Untold: Lawyering Theory Analyses of the First Rodney King Assault Trial*, 12 CLINICAL L. REV. 1, 20 (2005).

101. Pamela A. Wilkins, *Confronting the Invisible Witness: The Use of Narrative to Neutralize Capital Jurors' Implicit Racial Biases*, 115 W. VA. L. REV. 305, 349 (2012).

102. *Id.* at 355.

103. *See* Charles J. Ogletree, *Beyond Justifications: Seeking Motivations to Sustain Public Defenders*, 106 HARV. L. REV. 1239, 1241 (1993).

104. *See* Angel Rabasa et al., COUNTERNETWORK: COUNTERING THE EXPANSION OF TRANSLATIONAL CRIMINAL NETWORKS 45 (2017). *See also* United States v. Sinhue Mellado-Aceves, CR-12-2332-TUC-RCC (2013) (testimony of Peter Chalk during jury trial, Day 1, p. 13940, 150).

105. *See* Mark Overmyer-Velazquez, *Introduction: Histories and Historiographies of Greater Mexico, Beyond La Frontera*: THE HISTORY OF MEXICO-U.S. MIGRATION xix, xix (Mark Overmyer-Velazquez ed., 2011).

106. *See* Ellen A. C. Raaijmakers et al., *Why Longer Prison Terms Fail to Serve a Specific Deterrent Effect: An Empirical Assessment on the Remembered Severity of Imprisonment*, 23 PSYCHOL., CRIME & L. 32, 33 (2017).

107. *See* Kyle C. Velte, *A Tale of Two Outcomes Justice Found and Lost for Colorado's Schoolchildren*, 12 LEGAL COMM. & RHETORIC 115, (2015).

108. *See* Walter I. Gonçalves, Jr., *Busted at the Border: Duress and Blind Mule Defenses in Border-Crossing Cases*, THE CHAMPION 46, 50 (2018).

109. *See* FRANCISCO CANTU, THE LINE BECOMES A RIVER: DISPATCHES FROM THE BORDER (2018).

110. *See* Neda Mahmoudzadeh, *Love Them, Love Them Not: The Reflection of Anti-Immigrant Attitudes in Undocumented Immigrant Health Care Law*, 9 SCHOLAR 465, 468 (2007).

111. *See* Jenifer M. Bosco, *Undocumented Immigrants, Economic Justice, and Welfare Reform in California*, 8 GEO. IMMGR. L.J. 71, 80 (1994).

112. *See* John Fraser, *Preventing and Combating the Employment of Foreigners in Irregular Situation in the United States in* COMBATING THE ILLEGAL EMPLOYMENT OF FOREIGN WORKERS 101 (2000).

113. *See* Fran Ansley, *Inclusive Boundaries and Other (Im)possible Paths Toward Community Development in A Global World*, 150 U. PA. L. REV. 353, 397, 417 (2001) (citing RUTH MILKMAN, INTRODUCTION TO ORGANIZING IMMIGRANTS: THE CHALLENGE FOR UNIONS IN CONTEMPORARY CALIFORNIA 1, 11 (Ruth Milkman ed., 2000)).

114. *See* Ezra Rosser, *Immigrant Remittances*, 41 CONN. L. REV. 1 (2008) (remittances should be understood as an anti-poverty tool, but not as a route to development).

115. *See* Cynthia Lee, *Cultural Convergence: Interest Convergence Theory Meets the Cultural Defense*, 49 ARIZ. L. REV. 911, 916 (2007) (citing Michaël Fischer, *Note, The Human Rights Implications of a "Cultural Defense*," 6 S. CAL. INTERDISC. L.J. 663, 669 (1998)).

116. Professor Lee describes three examples of successful use of culture in criminal cases and argues that some cultural defenses are easier to get than others. Cynthia Lee, *Cultural Convergence: Interest Convergence Theory Meets the Cultural Defense*, 49 ARIZ. L. REV. 911, 941, 958 (2007)

117. *See The Cultural Defense in the Criminal Law*, 99 HARV. L. REV. 1293 (1986).

118. *See* Thomas F. Pettigrew & Linda Thorpe, *A Meta-Analytic Test of Intergroup Contact Theory*, 90 J. PERSONALITY & SOC. PSYCH. 751 (2006).

119. *See* Irene V. Blair, *The Malleability of Automatic Stereotypes and Prejudice*, 6 PERSONALITY & SOC. PSYCHOL. REV. 242, 25052 (2002); *see also* Patricia G. Devine et al., *Long-Term*

Reduction in Implicit Race Bias: A Prejudice Habit-Breaking Intervention, 48 J. Experimental Soc. Psych. 1267 (2013).

120. *See* Patricia M. Hernandez, *The Myth of Machismo: An Everyday Reality for Latin American Women*, 15 St. Thomas L. Rev. 859, 862 (2003).

121. *See* Diana Palaversich, *(Dis)locating Masculinity in Latin(o) America*, 7 GLQ: J. Lesbian & Gay Stud. 645 (2001).

122. *See* Chad Broughton, *Migration as Engendered Practice: Mexican Men, Masculinity, and Northward Migration*, 22 Gender & Soc'y 568, 571–73 (2008).

123. *See* Erica Campbell, *Racializing Intimate Partner Violence Among Black, Native American, Asian American, and Latina Women*, 12 Int'l J. Progressive Educ. 73 (2016).

124. *See* Frances Cleaver, *Men and Masculinities: New Directions in Gender and Development in* Masculinities Matter: Men, Gender, and Development (Frances Cleaver ed., 2002).

125. *See* Craig A. Field & Raul Caetano, *Longitudinal Model Predicting Partner Violence Among White, Black, and Hispanic Couples in the United States*, 27 Alcoholism: Clinical & Experimental Research 1451 (2006).

126. *See, e.g.,* Jasmine B. Gonzales Rose, *Language Disenfranchisement in Juries: A Call for Constitutional Remediation*, 65 Hastings L.J. 811, 826, 828 (2014); Zoe Flowers, From Ashes to Angel's Dust: A Journey Through Womanhood (2017). An expert on "machismo" can address many topics. Some applicable to victims of domestic violence in a "machista" context are the following: (1) Victims have a skepticism and distrust that shelters and intervention services are not culturally or linguistically competent. (2) Victims often defer to family unity and strength as opposed to their individual needs. (3) Victims have a strong personal identification based on familial structure/hierarchy, patriarchal elements, and cultural identity. (4) Religious beliefs reinforce a woman's victimization and legitimize the abuser's behavior. (5) Victims are guarded and reluctant to discuss private matters. (6) Victims fear rejection from family, friends, congregation, and community. (7) Victims distrust law enforcement (fear subjecting loved ones to a criminal and civil justice system they see as sexist, and/or racially and culturally biased.

127. *Interview with Supervisory Assistant Federal Public Defender Victoria Brambl* at Federal Public Defender, District of Arizona, Tucson, Arizona (Sept. 7, 2018).

128. *See* Silvio Torres-Saillant, *The Indian in the Latino: Genealogies of Ethnicity*, 10 S. Lat. Stud. 587 (2012).

129. *See* Rachael M. Byrd, *Rest in Place: Understanding Traumatic Death Along the Roadsides of the Southwestern United States*, 26 Ariz. Anthropologist 53 (2016).

130. *See* Marianne Lafrance & Clara Mayo, *Racial Differences in Gaze Behavior During Conversations: Two Systematic Observational Studies*, 33 J. Personality & Soc. Psychol. 547 (1976).

131. *See* Shawn C. Marsh, *The Lens of Implicit Bias,* Juvenile & Family Justice Today 19 (Summer 2009), https://www.ncjfcj.org/wp-content/uploads/2012/09/The-Lens-of-Implicit-Bias_0.pdf

132. *Id.*

133. The Federal Defenders of San Diego have an excellent outline for defending illegal entry cases. The Arizona office has a similar outline, and others, to defend drug busts and duress cases.

134. *See* Pilar Margarita Hernández Escontrías et. al., *The Future of Latinos in the United States: Law, Mobility, and Opportunity* (A Project of the American Bar Foundation), Prof. Law. 2017 at 21, 23 (2017).

135. *See, e.g.,* David B. Mustard, *Racial, Ethnic, and Gender Disparities in Sentencing: Evidence from the U.S. Federal Courts*, 44 J. L. & Econ. 285, 306 (2001).

TEN

Pain, Power, and Courage

An Interview on the Role of Judges in Addressing Bias

The Honorable Bernice B. Donald, U.S. Court of Appeals, Sixth Circuit
The Honorable Steven C. González, Chief Justice, Washington State Supreme Court
Professor Sarah E. Redfield, University of New Hampshire

A Note from the Editor: From Sarah: It is with both joy and great respect that I add this interview to the book. The idea grew out of a panel I moderated for the State and Local Government Section of the American Bar Association called *The Pain and Power of Judging*. Justice González was on that panel together with Judge Benita Y. Pearson, United States District Court for the Northern District of Ohio, and Judge Robert B. Foster, Massachusetts Land Court. It was an inspiring session, and I wanted to continue its momentum here.

Chief Justice González and Judge Donald are extraordinary thought and action leaders. Each of them stands as an example of lives fully committed to achieving equal justice for all. In this interview they share insights from both their personal backgrounds and professional experience as to how they have worked and continue to work to these ends. Both of these jurists are my heroes, and I am hugely honored to have had this opportunity to talk with them and pass their insight on to our readers. I am confident that readers will take away not only specific strategic ideas for their own work but also hope and inspiration.

Professor Redfield: Short bios are included at the end of this Chapter, but I would like to start by asking each of you to further introduce yourselves and explain what in your backgrounds and work led to your interest in implicit bias. Justice González, we will start with you.

Chief Justice González: Thank you, glad to be here. I'm Steve González, Chief Justice of the Washington Supreme Court, now, for all of seven months. I've been on the Court for ten years and was a trial judge for ten years before that. But I have experienced the effect of explicit and implicit bias throughout my life and also in my professional career. I think if we are going to be true to our principles and actually create a justice system that is open to everyone, we have to address this issue. It may be currently "in vogue" in some circles, but if we are to see change, we need to talk about implicit bias meaningfully and not just while it is popular to do so.

Professor Redfield: Judge Donald?

Judge Donald: I'm currently on the U.S. Court of Appeals for the Sixth Circuit, my fourth judicial position. I began my judicial career as a limited-jurisdiction trial court judge dealing with criminal cases only. I then served as a bankruptcy court judge on the U.S. Bankruptcy Court for the Western District of Tennessee—another high-volume court. Then I served on the United States District Court for the Western District of Tennessee, and now on the Sixth Circuit.

But before that, I guess my awareness goes back to my upbringing, because I was born pre-*Brown v. Board of Education*. I was born in 1951, a few months after *Brown* was filed. I was three years old when the case was decided and four years old when the remedies phase came down. Even though the highest court had said that "separate but equal is inherently unequal," the conditions in my life and in my community did not change.

I began school in a two-room cinderblock school, with Grades 1 and 2 in one room and Grade 3 in another room. There were two teachers teaching two classes in one room with no partition. The children in the upper school went to a Black church where pupils were pooled together to form the classrooms and all the of the teachers in Grade 4–8 taught in that one open room. In my community at that time, the school for Black kids did not go beyond Grade 8. I am not sure where those who wanted to go ahead and graduate from high school went. As for me, each and every day, I would open books that had names written in them that were unfamiliar to me. These were the books from the White school that were handed down to the Black schools after they were either out of date or no longer useful to them because of their poor condition. As I said, the school had no facilities. We were living under the law of the land that said, "separate but equal is inherently unequal," but our lives were, in fact, not equal. And when I look back, there were no places that I could see where the law had really affected change in and of itself. That's why I remind people always that laws are not self-executing. The *Brown*-ordered remedy did not come to Mississippi until 1966 when the schools began to be desegregated.

The inequality I saw was not just in schools. I also saw it in working conditions under which my parents existed, and I saw it in social settings. I saw it in the community where Black kids could only go to the zoo one day a week. I saw that Blacks who shopped in stores could not try on clothing; they took their items home and tried them on, and if they didn't fit, there was a no-return policy. So, there were all kinds of things that I was aware of. And most of these things were explicit biases. But even when we became enlightened in an era where things had become desegregated, I still noticed a difference in attitudes and actions toward people of color, and, especially in my community—African Americans. I finally learned that there was a term that encompassed that, and that was "implicit bias."

I have been committed all of my life to try to get to that "equal justice," which is a term that we strive for, but I do not know that we have achieved. That is what got me in it, and what keeps me passionate about it, day in and day out.

Professor Redfield: Thank you, Judge Donald. I suspect it is hard for anyone to hear this and not be inspired to follow your lead. Justice González, would you like to respond to Judge Donald or add something more from your background?

Chief Justice González: I grew up in Southern California, in a family with a mixed background. Growing up, it was interesting to see the contrasts in the families, to see the difference where the Latino families lived and where the rest of the community lived. It was interesting to watch the segregation that existed in a college town. The same *Brown v. Board* struggle had occurred where there were segregated schools in California, with some of the same players involved. My grandmother went to the same elementary school that my father and I did. When she went there, it was segregated, and when my father was there, the school was integrated. Some of the same teachers that taught in segregated classes were still teaching when I attended that elementary school. We think about segregation in the South, but it happened in the West as well. In the West, it was based on national origin not on race, but the same arguments were made.

If we are talking about an epiphany, I do not need to talk too much about my personal experiences—I had a number of them. But what I think they illustrate, and what I think happens, is that we tend to land on policies and decisions that make the majority comfortable, because the majority is in charge. There was an interesting story on the radio this morning about the first blood bank and how Blacks were not allowed to donate blood because Whites were uncomfortable getting a donation of blood that came from a Black person. That decision was not a scientific decision—it was a decision to make the majority comfortable. I think, frankly, in order to make progress, we are going to have to start making some decisions that may make the majority uncomfortable. That focus is the long focus, and it is conservative. And I do not mean conservative in a party sense, I mean conservative as in "anti-progress." We need to start having difficult discussions, being comfortable with discomfort, and making decisions based on the science, not based on implicit bias. The blood-bank story is representative of the kinds of decisions we are still making today, and it is time for us to stop.

Judge Donald: Justice González, when you talk about the story about people not of color refusing blood from an African American, I am thinking that a lot of this goes back to things, as you say, that were sanctioned by law. As you know, there was a time when the law said if you had a certain number of drops of Black blood, you had to be classified as Black. While obviously that did not refer to transfusions, the memory of that standard is still part of the cultural fabric that forms, informs, and fuels some of the bias, and really, some of the irrational decisions that I think we see resulting. But I agree with you—we have to become comfortable with discomfort.

Professor Redfield: I know from both your lives and your work that you stand committed to the rule of law. In this interview, we are talking about the role of law in relation to explicit and implicit bias. I want to focus more on the role of courts in this area. I know that at the time of the George Floyd murder many courts issued statements on equity and our right to equal justice under law. I know that both of you were involved in some of those statements, and I am wondering if you could talk about the genesis of those and also about whether you think they have had any effect. Justice González, we will start with you.

Chief Justice González: Our court did respond. On June 4, 2020, we issued a very strong letter, in which we acknowledged that we have been part of a system that has devalued Black lives.* We said this explicitly, not trying to talk in veiled terms about what we want to confront. We cited some opinions that are still on our books that addressed Native Americans and African Americans in derogatory terms. Those are published cases, part of our common law here in the State of Washington. We acknowledged that we have inherited this structure; and, even if we weren't the ones who built it initially, we acknowledged that we are the ones responsible for it now. The June 4th letter came about through a discussion here at the Court, starting with the discussion about whether we should issue such a letter at all. My initial response was to say we should not issue a statement if we were not actually going to live up to it. I didn't want us to say pretty, atmospheric things about justice and then just go back to work as normal.

I believe that if we are going to call out those derogatory opinions, we need to address them directly, and we have done that. Our letter has also been an impetus for trial court judges to feel freer to address directly those issues, because we, as the Supreme Court, gave them coverage and said it's alright to acknowledge the institutional bias that exists in some structures that we built, and to acknowledge our responsibilities to do something about it, and not be a passive reactive branch of government. We certainly do take an active role in the cases that come before us. But judges do more than just decide cases. We set the rules, we convene the discussions,

---

* This letter is included in the Appendix.

we are the administrators of the of judicial branch. And every time we make a new policy or change a rule, we have to think about effects that it might have.

Professor Redfield: Could you give us some examples of approaches taken in Washington State?

Chief Justice González: The State has adopted a new requirement for new statutes that they go through something like a fiscal note, but instead of evaluating the fiscal impact of the new statute, they have to evaluate the disproportionality that might flow from its enactment. So, even if it is neutral on its face, there needs to be a study of what the outcome is going to be of its adoption. We have also passed a statute to have counsel appointed for people in eviction proceedings. Even though it is not a full civil *Gideon*, you have a right to be appointed counsel if you get notice from your landlord that you will be evicted, and that is even before the case is filed.

For the Court itself, we have done a number of things. We have repudiated a few of our decisions.[†] We overturned one that had to do with the conviction of a Yakama tribe member for fishing on traditional tribal land and repudiated its racist language. We also overturned a case that upheld the right of a cemetery to refuse burial to a Black family and their child who had passed. In that case, not only was the law wrong, but there was explicit racist language denigrating Blacks and the civil rights movement. We think it is our job to repudiate these cases even though the justices who wrote them are not here to defend themselves. Those cases are our cases, we have inherited them, and it is our responsibility to say what we do and don't support in those cases.

Professor Redfield: You have also adopted some court rules to deal with bias, yes?

Chief Justice González: Yes. We have adopted a number of rules: we no longer allow immigration status to be discoverable in pretrial discovery, unless a specific showing can be made as to why it is necessary in that case. But the presumption is that you do not get to ask that of litigants. We have also asked ICE to treat our courthouses as sensitive areas and not to affect the execution of civil warrants in courthouses so that people would feel free to adjudicate under the rule of law regardless of their immigration status.

We have adopted a new general rule on jury selection, to strengthen *Batson*, acknowledging that *Batson* has failed to eliminate implicit bias in jury selection.

---

† State v. Towessnute, 197 Wash. 2d 574, 575, 486 P.3d 111, 111 (2020) (recalling order and vacating conviction State v. Towessnute, 89 Wash. 478 (1916)); Price v. Evergreen Cemetery Company of Seattle, 57 Wash. 2d 352 (1960), *overruled by* Garfield Cty. Transp. Auth. v. State, 196 Wash. 2d 378, 390 n.1, 473 P.3d 1205 (2020). *Towessnute* is included in the Appendix to Chapter 6.

Professor Redfield: Before we go on, can you speak a bit more about this. Some of the other authors in the book have discussed *Batson*, and I think having your perspective will be useful.

Chief Justice González: Yes, we, as a court, recognized that the *Batson* test was not working to eliminate bias in jury selection. We convened a work group to present and propose a rule that might improve the situation. We ended up with competing proposals, and we went with the stronger of the two. Our rule now says that a juror may not be removed by use of a peremptory strike if an objective observer could conclude that race was a factor in the exercise of that challenge. There was great concern that the sky was falling when we passed that Rule. But, in application, it has been a fairly sleepy affair. The Rule gets applied, people of color are less likely to be removed and therefore more likely to sit, and we therefore have more diverse juries.

Professor Redfield: We know from the science that heterogenous juries make better decisions than homogeneous ones do. They might take a little bit longer from time to time, but they are more likely to follow the judge's orders; they are more likely to review the evidence with each other; they are more likely discuss the case carefully before reaching a decision. And we also know that it is not just the additional input from diverse jurors that matters but that majority jurors also change their behavior in the presence of diverse co-jurors. So, I take it you are pleased with how it is going.

Chief Justice González: Yes, it was a bold step to eliminate a real problem. For the litigants, they have a right to be tried by a fair and impartial jury. And each juror who comes to serve has the right, maybe not to sit on any given case, but the right to not be removed for a racist reason. We are not just protecting the integrity of the system, we are respecting the rights of each person who answers the call and comes to serve.

Professor Redfield: I think that California has now adopted a similar requirement, but I am not sure if other states have as well. It's an example of something that a court has done that other courts can learn from. Anything else?

Chief Justice González: We have begun doing land acknowledgments at the beginning of each term of the Supreme Court, three times a year. Despite some resistance to this, I don't think it is a political statement at all. I think that it is a fair acknowledgment about the past and where we sit in this Court.

We have also done a harassment survey—not just for our trial courts but also for our clerks, our Office of Public Defense, the Office of Civil Legal Aid—to ask people about their experiences with harassment and bias in the workplace. We want to know how we are doing; we want to evaluate ourselves. What the study discovered is tremendous intersectionality where race, gender, orientation, and ability all seem to compound the problem. The numbers are not flattering for us, but that means we need to double our efforts to eliminate that sort of conduct in our own workplaces.

We have also formed a Racial Justice Consortium to study the judicial branch itself and to make recommendations about how we can eliminate implicit bias in the justice system. And I have been on the Board for decades of the Northwest Minority Job Fair where we have been encouraging people to recruit and find diverse applicants, to make sure we are casting a broad net when we are looking for people for openings that we have in our court system.

Professor Redfield: You know we did not ask you to do this interview by accident. We were familiar with some but not all of the things that are going on in Washington State and have gone on there for quite some time. You are an impressive State, and you are an impressive leader. You've made a lot of significant commitments in terms of change. Judge Donald?

Judge Donald: I want to certainly echo Professor Redfield's comments. Times like these require bold action. It requires thinking outside of the box but still within the ethical constraints that govern judges. That's important. So many times we see those who want to say our job is just to call balls and strikes. But I think in unusual circumstances, and if we are really going to address the cause of injustice and try to get to equal justice under law for all people, it sometimes takes going beyond balls and strikes. It requires examining societal infrastructure. I commend you for the leadership you've shown, and I believe what is happening in your State really counters those people who say that if we really want to incorporate diversity, equity, and inclusion, we have to lower standards and reassign values. You're saying "not so," and you are moving forward. I applaud and appreciate your stand.

Now, I am in Tennessee, and I cannot give a laundry list that would rival what you said. Our state court did not make a similar statement after the George Floyd case. Our federal court did respond by creating an entity to create greater awareness of bias and try to address it and to have conversations about it. We created an organization called Inclusion, Diversity, Equity, and Accessibility ("IDEA"), and it has been a wonderful opportunity for employees and judges and all court stakeholders and leaders to have conversations led by prominent people in the field. We developed a reading list; we are trying to learn more about implicit bias. We encourage people to take the Implicit Bias Association Test ("IAT"). We are always encouraging people to put together more diverse teams and cautioning them about the risks that arise from a lack of diversity.

Professor Redfield: What's next for your courts, Judge Donald?

Judge Donald: We still have not achieved the kind of success that I would hope for. Our current chief judge is involved in a consortium to try and address the issue of the lack of diversity in judicial law clerks. There has been a survey instrument developed, and they are soon going to start gathering data via that instrument. But we have some way to go.

We are acutely aware that we have an obligation to further diversity, equity, and inclusion, because, without that, we will have more difficulty creating an environment where people feel that the system is fair. And I just want to say again that the perception of justice often becomes as important as the reality of justice. People look at their situations, and their sense of justice is negatively impacted if they do not see people who look like them or if they see judges who they feel do not value their humanity. Whatever decision comes in an environment like that, people are dissatisfied and skeptical of the results. I believe that it is important for us to create inclusive environments so that every individual coming in the courtroom not only feels heard, but feels respected, feels valued, and feels that they have their dignity respected in that process. Beyond that, we must become leaders from our vantage point in the communities, doing those things that really create a fair and just judicial and legal system.

Chief Justice González: Thank you, Judge Donald. I agree with you a hundred percent. If I could just respond to a couple of things: First, I would stay I am the titular head of the state judicial branch as the Chief, but I've only been Chief for seven months, so I am taking credit for the work that many people have done. I get to take credit for some of it because of that position, but it is not me doing all the work; it is the State coming together and a variety of people helping us achieve this.

As for the study of implicit bias, I think it is critical that we study and understand it, but even proponents of this work are saying that simply studying it can be counterproductive if you do not actually take action steps then to remedy it. So I want to caution people: It is not enough just to read a book about implicit bias or take the IAT test, or go to a training, and then pat yourself on the back for being aware. That can actually result to just going back to your old ways and thinking that you are better because you studied it. We need to make sure we take studying to a series of next action steps. Finally, on the sports analogy of balls and strikes: I don't think we can really explain what we do with sports analogies, but given how rampant these analogies are, I'm going to use one. I think we do have balls and strikes, but we have to also acknowledge that we set the very strike zone itself. We decide what the rules are and then we implement those rules.

Judge Donald: Absolutely, and I thank you for adding to my sports reference. I want to add another thing also. I want to specifically applaud your Court for the case that you mentioned where you went back to get rid of some of the racist language. The first time I heard you talk about that case, I was very moved and thought your approach was wonderful and courageous. Words matter, words have power, and even though they were spoken a long time ago, if it was wrong, it is just wrong. This brings me again to an example in federal law. I know that *Dred Scott* was decided a long time ago, but its language is still there. The language from the Chief Justice, every time I read it, every time I speak it, it inflicts pain anew. The Court said in that case, as you know, that a "Black man has no rights that a White man is bound to respect." That language is still there and valid today. I hope that one day the Supreme Court will have the courage and the opportunity to do as you did and go back and say, "well, that may have been said, but it was wrong!"

Professor Redfield: Thank you both. I think what you have said thus far is a good lead in for my next question, which is to ask you to focus on things unique to your role as judges. We all know you write opinions; we all know you adopt rules; we all know you are in charge of the administration of your courts. I am hoping you might talk a little bit about some specific ways, in addition to what you have already said, that your unique role as judges allows you to do to address both explicit and implicit bias. Justice González?

Chief Justice González: Judicial education is very important. We have seen the retirement of a number of judicial officers, which means we have an influx of new judges. It is a great opportunity to evaluate how we bring new judges on board, what resources we provide to them, and what training we offer. For example, we are paying attention to training our new judges on how to use interpreters and how to advocate for funding for interpreters to make sure that those who supply the court with a budget are thinking about things like that. We are also focused on training on the proper appointment of counsel and on de-escalation techniques. And of course, we are including implicit bias training, which, every time, includes a list of steps that we are encouraging the new judges to take to make sure that they are not just understanding it, but they are doing their best to eliminate it from their courtroom.

In addition to judicial education and training for new judicial officers, we see ourselves as the convenors of the discussion for the branch. So, we are making sure that we do things like have a forum on legal and financial obligations, or juvenile justice, or bail reform. And we are bringing together the stakeholders—the prosecutors, the defenders, the funders, the lawmakers, and the executives—to sit down and to hear the best information so we are all operating not just from a kneejerk reaction, but from actual data, grounded in the research. We can come together and build an actual consensus about what we see as a just system and how we can work to be closer to that. I understand that we are never going to be perfect, but we have to every day be working to get closer to perfection. Otherwise, I do not think that we are doing our job.

Professor Redfield: The professor in me loves to hear you talk about that approach, which is one of learning and of basing your learning on the data and bringing people up to speed on the data. From my whole life's training, I recognize the significance of that, in changing or helping people change their views, which might otherwise have been pretty stereotypical.

Judge Donald: I can't tick off a list as Justice González did. On the Circuit Court, I can't say that we have done much—obviously because we are hearing appeals and dealing with lawyers with fifteen minutes per side with questions from the judges. But I will reflect back on some of the things that I did at the trial level to help ensure that we interrupt bias and not allow people to be abused as a result of being in the trial court system.

There was a history in Shelby County, where I am, of overt, explicit bias. Judges would not address African American lawyers professionally, would not give them the respect of a courtesy title—they certainly would not give their clients that respect and actually used offensive slurs in acknowledging clients. That changed over time, but still, people would be very informal when referring to witnesses. When I came on the federal trial bench, I developed in my judicial protocols, a set of rules of conduct in courts: lawyers may not address clients without the use of a courtesy title, unless it is a child; lawyers may not address another lawyer by first name in the proceedings. I published a set of rules in an effort to make certain that people did not do those things to undermine an individual's clout or to undermine their person by engaging in biased conduct. I think that was helpful.

The other thing was to try to make sure that the court was very much open to people. We know there is a huge bias when it comes to socioeconomic status. If you take care of the cases of all the private paid lawyers first, and you put the public defender clients and other people to the back of line, the individual who is experiencing marginal employment and who has to take off to come to court, that person is more at risk of losing that job. So, I changed that. We did not categorically put certain people to the back of line and others upfront. I also stopped requiring defendants to be in court for biweekly report dates when all that happened was their lawyer would say "I need more time." Again, the client has had to take time off work to be there, and employers need their employees on the job. For these same reasons, I started early on, even before the pandemic, requiring lawyers to do some of the hearings by telephone, for things we weren't making a record of anyway. That way, if they wanted a continuance, they didn't have to drive downtown and bill an hour to take five minutes and ask for a continuance. I put in efficiency rules that helped the whole process, and it certainly helped on the socioeconomic bias issue.

A final thing I will mention. I have been working to try to make certain that we provide judicial education and some implementation strategies with our judges around the issue of bias. In our judicial conference, I put together a whole day about the science and implementation measures, producing the literature and information on how our rules and actions could be enhanced by making certain that we factor in consideration of implicit bias. We brought in people from across the country—Dr. Eberhardt, Eva Paterson out of San Francisco, Jeff Rachlinski, and others. Unfortunately, there was pushback on that first day. Very few of the White judges—and this was open to circuit and district court judges—very few came on the first day, which is when we had all of the bias information. On the second day, we went back to the more traditional things like evidence and rules, and that is when people appeared. We are still struggling with acknowledgment of the reality, and that's a work in progress. That's what I've been trying. Sometimes it's like water on stone. I have been listening intently to Justice González and taking notes.

Chief Justice González: As I listen, I'm prompted to suggest an approach: If you're going to have folks avoiding the subject, an approach is to integrate it into the other subjects. So, if you are giving a presentation on evidence, make it be about evidence and include implicit bias questions in the evidentiary questions. You might talk about whether immigration status should be discoverable, that is an evidentiary rule discussion. If you integrate it into the more general topics, you will get the audience there.

Judge Donald: Thank you.

Professor Redfield: Judge Donald, I am wondering if you can talk about the ethics standards that are involved in the issues that you both have been talking about.

Judge Donald: Well, I can talk a little bit about many states that are passing these rules and requirements that lawyers engage in some training on bias and as a part of ethics rule. In fact, the American Bar Association passed ABA Model Rule 8.4(g).‡ I think lawyers must have that training, and I think it is actually helpful.

Professor Redfield: Thank you for that reminder. I am regretting that we do not have more time together. For now, I would like to bring our interview to a close by asking each of you to give advice to your fellow judges. Of the experiences you've had and the work you've done, what would you want them to pay most attention to or to perhaps set as a priority, to achieve the kind of equity that we have been talking about under the law? Justice González.

Chief Justice González: Attorneys and judges as a group tend to be cautious and backward-looking. And that's because we have been trained to be careful and to make our decisions based on precedent. But I think there are times when we need to turn around and look forward instead. That is particularly true when we are talking about our role as administrators of the branch, as the ones who decide on the rules.

---

‡ It is professional misconduct for a lawyer to: (g) engage in conduct that the lawyer knows or reasonably should know is harassment or discrimination on the basis of race, sex, religion, national origin, ethnicity, disability, age, sexual orientation, gender identity, marital status or socioeconomic status in conduct related to the practice of law. This paragraph does not limit the ability of a lawyer to accept, decline or withdraw from a representation in accordance with Rule 1.16. This paragraph does not preclude legitimate advice or advocacy consistent with these Rules.

There are all kinds of things that can be done, starting from small to big. One thing to do is to go through all of your rules and look for gender-biased language. We did this here. We went through our civil rules, we looked at the reference to Sheriff for example, and it always said "he, him, he shall serve the summons," etc. This is something we can change; we don't have to have a gender bias in our rules. Have a law student do it as a project, but make those changes. It is a small thing but language has consequences as we all know.

Then be willing to step out of your comfort zone a bit and convene discussions on what can be hard but necessary topics. This is a great nation, and the principles upon which it is founded are superb, but they don't mean anything unless we actually apply them, unless we make them apply to everything every day. Our job is to make sure that we are being honest with ourselves and really living up to that. If we say that everyone has a chance at justice, let's make sure that's true. Why not have an expert evaluate your website? Pretend that they are somebody without a legal education trying to figure out how to file for dissolution. Are they going to find the forms that they need? Can they find the help that they need? Let us have an honest evaluation of that website and make it user friendly. Let's update it. These are some small things, but there are lists and lists of ideas of things that can be done. It is our job to be leaders and to make sure we actually live up to our ideals.

Professor Redfield: Thank you. All good ideas to encourage us to focus on our messaging—and beyond. Judge Donald?

Judge Donald: For the judges and lawyers, I would say, first of all, embrace the fact that all of us as humans have biases ingrained in us. Once you acknowledge this, then get to the next step: "What do I do about it?" Learn everything you can and then try to become aware of the biases when you are making decisions that might be impacted by them.

The science says that where we have the greatest amount of discretion is where there is the greatest opportunity for bias to intervene. As judges, that is our essence—discretion. Even when we are limited, there is discretion within those limits. We need to make certain that we are mindful that there is potential for bias, and, when we make a decision, try to step back as best as we can, and be candid about the factors that drove us. Ask yourself whether or not bias played a role. Ask yourself if the parties were different, if the socioeconomic status were different, would the result have been the same.

For example, we have an opportunity to look at our actions with respect to motions. We are closing the court's doors to a lot of individuals by applying the *Twombly* and *Iqbal* standards of plausibility. As judges, we should recognize that plausibility is not an objective standard and is a place that can be rife with the influence of bias. On issues of bail and detention, on length of sentences, on summary judgment motions, on qualified immunity, on eviction issues—sometimes we get so in the habit of going through and deciding that we lose sight of the objects or aims of these cases. We need to make certain that we look at the goals our rules and statutes are supposed to serve and not elevate that form over the basic cause of those who are standing and seeking justice.

I remember there was a part from Aesop's Fables about a bird who hatched a number of birdlings, and the bird built a nest under the eaves of the courthouse. The mother bird went off one day to get food for the birdlings, and a snake had come by and eaten the babies. Upon learning that her birds were gone, the mother started to wail and cry. People came to her and said, "You're not the first bird to have lost your young." According to Aesop's Fables, the mother bird said, "I don't wail because I lost my young, but I wail because it happened under the eaves where the injured fly for justice." Our courts are the place where the injured come for justice. We need to make certain, if there are any barriers of any kind preventing them from having a reasonable expectation of having justice, that we remove them. That is our job, and we must have fidelity to that job. Thank you.

Professor Redfield: Very tempting to end on the note of Aesop's Fables. But I do want to ask you if either one of you wants to add something that I didn't have the foresight to ask about. So, please take a minute.

Chief Justice González: Just one thing. We've heard Judge Donald talk about discretion. She is absolutely right—that's what we exercise as a court. And there is a temptation for us to try to be scientific, and I applaud that, I think we want to be evidence-based. But one of the steps that some courts are taking is to move to what I call actuarial justice. To delegate the discretion and authority that they have to a tool, a metric that gives you a number to help decide if somebody should be released or not. I think we have to be very careful of those tools. At the same time if we are going to keep the discretion that we have, we must use it wisely in a way that is not disproportional.

I would urge every court to study what you are doing, and you will find that what you think you are doing might not always be what you are actually doing. There have been studies that found that judges are lenient in the morning and then strict on decisions towards the lunch hour. Maybe it's because they are tired, maybe it's because they are hungry, but if you do not study what you are doing, you won't be able to fix it. I urge you to be honest with yourselves, to do the study and then to avoid the temptation to pretend like there is some formula that you can use that is going to come to a better decision than humans will. We will always come to a better decision, assuming we are well-educated and careful about what we are doing. Thank you.

Professor Redfield: This has been a total joy. Thank you both.

Appendix

The Supreme Court
State of Washington

June 4, 2020

Dear Members of the Judiciary and the Legal Community:

We are compelled by recent events to join other state supreme courts around the nation in addressing our legal community.

The devaluation and degradation of black lives is not a recent event. It is a persistent and systemic injustice that predates this nation's founding. But recent events have brought to the forefront of our collective consciousness a painful fact that is, for too many of our citizens, common knowledge: the injustices faced by black Americans are not relics of the past. We continue to see racialized policing and the overrepresentation of black Americans in every stage of our criminal and juvenile justice systems. Our institutions remain affected by the vestiges of slavery: Jim Crow laws that were never dismantled and racist court decisions that were never disavowed.

The legal community must recognize that we all bear responsibility for this on-going injustice, and that we are capable of taking steps to address it, if only we have the courage and the will. The injustice still plaguing our country has its roots in the individual and collective actions of many, and it cannot be addressed without the individual and collective actions of us all.

As judges, we must recognize the role we have played in devaluing black lives. This very court once held that a cemetery could lawfully deny grieving black parents the right to bury their infant. We cannot undo this wrong—but we can recognize our ability to do better in the future. We can develop a greater awareness of our own conscious and unconscious biases in order to make just decisions in individual cases, and we can administer justice and support court rules in a way that brings greater racial justice to our system as a whole.

As lawyers and members of the bar, we must recognize the harms that are caused when meritorious claims go unaddressed due to systemic inequities or the lack of financial, personal, or systemic support. And we must also recognize that this is not how a *justice* system must operate. Too often in the legal profession, we feel bound by tradition and the way things have "always" been. We must remember that even the most venerable precedent must be struck down when it is incorrect and harmful. The systemic oppression of black Americans is not merely incorrect and harmful; it is shameful and deadly.

Members of the Judiciary and the Legal Community – June 4, 2020 Page 2

Finally, as individuals, we must recognize that systemic racial injustice against black Americans is not an omnipresent specter that will inevitably persist. It is the collective product of each of our individual actions—every action, every day. It is only by carefully reflecting on our actions, taking individual responsibility for them, and constantly striving for better that we can address the shameful legacy we inherit. We call on every member of our legal community to reflect on this moment and ask ourselves how we may work together to eradicate racism.

As we lean in to do this hard and necessary work, may we also remember to support our black colleagues by lifting their voices. Listening to and acknowledging their experiences will enrich and inform our shared cause of dismantling systemic racism.

We go by the title of "Justice" and we reaffirm our deepest level of commitment to achieving justice by ending racism. We urge you to join us in these efforts. This is our moral imperative.

Sincerely,

Debra L. Stephens,
Chief Justice

Charles W. Johnson,
Justice

Barbara A. Madsen,
Justice

Susan Owens, Justice

Steven C. González,
Justice

Sheryl Gordon McCloud,
Justice

Mary I. Yu, Justice

Raquel Montoya-Lewis,
Justice

G. Helen Whitener, Justice

ELEVEN

Judicial Education on Implicit Bias
Instilling a Lifelong Pursuit of Fairness

The Honorable Reba Ann Page, U.S. Armed Services Board of Contract Appeals

The Honorable Benes Z. Aldana, National Judicial College[*]

A Note from the Editors: The National Judicial College (the NJC) is a nonprofit and nonpartisan institution dedicated to providing comprehensive judicial education. The NJC faculty members are excellent and thoughtful educators, and their collective experience and advice is invaluable. Several other chapters in the book speak to education as a necessary (though not sufficient) building block for interrupting implicit bias. We welcome these two very knowledgeable and experienced authors to our book family. The insights they offer into judicial thinking and learning on this topic is a valuable guide for the judicial community and beyond as we develop strategies to limit the impacts of implicit bias.

CHAPTER HIGHLIGHTS

- Tracing the history of judicially sanctioned prejudice against various groups gives insight into the biases being fought today in our pursuit of impartiality.

- Judges' experiences show that implicit bias remains a problem even for those who are responsible for the unbiased and fair treatment of others.

---

[*] The views expressed herein are solely those of the authors and do not represent the United States government. The authors thank Dr. Lois S. Cronholm for her invaluable editorial assistance, as well as J.D. Page, Esq., Joy D. Lyngar, Esq., Edward Cohen, and Dr. Brian Lee.

- Bias education involves the steps taken in both individual jurisdictions and the national and international arenas, using methodologies centered on academic traditions of coursework, teaching, and learning.
- The content and methodology for bias education, as for all modern curriculum development, must be developed in concert with the sciences that explain the input, storage, and access of information in the brain.

CHAPTER CONTENTS

Introduction

1. The Urgency of Equal Justice for All
2. Lingering Legacies: Explicit Bias and the Evolution of Implicit Bias in the Judiciary
    A. The Difficulties of Assessing the Persistent Influence of Bias
    B. Echoes of Yesteryear: Today's Challenges of Implicit Bias in Race, National Origin/Ethnicity, and Gender
3. Views from the Bench
    A. Conversations Regarding Implicit Bias with Jurists and Their Recommendations
    B. Compiled Responses and Recommendations for Combatting Implicit Bias and Judicial Education
    C. Responses to The National Judicial College's Surveys of Judges on Implicit Bias
4. *You've Got to be Carefully Taught*: Means and Methods of Judicial Education in Overcoming Implicit Bias
    A. Sources of Judicial Education on Implicit Bias
    B. The National Judicial College's Efforts at Overcoming Implicit Bias
5. Measuring, Managing, and Responding to Questions of Judicial Ethics and Implicit Bias

Conclusion

Introduction

Today's judiciary must decide heavy caseloads of legally complex matters in a timely manner that affords due process and fundamental fairness to everyone, all with public scrutiny. Ensuring that the proceedings remain untainted by bias or prejudice adds to the courts' challenge of affording equal protection. Explicit biases (positive or negative conscious preferences for a category) may be more apparent because they are overt, but implicit biases (positive or negative preferences for a category that operate outside of our awareness) are by definition more difficult to discern.[1] The risk that bias poses to justice is massive—poisoning judicial processes and robbing the targets of the fair result that is the intended goal of our judicial system. The difficult questions confronting the court system are: how pervasive is judicial bias, and how do we combat an unseen or unacknowledged threat that undermines the fundamentals of our democracy?

While implicit bias is an often unacknowledged phenomenon, judicial and legal scholars' recognition of it is so well known that it would take volumes to give full treatment to the numerous books and articles on this subject. This Chapter focuses on recognizing the urgency of overcoming bias; examines lingering legacies of historic decisions that echo in today's most pressing social inequities; relates views from the bench on the impact of implicit bias and efficacy of anti-bias measures; tells how we must be carefully taught to overcome prejudice; reminds judges of relevant ethical obligations; and concludes by calling for all members of the justice system to forge a path forward for overcoming implicit bias.

1. The Urgency of Equal Justice for All

Although equal justice is always a timely cause, it is especially urgent now. That is why this Chapter recommends judicial education to raise awareness of bias and its consequences. At this writing in 2021, the United States has been through a period of considerable upheaval in which public health, racial unrest, and political events collided and shook the foundations of our society. The response to the Covid-19 viral pandemic spilled over into consequences that greatly influenced the treatment of classes of citizens long recognized as the subject of societal bias.[2] Violence against Asians has followed former President Trump's dubbing of the Covid-19 virus as "the Chinese virus" or the "kung flu."[3] The results of the 2020 election led to state legislation restricting voting that some believe targeted the participation of specific social groups.

Exacerbating racial unrest and challenges to governmental administration of the law was the May 2020 death of a Black man, George Floyd, at the hands of White police officer Derek Chauvin. Mr. Chauvin was convicted a year later of unintentional second-degree murder, third-degree murder, and second-degree manslaughter.[4] Yet, despite these prejudices, United States Senator and former California Attorney General Kamala Harris, the biracial daughter of Asian (Indian Subcontinent) and Black Jamaican immigrants, was elected the first female Vice President of the United States.[5]

Notwithstanding the devastating history and current events, this Chapter is written in the spirit of optimism and abiding faith in the United States, its people, and its institutions. As this Chapter focuses on using education to eliminate implicit bias within the judiciary, we reflect upon progress to date and upon key aspects of this multifaceted challenge.

2. Lingering Legacies: Explicit Bias and the Evolution of Implicit Bias in the Judiciary

The adage "history repeats itself" lives on because it serves as a signpost, a warning, to review the past as a guide to flawed paths going forward. Tracing the history of judicially sanctioned prejudice against various groups gives insight into the biases being fought today in our pursuit of impartiality. These lingering legacies are not recalled as excuses for disparate treatment but as meaningful explanations of today's state of affairs. Our purpose is to add an essential element to understanding the problem as a predicate to devising remedies.

A. The Difficulties of Assessing the Persistent Influence of Bias

The United States Supreme Court has recognized the persistent influence of American history and lingering racial biases upon today's society. In *McCleskey v. Kemp*, 481 U.S. 279 (1987), a decision criticized by some as akin to *Dred Scott v. Sandford*, 60 U.S. 393 (1857), the Court rejected the petition for habeas corpus of a Georgia death row prisoner.[6] The majority acknowledged that Mr. McCleskey, a Black man convicted of killing a White police officer during the commission of an armed robbery, produced evidence of a scientific study that statistically showed disproportionate punishment of Blacks under similar circumstances. But this statistical showing was deemed insufficient.[7] Instead, the Court insisted that the defendant "must prove that the decisionmakers in his case acted with discriminatory purpose." Justice Powell agreed that others had successfully proven bias using statistical analyses but said: "McCleskey's claim that these statistics are sufficient proof of discrimination, without regard to the facts of a particular case, would extend to all capital cases in Georgia, at least where the victim was white and the defendant is black."[8]

As Justice Brennan memorably observed in his dissent in *McCleskey*, the majority's arguments "suggest a fear of too much justice."[9] He recounted how the country in "recent times" has "sought to free ourselves from the burden" of historically discriminatory decisions. Justice Brennan cited *Dred Scott* and condemned Chief Justice Roger Taney's derogatory comments about Blacks' lack of rights.[10] He referenced *Plessy v.*

Ferguson, in which "A mere three generations ago, this Court sanctioned racial segregation, stating that '[i]f one race be inferior to the other socially, the Constitution of the United States cannot put them upon the same plane.'"[11] Justice Brennan praised the "honorable steps" taken to "free ourselves from the burden of this history" yet remonstrated that we ignore evidence of persistent racism "at our peril, for we remain imprisoned by the past as long as we deny its influence on the present."[12]

The dissenters in *McCleskey*, and those who believe in the value of scientific research as an indicator of bias (explicit or implicit), later saw greater acceptance of these approaches. Compare two decisions dealing with proof of bias: In *Texas Dep't of Housing and Cmty. Affairs v. Inclusive Communities Project*, 576 U.S. 519 (2015), the Court recognized the utility of statistical analyses in inferring bias but cautioned that "[i]f a statistical discrepancy is caused by factors other than the defendant's policy, a plaintiff cannot establish a prima facie case, and there is no liability."[13] Previously, the Court ruled in a split decision in *Watson v. Fort Worth Bank & Trust*, 487 U.S. 989 (1988), that a "disparate impact analysis may be applied to subjective as well as to objective practices" in claims involving Title VII of the Civil Rights Act of 1964, but that more is required than just "statistical disparities."[14]

B. Echoes of Yesteryear: Today's Challenges of Implicit Bias in Race, National Origin/Ethnicity, and Gender

At this writing, the country confronts a deadly global pandemic while simultaneously attempting to come to grips with racial unrest across the country. These are virtually the same overwhelming problems (a flu pandemic and racial terrorism in the Jim Crow South and beyond) that challenged the United States a hundred years ago.[15]

Consider Chief Justice Taney's damnable language in *Dred Scott*. In what is generally regarded as the worst decision ever rendered by the U.S. Supreme Court, the enslaved Mr. Scott and his family were denied their freedom. African Americans were told they "had no rights which the white man was bound to respect." As Chief Justice Taney described their status (or lack thereof):

> [T]he negro might justly and lawfully be reduced to slavery for his benefit. He was bought and sold, and treated as an ordinary article of merchandise and traffic, whenever a profit could be made by it. This opinion was at that time fixed and universal in the civilized portion of the white race. It was regarded as an axiom in morals as well as in politics, which no one thought of disputing, or supposed to be open to dispute; and men in every grade and position in society daily and habitually acted upon it in their private pursuits, as well as in matters of public concern, without doubting for a moment the correctness of this opinion.[16]

This sweeping denial of civil rights to those of African ancestry was overturned by the post-Civil War 13th, 14th, and 15th constitutional amendments, which respectively abolished slavery, guaranteed due process of law and fundamental fairness, and enshrined the right of all men to vote. However, this tide of progress was thwarted by *Plessy v. Ferguson*, 163 U.S. 537 (1896),[17] in which the Court re-established racial discrimination as a lawful and arguably desirable way of life, and it remained the law of the land until it was overturned in *Brown v. Board of Education*, 347 U.S. 483 (1954). There are a number of important Supreme Court rulings in the categories of most concern for implicit bias. Here is a brief timeline of select decisions that dealt with race, national origin, gender, and LGBTQIA+ issues; voting rights are included as an area in which bias spans these categories in affecting civil rights:

1873   In *Bradwell v. Illinois*, 83 U.S. 130 (1873), the Court rejected a woman's right to be licensed to practice law.

1874   In *Minor v. Happersett*, 88 U.S. 162 (1874), the Court upheld state laws denying women the right to vote on the basis that the Constitution did not confer a universal right of suffrage.

1875   In *United States v. Cruikshank*, 92 U.S. 542 (1875), the Courtdevastated those seeking protection of voting rights by declining to incorporate the Bill of Rights against the states.

1886   In *Yick Wo v. Hopkins*, 118 U.S. 356 (1886),the Court held that facially-neutral but disparately-applied laws were unconstitutional.

1898   In *United States v. Wong Kim Ark*, 169 U.S. 649 (1898), the Court found that the American-born son of Chinese immigrants qualified as a citizen under the birthright provision of the 14th amendment.

1915   In *Guinn v. United States*, 238 U.S. 347 (1915), the Court ruled against Oklahoma's voter-suppression measures (such as the "grandfather clause").

1927   In *Gong Lum v. Rice*, 275 U.S. 78 (1927), the Court rejected the petition of a Chinese parent to have his daughter admitted to a Whites-only school in Rosedale, Mississippi.

1944   In *Korematsu v. United States*, 323 U.S. 214 (1944), the Court upheld the internment of persons of "Japanese ancestry," including Japanese Americans during World War II.

1950   In *Sweatt v. Painter*, 339 U.S. 637 (1950), the Court rejected Texas's attempt to create a segregated, "separate but equal" law school.

1954   *Brown v. Board of Education*, 347 U.S. 483 (1954), the Court effectively overturned Plessy's pernicious "separate but equal" doctrine.

1960 In *Gomillion v. Lightfoot*, 364 U.S. 339 (1960), the Court rejected gerrymandering that attempted to redefine voting boundaries according to race in Tuskegee, Alabama.

1973 In *Keyes v. Denver School District* No. 1, 413 U.S. 189 (1973), the Court supported Hispanic/Latinx parents against segregated schools.

2015 In *Obergefell v. Hodges*, 576 U.S. 644 (2015), the Court recognized the right of same-sex couples to marry.

With this brief historical review, we move to our discussion of current-day judicial insight.

3. Views from the Bench

Because judges are especially well positioned to assess the adverse impact of implicit bias, The National Judicial College (the NJC) sought their input in two direct ways. The first was through interviews with a select group of jurists, who shared their personal experiences and thoughts regarding the effect of implicit bias upon the judicial system. The second was through two "one-question" surveys, which explored using judicial education as one antidote to the bias that leads to racism and other forms of bias.

A. Conversations Regarding Implicit Bias with Jurists and Their Recommendations

Four judges were interviewed about their experiences with implicit bias on and off the bench. At the time of the interviews they held the following positions: Judge Reggie B. Walton, an African American, is a Senior Judge of the United States District Court for the District of Columbia.[18] Justice Robert J. Torres, an Asian Pacific American, is an Associate Justice and former Chief Justice of the Supreme Court of Guam.[19] Judge Veronica A. Galván, who is of Hispanic/Latina[20] heritage, sits on the King County Superior Court in Washington State.[21] Judge Kristin L. Rosi, a member of the LGBTQIA+ community, is the Chief Administrative Law Judge for the California Department of Insurance. They were each asked the following questions:

1. Could you please describe the implicit biases you have experienced both on the bench and off?
2. Speaking both professionally and personally, what do you find most effective in combatting implicit biases?
3. With the goal of addressing implicit bias in the judiciary, what measures do you recommend for judicial education?

The judges' responses to these questions show the degree to which each has faced bias that continues despite their accomplishments and the honors they have received. Their experiences show that implicit bias remains a problem even for those who are responsible for the unbiased treatment of others and who are respected and successful in achieving that goal. This section summarizes an account shared by each judge, then compiles their overall recommendations for overcoming implicit bias through education and action.[22]

i. Judge Reggie B. Walton

Tragically, Judge Walton's family is among those who have suffered from racially motivated violence. His mother's family fled Georgia after her father was murdered by a White man for refusing to step off the curb when a White woman approached. Although the killer was known, he was not held accountable. Judge Walton himself faced the dangerous situation notoriously confronting Black males when visiting his parents in western Pennsylvania. As a young assistant United States attorney, he was driving a new Corvette when he was stopped at gunpoint by White police officers, who demanded to know how he had gotten the car. After he cautiously showed them his Department of Justice credentials, the officers fled. Why else would he have been stopped but for the officers' bias, probably implicit and explicit?

Despite—or maybe because of—such experiences, Judge Walton is careful to avoid bias in his own actions. He begins with the premise that everyone has biases and that we should acknowledge this as a first step to combatting them. Judge Walton believes that the most profound way to combat bias is through self-education and getting to know people who are different. Developing these relationships allows us to dispel stereotypes and understand that we may have perceptions that are not grounded in reality. He encourages self-assessment, such as taking the well-known Implicit Association Test (IAT), and greater self-awareness of the biases each of us has. Judge Walton spoke of being mindful on the bench, particularly in sentencing, and taking the time to ensure that he treats all defendants fairly.

ii. Justice Robert J. Torres, Jr.

Justice Torres expressed concern over the many steps in the legal process where decisions influenced by implicit biases can skew the outcome: there are multiple opportunities, from arrest to arraignment to bail to trial to sentencing and in between. At each point, the implicit biases of those involved can affect whether justice is delivered. This is true whether the person involved is law enforcement, counsel, a parole officer, a corrections official, a judge, or anyone else involved in the process.

Justice Torres reflected upon the impact of implicit bias on the work of Bryan Stevenson, Esq., a classmate at Harvard Law School. In 1989, Mr. Stevenson founded the nonprofit Equal Justice Initiative (EJI) in Montgomery, Alabama. EJI is "committed to ending mass incarceration and excessive punishment in the United States, to challenging racial and economic injustice, and to protecting basic human rights for the most vulnerable people in America."[23] Stevenson's efforts have disclosed shocking inequities in our criminal justice system, particularly for the indigent. Justice Torres queried what an analysis (a "deconstruction") of the cases undertaken by EJI (or similar verdicts by other courts) would disclose: from arrest to sentencing, what implicit biases resulted in injustice?

iii. Judge Veronica A. Galván

Judge Galván's straightforward response to the comment "you don't look like a judge" was to create the social media hashtag "#whatdoesajudgelooklike?" To Judge Galván, woman and a Latina, that remark reflected multiple layers of bias about who fits the mold to be a judge. We know that for hundreds of years in this country, neither women nor Latinas nor persons of color were allowed to hold such positions of authority. These and other historic exclusionary legal practices and precedents continue to inform today's perspectives, even though the rulings may have been forgotten or abrogated. It is imperative to acknowledge that we all have biases and to work on a continuous basis to banish its effects. Judge Galván described our obligation to do so by using the analogy of occupying an old house with lead pipes or outdated wiring. You may not have put them there, but the resulting problems are yours—and society's—until you deal with them.

As the former dean of the Washington State Judicial College and teacher on implicit bias, Judge Galván believes in mandatory and regular education on the topic. Washington has adopted a strong educational program dealing with bias and developed such measures as General Rule 37 Jury Selection, which requires judicial officers to take a proactive approach to ensuring fairness. She is a strong proponent of individual and organizational efforts to acknowledge, understand, and work cooperatively to eliminate the unjust effects of implicit bias. She urges that it be done with empathy to be effective. Judge Galván does not regard implicit bias as a political issue but as a substantive area of law with broad impact.

iv. Judge Kristin L. Rosi

Judge Rosi acknowledges that she enjoys a certain degree of privilege as the result of her position, race (White), Ivy League education, and the fact that she presents in her physical appearance as a woman and not necessarily as the advocate for the LGBTQIA+ community that she is. Although these attributes allow her ready access to people, places, and situations denied to others, Judge Rosi regards these as providing her a platform for furthering civil rights. Despite the success she enjoys today, she knows what it is to be vulnerable and alone, and she is fierce about speaking out for those who cannot effectively do so for themselves.

In Judge Rosi's opinion, overcoming implicit bias is all about establishing relationships, especially relationships formed with those different from herself. This method was recommended by each judge interviewed. Not unlike civil rights leader John Lewis's belief in creating "good trouble," Judge Rosi urges the challenge of "purposeful discomfort," of engaging with people of unlike backgrounds on a regular and consistent basis. Eliminating discriminatory laws that leave LGBTQIA+ members unsafe or excluded is a high priority. She eschews the notion that implicit bias can be overcome by a one-and-done training session. She argues that it must be lived daily. We must hold one another to account. As Judge Rosi points out, George Floyd was murdered by a police officer who had attended implicit bias training the week before. As Judge Rosi also points out: overcoming prejudice is not simply a matter of attending a class but living in an uncompromising and consistent way that respects and prioritizes the rights of others.

B. Compiled Responses and Recommendations for Combatting Implicit Bias and Judicial Education

The judges we interviewed expressed strong views supporting the necessity of combatting implicit bias both on and off the bench. They suggested strategies for well-designed judicial education and measures everyone should take to overcome personal and institutional biases. While there were many commonalities, each provided unique insights into their court as well as the communities they are a part of (i.e., African American, Asian Pacific American, Hispanic/Latinx, and Sexual Orientation/LGBTQIA+).

i. Responses to Question 2: Speaking both professionally and personally, what do you find most effective in combatting implicit biases?

- Acknowledge that everyone (including yourself) has implicit biases.
- Engage in self-assessment to discover and understand your implicit biases.
- Devise deliberate strategies for overcoming your individual implicit biases as well as those in your court.
- Do not ignore bias: respond appropriately, and use the occasion to overcome it.
- Empathy for others is essential in overcoming implicit bias.
- Accept that there will be growing pains in overcoming individual and institutional biases.
- Make thoughtful, well-considered rulings: avoid "acting fast" on assumptions, perceptions, and biases.

- Become more "culturally literate": get acquainted with those who are unlike you so they will no longer be "the other."
- Understand that biases of the past (such as exclusion of minorities from popular culture and segregated schooling) affect us today.
- Review decisions at each stage of litigation to ensure that these are not affected by implicit biases, especially those involving economic and social status. These include jury selection, pretrial release, sentencing,[24] considering parole, ruling on motions and on objections during proceedings, fact-finding, and decision-writing.
- Consider alternative results in writing decisions: what would be the effect of a different ruling?
- Gather more data: make use of information available from automated case-management systems; encourage further study of implicit bias in particular jurisdictions and areas of the law; devise and implement solutions based upon credible data.
- Consider on an ongoing basis for both individual judges and courts whether certain groups are statistically over- (or under-) represented in arrests and convictions and/or are disparately punished.

ii. *Responses to Question 3: With the goal of addressing implicit bias in the judiciary, what measures do you recommend for judicial education?*

- Education must be done in a forthright but nonconfrontational manner to ensure that judges do not become self-defensive and resist understanding the need to acknowledge and eliminate implicit bias.
- Education on implicit bias should be mandatory, even though it may be resisted by some.
- Emphasize that attending training does not complete the task of overcoming implicit bias.
- Provide self-assessment tools such as the IAT and other instruments that disclose the nature and scope of individual biases.
- Develop a holistic approach: devise programs that address implicit bias at every stage and by every participant in the judicial process. Consider how to overcome bias by education and amended procedures, including training for judges as well as law enforcement, prosecutors, defense counsel, jurors, marshals, clerks, parole officers, and administrative & support staff.

- Provide both "education" (i.e., scientific and legal theory) as well as "training" (actual or simulated clinical experience) regarding the origin and impact of implicit biases.

- "Training" could include having judges (1) review hypothetical situations as well as cases that have been adjudicated to ascertain whether and where there is evidence of implicit bias; and (2) compare decisions based upon similar facts to discern whether bias was a factor in the outcome.

- Teach judges how to defuse situations in which implicit bias has been or is becoming a problem.

- Ensure learning experiences are interesting and effective. This includes: having knowledgeable instructors who communicate well; developing and making available take-away resources such as bench cards, bench books, and relevant references; using multidisciplinary approaches that incorporate science and the law; and providing interesting instruction making good use of film, literature, and the arts.

These interviews uniformly show the value these judges place on implicit bias training that is well-designed and provided by instructors who are knowledgeable about current law and science underlying this problem. Each judge criticized the notion that a one-time session is sufficient to produce meaningful results: quality counts, and a "one-shot deal" is not enough. Although it is uncomfortable to acknowledge our biases, especially for judges who believe themselves to be fair and impartial, that is likely the easy part in overcoming prejudice. Sustained work is necessary to divest oneself of these harmful perceptions, with repeated reflection on whether these biases discovered (or new ones) are lodged in our thoughts. This underscores the importance of repeated training by highly-competent instructors and the learner's dedication to the ultimate goal of ensuring fairness.[25]

In addition to training and education, the judges interviewed recommended other approaches, many of which can be undertaken by the individual judge or by the court as a whole. These include: "deconstructing" cases to detect instances where bias may have affected the outcome; reviewing and comparing decisions to ensure they are not tainted by bias, and examining data to discern patterns of bias that might not otherwise be apparent.

C. Responses to The National Judicial College's Surveys of Judges on Implicit Bias

Each month, The National Judicial College emails an "informal, non-scientific one-question survey" to its more than 12,000 judicial alumni across the United States and abroad. These provide for objective choices (*e.g.*, yes/no, agree/disagree, multiple choice). Responders are also invited to provide further comment to elaborate upon the position taken or suggest additional inquiry into the issue. The College makes clear that these opt-in survey results "are not intended to be characterized as conclusive research findings."[26] Despite these disclaimers, the results of the surveys have proven to be of great interest, as demonstrated by further research on the topics, media attention to the results, and the popularity of courses addressing implicit bias offered by the NJC and other providers of judicial education.

Relevant to this Chapter are two questions posed in 2020 and 2021. In July 2020, the NJC queried its alumni regarding their opinions about systemic racism, and in July 2021 the College asked about the efficacy of judicial education in overcoming implicit bias. As well documented in this book and other publications and in numerous court decisions, there is ample empirical data regarding the prevalence and persistence of implicit bias.[27] The responses to these questions, which are discussed below, offer quantifiable information regarding individual judges' perspectives on these important questions.

i. July 2020 One-Question Survey

Posed only a few weeks after the death of George Floyd, the NJC's one-question survey emailed to its alumni in the first week of July 2020 asked for a "yes/no" response to this question: "Do you believe that systemic racism exists in the criminal justice system?" Of the 634 judges responding, 65% replied in the affirmative—a significant, majority consensus that racism remains an issue.

One respondent called for action: "Of course it does. The data doesn't (sic) lie. The burden on us judges is to, first, acknowledge the problem and then to work diligently to eradicate the problem."[28] Another judge insisted that a lack of awareness of implicit bias is no excuse. This anonymous judge emphasized the need for judicial education and squarely placed the onus on each judge to understand the real-world impact of such prejudices: "Any judge who is not educated on the reality of systemic racism and implicit bias and aware of the consequences of these issues should not be on the Bench." A different judge suggested that the high incarceration rates of Blacks and other minorities (proportionally greater than Whites) was attributable to systemic racism. This judge commented: "Most of the judges I know are not overtly racist and sincerely seek to treat all people equally, but I suspect that our implicit biases impact our decision-making more than we realize."[29]

Among the judges who disagreed that systemic racism exists in the judiciary, one questioned whether individual prejudices necessarily showed a systemic problem: "Our system isn't perfect and individual actors may harbor prejudices based on race. But those that do are vastly outnumbered by those who go about their work conscientiously and evenhandedly. I see no evidentiary basis for the contention that it is a systemic problem." Another blamed the national news media for advancing "a false narrative as a way to continue to divide this nation and discredit the thousands of good, fair judges and court employees in the United States."[30]

ii. July 2021 One-Question Survey

In anticipation of this Chapter, the NJC emailed this one-question survey to its alumni in July 2021: "Do you think judicial education can help rid the courts of implicit bias?" Although the monthly survey queries only judges, the question was broadly stated to encompass implicit bias throughout the court system. Part of the purpose for that was to ascertain (on an informal basis) whether judges educated in recognizing and overcoming implicit bias can/are taking a leadership role in eliminating bias and in assisting others involved in the court system in doing so.

Of the 489 judges who responded, 68% (similar to the 2020 results) answered "yes." One judge observed that "[w]ithout judicial education, many of us would be unaware of our implicit biases and, therefore, unequipped to combat them." Other judges expressed concern about implementation. As one anonymously stated: "Just being educated that we have biases is not enough. It requires action on the part of each judge."[31]

Two judges who responded "no" to the survey were even more skeptical. One said, "We can educate people on judicial topics and behavioral science all we want. That does not mean we can control each person's attitude or thought process that's been engrained since birth."

4. *You've Got to Be Carefully Taught*: Means and Methods of Judicial Education in Overcoming Implicit Bias

The lyrics of a popular song from the 1949 musical *South Pacific* show the insidious effect of learned bias:

> *You've got to be taught*
> *To hate and fear, you've got to be taught from year to year*
> *It's got to be drummed in your dear little ear*
> *You've got to be carefully taught.*
> *You've got to be taught*
> *To be afraid of people*
> *Whose eyes are oddly made*
> *And people whose skin is a different shade*
> *You've got to be carefully taught.*

Rodgers & Hammerstein's message[32] resonates today as we look to overcome bias in the judiciary. While serving as a reminder that "you've got to be carefully taught" to fear and distrust those unlike you, it offers encouragement that these reactions and behaviors can also be "unlearned" and replaced by those that are fair and unbiased. This section focuses on measures to achieve the latter.

Judges' work is achieved in numerous ways, ranging from landmark opinions of federal and state supreme courts to the quotidian workings at the trial and appellate levels. Each step of litigation offers an opportunity to reinforce or deny fundamental fairness, and various judicial and professional organizations are dedicated to educating judges to ensure that our courts provide fair justice for all. This section examines what is being done by select programs and providers to decrease the negative impacts of bias. At the outset, we acknowledge the perspicacity of judicial education professionals who, with the foresight of going beyond offerings on black-letter law, laid the foundation for including topics such as overcoming bias as an essential aspect of a sound court system. We applaud the visionaries of today who constantly examine the effectiveness of teaching methods and devise new measures that better meet society's needs, as judicial education is an ongoing and continuous process that must address the requirements of beginner and advanced student alike.

A. Sources of Judicial Education on Implicit Bias

A large number of distinguished organizations provide judicial education, which signals the importance of the issue. In addition to the American Bar Association (ABA), there are academic programs at various colleges and universities, national associations for judges and court professionals, and bar associations at all levels that are all engaged in the work. The ABA and the National Center for State Courts (NCSC), two important examples of such organizations' contributions in combatting implicit bias, are discussed in this Chapter as is the Iowa Judicial Branch.

i. The American Bar Association

Adopted in August of 2020, the ABA's groundbreaking Resolution 116G urged that "all states, territories and tribes require that lawyers, judges, commissioners, referees, probation officers, and court personnel receive periodic training regarding implicit biases," and that such training address "at minimum, the following subjects: sex, race, color, religion, ancestry, national origin, ethnic group identification, age, disability, medical condition, genetic information, marital status, sexual orientation, gender expression and gender identity."[33] The Resolution was accompanied by a report (ABA 116G Report), which discussed the history, rationale and context for supporting implicit bias training. The result of a years-long effort by multiple sections of the ABA, the Report credited the work of other organizations striving to achieve the same outcome and emphasized the importance of judicial precedent from the United States Supreme Court in acknowledging the harmful repercussions of implicit bias.[34]

ii. The National Center for State Courts

The National Center for State Courts (NCSC) assists courts nationally and around the world as it "play[s] a key role in the development of court administration."[35] It also provides information regarding judicial ethics through its Center for Judicial Ethics (CJE), which is a "clearinghouse for information about judicial ethics and discipline."[36] Although NCSC is oriented to state courts, its research and recommendations are useful to anyone seeking to better understand the origins and effects of implicit bias on the tribunals and the communities they serve.

In working to overcome implicit bias, the NCSC has brought together resources from organizations such as the Open Society Institute, the State Justice Institute, and others. The NCSC has been a leader in this arena, publishing an early *Primer* by UCLA law professor Jerry Kang as well as key reports about the genesis of implicit bias and eliminating its effects.[37] Its 2012 report "The Evolving Science on Implicit Bias: An Updated Resource for the State Court Community," was updated in March 2021 (NCSC 2021 Report).[38]

Acknowledging the tumult of 2020, the 2021 revisions support the unanimous Resolution passed by the Conference of Chief Justices and the Conference of State Court Administrators to

> continue and intensify efforts to combat racial prejudice within the justice system, both explicit and implicit, and to recommit to examine what systemic change is needed to make equality under the law an enduring reality for all, so that justice is not only fair to all but also is recognized by all to be fair.[39]

Another NCSC report, which is of special interest here, is *Helping Courts Address Implicit Bias: Resources for Education* (NCSC 2012 Report).[40] In addition to providing an overview of implicit bias and its consequences to the justice system and recommending general references, the report looked at judicial education programs in various states and relayed feedback on these from judges and court administrators. Based on its review, the NCSC urged pre-program planning and providing information on implicit bias using "specific curriculum delivery strategies" such as conferences, lectures, interactions with subject-matter experts, opportunities for self-assessment, and small group discussions.[41] Based upon the experiences of the states it surveyed, the NCSC presented six "lessons learned" that can aid any court seeking to develop a program to address implicit bias. The surveys found: (1) court audiences are receptive to implicit bias information; (2) the complexity of the implicit bias subject matter demands time and expertise; (3) implicit bias programs should be tailored to specific audiences; (4) content delivery methods affect participant understanding and satisfaction; (5) institutions should dedicate time to discuss and practice strategies to address the influence of implicit bias; and (6) development of an evaluation assessment with the faculty is essential.[42]

iii. The Innovative Response of the Iowa Judicial Branch to Implicit Bias

Many judicial branches and bar associations have developed programs to educate their judiciary, court administrators, and counsel on recognizing and combatting implicit bias. As it is beyond the remit of this Chapter to review them all, we focus on Iowa as an exemplar for overcoming inherent prejudice in its trial system. We acknowledge the work of the late Chief Justice Mark S. Cady, whose strategies are instructive for other jurisdictions.[43] Justice Cady delivered a clarion call that resonates today.[44] He cautioned there was "something that can adversely impact our fundamental values and our process of justice: implicit bias," which inhibits efforts to overcome racism:

> I do this because any form of bias interferes with justice, and we must work to identify implicit bias and remove it from our system of justice, just as we have done with explicit bias. And we must do the same throughout society.
>
> Implicit bias is almost always at the heart of the racial disparities that we continue to discover. We will only truly confront racial disparities when we confront our implicit bias.
>
> Yet as important as it is to confront implicit bias, it can be difficult to discuss. It can be difficult because to talk about our implicit bias can often be mistaken for accusations of being prejudiced or being biased. And can give rise to claims that we should be talking less about it.
>
> The truth is just the opposite. We should be talking more about implicit bias. We need to talk more about implicit bias, but in a respectful and thoughtful way. And we need to talk about the racial disparities in our society without feeling that it's a putdown to anyone. It is none of these things.
>
> We must remember that when we talk about implicit bias, we are talking about how our brains work, unconsciously. And how it stores up our past, and how it can be often used instinctively to make negative associations about individuals that are not truth.
>
> So we must be careful to accept that the implicit bias that we all have is not racism. It is not bigotry. It is instinctive, unconscious thinking, and can even involve thinking that runs counter to our stated values. But it can result in unintended bias.

Justice Cady's summary entitled *A Justice System's Response to Implicit Bias*[45] is useful to other jurisdictions in understanding the link between injustice and neurology. As Justice Cady notes, the courts have a duty to both uphold justice and remove injustice, and advancements in social science and "brain science" have "helped to reveal injustice by giving greater understanding" to fundamental concepts of law. To focus on ways of curbing bias in the judicial system, Justice Cady lists the following examples: affording due process in juvenile court proceedings; understanding the realities of "cruel and unusual punishment" as stated in the United States Constitution; and better effectuating "equal protection." And Justice Cady lists "action steps" to overcome implicit bias such as training; reviewing decision-making points including jury selection and jury instructions; establishing groups to devise solutions; and structuring courts to better address the problem. All these methods can be transferred across jurisdictions to state and federal courts to reduce the impact of bias in their daily operations.

B. The National Judicial College's Efforts at Overcoming Implicit Bias

i. The NJC's Work Generally Speaking

Founded in 1963, The National Judicial College is the United States' oldest, largest, and most widely attended institution for judicial education. A unique nonprofit and nonpartisan institution, the NJC serves a comprehensive breadth of our judiciary: the categories of judges it educates decide more than 95% of all cases in the United States. It is singular in that it teaches courtroom skills to judges from across the nation, Indian Country, and international jurisdictions.[46] The NJC also offers elective courses that are approved as part of the University of Nevada, Reno Master's and Ph.D. programs in Judicial Studies.[47]

The NJC is committed to a prominent role in the cause of justice by teaching judges how they may best serve society and the law, particularly in the array of jurisdictions in which they sit. Its enduring mission of racial justice is reinforced by the College's multidisciplinary and multimodal approaches to judicial education, with a comprehensive focus on the issue of implicit bias and the means of overcoming bias that may contaminate judicial actions. The NJC's expansive scope and diverse outreach and academic programs link it uniquely to critical legal issues with extensive impacts on our nation and the collaborative global world. It seeks and defines ways to enhance the aptitudes of the courts as institutions, and the judiciary as individuals of singular responsibility in upholding the law.

The College provides abundant online material related to judicial ethics and bias. For example, a series of webinars recorded in 2020 aims to enable "America's judges [to] confront the system's culpability for racial injustice and mount a search for solutions." The website includes a link to a list of *Twenty Actions Judges Can Take to Combat Racial Injustice*, which are drawn from the NJC's *Conversations on Racial Justice* webinars presented in the wake of the George Floyd killing. There is also a template from the NCSC to facilitate a "survey of all who pass through your courts about their perception of its access and fairness."[48]

ii. The NJC's Work on Implicit Bias in Particular

Substantial studies in neuroscience and social science demonstrate that there are multiple lifetime drivers of bias, which may surface in judicial decisions and which legal history demonstrates are problematic in achieving social justice.[49] In this context, and knowing that it is hard to recognize biases within ourselves, the NJC relies on a diverse faculty with a rich variety of backgrounds and experiences and offers a range of methods and courses.[50] In addition to general courses that provide essential bench skills that are of value in addressing implicit bias,[51] the NJC conducts highly-regarded specialized courses that target the effects of bias on the judiciary in particular and society as a whole.[52] Among these is *When Justice Fails: Threats to the Independence of the Judiciary*, a course that has variously examined case studies from the Holocaust, the incarceration of Japanese Americans during World War II, and other struggles involving racial equality and civil rights.[53] Similarly, the NJC offers specialized symposia such as *Judging the Book by More Than Its Cover: A Symposium on Juries, Implicit Bias, and the Justice System's Response* The accompanying report summarizes research on implicit bias as it relates to jury trials and provides "takeaways" describing helpful approaches adopted by various courts and juries to address the problem.[54]

In its offerings, the NJC uses proven teaching methods—visual, aural, print, tactile, interactive, and kinesthetic—and a variety of approaches. Judges engage in lectures grounded in thorough research; study stories, film, and literature to enhance interest and lesson retention; participate in learning circles, an approach adapted from tribal practices in which participants share experiences and interpretation; and receive takeaways such as topical bench cards, bench books, research, and reference resources. Instructors endeavor to make the classes engaging and memorable and are mindful to create a safe space for vulnerability, an important consideration for sensitive topics such as implicit bias.

5. Measuring, Managing, and Responding to Questions of Judicial Ethics and Implicit Bias

The sanctity of the judicial system itself lies at the very heart and purpose of judicial education on implicit bias: if the judges making decisions fail to adhere to the highest standards, the fabric of the law is rendered asunder, threatening the society that devised a legal system to protect its sanctity. The ABA Model Code of Judicial Conduct (MCJC), adopted by many states, clarifies each judge's obligation to ensure the integrity of law through the avoidance of even the appearance of impropriety. Canon 2.3 directly forbids bias, whether actual, apparent, explicit, or implicit:

Canon 2.3 Bias, Prejudice, and Harassment

2.3(A) A judge shall perform the duties of judicial office, including administrative duties, without bias or prejudice.

2.3(B) A judge shall not, in the performance of judicial duties, by words or conduct manifest bias or prejudice, or engage in harassment, including but not limited to bias, prejudice, or harassment based upon race, sex, gender, religion, national origin, ethnicity, disability, age, sexual orientation, marital status, socioeconomic status, or political affiliation, and shall not permit court staff, court officials, or others subject to the judge's direction and control to do so.[55]

Various state codes of judicial conduct instruct judges in meeting ethical obligations. For example, California's Code of Judicial Ethics specifically provides, in addition to general requirements to uphold the integrity and independence of the judiciary, the following strictures on performing judicial duties:

Judges must perform their judicial duties without bias or prejudice. They must not, in the performance of their judicial duties, engage in speech, gestures, or other conduct that would reasonably be perceived as bias, prejudice, or harassment, including, but not limited to, bias, prejudice, or harassment based on race, sex, gender, gender identity, gender expression, religion, national origin, ethnicity, disability, age, sexual orientation, marital status, socioeconomic status, political affiliation, or sexual harassment.[56]

Echoing MCJC Canon 2.3(B), California places an affirmative duty upon judges to ensure that attorneys in proceedings before them refrain from similar objectionable conduct. This includes "unconscious as well as conscious bias or prejudice" based upon the categories above. "Judicial officers" are told to "take steps to help reduce [such] incivility by calling [it] out for what it is and insisting that it not be repeated." In an extreme case, judges are authorized to "report the offending attorney to the State Bar."[57]

Today society places demands upon the judiciary in light of heightened social and political unrest. It is crucially important whether judges may appropriately respond to social justice issues, and if so, what limits are placed upon propriety. While codes of judicial conduct help guide judges in the performance of their official duties, what sets bounds for their actions off the bench that may affect how they are regarded while on the bench?

Conclusion: A Path Forward in Overcoming Implicit Bias

This Chapter surveys the pervasive problem of implicit bias confronting the judiciary and the extensive efforts of those engaged in reversing its negative impacts. Bias is documented for its cause and effect throughout our legal history. This review and analysis is systematic, including both judges and the institutions of the judiciary. It recognizes that self-awareness is a crucial first step, the prompt to judges to consider their own judicial practice to resolve the crisis of implicit bias and overcome this inhibitor to the justice system.

Implicit bias involves not only judicial decisions but the publications and orations made by judges, often relied on as members of our learned society. But the analysis is not limited to judges or to a particular subject. Decisions that may be affected by bias extend from property to tort to contract to employment law and to virtually every type of criminal/civil/human rights issue. Bias results in varied consequences in the several roles of court administrators and personnel, parties witnesses, and jurors.

While recognizing the depressive effects of a cause of the miscarriage of justice, the efforts by those dedicated to fair judicial practice are encouraging. Several institutions and courts have implemented a comprehensive educational design to reverse this stain on the integrity of the judicial system. Bias education involves both the steps taken in individual jurisdictions and in the national and international arenas, using methodologies centered on academic traditions of coursework, teaching, and learning. As for all modern curriculum development, content and methodology must be developed in concert with the sciences that explain the input, storage, and access of information in the brain. Those are the processes that both create bias and are available to combat bias through education. There is naught to contradict the need to continually remind the judiciary of this problem, and update all effective forms of judicial education: local, regional, national, international.

As for all modern curriculum development, content and methodology must be developed in concert with the sciences that explain the input, storage, and access of information in the brain. This Chapter contains recommendations for overcoming implicit bias that have been generated by scholars, scientists, and those in the legal profession. The measures proposed by the jurists in Section 3.A. are of special value, since those who were interviewed are among the most respected members of the judiciary and represent groups that have been particularly targeted by implicit bias. Ensuring a fair and just society relies upon doing so; let it not be said, this was where justice failed.

So, You'd Like to Know More

- Jerry Kang, What Judges Can Do about Implicit Bias, 57 Ct. Rev. 78 (2021).
- Debra Stephens & Veronica Galván, Why Judges Should Not Mistake the Norm for the Neutral, 57 Ct. Rev. 92 (2021).
- Reba Ann Page & Robert J. Torres, As Judge and Citizen: An Ethical Path to Racial Justice, 57 Ct. Rev. 72 (2021).
- Justin D. Levinson, Mark W. Bennett & Koichi Hioki, Judging Implicit Bias: A National Empirical Study of Judicial Stereotypes, 69 Fla. L. Rev. 63 (2017).
- Shawn C. Marsh, The Lens of Implicit Bias, Juvenile and Family Justice Today, Summer 2009, https://www.ncifci.org/sites/default/files/Implicit Bias.pdf.
- Shawn C. Marsh & Diane C. Marsh, Being Explicit about Implicit Bias Education for the Judiciary, 56 Ct. Rev. 92, (2020).
- Jeffrey L. Rachlinski, Sheri Johnson, Andrew J. Wistrich & Chris Guthrie, Does Unconscious Racial Bias Affect Trial Judges? 84 Notre Dame L. Rev. 1196 (2008–2009).
- Katheryn L. Yetter & Brian M. Lee, Judging the Book by More Than Its Cover: A Symposium on Juries, Implicit Bias, and the Justice System's Response (The National Judicial College, 2020), https://www.judges.org/resources/judging-the-book-by-more-than-its-cover/.

Note from the Editors: many of the reports and publications referred to in this Chapter appear or are referenced in other Chapters.

About the Authors

Benes Z. Aldana (B.A., J.D.) is President and Chief Executive Officer of The National Judicial College. He is the former chief trial judge of the United States Coast Guard. Judge Aldana earned his B.A. degree from Seattle University and his J.D. from the University of Washington School of Law.

Reba Ann Page (J.D., Ph.D.) is a judge on the United States Armed Services Board of Contract Appeals; the opinions expressed herein are solely hers, and do not represent the United States government. Judge Page earned her B.A. and M.S. degrees in Biology and J.D. from the University of Louisville, and her Masters and Ph.D. in Judicial Studies from University of Nevada, Reno.

Endnotes

1. These definitions were drawn from Shawn C. Marsh, *The Lens of Implicit Bias*, Juvenile and Family Justice Today, 16–19, (2009) https://www.ncjfcj.org/wp-content/uploads/2012/09/The-Lens-of-Implicit-Bias_0.pdf.

2. Dan Balz, *After a Year of Pandemic and Protest, and a Big Election, America is as Divided as Ever*, Wash. Post, Dec. 27, 2020, https://www.washingtonpost.com/graphics/2020/politics/elections-reckoning/.

3. David Nakamura, *With 'Kung Flu,' Trump Sparks Backlash over Racist Language – and a Rallying Cry for Supporters*, Wash. Post, June 24, 2020, https://www.washingtonpost.com/politics/with-kung-flu-trump-sparks-backlash-over-racist-language--and-a-rallying-cry-for-supporters/2020/06/24/485d151e-b620-11ea-aca5-ebb63d27e1ff_story.html.

4. Tim Arango, *Derek Chauvin Receives 22 and a Half Years for Murder of George Floyd*, N.Y. Times, June 25, 2021, https://www.nytimes.com/2021/06/25/us/derek-chauvin-22-and-a-half-years-george-floyd.html.

5. Joanna Slater, *As Kamala D. Harris Breaks Barriers, India and Jamaica Celebrate*, Wash. Post, Nov. 7, 2020, https://www.washingtonpost.com/world/asia_pacific/kamala-harris-india-vice-president/2020/11/07/e7842736-1ecb-11eb-ad53-4c1fda49907d_story.html.

6. *See* Equal Justice Initiative, Lynching in America: Confronting the Legacy of Racial Terror (3d. ed., 2017). The EJI criticized the decision in *McCleskey v. Kemp*, 481 U.S. 279 (1987) noting that although "the Supreme Court considered statistical evidence demonstrating that Georgia decisionmakers were more than four times as likely to impose death for the killing of a white person than a black person" and accepted "the data as accurate, the Court described racial bias in sentencing as 'an inevitable part of our criminal justice system.'" Still, the justices upheld Mr. McCleskey's "death sentence because he had failed to identify a 'constitutionally significant risk of racial bias.'" *Id.* at 64 (further citation omitted).

7. In the "Baldus Report," Professor Baldus performed a sophisticated analysis of over 2,000 murders that took place in Georgia in the 1970s and looked at 230 different variables in calculating whether the death penalty was likely to be imposed. As noted by the Court, "The raw numbers collected by Professor Baldus indicate that defendants charged with killing white persons received the death penalty in 11% of the cases, but defendants charged with killing blacks received the death penalty in only 1% of the cases." *McCleskey*, 481 U.S. at 286.

8. *McCleskey*, 481 U.S. at 339. For further discussion of the use of statistics to establish racial bias, *see, e.g.,* Marc Price Wolf, *Proving Race Discrimination in Criminal Cases Using Statistical Evidence*, Hastings Race & Poverty L.J. 39 (2007).

9. *McCleskey*, 481 U.S. at 343 (citing Dred Scott v. Sandford, 60 U.S. 393, 407 (1856).

10. *Id.*

11. *Id.* at 344 (citing Plessy v. Ferguson, 163 U.S. 537, 552 (1896).

12. *Id.*

13. Texas Dep't of Housing and Cmty. Affairs v. Inclusive Communities Project, Inc., 576 U.S. 519, 527 (2015).

14. Watson v. Fort Worth Bank & Trust, 487 U.S. 977, 933–94 (1988).

15. *See, e.g.,* Jennifer D. Roberts, *Pandemics and Protests: America Has Experienced Racism Like This Before*, Brookings Inst., June 9, 2021, https://www.brookings.edu/blog/how-we-rise/2021/06/09/pandemics-and-protests-america-has-experienced-racism-like-this-before/.

16. *Dred Scott*, 60 U.S. at 407.

17. *Plessy*, 163 U.S. at 537.

18. *See Senior Judge Reggie B. Walton*, D. CT. D.C., https://www.dcd.uscourts.gov/content/senior-judge-reggie-b-walton (last visited Oct. 19, 2021).

19. *See Robert R. Torres, Jr., Associate Justice*, GUAM SUP. CT., http://guamsupremecourt.com/Justices/Honorable_Robert_J_Torres_Jr.html (last visited Oct. 19, 2021).

20. Unlike African Americans or Asian Americans, Hispanics/Latinos are defined by national origin and not by race. The broadly-based identity of the Hispanic/Latino community is recognized in U.S. CENSUS BUREAU, OVERVIEW OF RACE AND HISPANIC ORIGIN, 2010 CENSUS BRIEFS. The term "Latinx" is used as a non-gender specific reference.

21. *See* KING CNTY, *Judge Veronica Galván*, https://kingcounty.gov/~/media/courts/superior-court/docs/judges/Galván-bio.ashx?la=en (last visited Oct 19, 2021).

22. Access to their Zoom interviews and a transcript of their remarks is available at Judges.org/Judicial-Bias-Interviews.

23. *See* About EJI, EQUAL JUST. INITIATIVE, https://eji.org/about (last visited Oct 19, 2021). *See also* BRYAN STEVENSON, JUST MERCY (2014). The best-selling book, which relates some of the author's work with death row inmates, was made into an award-winning feature film.

24. *See* Michael Spezio, *Automating Incarceration*, 373 SCI. MAG. 287 (2021), https://science.sciencemag.org/content/373/6552/287, for a review of CHRISTOPHER SLOBOGIN, JUST ALGORITHMS (2021), in which the author advocates using artificial intelligence in determining the nature and duration of sentences for criminal conduct.

25. SARAH E. REDFIELD ET AL., IMPLICIT BIAS IS REAL, IMPLICIT BIAS TRAINING MATTERS: RESPONDING TO THE NEGATIVE PRESS (Social Science Research Network, 2020) https://ssrn.com/abstract=3686762 or http://dx.doi.org/10.2139/ssrn.3686762.

26. Anna-Leigh Firth, *Most Judges Believe the Criminal Justice System Suffers from Racism*, JUD. EDGE (July 14, 2020), https://www.judges.org/news-and-info/most-judges-believe-the-criminal-justice-system-suffers-from-racism/.

27. *See, e.g.*, Jeffrey L. Rachlinski, Sheri Johnson, Andrew J. Wistrich & Chris Guthrie, *Does Unconscious Racial Bias Affect Trial Judges?*, 84 NOTRE DAME L. REV. 1196 (2008–2009).

28. *Id.*

29. *Id.*

30. *Id.*

31. Autumn King, *Most Judges Believe this Tactic Can Help Eliminate Implicit Bias in Court*, JUD. EDGE (July 16, 2021), https://www.judges.org/news-and-info/judges-believe-this-tactic-can-help-eliminate-implicit-bias-in-court/.

32. At the time, some criticized composer Richard Rodgers and lyricist Oscar Hammerstein for their thought-provoking production. A group of Georgia state legislators even introduced a bill to ban a touring performance, which they claimed had "an underlying philosophy inspired by Moscow." *See, e.g.*, Andrea Most, *"You've Got to Be Carefully Taught": The Politics of Race in Rodgers and Hammerstein's South Pacific*, 52 THEATER J. 307 (2000).

33. *See* AM. BAR ASS'N, ABA RESOLUTION 116G, https://www.americanbar.org/content/dam/aba/directories/policy/annual-2020/116g-annual-2020.pdf.

34. *See* Texas Dep't of Housing and Cmty. Affairs, 576 U.S. 519 (2015) and *Watson*, 487 U.S. 977 (1988), *supra* notes 14, 15.

35. *See Mission & History*, NAT'L CTR. FOR STATE COURTS, https://www.ncsc.org/about-us/mission-and-history (last visited Oct. 19, 2021).

36. The NCSC/CJE website provides a wealth of resources for those interested in judicial ethics. *See, e.g.,* https://ncsc-search.squiz.cloud/s/search.html?collection=ncsc-meta&profile=_default&query=cje. CJE Director Cynthia Gray publishes frequently about judicial ethics; *see, e.g.,* CYNTHIA GRAY, A STUDY OF STATE JUDICIAL DISCIPLINE SANCTIONS (2002); *also* Cynthia Gray, *The Center for Judicial Ethics: An Evolving Clearinghouse*, 96 JUDICATURE 305 (2013); and Cynthia Gray, "How Judicial Commissions Work," 28 JUST. SYS. J. 405 (2007).

37. JERRY KANG, IMPLICIT BIAS - A PRIMER FOR COURTS (Aug. 2009), http://wp.jerrykang.net.s110363.gridserver.com/wp-content/uploads/2010/10/kang-Implicit-Bias-Primer-for-courts-09.pdf.

38. JENNIFER K. ELEK & ANDREA L. MILLER, THE EVOLVING SCIENCE ON IMPLICIT BIAS: AN UPDATED RESOURCE FOR THE STATE COURT COMMUNITY (National Center for State Courts, 2021), https://ncsc.contentdm.oclc.org/digital/collection/accessfair/id/911.

39. A link to this Resolution is provided at https://www.judges.org/racial-justice/.

40. PAMELA M. CASEY ET AL., HELPING COURTS ADDRESS IMPLICIT BIAS: RESOURCES FOR EDUCATION (National Center for State Courts, 2012), https://ncsc.contentdm.oclc.org/digital/collection/accessfair/id/246/. The report grew from the "National Campaign to Ensure the Racial and Ethnic Fairness of America's State Courts," which was mobilized in 2006 to bring together the "significant expertise, experience, and commitment of state court judges and court officers to ensure both the perception and reality of racial and ethnic fairness in the nation's state courts."

41. *Id.* at 7.

42. *Id.* at 21–31.

43. *See also* JENNIFER JUHLER & MARK CADY, MORALITY, DECISION-MAKING, AND JUDICIAL ETHICS (Am. Bar Ass'n, n.d.), https://www.americanbar.org/content/dam/aba/administrative/professional_responsibility/judicialethics/resources/comm_code_cady_undated.pdf.

44. Justice Cady's remarks were made at the 2016 Iowa Summit on Justice and Disparities, which was sponsored by the Iowa-Nebraska Conference of the NAACP.

45. MARK S. CADY, A JUSTICE SYSTEM'S RESPONSE TO IMPLICIT BIAS (Omaha Bar Ass'n, 2017), https://cdn.ymaws.com/www.omahabarassociation.com/resource/resmgr/cle/Handout_for_CJ_Cady_Presenta.pdf.

46. The Federal Judicial Center serves federal judges on Article III courts, https://www.judges.org/about/.

47. The success of its programs and wide scope of the NJC's ongoing efforts to engage judges, other legal professionals as well as those in related disciplines, academics, and members of affected communities can be viewed by perusing its website, found at https://www/judges.org.

48. *See generally Conversations on Racial Justice,* judges.org/racial-justice/.

49. The book ENHANCING JUSTICE: REDUCING BIAS (Sarah E. Redfield ed., American Bar Association, 2017) examines the extremely complex relationship between neurological and the social roots of bias. Contributing authors explore causes, effects, and proposed recommended strategies for reducing bias; *see also* Nicole E. Negowetti, *Navigating the Pitfalls of Implicit Bias: A Cognitive Science Primer for Civil Litigators*, 4 ST. MARY'S J. LEGAL MAL. & ETHICS 278 (2014).

50. For instance, judges studying implicit bias are taught about testing commonly used in the field, such as the Implicit Assessment Test (IAT), which is widely used by psychologists, social scientists, and other researchers. *See, e.g.*, Anthony G. Greenwald & Linda Hamilton Krieger, *Implicit Bias: Scientific Foundations*, 94 CAL. L. REV. 945 (2006); Christine Jolls & Cass R. Sunstein, *The Law of Implicit Bias*, 94 CAL. L. REV. 969 (2006); Renee Clary, James Wandersee & Janet Schexnayder Elias, *Does Color-Coding of Examination Versions Affect College Science Students' Test Performance? Countering Claims of Bias*, 37 JOURNAL OF COLLEGE SCIENCE TEACHING 40 (2007).

51. Among the general courses are *Ethics and Judging, Reaching Higher Ground*; *Taking the Bench*, a series of interactive courses tailored to general jurisdiction, administrative law, specialized courts, and tribal judges; *Mindfulness for Judges*; *Conducting the Trial*; *Judicial Writing*; *Ethics, Fairness and Security in Your Courtroom and Community*; and *Decision Making*.

52. The NJC trains its faculty to use many instructional methods that are designed to best reach audiences of varying skills and preferences; *see, e.g., Designing and Presenting: A Faculty Development Workshop*, THE NATIONAL JUDICIAL COLLEGE, https://www.judges.org/courses/designing-and-presenting-a-faculty-development-workshop/.

53. Other specialized courses educating judges on addressing bias include *A Thoughtful Approach to Racially Impartial, Research-Based Sentencing* and *An Overview of Afrocentric Facial Feature and Skin Tone Bias in Criminal Law*.

54. This program is discussed in KATHERYN L. YETTER & BRIAN M. LEE, JUDGING THE BOOK BY MORE THAN ITS COVER: A SYMPOSIUM ON JURIES, IMPLICIT BIAS, AND THE JUSTICE SYSTEM'S RESPONSE (NJC 2020), https://www.judges.org/resources/judging-the-book-by-more-than-its-cover/. *See also* Chad Schmucker & Joseph Sawyer, *Decision Making, Implicit Bias, and Judges: Is This Blindfold Really Working?*, *in* ENHANCING JUSTICE: REDUCING BIAS (Sarah E. Redfield ed. 2017) at 1–4.

55. Excerpted from the ABA Model Code of Justice, https://www.americanbar.org/groups/professional_responsibility/publications/model_code_of_judicial_conduct/model_code_of_judicial_conduct_canon_2/rule2_3biasprejudiceandharassment/. *See also* ABA Model Rules of Professional Responsibility, Rule 8.4: "It is professional misconduct for a lawyer to:... g) engage in conduct that the lawyer knows or reasonably should know is harassment or discrimination on the basis of race, sex, religion, national origin, ethnicity, disability, age, sexual orientation, gender identity, marital status or socioeconomic status in conduct related to the practice of law..."

56. CAL. JUDGES BENCHBOOK CIV. PROC. TRIAL § 1.5 (2021).

57. *Id.*

TWELVE

The Past, Present, and Future Trajectory of Implicit Bias Education for the Judiciary

Tyler N. Livingston, Angelo State University, San Angelo, TX
Shawn C. Marsh, University of Nevada, Reno, NV
The Honorable John H. Larsen, California Public Utilities Commission

Note from the Editors: Dr. Marsh was a contributor to *Enhancing Justice: Reducing Bias*, and we are very grateful that he has joined *Extending Justice* as well. He is a long-time thinker, researcher, trainer, and writer about implicit bias and the justice system and one of the most insightful professors we know. In this Chapter, he is joined by two co-authors who also have extensive academic and hands-on experience educating around and working to interrupt implicit bias. It perhaps goes without saying that all work to assure a judiciary that is and is perceived as being fair and equitable is critical to the ongoing viability of our judicial system; and training the judiciary to recognize their implicit biases is critical to this end. Our own experience as trainers has shown over and over that judges, who see the very definition of their work as being fair, are eager to understand the scientific basis of the implicit bias research and to learn to interrupt that bias and limit its negative manifestations.

In addition to reviewing the trajectory of judicial education on implicit bias, the authors consider the criticism that implicit bias training doesn't work, a subject near and dear to our hearts—believing as we do from our own research and lived-experience that well-constructed training does work to change individuals and norms. The authors' honest insights as to the path and importance of judicial training and education should help us all think through how to intervene most usefully to achieve awareness of implicit bias and change norms based on that awareness.

CHAPTER HIGHLIGHTS

- Implicit bias education for the judiciary represents an opportunity to benefit all who contact the courts.
- This Chapter reviews the past, present, and future of implicit bias research and education and reflects on initial promise, recent controversy, and future innovation.
- Implicit bias reduction at each decision point in the legal system remains a critically important effort requiring collaboration between researchers, educators, and judges.

CHAPTER CONTENTS

Introductory Note

1. The General Trajectory of Implicit Bias as a Topic of Judicial Education
2. Past: Initial Promise and Adoption
    A. Research: The IAT Uncovers the Implicit Social Mind
    B. Education: Legal Scholars Embrace Self-Insight
3. Present: Controversy and Criticism
    A. Research: Thrust into the Popular Culture and Associated Attention
    B. Education: Disparate Methods and Varied Success
    C. A Note on Positionality: Effects of Judicial Attitudes on Judicial Decision-Making
4. Future: Preserving the Best and Improving the Rest
    A. Research: Future Directions More Apparent Under Pressure
    B. Education: Recent Insights Fuel Future Innovation

Conclusion

Introductory Note

We wrote this chapter as multiple and intertwined crises dominated national attention in the U.S. One of the most serious pandemics in modern history had killed over 200,000 people in our country since the start of 2020, leaving us with some of the highest Covid-19-related infection and death rates in the world. The total number of fatalities in the U.S. has since surpassed 600,000. Masks and social distancing were our primary tools to fight the virus as we awaited development and testing of a vaccine, but both had become highly controversial and politicized. Political polarization of the vaccine has not ceased since its deployment. In the midst of this pandemic, racial inequalities existed in access to healthcare and overall infection and death rates.[1]

The chaos introduced by Covid-19 was not the nation's only crisis. Former president Trump left a legacy of division and conflict in the U.S. that fell along major party lines, including impeachment proceedings, controversial appointments to the Supreme Court, chaotic presidential debates, accusations of internal systemic voting fraud and suppression, and unaddressed foreign interference in American elections. These conflicts culminated in a riotous and ultimately deadly attempt at insurrection at the U.S. Capitol on January 6, 2021. Overlying this toxic political landscape was the issue of climate change—an environmental issue not acknowledged by the former president—and its proposed connections to natural disasters such as the droughts and wildfires that continue to ravage western states.

During these unprecedented times, perhaps the most notable stressor given our history and given that it permeates these other crises/social issues was the civil and racial unrest associated with myriad deaths of Black citizens, such as George Floyd and Breonna Taylor, at the hands of police. These events led to protests, looting, and calls for comprehensive police reform. Again, the various sides to these issues were politicized and often fell along party lines. There was some evidence that radical rightwing and leftwing ideologies (e.g., Proud Boys, Antifa) usurped peaceful demonstrations and contributed to violence.

Race remains a central issue in our country. Noted crises serve to highlight the insidious nature of systemic and institutional racism that has recently been characterized as a caste system.[2] Citizens are not alone in struggling with what is next for this nation. Systems of education, health, justice, and others are revisiting best practices in the face of racial tension and clearer need for reform. Although our current reform debate in the U.S. is focused on law enforcement and reducing racism/violence, judges are critical actors in pursuing equal and fair access to justice given their role and status in our justice system.

Central to this discussion of race and other identity characteristics is the concept of implicit bias and how it might impact decisions. *Implicit bias* refers to a cognitive process that occurs outside of a person's awareness and that unduly shifts decision-making toward a particular outcome.[3] Well-intended decisions might be infused with implicit bias based on race, gender, or other demographic variables. Not surprisingly, education regarding social cognition and bias is a major tenet of systemic efforts to combat racism and encourage diversity and inclusion. It is not without critics, including former president Trump, who issued an executive order banning race/sex training workshops based on "divisive concepts" in Federal agencies, and other public figures who insist there is no issue of racism in our country.[4]

This stance is in sharp contrast to a recent Harvard Law School report that revealed how institutional racism permeates the criminal justice system and contributes to racial disparities in incarceration rates.[5]

Indeed, judicial education has focused on implicit bias in recent decades[6] under the belief that along with other known challenges (e.g., institutional) such bias does influence equity and fairness in the pursuit of justice and that better understanding of its form and function individually and collectively will improve practice and outcomes (e.g., reduce disparate outcomes, reduce disproportionate confinement, ensure fairness).[7] As issues such as racism, bias, discrimination, diversity, inclusion, equality, equity, and related others dominate the larger public conversation, the present time in history poses the question: What is next for judicial education on the topic of implicit bias given the role of judges in our justice system?

1. The General Trajectory of Implicit Bias as a Topic in Judicial Education

This Chapter suggests answers to the question of what is next for the judiciary in terms of bias education. We review the past, present, and future milestones in implicit bias *research* and *education*. Early forms of implicit bias research gained widespread attention and generated novel educational approaches targeted at the judiciary. Over time, constructive skeptics and obstructive cynics, respectively, aimed to improve or reject implicit bias research and education. This crossroads resulted in diverse contemporary perspectives on the merits of implicit bias education. We argue in favor of a nuanced view of implicit bias education into the future that addresses shortcomings and expands on observed effects. We suggest next steps that integrate findings from a recent survey of judicial educators on this topic. As our country can emerge stronger after crisis, we believe implicit bias education can emerge improved after criticism.

In presenting our history and suggestions for what comes next, we acknowledge several assumptions. First, we assume implicit bias exists, despite an ongoing yet constructive academic debate as to the nature and implications of this psychological construct. Second, we assume there is inherent value to learning about how the human brain processes social information. Third, we assume a devotion to the scientific method and empiricism. Fourth, we assume most people who work to educate others about implicit bias have meritorious intentions and desire beneficial progress. Fifth, although in the context of judges and specific to their experiences, we assume there are lessons here for others in the justice field seeking to improve education, practice, and policy. Lastly, we assume appreciation for the complexity of this topic while remaining positive that people and systems can and do change and become less biased in practice with thoughtful intervention.

Since its conception as a topic of judicial education, implicit bias has engaged researchers, educators, and professionals in a continuous process of innovation and refinement. The initial promise of implicit bias education to improve judicial practice inspired great attention and excitement from the judiciary. More recently, education on implicit bias reached a critical point of reflection and retooling in response to methodological criticisms from psychologists and practical concerns from practitioners. The future provides boundless opportunity for stakeholders to leverage newfound technologies and insights to deliver on the fundamental promises of implicit bias education: to enhance justice for all who contact the judicial system.

2. Past: Initial Promise and Adoption

The storied past of implicit bias research and education began in earnest in the 1980s. This decade saw social psychologists adapt existing methods from cognitive psychology to document an unconscious, *implicit* process of social categorization that occurred automatically in interpersonal interaction. The creation of the Implicit Association Test (IAT) allowed researchers to measure the magnitude and direction of implicit bias and spawned dozens of early research studies examining implicit social cognition. Simultaneous to these empirical developments, visionary legal thinkers theorized about the potential for collective racism, embedded in culture and reinforced subtly, to explain differential legal outcomes for people of color. These developments converged in the early 2000s to produce the first widespread curricula for judicial education on implicit bias.

A. Research: The IAT Uncovers the Implicit Social Mind

Prominent cognitive psychologist George A. Miller speculated that people are consciously aware only of the *result* of their thinking, but not the process contributing to that result.[8] This hypothesis suggested that variables outside of a decision-maker's awareness could influence behavior. By the 1980s, early researchers of the implicit mind began to illuminate the decision-making process to identify the unconscious underlying factors proposed by Miller. In a now-classic study of implicit association, research participants who first read words associated with pleasant meanings (e.g., *music*) later categorized other positive-sounding words (e.g., *delightful*) more quickly than they categorized negative-sounding words (e.g., *repulsive*).[9] The same pattern emerged for participants who first read words associated with unpleasant meanings (e.g., *death*), and who were subsequently quicker to categorize negative-sounding words. These findings evidenced an implicit process whereby exposure to a given concept (i.e., music, death) could facilitate or inhibit subsequent behavior (i.e., response times). A natural extension of these findings was to social situations.

Following initial investigations of implicit association, researchers in the 1990s and early 2000s applied principles of implicit cognition to social decision-making.[10] If automatic word associations were measurable and could affect categorization decisions, it stood to reason that similarly automatic associations with identity groups (e.g., based on race or gender or other categories) might exist and exert bias on social behavior. Researchers suspected that biases based in social categories, deeply ingrained via culture and upbringing, could greatly influence interpersonal evaluations.[11] The IAT, which uses computer software to assess response times to social stimuli, quickly became the most prominent tool to measure implicit bias in social cognition.[12] The IAT presents participants with a target word (e.g., *happy, awful*) or picture (e.g., a Black face or a White face) and instructs participants to quickly assign the target to one of two categories (e.g., *good, bad*). In the aggregate, participants more quickly and accurately assign words like *happy* and pictures of White faces to categories that contain the word *good*. Such a response pattern reveals implicit bias to more readily pair White faces, compared to Black faces, with positive categories. A common interpretation of this result is that participants harbor an automatic preference for White faces over Black faces.

The IAT quickly gained attention as the premiere measure of implicit bias due to its simplicity and provocative results (to take an IAT online for free, visit https://implicit.harvard.edu/implicit/takeatest.html). Contrary to self-reports that can vary depending on respondents' perceptions of experimenter expectations or social desirability, implicit attitudes are beyond awareness and less susceptible to self-censorship. Many participants found that their IAT results conflicted with their explicitly held egalitarian beliefs, and even some Black participants demonstrated a bias against their own race. These striking findings intrigued researchers studying prejudice and discrimination. Continued examination indicated that although self-report data showed a year-over-year reduction in explicit racial and gender bias,[13] implicit bias remained prevalent in indirect measures such as the IAT. Researchers believed they had devised a novel measure of bias existent in the mind but previously hidden from direct observation. Early implicit bias research suggested that prejudice in the modern era was more covert but as pervasive as ever.[14] Methods of education regarding implicit bias quickly arose with the intent to enhance awareness of implicit biases and reduce their influence on behavior.

B. Education: Legal Scholars Embrace Self-Insight

Around the same time that psychologists conducted the first experimental studies of implicit bias, legal scholars theorized about unconscious sources of discrimination that might affect the legal profession. Professor Charles R. Lawrence III suggested in 1987 that racial discrimination can occur unintentionally in the application of the law due to collective attitudes and beliefs associated with race.[15]

His understanding of implicit bias informed his assertion that "we are all racists" who are largely "unaware of our racism."[16] Lawrence's articulation of implicit bias in the law influenced a generation of legal scholars and critical race theorists[17] and contributed to a groundswell of interest in judicial education on these issues. The notion of implicit bias in the judiciary reached critical mass in the two decades following Lawrence's original publication. Legal scholars began to examine how implicit bias operates in the judiciary and conceptualized opportunities for education.

By 2009, Professor Charles Ogletree famously called for the inclusion of implicit bias training in judicial education as a means of reducing the disproportionate incarceration of people of color.[18] Ogletree believed that social psychological research applied to legal decisions could deliver justice to more people. Judicial education regarding implicit bias took hold around this time, leading to the first scholarly papers aimed at proposing remedies for implicit bias in judicial decision-making.[19] Many of these papers emphasized the potential for implicit bias to accumulate at decision points throughout the legal process, from initial contact with the justice system to case resolution.[20] A sense that education regarding implicit bias could solve the problem of racial disparities in legal outcomes prevailed throughout the judiciary, fueled in part by concurrent empirical research conducted with trial judges.

One landmark study by Professor Jeff Rachlinski and his colleagues demonstrated that trial judges held implicit racial biases at rates similar to, and sometimes greater than, the general population.[21] Among 85 participating White judges, 87.1% demonstrated a preference for White versus Black faces. By contrast, a sample of White non-judge participants from the general population demonstrated a weaker preference for White versus Black faces. Some Black judges also expressed implicit biases favoring White faces, but this preference was less consistent and no stronger than that of the general population of Black non-judges. Though potentially detrimental to the notion of the fair and impartial judge at first glance, findings also indicated that judges who are aware of potential bias mechanisms and motivated to provide equal treatment to all litigants could overwhelm their biases to produce fairer decisions.[22] Data from White judges in particular prompted these authors to recommend that new judges complete an IAT for the tandem purposes of self-reflection and education: self-reflection could alert judges of their potential to act with bias and simultaneously generate interest in curbing bias.

Professors Christine Jolls and Cass R. Sunstein suggested that although the law insulated outcomes from the effects of bias and explicitly prohibited discrimination (e.g., in hiring), implicit bias largely operated unfettered because it is difficult to detect.[23] These authors identified "indirect debiasing" strategies to limit the expression of implicit bias,[24] such as promoting diversity among judges and court staff and commemorating revered members of underrepresented groups (e.g., Dr. Martin

Luther King, Jr.) in the physical environment. In collaboration with the National Center for State Courts (NCSC), Professor Jerry Kang placed similar emphasis on the "malleability" of implicit biases in his introduction to implicit bias for judges.[25] Kang supported some of the strategies offered by Jolls and Sunstein and recommended additional methods to change the content of implicit biases. These methods included encouraging regular interaction with people of diverse backgrounds and committing to predetermined criteria before making decisions (thus reducing reliance on unconscious cues to inform legal judgments). Individual judges relatively easily implemented such strategies, but the challenge to formalize education with a view toward systemic reform remained.

Official guidance on implicit bias reduction soon emerged. The National Judicial College (NJC) incorporated social science findings in its model curriculum for judges to increase awareness as to how judges' backgrounds and personal experiences affect decision-making.[26] Trainings engaged judges in interactive modules designed to enhance mindfulness of automatic stereotypes and minimize their influence on decisions. Proponents of such trainings were careful to specify that the purpose of judicial education on implicit bias was to broaden judges' cross-cultural perspectives—not to impose a particular point of view.[27] Enthusiasm for such curricula grew in the ensuing decade and resulted in a wider array of educational approaches for the judiciary.

3. Present: Controversy and Criticism

The immense success of implicit bias research and early education garnered praise and critique. Although the IAT and other assessments of implicit bias clearly measured *something*, the extent to which implicit bias correlated with explicit bias or affected behavior and could be reduced via education became increasingly disputed. Methodological critiques seemed to undermine some bases of implicit bias research and strengthen others, resulting in rigorous but sometimes chaotic science. Perhaps sensing weakness in implicit bias as a construct, skeptics of education on the topic maligned aspects of curricula as driven by political correctness or hiding a racially divisive agenda. Proponents of implicit bias research and education continued to improve their work under this pressure, setting up for a prosperous future for judicial education on this important topic.

A. Research: Thrust into the Popular Culture and Associated Attention

The initial success of implicit bias research and education, and the proliferation of the concept into popular culture, was met with recent criticism. Those who are skeptical about the significance of implicit bias ask tough but valuable questions to fortify the construct; cynics lodge grievances to cast doubt on implicit bias as a topic of social science inquiry. Skeptics have identified substantive criticisms of the validity and reliability of implicit bias measures such as the IAT. Cynics have expressed incredulity at the mere existence of implicit bias, perhaps uncomfortable with the notion of covert negative influences on behavior. Present controversy and criticism related to implicit bias represent a marked shift in the trajectory of research on the topic and an opportunity for improvement.

The concept of implicit bias has uniquely interested laypeople and professionals outside of social science. Most major news and popular media publications in the U.S. have published articles describing potential influences of implicit bias in a variety of domains such as health care, policing, education, and employment. The great extent to which the notion of implicit bias has entered the mainstream is evident in recent statements by politicians including Hillary Clinton, who argued during a 2016 presidential debate that "implicit bias is a problem for everyone, not just police,"[28] and then-Senator Kamala Harris, who stated during the 2020 vice presidential debate that "Joe Biden and I recognize that implicit bias does exist."[29] Although implicit bias has achieved cultural acknowledgement, researchers continue to elucidate the construct and debate its validity and reliability.

Implicit bias remains a popular topic of research in 2021. The academic content database OneSearch yielded nearly 2,000 journal articles containing the term "implicit bias" published in the year 2020 alone. More than 700 of these journal articles pertained specifically to law. Within this vast literature, a theme of criticism emerged starting in 2006 that questioned the nature of implicit bias and its measurement.[30] Scholarly criticism of implicit bias has peaked in recent years, but perhaps so has its cultural salience and popularity as a topic of research.

Though the complete history of the lively academic debate related to implicit bias is beyond the scope of this Chapter, concerns about the extent to which measures of implicit bias predict behavior and yield consistent scores at multiple time points dominate the controversy.[31] Regarding behavioral prediction (i.e., a measure of validity), the correlations between measures of implicit bias and behavior are weak to moderate.[32] Among other possibilities, these relationships could indicate that implicit and explicit measures quantify fundamentally different constructs or that one measure is invalid (i.e., it does not assess its purported construct).[33] The IAT is the main target of the latter contention because its scores do not consistently indicate who, in real-world situations, will engage in discrimination.[34] Some prominent writers on these issues have recommended abandoning the IAT altogether.[35] However, the IAT remains a valuable instrument because predictions of behavior are most accurate when implicit and explicit measures correlate strongly.[36]

Regarding consistency, recent research indicates weak correlations between a person's scores on implicit measures at separate time points.[37] These correlations are notably weaker than correlations between explicit measures at separate time points, further cementing some scholars' preference for explicit measures of bias.[38] Despite these methodological concerns, implicit measures at the aggregate (vs. individual) level can provide valuable information regarding the extent of bias present in a population and targeted at particular social groups.[39]

B. Education: Disparate Methods and Varied Success

Educational offerings to reduce implicit bias expanded between 2010 and 2021 and became commonplace in many of America's large corporations,[40] law enforcement agencies,[41] educational institutions,[42] and health care settings.[43] The proliferation of implicit bias education into popular culture attracted criticism aimed largely at the unclear motivations and effectiveness of bias-reduction initiatives. Skeptics have questioned whether organizations offer (or, in some cases, mandate) implicit bias education to their personnel to avoid legal liability in circumstances of alleged discrimination,[44] regardless of whether the education program works.[45]

The Supreme Court's decision in *Kolstad v. American Dental Association* (1999) held that employers who made an effort to educate employees regarding harassment and discrimination could avoid punitive damages in relevant civil cases. This ruling has contributed to the growth of a lucrative consulting industry offering an assortment of trainings that vary in scientific merit.[46] Some psychologists have grown increasingly concerned about potential deleterious effects of implicit bias education conducted improperly, including normalizing or enhancing bias expression.[47] Education materials that simply emphasize the high prevalence of implicit bias might lead some people to mistakenly believe that any effort to reduce their own bias would be futile.[48] The present era of implicit bias education is characterized simultaneously by wide adoption and uncertainty.

Perhaps some criticism of implicit bias education stems from specific methods applied in workshops. Whereas the NJC has recommended self-reflection and interactive discussion regarding biased assumptions,[49] other more stressful and controversial training activities categorize attendees according to their experienced hardship. The Privilege Walk activity, based on Peggy McIntosh's concept of White privilege[50] and at times deployed in new judge orientations,[51] requires a facilitator to prompt attendees about their life experiences. Initially standing in a group in the middle of the room, attendees take a step forward or backward in response to a series of statements such as, "If English is your first language, take a step forward" and "If you grew up in an urban setting, take a step backward." Often, the Privilege Walk activity results in White men occupying the front half of the room, and women and people of color occupying the back half. The activity results in a stark visual representation of privilege and inspires discussion of how individual characteristics are associated with disparities. However, it can also create a sense of public shaming and division, and more than a few educators challenge the notion the activity has anything to do with implicit bias and assert that it is actually detrimental to effective implicit bias education. Negative outcomes of this activity might be especially likely when trainers who lack sufficient expertise lead education workshops, highlighting the importance of subject-matter experts' involvement in judicial education.[52]

Attitudes among judicial educators toward implicit bias education remain mixed due in part to similar concerns that have accumulated over the past decade. A recent survey of 238 judges and judicial educators revealed that 63% had been involved in implicit bias education in the last 5 years, and 48% were aware of controversy or criticism surrounding the topic.[53] Some of these educators doubted the validity of the construct itself, its measurement, and its application to the courts. In fact, a minority of respondents (22%) believed judicial education regarding implicit bas was "very effective" or "extremely effective."[54] These figures indicated that unanswered empirical questions and inconsistent training might have taken a toll on the reputation of implicit bias education in recent years. Although stakeholders might be wary of the future of implicit bias education, we believe that research and training in this area is yet nascent and stands to contribute greatly to the judiciary and those it serves. A consideration of future directions for research and education indicates that the ensuing decade will bring increased clarity to a currently fraught topic.

C. A Note on Positionality: Effects of Judicial Attitudes on Judicial Decision-Making

The criticism that implicit bias education amounts to political correctness raises the need to consider the effects of judicial attitudes on judicial decision-making.[55] The U.S. was founded upon the principle of equality embedded in the 14th Amendment of the Constitution amidst the contradictory reality of slavery. The struggle to end the American caste system established by slavery[56] continued after the civil war, through the Jim Crow era, to the present state of disparate treatment of African Americans and other disenfranchised groups.[57] Despite decisions such as *Brown v. Board of Education*[58] that held racially segregated schools to be unconstitutional and calls for continued reform, judges do not agree on the extent to which social justice reforms should be implemented.[59] American citizens, who elect some judges as well as the members of the legislative and executive branches who appoint other judges, will determine the extent to which systems of education, health, and justice will achieve equality. Whether greater equality is achieved in a certain area of society will be impacted by laws that are passed and how they are applied by judges.

The study of implicit bias in judicial decision-making involves an application of social science to the study of the judicial system and the *judicial decision-making process*, which is *not* a science. Science cannot determine what is just: rather, science is a tool on which the law must sometimes rely to do the fair and just thing.[60] Ideally, the legislative and executive branches of our democratic government will pass laws for the benefit of all Americans and judges will implement them. However, studies suggest that the myriad attitudes of judges embedded within a given court culture play a significant role in judicial decision-making.[61] For better or for worse, cases illustrating the influence of judicial attitude on judicial decision-making indicate how implicit bias creeps into the judicial system. For example, in 1965, federal courts in the South began abandoning the policy of taking a "hands off" approach to allegations of unconstitutional prison conditions and began reforming prison operations. They did so largely because their attitude toward hearing prisoners' appeals changed.[62] These cases indicate that judicial attitudes can have a positive effect on decision-making, but also a negative one.

From such examples, one can infer that effectiveness of implicit bias education for judges might be influenced by their explicit attitudes or internalized beliefs as well. Some judges may enthusiastically incorporate training to reduce the effects of biases because they believe in the goals of the training. Some judges may consciously disagree with calls for reforming the criminal justice system. In between these two cohorts, a large group of judges may agree that criminal justice reform is needed, but they may still harbor biases that unjustly impact their decision-making. In other words, to evaluate the effectiveness of implicit bias training, researchers might have to consider whether judges consciously or unconsciously disagree with the goals of the training within a larger societal context. Consequently, to be most effective, implicit bias education/research might need to better assess and address judges' attitudes toward criminal justice and other social reforms and their willingness to consider how their biases can affect their decision-making.

4. Future: Preserving the Best and Improving the Rest

Social scientists and practitioners continue to identify new pathways by which implicit bias research and education can enhance social life. In the wake of recent criticism and public attention, coupled with enormous advancements in neuroscience, technology, and our subsequent understanding of the brain, research of the near future will be more rigorous than ever. Important questions remain for examination, such as how the person and the social environment interact to influence the expression (or inhibition) of implicit biases. The progress of future research will be met with equal advancements in education. Recent transitions to remote operations in response to the Covid-19 pandemic inspire new opportunities to deliver effective implicit bias education to larger groups while expanding beneficial social interaction between attendees. The future of implicit bias education for the judiciary will rely on synergy between researchers, educators, and legal practitioners made possible by newfound technology and a persistent desire to enhance justice by reducing bias.

A. Research: Future Directions More Apparent Under Pressure

The future of implicit bias research will likely be as vibrant and controversial as its past. A topic that engenders healthy debate among scientists and possesses the potential to dramatically improve social processes and outcomes for a diverse population is unlikely to fade from public discourse. It is the responsibility of researchers to continually improve a collective empirical understanding of the construct and convey its merits to the broader public. In so doing, future research should answer fundamental questions that remain about which components of the implicit bias construct are sound and which might require reformulation to achieve their full potential in explaining social behavior and decision-making. Future research should further explicate the relationship between implicit bias and observable behavior, identify interventions that effectively reduce observable bias, and deploy and consistently evaluate those interventions to ensure their effects remain over time. These pursuits will ensure implicit bias research emerges more rigorous and informative after recent controversy.

To explicate the relationship between implicit bias and behavior, researchers and educators should conceptualize bias as a product of the interaction between the person and the environment rather than a stable feature of personality. Person-environment interactions have long been the focus of social psychology because they explain more of human behavior than either variable alone.[63] The IAT and other measures of implicit bias might seem to lack validity and reliability due to differences in the social context under which behavior or subsequent measures take place, rather than due to flaws in the underlying construct. The context-based approach suggests that implicit bias is a feature of the situation rather than of the individual, and that particular situations can encourage greater (or lesser) expression of bias.[64] This approach places less of the burden for bias on individuals, thereby reducing the likelihood that people feel privately or publicly shamed. It also accounts for features of the person and the environment to make more informed, multivariate predictions.[65] With some of the taboo removed from the results of an implicit bias measure, people and organizations can concentrate efforts on adjusting their context (e.g., displaying, in government buildings, revered members of historically marginalized groups) as a primary means of minimizing the expression of bias in decision-making.

Studies of person-environment interactions and their effects on implicit bias will have implications for behavioral interventions that adjust the context of decision-making. If bias manifests due to situational variables, altering the context of decision-making might reduce the expression of bias.[66] A pertinent avenue for future research is to identify features of the situation that can activate bias and develop strategies to eliminate those features. Some researchers hypothesize that reminders of inequality, such as monuments dedicated to Confederate leaders, can prompt the expression of bias; thus, removing these monuments from public spaces might inhibit implicit bias.[67] Prompting decision-makers to intentionally consider the benefits of equality between demographic groups at the time of the decision might further reduce implicit bias.[68] Extant studies empirically examining these hypotheses have thus far shown null effects,[69] but ongoing research suggests that the timing of these techniques might improve their effectiveness.[70] The future of implicit bias research lies in examining interactions between the person and the environment to identify and test practical interventions. Continued empirical testing of the context-based approach can enhance behavioral prediction and identify strategies for effective education.

Future research should identify interventions that produce long-term reductions in implicit bias. Though targeted modifications of the decision-making environment can limit the short-term expression of bias, these interventions and others have yet to consistently demonstrate lasting change to implicit attitudes. A test of nine bias-reduction methods demonstrated that implicit biases rebounded fewer than four days after an initial intervention (e.g., prompting decision-makers to consider egalitarian beliefs or counter-stereotypical exemplars).[71] Few other studies have conducted follow-up tests to examine the persistence of individual implicit bias after a delay or at what point an intervention at an aggregate level impacts bias in a system, indicating a need for more research in this area. The dearth of data on the long-term persistence of implicit bias reduction individually and collectively suggests that interventions that produce lasting change need more testing and that implicit biases might be difficult to limit or erase. However, there also is evidence of successes, with extended training procedures showing the most promise, including repeated bias-reduction exercises[72] and consistent positive interaction with dissimilar others.[73] Researchers should continue to explore these possibilities using the most rigorous methods of experimentation and evaluation.[74] It is imperative that future research employs longitudinal methods to evaluate the effectiveness of bias-reduction interventions over time and incorporates necessary adjustments to achieve lasting change.

B. Education: Recent Insights Fuel Future Innovation

Past optimism and current controversy will motivate the targeted and rigorous approaches to implicit bias education necessary for the future. Ongoing research and practice illuminate a promising trajectory for education that will include judges' input in the delivery of education, recognize the need for constant improvement, and leverage opportunities associated with remote operations. These developments can renew confidence in the value of implicit bias education. The topic is especially important to a changing world in which bias and the need to address it is more salient than ever before.

Implicit bias curricula of the future should solicit and incorporate judges' input. The aforementioned recent survey of judges and judicial educators revealed that the majority (71%) preferred an approach to education that teamed a judge with a subject-matter expert (e.g., a social scientist specializing in intergroup relations).[75] This approach can inform more effective procedures that reflect a joint understanding of court practice and cutting-edge theory and research, thereby reducing the conceptual disconnect between knowledge of implicit bias and its effects on legal judgments. Team formats allow participants to develop the rapport necessary to address common misconceptions regarding implicit bias education, such as the notion that it is a pseudoscientific vehicle for a politically motivated agenda. Educators should utilize working relationships with judges to gather information about how to improve curricula. For instance, interactive small group discussions lasting 50–90 minutes might be preferable to self-study programs.[76]

Educators and courts should resolve to constantly improve curricula. Stakeholders must recognize that education is not a "one-and-done" effort, but instead a continuous process of implementation and adjustment that requires motivation and active effort on the part of participants. The current academic climate regarding implicit bias, and the sociopolitical climate regarding race and other identity characteristics, provides a unique opportunity to reflect and retool education to address contemporary issues using the most rigorous methods of assessment. Although many judges and judicial educators believe implicit bias education is highly important, relatively few believe it is broadly effective in its current formulation.[77] Fidelity assessments—which measure whether participants adhered to the curricula as instructed[78]—will help to address this concern and inform future approaches to judicial education, especially if participation occurs virtually in light of recent transitions to remote operations. Education modules should at minimum assess fidelity by asking participants whether they completed assignments, but more comprehensive strategies for assessment might include direct observation of judicial practice following education.[79] Education interventions with high fidelity are most likely to be successful at reducing implicit bias.

Remote operations such as those introduced by the pandemic facilitate easier dissemination of educational materials but introduce new challenges, such as maintaining participants' engagement. Educators should use fidelity assessment data to adjust curricula for online delivery. Consistent check-ins with participants will help educators to identify the components of curricula that garner the greatest adherence among judges and emphasize those in improved implicit bias training. As the courts move beyond the Covid-19 pandemic and acclimate to a future that will likely include continued emphasis on remote operations, implicit bias education should incorporate telecommunication and virtual instruction. The IAT, a fully computerized test, is easily completed online using participants' personal computers during virtual education lessons. Implicit bias curricula can continue to utilize the IAT as a tool for self-insight, group discussion content, and pre-/post-instruction comparisons. Opportunities to deliver implicit bias education online allow for a larger number of participants in a single session, as well as for participants from different locations to meet simultaneously.

Online instruction can facilitate interaction between participants who might not have the opportunity otherwise to share their diverse experiences with issues related to implicit bias. Additionally, educators can honor judges' preferences for small group discussions by temporarily segmenting participants online into teams that include a subject-matter expert for more specific and intimate discussion of sensitive topics (e.g., personal experiences with bias or IAT scores). Related results of a recent NJC Jury *Question of the Month* illuminated judges' thinking, suggesting that informal interactions with diverse communities—a task that could be completed virtually—might reduce judges' implicit bias and assist educational efforts.[80] Courts and educators should leverage newfound familiarity with online tools for telecommunication to develop innovative methods of implicit bias education.

Conclusion

Crises in our nation underscore the need for meaningful conversations and change regarding disparities across systems and society. Responding to these crises are social scientists and leaders in the legal profession.[81] Disproportionate and disparate outcomes for persons of color (and others) in terms of health, justice, and economics suggest the need for a "racial justice moon shot" effort in our country. To make progress toward racial justice and justice for other marginalized groups, researchers and practitioners should embrace the scientific method rather than hunches or anecdote.

Even if implicit bias is an imperfect construct not yet fully understood and often misunderstood, there is little direct evidence to suggest that teaching on it is harmful—and, in fact, findings suggest it is beneficial if done correctly to lay a foundation for more in-depth discussion and change even if small. Scholars and practitioners should redouble their efforts to build on the substantial progress to date on this topic: toward research to understand how even the trained decision-maker can succumb to influences of implicit bias, and toward education to identify and eliminate sources of undue bias. The necessity of these efforts is more salient now than perhaps any time in modern history, and professionals now have the experience and tools to develop, assess, and refine productive judicial education. Self-insight through education can manifest consistently at each decision point in the judicial system to create positive change for those who would benefit from it most.

So, You'd Like to Know More

- Lindsay M. Perez, Monica K. Miller, Alicia Summers & Shawn C. Marsh, Assessing Interventions to Reduce Judicial Bias: Fighting Implicit Bias—What Judges and Lawyers can Do, in Enhancing Justice: Reducing Bias 317 (Sarah E. Redfield ed. 2017).
- Shawn C. Marsh & Diane C. Marsh, Being Explicit about Implicit Bias Education for the Judiciary, 56 Court Review 92 (2020).

About the Authors

Tyler N. Livingston, Ph.D., is an Assistant Professor in the Department of Psychology at Angelo State University, San Angelo, TX.

Shawn C. Marsh, Ph.D., is the Director of the Judicial Studies Graduate Degree Program and Associate Professor of Judicial Studies, Communication Studies, and Social Psychology at the University of Nevada, Reno.

Honorable John H. Larsen, J.D., MJS, is an administrative law judge for the California Public Utilities Commission and doctoral candidate in Judicial Studies at the University of Nevada, Reno.

Endnotes

1. Centers for Disease Control, *Covid-19 Hospitalization and Death Rates by Race/Ethnicity* (August 18, 2020). https://www.cdc.gov/coronavirus/2019-ncov/covid-data/investigations-discovery/hospitalization-death-by-race-ethnicity.html.

2. Isabel Wilkerson, Caste: The Origins of Our Discontents (2020).

3. Anthony G. Greenwald & Linda Hamilton Krieger, *Implicit Bias: Scientific Foundations*, 94 Cal. L. Rev. 945 (2006).

4. *Executive Order on Combatting Race and Sex Stereotyping* (2020 September 22), https://www.whitehouse.gov/presidential-actions/executive-order-combating-race-sex-stereotyping/.

5. Elizabeth Tsai Bishop, Brook Hopkins, Chijindu Obiofuma & Felix Owusu, *Racial Disparities in the Massachusetts Criminal System, A Report by The Criminal Justice Policy Program* (submitted to Chief Justice Ralph D. Gants, Supreme Judicial Court of Massachusetts September 2020).

6. *See* Jerry Kang, Implicit Bias: A Primer for Courts 4 (August 2009). https://www.ncsc.org/__data/assets/pdf_file/0025/14875/kangibprimer.pdf; The National Judicial College, Model Curriculum for Judges Faculty Manual 1 (2005).

7. Shawn C. Marsh, *The Lens of Implicit Bias*, JUVENILE & FAMILY JUSTICE TODAY 17 (2009).

8. GEORGE A. MILLER, PSYCHOLOGY: THE SCIENCE OF MENTAL LIFE 56 (1962).

9. Russell H. Fazio, David M. Sanbonmatsu, Martha C. Powell & Frank R. Kardes, *On the Automatic Activation of Attitudes*, 50 J. PERSONALITY & SOC. PSYCHOL. 229 (1986).

10. Anthony G. Greenwald, Mahzarin R. Banaji, Laurie A. Rudman, Shelly D. Farnham, Brian A. Nosek & Deborah S. Mellott, *A Unified Theory of Implicit Attitudes, Stereotypes, Self-Esteem, and Self-Concept*, 109 PSYCHOL. REV. 3 (2002).

11. Anthony G. Greenwald & Linda Hamilton Krieger, *Implicit Bias: Scientific Foundations*, 94 CAL. L. REV. 945 (2006).

12. Anthony G. Greenwald, Debbie E. McGhee & Jordan L. K. Schwartz, *Measuring Individual Differences in Implicit Cognition: The Implicit Association Test*, 74 J. PERSONALITY & SOC. PSYCHOL. 1464 (1998).

13. GALLUP, THE PRESIDENCY, https://news.gallup.com/poll/4729/presidency.aspx

14. Paul C. Taylor, Linda Martín Alcoff & Luvell Anderson, *The Routledge Companion to Philosophy of Race*, 266 (2017).

15. Charles R. Lawrence III, *The Id, the Ego, and Equal Protection: Reckoning with Unconscious Racism*, 39 STANFORD L. REV. 317 (1987).

16. *Id.* at 322.

17. Charles R. Lawrence III, *Unconscious Racism Revisited: Reflections on the Impact and Origins of "The Id, the Ego, and Equal Protection,"* 40 CONN. L. REV. 931 (2008).

18. The American Bar Association, *Three Questions with Charles Ogletree*, 17 CRIM. J. NEWSLETTER 5 (2009).

19. *See* Christine Jolls & Cass R. Sunstein, *The Law of Implicit Bias*, 94 CAL. L. REV. 969 (2006); Chris Guthrie, Jeffrey J. Rachlinski & Andrew J. Wistrich, *Blinking on the Bench: How Judges Decide Cases*, 93 CORNELL L. REV. 1 (2007); Mary Kreiner Ramirez, *Into the Twilight Zone: Informing Judicial Discretion in Federal Sentencing*, 57 DRAKE L. REV. 591 (2008); Jeffrey J. Rachlinski, Sheri Lynn Johnson, Andrew J. Wistrich & Chris Guthrie, *Does Unconscious Racial Bias Affect Trial Judges?*, 84 NOTRE DAME L. REV. 1195 (2009); Shawn C. Marsh, *The Lens of Implicit Bias*, JUVENILE & FAMILY JUSTICE TODAY 17 (2009).

20. *See, e.g., id.*, Marsh at 16.

21. Jeffrey J. Rachilinski, Sheri Lynn Johnson, Andrew J. Wistrich & Chris Guthrie, *Does Unconscious Racial Bias Affect Trial Judges?*, 84 NOTRE DAME L. REV. 1195 (2009).

22. *Id.*

23. Jolls & Sunstein, *The Law of Implicit Bias*, 94 CAL. L. REV. at 989.

24. *Id.* at 986.

25. JERRY KANG, IMPLICIT BIAS: A PRIMER FOR COURTS 4 (August 2009).

26. *Id.*

27. Mary Kreiner Ramirez, *Into the Twilight Zone: Informing Judicial Discretion in Federal Sentencing*, 57 DRAKE L. REV. 591, 630 (2008).

28. Mark Hensch, *Clinton: We Must Fight "Implicit Bias,"* THE HILL (Sept. 26, 2016). https://thehill.com/blogs/ballot-box/presidential-races/297939-clinton-i-think-implicit-bias-is-a-problem-for-everyone.

29. Steven Nelson, *Mike Pence Slams Kamala Harris for Her Racial Disparities as Prosecutor*, N.Y. POST (Oct. 7, 2020), https://nypost.com/2020/10/07/pence-berates-kamala-harris-for-her-racial-disparities-as-prosecutor/.

30. Hart Blanton & James Jaccard, *Arbitrary Metrics Redux*, 61 AM. PSYCHOL. 62 (2006); Anthony G. Greenwald, Brian A. Nosek & N. Sriram, *Consequential Validity of the Implicit Association Test*, 61 AMERICAN PSYCHOLOGIST 56 (2006) for response to criticism; *See* Cherly Staats, Kelly Capatosto, Lena Tenney & Sarah Mamo, *State of the Science: Implicit Bias Review* (Kirwan Institute for the Study of Race and Ethnicity at The Ohio State University 2017) for a detailed history of controversy.

31. Michael Brownstein, Alex Madva & Bertram Gawronski, *Understanding Implicit Bias: Putting the Criticism into Perspective*, 101 PACIFIC PHILOSOPHICAL Q. 276 (2020).

32. *See* C. Daryl Cameron, Jazmin L. Brown-Iannuzzi & B. Keith Payne, *Sequential Priming Measures of Implicit Social Cognition: A Meta-Analysis of Associations with Behavior and Explicit Attitudes*, 16 Personality & Soc. Psychol. Rev. 330 (2012); Frederick L. Oswald, Gregory Mitchell, Hart Blanton, James Jaccard & Philip E. Tetlock, *Predicting Ethnic and Racial Discrimination: A Meta-Analysis of IAT Criterion Studies*, 105 J. PERSONALITY & SOC. PSYCHOL. 171 (2013); Benedek Kurdi, Allison E. Seitchik, Jordan R. Axt, Timothy J. Carroll, Arpi Karapetyan, Neela Kaushik, Diana Tomezsko, Anthony G. Greenwald & Mahzarin R. Banaji, *Relationship Between the Implicit Association Test and Intergroup Behavior: A Meta-Analysis*, 74 AM. PSYCH. 569.

33. Anthony G. Greenwald & Mahzarin R. Banaji, *The Implicit Revolution: Reconceiving the Relationship between the Conscious and Unconscious*, 72 AM. PSYCHOL. 861 (2017).

34. Michael Brownstein, Alex Madva & Bertram Gawronski, *Understanding Implicit Bias: Putting the Criticism into Perspective*, 101 PACIFIC PHILOSOPHICAL Q. 276 (2020).

35. Jesse Singal, *Psychology's Favorite Tool for Measuring Racism Isn't Up to the Job*, THE CUT (2017) https://www.thecut.com/2017/01/psychologys-racism-measuring-tool-isnt-up-to-the-job.html; Tom Bartlett, *Can We Really Measure Implicit Bias? Maybe Not*, CHRONICLE HIGHER EDUC. (Jan. 5, 2017, https://www.chronicle.com/article/can-we-really-measure-implicit-bias-maybe-not/

36. Anthony G. Greenwald, T. Andrew Poehlman, Eric Luis Uhlmann & Mahzarin R. Banaji, *Understanding and Using the Implicit Association Test: III. Meta-Analysis of Predictive Validity*, 97 J. PERSONALITY & SOC. PSYCHOL. 17 (2009).

37. Bertram Gawronski, Mike Morrison, Curtis E. Phills & Silvia Galdi, *Temporal Stability of Implicit and Explicit Measures: A Longitudinal Analysis*, 43 PERSONALITY & SOC. PSYCHOL. BULL. 300 (2017).

38. *Id.*

39. Heidi A. Vuletich & B. Keith Payne, *Stability and Change in Implicit Bias*, 30 PSYCHOL. SCI. 854 (2019).

40. Edward H. Chang, Katherine L. Milkman, Laura J. Zarrow, Kasandra Brabaw, Dena M. Gromet, Reb Rebele, Cade Massey, Angela L. Duckworth & Adam Grant, *Does Diversity Training Work the Way It's Supposed To?*, HARV. BUS. REV. (July 2019), https://hbr.org/2019/07/does-diversity-training-work-the-way-its-supposed-to.

41. Robert J. Smith, *Reducing Racially Disparate Policing Outcomes: Is Implicit Bias Training the Answer?*, 37 U. HAWAI'I L. REV. 295 (2015).

42. Jason A. Okonofua, David Paunesku & Gregory M. Walton, *Brief Intervention to Encourage Empathetic Discipline Cuts Suspension Rates in Half among Adolescents*, 113 PNAS 5221; Denise K. Whitford & Andrea M. Emerson, *Empathy Intervention to Reduce Implicit Bias in Pre-Service Teachers*, 122 PSYCHOL. REPORTS 670 (2019).

43. Cayla R. Teal, Anne C. Gill, Alexander R. Green & Sonia Crandall, *Helping Medical Learners Recognise and Manage Unconscious Bias toward Certain Patient Groups*, 46 MED. EDUC. 80 (2012).

44. *Kolstad v. American Dental Association*, 527 U.S. 526 (1999). The Court held that employers who demonstrated efforts to prevent discrimination and harassment could avoid punitive damages in discrimination and harassment cases.

45. Frank Dobbin & Alexandra Kalev, *Why Doesn't Diversity Training Work? The Challenge for Industry and Academia*, 10 ANTHROPOLOGY NOW 48 (2018).

46. Heather MacDonald, *The False 'Science' of Implicit Bias*, WALLSTREET J. (October 9, 2017). https://www.wsj.com/articles/the-false-science-of-implicit-bias-1507590908.

47. Michelle M. Duguid & Melissa C. Thomas-Hunt, *Condoning Stereotyping? How Awareness of Stereotyping Prevalence Impacts Expression of Stereotypes*, 100 J. APPLIED PSYCHOL. 343 (2015).

48. *Id.*

49. THE NATIONAL JUDICIAL COLLEGE, MODEL CURRICULUM FOR JUDGES FACULTY MANUAL 1 (2005).

50. PEGGY MCINTOSH, WHITE PRIVILEGE: UNPACKING THE INVISIBLE KNAPSACK, 147 (1989).

51. Municipal Judge Education, Missouri Courts https://www.courts.mo.gov/page.jsp?id=1805

52. Shawn C. Marsh & Diane C. Marsh, *Being Explicit about Implicit Bias Education for the Judiciary*, 56 Court Rev. 92 (2020).

53. *Id.*

54. *Id.* at 95.

55. MALCOLM M. FEELY & EDWARD L. RUBIN, JUDICIAL POLICY MAKING AND THE MODERN STATE: HOW THE COURTS REFORMED AMERICA'S PRISONS (1999).

56. Brown v. Board of Education, 347 U.S. 483 (1954).

57. *See, e.g.,* MICHELLE ALEXANDER, THE NEW JIM CROW: MASS INCARCERATION IN THE AGE OF COLORBLINDNESS (2010).

58. ISABEL WILKERSON, CASTE: THE ORIGINS OF OUR DISCONTENTS (2020).

59. ANTHONY AMSTERDAM & JEROME BRUNER, MINDING THE LAW 246 (2000).

60. DAVID L. FAIGMAN, LEGAL ALCHEMY: THE USE AND MISUSE OF SCIENCE IN THE LAW 294 (1999).

61. MALCOLM M. FEELY & EDWARD L. RUBIN, JUDICIAL POLICY MAKING AND THE MODERN STATE: HOW THE COURTS REFORMED AMERICA'S PRISONS 336 (1999).

62. *Id.* at 36.

63. GORDON W. ALLPORT, THE HANDBOOK OF SOCIAL PSYCHOLOGY 5 (1985).

64. Heidi A. Vuletich & B. Keith Payne, *Stability and Change in Implicit Bias*, 30 PSYCHOL. SCI. 854 (2019).

65. Benedek Kurdi, Allison E. Seitchik, Jordan R. Axt, Timothy J. Carroll, Arpi Karapetyan, Neela Kaushik, Diana Tomexsko, Anthony G. Greenwald & Mahzarin R. Banaji, *Relationship between the Implicit Association Test and Intergroup Behavior: A Meta-Analysis*, 74 AM. PSYCHOL. 569 (2019) demonstrated that the IAT is uniquely predictive of behavior beyond explicit measures; Yoav Bar-Anan & Michelangelo Vianello, *A Multi-Method Multi-Trait Test of the Dual-Attitude Perspective*, 147 J. EXPERIMENTAL PSYCHOL.: GEN. 1264 (2018) demonstrated enhanced predictive power of a dual-construct model incorporating implicit and explicit measures compared to single-construct models.

66. Heidi A. Vuletich & B. Keith Payne, *Stability and Change in Implicit Bias*, 30 Psychol. Sci. 854 (2019).

67. *Id.*

68. Calvin K. Lai et al., *Reducing Implicit Racial Preferences: II. Intervention Effectiveness Across Time*, 145 J. Experimental Psychol.: Gen. 1001 (2016) found no effect of egalitarian priming, but Vuletich & Payne, hypothesize that such an intervention could be effective if employed immediately prior to decision-making.

69. *Id.*

70. Heidi A. Vuletich & B. Keith Payne, *Stability and Change in Implicit Bias*, 30 Psychol. Sci. 854 (2019).

71. Calvin K. Lai et al., *Reducing Implicit Racial Preferences: II. Intervention Effectiveness Across Time*, 145 J. Experimental Psychol.: Gen. 1001 (2016)

72. Patricia G. Devine, Patrick S. Forscher, Anthony J. Austin & William T. L. Cox, *Long-term Reduction in Implicit Race Bias: A Prejudice Habit-Breaking Intervention* 48 J. Experimental Soc. Psychol. 1267 (2012).

73. Natalie J. Shook & Russell H. Fazio, *Interracial Roommate Relationships: An Experimental Field Test of the Contact Hypothesis*, 19 Psychol. Sci. 717 (2008).

74. *See* Lindsay M. Perez, Monica K. Miller, Alicia Summers & Shawn C. Marsh, *Assessing Interventions to Reduce Judicial Bias: Fighting Implicit Bias—What Judges and Lawyers Can Do*, in Enhancing Justice: Reducing Bias 317 (Sarah E. Redfield ed. 2017).

75. Shawn C. Marsh & Diane C. Marsh, *Being Explicit about Implicit Bias Education for the Judiciary*, 56 Court Rev. 92 (2020).

76. *Id.*

77. *Id.*

78. Carol T. Mowbray, Mark C. Holter, Gregory B. Teague & Deborah Bybee, *Fidelity Criteria: Development, Measurement, and Validation*, 24 Am. J. Evaluation 315, 316 (2003).

79. Lindsay M. Perez, Monica K. Miller, Alicia Summers & Shawn C. Marsh, *Assessing Interventions to Reduce Judicial Bias: Fighting Implicit Bias—What Judges and Lawyers Can Do.*

80. Autumn King, *Most Judges Believe this Tactic can Help Eliminate Implicit Bias in Court*, NJC (July 16, 2021). https://www.judges.org/news-and-info/judges-believe-this-tactic-can-help-eliminate-implicit-bias-in-court/,

81. *See* California Lawyers Association, *Supreme Court of California Statement on Equality* (June 11, 2020). https://calawyers.org/litigation/supreme-court-of-california-statement-on-equality/; Bernice B. Donald, Jeffrey Rachlinski & Andrew J. Wistrich, *Getting Explicit About Implicit Bias*, 104 Judicature 75 (2020).

THIRTEEN

Leveraging and Interrupting Implicit Biases Concerning Women Trial Lawyers

Cynthia Eva Hujar Orr, Goldstein & Orr, San Antonio, TX

A Note from the Editors: We know Attorney Orr primarily through our joint work with the American Bar Association Criminal Justice Section (where both she and Judge Donald have served as Chair). She is an exceedingly competent defense lawyer who is a thought leader in the field of criminal justice. When we asked Ms. Orr to write a chapter for this book, we thought she would write about white collar crime, an area of her expertise; instead she chose to write about another area of her expertise—implicit bias and women lawyers. The book is all the better for this. As women—one judge, one professor; one person of color, one White; one abled person, one with a disability—we, like Cynthia, of course, bring our own lived and complex experiences to this topic. We note that Attorney Orr recognizes this complexity and nuance when she advises that favorable biases can be leveraged just as unfavorable ones can be ameliorated. We are grateful to Attorney Orr for her work in criminal justice writ large and for her willingness to share with us her research and practical, successful experience. This is a thought-provoking Chapter from which all groups can learn.

CHAPTER HIGHLIGHTS

- Great trial lawyers are aware of implicit biases but need to learn about and understand these biases particularly as they concern women lawyers. This knowledge benefits the client and all members of a litigation team.

- A woman lawyer and her team should know how women lawyers are perceived by jurors, the judge, and other litigants.

- Use of and interruption of these assumptions and stereotypes that favor and disfavor women lawyers are crucial tools in trials. These stereotypes and biases are as important in a case as the facts and the law. This is because these implicit assumptions influence outcomes with opposing counsel, judges, and jurors.

- Favorable biases may be leveraged and unfavorable biases ameliorated if known and used or addressed.

CHAPTER CONTENTS

Introduction

1. Defining the Context: Implicit or Unconscious Bias

   A. Confirmation Bias and Ingroups

   B. Male Lawyers as the Apex Ingroup

2. A Possible Solution: Bringing the Research Together

   A. Forming Ingroups to Neutralize Our Biases

   B. Enhancing Affinity

Conclusion

Introduction

I ask no favor for my sex. All I ask of our brethren is that they take their feet off our necks.

Ruth Bader Ginsburg[1]

This Chapter discusses lived experience, studies, and research concerning implicit biases about women lawyers, and it indicates where further study is necessary. It also suggests ways that the negative manifestations of implicit biases we have been able to identify as prevalent can be defeated through expanding our profession's ingroups or utilizing implicit biases in favor of the woman lawyer as leverage in a trial setting.

1. Defining the Context: Implicit or Unconscious Bias

In 1995, Drs. Mahzarin Banaji and Anthony Greenwald published a paper reviewing what they called implicit social cognition (i.e., implicit or unconscious "knowing and awareness, such as perceiving, conceiving, remembering, reasoning, judging, imagining, and problem solving").[2] Discussing how such implicit thinking was not known to the individual, they observed that indirect measurement would be necessary.[3] Three years later, Dr. Greenwald and his colleauges Debbie McGhee and Jordan Schwartz published their paper on a method for such measurement, the Implicit Association Test (IAT).[4] Writing in 2021, Professor Greenwald and his colleagues observed that since then more than 3,000 peer reviewed articles had been published about the IAT.[5] And it is clear the terminology *implicit bias* has entered the national lexicon.

Dr. Greenwald and his colleagues defined implicit social cognition as thinking or behavior influenced by unconscious associations and judgments. These associations and judgments, they explained, are developed by each of us over time, based on our cultural backgrounds, our environments, and our life experiences.[6] For lawyers, a good illustration of how our culture, background, environment, and experiences produce our assumptions is how we have interacted with and have used the phrase *all men are created equal* over time. At the time that phrase was written by our founding fathers in the United States Declaration of Independence, they meant what they said.[7] But in their culture the "all men" to whom they accorded equality did not include African American men. It did not include women. Encompassed in what these revolutionary mavericks[8] deemed as a generous all-encompassing description of their aspirations for their new country was, regrettably, exclusion, denigration, and devaluation of whole segments of humankind. In our current culture, most of us use the phrase *all men are created equal* to include everyone. We aspire to seeing that all persons, with all of their differences, deserve equal respect. While their rights might vary based upon citizenship or other factors such as criminal convictions, they are each respected as human beings.

Despite the current use of *all men are created equal* to express the near universal belief in equality in the United States, this is not how we act. The work done by Dr. Greenwald and his colleagues offers an explanation for this disconnect. The IAT and other indirect measures, coupled with other supporting research in neuroscience and social psychology, demonstrate that our behaviors—even when we have explicit egalitarian motives—can be based in unconscious implicit responses. Perhaps the most confounding point for lawyers is that both views can be true. We can honestly and explicitly hold and articulate unbiased views at the very same time that our decisions are influenced by implicit and unintended biased associations.[9] We need these implicit associations—sometimes described as schema, heuristics, or mental shortcuts—to efficiently move through our lives. But while often correct, sometimes they are not.[10] Dr. Banaji calls them "brain bugs," I suppose because, like computer software bugs, they are misfires that lead us astray in our perceptions, decisions, and actions.[11]

A. Confirmation Bias and Ingroups

Dr. Banaji's brain bugs were recognized as a part of the human condition long before pioneering social scientists brought the problems accompanying these implicit biases to our attention. In 1620, Francis Bacon described one type of implicit bias, confirmation bias:

> [T]he human understanding when it has once adopted an opinion draws all things else to support and agree with it. Although there be a greater number and weight of instances to be found on the other side, yet these it either neglects or despises, or else by some distinction sets asides and rejects, in order that... the authority of its former conclusions may remain inviolate.[12]

In 1921, Clarence Darrow talked about a second major type of implicit bias, affinity bias, when he observed, "Jurymen seldom convict a person they like, or acquit one that they dislike. The main work of a trial lawyer is to make a jury like his client, or, at least, to feel sympathy for him; facts regarding the crime are relatively unimportant."[13]

As described above, unconscious confirmation bias is a conclusion or belief that confirms what a person already believes to be true regardless of information and evidence to the contrary.[14] Confirmation of information is often coupled with confirmation of affinity bias as to what we believe to be true about groups of people. For example, I worked on a Texas case where we saw IRS and FBI agents, who had identified bribery and corruption involving a federal medical services contract, too quickly generalize their findings to another defendant. In doing so, they ignored information that disproved his guilt, including the fact that contracts to provide these specialized services pre-existed any relationship between the alleged bribe payor and alleged bribe recipient.[15]

Confirmation bias occurs where a person is primed to believe something,[16] holds a belief in which the person is invested,[17] or where a person is influenced by his or her group.[18] In this last circumstance, the person will generally favor others in their ingroup or ingroups.[19] That is, we generally prefer what we perceive to be our own, even where the ingroup is artificially or minimally constituted—for example, wearing T-shirts the same color or wearing similarly styled shoes. Experiments with such groups have shown ingroup favoritism is strong, to the point of disadvantaging an outgroup.[20] Such group loyalty and ingroup favoritism are formed by belonging, joining, or supporting a group and are also driven by the desire to exercise power or achieve success.

B. Male Lawyers as the Apex[21] Ingroup

Manifestations of implicit gender bias are rampant in the legal profession. More women graduate from law school, but few women lead. This is a time when women have comprised forty percent of law graduates over the last three decades. And during the last five years, more women than men have attended and graduated from law schools.[22] But the practice remains disproportionate.

Since 2006 the National Association of Women Lawyers (NAWL) has published a survey concerning the leadership status of women lawyers in private practice.[23] The NAWL 2009 survey found that women accounted for fewer than 16% of equity partners (defined as "those lawyers who hold an ownership interest in their firms and occupy the most prestigious, powerful and best-paid positions") and 6% of managing partners. Summarizing, NAWL observed that "[i]n spite of more than two decades in which women have graduated from law schools and started careers in private practice at about the same rate as men," women "continue to be markedly underrepresented in the leadership ranks of firms."[24] Ten years later, NAWL found similarly that women "remain about 20% of all equity partners, with this representation holding steady for the last three years," and "are largely unrepresented as firm managing partners."[25] By 2020, NAWL summarized partnership progress as slow and threatened:

> On the whole, the numerical results of the 2020 survey are a near exact replication of those from 2017 to 2019. The progress made by women in law firms over the last decade has been slow and incremental at best, and law firms continue to face challenges with respect to supporting and promoting women. Despite approaching near universal adoption of diversity initiatives, including diversity committees and dedicated diversity officers, and increased awareness of the challenges women and diverse attorneys face in their advancement through the law firm, there has been little progress made in recent years that is reflected in noticeable increases in representation of women and diverse attorneys, particularly at the more senior levels of the law firm.[26]

Like the NAWL firm leadership data, empirical data show that about 25% or fewer of lead counsel and trial counsel in civil cases are women. In criminal cases, where most cases are defended by one lawyer, the percentage of women lead counsel increases slightly to 33%.[27] It is also interesting that most of the women who were lead counsel in criminal cases were employed by the government; they were prosecutors.[28]

In my experience, the prevalence of male lead trial lawyers is driven by clients who choose male lawyers over women lawyers;[29] by male partners who chose someone "like me" as first chairs; and by negative stereotypical comments and conduct by judges, opposing counsel, and even co-counsel in the courtroom.[30] Falling into these stereotypes can be costly. For example, some analysts have reported that "On average, a male-female trial team outperformed a male-male trial team, winning more often and making fewer decision errors. For defendants, the average cost of these errors was a stunning $2.6 million average reduction in defendant liability."[31]

The partnership and trial counsel data is mirrored to a somewhat lesser extent in other areas of practice. Statistics show that women account for about 28% of federal judges, 39% of state court judges, 41% of law school deans,[32] and 36% of the law school tenured faculty.[33] Law student stereotypes concerning the legal profession were found to show similar status differences that favored men. The students were more likely to associate women with paralegal and men with judge.[34] (There was a positive note—these law students were found less likely to act consistent with their biases than previously tested groups.[35] They knew how to interrupt or neutralize their biases.)

These datasets illustrate the manifestation of implicit bias in practice. I believe that if we asked the leaders represented in this data if they were biased against women lawyers, if they thought women were less brilliant than men,[36] they would answer, of course not, of course not. So, what explains the numbers and their intransigence? The reality that these numbers and observations manifest is that persons practicing law are affected by negative implicit biases toward women,[37] particularly women of color. They must contend with double stereotypes, those associating women with paralegals and those discounting persons of color as less able.[38]

These data and research provides support for further inquiry on at least two points. First, in regard to the difference between government and private employment, it would be valuable to consider whether government regulation and laws against discrimination may have had a positive effect on advancing women leaders in the profession. Identifying the reasons that a greater percentage of women occupy leadership roles in government might help resolve their under-utilization as leaders generally in litigation when they possess the talent and skill to lead. Second, further study of how it is that the law students studied above knew to act against their unconscious biases would be helpful. Was it because the phenomenon of implicit bias has become general knowledge and acting without bias or assumptions has become a life goal? If so, this has not yet translated into improved status in practice, where few women progress to partner and senior partner and where other patterns of devaluing women continue to exist throughout the legal sector.

Many conclude that implicit gender stereotypes and biases are responsible for these disparities. But it is also the case that patent discrimination fostered many of the disparate results. The military is an example. When women were first permitted to serve in the U.S. military, their roles were limited.[39] Today, women have been integrated into every military function, including combat positions. And it has proven to be true that women perform very well in these roles.[40] In some cases, actual laws held us back. In other instances, gender stereotypes work a disservice to women.

2. A Possible Solution: Bringing the Research on Women and Ingroups Together

A main truth about ingroups—that we can shape our ingroups—may lead us to a solution, bringing the research on women and ingroups together to strengthen women's roles in the law. One of the leading evidence-based strategies for interrupting implicit bias is to increase diverse contact.[41] Law professor Sarah Redfield often describes this by saying "if you want to change the way you think, work to change the way you see, to change what you will comfortably consider your own."[42] This strategy can work in two directions to interrupt the implicit biases that are limiting women's roles in the profession. Women and men can work to change what the ingroup looks like for a litigation/leadership team, changing what they see and what is seen. As I mentioned above, even artificially created ingroups are composed of people who act in favor of the ingroup.[43] Expanding one's ingroup teaches empathy and understanding of others. This leads to inclusion and support of these others, who are no longer others; but are now included in the ingroup.

A. Forming Ingroups to Neutralize Our Biases

A great illustration of how diverse contact works is the true story of Derek Black and Matthew Stevenson, two students at the New College of Florida. Derek came from a White nationalist upbringing of some notoriety[44] and Matthew from an Orthodox Jewish family. When Derek's White nationalism was exposed at school, he was ostracized by many on campus. But Matthew did something extraordinary and unexpected. He invited Derek to his weekly Shabbat dinners. No one attending dinner was permitted to attack Derek for his White nationalist beliefs. In fact, for two years most dinner conversation was about organized religions and other topics. At first, Matthew's usual Shabbat dinner guests stayed away. But over time they started to attend again.

Derek said of the experience that he was accustomed to defending his separation of races and White protectionist theories in debates. He would—he now says—misuse statistics and social science to prove his views were correct.[45] But this is not what he did at these dinners. Since he was not under attack, Derek listened and made friends with Matthew. Derek learned that, even though he was not doing anything to others when he attended White nationalist meetings, he was, in fact, harming others. He concluded that his views were not just supportive of the White race but that they constituted hatred and espoused the exclusion of entire groups of humanity. He eventually wrote a letter about his evolution and condemned White nationalism. And he described his transformation as expanding his ingroup to a more inclusive group:[46] "And it really was empathizing with people who were not 'supposed' to be part of my group and increasing the number of people who were in my group. That's the universal thing that I think came out of what I learned from coming through that...."[47]

I have to believe that if Derek and Matthew can form a new ingroup, the rest of us can as well. The research is very clear that diverse teams produce better, more creative, and more profitable results.[48] In addition to the research, my own lived experience is that trial teams of diverse groups of lawyers readily accept and follow women lead counsel with favorable results. Various studies and reports support the suggestion that we can interrupt implicit bias based on gender stereotypes and improve the participation of women in all aspects of the profession. Getting comfortable with women lawyers leading and trying cases will allow male lawyers, clients, opposing counsel, and judges to learn that women are frequently the superior lawyers on the team. They are much better at collaboration than their male counterparts.[49] Ego and competition within a team play less of a role,[50] allowing for better focus on the issues and challenges in the litigation.

B. Enhancing Affinity

Research has shown that men can have greater affinity with women than with men, and this is a possible basis for change. We have heard the phrase "it's a man's world,"[51] and many believe it is still true that men are perceived as the ingroup that possesses more power and resources. Therefore, life is more difficult for women, the reasoning goes. However, empirical data show that it might be otherwise. Psychologists Laurie Rudman and Stephanie Goodwin studied the comparative ingroup response for men and women and concluded that in "women's automatic in-group bias is remarkably stronger than men's,"[52] suggesting that, not only are women closer to women than men are to men, but many men are actually also closer to women than they are to men.

Drs. Rudman and Goodwin also found that men who had more intimate relationships with women come to have a greater affinity with them, considering them as among their ingroup over other men.[53] This part of their study only examined circumstances in which these men had romantic relationships with women. It did not study business or professional relationships. But it provides encouragement for the view that inclusion of women in trial team ingroups will neutralize negative unconscious biases against them. Inclusion of women will be further motivated when, through this process, male lawyers learn that women lead and trial counsel have strong skills that lead the group to success.

By building on the research that shows that gender is not as subject to implicit automaticity of ingroups as we might expect, we can develop groups that are more inclusive of women and women of color in private firms and other professional settings. In addition to the diversity advantages discussed earlier, this would give male lawyers the opportunity to listen and discover the fact that women lawyers offer a great deal to any litigation team.⁵⁴ In my own work, I have found that male and women trial lawyers are cooperative and readily follow a woman lead counsel. They each will join the team in whatever capacity delineated by lead counsel and add strength to the team. Likewise, I have not experienced a lack of cooperation when I lead a trial team. Whether in a white-collar case or defending a blue-collar crime, my experience is that lawyers work well under the leadership of women.

Further, having women lead counsel is an advantage because jurors believe and trust women lawyers more so than male lawyers.⁵⁵ Women lawyers are effective—even more effective than male lawyers.⁵⁶ Women are often in the majority on juries, thus they relate to women lawyers more so than they do male lawyers.⁵⁷ Women lawyers are also perceived as especially effective and persuasive in any matter involving what is seen as any traditional woman's issue. And merely explaining the reason for anger in a proceeding, and women lawyers gain equal persuasion footing with men explaining the reason for anger in a proceeding and thus by interrupting the incorrect stereotypical assumption that they are merely exhibiting lack of emotional control.⁵⁸

Conclusion

The real solution to the poor promotion and advancement of women in law is to include them in our ingroups. Women should suggest themselves for lead roles or take the lead. Women should mentor one another and give other women a step up by promoting them and including them on trial teams. When a young woman associate has written a motion and knows more about it than lead counsel does, lead counsel should give her the opportunity to present the matter in court. "Just do it"⁵⁹ is not just a good ad slogan for Nike sneakers, it is what we must do to help the capable women lawyers in our profession succeed. Always add a woman or two or three to your trial team. Once women lawyers are routinely included in the leadership position on trial teams, they will be on the teams' ingroups. Support, cohesion, collaboration, empathy, and success will naturally follow. By expanding our ingroups to more inclusive ones, we learn empathy and develop affinity with others. In this way, stereotypes fall away and we begin to support and promote each other for the benefit of the entire group.

So, You'd Like to Know More

- Lara Bazelon, What it Takes to be a Trial Lawyer If You're Not a Man, The Atlantic, Sept. 2018.
- NAWL, Survey Report on Promotion and Retention of Women in Law Firms (2019).

- NAWL, Survey Report on Promotion and Retention of Women in Law Firms (2020).

About the Author

Cynthia E. Hujar Orr is the managing partner at Goldstein & Orr in San Antonio, Texas. She has attained national prominence defending citizens and entities in state and federal trial and appellate courts. She served as Chair of the American Bar Association Criminal Justice Section in 2014 and is currently President of the International Society for the Reform of Criminal Law. Attorney Orr is a graduate of the University of Texas at Austin and St. Mary's University Law School.

Endnotes

1. Justice Ginsburg borrowed the quote from Angelina Emily Grimke, one of the first female agents of the American Anti-Slavery Society and a feminist activist. On July 17, 1837, Grimke wrote in a letter to her sister and fellow activist: "Even admitting that Eve was the greater sinner, it seems to me man might be satisfied with the dominion he has claimed and exercised for nearly 6,000 years, and that more true nobility would be manifested by endeavoring to raise the fallen and invigorate the weak, then by keeping women in subjection. But I ask no favors for my sex. I surrender not our claim to equality. All I ask of our brethren is, that they will take their feet from off our necks, and permit us to stand upright on that ground which God designed us to occupy."

2. *Cognition*, Am. Psychol. Ass'n APA Dictionary of Psychol. (2020), https://dictionary.apa.org/cognition.

3. Anthony G. Greenwald & Mahzarin R. Banaji, *Implicit Social Cognition: Attitudes, Self-esteem, and Stereotypes*, 102 Psychol. Rev. 4, 8 (1995). Dr. Banaji is a long-time leading expert in discrimination. She describes an experience of her friend and colleague Carla Kaplan as influencing her thinking. As the story goes, Kaplan, who was both an avid quilter and a Yale professor, was being treated for a hand injury at Yale-New Haven Hospital. At first, the doctor treating Kaplan said just stitches would be needed, but when one of her students called out to her as Professor Kaplan, and her doctor realized she was a Yale professor, the doctor arranged for intensive and specialized surgery. It was the act of kindness and special attention her colleague received as an ingroup member that struck Banaji and made her realize that discrimination was comprised of subconscious acts of omission as well as the more obvious acts of commission associated with patent discrimination. Shankar Vedantam, Rhaina Cohen, Thomas Lu, Tara Boyle, Parth Shaw & Cat Schuknecht, *Playing Favorites: When Kindness Toward Some Means Callousness Toward Others*, NPR Hidden Brain (June 8, 2020); *see also* Mahzarin Banaji & Anthony Greenwald, Blindspot: Hidden Biases of Good People (2013); Anthony G. Greenwald & Thomas F. Pettigrew, *With Malice Toward None and Charity for Some: Ingroup Favoritism Enables Discrimination*, 69 Am. Psychologist 669 (2014).

4. Anthony G. Greenwald, Debbie E. McGhee & Jordan L.K. Schwartz, *Measuring Individual Differences in Implicit Cognition: The Implicit Association Test*, 74 J. Personality & Soc. Psychol. 1464, 1465 (1998).

5. Anthony G. Greenwald & 20 others, *Best Research Practices for Using the Implicit Association Test*, Behav. Res. Methods, Online 2021.

6. *See* Anthony G. Greenwald & Mahzarin R. Banaji, *Implicit Social Cognition: Attitudes, Self-esteem, and Stereotypes,* 102 Psychol. Rev. 4, 8 (1995).

7. A truth that my law partner, Gerald Goldstein, calls to our attention almost every time he speaks publicly. Therefore, I am crediting his observation here.

8. A maverick is a person whose ideas and behaviors are different from others. "Maverick is an eponym, a word derived from someone's name. It originally meant an unbranded calf and comes from a Texas rancher called Samuel A. Maverick (1803–70) who did not brand his cattle." *Word of the Day*, Macmillan Dictionary, https://www.macmillandictionaryblog.com/maverick. The Maverick family ancestors were iconoclasts who promoted education, independence, inclusion, and diversity historically. Samuel, a Yale educated lawyer, signed the Texas Declaration of Independence. Maverick Family, A Guide to the Maverick Family Papers (1840–1980), https://legacy.lib.utexas.edu/taro/drtsa/00117/drt-00117.html.

9. Enhancing Justice: Reducing Bias 44 (Sarah E. Redfield ed., 2017); *see also* Brian A. Nosek & Rachel G. Riskind, *Policy Implications of Implicit Social Cognition*, 6 Soc. Issues & Pol'y Rev. 113 (2012); Mahzarin Banaji & Anthony Greenwald, Blindspot: Hidden Biases of Good People (2013).

10. *See* Jennifer K. Elek & Andrea L. Miller, National Center for State Courts, The Evolving Science on Implicit Bias: An Updated Resource for the State Court Community 23 (2021); *see also* Stanley O. Gaines, Jr., *The Ultimate Attribution Error in the Killing of George Floyd: Derek Chauvin's Behavior Reflects His Own Stereotypes, Not George Floyd's Acts*, Deep Focus, Psychology Today, June 9, 2020.

11. Mahzarin Banaji & Anthony Greenwald, Blindspot: Hidden Biases of Good People (2013).

12. Lord Bacon, Novum Organum (1620).

13. As quoted in Edwin H. Sutherland & Donald R. Cressey, Principles of Criminology 431 (8th ed. 1992).

14. *See generally, e.g.,* Raymond S. Nickerson, *Confirmation Bias: A Ubiquitous Phenomenon In Many Guises*, 2 Rev. Gen. Psychol. 175 (1998).

15. *See* Patrick Danner, *Jury Acquits Uresti Co-Defendant in Bribery Case*, Express News, Nov. 9, 2019.

16. An example is when law enforcement sends a report or a prosecutor coveys the prosecution theory to a forensic scientist. The scientist will, thus, be primed to find results from scientific testing consistent with the report or theory previously conveyed and may miss a contrary or inconsistent result that the prevalence of scientific data indicates.

17. An example is the belief that wearing masks or taking vaccines that are approved for emergency use are or are not effective in interrupting the spread and serious health consequences of a virus that has reached pandemic proportions.

18. These groups may be based on gender, race, community, school attendance, geographic location, sexual orientation, or any other factor, including groups formed by artificial means instead of personal affinity. An ingroup is a group a person has joined or in which they belong. An outgroup is a group in which a person does not belong or has not joined.

19. An ingroup is a group whose members share characteristics with each other; they may be artificially created, that is, formed by others for their own purposes. These can be groups formed by teachers in schools, seminar or program chairs, and even social scientists for several reasons. A good example of ingroups based on affinity is a group of sports fans of one team, say the Green Bay Packers. An outgroup from Packers' fans would be New Orleans Saints' football fans.

20. *See, e.g.*, Rebecca S. Bigler, Lecianna C. Jones & Debra B. Lobliner, *Social Categorization and the Formulation of Intergroup Attitudes in Children*, 68 CHILD DEV. 530 (1997); NCSC, THE EVOLVING SCIENCE ON IMPLICIT BIAS: AN UPDATED RESOURCE FOR THE STATE COURT COMMUNITY 5 (2021).

21. *Apex*, MERRIAM WEBSTER, https://www.merriam-webster.com/dictionary/apex (defining "apex" to mean the uppermost or highest point).

22. *Law School Rankings by Female Enrollment (2020)*, ENJURIS, https://www.enjuris.com/students/law-school-women-enrollment-2020.html (last visited October 12, 2021); Lara Bazelon, *What it Takes to be a Trial Lawyer if You're not a Man*, THE ATLANTIC, Sept. 2018.

23. NAWL, SURVEY REPORT ON PROMOTION AND RETENTION OF WOMEN IN LAW FIRMS 1 (2006), available through the links at https://www.nawl.org/p/cm/ld/fid=2019.

24. NAWL, SURVEY REPORT ON PROMOTION AND RETENTION OF WOMEN IN LAW FIRMS (2009).

25. NAWL, SURVEY REPORT ON PROMOTION AND RETENTION OF WOMEN IN LAW FIRMS (2019).

26. NAWL, SURVEY REPORT ON PROMOTION AND RETENTION OF WOMEN IN LAW FIRMS (2020).

27. *Id.*

28. *Id.* "Of men appearing as lead counsel in criminal cases, 34% appear for the government and 66% appear for defendants. Of women appearing as lead counsel in criminal cases, the ratio is reversed: 69% appear for the government and 31% appear for defendants." *Id.* at 4.

29. Researchers have reported similarly that male clients are a third less likely than female clients to choose female lead partners from their law firms. *See* Acritas, *Gender Diverse Legal Teams Outperform Single Gender Teams* (2017), https://www.acritas.com/news/gender-diverse-legal-teams-outperform-single-gender-teams. Lisa Hart Shepherd, Acritas CEO, frames it this way: "The challenge for firms is that their male clients will be more likely to bring work to their male partners and the majority of clients are male. If clients, both male and female, can start to apply quotas in their work allocation – giving at least one in three matters to a female lead partner and demand gender diverse teams, this will start to balance the power and increase the chances of equity for women. At the same time, if law firms can field gender diverse teams and push their female lawyers to the forefront of relationships, this will help to balance out the gender gap. For both sides, these efforts will be rewarded with a better result – a more satisfying service for clients and stronger, more loyal relationships for firms."

30. STEPHANIE A. SCHARF & ROBERTA D. LIEBENBERG, THE PARTICIPATION OF WOMEN LAWYERS AS LEAD COUNSEL AND TRIAL COUNSEL IN LITIGATION 3. (2015). Women lawyers were called "honey," "dear," or by their first names. *Id.*; *See also* MARYAM AHRANJANI, PULLING BACK THE CURTAIN: A FOLLOW-UP REPORT FROM THE ABA CRIMINAL JUSTICE SECTION WOMEN IN CRIMINAL JUSTICE TASK FORCE (TF) (ABA Crim. Just. Sec., Oct. 5, 2021).

31. Yvonne Nath & Evan Parker, *Nothing Not to Like: Diversity and Law Firm Profitability*, LEGAL EVOLUTION, June 27, 2021 (referencing Randy Kiser); Bill Henderson, *American Law*

Firms in Transition: Trends, Threats, and Strategies (also citing Kiser, Beyond Right and Wrong 81–83 (2010); Premonition, Women in Law: Who Makes the Better Lawyer? Male or Female? (2018)).

32. ABA, Profile of the Legal Profession, Women in the Legal Profession (2021), https://www.abalegalprofile.com/women/women; *see also* Danielle Root, Jake Faleschini & Grace Oyenubi, Building a More Inclusive Federal Judiciary (2019), https://www.americanprogress.org/issues/courts/reports/2019/10/03/475359/building-inclusive-federal-judiciary/; NAWJ, 2019 US State Court Women Judges (2019), https://www.nawj.org/statistics/2019-us-state-court-women-judges.

33. Kristen K. Tiscione, *Gender Inequity Throughout the Legal Academy: A Quick Look at the (Surprisingly Limited) Data*, 69 J. Legal Educ. 116 (2019); *see also* Justin D. Levinson & Danielle Young, *Implicit Gender Bias in the Legal Profession: An Empirical Study*, 18 Duke J. Gender L. & Pol'y 1 (2010).

34. Implicit Racial Bias Across The Law 18 (Justin D. Levinson & Robert J. Smith eds., 2012).

35. *Id.*

36. *See generally* Daniel Storage, Tessa E. S. Charlesworth, Mahzarin R. Banaji & Andrei Cimpian, *Adults and Children Implicitly Associate Brilliance with Men More than Women*, 90 J. Experimental Soc. Psychol. 104020 (2020).

37. Stephanie A. Scharf & Roberta D. Liebenberg, The Participation of Women Lawyers as Lead Counsel and Trial Counsel in Litigation 3. (2015); *see also generally* Stephanie Scharf & Roberta Liebenberg, Practicing Law in the Pandemic and Moving Forward: Results and Best Practices From a Nationwide Survey of the Legal Profession (2021).

38. Enhancing Justice: Reducing Bias 44 (Sarah E. Redfield ed., 2017).

39. Bettie J. Morden, *The Woman's Army Corps*, 1945–1978, U.S. Army Center of Military History 48–55 (Oct. 12, 2021), History.army.mil.

40. U.S. Army Center of Military History, "Trust Transcends Gender," Gender Integration Initiative, https://history.army.mil/genderintegration/index.html.

41. *See, e.g.,* Jerry Kang, *What Judges Can Do about Implicit Bias*, 57 Ct. Rev. 78 (2021); Nilanjana Dasgupta & Shaki Asgari, *Seeing Is Believing: Exposure to Counterstereotypic Women Leaders and Its Effect on the Malleability of Automatic Gender Stereotypes*, 40 J. Experimental. Soc. Psychol. 642 (2004).

42. Personal interview with Professor Sarah Redfield (Oct. 17, 2021); *see also* Adam Brandenburger, *To Change the Way You Think, Change the Way You See*, Harv. Bus. Rev., Apr. 16, 2019.

43. Enhancing Justice: Reducing Bias (Sarah E. Redfield ed., 2017).

44. David Duke was his godfather, even though Derek's parents were both atheists.

45. At the time, he knew he was right about his beliefs and that statistics and social science backed him up. He was not attacking others. He was protecting the rights of Whites.

46. Derek Black & Matthew Stevenson, *Befriending Radical Disagreement,* May 17, 2018; *see generally* Ely Saslow, Rising Out of Hatred: The Awakening of a Former White Nationalist (2018) (Pulitzer Prize winner).

47. "I — the only lesson that I think that I took from my experience that I feel is fairly universal is that it was grounded in empathy; that the reason why I was not willing to listen to

the argument that sounded very straightforward — that we should work towards inclusion, not separation — was because I didn't empathize with people who weren't part of my ingroup. And I thought I wasn't necessarily doing anything bad to them, but it was also, the priority was the people who were within my ingroup. And what changed was feeling that people who were not in my ingroup were being negatively impacted by my actions and that I should care about that. And trying to reconcile that I should care about people who are negatively impacted by my actions, and I'm still doing the actions, became very difficult." *Id.* (Black)

48. *See generally e.g.*, Sundiatu Dixon-Fyle, Kevin Dolan, Vivian Hunt & Sara Prince,, McKinsey & Company, Diversity Wins: How Inclusion Matters (2020) ("The business case for inclusion and diversity is stronger than ever."); Scott Page, The Diversity Bonus: How Great Teams Pay Off in the Knowledge Economy (2019).

49. *See, e.g.,* David Shindler, *Are Women More Collaborative and Men More Competitive?* (Oct. 2, 2018), https://www.linkedin.com/pulse/women-more-collaborative-men-competitive-david-shindler/.

50. *Id.*

51. James Brown sang, *It's a Man's World*, written by his girlfriend Betty Jean Newsome in 1966.

52. Laurie A. Rudman & Stephanie A. Goodwin, *Gender Differences in Automatic Ingroup Bias: Why Do Women Like Women More Than Men Like Men?* 87 J. Pers. Soc. Psychol. 494 (Oct. 2004).

53. *Id.*

54. Stephanie A. Scharf & Roberta D. Liebenberg, The Participation of Women Lawyers as Lead Counsel and Trial Counsel in Litigation (2015).

55. *Id.*

56. *Id.*

57. *Id.*

58. *See also* Lara Bazelon, *What it Takes to be a Trial Lawyer if You're Not a Man*, The Atlantic, Sept. 2018.

59. Nike recently released an ad promoting women with the phrase: "If they think your dreams are crazy, show them what crazy dreams can do. Just do it." *Dream Crazier,* https://www.usatoday.com/story/sports/2019/02/24/serena-williams-nike-ad-dream-crazier/2973700002/, https://www.youtube.com/watch?v=5Mc06cIrvXE

FOURTEEN

Confronting Implicit Bias in the Nonprofit Sector

A Personal Perspective

Angelic Young

A Note from the Editors: One of the things we sought with this second book was to hear from more sectors and more and more diverse voices. We first met Ms. Young because of her work with the Anti-Defamation League, where she generously invited us to observe a session of their trainings. Knowing that many communities are striving to reduce the negative manifestations of implicit bias and that we all have much to learn from each other, we reached out to her to contribute her thoughts. Here she writes in a very personal voice about her work in the nonprofit sector. She highlights her own journey and also calls attention to much of the research on the extent and reasons for disproportionality between women, especially women of color, and men. Ms. Young also offers us some blunt and honest strategies for developing and implementing an action plan for more inclusive language and more inclusive decision-making. We are struck by the common ground between the nonprofit sector and others and inspired to put much of what we have learned from Ms. Young in practice in our own lives.

CHAPTER HIGHLIGHTS

- DEI initiatives that don't address culture allow people and organizations to avoid accountability for key behavioral changes.
- The burden of eliminating exclusionary language lies with those with privilege rather than those who are impacted by hurtful, exclusionary words.

- Whether consciously or not, nonprofit culture often treats women, Black, Indigenous, People of Color (BIPOC), and other identities as liabilities to be managed or overcome—further entrenching systems of oppression.
- Focusing on eliminating fragility (emotional responses to critiques) can often be performative and not useful; instead, we must focus on changing behaviors.
- Meaningful progress at a mission level requires a board and donor base that prioritizes DEI—diversification of both is critical.
- Developing an action plan with measurable benchmarks is critical to lasting change.

CHAPTER CONTENTS

Introduction

1. Industry Profile
2. Focus on Diversity, Equity, and Inclusion (DEI) Initiatives
    A. Representation, Voice, and Agency in Nonprofit Organizations
    B. The Dangers of Performative Allyship
    C. The Importance of Agency and Accountability in Nonprofits
    D. Exclusionary Language
    E. Identity as a Liability
    F. White (or Male) Fragility as a Crutch
3. Leadership and Organizational Action
    A. Fit as Bias, Bias Disguised as Protectionism
    B. Burden-Shifting
    C. Mission Formulation for Nonprofits to Achieve DEI
4. Developing an Action Plan
    A. Everyday Actions Leaders Can Take to Foster Inclusive Decision-Making in the Workplace
    B. Everyday Actions Leaders Can Take to Foster Inclusive Language in the Workplace
    C. Everyday Actions Leaders Can Take to Foster Inclusive Culture
    D. Track Your Progress

Conclusion

Introduction

I've worked in the field of diversity, equity, and inclusion (DEI) for over a decade. Most recently, at the Anti-Defamation League, I've designed training programs to help law enforcement reduce the influence of bias on their work and build skills to respond more effectively and inclusively to hate crimes and violent extremism. I've long been passionate about the DEI space generally and about tackling bias specifically. Still, during the summer of 2020, when it felt like discussions about racism and White supremacy reached peak awareness, I was forced to reckon with the gut-punching reality that I, too, reinforce White supremacy.

I was in a meeting with peers, all of whom are experts in anti-bias work.[1] It had been a particularly tough work week, and when someone asked what song we should play while waiting for the meeting to start, I suggested *It's the end of the world as we know it (and I feel fine)* by REM. A handful of colleagues indicated their unfamiliarity with the song. Several others responded by poking fun at me for "dating myself" in a room comprised mainly of people younger than I. However, one person pointed out that age was not the only reason that many in the room were unfamiliar with the song.

While the meeting continued, I remained focused on that comment. Baked into my assumption that this one song would be a universal reference that everyone in the room would "get" was my Whiteness. The song debuted in 1987 before several of the individuals in the meeting were born, but nearly all the White people in the room recognized it regardless of age. Aside from the chorus, which is simply the repeated phrase, *It's the end of the world as we know it, and I feel fine,* the lyrics are more stream of consciousness than particularly insightful. There was little meaningful relevance to the meeting agenda. Yet culturally, I presumed that the title and chorus carried weight in a room dominated by White people.

Suppose I wanted to convey a general sense of impending doom. In that case, I could have proposed the more lyrically coherent *Sign o' the Times* by Prince, released the same year, which touches on AIDS, guns, poverty, and war, among other serious themes. Or, given that the focus of my work is law enforcement, I could've proposed a song from *Straight Outta Compton* by N.W.A.—a landmark album in the evolution of rap which includes the track *F**k tha Police*, a song protesting police brutality and racial profiling. All of these would have been much more pointedly relevant to my work and mood. Instead, I proposed a piece that I don't even particularly like because I assumed that the cultural reference would be universal—and there lies the intransigence of White supremacy.

The gut-punch this represented hit hard. And there's no small amount of irony in that for me. I design and lead programs related to tackling bias for law enforcement. The objective of those initiatives is to create more inclusive and equitable approaches to public safety. As a result, I spend a great deal of time talking about the danger of hidden biases. I often use myself as an example, noting that those who work in this field are susceptible to hidden biases, beginning to believe our own narrative about our role in dismantling (rather than perpetuating) systemic racism. And yet, here I was, oblivious to my hidden biases, centering on the *we* in *we know it,* centering my Whiteness in a meeting about anti-bias work.

Ultimately, very few people working in the nonprofit sector, especially those working on issues of social justice, woke up one day in 2020, realizing, for the very first time, that structural racism and male superiority continue to shape our culture. That BIPOC and women don't occupy enough leadership roles, are marginalized in strategic conversations, and continue to experience bias in the workplace are well-established facts. Yet awareness, in and of itself, is seemingly insufficient to prompt meaningful changes in behavior. Many are willing to learn, talk, read and listen—but few are willing to *do.*

This Chapter will briefly explore the nonprofit sector's financial profile and demographics. It will then examine the influence and impact of bias in the nonprofit sector. Examples are highlighted of both racism and sexism, noting that it's essential to be mindful that it can be easier, for some, to lament the influence of sexism while simultaneously reinforcing racism. While the experiences are not the same, understanding how these and other systems of oppression buttress each other to keep White men in power is crucial. Throughout, specific examples of everyday actions one can take to mitigate the influence of bias are provided.

1. Industry Profile

Focus on a social cause, advocacy, or mission-driven work typically defines the nonprofit sector. Regarding issue focus and overall dollars, the largest portion of the sector is dedicated to health, including nonprofit hospitals. Education is the second-largest component of the industry, including universities, colleges, and research institutions. Next come social and legal services, then social advocacy, followed by international relations organizations focusing on foreign policy, international peace and security, and global human rights. Closing out the bottom of the list are organizations dedicated to art and culture.[2]

The nonprofit sector is big business, and it is getting bigger. Approximately 1.54 million nonprofit organizations were registered with the Internal Revenue Service, and the industry contributed over $1 trillion to the U.S. economy (about 5.6% of the GDP) in 2016. According to Giving USA, total charitable giving rose for consecutive years from 2014 to 2017, making 2017, at $390.05 billion, the most significant single year for private charitable giving (adjusted for inflation).[3]

Briefly, let's talk about the demographics and representational diversity challenges illustrated by industry data. White people hold most of the top nonprofit positions, including executive leadership and board leadership roles. The same is true of the corporate world—where Black professionals hold just 3.3% of all executive or senior leadership roles and where 37% of companies don't have a single Black board member.[4]

BIPOC experience barriers to promotion to leadership for a host of reasons, including lack of role models, mentorship, and support from nonprofit managers and executives, as well as leaders' tendency to recruit from their own homogenous professional networks. BIPOC also continue to experience pay inequity coupled with a greater statistical likelihood of external financial pressures.[5] Even as our country has become increasingly diverse and more attention has focused on the importance of DEI, the percentage of BIPOC in leadership roles has remained stagnant for fifteen years.[6]

In this data, culture is the White supremacy through-line—impacting everything from recruitment and hiring to retention, promotion, pay, and benefits. Culture is a collection of our experiences, knowledge, beliefs, practices, attitudes (and so much more) and shapes how we see and communicate with each other. White supremacy culture integrates a complex web of biases—both explicit and implicit—into our understanding of one another. Through culture, we assign value and normality to Whiteness and maleness, and that plays out in the workplace to an alarming degree.[7]

Further complicating matters is nonprofit leaders' tendency to tokenize BIPOC, especially in diversity, equity, and inclusion (DEI).[8] To be clear: This is not to say that BIPOC are not interested or qualified to lead DEI initiatives. Yet it remains common to see organizations temporarily lift the voices of their BIPOC staff for the all-important-public-panel on DEI, seemingly to demonstrate their attention visibly to the issue—only to see those employees once again fade into the background when attention shifts. Often, BIPOC are asked for significant unpaid labor to support public-facing efforts (frequently shorter-term in nature), but are otherwise overlooked, unheard, and pushed to the margins in longer-term strategic conversations. For example, a nonprofit leader might ask BIPOC colleagues to review writing to help eradicate traces of implicit bias in language. The objective is great; asking them to do so for free is not—editing is a job that ought to pay. Similarly, organizations often lean on their BIPOC staff to lead internal conversations or training workshops on bias (especially in the aftermath of George Floyd's murder), even when internally focused DEI work is not part of their job description. When organizations lean on their BIPOC staff to lead DEI initiatives without compensating them for the added time and energy such work entails, they're asking for unpaid labor.

Gender gaps still exist, too. Women comprise a staggering 73% of the nonprofit workforce, yet less than half of board members are women, and less than a quarter of executive directors and CEOs of large nonprofits are women.[9] For women of color, the gap is even more significant—they comprise less than 10% of nonprofits CEOs/executives.[10] The numbers in the private sector are comparable.[11]

Representational diversity matters. Closed networks that lack BIPOC or women make it significantly more challenging to attract, recruit, and retain diverse candidates, simply entrenching the cycle of ingroup hiring and promotion. Further, many studies suggest that diversity is good for business—increasing innovation and positively impacting the bottom line.[12]

Nonetheless, while representational diversity is an important issue, attaining this diversity will not be sufficient. There is a tendency to think that when BIPOC and women are visibly present, the DEI effort is "mission accomplished." The reality is that representation alone is not inclusion. It does not necessarily demonstrate a long-term commitment to meaningful integration of BIPOC voices in the nonprofit sector's leadership.

2. Focus on Diversity, Equity, and Inclusion (DEI) Initiatives

Most large companies have some sort of DEI initiative, these having gained popularity in the corporate sector in the late 1980s and early 1990s[13] and remaining so today. Before we dig into the content of different types of DEI initiatives, let's address the very framing of these efforts as *initiatives*, which is itself problematic. Merriam-Webster defines initiative as "an introductory step," and the Cambridge Dictionary, as a "new plan or process to achieve something or solve a problem."[14] As these definitions would suggest, rather than focusing on transforming the cultural lens through which we work, DEI initiatives are often discrete, time-bound exercises. They tend to be narrowly construed, discretely focused, and minimally impactful on either internal, organizational issues or on broader societal culture.

Among these large companies, 65% have turned to DEI training to combat the disproportionality of White leaders and the prevalence of bias in the workplace.[15] Yet, DEI training appears to fall short, potentially contributing to complacency about bias and lack of individual responsibility.[16] Often, that's because the training content doesn't address the DEI initiative objectives. That is, while many DEI initiatives prioritize representational diversification of boards, staff, or the organization, training workshops tend to lack skills-building explicitly related to recruitment, retention, and promotion tactics that might lead to representational diversification. Instead, they tend to focus on defining terms and increasing so-called "cultural awareness" or strengthening one's ability to recognize and manage the influence of implicit and explicit bias or understanding privilege and fragility. While increased awareness of how bias plays out on the job in these and other ways is essential to long-term reduction of toxicity in the workplace, these focus points do not necessarily lead to tangible growth in the representation of BIPOC or women at leadership levels. For that, explicit, measurable targets to which leaders are held accountable are needed.

An additional problem with much of the training currently offered to nonprofit organizations is that BIPOC and White people experience these kinds of programs differently. White people tend to report more positive engagement in such training programs than BIPOC. That White people feel more positively about such training programs isn't surprising, given that these programs primarily aim to help White people unpack their biases and increase awareness. White people walk away self-satisfied and even complacent; when satisfied they've "acted," they tend not to look for further action to take. Unfortunately, the data tells us that training and education aren't likely to create a better workplace for BIPOC or women without a concrete action plan. Because such programs don't place responsibility on leadership to *address* bias once they have become aware, the burden of challenging White supremacy and male superiority is left to fall primarily on BIPOC and women's shoulders.

Even where DEI training programs achieve some long-term representational diversification, they still may lack meaningful impact. Part of the difficulty is that the terms diversity, equity, inclusion, and equality are (mis)used as interchangeable objectives. Thus, few meaningful steps are taken to embrace the diversity of experience and thought to the same degree as white-centric experience and thought. We mistake diversity for inclusion and characterize it as the end-goal rather than a means to an end. We presume equality to be the same as equity and consider it accomplished with representational diversity. Just like that, DEI becomes synonymous with a checklist of entry-level training learning objectives aimed at the individual rather than the organization. For DEI initiatives to work, decision-makers must have the will to change *behaviors* rather than just minds. That is, they must understand that merely hiring more BIPOC or women doesn't automatically translate to a diversified, bias-free inclusive workplace. As noted previously, women comprise most of the nonprofit workforce but still struggle to attain equal representation in the C-suite. Representational diversity of the overall workforce alone won't eliminate bias or make for a more inclusive workplace. Being granted a seat at the table does not always come with a microphone—one can be present and still lack voice and agency.

This focus on "will" brings us back to the beginning—if awareness is not enough, if the abundance of data doesn't make a compelling case that we have a systemic racism and White supremacy problem, what is it that we do need? What makes leaders change behavior in ways that meaningfully benefit BIPOC in the workplace? How do we translate individual behavioral shifts into meaningful, positive cultural transformation in our communities—bettering our very humanity?

The example shared earlier, of a musical choice, probably felt a bit frivolous compared to the many more grave and stark examples of *isms that BIPOC or women have experienced in the workplace—and it may be. Yet, caution is required when considering dismissing such micromessages as de minimis or *just kidding*, letting them go as inconsequential or unintentional and brushing them off. Instead, focusing on both small and large messages, dividing things into macro and microaggressions, or explicit and implicit bias, allows people to contextualize the acts they commit and see how they reinforce White or male supremacy in their organizations. Not paying attention enables individuals to continue to duck responsibility for their role in these structures and systems. When the focus is solely on individuals, rather than culture—which exists regardless of specific acts or failures to act—it allows people and organizations to continue to define others as racists or sexists and themselves as feminists and anti-racists. Taking responsibility for how both individuals and organizations uphold these systems and subsequently change behavior is the only way to have a personal, measurable impact.

A. Representation, Voice, and Agency in Nonprofit Organizations

Nonprofit organizations, even those engaged in social justice work, continue to struggle to achieve DEI. This is evident in the statistics cited above, but also in other ways. Speaker lists and opportunities are an example. It is still common in this field for those lists to start predominantly White or male and be altered only after someone points out that the list excludes BIPOC or women. Whiteness, and sometimes maleness, is still the beginning point, the baseline point of reference. That this is so reflects the importance of transforming culture.[17] While it is also increasingly common to see organizations or leaders called out for such a lack of diversity, rarely is the call-out accompanied with an offer to roll up one's sleeves and do the work needed to identify participants that can diversify an attendee or speaker list. For every meeting in which one may consciously work not to center oneself or dominate the conversation, there are likely at least two others in which we do take the center and fail to do the work (in the same way, calling on those who are already in our ingroups, those most familiar to us). For most, when not directly contributing to biased behavior, at best the engagement is superficial or performative.

Some months ago, I was asked to contribute to a meeting about the role of law enforcement in schools. I pointed out to the organizers that there weren't any BIPOC names on the invitee list. I followed up with suggestions of individuals from my network who could contribute to the conversation. The organizers selected one of my recommendations.

After congratulating myself for ensuring representational diversity at this meeting, I participated, intending to find ways to elevate my BIPOC colleague's contributions. My good intent lasted only until I missed the sound of my own voice.

Midway through the meeting, I found myself inexplicably interrupting the colleague I meant to elevate to deliver my thoughts on the topic. In my mind, I was reframing what the other woman had said to indicate my agreement. But in doing so, I assumed that others wouldn't "hear" her—and ironically I ended up being the voice that crowded hers out.

This is the rub: Getting my colleague invited to the meeting (representational diversity) was essential, but it is only the first step. Being invited didn't guarantee her voice was heard or her agency valued. I fell short on the second part. Recognizing that elevating someone else's voice may well require limiting one's own is a hard lesson to learn. On the other hand, recognizing that you didn't necessarily earn your voice and agency and that you might only be "giving" what your Whiteness or maleness has gifted to you helps make the case clearer.

So, the task is threefold: to commit to representational diversity, elevate marginalized voices, and ensure they have agency within nonprofit organizations, events, meetings, and gatherings. Next, let's explore how to fully commit to both changing behavior and challenging others.

B. The Dangers of Performative Allyship

Allyship is "an active, consistent, and arduous practice of unlearning and re-evaluating, which a person in a position of privilege and power seeks to operate in solidarity with a marginalized group." *Transformative* allyship is not an identity nor is it self-defined.[18] On the other hand, *performative* allyship is behavior designed primarily to generate positive social feedback for one's self through surface-level, often short-lived, public demonstrations of solidarity. While both transformative and performative approaches can create a positive impact, performative allyship has no lasting power—it's a tweet with the right hashtag; a short-lived public intervention with no follow-through—largely self-serving. In the workplace context, performative allyship might be showing up at a meeting and grabbing the mike to call out the organizers for failing to elevate marginalized perspectives. Transformative allyship would have helped plan the meeting, calling in the organizers and working with them to identify ways to promote marginalized perspectives.

As these examples suggest, performative behavior materializes in many ways. I've found myself sitting in meetings analyzing what others are saying, looking for a mistake to edit. I eagerly await the moment to be the anti-racism police and intervene on behalf of BIPOC everywhere to point out the way some other White woman just screwed up. Now, intervention is not a bad thing—it can be enormously powerful to use one's privilege to connect with other people who share the same privilege. Still, it's important not to focus *only* on the behavior of others but simultaneously to check one's own behaviors.

Looking back at the meeting where one of my colleagues was invited but not fairly heard, it would have been easy for me to evade responsibility or defer to someone else when responsibility for the meeting, event, invitee, or speaker list didn't belong to me. So, as a person in a position of privilege/power, the first step is to take responsibility for checking other White colleagues' behavior. Silence is complicity and just as much a part of upholding White—or male—supremacy as any other action. But the second step is also vital: coupling the desire to target others' behavior with responsibility for one's own actions. Instead of gravitating toward *"what can I do about other people's bad behavior,"* focus on *"what can I do about other people's bad behavior AND how do I fix my behavior."* In my meeting example, dismantling White and male supremacy would have meant that I maintained a laser focus on opportunities to elevate voices rather than moments to silence voices.

One approach seeks positive opportunities for change; the other can quickly become little more than gossipy sniping. If the purpose in speaking up is to be heard rather than to transform—reconsider the intervention or adjust the manner of the intervention. Suppose the risk is immediate, meaning failure to intervene means someone will drown out a BIPOC voice. In that case, one might interject by identifying the BIPOC voice, relating that you believe that person has something to contribute, and then giving them the floor stating that you'd like to hear that person's thoughts. This can as simple as *"Diane is an expert on this, I'd like to be sure we hear what she has to say."* In other words, literally grabbing the microphone and then immediately handing it off. However, if the risk is not urgent, but you believe you have constructive feedback to provide to another person in the meeting (someone unaware of their behavior), intervene afterward in an environment conducive to conversation and learning.

The critical question to ask, always, is if the intervention places a spotlight on you rather than the person whose voice you intend to elevate. If so, it's likely only performative.

C. The Importance of Agency and Accountability in Nonprofits

In the larger perspective, it is simply easier and more comfortable to gravitate to those we know. We have an affinity bias and without any malice for those in the outgroup, we will do good for those who are in our ingroup. [19] It's easy to see how this bias is both contagious and self-perpetuating.[20] When all panelists or participants look alike, we think all experts must look like that. As the earlier discussion of the advantages of diversity suggests, it can mean we miss important viewpoints and information; for those excluded, it is painful.[21] When critical conversations lack BIPOC or women's perspectives, they miss vital contributions that matter to the end results of the work, something especially important when the work focuses on social justice. It is important to remember that the tendency toward our own need not always be the end result—we can interrupt these biases, and we will interrupt them when we are held accountable.

The niche nonprofit field of women, peace, and security offers an example. Here most experts are women, and most conferences and events are primarily attended by women, women gravitating to those they know in a field they know. The founder of one organization working in this arena, however, prioritized the inclusion of men. Each time that her organization held an event, she gave her staff the same mandate: ensure that men constituted a significant presence. They kept track, and she held them accountable if they weren't reaching their target. The notion that any one of them couldn't find men interested in attending wasn't acceptable. They got creative. They expanded their networks. They were bold. They hustled. If they invited a female colleague, they asked that colleague to identify at least one man to bring with her to the event. And it worked. When given a clear objective and held accountable for meeting that goal, they all found ways to execute. Intentionality was the key to success in this example. The DEI goal was not just a "nice-to-have," rather it was a "must-have." The organization's leader would be counting, and there was no room for failure in this example—it simply was not an option. When setting up meetings, events, or projects, it's essential to ensure that contributor, speaker, and invitee lists are diverse and to proactively solicit input on the agenda and project or program from BIPOC or women.

Integrating voices of BIPOC and women isn't just the right thing to do, it's the smart thing to do. Leaders in the nonprofit space who find themselves with a homogenous list of invitees, speakers, or panelists cannot make excuses and must hold themselves accountable. If you don't know a BIPOC or woman to whom you could reach out, then do some research. The lack of diversity in your professional network is most certainly not because BIPOC or female expertise on the topic is lacking. Accountability starts with proactively expanding that network rather than waiting for the next meeting or event.

Focusing on agency is also critical lest leaders claim DEI victory once they've achieved representational diversity. Agency is the combination of representational diversity, voice, and inclusive culture. It's having a seat at the table, a microphone you can turn on and off at will, and an audience that is listening when you speak. It's the thread that runs through the entire meeting, event, or project. Agency isn't present, or not to a significant degree, in an organization heavily dominated by White supremacy culture. For example, a culture of urgency (meaning a set of practices that prioritize quick decisions in response to often arbitrary deadlines) that disallows inclusive decision-making processes or seeks visible short-term gains at the expense of long-term transformative change may indicate a lack of agency and predominance of White supremacy culture.[22]

A culture of urgency, in practice, can show up in subtle ways. One example is the tendency of organizations to rush to publish written work or adopt policy, without consulting a diverse group of practitioners on the content or aims of the work. When we only include BIPOC and women's voices after the primary aims of the policy initiative or content have been identified, after the most critical stage of strategy formulation is complete, we miss the point of inclusion. For example, early on in my career, I worked on a project to increase women's participation in law enforcement in another country. I desperately wanted to deploy female police advisers to serve as mentors on the ground for the project. I asked the contractor providing personnel to identify more women; they told me women weren't typically interested in these kinds of missions. We began to strategize how to increase interest, focusing heavily on our recruitment materials and the message those materials conveyed. But we didn't initially ask any women why they might be less inclined to participate; only later did we discover that one of the most significant barriers had little to do with a lack of interest—and everything to do with one of the project's physical fitness tests. During that test, candidates were required to run an obstacle course in fully body armor within a certain amount of time. But the body armor that was issued was too large for most of the women—and many men—to comfortably run in, slowing them down. Had we begun by asking the women if our baseline assumption (the problem is women's interest) was correct, we could've saved significant time in developing a solution.

Accountability can also be challenging because of corporate perfectionism—both in and of itself and wrapped up in White supremacy culture. In such a culture, we may misattribute mistakes or see them as failures rather than learning opportunities. The result is that nonprofit leaders miss ideas that have merit, approaches that may be effective with refinement, and lose people that have potential. Instead of valuing contributions, efforts, and work, the nonprofit sector's culture centers on valuing results. This kind of corporate perfectionism can lead to groupthink and risk aversion.[23] Organizations succeed, but only at what they already know how to do—they don't grow, improve, or evolve. Setting measurable goals for reducing bias and transforming organizational culture becomes difficult in such an environment—if they miss, they'll take it personally; blame will be laid. Thus, the inclination is to shy away from such measures because nonprofit leaders can't afford to fail. Instead of falling back on corporate perfectionism, consider developing, as anti-racism educators Kenneth Jones and Tema Okun write, a culture of appreciation, learning, and feedback.[24]

Lastly, let's focus on one final note about intentionality and its relationship to cultural change. White supremacy, ultimately, relies upon the tendency to fall back on old routines when change seems too hard. We name goals without accountability measures and make mistakes without capitalizing on the learning opportunities they present. For example, I've been guilty of breaking my own DEI rules (e.g., refusing to speak on panels that lack diversity) when time is short, or the opportunity is too good to miss. I tend to fall back into my old routines of doing the work when it's easy, but not when it's hard. These are examples of the lack of intentionality to make meaningful shifts in behavior.

D. Exclusionary Language

Racist and misogynistic culture and their related systems of communication can serve as a barrier to inclusion. Nonprofits' use of language can welcome or exclude, convey insider or outsider status. Similarly language can remind individuals how aspects of their identity are a liability rather than an asset. White supremacy flavors so much of our language. Language, voice, and attitude are no less weaponized than their consciously-biased counterparts.

For example, during a workshop I participated in focused on language, the facilitator asked us to think about words for which meaning has changed over time or which had come to be recognized as informed by racism/White supremacy. The facilitator provided a list of examples and instructed us to either select a word from the list that surprised us or add words or terms. I struggled. I reviewed the provided list and thought, to myself, *Well, these are all terms I'm quite familiar with—nothing on here really surprises me.* I joined the conversation with the attitude of someone very conscious of my own language who had little learning to do—and said as much to my partner. He nodded and then added the term *master bedroom*. The shame blossomed across my face with discernible heat. How had I never reflected on a term like this without considering the word "master" and its history? The inability to recognize how language plays out stems from the same set of unconscious biases that feed White supremacy culture.

The list of words and phrases to learn and eliminate from our discourse is endless. People use the term "grandfathering"[25] regularly without awareness of its origins or without fully acknowledging the importance of eliminating the term from their vocabulary, even once they understood the history. Others fail to recognize the importance of using pronouns and normalizing such usage by integrating them into their introductions and bios. I've referred to groups of people in an unnecessarily gendered or binary manner, e.g., *guys, listen up* or *the men and women of this organization*. Worse, I've introduced or spoken about BIPOC peers to others with language that designates their identity as a liability. For example, *we should include Ed; he does a great job of maintaining neutrality and calm, even as a Black man in the face of pushback*. I say this as a positive but as though these attributes are unique or surprising, for a Black man.

I share these examples, not for the purpose of self-flagellation but rather to acknowledge and own that implicitly biased language has been one of the most challenging areas for me and one of the ways in which systems of oppression are most regularly reinforced. I love to talk and write quickly and have oft-played the *my mouth/fingers move(s) faster than my brain* card. When I do this, I fail to recognize that the sense of urgency to dominate a conversation or written space is wrapped up in White supremacy culture: If I don't have enough time to be thoughtful, to consult others on my words and their impact, then I must reconsider whether I have the time to speak or write. Again, the burden to adapt and adjust should not rest with those impacted by my language, the burden should rest with me, with those of us with agency to spare.

E. Identity as a Liability

When I share my background with others, the most frequently asked question I receive is how much of an impediment my gender has been to my ability to run law enforcement programs. Male colleagues have offered to take my place as the lead in important meetings because my counterparts *probably wouldn't take me seriously, as a woman.* I've been introduced in professional settings by men to other men with a qualifier such as, *She doesn't look like someone you would expect to have that background, does she?*

These anecdotes illustrate that the expectations created by intersecting oppressive systems are centered around cultural norms that value specific conceptions of maleness and Whiteness. These value systems play out in various ways. We see them in explicit and implicit biases related to notions of gender identity that impact those who are transgender or non-binary (e.g., failing to adopt the usage of pronouns, gender-segregated bathrooms).We also see them play out in our implicit and explicit biases related to our concepts of what it means to be professional concerning work attire, grooming, speech, and accent patterns (e.g., bias against those with "natural" hairstyles or those who have particular regional or foreign accents or those who speak Black Vernacular English (BVE)). Within these systems, identities perceived to be other than "the norm," e.g., women, BIPOC, members of the LGBTQ+ community, and those who are neurodiverse or differently-abled, are perceived (consciously or not) as liabilities—to be managed or overcome.

When we treat identity just as something to be managed, it paves the way for colleagues, who, after all, only want to get the work done, to speak for me or others, and entrenches these systems of oppression. The career paths of those whose identity is not White and male are harmed. Black women specifically are significantly impacted. In a recent report, 48% indicated that their race had been a barrier to career advancement.[26] More generally, we know that women are aware that they cannot engage as aggressively as their male counterparts without repercussions.[27] Engaging with colleagues loudly, confidently, and forcefully will often mean being heard as angry, aggressive, and difficult. Women who work in fields in which casual banter often includes profanity must still carefully manage their language because, as a woman, profanity isn't typically acceptable professionally.[28] Male colleagues adjust their language around women as they acknowledge *the ladies in the room* or refer to female colleagues formally, carefully (first name or title) and male colleagues informally, jovially (last name, nickname) or the reverse, female first names, male titles. These differences serve as reminders that women are different from the norm (White men). To succeed, they must adjust their language, dress, and behavior to fit the accepted cultural standards. If they slip, their work will be devalued—they'll be taken less seriously.[29]

BIPOC colleagues experience similar identity threats and questions. They are oft-introduced by White people to other White people with qualifiers such as: *He's so incredibly articulate* or *She's so amazing, you know—she manages to be direct without being aggressive.* They receive pushback when they address issues of racism directly in conversation, just as I receive pushback when I address issues of gender bias. They're described or evaluated in relation to the White male norm. When described as articulate, for example, the implied expectation is that the ability to articulate language clearly is not part of the BIPOC identity. Yet even the very construct of what it means to be articulate is centered around norms about how White people speak and pronounce words and excludes dialects like BVE or Native American English. Again, the entire cultural frame centers around Whiteness and maleness.

In situations like those described here, BIPOC and women must endure skepticism and pushback to avoid the multitude of stereotypes assigned to them. They collectively work overtime to adapt their identities (or at least the identities they show in their work settings) and to adjust to a linguistic culture that centers around Whiteness and maleness. This work takes an enormous emotional toll on individuals and the drain of this energy takes an enormous emotional toll from their nonprofit organization. Individuals are sidelined, minimized, or tokenized. Others take on the burden of code-switching, working overtime to adjust to cultural expectations. Data illustrates the cost of the emotional labor that Black women face in regulating their responses to avoid being perceived as *angry* and making people feel *uncomfortable*.[30] These daily experiences of bias produce traumatized employees, reduce employee engagement, increase employee turnover, increase absenteeism for health reasons, all of which decrease productivity, and make it challenging to recruit the best candidates.[31]

F. White (or Male) Fragility as a Crutch

Oh, Robin DiAngelo, how we White ladies love you and your popular mainstream book *White Fragility*.[32] We love to use you to call each other out for instances of fragility or tears. We focus on self-reflection, learn to breathe, remember to check emotional reactions, and learn not to cry, learn to do our research, and how not to rely upon BIPOC in our journey. If we react with emotion to a challenge of our behavior—we learn to label our reaction, shame it appropriately in ourselves or others, and thus in so doing—our work is done. We learn to sit with our discomfort and encourage others to do the same. We learn that so much of unpacking White supremacy is recognizing our internal fragility and propensity (if women) to weaponize our tears. We learn to battle against it all through reflection and personal growth. I recall suggesting once to a colleague, as a joke, that we ought to have t-shirts that said *If you aren't uncomfortable, we're not doing our job.*

Fragility is an important and valuable concept; self-reflection is vital, and so much of *White Fragility* has influenced many. But should we love DiAngelo? Has her conceptualization of issues helped us achieve meaningful change? Does awareness of fragility mean we must eradicate all emotions during conversations about race and racism? Or is it more likely that it's easier for self-reflection to become the journey, a journey without change in the end. Over the past year, I've found that in trying to embrace what I learned from DiAngelo, I may be doing more harm than good, or at the very least, I'm not doing anything proactive as I follow her credo.

A little over a year ago, I led a particularly grueling multi-day training session. After several hours of difficult conversations around the history of and relationship between law enforcement and communities, a participant asked me a series of questions about a scenario in the curriculum that involved a BIPOC teen experiencing a frightening encounter with a law enforcement officer. In the scenario, meant to help illustrate how bias can play out in interactions with law enforcement, the teen was presumed to have committed a crime, and the law enforcement officer drew his gun. The scenario concluded with a phrase to the effect of *the situation ends without violence, peacefully.* My colleagues objected to the notion that I characterized a situation like this as non-violent. For the teen in this hypothetical situation, a gun was drawn and pointed at him—violence was most certainly committed.

It was a scenario I had designed, and I became emotional in response. I was exhausted, hungry, and frustrated. I was significantly behind schedule. I took the feedback as criticism of my work and was unable, in the moment, to acknowledge it unemotionally. It seemed that months of work were unraveling before my eyes. I decided to take a break and re-center myself. I escaped outside to find a quiet space to let myself cry some frustrated tears, intending to do so alone. Alas, another White woman followed me to check in on me and hand me some tissues. Later, we agreed as a group that it was important that I acknowledge that I cried some White tears—demonstrating White fragility—and that this White woman had enabled me, compounding the matter. Though I had intended to avoid my emotions being the center of response to the critique, my actions had the opposite impact. Everyone was aware that I cried. The focus of the group became my feelings rather than the critical piece of feedback. I could—and should—have asked the colleague with tissues to go back to the room and declined the comfort that reinforced and centered my fragility. Or even better—I could've heard the critique for what it was: valuable, constructive feedback.

I resolved to do better the next day, meaning to ensure that my own emotions would not be the center of the conversation, even if I received challenging feedback. I harangued myself internally for the display of tears and fragility. I called myself out externally, using this example as a sort of self-naming and shaming exercise. My colleagues symbolically patted me on the back for the good internal reflective work I'd done and the example I'd made of myself. I agreed publicly, but privately, I returned from the trip exhausted, depleted, and demotivated. I questioned whether I ought to be working in this field, whether my Whiteness would always be too much present; I certainly lost track of my accomplishments and was slow to feel like focusing on the curriculum again.

How did any of this accrue to the goals of my work; how did it benefit BIPOC? Perhaps the acknowledgment of fragility at the moment, publicly, was beneficial emotionally to the BIPOC in the room. But more likely not. To be clear, I'm not advocating that it's ok to respond to pushback with fragility. Rather, I'm asserting that fixing the underlying error that generated the pushback is more important than castigating the fragility embodied by the initial response. I guess that few would've prioritized an apology for my tears over action. The self-flagellation that our focus on White fragility and tears has become is designed to change internalized emotional reactions rather than external actions and behavior. It is performative art, not demonstrable change. In that vein, what likely would've been more meaningful is if I'd made the curriculum adjustments that were the genesis of the conversation immediately rather than nearly a year later.

How can we move, then, beyond the performative to the constructive? What is the line between fragility and self-reflection or flagellation and accountability? Is it ever enough to just reflect? I think not. The lesson I learned from this experience was invaluable: don't focus on scoring points by highlighting the fragility of a colleague (or yourself). Instead, focus on how to mitigate the impact of the fragility or change the behavior itself. Unless highlighting the fragility somehow results in positive, tangible action or benefit for BIPOC, it's likely performative, not meaningful. If there is no benefit to BIPOC and nobody has asked someone to do this, we ought to question whether our underlying motivation is self-centered.

To be clear, this is not a zero-sum exercise. We can self-reflect and seek to change how we emotionally respond to criticism or questions while also identifying tangible steps we can take to disrupt oppressive systems. That is, I can share examples of my behavior to help others learn. But, instead of prioritizing the naming and shaming of White fragility, prioritize changing the behavior that generated the criticism (to which you or someone else may have responded with fragility) first. Fragility is a symptom and thus secondary. It demonstrates our emotional connection to some aspect of White or male supremacy that we don't want to give up, admit, or change in ourselves. The key is to focus on what caused the reaction in the first place.

Understanding this critique and making the necessary adjustments to the scenario was the meaningful, tangible action I could and did (eventually) take. My emotional response to the critique was perhaps inappropriate, but ending my tears was not nearly so important as making the requisite edits in the curriculum. Focusing on the fragility allows me to avoid focusing on meaningful behavioral adjustments.

3. Leadership and Organizational Action

As previously discussed, women make up 73% of the nonprofit workforce in the U.S., but less than half of all nonprofits have women executives, and for larger nonprofits with budgets over $50M, it's less than a quarter.[33] And those CEOs who are women tend to make less than men: Women leading large nonprofits with budgets exceeding $50M earned 20% less than their male counterparts; those leading smaller organizations, 5% less.[34] What is it that makes these numbers so hard to change?

Throughout my career, I have worked primarily with other women. Nearly every team I've worked on has been staffed mainly by women and led mostly by men. Two of these men provided invaluable support at difficult points in my career; one was an excellent listener who sought and integrated my input and took opportunities to elevate my profile. The other never hesitated to throw me into the deep end. His faith that I'd swim rather than sink was never in question. The courage his confidence provided me empowered me to take more strategic risks, lead more boldly, and accomplish more tangibly. Still, I've worked with many others whose leadership undermined rather than provided a pathway for my success.

Leaders that implicitly reinforce biased behavior and attitudes erect or steepen barriers to BIPOC and women's ability to advance within the nonprofit sector. Statements that reflect a commitment to DEI values are insufficient, absent concrete action, to transform culture. There are many behaviors that well-intentioned leaders engage in that contribute to, rather than eliminate, toxicity in the workplace, such as protectionism, burden-shifting, and failing to integrate DEI objectives into mission formulation.

A. *Fit* as Bias, Bias Disguised as Protectionism

Many years ago, the evening before I was to leave on a trip during which I would lead a complex negotiation along with another female colleague, a senior manager in my organization called me into his office. He informed me he'd decided to cancel the trip because he didn't want *two little girls to get rolled* by the person with whom we were supposed to negotiate. Both in our late twenties, we were, most assuredly, not "little girls." It was crushing, not to mention inappropriate.

As this story illustrates, one of the biggest mistakes that leaders make is to be protectionist. It's the perfect foil: *I'm going to take this meeting or call or intervene on your behalf, not because I don't think you can handle it, but because I don't want to see you hurt.* The message is that I am delicate, vulnerable, and need protection to succeed. It's also a way of signaling, for the offender, that it is not they who are biased but everyone else. Either way, the underlying message is that your identity is the problem; it's a liability, not an asset. To change this view, instead of shielding BIPOC or women from potential harm, supervisors and other leaders need to focus on eliminating the dangers and making the workplace a safer environment.

Recently, a colleague working in a leadership role at a nonprofit organization shared a similar story. She was awaiting the outcome of a critical programmatic decision. Her supervisor told her that senior leadership in the organization appreciated her, she was well-regarded, and praise for her work was effusive. But they weren't willing to let her lead the program because they weren't confident *others* in the organization would follow her direction. While they made no specific reference to gender or race, despite having the title, formal responsibility, and excellent performance record, leadership lacked confidence in her actual ability to direct work. Put another way, in their view, she perhaps had the credentials but not the gravitas.

The lack of some intangible quality is something with which many BIPOC and women are familiar as an obstacle to professional growth. It's either something you are that isn't valued or something you aren't that is. For me it's the response I frequently experience when I share details of my background—people are apparently shocked that someone who *looks like me* has worked with law enforcement in war zones. Often, leaders will justify their decisions on others' expected bad behavior. *It's not that I feel that way—it's just how it is—you know how the rest of the organization will react.* Or, they justify it on culture: *They just don't feel like a fit.*

Try this exercise: Give yourself two minutes to quickly jot down a list of desirable attributes in a leader. When you finish, review the attributes and consider how many are more commonly associated (stereotypes) with a specific gender, race, ethnicity, or another such aspect of identity. Compare your list to those found in this 2018 study of the relevant frequency of attributes assigned to male and female service members in performance reviews. Positive attributes used to describe men included analytical, competent, dependable, confident, versatile, articulate, logical, and practical. Positive attributes used to describe women included compassionate, organized, enthusiastic, and energetic. Negative attributes used to describe men were limited to arrogant and irresponsible; negative attributes used to describe women included frivolous, passive, gossipy, opportunistic, vain, panicky, temperamental, and indecisive.[35] Google saw similar results when it polled its employees about the attributes that make a good manager: 71% of attributes that employees characterized as positive managerial characteristics were associated with men versus just 10% with women.[36]

These differences are often the underlying basis for a determination about who is a good "fit" for a particular position or project. When leaders and managers rely on so-called gut instinct or other such intangibles when assessing a potential new hire, promotion candidate, or project leader, when they reject someone as not a good fit, they're most likely relying on bias, even if unconsciously—implicit bias. When leaders deny the influence of bias by naming decisions as influenced by *culture* and *fit*, they simply further entrench White and male supremacy culture. When leaders and managers decline to offer BIPOC and women opportunities out of a fear that others won't take those individuals seriously, they're not protecting those staff—they're undermining them and denying their organizations the benefit of diverse expertise. Both behaviors, protectionism and devolving to stereotype and fit, are close cousins to gaslighting. These kinds of actions invalidate the experience of those impacted by bias while simultaneously validating discriminatory behavior and attitudes.

B. Burden-Shifting

Another mistake that prevents achieving more diversity in nonprofit leadership is placing the burden on the employee to handled biased behavior. A colleague recently participated in a training program that focused on communication skills to tackle bias. Over several weeks, they learned tactics to improve their ability to listen, rephrase, and challenge bias. While useful on many levels, the training did not adequately assess the burdens that might be involved. During one of the final sessions, they participated in an exercise in which they were to relive a difficult conversation involving bias and use their newfound skills to challenge the offender. The activity worked like this: First, the employee described an experience of bias from their past; then, the employee would reenact the incident with the facilitator, who would play the offender's role. The employee's task was to use their new skills to challenge the bias. The exercise re-traumatized a BIPOC woman in their group. By the time she got to the part of the exercise where she was to use her training to challenge the bias, she was already in tears.

The organization could've trained its staff on reducing personal bias or being an ally to those who experience bias. Instead, they supported the message that, rather than potential perpetrators learning to interrupt their bias, the burden of challenging bias belongs to the victim of bias: As the recipient of biased treatment or communication, your newfound skills would allow you to shoulder that burden with grace, professionally, and tactfully. In other words—your identity is the liability, and thus you must learn to manage the bias that will inevitably come your way—instead of the bias being the liability and unacceptable behavior.

No doubt those who sought and organized this training had the best of intentions. We all recognize that communication skills are valuable assets and that handling a difficult conversation is undoubtedly a worthwhile skill. But care needs to be taken to couple such approaches to tackling bias with visible, accessible accountability frameworks.

This isn't to suggest that there's zero value in training and education. Developing broader self-awareness and the skills to challenge bias is essential. However, the research indicates that this work can be, without a proper institutional framework, primarily self-serving. When not coupled with a structure for responsibility and accountability, such efforts may become check-the-box exercises that serve to provide cover rather than spur action. You can provide your employees with the skills to challenge biased language and behavior through conversation and action. For example, you can teach implicit bias reduction strategies such as counter-stereotyping, exposure or individuation, that put the onus on employees to self-reflect, identify and actively work to reduce their reliance on bias. You can coach your employees to become better allies and effectively challenge explicit bias through questioning and communicating the impact of bias. Above all, however, you must send the message that the biased behavior or language is unprofessional.

In all of this, leadership is critical. Leaders identify, acknowledge, and address power imbalances and take responsibility for tackling cultural barriers to advancement within their organizations. Leaders don't shift burdens downwards; they shoulder them. The presence of bias within an organization is not something to be addressed by those most significantly impacted but by those with the voice and agency to hold bad actors accountable.

C. Mission Formulation for Nonprofits to Achieve DEI

Another area of potential weakness in achieving DEI is in the organization's mission and resources. A little more than half of nonprofits have a formal diversity statement or mission.[37] Even for those that do, we should consider who the board membership and leaders (and donors) are who influence those statements. According to a 2018 study, nonprofit boards are Whiter and older than the population, at 78.6% White and 83.1% older than 40.[38] Sixty-five percent of CEOs, according to Boardsource, report being unhappy with their organization's progress on DEI compared to 41% of board chairs—which suggests that DEI isn't nearly so much a priority for board leadership.[39] If your board lacks diversity, it's unrealistic to expect that you will develop your mission through an equity lens. As a Latinx respondent to a 2017 study of the nonprofit racial leadership gap said, *My White upper-class directors often bond over experiences, about places, and relationships from their personal and family histories. Staff conversations are very exclusive.*[40]

Let's presume that there are three goals for most DEI initiatives: (1) to increase representational diversity; (2) to transform work environments to be more culturally inclusive; and (3) to reap the benefits that accrue from a diverse, equitable, and inclusive environment. As previously discussed, some research has found that programs that aim to reduce bias solely through education have minimal positive and possibly even negative impacts.[41] Networking seems to have a modest effect, at best, for Black women; mentoring and coaching programs, on the other hand, have demonstrated some ability to facilitate career development. However, such programs seem to work best when combined with programs that assign responsibility and hold leaders accountable for change.

For nonprofits, the dollars drive the goals and programs. If you want to prioritize equitable mission and program development, you need a board and donor base that prioritizes DEI. Without this, diversity efforts will remain stagnant. As it is now, the lack of appreciation for the optics alone of a majority White, male board setting priorities for a primarily White, male-led organization funded by mostly White, male donors to solve problems on behalf of marginalized groups never fails to amaze. Setting institutional responsibility and accountability to address this disconnect is a critical response. Some suggest[42] taking lessons from other sectors, such as the so-called Rooney Rule from the National Football League, requiring that job searches for leadership positions must include interviews with at least one candidate of color.[43] Though it's difficult to prove a causal link, since adopting the so-called Rooney Rule, the NFL has seen significant improvement on this front. Regardless, identifying and holding your senior leadership, board leadership, and development directors accountable to DEI benchmarks is vital.

4. Developing an Action Plan

Keeping our focus on steps towards effecting measurable behavioral changes, let's discuss the importance of developing an action plan with specific goals and targets and being intentional about implementation. Think of it this way: If you decide you'd like to eat healthier, what's most effective? An amorphous "eat healthier" goal or a specific "add at least one vegetable to every meal I eat for the next three weeks" action plan? Developing a detailed action plan helps you become more intentional about changes you aim to make in your behavior and the behavior of those you manage. Some researchers frame this as developing implementation intentions.[44] For example, when seeking to expand one's professional network, set out an intention to identify and connect with at least one new BIPOC voice per month who writes, speaks, or otherwise engages on topics in your field. Commit to reading that person's research, contributing to amplifying their voice on social media, and recommending their work to others. Developing such an action plan—a concrete reminder of your implementation intention—provides you with a means of holding yourself accountable. Otherwise, the tendency to fall back on old routines will creep in, even if you're not aware of it when it happens.

The following recommendations are simple, tangible ways to change behavior. Some studies indicate that intentionally and regularly using strategies designed to reduce implicit bias can have a long-lasting impact and break prejudice-related habits.[45] Seek not only to break prejudiced habits but to form new, inclusive habits. Here are some suggestions for everyday actions that leaders can take to effect change in the areas discussed above.

A. Everyday Actions Leaders Can Take to Foster Inclusive Decision-Making in the Workplace

- Assess professional network diversity and determine how many of your trusted colleagues are White, male, or both.
- Reflect on the extent diversity in your network has influenced your perspective. If you don't know the BIPOC or women's voices in your area of expertise, you're not dismantling White or male supremacy; you're helping maintain it. Do the work to identify BIPOC and women's voices in your field, read their research, follow them on social media, and elevate their work and voices.
- Set ambitious targets for representational diversity at events or meetings you organize or co-organize and hold yourself and those you manage accountable for meeting them. Write representational diversity goals into your performance plan and the plans of those you manage.
- When you organize meetings, events, or projects, consider whether you consulted BIPOC and women experts, and if so, whether you meaningfully integrated their input. If you did integrate their input, check whether you visibly credited their contributions. If you didn't, and it's rectifiable, take immediate corrective action. If the moment has passed, note that you missed the target and identify steps to ensure you do not do so next time. If your ability to secure, integrate and credit diverse voices in your work is not part of your performance plan or those you manage, add it.
- Pledge not to speak at or moderate panel discussions or events which exclude BIPOC or women's voices.
- When invited to representationally diverse events, ask yourself whether your voice is the voice that needs to be heard at this moment on this topic. When you opt not to participate, don't just decline—take the time to recommend a BIPOC or woman colleague with similar expertise. When you choose to participate, use your agency to recommend a BIPOC or woman colleague with similar expertise to join you. Look for opportunities to elevate others with whom organizers might not be familiar.

- When participating in meetings where BIPOC or women's voices are ignored or spoken over, intervene to amplify their voice, not yours. Ask yourself: Does your effort to elevate their voice result in boosting yours, or the other way around? (If your purpose in speaking up is to validate the voice of a BIPOC or woman colleague, but it takes you more than a few moments to do so, there's a decent chance you're centering yourself.) It takes me just four seconds to say: *Let's let her finish*, or, *I think what Brenda had to say is vital, and I agree with her.*
- Assess how much time is allowed for inclusive decision-making processes to play out. Consider how many projects or activities you complete or lead the completion of on an urgent basis, such as to exclude the potential for broader input and reflection on design through a gender or race lens.
- Observe who participates in crucial parts of decision-making processes and reflect on whose voices seem to have the most significant impact and whether that impact appears linked to identity.
- Examine organizational goals and results, reflecting on whether you measure most projects by visible, quantifiable short-term gains versus long-term transformative impact.
- Reflect on the extent to which internal organization policies and practices conform with principles of equity. For example, assess your organization's wage ratio (the difference between your highest and lowest paid employees) and whether it might contribute to internal BIPOC or gender pay gaps.

B. Everyday Actions Leaders Can Take Foster Inclusive Language in the Workplace

- Deliberate on and regularly reframe the words you choose to speak or write. If you're not sure about a term or phrase, take the time to do research. If using appropriate terminology or phrases feels awkward, sit with that discomfort. It will improve over time. For example, some struggle to adjust to using "they" or "them" when referring to non-binary individuals, but it becomes natural with practice. Remember that implicit bias is wired into your brain; you must consciously break associations to overcome it; you have to work at it.
- Be open to and seek out feedback from others on your words, but don't expect BIPOC and women to review your work for cultural competence without consideration. It isn't their job to educate you or to serve as your editor.

- Remember that taking the time to review your language is minimally inconvenient but significantly impactful. Eliminating exclusionary language sets the tone for a more welcoming culture.
- Be willing to take risks and fail. Acknowledge that you will make mistakes in the process of learning. Don't hide them or minimize their impact, but don't become paralyzed from the fear of erring. Acknowledge and own your failures, apologize, learn, and do better. But don't make your emotions the center where they are not justifiably so.
- Check your motives when challenging others' behavior. If you're about to call yourself or someone else out, ask yourself honestly: Is this more likely to generate positive feedback for you than positive behavior change to benefit BIPOC or women?
- Focus on action. Whether you've decided your motives are suspect or not, make sure to identify what action you'll take beyond simply owning your fragility (or helping someone else own theirs).

C. Everyday Actions Leaders Can Take to Foster Inclusive Culture

- Reflect on how frequently individuals within your organization are assessed based on some intangible measure, such as *gravitas* or *cultural fit*. If you find yourself or others using such phrases or standards, stop.
- Don't engage in protectionism, period. If you believe that a project or opportunity might place a colleague at risk of being impacted by bias, rather than "protecting" them, challenge the bias directly or support them in challenging it.
- Establish responsibility and accountability for DEI objectives, and invest in talent and resources to lead such efforts. Organizations must imbue DEI leadership roles with the same level of power/authority as other senior roles.
- Avoid tokenism. If your DEI team relies upon your BIPOC staff's unpaid labor (e.g., volunteers or appointments with full-time jobs outside the DEI initiative), that's a red flag.
- Task your HR department with reviewing recruitment, professional development, promotion, and pay practices and policies and make explicit that *I can't control the fact that mostly White men are applying* is not an acceptable excuse for failure to meet hiring and promotion targets. Ask them to analyze and report to you the following to start:
    - When job announcements are shared—where are they shared? Do your HR leaders know where to advertise to attract diverse candidates?

- Are criteria set out in advance?
- How significant are personal recommendations/networking in the recruitment process for senior leadership roles? If significant, do the networks of those conducting outreach included BIPOC and women?
- What kind of reputation does your organization have in communities from which you hope to attract candidates?
- How are job descriptions and minimum requirements crafted? Have they been reviewed with an equity lens? Is there exclusionary language included within the description?
- What's your organization's wage ratio? If senior leaders are paid exponentially more than middle managers or entry-level employees, and you lack diversity at senior levels, take steps to introduce equitable pay policies.

- Examine your board's diversity and report the results to your board and your staff on a regular basis, coupled with a time-bound measurable commitment to improvement.
- Examine the diversity of your donor base. If most of your resources come from organizations that themselves lack diversity at leadership levels, recognize and acknowledge the impact on your mission. Seek funders that prioritize DEI and set a time-bound measurable objective on which you'll commit to reporting progress to your staff.
- Examine the diversity of the organizations or individuals where you provide grants or other resources. If most of your grantees or recipients are organizations that lack diversity at leadership levels, recognize and acknowledge your role in upholding White supremacy funding culture. Seek to support your grantees DEI work and see to provide resources to organizations that also prioritize DEI by setting time-bound measurable diversification of funding objectives.

D. Track Your Progress

- The last step in developing your plan is to set targets. Reflecting on your progress, or lack thereof, through regular benchmarking and measurement helps ensure you remain committed to meaningful action rather than platitudes. For example, at the end of each week, month, or quarter, you could assess:
  - How frequently you took direct action to review and adjust your language, seek and incorporate feedback, make and learn from mistakes and challenge exclusionary behaviors.

- The percentage of time you dedicated toward improving your language versus correcting others—e.g., how much time you spent calling others out for mistakes versus addressing your own, and the success rate of your interventions in others behavior.
- How many times you took direct action to elevate BIPOC or women's perspectives without centering yours.
- How carefully you checked your behavior when leading events, meetings, or projects—as well as when invited to consult or speak.
- How many times you took direct action to elevate DEI priorities at the leadership level. If you offer training (related to DEI), consider whether it was accompanied by an action or accountability plan, and whether it placed the burden of adjusting language and behavior on victims of bias, perpetrators, or managers.
- What tangible steps you took to increase the diversity of your staff, leadership, board, donors, or funding recipients.
- If or how frequently you reported on the progress of DEI initiatives, including to your staff.
- Continue to use these regular check-ups to reflect on your progress, adjust what isn't working and highlight your commitment to future improvement.

Conclusion

At the beginning of this Chapter, I shared a story about assuming a particular song would resonate with colleagues as a common cultural reference. My story demonstrates how pervasive implicit bias can be in reinforcing White supremacy culture. It's not just a song; really, it's an assumption of shared experience, beliefs, and expectations that misses the mark and serves to exclude identities other than my own. The gut-punch, in this case, however painful at the moment, was an important wake-up call to how I've grown lazy over the years in seeking to advance DEI objectives.

A former colleague recently shared a piece that deeply resonated with me, listing twenty-plus ways organizations and foundations, however well-intentioned, perpetuate injustice.[46] As I read through the list, the majority of the points were easy to recognize and appreciate. E.g., *You center the feelings of White donors and avoid anything that could make them uncomfortable.* I read and acknowledge how I've previously done this and commit to NOT doing this in the future. But here I am again, working to check off the boxes on my list to performatively demonstrate to readers how I've done the work. As I seek to refine my own personal action plan, I'm going to focus on the point that stuck in my craw; the one that I can't read without cringing, *You help marginalized people and organizations survive and compete in inequitable systems instead of working with them to dismantle those systems.* This item makes me uncomfortable because this is precisely what I've spent most of my career doing. I've worked with law enforcement for twenty years. It's fair to say that until recently, I didn't even consider the option of working to dismantle our inequitable criminal justice system, built on the foundations of racism and misogyny. As I awaken to the recognition that dismantling must become a necessary part of my mission, I still struggle with what that means. I wrestle with how such a shift in purpose impacts my career in contrast with how it might best achieve equity and positively impact the lives of the BIPOC communities I seek to support. Dismantling the criminal justice system might mean putting people out of work, including me. It would undoubtedly mean acknowledging not just the harm caused by individual bad actors but the harm caused by the institution itself. All of this circles back to recognizing that shifting culture requires intentionality, even when it's hard—otherwise, I'm once again falling back on behaviors shaped by White supremacy and patriarchy.

I share this internal dissonance not because I have an easy answer or recommendation on stopping engaging in this harmful behavior. I don't, not yet. But the worst thing I could do is review that list of 20+ actions, consume just the palatable ones, and discard the rest. Instead, I need to read and reread this list and force myself to evaluate the validity of the points made, acknowledge why I am uncomfortable—until I develop an answer and a path for what comes next. And that, ultimately, is what I encourage leaders in the nonprofit sector to do. Evaluate with focused intentionality, acknowledge what feels comfortable, but highlight what feels hard. Embrace the discomfort that comes with recognizing your complicity in White and male supremacy and developing a set of goals and benchmarks to help you do better. Make a list, not to check things off, but to capture your commitments, especially those you don't yet know how to accomplish.

So, You'd Like to Know More

- David Sipress, *The subject of tonight's discussion is: Why are there no women on this panel,* New Yorker Cartoon, November 9, 2009 (with a panel of five men), available at https://www.art.com/products/p15064006211-sa-i6861177/david-sipress-the-subject-of-tonight-s-discussion-is-why-are-there-no-women-on-this-panel-new-yorker-cartoon.htm.
- Dismantling Racism Works (dRworks), White Supremacy Culture, https://www.whitesupremacyculture.info.

- Nonprofit AF (blog by Vu Le) https://nonprofitaf.com/.
- Zulekha Nathoo, Why Ineffective Diversity Training Won't Go Away (BBC), Worklife, https://www.bbc.com/worklife/article/20210614-why-ineffective-diversity-training-wont-go-away" https://www.bbc.com/worklife/article/20210614-why-ineffective-diversity-training-wont-go-away.
- John McWhorter, The Dehumanizing Condescension of White Fragility, The Atlantic, https://www.theatlantic.com/ideas/archive/2020/07/dehumanizing-condescension-white-fragility/614146/.
- Nonprofit Quarterly, Race and Power, https://nonprofitquarterly.org/tag/race-and-power-racial-justice/.

About the Author

Angelic Young leads professional development and education programs on hate crimes, violent extremism, and inclusive policing for law enforcement. She has worked in the public and nonprofit sector for 20 years, including a decade managing police training and assistance programs in conflict-affected countries at the U.S. Department of State. Ms. Young received her B.A. from Willamette University, her J.D. from Chicago-Kent College of Law, and is a Truman National Security Fellow. Angelic dedicates this Chapter to Danika Manso-Brown, a friend, colleague and thought partner whose guidance and encouragement during this writing journey was invaluable.

Endnotes

1. *Anti-bias education* is "an approach to teaching and learning designed to increase understanding of differences and their value to a respect and civil society, and to actively challenge bias, stereotyping and all forms of discrimination." ANTI-DEFAMATION LEAGUE, WHAT IS ANTI-BIAS EDUCATION?, https://www.adl.org/education/resources/glossary-terms/what-is-anti-bias-education.

2. LESTER M. SALAMON, BROOKINGS INSTITUTE, THE STATE OF NONPROFIT AMERICA, CH. 1 (2012), https://www.brookings.edu/book/the-state-of-nonprofit-america.

3. NATIONAL CENTER FOR CHARITABLE STATISTICS, THE NONPROFIT SECTOR IN BRIEF, https://nccs.urban.org/project/nonprofit-sector-brief.

4. Jeanne Sahadi, *After Years of Talking About Diversity, The Number of Black Leaders at US Companies Is Still Dismal* CNN, June 2, 2020, https://www.cnn.com/2020/06/02/success/diversity-and-black-leadership-in-corporate-america/index.html.

5. Julie Hayes, *Is the Nonprofit Sector Doing Enough for Diversity?*, DIVERSITY J. (Nov. 9, 2012), https://diversityjournal.com/9897-is-the-nonprofit-sector-doing-enough-for-diversity.

6. Frances Kunreuther & Sean Thomas-Breitfeld, Race to Lead, Confronting the Nonprofit Racial Leadership Gap (2017), https://racetolead.org/race-to-lead/ (last visited February 25, 2021).

7. Dismantling Racism Works (dRworks), https://www.whitesupremacyculture.info/ (last visited July 25, 2021).

8. Helen Kim Ho, *8 Ways People of Color Are Tokenized in White Supremacy Culture Nonprofits*, Medium, Sept. 18, 2017, https://medium.com/the-nonprofit-revolution/8-ways-people-of-color-are-tokenized-in-nonprofits-32138d0860c1.

9. Atokatha Ashmond Brew, *Why Women Are Still Underrepresented in Nonprofit Leadership and What We Can Do About It*, Nonprofit HR, Sept. 6, 2017, https://www.nonprofithr.com/women-underrepresented-nonprofit-leadership/.

10. Tessie Castillo, *Will Women of Color Leading Nonprofits Drive Deeper Equity?*, Feb. 28, 2019, Filter, https://filtermag.org/will-women-of-color-leading-nonprofits-drive-deeper-equity.

11. Women in the Workplace, McKinsey, https://www.mckinsey.com/featured-insights/diversity-and-inclusion/women-in-the-workplace# (last visited February 25, 2021).

12. *See, e.g.,* Sara Garlick Lundberg, *You Should Be Hiring More Women: Here's Why*, DRG (Feb. 26, 2019), https://drgsearch.com/hiring-women-heres/#; *4 Ways Diversity & Inclusion Is Good for Business*, Galvánize (Jan. 9, 2020); Vijay Eswaran, *The Business Case for Diversity Is Now Overwhelming. Here's Why*, World Economic Forum, https://www.weforum.org/agenda/2019/04/business-case-for-diversity-in-the-workplace/ (Apr. 9, 2019).

13. Matt Krentz, *Survey: What Diversity and Inclusion Policies Do Employees Actually Want?* Harv. Bus. Rev. (Feb. 5, 2019); *The History of Diversity Training and Its Pioneers*, Diversity Officer Magazine, https://diversityofficermagazine.com/diversity-inclusion/the-history-of-diversity-training-its-pioneers/.

14. *Initiative*, Merriam Webster, https://www.merriam-webster.com/dictionary/initiative (last visited February 25, 2021) and Cambridge, https://dictionary.cambridge.org/us/dictionary/english/initiative (last visited February 25, 2021).

15. Frank Dobbin & Alexandra Kalev, *Why Doesn't Diversity Training Work? The Challenge for Industry and Academia*, 10 Anthropology Now 48, 51 (2018).

16. Alexandra Kalev, Frank Dobbin & Erin Kelly, *Best Practices or Best Guesses? Assessing the Efficacy of Corporate Affirmative Action and Diversity Policies*, 71 Am. Soc. Rev. 589 (2006).

17. *See generally* Jo Handelsman & Arturo Casdevall, *The Presence of Female Conveners Correlates with a Higher Proportion of Female Speakers at Scientific Symposia*, 5 Mbio #1 (2014); Jory Lerback & Brooks Hanson, *Too Few*, Nature, Jan. 26, 2018.

18. *Allyship*, The Anti-Oppression Network, https://theantioppressionnetwork.com/allyship/.

19. *See, e.g.,* Anthony G. Greenwald & Thomas F. Pettigrew, *With Malice Toward None and Charity for Some: Ingroup Favoritism Enables Discrimination*, 69 Am. Psychologist 669 (2014); Nicole Shelton, Jennifer A. Richeson, Jessica Salvatore & Sophie Trawalter, *Ironic Effects of Racial Bias During Interracial Interactions*, 16 Psychol. Sci. (2005).

20. *See* Jennifer K. Elek & Andrea L. Miller, Nat'l Center for State Courts, The Evolving Science on Implicit Bias: An Updated Resource for the State Court Community (2021) (Included as Chapter 2, this book); Allison L. Skinner & Sylvia Perry, *Are Attitudes Contagious*, 46 Personality & Soc. Psychol. Bull. 514 (2020).

21. Lilia M. Cortina, M. Sandy Hershcovis & Kathryn B. Clancy, *The Embodiment of Insult: A Theory of Biobehavioral Response to Workplace Incivility*, 48 J. MANAGEMENT 738 (2022).

22. *White Supremacy Culture Characteristics*, SHOWING UP FOR RACIAL JUSTICE, https://www.showingupforracialjustice.org/white-supremacy-culture-characteristics.html.

23. Irving L. Janis, *Groupthink*, PSYCHOL. TODAY (1971).

24. Kenneth Jones & Tema Okun, *White Supremacy Culture Characteristics*, SHOWING UP FOR RACIAL JUSTICE, https://www.showingupforracialjustice.org/white-supremacy-culture-characteristics.html.

25. Alan Greenblatt, *The Racial History of the 'Grandfather Clause'*, NPR, Oct. 22, 2013, https://www.npr.org/sections/codeswitch/2013/-10/21/239081586/the-racial-history-of-the-grandfather-clause.

26. RACE TO LEAD: WOMEN OF COLOR IN THE NONPROFIT SECTOR, https://buildingmovement.org/reports/race-to-lead-women-of-color-in-the-nonprofit-sector/.

27. Pratima Rao Gluckman, *When Women Are Called 'Aggressive' at Work*, FORBES, https://www.forbes.com/sites/nextavenue/2018/08/28/when-women-are-called-aggressive-at-work/?sh=55baab677bc8.

28. Karen Tumulty, *Republicans Suddenly Discover They Don't like Naughty Words*, WASH. POST, Dec. 17, 2020, https://www.washingtonpost.com/opinions/2020/12/17/omalley-dillon-marco-rubio-swearing-biden/.

29. *See generally* Joan C. Williams, Katherine W. Phillips & Erika V. Hall, *Tools for Change: Boosting the Retention of Women in the STEM Pipeline*, 6 J. RESEARCH IN GENDER STUDIES 65 (2016).

30. J.C. Walley-Jean, *Debunking the Myth of the "Angry Black Woman:" An Exploration of Anger in Young African-American Women*, BLACK WOMEN, GENDER & FAMILIES (2009).

31. Tanya Prive, *4 Devastating Consequences of a Toxic Workplace Culture*, inc.om, https://www.inc.com/tanya-prive/4-devastating-consequences-of-a-toxic-workplace-culture.html (last visited February 25, 2021); *see also* Lilia M. Cortina, Vicki J. Magley, Kerri Nelson & Dana Kabat-Farr, *Researching Rudeness: The Past, Present, and Future of the Science of Incivility*, 20 J. OCCUPATIONAL HEALTH PSYCHOL. 299 (2017).

32. ROBIN J. DIANGELO, WHITE FRAGILITY (2018).

33. Erin Shankie, *Women in Power-Or, Not So Much: Gender in the Nonprofit Sector*, NONPROFIT QUARTERLY, Jan. 21, 2015, https://nonprofitquarterly.org/women-in-power-or-not-so-much-gender-in-the-nonprofit-sector/.

34. Michael Theis, *Midsize Nonprofits Show Greatest Progress Closing CEO Gender Pay and Leadership Gaps, Study Shows*, COP, Sept. 24, 2019, https://www.philanthropy.com/article/midsize-nonprofits-show-greatest-progress-closing-ceo-gender-pay-and-leadership-gaps-study-shows/.

35. David G. Smith, Judith E. Rosenstein & Margaret C. Nikolov, *The Different Words We Use to Describe Male and Female Leaders*, HARV. BUS. REV. (May 25, 2018), https://hbr.org/2018/05/the-different-words-we-use-todescribe-male-and-female-leaders (discussing David Smith et al. *The Power of Language: Gender, Status, and Agency in Performance Evaluations*, 80 SEX ROLES 159 (2019); AMARETTE FILUT, ANNA KAATZ & MOLLY CARNES, THE SASKAWA PEACE FOUNDATION EXPERT REVIEWS SERIES ON ADVANCING WOMEN'S EMPOWERMENT THE IMPACT OF UNCONSCIOUS BIAS ON WOMEN'S CAREER ADVANCEMENT (2017).

36. *Re:Work*, Google, https://rework.withgoogle.com/print/guides/5079604133888000/; *see also* Naomi Ellemers, *Gender Stereotypes*, 69 Ann. Rev. Psychol. 275 (2018).

37. *2019 Non Profit Diversity Practices*, Non Profit HR, https://www.nonprofithr.com/wp-content/uploads/2019/11/New-Report-Published-Nonprofit-Diversity-Practices-Report-Published2019.pdf.

38. Una Osili, *The Impact of Diversity: Understanding How Nonprofit Board Diversity Affects Philanthropy, Leadership, and Board Engagement*, IUPUI, (2018), https://scholarworks.iupui.edu/handle/1805/15239.

39. *Id.*

40. Ofronama Biu, Race to Lead: Women of Color in the Nonprofit Sector (2019), https://buildingmovement.org/reports/race-to-lead-women-of-color-in-the-nonprofit-sector/.

41. Gretchen R. Webber & Patti Giuffre, *Women's Relationships with Women at Work: Barriers to Solidarity*, 13 Sociology Compass (2019); Lucia Osborne-Crowley, *Queen Bee Syndrome Debunked: Women Aren't Kicking the Ladder Out After All*, Women's Agenda, June 10, 2015.

42. Elizabeth A. Castillo, *Why Are We Still Struggling with Diversity, Equity, and Inclusion in Nonprofit Governance?*, Nonprofit Quarterly mag.

43. Adam Sites, *NFL's Rooney Rule: What Is It and How Does It Work?*, Jan. 6, 2018, SBNation.com, https://www.sbnation.com/2018/1/6/16856550/rooney-rule-nfl-explained-how-it-works-coaches.

44. Saaid A. Mendoza, Peter M. Gollwitzer & David M. Amodio, *Reducing the Expression of Implicit Stereotypes: Reflexive Control Through Implementation Intentions*, 36 Personality & Soc. Psychol. Bull. 512 (2010).

45. Patricia G. Devine, Patrick S. Forscher, Anthony J. Austin & William T.L. Cox, *Long-Term Reduction in Implicit Bias: A Prejudice Habit-Breaking Intervention*, 48 J. Experimental Soc. Psychol. 1267 (2012).

46. Vu, *21 Signs You or Your Organization May Be the White Moderate Dr. King Warned About*, Nonprofit AF (Jan. 12, 2021), https://nonprofitaf.com/2021/01/21-signs-you-or-your-organization-may-be-the-white-moderate-dr-king-warned-about/?fbclid=IwAR0tJOlHZIQlRhzPdAgkSSs_W5YGbDWe_sutKQaiGxdpLlU7BZK6NPutI3g#more-7059.

FIFTEEN

Gender and Evaluation

Dr. Virginia Valian, Hunter College and CUNY Graduate Center, NY

A Note from the Editors: From us both: While this Chapter finds its focus in examples from the academy, the principles and questions identified play out in other arenas both in law schools and beyond. For example, presenting at major bar or medical conferences is seen as a way to network and to advance one's reputation in many fields; or, lawyers might be thinking here about how to put teams together for a pitch to a client; and all employers can find useful approaches here. Similarly, Professor Valian's discussion on moral licensing (and how it frees us to make a more biased decision later) is an important thought point. All told, Professor Valian's explanation of difference rings true in many settings, and her pointers on how to interrupt bias are useful wherever people are evaluating other people. An additional note from Sarah: I think of Professor Valian as one of my heroes, albeit until recently someone I just knew as a reader of her writings. In 1998, when I was myself reflecting on my own career, Dr. Valian wrote a book called *Why So Slow: The Advancement of Women*. If only I had read the book then, instead of many years later, my career path might well have been different; it certainly would have been easier. I would have more readily seen my commonality with other women faculty and felt less that negative messages I received were about me, about my failure to be "as good." In any case, I'm glad to be able to welcome Dr. Valian to this book and encourage our readers to consider her message as one that is broadly applicable. I especially encourage our women readers to take note of the research that supports the way schemas can work against us in evaluative situations.

CHAPTER HIGHLIGHTS

- Evaluations are integral to academic and professional success, but they can be inaccurate, even when the evaluator has every intention of being fair.

- Evaluations are affected by schemas—mental models that categorize objects, people, and roles; gender schemas lead to small but consistent overvaluations of men's accomplishments and undervaluations of women's accomplishments.

- Small advantages accumulate over time to create widening differences in male and female careers. The answer to "Don't make a mountain out of a molehill" is "Mountains *are* molehills, piled one on top of the other."

- Understanding how and why our minds use schemas is critical if we want to judge people fairly.

- The content of gender schemas varies somewhat depending on race and ethnicity.

CHAPTER CONTENTS

Introduction

1. Men's and women's achievements are recognized and evaluated differently.
    A. Three Small Local Phenomena
    B. A Large-Scale Phenomenon
    C. Laboratory Experiments and Audit Studies
    D. Putting the Data Together
2. The way our minds take shortcuts (schemas) explains the differences.
    A. Schemas
    B. Generality of Schemas
    C. How Schemas Work
3. Schemas can mesh or clash and can do so within or outside of awareness.
    A. Accumulation of Advantage
    B. Flawed Decision-Making
    C. Moral Licensing
4. How can we achieve change such that evaluations will be more equitable?
    A. The Individual Level: Education
    B. The Individual Level: Intervention and Prevention
    C. The Institutional Level: Policies and Procedures

Conclusion

Introduction

Evaluation is a constant and ubiquitous feature in work life. People judge and are judged. How do people decide whom to invite to give a talk? How do people decide which authors to read on subjects that interest them? How do faculty decide which authors their students will read? How do college students decide which of their professors is competent and knowledgeable? How do people decide whether they will pay attention to a suggestion that someone makes in a meeting? How do employers decide who to hire and promote? People judge and are judged. This Chapter focuses on evaluations of merit and ability and the role of gender schemas in making those evaluations.

1. Men's and women's achievements are recognized and evaluated differently.

There are three kinds of data we can use to answer our questions about evaluations—small local phenomena, large-scale phenomena, and laboratory experiments. Each form has advantages and disadvantages. Consider these examples of data on the way achievements are recognized—recognition being one aspect of positive evaluations that helps determine the trajectory of someone's career.

A. Three Small Local Phenomena

Research, writing, and presenting one's work at colloquia and conferences are significant markers for a successful career in the academy (and in analogous ways in other professions). At major research universities, and increasingly at smaller universities and colleges as well, one's progress through the ranks depends on the quality and quantity of one's research. While teaching is valued in all academic institutions, and at some colleges is the major determinant of promotion, research is the principal determinant of success in one's field. Grants and fellowships are awarded based on one's research. Invitations to be a keynote speaker at a professional conference are based on one's research. A national and international reputation is developed through one's research. Prizes and awards from professional societies are given based on one's research.

Both small and large measures of recognition matter. Consider the following example that a colleague offered: She had told her chair that she was giving the annual keynote at an upcoming conference in her field—the major conference. Her department's website had a section where faculty achievements were posted. She waited a few days, but did not see her keynote on the website. She spoke to the chair again, and he said he would take care of it. Her keynote went up as a feature. A couple of days later it was replaced by a notice of a male colleague's presentation—not a keynote—at a minor conference several months away. Her colleague's notice stayed up for weeks.

What may not at first seem such a large matter often turns out to be so. Consider the example of listing authors. Since more and more research is conducted by teams, one's placement in the list of authors is a signal of the importance of one's contribution. The first author is the major contributor and the person who will most often be cited and credited with the research. In the natural sciences (and more and more in psychology and other social sciences), the last author in a group of several authors will commonly be the senior person in whose laboratory the research was conducted. One colleague at a law school reported being told by her Dean that being the second (of two) authors meant her publication would not be considered a positive contribution in her annual evaluation.

Deans are not alone in this attitude. Justin Wolpers, an economist writing in the *New York Times* in 2015, noticed a small phenomenon—how four journalists recognized the same newsworthy research by economists.[1] David Plotz, writing in *Slate*, an online magazine, referred to research by "Nobel Prize-winning economist Angus Deaton and Anne Case, who is *his wife*, and *also a researcher.*" Ross Douthat, writing in the *New York Times*, referred to the same research by "Nobel Laureate Angus Deaton and *his wife*, Anne Case." Gina Kolata, writing in the *New York Times*, mentioned "the Deaton-Case analysis." Paul Krugman, in the *New York Times*, talked about "a new paper by the economists Angus Deaton (who just won a Nobel) and Anne Case." One might wonder who Anne Case is, other than a wife. One certainly wouldn't think she was the lead author. Dr. Case is a professor of economics and public affairs at Princeton; she is a fellow of the Econometric Society. Wolpers calls her one of the leading health economists of her generation. Most striking, she is the first author of the paper being described. Of the four journalists, one is a woman, one leans to the right, and two lean to the left. All four are White, as are Case and Deaton. Neither gender nor political persuasion immunizes one from underrating women's accomplishments.

In the first and second cases, we are hearing an anecdote. In the third, we have a slightly broader phenomenon, but it is still just an example. Only data on a larger scale can tell us how often sex disparities in recognition occur, and only data incorporating various controls can tell us whether the unequal recognition is inappropriate.

B. A Large-Scale Phenomenon

A study on who speaks at university colloquia suggests that sex disparities in recognition occur on a large scale—and inappropriately. By "inappropriately" I mean that the disproportionality cannot be explained by there being more men at a given rank in the field or by more women choosing not to participate. This study examined gender differences in colloquium speakers at fifty prestigious U.S. colleges and universities in 2013–2014.[2] It used archival data to analyze 3,652 talks in six academic disciplines: biology, bioengineering, political science, psychology, sociology, and history. Those disciplines span broad areas in academia, and the percentage of women in the fields ranges from 22% to 47%. (Race and ethnicity information was not collected.)

Men gave twice as many talks as women did. One explanation might be that the numbers favor men in all of the fields. If fields have few women, one would not expect many female speakers. The study thus calculated the possible pool of speakers by looking at the percentage of women in each field across one hundred institutions where the colloquium speakers worked. Another control incorporated the rank of the speaker; most speakers are full professors, and that rank has the smallest percentage of women. It might be possible, then, for an imbalance of men and women at different ranks to be responsible for more men giving talks. Even after both important controls were introduced, however, men were significantly more likely than women to be colloquium speakers.

Another possible explanation is that schools invited women to talk at rates proportional to their representation in the field, but women refused invitations more often than men did. Women might care less than men do about public recognition, or they might find it more difficult to accept a speaking invitation because they have greater home and childcare responsibilities than do men. To eliminate those possibilities, the study surveyed men and women who were colleagues at the same institutions as actual speakers to find out how interested those potential speakers were in giving colloquia and how often they accepted invitations. Men and women showed an equal interest in giving talks and indicated the same acceptance rates. The large-scale data, then, suggest that there must be another reason that women's accomplishments are under-recognized. Although colloquium committees may deliberately exclude women, I suggest that exclusion is, typically, neither deliberate nor intentional. Rather, exclusion occurs because our ability to evaluate others is flawed.

One virtue of the small- and large-scale data just reviewed is that they are "ecologically valid." They look at real-world events that have real-world consequences. Recognition begets more recognition and influence in one's field. The disadvantage of such studies is that it is impossible to fully control for every variable. In the large-scale study just described, even after all the controls that were used, it could be argued that women researchers might be doing less important work than men researchers, even if they are at the same institution and at the same rank.

C. Laboratory Experiments and Audit Studies

Laboratory experiments offer more control. In the laboratory, researchers can ensure that qualifications are equal and only gender varies. That allows a more direct—if slightly artificial—look at the sources of people's judgments and choices. Consider, for example, a study that asked physicists, biologists, and chemists to read the résumé of a (fictitious) recent college graduate applying for a job as lab manager and rate the applicant on how competent and hireable they were and also to say how interested they would be in mentoring the applicant.[3] Half the participants received a résumé with a male name at the top, and the other half received the same résumé with a female name at the top. There were no other differences between the applicants and no other demographic information was provided. Faculty—male and female alike—rated the male applicant as more competent and hireable, and they showed more interest in mentoring the male candidate.

That wasn't all. Participants also answered questions that probed their beliefs about whether disadvantages that women have experienced are largely in the past. People who thought there was no longer a gender problem tended to rate the male applicant more highly (or the female applicant less highly, depending on condition). People feel freer to indulge their beliefs—that a man would make a better lab manager—if they believe gender inequality does not exist. Other data suggest political party differences in the likelihood of belief in gender inequality. A survey in 2019 of over 1,900 likely voters found substantial differences in the extent to which different political, gender, and ethnic groups thought there was full equality for women in work, life, and politics.[4] For example, 88% percent of Democratic women and 79% of Democratic men thought there was still work to be done, compared to 46% of Republican women and 23% of Republican men.

Gender is not the only characteristic that evaluators attend to, and the academy is not the only setting where people show preferences that are orthogonal to merit. An audit study investigated how firms responded to applicants for job postings.[5] (An audit study, also called a correspondence study when conducted via written materials only, is a field experiment in which researchers send fictitious materials to actual firms or individuals, varying gender, race, or other demographic features and observe responses to the materials.)[6] Identical materials that varied the apparent race, gender, and prestige of the college the person had graduated from were sent to companies that had advertised openings for recent college graduates. Race and gender were signaled via the person's name; Jamal and Ebony, for example, were used to suggest a Black male and a Black female, while Ronny and Anne were used to suggest a White male and White female. The résumés indicated graduation from a high-prestige school like Harvard or a lower-prestige school like the University of Massachusetts.

Companies responded more often to White than Black applicants and more often to putative Harvard than putative UMass graduates. There were no gender differences. Most interesting was the interaction between race and prestige. Jamal from Harvard received more responses than Jamal from UMass, but Jamal from Harvard received only as many responses as did Ronny from UMass. Prestige helped Black applicants but still did not make them equal to White applicants.

D. Putting the Data Together

Taken together, the different kinds of data that I have presented tell a coherent and consistent story: women's qualifications are rated less highly than men's. When data converge, we have more confidence in the results. All studies leave questions behind that later work tries to answer, and all studies draw conclusions that later work may challenge or amplify. For example, a real-world analysis of awards from professional societies to neuroscience faculty found that men received more awards than women.[7] The gender gap remained after controls for institutional prestige, year of degree, and total publications were implemented. After controlling for total citations, however, no gender difference in awards appeared. If citations are a good measure of the value of someone's research, one could argue that men deserve to get more awards.

Are citations a good measure of quality? Perhaps not. The same downgrading processes that are hypothesized to play a role in women's lack of awards and invitations to give colloquium talks might also play a role in their lack of citations. A study of the reference lists of neuroscience papers in major journals has analyzed who is cited and who cites whom and provides helpful data.[8] Neuroscience papers are typically multi-authored. Both the first author and the last author are the ones with major responsibility for the work, the first author for obvious reasons and the last author because that is generally the person in whose laboratory the research was conducted. The analysis examined how often male-male, male-female, female-male, and female-female pairs were cited in five major journals over a twenty-two-year period. Roughly 50% of the published papers were by male-male pairs; the other 50% included a female first or last author.

Male-male papers in the five journals were cited more often than would be predicted after various controls (such as the number of papers authored by different combinations and the seniority of investigators) were instituted, while papers from each of the other three combinations were cited less often than would be expected. Papers by women authors, whether women were one of the two authors or both authors, were under-cited.

More interesting was who cited whom. Male-male pairs cited male-male papers significantly more often than would be expected and cited papers with a female author significantly less often than would be expected. In contrast, pairs with a female author cited papers from different combinations at roughly the predicted rate. Only female-female pairs cited female-female papers more often than would be expected.

Since the analysis examined citation patterns over two decades, it was possible to see whether the over-citation of male-male papers by male-male authors receded as more women entered the field. To the contrary, it increased over time. Time will not automatically heal the over-citation of men. Over-citation matters, as citation rates appear to be an important driver of prestigious professional awards.

A similar imbalance occurs in the course reading lists of professors of social psychology.[9] An analysis of seventy-two reading lists found that female first authors were included less often than would be predicted given the availability of female-led articles in the top two social psychology journals. Even reading lists created after 2010 had fewer female-led papers than would be expected.

2. The way our minds take shortcuts (schemas) explains the differences.

As discussed in the preceding section, data from a variety of sources confirm that women receive less recognition than men.[10] Since most academics, and most professionals in every field, sincerely espouse the merit principle, the question naturally arises: why do women continue to be less positively evaluated than men? Although it is impossible to rule out intentional discrimination, especially since we know that overt bigotry exists, the path I will follow here assumes that people overall intend to judge fairly. Indeed, as we will see, it is in part because people believe so firmly in the sufficiency of their good intentions that their tendencies to underrate women are given free rein. But, first, we need to understand the role of schemas in categorizing, remembering, and evaluating people.

A. Schemas

The first concept I will concentrate on here is schemas. Schemas are cognitive constructs—largely but not completely nonconscious—that organize beliefs and knowledge about members of a category in schematic form. The category can range from inanimate objects like skyscrapers to social categories, like woman, to professional positions, like scientist. We tend to pay attention to information that is consistent with our categories and discount or ignore other information.

Schemas are similar to stereotypes, but to most people the idea of a stereotype suggests a negative attitude, whereas schemas are in principle neutral. Schemas are critical for efficient understanding of all the objects, people, and situations that we encounter in the course of a day. People are cognitive misers, taking shortcuts whenever possible.[11] We cannot treat every object and person that we encounter as if we know nothing about the category to which they belong, because their category is at least partially diagnostic. Schemas help us know what to expect and predict and help us make interpretations and judgments. And, often, our schemas are accurate. For example, schemas portray women as shorter than men on average, which they are.

Both men and women hold gender schemas—schematic views of men and women. Schemas are cognitive constructs that portray men as capable of independent action (agentic), as doing things for a reason (instrumental), and as being oriented to the task at hand (task-oriented). Men look right for jobs that are thought to require focus, unemotional reasoning, and ambition—jobs like science, finance, technology. In fact, men look *so* right for such jobs that both men and women rate men higher than their performance warrants.[12] Schemas portray women as being concerned about and helping others (nurturant), caring about the common good (communal), and expressive of their feelings. Women look right for the job—and feel right for the job—of taking care of others, of laboring for love. Such schema characteristics continue to be seen as broadly descriptive of men and women.[13] In addition to attributing different psychological qualities to men and women, people attribute different cognitive characteristics. In particular, men are perceived as "brilliant," women not so much.[14]

B. Generality of Schemas

Although I have used the terms "men" and "women" as if they apply generally and universally, the reality is that in many experiments, the individuals who are doing the evaluating are primarily White, thus restricting their generality. Most of the existing data either does not specify the race or ethnicity of the individuals who are being evaluated or assumes a White target. Similarly, social class, sexual orientation, religion, political affiliation, and other demographic categories are usually not specified.

Studies that specifically incorporate race as a variable along with gender may show gender commonalities or gender differences across race, depending on what is being measured. Consider who gets PhDs in the sciences in the United States. Among Whites and Asians, more men than women get science PhDs; but among Latinx individuals and African Americans, more women get science PhDs.[15]

A different example, an experiment with primarily White participants, shows both gender commonalities and gender differences. Both White and Black women were perceived as less feminine if they had a neutral facial expression rather than a smiling face. Smiling enhances femininity for both White and Black women. But

Black women with a neutral face were seen as less feminine than White women with a neutral face.[16]

The term "intersectionality" is used in two different ways in research. In its original form, intersectionality was intended to refer to a system of discrimination.[17] Black women, in particular, have lost antidiscrimination cases because they have not had standing as Black women, but only as either Black or as female. Professor Kimberlé Crenshaw, who coined the term intersectionality, notes that White women have been seen by courts as representing the class of *women*, because women's race as White is taken for granted. But Black women have not been seen as capable of simultaneously representing both women and Blacks. White women are as much of a "hybrid" as Black women, but because the law has taken Whiteness as the norm, White women are viewed as representing all women.

In Crenshaw's formulation, Black women could be analogized as in the middle of a traffic intersection, with cars coming from multiple directions, any one or several of which could cause injury to the person in the middle. As Crenshaw puts it:

> Black women sometimes experience discrimination in ways similar to White women's experiences; sometimes they share very similar experiences with Black men. Yet often they experience double-discrimination—the combined effects of practices which discriminate on the basis of race, and on the basis of sex. And sometimes, they experience discrimination as Black women—not the sum of race and sex discrimination, but as Black women.

Crenshaw goes on to say:

> Neither Black liberationist politics nor feminist theory can ignore the intersectional experiences of those whom the movements claim as their respective constituents. In order to include Black women, both movements must distance themselves from earlier approaches in which experiences are relevant only when they are related to certain clearly identifiable causes (for example, the oppression of Blacks is significant when based on race, of women when based on gender).[18]

Within psychology, intersectionality is often interpreted primarily in terms of identities, rather than in terms of the effects of social policies as a function of identities.[19] For example, assertiveness, which is generally seen more negatively when displayed by White women compared to White men, may not elicit as much of a penalty when displayed by Black women.[20]

Since we continue to lack a genuinely diverse set of participants and a genuinely diverse set of experimental materials in laboratory studies, the reader should keep in mind the limitations, assumptions, and uncertainties.

C. How Schemas Work

Schemas are like miniature hypotheses that explain the world. As I have pointed out, they are useful, even necessary. They are sometimes correct, but also lead us astray, in part because of their automaticity and accessibility. Since schemas are activated almost automatically, we are largely unaware of their operation.

Schemas lead to overvaluations of men and undervaluations of women in professional settings because the schema for men and the schema for high achievement mesh well, while the schema for women and the schema for high achievement do not fit well.[21] Consider, for example, an observational study of the success of male and female founding chief executive officers (CEOs) in raising initial funds for their equivalently-rated companies.[22] One way to investigate this is to compare companies that can be classified as male- or female-dominated, based on the percentage of women employed in a given industry. Women look more appropriate as a CEO for female-dominated companies, so we would expect them to raise more money as CEOs there than as CEOs of male-dominated companies. For men, predictions are less clear, since men might look appropriate as a CEO, whether it is for male- or female-dominated companies.

Women raised almost seven times more money if they were leaders of a female-dominated industry than if they were leaders of a male-dominated industry. Men raised the same amount of money whether they were CEO of a female- or male-dominated company. If we focus on female-dominated companies and compare men and women, we find that they were equally successful in fund-raising. For male-dominated companies, in contrast, men raised about ten times more money than women. Women fit as leaders of companies that are female-dominated, but not as leaders of companies that are male-dominated; men fit as leaders regardless of industry type.

Observational studies, as already mentioned, are limited by lack of control. In this case, the observational study was paired with an experimental study with roughly one hundred real-world investors as participants. Two-thirds were men, and almost 90% were White. The participants read four vignettes, two that described male-dominated industries and two that described female-dominated industries. In each industry type, one vignette had a woman's name and one had a man's name. The investors were told they had $400,000 to invest across the four companies. Mirroring the observational study, the investors allocated more money to women where the fit was good and allocated the same amount to men regardless of industry type. Participants separately indicated that they perceived a better fit between the woman CEO and a female-dominated industry compared to the male-dominated industry. Participants did not see a fit difference for men. The gender of participants did not play a role; as is the case in most studies, men and women rate other men and women the same way.

3. Schemas can mesh or clash and can do so within or outside of awareness.

Schemas are descriptive in the sense that they summarize the relevant dimensions of categories—how things are, or at least how they appear to us. In the social world, people can also use schemas prescriptively, to summarize what traits children and adults ought to have. The absence of those traits—such as a woman not being particularly nice or a man not being particularly assertive—signifies that someone is failing to live up to the norms that are expected; they are not performing in the prescribed mode. Beyond prescription is proscription, when a child or adult displays a trait that is contra-indicated for their apparent gender. When an adult tells a boy who is crying, "Boys don't cry," they are not just uttering a generalization, but giving the boy an instruction to stop crying; crying is proscribed for boys and men. By the time adulthood rolls around, a boy's tears are largely a thing of the past, while girls are allowed to continue to cry when emotion overwhelms them.

One laboratory study asked different groups of adults (80% of whom were White) to indicate how typical or desirable ninety-six traits, behaviors, and preferences were for three-year-old girls or boys.[23] If a characteristic was rated as not desirable for a girl or a boy, it was considered a proscribed characteristic for that gender. For instance, "Enjoys wearing skirts and dresses" was seen as descriptive for girls, desirable (and hence prescribed) for girls, not descriptive for boys, and not desirable (and hence proscribed) for boys. "Likes to pretend to be a soldier" was rated as descriptive for boys, desirable for boys, not descriptive for girls, and not desirable for girls. People might fail to demonstrate a prescribed trait, might display a proscribed trait, or might fail to balance traits appropriately.[24] Deviating from a gender norm is costly. Laboratory studies on backlash show that participants range from thinking ill of those who deviate to punishing them. In some contexts there is occasionally no penalty. For example, women who adopt a strong leadership role can "neutralize" it by being conspicuously communal and warm.[25]

To summarize the research discussed thus far, gender schemas portray men and women as having distinctive areas of specialization, while of course also having many overlapping traits. In consequential areas, such as professional recognition, men fare better, even when, to the extent possible, we have controlled for variables other than gender.

A. Accumulation of Advantage

Up to this point we have discussed clearly consequential areas where men have an advantage: men accrue more prizes and awards, more citations, more invitations to talk; men can raise money more easily in male-dominated fields. We have not yet discussed seemingly inconsequential areas. One example that might seem trivial is how people are introduced before a talk at a meeting. In one analysis of talks at an oncology meeting, women were more likely than men to be introduced by their first name than as Doctor or Professor So-and-So.[26] Adding to the impression that the example is trivial is the fact that it is not universally the case: there is variability in the extent to which women experience small indignities.[27]

Another small example occurs at meetings: a woman makes a suggestion and it is ignored; ten minutes later a man makes the same suggestion and the group discusses it and credits the man with it. As with introductions, this doesn't happen every time a woman speaks; it is variable. But it happened often enough in the early days of the Obama administration that women in meetings decided to amplify their female colleagues' voices: "When a woman made a key point, other women would repeat it, giving credit to its author."[28]

Although these examples are minor and variable, they happen to women more than they happen to men. How important are such small events? Well-meaning observers may tell a woman who notices that her suggestion was ignored not to make a mountain out of a molehill, to pick her battles. That is where the notion of the accumulation of advantage (also known as the Matthew effect[29]) comes in. It is the message of compound interest: no matter how small the difference is between the interest on a loan from one bank and the interest from another bank, the savvy borrower will choose the bank with smaller interest rates on loans, just as the savvy investor will choose the bank with higher interest on savings accounts. Over time, it matters. Small differences, if consistently encountered, add up to create more and more advantage for one group and less and less advantage for the other group.

Success is largely the accumulation of advantage, exploiting small gains to get bigger ones. A computer simulation demonstrates how the accumulation of advantage works.[30] The researchers simulated an eight-level hierarchical institution, with a pyramidal structure. They staffed this hypothetical institution with equal numbers of men and women. The model assumed a tiny bias in favor of promoting men, a bias accounting for only 1% of the variability in promotion. That is an amount of bias that most people would consider negligible. They iterated the promotion process until they had completely turned the organization over. At that point, the top level was 65% male. Even very small amounts of disadvantage accumulate. The answer to "Don't make a mountain out of a molehill" is "Mountains *are* molehills, piled one on top of the other."

Now we can put the two concepts of gender schemas and the accumulation of advantage together. Schemas lay the groundwork for understanding why women receive less recognition than men. The accumulation of advantage explains why male and female careers are increasingly divergent over time. In many small ways that add up and compound over time, women receive less recognition than men. Both men and women have largely the same gender schemas and, in most laboratory experiments, do not differ in how they evaluate other men and women.

B. Flawed Decision-Making

Gender schemas and the accumulation of advantage are not, however, the only processes at work. Human decision-making is flawed, even when gender is not in the picture. Gender exacerbates the flaws.

Consider, first, people's confidence in their own objectivity and their own good judgment. It's understandable. It would be hard to get along in the world if one were constantly second-guessing one's judgments. But belief in one's objectivity leads to misplaced confidence in the accuracy of one's judgments. Consider a study that examined the effects of giving people a five-item questionnaire that encouraged them to think they were objective.[31] A sample question was "When forming an opinion, I try to objectively consider all of the facts." People already think they are objective; this questionnaire made that view of themselves salient. Another group of participants did not fill out the questionnaire. The participants who were encouraged to think that they were objective were more likely to think they were objective when they were actually discriminating on the basis of age discrimination than were the participants who had no encouragement to think they were objective. (Interestingly, it proved almost impossible to prime people to think that they were biased. People are biased to think that they are objective.)

A related source of error is confidence in one's own expertise, a confidence that interacts with other errors of judgment. People in academia, for example, think that they are good at detecting intellectual excellence and that they bring that "expertise" to bear when evaluating job candidates. They may have limited ability to determine just how good their evaluations are, because they may not get data about whether they were right or wrong for quite some time.[32] They can even forget in the meantime what their judgment was. Confirmation bias makes matters worse.[33] We tend to count the correct evaluations we made—"I always knew that person would be a star"—and ignore the incorrect evaluations.

Not only can we misremember our predictions, but we can create the conditions that foster or discourage merit, thus falsely confirming our expertise. We can create a self-fulfilling prophecy.[34] When we treat people as if we think they are likely to succeed, they tend to become more successful, and when we treat them as if we think they are likely to fail, they tend to become less successful.

C. Moral Licensing

"I don't care who they are, I just want the best person."

Perhaps the most pernicious source of errors is the belief that one's good intentions are sufficient, in which we ignore the adage about what the road to hell is paved with. People not only have good intentions, they believe that their good intentions inoculate them from giving one group more benefits than another group. It appears that once individuals have announced their bona fides—they are good people, unbiased—they think they have demonstrated a lack of bias. Saying it makes it psychologically so.

A number of studies[35] find that suggestions to people that they are fair—such as if they endorsed Obama rather than McCain for president, compared to no suggestion—leads to their being unfair. For example, if someone indicated that they planned to vote for Obama, that intention served to reassure them that they were not racist. When then given the opportunity to choose a Black or White man as chief of police, they were *more*, rather than *less*, likely to choose the White man. By reminding themselves how "fair" they are, people feel licensed to be unfair without recognizing that they are being unfair. People want to be fair and pride themselves on being fair. One of the most common remarks people make is, "I don't care who they are, I just want the best person." People think that their good intentions inoculate them against unfairness. To understand what happens in inviting people to give keynote talks or colloquia, we can combine gender schemas that represent women as less competent with an understanding of how people's good intentions can backfire. People believe they are inviting the best people and they believe they are free from gender schemas, opening the door for their gender schemas to operate.

What is most sobering for evaluators who wish to be fair is that simply explicitly disagreeing with an overtly sexist statement makes it more likely that an individual will then go on to pick a man for a stereotypically male job.[36] People were asked to say whether a job in the construction industry—a job typically associated with men—would be better suited for men, better suited for women, or equally suited to either sex. One group of participants was first asked to agree or disagree with statements like "Most women are not very smart." Another group did not read any sexist statements ahead of time. A third group read statements like "Some women are not very smart." Male participants who read the statements about "most women" were likely to disagree with them; those participants were then more likely to choose a male for the construction job than the participants who had not read any statements.[37] (This is one of the few cases in which women were unaffected.)

As indicated earlier, a similar phenomenon happens with race. In February 2008, one group of undergraduates was asked to indicate who they would vote for, Obama or McCain. Another group was not asked to endorse anyone. Both groups then rated how suitable a Black or White person would be for a police force that was experiencing racial tension. Individuals who actively endorsed Obama were more likely than individuals who had not endorsed either candidate to strongly rate a White candidate as suitable compared to a Black candidate.[38]

After reassuring themselves of their lack of bias, people are more likely, in the next situation that activates gender or race schemas, to demonstrate bias. People can reassure themselves that their decision was made on the basis of merit because they have at hand judgments that they have recently made that suggests to themselves that they are free from bias. But their schemas are still alive and well and freer to operate if they are not concerned about demonstrating bias.

Since academics and professionals routinely espouse the merit principle, this moral "licensing" should give everyone pause. "I don't care who they are; I just want the best person" is a good set up for moral licensing. Once people have assured themselves that they judge fairly, and that women and people of color are not at a disadvantage in their evaluation process, they are less concerned about their behavior in any particular case and their schemas can operate more freely.

The literature on moral licensing teaches us to be humble about our good intentions, not to pat ourselves on the back because we have them.

4. How can we achieve change such that evaluations will be more equitable?

Although we have much further to go to create a genuine meritocracy, we have made progress. Progress is still too slow, and the experiences of professional women during the Covid-19 pandemic show the fragility of progress,[39] but we have made progress. For example, more and more women are entering professional fields. Further change is possible at the individual level and the institutional level.

A. The Individual Level: Education

People can educate themselves about how schemas work, by reading, for example, the sources used in this Chapter. One real-world study found that a one-time intervention with science-based data changed the attitudes, though not the behaviors, of individuals who were less supportive of women; the intervention also changed some of the behaviors of individuals who were more supportive of women. Education is thus a good start but it is not enough by itself.[40]

B. The Individual Level: Intervention and Prevention

People can usefully intervene in ordinary situations by being alert to schemas in action. For example, if women or people of color are being ignored, or interrupted, or treated dismissively, one can be a useful bystander by bringing attention to their point and crediting them. One can stop inappropriate comments: "Oh, I want to hear the rest of Sophie's suggestion" or "I think Sophie said that earlier; Sophie, could you elaborate?"

Or take the following extreme (putatively true) story of an older man interviewing a young woman for a philosophy job.[41] The man asked, "suppose I wanted to slap you, and suppose I wanted to slap you because I thought you were giving us really bad answers, and I mistakenly believed that by slapping you I'll bring out the best in you. Am I blameworthy?" That interviewer may have thought he was posing, in a provocative way, a question about whether an ostensibly bad action could be deemed good if good motives were behind it. And he may have posed the question to women and men alike. Nevertheless, it is a bad question, in part because it is likely to be more disturbing to some candidates than others. A co-interviewer could usefully step in and say, "Maybe there is a better way of posing the question. How should we treat people who commit a bad action with good motives?"

More importantly, an interview like the one I just described should not occur to begin with. To create institutions that bring out the best work people can do, we need to interview people in a way that allows them to demonstrate their potential. Individuals can help develop procedures that will prevent the bad situations they observe. Individual understanding and individual action count, but they are not enough. Changes in how institutions hire, promote, recognize, and treat their employees on a day-to-day level are necessary for long-lasting change. I turn now to policies and procedures.

C. The Institutional Level: Policies and Procedures

There is an interplay between individuals and institutions. Individuals can encourage institutions to change practices that inappropriately benefit some individuals over others; institutions can establish norms and guidelines that affect individuals' behavior.

Consider fairness in hiring and evaluating candidates. Fairness will improve if criteria are thoughtfully discussed, agreed to, and adhered to. The point of establishing criteria and adhering to them is to buffer evaluators from the errors that schemas and reasoning flaws would otherwise lead to. By lashing ourselves to the mast, we resist the siren's call to indulge our preferences. Each step in the process is important. A wide-ranging discussion about criteria, with input from a broad range of people, will help establish which criteria are important and serve the goals of the department or organization. Examination of criteria that similar institutions are using may be helpful; increasingly, for example, institutions are asking candidates to indicate in their applications how they will contribute to diversity. Agreement on the criteria promotes a sense of fairness among members of the institution. Adherence to the criteria ensures that powerful members of the institution cannot indulge their preferences when those preferences are at variance with the criteria.

Professional organizations are another source of change and, like other institutions, are themselves changed by pressure from members.[42] Professional societies implicitly articulate norms by tacitly accepting or disallowing certain forms of behavior. They sometimes explicitly articulate norms by setting out expectations and requirements. While our focus has been on the cognitions that underlay incorrect evaluations, a focus on procedures and norms helps instill good behavior. Women, particularly women of color, are more likely to experience harassment and abuse than are White men.[43] Those experiences lead to attrition.

The National Academy of Sciences (NAS) is an example of an organization that has (belatedly) addressed harassment and bullying. Membership in the NAS is by election; it honors a scientist's work. In December 2018, the NAS revised its code of conduct for members to include treatment of others: "NAS members must refrain from all forms of discrimination, harassment, and bullying in their professional encounters, especially when they involve power differentials, as these behaviors have adverse impacts on the careers of scientists and the proper conduct of science."[44] The code further spells out what counts as discrimination, harassment, and bullying. In 2021, the NAS amended the bylaws to provide for rescinding membership of scientists who violated the code of conduct. Shortly thereafter, the NAS expelled two male scientists whose institutions found that they had harassed women. Although it took the NAS a little more than two years to act after it had spelled out a code of conduct, it did act.

Conclusion

Schemas are slow to change. What will it take for journalists to give credit appropriately, for academics to invite women speakers at appropriate rates, for investors to recognize women CEOs? The data presented in this Chapter suggest that active intervention is necessary to improve the participation and recognition of women in the professions. The flaws in human judgment, from overconfidence in one's expertise to misplaced beliefs in the sufficiency of one's good intentions, make it difficult to eliminate the effects of schemas on evaluations. Understanding the social science data and theory that create and maintain incorrect evaluations is a first step; changing policies and procedures is the next step.

So, You'd Like to Know More

- The book I co-authored with Abigail Stewart, An Inclusive Academy: Achieving Diversity and Excellence, provides more extensive discussion of schemas and, particularly, detailed suggestions about how to improve hiring, retention, promotion, and recognition of women.

- A summary of sexual and gender harassment can be found in Sexual Harassment of Women: Climate, Culture, and Consequences in Academic Sciences, Engineering, and Medicine (Paula A. Johnson, Sheila E. Widnall & Frazier F. Benya eds., 2018).

About the Author

Virginia Valian is Distinguished Professor of Psychology at Hunter College – CUNY, and is a member of the doctoral faculties of Psychology, Linguistics, and Speech-Language-Hearing Sciences at the CUNY Graduate Center. She directs the Language Acquisition Research Center at Hunter College, which studies the acquisition of syntax in young children and the relation between bilingualism and cognition in adults. She is co-founder and director of Hunter's Gender Equity Project. In her work on gender equity, Dr. Valian performs research on the reasons behind women's slow advancement in the professions and proposes remedies for individuals and institutions. She is the author of *Why So Slow? The Advancement of Women* (1998, MIT Press) and is co-author, with Abigail Stewart, of *An Inclusive Academy: Achieving Diversity and Excellence* (2018, MIT Press). Dr. Valian's recent work on gender includes an opinion piece on sexual harassment (*Nature*, 2019), a co-authored policy article on gender in science (*Science*, 2019), and co-authored empirical papers on the gender of speakers at university colloquia, awards to men and women in academia, and reactions to male and female presidential candidates. Dr. Valian speaks to institutions and organizations in Australia, Canada, Europe, the United Kingdom, and the United States on improving gender equity in hiring, promotion, and recognition.

Endnotes

1. Other examples from the Wolpers article: Adam Davidson wrote in the *New York Times*: "Lawrence Katz, a professor at Harvard and a leading scholar of education economics, co-wrote a paper a few years ago with Claudia Goldin..." Claudia Goldin is a professor at Harvard and a leading scholar of education economics—and the first author on the cited paper. Anne Marie Slaughter wrote in *The Atlantic* in 2012: "The economists Justin Wolfers and Betsey Stevenson have shown that women are less happy today than their predecessors were in 1972, both in absolute terms and relative to men." Betsey Stevenson is Chief Economist [at the time of writing] at the U.S. Department of Labor—and the first author on the cited paper.

2. Christine L. Nittrouer, Michelle R. Hebl, Leslie Ashburn-Nardo, Rachel C. E. Trump-Steele, David M. Lane & Virginia V. Valian, *Gender Disparities in Colloquium Speakers at Top Universities*, 115 PNAS 104 (2018).

3. Corinne A. Moss-Racusin, John F. Dovidio, Victoria L. Brescoli, Mark J. Graham & Jo Handelsman, *Science Faculty's Subtle Gender Biases Favor Male Students*, 109 PNAS 16474, 16479 (2012).

4. *Gender Equality, the Status of Women and the 2020 Elections*, SUPERMAJORITY / PERRYUNDEM NATIONAL SURVEY (Aug. 19, 2019).

5. S. Michael Gaddis, *Discrimination in the Credential Society: An Audit Study of Race and College Selectivity in the Labor Market*, 93 SOC. FORCES 1451 (2015).

6. S. Michael Gaddis, *An Introduction to Audit Studies in the Social Sciences*, in AUDIT STUDIES: BEHIND THE SCENES WITH THEORY, METHOD, AND NUANCE 3 (S. Michael Gaddis ed., 2018); Marianne Bertrand & Sendhil Mullainathan, *Are Emily and Greg More Employable than Lakisha and Jamal?*, 94 AM. ECON. REV. 991 (2004); Stijn Baert, *Hiring Discrimination: An Overview of (Almost) All Correspondence Experiments Since 2005*, in AUDIT STUDIES: BEHIND THE SCENES WITH THEORY, METHOD, AND NUANCE 63 (S. Michael Gaddis ed., 2018).

7. David E. Melnikoff & Virginia V. Valian, *Gender Disparities in Awards to Neuroscience Researchers*, 7 ARCHIVES OF SCI. PSYCHOL. 4 (2019).

8. Jordan D. Dworkin, Kristin A. Linn, Erin G. Teich, Perry Zurn, Russell T. Shinohara & Danielle S. Bassett, *The Extent and Drivers of Gender Imbalance in Neuroscience Reference Lists*, 23 NATURE NEUROSCIENCE 918 (2020).

9. Linda J. Skitka, Zachary J. Melton, Allison B. Mueller & Kevin Y. Wei, *The Gender Gap: Who Is (And Is Not) Included on Graduate-Level Syllabi in Social/Personality Psychology*, 47 PERSONALITY & SOC. PSYCHOL. BULL. 863 (2021).

10. For review and additional data, see ABIGAIL J. STEWART & VIRGINIA VALIAN, AN INCLUSIVE ACADEMY (2018).

11. SUSAN T. FISKE & SHELLY E. TAYLOR, SOCIAL COGNITION (1984).

12. Ernesto Reuben, Pedro Rey-Biel, Paola Sapienza & Luigi Zingales, *The Emergence of Male Leadership in Competitive Environments*, 83 J. ECON. BEHAV. & ORG. 111 (2012).

13. Elizabeth L. Haines, Kay Deaux & Nicole Lofaro, *The Times They Are A-Changing... Or Are They Not? A Comparison of Gender Stereotypes, 1983–2014*, 40 PSYCHOL. OF WOMEN 353 (2016); Tanja Hentschel, Madeline E. Heilman & Claudia V. Peus, *The Multiple Dimensions of Gender Stereotypes: A Current Look at Men's and Women's Characterizations of Others and Themselves*, 10 FRONTIERS IN PSYCHOL. 11 (2019).

14. Daniel Storage, Tessa E. S. Charlesworth, Mahzarin R. Banaji & Andrei Cimpian, *Adults and Children Implicitly Associate Brilliance with Men More than Women*, 90 J. EXPERIMENTAL SOC. PSYCHOL. 104020 (2020).

15. ABIGAIL J. STEWART & VIRGINIA VALIAN, AN INCLUSIVE ACADEMY (2018).

16. Erin Cooley, Hannah Winslow, Andrew Vojt, Jonathan Shein & Jennifer Ho, *Bias at the Intersection of Identity: Conflicting Social Stereotypes of Gender and Race Augment the Perceived Femininity and Interpersonal Warmth of Smiling Black Women*, 74 J. EXPERIMENTAL SOC. PSYCHOL. 43 (2018).

17. Kimberlé Crenshaw, *Demarginalizing the Intersection of Race and Sex: A Black Feminist Critique of Antidiscrimination Doctrine, Feminist Theory and Antiracist Politics*, 89 U. CHI. LEGAL F. 139 (1989).

18. *Id.* at 149, 166.

19. Elizabeth R. Cole, *Demarginalizing Women of Color in Intersectionality Scholarship in Psychology: A Black Feminist Critique*, 76 J. Soc. Issues 1036 (2020); Rachel E. Luft & Jane Ward, *Toward an Intersectionality Just Out of Reach: Confronting Challenges to Intersectional Practice*, in 13 Perceiving Gender Locally, Globally, and Intersection-Ally 9 (V. Demos & M. Texler Segal eds., 2009).

20. Robert W. Livingston, Ashleigh S. Rosette & Ella F. Washington, *Can an Agentic Black Woman Get Ahead? The Impact of Race and Interpersonal Dominance on Perceptions of Female Leaders*, 23 Psychol. Sci. 354 (2012).

21. Madeline E. Heilman, *Sex Bias in Work Settings: The Lack of Fit Model*, 5 Res. in Org. Behav. 269 (1983); Madeline E. Heilman & Suzette Caleo, *Combatting Gender Discrimination: A Lack of Fit Framework*, 21 Group Processes & Intergroup Rel. 725 (2018).

22. Dana Kanze, Mark A. Conley, Tyler G. Okimoto, Damon J. Phillips & Jennifer Merluzzi, *Evidence That Investors Penalize Female Founders for Lack of Industry Fit*, 6 Sci. Advances (2020).

23. Deborah A. Prentice & Erica Carranza, *What Women and Men Should Be, Shouldn't Be, Are Allowed To Be, and Don't Have To Be: The Contents of Prescriptive Gender Stereotypes*, 26 Psychol. of Women Q. 269 (2002).

24. Laurie A. Rudman & Peter Glick, *Prescriptive Gender Stereotypes and Backlash Toward Agentic Women*, 57 J. Soc. Issues 743 (2001); Jessica Sullivan, Corinne Moss-Racusin, Michael Lopez & Katherine Williams, *Backlash Against Gender Stereotype-Violating Preschool Children*, 13 PloS One (2018); Madeline E. Heilman, Aaron S. Wallen, Daniella Fuchs & Melinda M. Tamkins, *Penalties for Success: Reactions to Women Who Succeed at Male Gender-Typed Tasks*, 89 J. Applied Psychol. 416 (2004); Elizabeth L. Haines & Steven J. Stroessner, *Role Prioritization Model: How Communal Men and Agentic Women Can (Sometimes) Have It All*, 13 Soc. & Personality Psychol. Compass e12504 (2019); Madeline E. Heilman & Aaron S. Wallen, *Wimpy and Undeserving of Respect: Penalties For Men's Gender-Inconsistent Success*, 46 J. of Experimental Soc. Psychol. 664 (2010).

25. Madeline Heilman & Tyler G. Okimoto, *Motherhood: A Potential Source of Bias in Employment Decisions*, 93 J. Applied Psychol. 189 (2008).

26. Camille L. Stewart and 10 others, *Unconscious Bias in Speaker Introductions at a Surgical Oncology Meeting: Hierarchy Reigns Over Gender*, 27 Annals of Surgical Oncology 3754 (2020).

27. *Id.;* Christina C. Huang, Kaitlyn Lapen, Kanan Shah, Jolie Kantor, Jillian Tsai, Miriam A. Knoll & Fumikoi Chino, *Evaluating Bias in Speaker Introductions at the American Society for Radiation Oncology Annual Meeting.* 110 Int'l J. of Radiation Oncology - Biology - Physics 303 (2021).

28. Juliet Eilperin, *White House Women Want to Be in the Room Where It Happens*, Wash. Post, Sept. 13, 2016.

29. Robert K. Merton, *The Matthew Effect in Science*, 159 Sci. 56 (1968).

30. Richard F. Martell, Mark Lane & Cynthia Emrich, *Male-female Differences: A Computer Simulation*, 51 Am. Psychol. 157 (1996).

31. Nicole M. Lindner, Alexander Graser & Brian A. Nosek, *Age-based Hiring Discrimination as a Function of Equity Norms and Self-Perceived Objectivity*, 9 PloS-one e84752 (2014).

32. Daniel Kahneman, Thinking Fast and Slow (2011).

33. Raymond S. Nickerson, *Confirmation Bias: A Ubiquitous Phenomenon in Many Guises*, 2 Rev. Gen. Psychol. 175 (1998).

34. Sarah Gentrup, Georg Lorenz, Cornelia Kristen & Irena Kogan, *Self-Fulfilling Prophecies In The Classroom: Teacher Expectations, Teacher Feedback And Student Achievement*, 66 LEARNING & INSTRUCTION 101296 (2020).

35. Daniel A. Effron, Jessica S. Cameron & Benoît Monin, *Endorsing Obama Licenses Favoring Whites*, 45 J. EXPERIMENTAL SOC. PSYCHOL. 590 (2009).

36. Anna C. Merritt, Daniel A. Effron & Benoît Monin, *Moral Self-Licensing: When Being Good Frees Us To Be Bad*, 4 SOC. & PERSONALITY PSYCHOL. COMPASS 344 (2010).

37. Benoît Monin & Dale T. Miller, *Moral Credentials and the Expression of Prejudice*, 81 J. PERSONALITY & SOC. PSYCHOL. 33 (2001).

38. Daniel A. Effron, Jessica S. Cameron & Benoît Monin, *Endorsing Obama Licenses Favoring Whites*, 45 J. EXPERIMENTAL SOC. PSYCHOL. 590 (2009).

39. For one of increasingly many papers describing the professional toll of the Covid-19 pandemic on women, *see* Caitlin Collins, Liana Christian Landivar, Leah Ruppanner & William J. Scarborough, *Covid-19 and the Gender Gap in Work Hours*, 28 GENDER, WORK & ORG. 101 (2021).

40. Edward H. Chang, Katherine L. Milkman, Laura J. Zarrow, Kasandra Brabaw, Dena M. Gromet, Reb Rebele, Cade Massey, Angela L. Duckworth & Adam Grant, *The Mixed Effects of Online Diversity Training*, 116 PNAS 7783 (2019).

41. Nomy Arpaly, N., *Is Polite Philosophical Discussion Possible?* DAILYNOUS (2016), https://dailynous.com/2016/04/28/is-polite-philosophical-discussion-possible/.

42. Rodrigo Perez-Ortega, *National Academy of Sciences Ejects Biologist Francisco Ayala in the Wake of Sexual Harassment Findings*, SCIENCE (2021), https://www.sciencemag.org/news/2021/06/national-academy-sciences-ejects-biologist-francisco-ayala-wake-sexual-harassment.

43. Emily A. Vargas, Sheila T. Brassel, Chithra R. Perumalswami, Timothy R.B. Johnson, Reshma Jagsi, Lilia M. Cortina & Isis H. Settles, *Incidence and Group Comparisons of Harassment Based on Gender, LGBTQ+ Identity, and Race at an Academic Medical Center*, 30 J. WOMEN'S HEALTH 789 (2021).

44. *NAS Code of Conduct*, NATIONAL ACADEMY OF SCIENCES, http://www.nasonline.org/about-nas/code-of-conduct/nas-code-of-conduct.pdf.

SIXTEEN

"Ducks Pick Ducks"

The Military's Institutionalized Unconscious Bias Challenge

Lieutenant Colonel Susan E. Upward, USMC

A Note from the Editors: We first met Lieutenant Colonel Upward as a fellow member of the ABA Criminal Justice Section's Task Force on Women in Criminal Justice. She has proven to be an extraordinary colleague as we have worked together to consider the reasons why women may leave the practice of criminal law and ways we might support efforts to prevent this. Here she writes about the military's approach and experience with issues of implicit bias. In many ways, the experience is like the more generalized experience, but the military and its command structure provide some unique perspectives. We introduced Susan to Judge Bennett and Judge Parker (who is doing interesting empirical work measuring the impact of implicit bias instructions in Dallas), and we certainly benefited from hearing them exchange views. We are confident that that kind of interaction will continue in this Chapter and beyond.

CHAPTER HIGHLIGHTS

- The military, an echo of the society it serves, has long faced both gender and racial divides. As in other parts of society, the military justice system shows marked disproportionality.
- The murder of George Floyd and the accompanying protests sharpened the military's attention to bias in the ranks.

- The military has moved quickly to address some issues of bias in ways which may offer a model for other institutions, but even these efforts may not be sustainable without a comprehensive battle plan that does not lose sight of either history or the implicit nature of bias.

CHAPTER CONTENTS

Introduction
1. Defining the Problem
    A. The Gender Divide
    B. The Racial Divide
    C. 2020: The Tipping Point
2. 2021 And Beyond: "Getting After" the Problem
    A. Judge Advocates Should Take the Lead
    B. Make Diversity AND Inclusion the Goal
    C. Training Must Be Mandatory and Meaningful
    D. Leaders Must Buy-In and Tie-In
    E. Learn from Others
    F. Use the Military's Professional Reading Lists
    G. Re-value Physical Fitness as a Valuation Metric
3. The System is Blinking Red…and Pink, Black, Brown, Yellow

Conclusion

Introduction

In an interview with CBS in March 2021, retired Navy Admiral Mike Mullen, who served as chairman of the Joint Chiefs of Staff during both the Bush and Obama administrations, was asked about the senior military ranks being almost completely White and male.[1] "Ducks pick ducks," he replied, describing the promotion and assignment selection system in the military. "I don't think it was conscious bias, but I think it was institutional bias, if you will…. And when you have White guys pickin,' they pick other White guys." Recognizing the bias, Admiral Mullen continued, "that's what the leadership has to break up to make sure that we're not in that kind of situation."[2]

In a few short sentences, Adm. Mullen captured the issue that the military has faced for several decades: the armed forces have long strived for diversity and inclusion, but have struggled with tackling the underlying biases that have hindered each of the services' success, particularly in the areas of race and gender, and regardless of whether the biases are intentional or unintentional.[3] There have been significant policy changes made in this area over the last decade, and especially in 2020, which may prove to be a watershed moment for the military in terms of tangible actions by leadership. But while the Department of Defense (DoD) has repeatedly stated its staunch commitment to diversity and inclusion, it has done little more than acknowledge the existence of unconscious bias as a roadblock to those goals. Until the military takes the problem of unintentional bias seriously and finds a way to effectively address it, it will continue to forego the benefits of not only a statistically diverse, but also a truly inclusive force.

As a starting point, the definition of institutional bias is:

> A tendency for the procedures and practices of particular institutions to operate in ways which result in certain social groups being advantaged or favored and others being disadvantaged or devalued. This need not be the result of any conscious prejudice or discrimination but rather of the majority simply following existing rules or norms.[4]

Under this rubric, it is clear that some of the military's ongoing struggle with diversity and inclusion can be directly traced to its track record of dragging its feet with implementing change.

1. Defining the Problem

History has shown the military's penchant for quickly labeling problems, but for only slowly executing change in internal policies and procedures especially where they are not aimed directly at warfighting and particularly in terms of equal opportunity.

A. The Gender Divide

The road to gender desegregation in the military has been a long and drawn-out process. The armed forces were officially and permanently gender-integrated in 1948, but the number of women who could serve on active duty was subject to a percentage ceiling until that provision was repealed in 1967.[5] It was not until 1993 that Congress repealed all laws prohibiting women from serving in any military unit or occupational specialty, or on combatant vessels and aircraft.[6] Even two decades following that legislation, the DoD continued excluding women from serving in any occupation or unit involved in direct ground combat. In January 2013, Secretary of Defense (SecDef) Leon Panetta announced the DoD was rescinding that rule and ordered the services to conduct a review to "expeditiously move forward in the integration of women into previously closed positions" no later than January 2016.[7]

Although the Pentagon delayed changing their policy for 20 years, leaders almost immediately recognized the need for unintentional bias training to combat the long-held and embedded beliefs of the military that were arguably personified by that delay itself. For instance, in 2014, as the Marine Corps began to prepare for opening jobs that were previously closed to women, the Marine Corps Force Innovation Office developed a commander's toolkit to aid units in the transition, including content on organizational change and unconscious bias.[8] The mandate that was given directly to unit commanders was that their "leadership and support are critical to successful gender integration. Utilization of the commander's toolkit will help develop a positive and inclusive command climate."[9] The toolkit included what appeared to be the hallmarks of a comprehensive and engaging training program, including discussion guides, suggested readings, interactive exercises, and scenarios.[10] But the training was not mandatory and was left to be "taught at the unit commander's discretion," if at all.[11]

Meanwhile, all of the services conducted their organizational review of policies and standards per the SecDef's guidance, and in September 2015, each of the service secretaries submitted their recommendations to facilitate the full integration of women into previously closed roles. The Commandant of the Marine Corps, however, was the only service chief to request exceptions to policy for both its ground combat units and the jobs therein.[12] The Secretary of the Navy (SecNav) summarily disapproved the Marine Corps' request, and in December 2015, SecDef Ash Carter ordered the armed forces to open all combat jobs to women.[13]

Although the integration of women was now a reality from a policy perspective, the die had been cast—the decision to make implicit bias training optional, coupled with the Marine Corps' leadership's public insistence to exclude women in the face of clear mandates to the contrary from both Congress and the SecDef, had set conditions for an institutional bias that the Marine Corps still struggles to cope with today. As a result, "[a]lthough many barriers representing conscious, explicit bias against women in the workplace have been removed, unconscious bias continues to affect women's opportunities and advancement in professional settings," not just in the Marine Corps, but across the services.[14] Consider in early 2016, as the Navy and Marine Corps began the transition to gender-neutral job titles and women began to be assigned to combat units, "a significant majority of male Marines at every rank" and, perhaps more surprisingly, "at least a third of female Marines" opposed the decision to gender-integrate ground combat units and jobs.[15] In response, the Corps appeared to react quickly, instituting two days of mandatory training on gender integration for all active duty Marines, to include guided discussions about gender-neutral physical standards.[16] But even at this critical juncture of a major cultural change for the Marine Corps, when "institutional resistance" was significant, the "subject of unconscious bias [was] a very minimal part of the planned discussions on how Marines, think, act and make decisions."[17]

In October 2016, President Barack Obama instructed the military and other federal agencies to "expand training on unconscious bias, inclusion, and flexible work policies," and made implicit bias training mandatory, but only for "senior leadership and management positions."[18] In turn, the Marine Corps mandated training on unconscious bias, sending out mobile training teams to teach course material at Marine Corps boot camp locations, schoolhouses, and commanders' courses.[19] Although the training was more comprehensive than its 2014 counterpart, the two-day seminar was aimed at only majors and lieutenant colonels, who were then expected to train their subordinates.[20] The mandate did not extend to the lower levels of the ranks, which is arguably where the damaging effects of bias are often felt the most.

The other services have not been immune from unconscious bias in the gender arena, despite policies that appear to be "standardized" in the hopes of leveling the gender playing field. In the wake of the Marines United scandal in 2017—and what should have been a wake-up call for culture change across the armed forces—the military instead made note of what, in hindsight, should have been an obvious symptom of bias: research showed that "many male service members [felt] women in the military are not worthy of respect because they [were] not required to be as strong and fast as men," and that the "double standards" for males and females only led dissension in the ranks because of the "negative perceptions about the capabilities of women."[21] Even a report produced for the Defense Advisory Committee on Women in the Services (DACOWITS) specifically addressing both conscious and unconscious gender bias recommended "eliminat[ing] gendered policies... especially ones that potentially reinforce gendered stereotypes [and] may create false limitations on gender... [because] policies and programs that are designed in gendered ways may continue to encourage gendered behavior, thus reinforcing common biases and stereotypes that counter equality."[22]

Instead of addressing why so much emphasis was being placed on physical fitness above all other attributes to assess the inherent value of individual servicemembers, the military concluded that the best course of action was to ignore the inherent physical differences between men and women and make a gender-neutral test. In 2018, the Army approved a new Combat Fitness Test (CFT) to "better predict a soldier's ability to perform in combat" that was both "age and gender-neutral, measuring every Soldier against the same standard."[23] During the rollout, Army Secretary Mark Esper publicly lauded the change "because the enemy does not specify who they're going to shoot and not shoot. Combat is combat."[24] But the message rang incredibly hollow, especially in a day and age where combat roles have changed dramatically, and where mental acumen and critical thinking are just as coveted in our servicemembers as physical prowess.²⁵ This purportedly gender-neutral standard not only failed to address the institutional bias and culture that fostered a gender-driven scandal like Marines United to occur, but also ignored the fact that the new standard would place women at a disadvantage for career advancement because it would still be scored on a scale, and the score itself is a major component in calculating promotion scores and "ranking" servicemembers against one another.

Not surprisingly, by early 2021, it was clear that while the Army did not intentionally "set out to build [a fitness test] that was skewed against women," its leaders had unconsciously done just that.²⁶ The initial data showed that 44-percent of women across the Army had failed the Combat Fitness Test, as compared to only 7-percent of males, and "the Army's attempt to create a fitter force is creating more barriers to success for women."²⁷ In January 2021, Congress ordered the Secretary of the Army to halt full implementation of the CFT until an organization independent of the DoD could research the test's gender disparities and its impact on retention and recruiting.²⁸ The Army responded by creating a new version of the CFT with "new scoring tiers for male and female soldiers meant to acknowledge their biological differences."²⁹ But Congress continued to show concern for the institutional bias that manifested itself in the creation of the test at the outset; at a House Appropriations Committee in May 2021, Congressional members were still questioning Army officials about the fitness test, as well as several other issues of gender bias, including ill-fitting equipment and parental leave. While Army leaders admitted that the service was already considering returning to a gender-specific standard and reviewing other policies to adequately address gender bias in the workplace, they did not address the underlying institutional bias that perhaps led them to ignore those issues in the first place.³⁰

B. The Racial Divide

Perhaps more disconcerting than the military's institutional bias in terms of gender is the disturbing trend of racial bias, especially within the military justice system.

In the same year that the military was gender-integrated, President Harry Truman ordered the complete racial desegregation of the military to "be put into effect as rapidly as possible, having due regard to the time required to effectuate any necessary changes without impairing efficiency or morale."³¹ The general assumption should be that an order from the commander-in-chief would be followed without delay. Yet, the last racially segregated active duty unit was not abolished until 1954, and some National Guard and Reserve units stayed segregated well into the 1960s.³² Mirroring the broader societal struggles with race that plagued the United States during this period, racial tensions likewise persisted in the military. Most are well-known and documented through the Vietnam Era and beyond. But perhaps less well-known is the full-blown race riot at Camp Lejeune, North Carolina, in July of 1969.[33] What that incident and many others should have made clear to military leaders was that total desegregation had not yet eliminated racism from the armed forces. Yet military leaders had remained obtusely and totally "unaware that institutionalized racism remained a problem."[34] Moreover, the Pentagon completely ignored their own role in "causing their own problem" in that, similar to gender integration, "Congressional and military panels made recommendations to reduce racial tensions, but changes were slow to come."[35] Reforms were eventually made to quell the racial unrest, but more than fifty years later, the services still struggle with the disparate treatment of the races in the military justice system.

In 2017, a group called Protect Our Defenders (POD), an organization that is "dedicated to exposing and eradicating bias within the military justice system," published a scathing report that analyzed previously unpublished data from 2006 to 2015 from each military service branch categorized by racial and ethical demographics.[36] The report found that "for every year reported and across all branches, black service members were substantially more likely than White service members to face military justice or disciplinary action, and these disparities failed to improve or *even increased* in recent years."[37] Like many of the pages of this book show, "racial disparities exist in criminal justice systems throughout the United States," so the "existence of racial disparities within the military justice system is not atypical" and should not come as shock to anyone—the military, in many ways, acts as an echo of the society it serves.[38] Yet, despite other "equalizing factors" such as rigorous entry screening, a standardized pay structure providing steady income, and regular drug testing, the report concluded that "[t]he persistence of racial disparities within the military may indicate the existence of racial bias or discrimination among decision-makers in the military justice system."[39]

In the face of such pejorative evidence, the services should have acted quickly to rectify the problem that was now clearly identified in black and white. In 2016, when the Air Force initially responded to POD's FOIA request for data, the Air Force responded that it had already formed a "cross-functional team led by diversity and inclusion experts [who] will collect and analyze the data and recommend policy changes, process modifications or additional study as appropriate."[40] In 2017, after the release of its report, the POD made another FOIA request for the outcomes of the Air Force's self-titled "disparity working group," but would eventually have to file a lawsuit to obtain the results after the delayed response was heavily redacted.[41] As a result, it was discovered that the working group, whose purpose was to "[p]rovide an overview of steps that could be taken to address potential implications of unconscious bias in the USAF military justice system," had made recommendations to include standardizing and institutionalizing unconscious bias training for commanders, first sergeants, supervisors, and judge advocates, and then analyzing the effect of that training post-implementation annually by reviewing the data of enlisted nonjudicial punishments and courts-martial.[42] But the court found that the DoD provided insufficient evidence "to determine whether the withheld information...is part of any real governmental decision process rather than simply an exercise which went nowhere" and that there was nothing to indicate that "any of the recommendations were adopted."[43]

While the damning POD report made little noise in the public eye, Congress did take notice. Six weeks after the publication of the POD report, Congress amended the National Defense Authorization Act for Fiscal Year 2018 and ordered the U.S. Government Accountability Office (GAO) to conduct its own investigation into "racial and gender disparities in the military justice system, and whether disparities have been studied by the DoD."[44] When the GAO's report was released in May 2019, it not only confirmed the POD Report from two years earlier, but also faulted the Pentagon for 1) not keeping consistent data on race and ethnicity in regards to military justice proceedings, and 2) for not investigating the causes of biases against minority troops in order to "better position [the Department of Defense] to identify actions to address disparities and help ensure the military justice system is fair and just."[45] In terms of the latter issue, the GAO purposefully found:

> [o]fficials from DoD and the military services acknowledged that they do not know the cause of the racial and gender disparities that have been identified in the military justice system...because they have not conducted a comprehensive evaluation to identify potential causes of these disparities and make recommendations about any appropriate corrective actions to remediate the cause(s) of disparities in the military justice system.[46]

Again, despite the adverse information in both the POD and GAO reports, there was little sense of urgency in implementing change. Without a forcing function, the services continued to form committees to talk about the critical issue of diversity and inclusion, but continued to fail to order any meaningful training or enacting changes to either the military justice system or the institution as a whole.

C. 2020: The Tipping Point

The summer of 2020 appears to be the tipping point for the military in finally coming to terms with its unintentional, but institutionalized bias. The protests that followed the tragic killing of George Floyd at the hands of a Minnesota police officer were not only felt on the global stage, but also left a mark on the psyche of the military writ large. There was a flurry of activity and uncharacteristically swift action in taking palpable steps to address institutional bias in its various forms.

Just days after the Floyd killing, the Commandant of the Marine Corps officially banned the public display of the Confederate battle flag aboard Marine Corps installations, and reiterated that "current events are a stark reminder that it is not enough for us to remove symbols that cause division—rather, we also must strive to eliminate division itself."[47] A few weeks later, SecDef Mark Esper addressed the entire force via video message and admitted that, despite the plethora of diversity and inclusion initiatives over many years, the United States military was still "not immune to the forces of bias and prejudice."[48] Calling for a "new era" in the DoD "marked by a reinvigorated effort to build a better U.S. military that pursues equal opportunity and aspires to true meritocracy with greater vigor and purpose," the SecDef announced three new initiatives for the DoD: 1) the creation of a new "Defense Board on Diversity and Inclusion in the Military" to conduct a six-month study and "develop concrete, actionable recommendations to increase racial diversity and ensure equal opportunity across all ranks;" 2) standing up the "Defense Advisory Committee on Diversity and Inclusion in the Armed Services," a more permanent committee to provide recommendations and advice to the SecDef; and 3) directing both civilian and uniformed leaders to bring changes that could be implemented immediately.[49] His clearly stated intent was "to effect an enterprise-wide, organizational and cultural shift."[50] He followed his video message up with a memorandum to all DoD personnel on June 23, 2020, reiterating that the military is "susceptible to the forces of bias and prejudice, whether seen or unseen, deliberate or unintentional."[51]

The Army acted quickly in response to the SecDef's direction and attacked an aspect of the military's promotion system that invited bias. On June 26, 2020, Secretary of the Army Ryan McCarthy issued a memo suspending the requirement for a promotion photo to be submitted for possible advancement to the next rank.[52] Moreover, he also ordered the redaction of data that could be used to identify race, gender, or ethnicity in a promotion selection board file, stating that "[d]iversity is critical to every aspect of talent management in our Army, but it is especially important in the selection board process. Our soldiers must be confident that equal opportunity exists at every stage of their career.... These changes will help ensure that selection boards are as fair and impartial as possible."[53] The Air Force also took immediate actions in the wake of the racial unrest by ordering an inspector general review of "racial imbalances in its justice system and career advancement opportunities," and producing "a new video on unconscious bias training."[54]

After receiving recommendations from military leaders, the SecDef concluded that some of the issues facing the military in this arena could be immediately addressed. He wasted no time in following the Army's lead and ordered the removal of promotion board photos across the services.[55] He also directed a review of policies that redacted identifiable and classification information to ensure the promotion and selection processes "are free from bias based on race, ethnicity, gender, or national origin."[56] He specifically called out unconscious bias as a threat to the services and ordered the development of "educational requirements for implementation across the military lifecycle to educate the force on unconscious bias," as well as a review of hairstyle, grooming, and appearance standards and policies to detect racial bias.[57]

In December 2020, the DoD Diversity and Inclusion Board made its final report to the SecDef, who in turn released a memorandum directing actions deriving from the Board's fifteen recommendations.[58] But unlike his July memo that clearly stated the threat of implicit bias within the ranks, the term is notably absent from this written set of directives. Indeed, some of the directives skirt the sub-contextual topics that directly relate to implicit bias—the need to "update recruiting content to represent all service members;" revaluating and removing military aptitude test "barriers that adversely impact diversity;" and "developing racially/ethnically diverse pools of candidates for consideration by non-statutory selection or selecting official for nominative assignments."[59] But for the most part, the directed actions focused more on intentional acts to ensure diversity in the ranks, instead of addressing the unconscious bias that pervades the organization.

2. 2021 and Beyond: "Getting After" the Problem

The events and actions of 2020 have widened the aperture on bias in the armed forces, but the question remains if the military will capitalize on the momentum, seize the initiative, implement tangible changes to address the underlying biases within the system, and sustain the transformation to positively affect the institution's culture in the long term.

In his initial planning guidance to the force and again in his comments in regards to banning the Confederate battle flag, the Marine Corps Commandant said, "anything that divides us, anything that threatens team cohesion, must be addressed head-on."[60] Indeed, the services have commenced a full-frontal assault on diversity, attacking the enemy head-on in the hopes of a quick and decisive victory. But as any basic military strategist will tell you, that methodology will often lead to unsustainable casualties and little tactical success. In military parlance, a better tactic would be to use its full assault on diversity in support of a separate flanking maneuver to attack the supply lines of unintentional bias that is, in turn, feeding the military's diversity problem.[61] While the attack must be deliberate, it would be foolhardy to believe that we can close with and destroy the enemy outright. Military leaders must accept that the battle against unintentional bias will be ongoing and persistent, and not a fire-and-forget fight.

As a starting point, the military has at least acknowledged that biases exist, but the path to a truly inclusive institution must attack the problem on several fronts:

A. Judge advocates should take the lead.

Military judge advocates are attorneys who perform legal duties while serving in their specific branch of the armed forces. Judge advocates can serve in a variety of billets that primarily cover three areas: 1) providing legal advice to a command as a Staff Judge Advocate (SJA); 2) providing legal services to multiple commands as a prosecutor, legal assistant, or specialty attorney, or 3) providing legal representation to servicemembers as a defense counsel.[62] As such, the Uniform Code of Military Justice demands that judge advocates play a central role in the court-martial process by not only ensuring that only qualified personnel litigate and preside over the proceedings, but also requiring commanders "at all times communicate directly with their [SJAs]... in matters relating to the administration of military justice."[63] In this context, the POD reports outlining the disparities in the military justice system, as well as recent and pending legislation to change the military justice process, has provided the military's judge advocate community a golden opportunity to lead from the front in the war on unintentional bias.

The report's data "strongly indicate the need for aggressive responses to address inequities" because, just like its civilian counterparts, "[a] system of justice is fundamentally unfair if, due to inherent bias, it fails to effectively deliver justice."[64] One such response was the recommendation to reform the military justice process "to empower legally trained military prosecutors, instead of commanders of the accused, to determine when to refer a case to court-martial, thereby reducing the potential for bias based on familiarity, friendship, race, or ethnicity."[65] Undoubtedly, the removal of convening authority from commanders has been a hot-button topic for many years, but in the context of sexual assaults and other special victim crimes.[66] Nonetheless, major changes in line with the POD report recommendations appear to be on the cusp of fruition. In December 2021, after years of debate, the National Defense Authorization Act for 2022 was enacted by President Joe Biden and indeed removes the decision for referring certain cases to court-martial from outside of the chain of command, placing it in a judge advocate who holds a grade no lower the O-7 and who is a prosecutor with "significant experience in military justice."[67] However, a provision requiring the Sec Def to increase "enhanced and specialized training to certain prosecutors on the proper conduct, presentation, and handling of sexual assault and domestic violence cases," which would have been a prime opportunity to train military prosecutors on the effects of implicit bias, was removed from the final version of the bill.[68]

But any cure that Congress can conceive of does not address the source of what is ailing the military at its core. Whether the recent changes will lead to more sexual assault prosecutions in the military remains to be seen, but removing the convening authority from a commander and placing it in a military prosecutor for any crime assumes that the military prosecutor will be free, or more free, from unconscious bias. The data of the POD report supports the notion that the military as a whole—whether it be the generals and admirals affecting policy, the commanders making referral decisions, or the relatively junior officers and enlisted members who make up a court-martial members panel—are all susceptible to unintentional bias. When POD sued the DoD under the FOIA for withheld and/or redacted military justice records, the U.S. District Court for the District of Connecticut made an analogous warning: "one's credentials are unlikely to shed much light on prosecutorial discretion misconduct based in unconscious bias. Where one went to law school or what positions one held will not particularly illuminate whether that individual harbors bias or discriminatory tendencies."[69] That is the blindspot—judge advocates are still military officers and are susceptible to the same institutional bias as commanders. They are not immune, just as prosecutors, defense counsel or judges are not immune, and staff judge advocates advising commanders are not immune.

Whether the military justice community is empowered to make decisions in this arena or not, the data collected from the POD report shows that it is essential that the judge advocate community take steps to mitigate unintentional bias in our courtrooms. The military can learn from its civilian counterparts and ensure each service's judge advocate school trains their attorneys by "incorporat[ing] unconscious bias concepts more comprehensively and organically into education and training provided to emerging leaders and [legal] professionals," just as "private sector corporations of varying sizes are working to equip their leaders at all level [sic] to act more inclusively and overcome biases in their talent management activities" and "public defenders and district attorneys in the civilian legal system are also incorporating unconscious bias-related training in efforts to improve their effectiveness and equity."[70]

The judge advocate community could set the example for the rest of the formal military education institutions by being particularly mindful and deliberate in designing this training. As other experts have noted, training in this area "can make a difference, but... is not a quick process accomplished fully by a two-hour diversity training program."[71] Like all continuing legal education, it must not devolve into a one-and-done period of instruction only offered at basic-level lawyer courses, but rather offered at intermediate and advanced courses, as well as during specialized advocacy courses and training for our military judges.

To that end, the military's judiciary also has an important role to play in mitigating unintentional bias in courts-martial. As of 2021, the only mention of bias in the Military Judge's Benchbook is implied bias in the context of member challenges during voir dire.[72] Because judges are expected to consider the totality of the circumstances to determine whether implied bias is present, that analysis should include an assessment of whether there is evidence that a member harbors an unintentional bias that could raise a question about that member's impartiality.[73] Under that rubric, military judges should ask preliminary questions themselves or allow counsel for both sides to delve into the topics of institutional and unintentional bias during voir dire.[74] Additionally, until such time as a standard, non-evidentiary instruction on this topic are included in the Benchbook, military judges should seriously consider and liberally grant motions from counsel for a novel instruction covering unintentional bias. While there is, of course, some argument concerning the effectiveness of an implicit bias instruction, it will at least raise the issue with the members so they are properly encouraged to evaluate only the evidence presented and can avoid making critical decisions based on "feelings, assumptions, perceptions, fears, and stereotypes."[75]*

B. Make diversity AND inclusion the goal.

While the issues identified in the POD reports are a harsh evaluation of the military justice system, they are just a microcosm of the problems the military institution is facing on the whole.

An all-too-common refrain in the military is that servicemembers do not see black or white because "we're all green."[76] Indeed, as Thomas E. Ricks observed in 2016, "combat can create life-long bonds between the most disparate groups, often overcoming social, economic, religious, and racial barriers" and reflecting a certain level of conformity, uniformity, and anonymity that is a prerequisite of military service.[77] But that mantra is as false as it is foolhardy. Not only is the military not in a constant state of combat, but the simple fact is that the U.S. military is as diverse as ever, with servicemen and women coming from a rich and varied mosaic of backgrounds.[78] As such, to ignore our differences in race, gender, sexual orientation, identity, background, experience, etcetera, is to neglect the vast cornucopia of perspectives that can be garnered from a diverse group and to imply "the deep-seated consequences of race in America have been vanquished by the unflappable moral character of a band of brothers forged in combat."[79] Clearly, the events of the summer of 2020 showed that they have not.

Accordingly, if the leadership of the armed forces is committed to winning the war in achieving diversity in the ranks, it cannot fall victim to the same malady that followed both racial desegregation and gender integration–it must recognize that "[d]iversity alone, without a climate that fosters it, does little to root out latent racism, sexual harassment, and other manifestations of bias."[80] To avoid that trap, the military must get after both diversity AND inclusion. While the two terms are often used interchangeably, they are separate and distinct. Diversity, sometimes called statistical diversity, is about the composition of a group, while inclusion is more about

---

* See also the discussion of jury instructions in *Implicit/Unconscious Bias in the Courtroom* by Judge Bennett; Susan E. Upward, Empaneling "Fair and Impartial" Members: The Case for Inclusion of an Implicit Bias Instruction at Courts-Martial, 32 S. Cal. Rev. L. & Soc. Just. (forthcoming Winter 2023).

ensuring its members feel like and are part of the team. More simply put, diversity is about numbers who have a seat at the table; inclusion is about an organization's culture and who has a voice once they get that seat at the table.[81]

In June 2021, Marine Corps leadership once again espoused the virtues of diversity to a warfighting organization, referring to the events of 2020 as "an opportunity to genuinely reflect on diversity, equality, and inclusion" and admitting "that real examples of racial and gender bias exist in our Corps."[82] But the programs that the Marine Corps currently has in place are primarily focused on statistical diversity, the intent being "to get after the goal of having all ranks be reflective of the diversity of the total force and to prevent incidents of real or perceived bias for all Marines," even though there is a recognition that "simply having a diverse organization does not guarantee success."[83]

An illustration of the sometimes complicated relationship among implicit bias, diversity, and inclusion can be seen in the service's struggles with the removal of photos and the redaction of demographic information from promotion files. In taking this approach, the Army sought to mitigate "the presence and impact of implicit bias" and the possibility that a promotion board would make snap judgments based on the photo alone. But the removal had two other unintended effects. First, it limited the ability to achieve statistical diversity because it is difficult to build a diverse team without knowing the metrics that make the talent pool so diverse in the first place. Secondly, it also limited the ability of selection boards to take into account earlier discrimination or bias;[84] especially considering that "career success is cumulative and that racial and ethnic minority officers, on average, were less likely to have achieved the early career milestones that are correlated with improved promotion prospects."[85] Given these issues, and only a few months after the Army completely removed photos, Army leaders clarified their service's policy, stating that while photos and identifying data will still not be used on promotion boards, the latter could be used "for assignment and slating processes... so that leaders can consider the information as they build their teams from the diverse talent seeking to serve in the Army, and from the diverse talent found in the Army."[86] Fast forward to 2021, and at least two of the services are already looking to reverse the promotion photo sea change altogether. In August 2021, the Chief of Naval Personnel opined that the Navy "should consider reinstating photos in selection board" because the data the Navy has collected over the last five years has shown that diversity decreased with the photos removed and "having a clear picture... just makes it easier" for promotion board to consider diversity.[87] The Marine Corps Director of Manpower Plans and Policy Division added that his service is still conducting a survey on the latest round of promotion and selection boards to find if bias played a role, but stated: "if we find out that there [are] disparities within the way we do business within the service, we need to be intellectually curious enough to ask why and figure out why and then figure out what we need to do."[88]

Whether the services return to the use of promotion photos or not, the root cause of a lack of diversity is the underlying bias. While the service's efforts in the diversity realm are to be lauded, military leaders must get out of the mindset that diversity equates inclusion—they are simply not the same, nor will victory in the battle of the former equate success in the war of the latter, as long as latent biases exist.

C. Training must be mandatory and meaningful.

Unintentional bias training for the armed forces is an absolute must—it must occur early and often in a military career, it must be meaningful, and it must be mandatory for all ranks. This is in line with every report and study that has been done in the last decade and has consistently recommended training in this area.[89]

Regardless of how each of the services intends to attack the issue of unintentional bias with its troops, mere awareness is the first step as a baseline—servicemembers must be exposed early on in their military career to the very existence of unintentional bias. If the preeminent solution that has been offered time and time again by military leadership is more diversity and inclusion training, then it must necessarily include implicit bias training so servicemembers understand how their brain processes these biases in a very unintentional way. Any training that omits this knowledge is likely to produce similar results to the training that has already been done, to limited noticeable effect.

Moreover, the critical thinking concepts that accompany unintentional bias training must be repeated at regular intervals throughout a servicemember's career, or the risk is that the skills gained will atrophy. On an annual basis, the military conducts training and tests to ensure that servicemembers are physically fit, can fire their weapon, can demonstrate basic survival skills such as the gas chamber or swim qualifications, and are trained in "soft" skills such as cyber awareness, insider threat awareness, and sexual assault prevention. Professional military education on unintentional bias can be seen no differently than these critical proficiencies and must be trained on a regular time interval.

Since President Obama's Executive Order in 2016, the services have mandated unintentional bias training at least at some level and mostly for leaders and supervisors. For instance, the Air Force has mandated unintentional bias training since 2016, just as the Marine Corps has provided "unconscious bias awareness education across Marine Corps formal schools and the Recruit Depots."[90] But as history has shown, this methodology has, so far, been unsuccessful. Unintentional bias training must be made mandatory for all ranks in every service—if everyone has bias, everyone should be trained to recognize it and mitigate its harmful effects. Of course, voluntary training is the preferred delivery method for knowledge rather than mandatory training because the latter can be counterproductive and can lead to backlash, as some experts contend.[91] Indeed, in 2014 when this kind of training for gender integration was just starting, Marine Corps officials were adamant that research shows "when you make this type of training mandatory, Marines don't necessarily take it as openly as they would as if it were optional and used at their own discretion."[92] But seven years after making unintentional training optional and then only mandatory for leaders, the culture in the Marine Corps, and the military writ large, is still broken. Consider that in February 2021, the Army requested a study to be conducted as part of SecDef Lloyd Austin's order to all the services "to take immediate action to address sexual harassment and sexual assault in the military."[93] In August 2021, the Rand Corporation released the results of their research into two complementary areas—they studied both the organizational characteristics related to the risk of sexual assault and sexual harassment, as well as examining the intersectionality of sexual harassment and gender discrimination in the Army.[94] What the research showed was the telltale hallmarks of bias—whether intentional or unintentional—that still pervades the ranks: 53 percent of the female soldiers surveyed reported that they experienced "being ignored, mistreated, or insulted because of their gender, and 45 percent indicated being told that women are not as good at their job as men are."[95] Perhaps the most eye-opening statistic from the research was the gender bias that was experienced *by men*—more than one-third of male soldiers responded "being told that they did not act like a man."[96]

Given these results, and the history of failed efforts to address them, implicit bias training needs to be made mandatory, at least until a point in time where the culture of the service is such that it is the norm to participate in that training. Carefully constructed, this training can avoid the pitfalls sometimes associated with mandatory training, and can be successful in achieving meaningful change.[97] Even as I write this, I can almost hear the collective groan from the majority of those who wear or have worn a uniform at even the mere mention of more mandatory training.[98] But as an institution, the military must reframe its thought process about mandatory education in this area. While having uncomfortable conversations about bias is perhaps not as appealing as field operations or live-fire drills, it is just as critical to mission accomplishment.[99] To that end, educating the force on unintentional bias cannot devolve into the laissez-faire, death-by-PowerPoint or online click-'til-completion, check-in-the-box training that required military training often becomes, especially when it is not combat-focused.[100] The biggest challenge facing the military as it continues to train on diversity, but also introduces training on unintentional bias and how it interacts with diversity, is finding a way to make this training impactful, meaningful, and lasting. Effective training should involve active participation and scenarios, open discussions about personal experiences for servicemembers of all ranks.[101] The military can direct leaders to start meaningful conversations about race with their subordinates, but it is an entirely different task to engage our most junior servicemen and women to "actively listen" and embrace the Marine Corps

Commandant's concept that "[b]y listening, we learn, by learning, we change" to hopefully achieve institutional transformation.[102]

D. Leaders must buy-in and tie-in.

Imperative to the success of unintentional bias training is that military leaders both visibly and actively participate, and also find some way to make the critical link from classroom to combat.

First, in an overtly hierarchical setting like the military, where leaders are expected to lead from the front and set the example for their subordinates, "endorsement or buy-in from upper management is critical... [because] researchers have found that diversity initiatives are most effective when organizational leaders directly take on responsibility for them."[103] Undoubtedly, this was the intent of the Marine Corps in providing a toolkit to commanders for gender integration in 2014; similarly, one of the recommendations from the Air Force working group in the wake of the POD report was to provide "tailored training in leadership preparation courses regarding unconscious bias and its potential implications for commanders' and supervisors' roles and strategies for reducing/managing unconscious bias."[104] Commanders are uniquely situated to know their troops and the best way to approach the often uncomfortable conversations that inevitably accompany discussions about bias—those are the very kinds of difficult dialogues that the rank and file need to hear, especially an acknowledgment that institution's own policies and procedures may have contributed to both the creation and perpetuation of those biases in the first place.

Like any other organization, change in the military will always bring conflict. In instituting new training and policies, there must be cognizance that there will be those who have a visceral reaction about this topic—ironically, there is a very real and palpable bias about unintentional bias, and the military is not exempt.[105] Commanders are best positioned and must be prepared to respond to those who think it is just a trendy topic or that it is a politically motivated topic—that is irrelevant.[106] What is relevant is that there is an issue of disparate treatment in the military of certain groups that is eating away at the fabric of cohesion within the institution, and "pervasive cultural biases... can contribute to interpersonal friction within military units and distract from the unit's ability to perform under stress."[107] Silence by commanders is not an option in this area because "bias or even the perception of bias thrives on silence," and issues that affect a unit's teamwork or effectiveness must be addressed by its leadership.[108] Moreover, commanders are the best situated to make training on unintentional bias a priority. Operational tempo is different at every unit, and competing requirements coupled with a finite amount of time do not always allow for comprehensive training. Only a commander can make time in the unit's schedule and ensure the importance of the topic receives the investment of time it deserves.

Secondly, research shows that facilitators leading unintentional bias training must also tie the training to mission accomplishment and how the training is relevant to the organization's identity.[109] In that context, perhaps reframing the problem in military parlance may help change the lens for servicemembers to look at unintentional bias from a different perspective in order to start the attack against it. For instance, the military establishment collectively shudders at the thought of "group think" when it comes to external decisions—assuming that one enemy is the same as another, or one battle will play out the same as a similar historical battle, is proverbial kryptonite to the military thinker.[110] Yet, when we ask servicemembers to turn 180 degrees and think about whether their unintentional bias might play into their decision about their fellow soldiers, sailors, airman, Marines, or guardians, it becomes almost an unbreachable taboo. Interestingly, some trainers on implicit bias topics specifically include discussion of implicit reactive devaluation bias and its relationship to groupthink.[111]

In fact, the term groupthink was coined in the after-action discussion following the United States' disastrous invasion of the Bay of Pigs where President Kennedy notably said, "How could we have been so stupid?"[112] As such, it is hardly surprising that the military has been using strategies to interrupt this kind of bias for decades. But few service members have been asked to look at unintentional bias through the lens of red teaming—imagine how much more amenable they might be to accept these concepts if they knew that the Army and Marine Corps had been looking at unintentional bias for years, albeit projected outwards to tactical, operational and strategic planning.[113] Red teaming is essentially organized role-playing of devil's advocate to "challenge explicit and implicit assumptions" and provide "a level of protection from the unseen biases and tendencies inherent in all of us."[114] During exercises and operational planning, a red cell is an ad hoc group independent from the rest of the staff and tasked with picking apart the prevailing notions or assumptions the staff has made in developing their recommended courses of action. But a red team is different—it is a primary duty for a servicemember and an integral member of a command's staff that casts a wider net, not just limited to wargaming or the planning process, but evaluating a unit's effectiveness on the whole.[115] To that end, there is no reason leaders cannot use that red team process to evaluate their own biases or point out the inherent biases in their subordinates, peers, or superiors alike, at any level or size of unit.

Again, it would be naïve to believe that some servicemembers will not have a bias toward unintentional bias training from the start. However, by studying red teaming and gaining an understanding of how the institution applies this analytical tool to assist in unit readiness projected outward toward operations, it might soften the blow in minimizing initial impressions and impulsive reactiveness when it comes time to turn the focus inward to review how our own individual biases may be affecting our operations as a team. Reframing the problem and labeling the red team context as a tactical tool to make us better warfighters, as well as address the unintentional bias in the institution, might be the catalyst to engage even the most junior members of the military.

E. Learn from others.

From 2019 to 2021, I was assigned as the Command Judge Advocate (CJA) at The Basic School (TBS) in Quantico, Virginia, where all new Marine Corps officers attend a six-month course before attending their specialized school in their Military Occupational Specialty. The mission of TBS is to train and educate every lieutenant "in the high standards of professional knowledge, esprit de corps, and leadership to prepare them for duty as company-grade officers in the operating forces, with particular emphasis on the duties, responsibilities, and warfighting skills required of a rifle platoon commander."[116] Part of that curriculum since 2017 has been a period of instruction on unintentional bias—a topic I was fortunate enough to teach during my tenure at TBS. In this context, I offer up the TBS way of doing business not as the model, but only as one method to "get after" this issue and hopefully provide other military units an example of how to tackle the topic of unintentional bias.

First and foremost, the TBS leadership visibly had "buy-in" on the topic—the TBS Commanding Officer and/or the Company Commander for each student company participated in the discussion groups or attended the class.[117] Even during the restrictive social-distancing requirements during the Covid-19 pandemic in 2020 when the majority of formal classes at TBS were moved online, the Commanding Officer ensured the unintentional bias class was adjusted to be taught in-person to facilitate open dialogue between students and staff, but also to impress upon the students the importance of the subject matter.[118]

In terms of scheduling, unintentional bias training was purposefully placed after classes on tactical planning, where students are introduced to the concepts of deliberate and hasty planning, and in the same week as other ethical decision-making classes.[119] The intent was to get the students to "unpack" their own decision-making process, "think about the way they think," and self-reflect to identify their own biases, while also providing tools to mitigate those biases. The curriculum included at least 2.5–3 hours of instruction, broken down into two separate segments.[120] The first portion was an hour-long discussion with the students in small groups and a staff member, usually of a higher rank, serving as a facilitator. The purpose of these discussion groups was merely to start the conversation—provide a more intimate setting and the right environment for students to start breaking down barriers or perceived concerns about openly discussing what can be an uncomfortable topic.

Facilitators were encouraged to share personal anecdotes to set the right conditions and help alleviate an individual's insecurities associated with their willingness to participate and hopefully generate meaningful discussion. The facilitator would also guide the discussion by prompting students with leading questions on topics such as what does the model Marine look like and why do we have that perception, but otherwise, the group was free to engage in open dialogue.

The second segment of the unintentional bias period of instruction occurred usually immediately following the small-group discussions and consisted of a more traditional, formal-learning class of approximately 300 students. The agenda for the 1.5–2-hour class was essentially broken down into four parts: defining unintentional bias, examining the implications of bias, providing methods to break bias, and then discussing with the students how bias interacts with the expectations of a Marine officer. From the outset, it was important to ensure students did not immediately view the term "bias" with a negative connotation, especially considering the "bias for action" we attempt to cultivate in all military leaders in tactical scenarios.[121] As such, the tie-in for students was tactical planning—discussing the concepts of System 1 and System 2 thinking from Daniel Kahneman's book *Thinking Fast and Slow*, and how that mirrors the concepts of planning hasty and deliberate attacks.[122] Similar to the red teaming tie-in suggested earlier, the goal was to make students understand how we use these analytical tools to evaluate our actions on external forces, so they would hopefully be able to turn around and use the same deliberate thinking processes to evaluate their own biases in performance reviews, awards, promotions, assignments, etcetera. The class also examined types of bias, such as confirmation bias, value attribution, and anchoring bias, and provided six methods for breaking bias:

1. Detect, Reflect, Reject—Detect the influence of stereotypes and biases, reflect on the source of the bias and the effects of stereotypes, reject the stereotype.
2. Seeking individualized information, instead of solely relying on a stereotype of a group.
3. Perspective Taking—Instead of viewing how you would react in a situation, consider a person's unique point of view based on their background and experiences and how that may affect their response in the same situation.
4. Consider Situational Explanations—Think about how a situation may have influenced a behavior more than a personal characteristic, and how something outside of a person as a possible explanation of behavior.
5. Committing to Standards—Determining a rubric before an evaluation to increase objectivity and minimize subjectivity, but be aware that the

standard itself might have an inherent bias (usually using the Army CFT as an example).

6. Increase Opportunities for Contact/Dimensions of Difference—Seek out greater interaction with other groups and exposure to people, things, and ideas from diverse backgrounds.

Finally, the class reminded students of the purpose of TBS, which is to train officers to observe, interact, and lead, and the potential roadblock unintentional bias may pose to effective leadership because it leads to nonobjective assessments and evaluations, and detrimentally affects unit cohesion.

Unlike other classes at TBS, there was no test or practical evaluation to gauge students comprehension or retention of the material presented in these periods of instruction—nor was that the intent. But as an instructor, I always had students who approached me after the class—sometimes to ask questions, sometimes to challenge an idea that they heard, and sometimes just to say that they had not considered their own thought processes in this way before. Regardless of their individual reactions, it was clear that students had at least contemplated the material in an introspective way, and therefore the unintentional bias curriculum at TBS accomplished what it set out to do and could be considered a success.[123]

F. Use the military's professional reading lists.

Even with a formal training session like the one at TBS, there must be a certain level of self-realization and reflection that is inherent to learning about and understanding unintentional bias. One of the Marine Corps' leadership principles is to "know yourself and seek self-improvement"—once a servicemember is aware of the existence of unintentional bias, it is incumbent on him/her to "examine yourself honestly, determine what biases you have and whether you have biases that favor or disfavor particular races, gender or sexual orientation. Emplace personal [Standard Operating Procedures] to minimize the effects of your biases. Read books about bias to assist you in your self-assessment and mitigation methods."[124]

Self-education through reading in this vein is not new to the military and provides another avenue for the armed forces to "get after" the issue of unintentional bias. All the services have at least one professional reading list that is intended to be utilized by all ranks and that is regularly updated to rotate in new titles[125] Units routinely house their own internal libraries with copies of these books. Service associations and organizations will provide leader discussion guides to facilitate small-group discussions on a book, while also offering E-books and audiobooks to increase the number of ways servicemembers can access these titles and cater to the younger and more technically savvy generation. And while these lists have historically been filled with books on combat leadership, courage under fire, and thinking about future war, in the past decade there has been a shift to add other titles that are specifically geared to thinking about implicit bias. For instance, the Navy's list recommends *How to be an Antiracist* by Ibram X. Kendi, the Air Force's list recommends *The Art of Thinking Clearly* by Rolf Dobelli, and the Marine Corps' list recommends *Thinking Fast and Slow* by Daniel Kahneman.

Not surprisingly, these additions to the reading lists have garnered scrutiny that perhaps is unwarranted. Partly motivated by the addition of Kendi's book to the Navy's list and the recommendation of *White Fragility* by Robin DiAngelo in the Navy's Second Fleet's book club, Senator Tom Cotton introduced the Combat Racist Training in the Military Act in April 2021, aimed at prohibiting theories like critical race theory from being taught to military members.[126] In June 2021, during a House Armed Service Committee on the National Defense Authorization Budget Request for FY22, Chief of Naval Operations Admiral Mike Gilday was questioned about the addition of Kendi's book to the voluntary reading list. In his response, Gilday did not shy away from the Navy's problem: "[T]here's racism in the Navy, just like there's racism in our country. And the way we're going to get after it is to be honest about it, not to sweep it under the rug, and to talk about it—and that's what we're doing. And that's one of the reasons the book is on the list."[127] General Mark Miley, Chairman of the Joint Chiefs of Staff, responded more pointedly to a similar question, but still conveyed the same message:

> I do think it's important, actually, for those of us in uniform to be open-minded and be widely read.... I've read Mao Zedong. I've read Karl Marx. I've read Lenin. That doesn't make me a communist. So what is wrong with understanding, having some situational understanding about the country for which we are here to defend. And I personally find it offensive that we are accusing the United States military—our general officers; our commissioned [and] non-commissioned officers of being quote "woke" or something else because we are studying some theories that are out there.[128]

The military cannot be deterred and should continue to add unconventional titles to these reading lists. Even if some disagree with the theories espoused in a book, a broader reading curriculum does not imply or equal an endorsement of the ideas contained in its pages. Rather, it broadens the reader's horizons and exposes servicemembers to a wide variety of ideas and viewpoints because "reading is the gateway to true self-evaluation"—a skill that is absolutely required both in the military as a profession and in the unintentional bias space.[129]

G. Re-value physical fitness as a valuation metric.

As seen by the Army CFT, relying on physical fitness is a constant unintentional bias trap in the military. Undoubtedly, the very nature of military service and combat requires a higher level of physical fitness than almost any other profession. But the tendency is to overvalue physical fitness to define what a "good" soldier, sailor, airman, Marine, or guardian is, and then to use a scored physical fitness test as a definitive metric to rank servicemembers, which inherently affects performance evaluations, promotions, and assignments. This disproportionate amount of value the military places on physical fitness, as opposed to other skill sets like critical thinking or problem solving or empathy, or any of the leadership traits we so vehemently espouse, is increasing opportunities for bias and decreasing our effectiveness and lethality as a military force.[130] Consider the following story that personifies and illustrates this trap:

> A young corporal joined our [Human Intelligence] team in Afghanistan; she's working on a problem that has existed for ten years. There was a Taliban commander, who had killed a lot of Marines between 2008–2014, and this young female corporal turns to this problem set, and dives deep, and dedicates herself to hunting this guy. I won't get into trade craft or anything, but she figures it out, and we dropped a bomb on him after hunting him for ten years. The credit for this strike was to this female [Human Intelligence] Marine, so when I hear about biased behaviors going on, I want to ask, you think you're a better Marine? Are you more lethal? Are you stronger, faster? Maybe. But she's an outstanding Marine with respect to lethality and capability. So how come you think you're a better Marine? Marines had been working on this for ten years, she figured it out in three months. If we don't value that, what business are we in? That's what vexes me.[131]

Similarly, the discussion of physical fitness came up in almost every Unintentional Bias class I taught at TBS. Lieutenants would invariably espouse the institution's preference for size and strength when it comes to combat arms jobs, such as infantry or artillery. My response always tried to shift their perspective on that thinking: if size and strength was the preeminent prerequisite to fill those combat roles, then how could they account for the "shortest, skinniest, and most limber men" who did not stand taller than 5'2 and who *volunteered* to go headlong into enemy tunnels in Vietnam, armed with only a pistol and a flashlight?[132] Moreover, if size and strength was the sole determiner for success in combat, then the Marine Corps would never have known the greatness of Lieutenant Lewis B. "Chesty" Puller, who is infamous for having the heart of a lion and is the most decorated Marine in history, but is perhaps less known for standing only a mere 5'2" tall.

The solution to mitigate the institutional bias in the military that accompanies physical fitness tests and is, in many cases, deliberate and intentional, is simple: stop scoring it. If the services set the *minimum* standard—whatever that standard might be—and make the evaluation pass/fail, then the standard could also be gender-neutral, which appears to be desired end state for at least the Army and the Marine

Corps. Specific military occupational specialties could have physical event requirements, as they do now, to be qualified to perform that job—not a separate scored test per se but, for instance, the infantry could require a minimum hike distance under a certain load weight, or pilots could require a certain level of swim qualification to ensure they can escape a water ditching. However, none of those events would be calculated into a score that would then factor into promotions or advancement. The spirit of camaraderie, esprit de corps, and competition that is often fostered during physical fitness events could still be attained through unit events, whether that be through exercising combat skills or playing team sports.

Instead of continually adjusting the test's events or the grading scale, the military needs to accept the fact that continued scoring of physical fitness tests will only lead to biased comparisons that are based on one metric alone, and not the whole-person concept that is paramount to achieving true diversity and inclusion in the ranks.

3. The System Is Blinking Red...and Pink, Black, Brown, Yellow

Following the terrorist attacks on the United States on September 11, 2001, one of the failures attributed to the intelligence community was that "the system was blinking red"—the signs were all pointing to a catastrophic event, but "no one looked at the bigger picture; no analytic work foresaw the lightning that could connect the thundercloud to the ground."[133] The military might be at a similar point with the internal threat that biases pose to the institution, especially in the realms of racial and gender discrimination. If the data points, research, and personal anecdotes collected up to and including 2020 were not enough, the events in the nation's capital on January 6, 2021, and the role that both active duty military members and veterans played in the riot, should have served as the ultimate warning sign—the lightning rod—for the leaders of the armed services.[134]

Indeed, following that event, SecDef Lloyd Austin immediately ordered a standdown to address extremism in the ranks—a decisive and timely move aimed at the immediate point of friction. Perhaps the standdown reflects that the services have finally learned the hard lessons from racial and gender segregation, and how the quick-to-label-but-slow-to-execute methodology only serves to hinder the institution's success in the long run. Unquestionably, dealing with the most extreme ideologies and intentional bias that still exists in the military needed to be aggressively addressed. Yet, when looked at from a broader perspective, it seems the standdown is just plugging another leak in the hose without cutting off the water supply—there needs to be just as much focus, time, and effort devoted to the implicit bias that pervades the institution, which is mostly undiagnosed and unbeknownst to those afflicted with it, or risk that these attitudes and beliefs will continue to fester in the rank and file.

In 2007, as a young lieutenant, I returned from my first tour in Fallujah, Iraq, to my unit's home base at Camp Pendleton, California. Part of our integration back into the unit in garrison was for each company-grade officer to be given a collateral billet beyond their primary military occupational specialty, with jobs in certain sections such as administration, training, intelligence, and logistics. As an enlisted Marine, I had already served as a personnel clerk responsible for correspondence and personnel records, so I requested for any of the other available billets to increase my knowledge in other fields. One day, as I was waiting for my collateral billet assignment with my peers, a male lieutenant approached me and asked me why I had not asked for the adjutant billet, that is the administrative assistant to the commanding officer. I explained my history in the administration field and my desire to broaden my areas of expertise. I then asked him the same question in return because I knew he had also requested not to be slated as the adjutant. He was visibly taken aback, guffawed, and simply said "that's a girl's job." In turn, I too was visibly taken aback and then proceeded to engage in a spirited conversation with my peer (which may have included language that is colloquially attributed to sailors on shore leave) about why that comment was both inappropriate and incorrect. "I'm not good at paperwork, and the adjutant has always been a girl" was his reply, as if his incompetence coupled with historical precedence brought credence to his opinion. I was therefore frustratingly disappointed, but not at all surprised when I was assigned the duties of the unit's adjutant. Shortly after taking on my new role, I went to my superior, a major and the unit's executive officer, and relayed the conversation I had with my peer. The major was at first upset, but when he and I went back in the unit's chronology and discovered that at least the past five unit's adjutants before me were female, he became dismayed. Until he looked at the data, he had no idea that the unit was unwittingly contributing and perpetuating that negative stereotype. Needless to say, after my tenure was complete as the unit's adjutant, my successor was a male.

In his memoir, former SecDef and revered Marine Corps General Jim Mattis said "[i]nstitutions get the behaviors they reward."[135] For too long, the military has been complicit in setting conditions for unintentional bias to fester in its ranks. In the last decade, and especially following the events of the summer of 2020, one would hope the military has finally come to realize that its own policies, practices, and procedures have facilitated unintentional, yet institutionally sanctioned, biases against its own members by its own members. These biases have manifested themselves in outright scandals, such as Marines United or the POD military justice report, but have also affected promotions, assignments, and career advancement opportunities for marginalized groups, especially along racial and gender lines, and has critically hindered the DoD's diversity goals.

372 Extending Justice

But those examples are just symptoms of a much larger and more devastating disease. The threat that biases pose to operational planning has long been known to military strategists, and the Army and Marine Corps have both used red teaming to counteract the harmful effects of groupthink when it comes to problems related to projecting military power externally on our enemies. But the military establishment has only recently acknowledged the internal threat—a lack of diversity is affecting our "strategic advantage on the global stage," but diversity alone is not enough; true inclusion is the key to a "diversity of thought and perspective," and remains frustratingly elusive.[136] That is a problem that can no longer be simply ignored or minimized merely as a talking point.

The services seem to be on the precipice of effecting real change within the ranks. The military has taken some of the small, necessary steps to "get after" the unconscious bias problem, but leaders must be in it for the long haul—this is not an easy or overnight fix that will be solved only with mandatory training. It will take dedication and persistence to call out and reflect on our own biases that effectively "acts like friendly fire. The possibility of friendly fire remains ever present, and the entire team must stay vigilant and work together as a team to limit its occurrence while mitigating the effects when it happens."[137]

Conclusion

Whether it be in court-martial deliberation rooms or promotion boards, until the very real threat that unconscious bias poses is taken seriously by the military and not considered the proverbial elephant in the room, it is unlikely that the ducks will pick geese or include them as valuable members of the flock any time soon.

So, You'd Like To Know More

- U.S. Dep't of Army, The Red Team Handbook (9th ed. 2020) available at https://usacac.army.mil/sites/default/files/documents/ufmcs/The_Red_Team_Handbook.pdf.
- Don Christensen & Yelena Tsilker, Protect our Def., Racial Disparities in Military Justice: Findings of Substantial and Persistent Racial Disparities Within the United States Military Justice System (May 5, 2017), https://www.protectourdefenders.com/wp-content/uploads/2017/05/Report_20.pdf.
- Rachel Gaddes et al., Conscious and Unconscious Gender Bias: Response to DACOWITS RFI 4, Def. Advisory Comm. on Women in the

Servs. (Dec. 2018), https://dacowits.defense.gov/Portals/48/Documents/General%20Documents/RFI%20Docs/Dec2018/Insight_RFI%204.pdf?ver=2018-12-08-000555-027.

- U.S. Gov't Accountability Off., GAO-19-344, Military Justice: DoD and the Coast Guard Need to Improve Their Capabilities to Assess Racial and Gender Disparities (May 2019).
- Pamela Fuller, et al., The Leader's Guide to Unconscious Bias: How to Reframe Bias, Cultivate Connection, and Create High-Performing Teams (2020).

About the Author

Lieutenant Colonel Susan E. Upward is a judge advocate in the United States Marine Corps. A native of Toronto, Canada, she enlisted in the Marine Corps in February 2004 and became a U.S. citizen in September of the same year. After commissioning in 2005, she spent seven years of her military career as an Air Support Control Officer, including two tours in support of Operation Iraqi Freedom, before she was selected to attend law school. She holds a B.A. in English from Valparaiso University; a M.A. in Military Studies from American Military University; a J.D. from Syracuse University; and an LL.M. in Homeland and National Security Law from Western Michigan University's Cooley Law School. She has served as a prosecutor, defense counsel, and as a CJA prior to her current role as the Legal Services Support Team Officer-in-Charge at Marine Corps Air Station Cherry Point, North Carolina.

In accordance with 5 CFR § 3601.108, the views and opinions expressed in this Chapter are those of the author and do not necessarily represent the views of the DoD or its components.

Endnotes

1. David Martin, *Race in the Ranks: Investigating Racial Bias in the U.S. Military*, CBS (March 21, 2021), https://www.cbsnews.com/news/us-military-racism-60-minutes-2021-03-21/.

2. Admiral (Ret.) Mike Mullen in *id.; see also* Kristy N. Kamarck, Cong. Rsch. Serv., R44321, Diversity, Inclusion, and Equal Opportunity in the Armed Services: Background and Issues for Congress 20 (2019) ((hereinafter "Kamarck, CRS, Diversity in the Armed Services") ("[T]he officer corps, and especially at the senior leadership level, racial and ethnic minorities are underrepresented relative to the enlisted corps and the U.S. population").

3. Other biases surely exist in the military, including those based on equal opportunity categories such as sexual orientation and religion, as well as military-specific biases based on rank and military occupational specialty, or even biases based on each of the services as entities on the whole. Although the most visible issues facing the armed forces are racial and gender biases, that is not to minimize the impact of other biases facing the military that can also be addressed through the proposed solutions offered here.

4. Daniel Chandler & Rod Munday, A Dictionary of Media and Communication (3rd ed. 2020), https://www.oxfordreference.com/view/10.1093/oi/authority.20110803100005347.

5. Kristy N. Kamarck, Cong. Rsch. Serv., R40275, Women in Combat: Issues for Congress 22 (2016) (citing The Women's Armed Services Integration Act of 1948, Pub. L. No. 80-625, 62 Stat. 356, *repealed by* Pub. L. No. 90-130, 81 Stat. 374 (1967) (hereinafter "Kamarck, Women in Combat"). The proportion of women in the military was limited to two percent of the enlisted ranks and ten percent of officers.

6. *Id.* at 6 (citing Pub. L. No. 103-160, 107 Stat. 1659 et. seq. (1993)).

7. *Id.* at 13–14 (citing Memorandum from the Chairman of the Joint Chiefs of Staff to the Secretary of Defense on Women in the Service Implementation (Jan. 9, 2013)).

8. Marine Administrative ("MARADMIN") Message, 589/14 (Nov. 12, 2014), https://www.marines.mil/News/Messages/Messages-Display/Article/896780/announcement-of-change-to-assignment-policy/.

9. *Id.* at ¶ 8B.

10. Rebecca Mukuna, *Unconscious Gender Bias: New Training Tool as the Marine Corps Prepares to Open New Positions to Women*, NATO Assoc. of Canada (Dec. 4, 2014), https://natoassociation.ca/unconscious-gender-bias-new-training-tool-as-the-u-s-marine-corps-prepares-to-open-new-positions-to-women/

11. *Id.*

12. Kamarck, Women in Combat at 14.

13. *Id.*

14. Rachel Gaddes et al., *Conscious and Unconscious Gender Bias: Response to DACOWITS RFI 4*, 14 Def. Advisory Comm. on Women in the Servs. (Dec. 2018), https://dacowits.defense.gov/Portals/48/Documents/General%20Documents/RFI%20Docs/Dec2018/Insight_RFI%204.pdf?ver=2018-12-08-000555-027 [hereinafter DACOWITS Report].

15. Mark D. Faram, *Navy Looks to Remove 'Man' from All Job Titles*, Navy Times (Jan. 7, 2016), https://www.navytimes.com/news/your-navy/2016/01/07/navy-looks-to-remove-man-from-all-job-titles/; Hope Hodge Seck, *All Marines to Get 'Unconscious Bias' Training as Women Join Infantry*, Military.com (Mar. 18, 2016), https://www.military.com/daily-news/2016/03/18/all-marines-unconscious-bias-training-women-join-infantry.html (citing an undisclosed Center for Naval Analysis survey of 54,000 Marines).

16. Jeff Schogol, *All Marines to Undergo 2-Day Training as Women Join Combat Units*, Marine Corps Times (June 16, 2016), https://www.marinecorpstimes.com/news/your-marine-corps/2016/06/16/all-marines-to-undergo-2-day-training-as-women-join-combat-units/.

17. *Id.* (internal quotations omitted); Hope Hodge Seck, *All Marines to Get 'Unconscious Bias' Training as Women Join Infantry*, Military.com (Mar. 18, 2016).

18. Pres. Memorandum on Promoting Diversity and Inclusion in the National Security Workforce, 81 Fed. Reg. 69993, 69996 (Oct. 7, 2016).

19. Hope Hodge Seck, *A Top Marine General Says "Unconscious Gender Bias" Will be Scrubbed From Official Documents in 2 Years*, TASK & PURPOSE (Oct. 3, 2018), https://taskandpurpose.com/news/marine-corps-publications-gender-bias/);Hope Hodge Seck, *All Marines to Get 'Unconscious Bias' Training as Women Join Infantry*, MILITARY.COM (Mar. 18, 2016).

20. Hope Hodge Seck, *All Marines to Get 'Unconscious Bias' Training as Women Join Infantry*, MILITARY.COM (Mar. 18, 2016).

21. The Marines United scandal involved a closed Facebook group of more than 30,000 members of the United States Armed Forces who were inappropriately sharing and commenting on hundreds of photos of females servicemembers online, to include nonconsensual nude photos and "revenge porn." Jeff Schogol, *Army's New Physical Fitness Test Will Be Gender-Neutral, Secretary Says*, TASK AND PURPOSE (Feb. 15, 2018), https://taskandpurpose.com/health-fitness/army-wants-gender-neutral-fitnes-test/.

22. DACOWITS Report, at 15.

23. The Army's old physical fitness test was comprised of three events: push-ups, sit-ups, and a two-mile run. The proposed new combat fitness test was comprised of six-events: deadlifts, standing power throws, hand-release push-ups, leg tucks, sprint-drag-carry, and a two-mile run to take place only after the other five events. However, the leg tuck has since been officially removed as an event. Jenni Fink, *Army Approves New Gender-, Age-Neutral Fitness Test*, NEWSWEEK (July 9, 2018), https://www.newsweek.com/army-approves-new-gender-age-neutral-fitnesstest-1014928; Haley Britzky, *The Leg Tuck is Officially Dead and Other ChangesComing to the Army Combat Fitness Test*, TASK & PURPOSE (Mar. 23, 2022), https://taskandpurpose.com/news/army-combat-fitness-test-rand-study/.

24. Jeff Schogol, *Army's New Physical Fitness Test Will Be Gender-Neutral, Secretary Says*, TASK AND PURPOSE (Feb. 15, 2018).

25. *See, e.g.*, Charles C. Krulak, *The Strategic Corporal: Leadership in the Three Block War*, MARINES MAGAZINE (Jan. 9, 1999) (describing modern warfare as complex, multi-faceted and rapidly evolving, requiring leaders at the lowest levels to have critical thinking skills in order to make independent decision that could have major consequences), available at https://apps.dtic.mil/sti/pdfs/ADA399413.pdf.

26. Hope Hodge Seck, *DoD Quietly Calls for Shutdown of 70-Year-Old Committee on Women in the Military*, MILITARY.COM (June 24, 2021) (quoting Captain (Ret.) Lory Manning), https://www.military.com/daily-news/2021/06/24/dod-quietly-calls-shutdown-of-70-year-old-committee-women-military.html?fbclid=IwAR2srt_W5GAIpRfjfZelwdXKrDHu34gNRQN325VTIx8J_wDhTFzSjbp4iS0.

27. Steven Beynon, *Nearly Half of Female Soldiers Still Failing New Army Fitness Test, While Males Pass Easily*, MILITARY.COM (May 10, 2021), https://www.military.com/daily-news/2021/05/10/nearly-half-of-female-soldiers-still-failing-new-army-fitness-test-while-males-pass-easily.html.

28. Nat'l Def. Authorization Act for Fiscal Year 2021, S. 4049, 116th Cong. § 592 (2020).

29. Corey Dickstein, *Army Rolls Out Latest Combat Fitness Test with Different Scoring Tiers for Male, Female Soldiers*, STARS AND STRIPES (Mar. 22, 2021), https://www.stripes.com/theaters/us/army-rolls-out-latest-combat-fitness-test-with-different-scoring-tiers-for-male-female-soldiers-1.666842 (internal quotation marks omitted).

30. Sarah Cammarata, *House Lawmaker Grills Army Officials on Gender Bias, Including 'Lopsided' Combat Fitness Test*, STARS AND STRIPES (May 25, 2021), https://www.stripes.com/branches/army/2021-05-24/ARMY-WOMEN-1576902.html.

31. Exec. Order No. 9981, 13 Fed. Reg. 4131 (July 29, 1948) (ordering the "equality of treatment and opportunity for all persons in the armed services without regard to race, color, religion, or national origin," but at the time, made no mention of gender or sexual orientation).

32. KAMARCK, WOMEN IN COMBAT at 15 (citing MORRIS J. MACGREGOR JR., INTEGRATION OF THE ARMED FORCES 1940–1965 518, 553 (1979)).

33. Jay Price, *In 1969, The Military Thought It Had Eliminated Racism In Its Ranks. Then Troops Began Rioting*, KPBS (Aug. 2, 2019), https://www.kpbs.org/news/2019/aug/02/1969-military-thought-it-had-eliminated-racism-its/; *see also* JAMES E. WESTHEIDER, FIGHTING ON TWO FRONTS: AFRICAN AMERICANS AND THE VIETNAM WAR (1999).

34. Jay Price, *In 1969, The Military Thought It Had Eliminated Racism In Its Ranks. Then Troops Began Rioting*, KPBS (Aug. 2, 2019).

35. *Id.*

36. Don Christensen & Yelena Tsilker, *Racial Disparities in Military Justice: Findings of Substantial and Persistent Racial Disparities Within the United States Military Justice System*, PROTECT OUR DEFENDERS (May 5, 2017), https://www.protectourdefenders.com/wp-content/uploads/2017/05/Report_20.pdf [hereinafter POD Report I]; *see generally* Protect Our Defenders, https://www.protectourdefenders.com/about/.

37. POD Report I (emphasis added) (The Navy only provided complete data from 2014–2015).

38. *Federal Lawsuit Reveals Air Force Cover Up: Racial Disparities in Military Justice Part II*, PROTECT OUR DEF. 15 (May 2020), https://www.protectourdefenders.com/downloads/POD_Disparity_Report_2020.pdf [hereinafter POD Report II].

39. POD Report I, at ii.

40. POD Report II, at 7.

41. *Id.* at 8.

42. *Protect Our Defs. v. Dep't of Def.*, 401 F. Supp. 3d 259, 279 (D. Conn. 2019).

43. *Id.*

44. U.S. GOV'T ACCOUNTABILITY OFF., GAO-19-344, MILITARY JUSTICE: DOD AND THE COAST GUARD NEED TO IMPROVE THEIR CAPABILITIES TO ASSESS RACIAL AND GENDER DISPARITIES (May 2019).

45. *Id.*

46. *Id.*

47. The Commandant initially announced his intent to ban Confederate-related items in February 2020, but did not officially order the removal until June 5, 2020. The Secretary of Defense expanded the ban to all DoD installations on 16 July 2020. MARADMIN Message, 331/20 (June 5, 2020), https://www.marines.mil/News/Messages/Messages-Display/Article/2210513/removal-public-displays-of-the-confederate-battle-flag/.

48. Sec'y of Def. Message to the Force on DoD Diversity and Inclusiveness (June 18, 2020), available at https://www.defense.gov/Newsroom/Transcripts/Transcript/Article/2224438/secretary-mark-t-esper-message-to-the-force-on-dod-diversity-and-inclusiveness/.

49. *Id.*

50. *Id.*

51. Memorandum from the Sec'y of Def. to All DoD Personnel, Message to the Force– Feedback on Diversity and Inclusion in the Military (June 23, 2020), available at https://media

.defense.gov/2020/Jun/25/2002321309/-1/-1/1/MESSAGE-TO-THE-FORCE-FEEDBACK-ON-DIVERSITY-AND-INCLUSION-IN-THE-MILITARY.PDF

52. Memorandum from the Sec'y of the Army & Army Chief of Staff, Elimination of Department of Army (DA) Photos, and Race, Ethnicity and Gender Identification Data for Officer, Warrant Officer, and Enlisted Selection Boards (Updated) (Jun. 26, 2020), available at https://www.soc.mil/swcs/DOTDP/_pdf/GRAD/Elimination%20of%20DA%20Photo%20and%20mRace%20Ethinicity%20Gender%20Data%20From%20Selection%20Board%2020200626.pdf

53. *Id.*

54. Stephen Losey, *Air Force Announces First Changes from Diversity Task Force*, AIR FORCE TIMES (July 9, 2020), https://www.airforcetimes.com/news/your-air-force/2020/07/09/air-force-announces-first-changes-from-diversity-task-force/.

55. Memorandum from the Sec'y of Def., Immediate Actions to Address Diversity, Inclusion and Equal Opportunity in the Military Services (July 14, 2020), available at https://media.defense.gov/2020/Jul/15/2002457268/-1/-1/1/Immediate_Actions_to_Address_Diversity_Inclusion_Equal_Opportunity_in_Military_Services.pdf.

56. *Id.*

57. *Id.*

58. Memorandum from the Sec'y of Def., Actions to Improve Racial and Ethnic Diversity and Inclusion in the U.S. Military (Dec. 17, 2020), available at https://media.defense.gov/2020/Dec/18/2002554854/-1/-1/0/ACTIONS-TO-IMPROVE-RACIAL-AND-ETHNIC-DIVERSITY-AND-INCLUSION-IN-THE-U.S.-MILITARY.PDF.

59. *Id.*

60. General David H. Berger, *A Letter from the Commandant*, MARINE CORPS GAZETTE 8 (June 2020), available at https://mca-marines.org/wp-content/uploads/CMC-Letter-R1.pdf.

61. *See* THE BASIC SCHOOL, RIFLE PLATOON IN THE ATTACK: B3J3718 STUDENT HANDOUT, available at https://www.trngcmd.marines.mil/Portals/207/Docs/TBS/B3J3718%20Rifle%20Platoon%20in%20the%20Attack.pdf.

62. In addition to criminal law, judge advocates practice in a number of areas to provide specialized advice to commanders, including in international, labor, contract, environmental, cyber, tort, and administrative law.

63. Uniform Code of Military Justice, 10 U.S.C. §§ 806, 826, 827 (2019).

64. POD Report I, at i, iii.

65. *Id.* at iii.

66. Senator Kirsten Gillibrand first introduced the concept of removing convening authority from commanders in the Military Justice Improvement Act of 2013, S. 967, 113th Cong. (2013).

67. S. 1605, 117th Cong., §532 (2021) (The grade of O-7 represents a rear admiral (lower half) in the Navy and Coast Guard, and a brigadier general in the Army, Air Force, Marine Coprs, and Space Force.).

68. Military Justice Improvement and Increasing Prevention Act of 2021, S. 1520, 177th Cong., § 7 (2021).

69. 401 F. Supp. 3d at 287 (POD sued under FOIA for records withheld and/or redacted by the DoD, including for the biographies of SJAs from each of the services. Despite the statement quoted here, the court found that SJAs had a relatively low privacy interest that was outweighed by the public interest in their disclosure and ordered the DoD to produce the SJAs biographies with only purely personal information redacted).

70. POD Report II, at Appendix K.

71. Judge Karen Arnold-Burger, Jean Mavrelis, & Phyllis B. Pickett, *Hearing All Voices: Challenges of Cultural Competence and Opportunities for Community Outreach*, in ENHANCING JUSTICE REDUCING BIAS 198 (Sarah E. Redfield ed., 2017) [hereinafter ENHANCING JUSTICE]; *see also* Victoria C. Plaut & Christina S. Carbone, *Considering Audience Psychology in the Design of Implicit Bias Education*, in ENHANCING JUSTICE at 274 ("[T]he notion that people can be debiased in a two-hour session on implicit bias is deeply misguided.").

72. U.S. Dep't of the Army, Pamphlet 27-9, *Military Judges' Benchbook* ch. 2-5-3 (2020) ("Implied bias exists when, despite a disclaimer, most people in the same position as the court member would be prejudiced").

73. *Id.*

74. *Id.* at ch. 2-5-1.

75. Cynthia Lee, *Awareness as a First Step Toward Overcoming Implicit Bias*, in ENHANCING JUSTICE at 291–292 (Some judges have started crafting specific instructions and warning jurors against deciding cases based on implicit biases, while in other jurisdictions, attorneys are using voir dire to educate jurors about implicit bias. While the limited research that has been done on the effectiveness of these approaches is that they are insufficient and may not have a significant effect on the results of trial, a sample instruction is provided in this reference that is used by a federal district court judge in Iowa).

76. Thomas E. Ricks & Sebastian J. Bae, *Racial inclusion and diversity in the armed forces: Some thoughts on today*, FOREIGN POLICY (Oct. 6, 2016), https://foreignpolicy.com/2016/10/06/racial-inclusion-and-diversity-in-the-armed-forces-some-thoughts-on-today/.

77. *Id.*; *see also* SEBASTIAN JUNGER, TRIBE: ON HOMECOMING AND BELONGING 125 (2016) ("In combat, soldiers all but ignore differences of race, religion, and politics within their platoon").

78. KAMARCK, CRS, DIVERSITY IN THE ARMED SERVICES at 20 ("The active duty enlisted corps is more racially diverse than the U.S. resident population with nonwhite servicemembers accounting for roughly one-third of all active duty enlisted and 23% of the total U.S. population ages 18–64").

79. Thomas E. Ricks & Sebastian J. Bae, *Racial inclusion and diversity in the armed forces: Some thoughts on today*, FOREIGN POLICY (Oct. 6, 2016).

80. Rand Rodriguez, *Bias: The Hidden Figure in Diversity*, WAR ROOM–U.S. ARMY WAR COLLEGE (July 26, 2018), https://warroom.armywarcollege.edu/articles/bias-hidden-figure/).

81. PAMELA FULLER, ET AL., THE LEADER'S GUIDE TO UNCONSCIOUS BIAS: HOW TO REFRAME BIAS, CULTIVATE CONNECTION, AND CREATE HIGH-PERFORMING TEAMS 77–78 (2020).

82. Lieutenant General David Ottignon & Brigadier General Jason Woodworth, *Diversity, Equity & Inclusion: Why This Is Important to the Corps as a Warfighting Organization*, MARINE CORPS GAZETTE WE38 (June 2021), available at https://mca-marines.org/wp-content/uploads/Diversity-Equity-Inclusion-1.pdf.

83. *Id.* at WE41 (The Marine Corps is currently studying the processes for both promotion and selection boards "to determine if, and to what extent, barriers exist for minorities and females." The service is also conducting similar studies into fitness reports, advancement/retention issues, and military occupational specialty assignments.).

84. Major Benjamin McClellan, *Address Implicit Racial Bias Found In Officer*, ASSOCIATION OF THE UNITED STATES ARMY (Jan. 5, 2021), https://www.ausa.org/articles/address-implicit-racial-bias-found-officer.

85. Kamarck, CRS, Diversity in the Armed Services at 22.

86. Memorandum from the Assistant Sec'y of the Army (Manpower and Reserve Affairs), Updated Guidance Regards the DA Photo and Use of Race, Ethnicity, and Gender Identifying Data in Assignment and Slating Processes (Oct. 19, 2020), available at https://va.ng.mil/Portals/55/Documents/Foxhole/DA-PhotoUpdate.pdf?ver=vdIkjyb0dPwVYE82etwQbA%3D%3D.

87. Diana Stancy Correll, *CNP: Removing Photos from Promotion Boards Has Hurt Diversity*, Navy Times (Aug. 3, 2021) (quoting Vice Admiral John Nowell Jr.), https://www.navytimes.com/news/your-navy/2021/08/03/cnp-removing-photos-from-promotion-boards-has-hurt-diversity/.

88. *Id.* (quoting Brigadier General Ahmed T. Williamson).

89. *E.g.*, U.S. Marine Corps, Commandant's Planning Guidance: 38th Commandant of the Marine Corps 21 (July 17, 2019), available at https://www.marines.mil/News/Publications/MCPEL/Electronic-Library-Display/Article/1907265/38th-commandants-planning-guidance/ ("We will emphasize the need to educate the force in area such as unconscious bias."); Memorandum from Sec'y of Def., Action to Improve Racial and Ethnic Diversity and Inclusion in the U.S. Military (Dec. 17, 2020) (Two of the SecDef's broad recommendations were the establishment of a "Diversity and Inclusion Center of Excellence" that would be tasked with developing and instituting "a DoD-wide curriculum on diversity, inclusion, and cultural awareness," as well as "developing and publishing standardized leadership and professional curriculum, to include modules and case studies explaining the value of fostering and cultivating a diverse and inclusive workforce").

90. U.S. Air Force, Fact Sheet: 2016 Diversity & Inclusion Initiatives, https://www.af.mil/Portals/1/documents/diversity/Attach2_2016%20Diversity%20and%20Inclusion%20Initatives%20Fact%20Sheet.pdf?ver=2016-09-30-111307-623; Department of Defense Board on Diversity and Inclusion, Recommendations to Improve Racial and Ethnic Diversity and Inclusion in the U.S. Military (Dec. 20), available at https://media.defense.gov/2020/Dec/18/2002554852/-1/-1/0/DOD-DIVERSITY-AND-INCLUSION-FINAL-BOARD-REPORT.PDF.

91. Interview by Lee Jussim with Dr. Mahzarin R. Banaji, *in Mandatory Implicit Bias Training Is a Bad Idea*, Psychology Today (Dec. 2, 2017), https://www.psychologytoday.com/us/blog/rabble-rouser/201712/mandatory-implicit-bias-training-is-bad-idea).

92. Major Martha Sullivan, *quoted in* Rebecca Mukuna, *Unconscious Gender Bias: New Training Tool as the Marine Corps Prepares to Open New Positions to Women*, NATO Assoc. of Canada (Dec. 4, 2014).

93. Avery Calkins et al., *Sexual Harassment and Gender Discrimination in the Active-Component Army; Variation in Most Serious Event Characteristics by Gender and Installation Risk*, Rand Corp. (2021), available at https://www.rand.org/pubs/research_reports/RRA1385-1.html; Memorandum from the Sec'y of Def., Immediate Actions to Counter Sexual Assault and Harassment and the Establishment of a 90-Day Independent Review Commission on Sexual Assault in the Military (Feb. 26, 2021), available at https://media.defense.gov/2021/Feb/26/2002590163/-1/-1/0/APPROVAL-OF-MEMO-DIRECTING-IMMEDIATE-ACTIONS-TO-COUNTER-SEXUAL-ASSAULT-AND-HARASSMENT.PDF.

94. Miriam Matthew et al., *Organizational Characteristics Associated with Risk of Sexual Assault and Sexual Harassment in the U.S. Army*, Rand Corp. (2021), available at https://www.rand.org/content/dam/rand/pubs/research_reports/RRA1000/RRA1013-1/RAND_RRA1013-1.pdf; Avery Calkins et al., *Sexual Harassment and Gender Discrimination in the Active-Com-

ponent Army; Variation in Most Serious Event Characteristics by Gender and Installation Risk, RAND CORP. (2021), available at https://www.rand.org/pubs/research_reports/RRA1385-1.html.

95. *Id.* (Calkins) at 14.

96. *Id.* at 37.

97. *See, e.g.,* AMARETTE FILUT, ANNA KAATZ & MOLLY CARNES, THE IMPACT OF UNCONSCIOUS BIAS ON WOMEN'S CAREER ADVANCEMENT, THE SASKAWA PEACE FOUNDATION EXPERT REVIEWS SERIES ON ADVANCING WOMEN'S EMPOWERMENT (2017) (summarizing research on unconscious bias and its successful interruption); Frank Dobbin & Alexandra Kalev, *Why Doesn't Diversity Training Work? The Challenge for Industry and Academia*, 10 ANTHROPOLOGY NOW 48, 52 (2018) ("The key to improving the effects of training is to make it part of a wider program of change").

98. *See* Lisa Saum-Manning et al., *Reducing the Time Burden of Army Company Leaders*, RAND CORP. 1 (2019) (Leaders at the company level face an "inherent tension between activities that develop combat readiness and other mandatory training.").

99. *See* Philip Athey, *A Diverse Corps Is Necessary to Implement Future Force Design, Top Official Says*, MARINE CORPS TIMES (Aug. 10, 2021) (quoting Williamson), https://www.marinecorpstimes.com/news/your-marine-corps/2021/08/10/a-diverse-corps-is-necessary-to-implement-future-force-design-top-official-says/ ("The Marine Corps need increased diversity to fully implement the force design changes required to face off against China, Russia or other potential threats.").

100. The Marine Corps does currently offer an online course on Unconscious Bias, but the intended audience is civilian DoD employees and their uniformed supervisors/managers. *See* U. S. MARINE CORPS, HUMAN RES. & ORGANIZATIONAL MGMT., *Unconscious Bias: Understanding Bias to Unleash Potential* available at https://www.hqmc.marines.mil/hrom/Sponsored-Training/Course-222/ and https://www.hqmc.marines.mil/hrom/Sponsored-Training/Course-223/.

101. Bernice B. Donald, Anthony Holloway & Sarah E. Redfield, *Implicit Bias is Real, Implicit Bias Training Matters: Responding to the Negative Press* (Sept. 2020) 6, 8–9, 13–14, available at https://ssrn.com/abstract=3686762 or http://dx.doi.org/10.2139/ssrn.3686762; *id.* at 6, 8, 9 (discussing aspects of successful training).

102. Press Release, U.S. Marine Corps, Message from the Commandant of the Marine Corps and the Sergeant Major of the Marine Corps (June 3, 2020), https://www.marines.mil/News/Press-Releases/Press-Release-Display/Article/2207572/message-from-the-commandant-of-the-marine-corps-and-the-sergeant-major-of-the-m/.

103. Victoria C. Plaut & Christina S. Carbone, *Considering Audience Psychology in the Design of Implicit Bias Education*, *in* ENHANCING JUSTICE at 272.

104. POD Report II, at Appendix K.

105. *See generally* David Rock & Heidi Grant Halvorson, *Is Your Company's Diversity Training Making You More Biased?*, 88 STRATEGY+BUSINESS (2017) (considering that even the idea of differences as being valuable can be a trigger for amygdala response/implicit bias).

106. PAMELA FULLER, ET AL., THE LEADER'S GUIDE TO UNCONSCIOUS BIAS: HOW TO REFRAME BIAS, CULTIVATE CONNECTION, AND CREATE HIGH-PERFORMING TEAMS 14 (2020); *see also* B. Keith Payne, Laura Niemi & John M. Doris, *How to Think About "Implicit Bias,"* SCI. AM., March 27, 2018.

107. KAMARCK, CRS, DIVERSITY IN THE ARMED SERVICES at 4.

108. Pamela Fuller, et al., The Leader's Guide to Unconscious Bias: How to Reframe Bias, Cultivate Connection, and Create High-Performing Teams 238 (2020).

109. Victoria C. Plaut & Christina S. Carbone, *Considering Audience Psychology in the Design of Implicit Bias Education*, in Enhancing Justice at 267 (Tying implicit bias training to "an organization's values, goals, and mission" and "framing the training as critical to an organization's purpose and function, [so] members of that organization may come to see the presentation as relevant and important to their jobs and, even further, their identity").

110. Lieutenant General David Ottignon & Brigadier General Jason Woodworth, *Diversity, Equity & Inclusion: Why This Is Important to the Corps as a Warfighting Organization*, Marine Corps Gazette WE38 (June 2021), available at https://mca-marines.org/wp-content/uploads/Diversity-Equity-Inclusion-1.pdf.("We all know that when faced with the challenge of combat–the same way of framing a problem, the same opinion or perspective–just will not do").

111. Interview with Professor Sarah Redfield (Sept. 4, 2021) (discussing these training topics); *see also* Lee Ross & Constance Stillinger, *Barriers to Conflict Resolution*, 8 Negotiation J. 389, 394 (1991) discussing how we are influenced by who the source is for our information); Irving L. Janis, *Groupthink*, Psychol. Today 84 (1971) (explaining Groupthink in the context of the Bay of Pigs decision); Kahlil Smith, The Business Case: *How Diversity Defeats Groupthink*, Neuroleadership Institute, 2019, at 5–6 ("The best way to prevent these kinds of groupthink fiascos is to assemble a team with meaningful diversity... and to promote an environment of inclusion.").

112. Irving L. Janis, *Groupthink*, Psychol. Today 84, 84 (1971).

113. In 2004, the Army Directed Studies Office stood up the first service-level red team to "help guard against the shortcomings" leading up to the 9/11 terrorist attacks. The Marine Corps followed the Army's lead and also formalized a service-level red team in 2011. Lieutenant Colonel Brendan Mulvaney, *Red Teams: Strengthening through challenge*, Marine Corps Gazette 63 (July 2012), available at https://www.hqmc.marines.mil/Portals/138/Docs/PL/PLU/Mulvaney.pdf.

114. U.S. Dep't of Army, The Red Team Handbook (9th ed. 2020), available at https://usacac.army.mil/sites/default/files/documents/ufmcs/The_Red_Team_Handbook.pdf.

115. Lieutenant Colonel Brendan Mulvaney, *Red Teams: Strengthening through challenge*, Marine Corps Gazette 112 (July 2012).

116. U.S. Marine Corps, The Basic School, https://www.trngcmd.marines.mil/Northeast/The-Basic-School/ (last visited Aug. 3, 2021).

117. On average, TBS matriculates seven companies of approximately 300 students annually–six companies of lieutenants and one company of newly appointed warrant officers.

118. On 22 Sept. 2020, President Trump ordered via Executive Order the halt to training on "divisive concepts" such as "critical race theory" or suggestions of "white privilege." To be clear, these topics were not part of the TBS unintentional bias period of instruction. However, the effect of the Executive Order was that all diversity training in the DoD essentially stopped while the services vetted their training programs to ensure they did not include the banned topics. For instance, the Marine Corps suspended all military and civilian personnel training relating to diversity and inclusion, to include unconscious bias training, until the Assistant Secretary of the Navy for Manpower & Reserve Affairs certified the training's compliance with the Executive Order. In some cases, that approval never came prior until the administration change, and all diversity and inclusion training was resumed without higher-level approval in March 2021. Exec. Order No. 13950, 85 C.F.R. § 60683 (Sept. 22, 2020) (Executive Order on Combating Race and Sex Stereotyping); MARADMIN Message, 706/20 (Nov. 23, 2020),

https://www.marines.mil/News/Messages/Messages-Display/Article/2424644/implementation-of-executive-order-on-combating-race-and-sex-stereotyping/; MARADMIN Message, 008/21 (Mar. 11, 2021), https://www.marines.mil/News/Messages/Messages-Display/Article/2533738/cancellation-of-maradmin-70620/.

119. THE BASIC SCHOOL, RIFLE PLATOON IN THE ATTACK: B3J3718 STUDENT HANDOUT, available at https://www.trngcmd.marines.mil/Portals/207/Docs/TBS/B3J3718%20Rifle%20Platoon%20in%20the%20Attack.pdf (Hasty attacks rely on intuitive decision-making; deliberate attacks rely on analytical decision-making).

120. The time fluctuated based on student participation–the staff wanted to ensure meaningful discussions were not cut short simply to meet a set time parameter.

121. THE BASIC SCHOOL, OFFICERSHIP FOUNDATIONS: B1X0856 STUDENT HANDOUT 10, available at https://www.trngcmd.marines.mil/Portals/207/Docs/TBS/B1X0856%20Officership%20Foundations.pdf?ver=2015-03-26-091435-550 (A Marine Corps officer "has a bias for action–seizes the initiative and acts instead of waiting for the perfect sight picture of direction from higher").

122. DANIEL KAHNEMAN, THINKING FAST AND SLOW (2013) (System 1 is fast, intuitive, and emotional thinking, while System 2 is slower, more deliberative, and more logical, analytical thinking).

123. The author would like to acknowledge the officers who were heavily involved in the development and execution of the Unintentional Bias curriculum at TBS: Colonel David R. Everly, Lieutenant Colonel Jerry A. Godfrey, and Lieutenant Colonel Patrick H. Murray.

124. THE BASIC SCHOOL, OFFICERSHIP FOUNDATIONS: B1X0856 STUDENT HANDOUT 6, available at https://www.trngcmd.marines.mil/Portals/207/Docs/TBS/B1X0856%20Officership%20Foundations.pdf?ver=2015-03-26-091435-550; Col. Christopher Shaw, *One Tribe Requires Inclusion: The Commandant's Directive to Talk Creates an Opportunity*, MARINE CORPS GAZETTE WE5, WE10 (Sept. 2020), available at https://mca-marines.org/wp-content/uploads/One-Tribe-Requires-Inclusion.pdf.

125. *See* CHIEF OF STAFF OF THE ARMY'S 21ST CENTURY READING LIST, https://www.army.mil/leaders/csa/readinglist/; CHIEF OF NAVAL OPERATIONS PROF'L READING PROGRAM, https://www.navy.mil/CNO-Professional-Reading-Program/; CHIEF OF STAFF OF THE AIR FORCE PROF'L READING LIST, https://static.dma.mil/usaf/csafreadinglist/; MARINE CORPS COMMANDANT'S PROF'L READING PROGRAM, https://mca-marines.org/commandants-professional-reading-list/; 2020 COAST GUARD PROF'L DEV. READING LIST, https://www.dcms.uscg.mil/Our-Organization/Assistant-Commandant-for-Human-Resources-CG-1/Civilian-Human-Resources-Diversity-and-Leadership-Directorate-CG-12/Office-of-Leadership-CG-128/Reading-List/ (last visited Aug. 3, 2021).

126. Press Release, Cotton Introduces Bill to Combat Racist Training in the Military Act (Mar. 25, 2021), https://www.cotton.senate.gov/news/press-releases/cotton-introduces-bill-to-combat-racist-training-in-the-military; Combating Racist Training in the Military Act of 2021, S. 968, 177th Cong. (2021).

127. *The Fiscal Year 2022 Nat'l Def. Authorization Budget Request from the Dep't of Def. Before the H. Armed Services Comm.*, 177th Cong. (June 23, 2021), https://armedservices.house.gov/2021/6/full-committee-hearing-the-fiscal-year-2022-national-defense-authorization-budget-request-from-the-department-of-defense.

128. *Id.*

129. ADMIRAL (RET.) JAMES STAVRIDIS & R. MANNING ANCELL, THE LEADER'S BOOKSHELF 3 (2017).

130. The Basic School, Officership Foundations: B1X0856 Student Handout 4–6, available at https://www.trngcmd.marines.mil/Portals/207/Docs/TBS/B1X0856%20Officership%20Foundations.pdf?ver=2015-03-26-091435-550 (Even though the Marine's Corps literature states that the 14 leadership traits "are tools that Marines use to judge leadership ability," physical fitness is not one of the enumerated traits Marines are required to memorize. They are bearing, courage, decisiveness, dependability, endurance, enthusiasm, initiative, integrity, judgment, justice, knowledge, loyalty, tact, and unselfishness).

131. Lieutenant General David Ottignon & Brigadier General Jason Woodworth, *Diversity, Equity & Inclusion: Why This Is Important to the Corps as a Warfighting Organization*, Marine Corps Gazette WE38 (June 2021) (quoting Major General Robert Turner), available at https://mca-marines.org/wp-content/uploads/Diversity-Equity-Inclusion-1.pdf.

132. Scarlett Mansfield, *10 Facts About Tunnel Rat Soldiers During the Vietnam War*, History Collection (Dec. 19, 2017), https://historycollection.com/10-crazy-things-never-knew-tunnel-rat-soldiers-vietnam-war/3/.

133. The 9/11 Commission Report: Final Report of the National Commission on Terrorist Attacks Upon the United States 277 (2004) (The phrase "the system was blinking red" was attributed to Director of Central Intelligence George Tenet).

134. Although early reports estimated that approximately 20–25 percent of the people involved in the Capitol riot were connected to the military, as of August 2021, only 11 percent of those charged are current or former military members, including only one active duty Marine and four reservists/National Guardsman. Clare Hymes et al., *Seven Months After the Capitol Siege, More Than 570 Defendants Have Been Arrested*, CBS News (Aug. 6, 2021), https://www.cbsnews.com/news/us-capitol-riot-arrests-latest-2021-08-06/; Simon Ostrovsky, *Exploring Hate: An Inside Look at Anti-Extremism Training in the Military*, PBS (Mar. 13, 2021), https://www.pbs.org/newshour/show/extremism-in-the-ranks-some-at-the-january-6-capitol-riot-were-police-active-military.

135. General (Ret.) Jim Mattis, Call Sign Chaos: Learning to Lead xii (2019).

136. Memorandum from the Assistant Sec'y of the Army (Manpower and Reserve Affairs), Updated Guidance Regards the DA Photo and Use of Race, Ethnicity, and Gender Identifying Data in Assignment and Slating Processes (Oct. 19, 2020).

137. Col. Christopher Shaw, *One Tribe Requires Inclusion: The Commandant's Directive to Talk Creates an Opportunity*, Marine Corps Gazette WE5 (Sept. 2020).

SEVENTEEN

Addressing Underrepresentation in the Legal Profession

Tannera Gibson, Burch Porter & Johnson, Memphis, TN
Terrence Reed, Managing Director of Employment Litigation,
    FedEx Express, Memphis, TN

A Note from the Editors: Enhancing Justice: Reducing Bias was geared to increasing awareness of implicit bias and its manifestations and sources. Not surprisingly, once readers and others became aware, they were looking for ways to interrupt that bias so as to lessen its negative impact. While the measurement of implicit bias using instruments like the Implicit Association Test (IAT) came to the fore in the mid-1990s, research on effective strategies for interrupting that bias is more recent and still emerging. Nevertheless, there is evidence demonstrating that well-constructed training approaches and other data-driven interventions can succeed in achieving a more diverse, inclusive, and equitable workplace. Attorneys Tannera Gibson and Terrence Reed, both leading practitioners in employment law, responded to our request to write about these strategies, and they have done so grounded in the research and their lived experiences. Readers will find here an excellent analysis and set of suggestions and resources that are well-informed, practiced, and practical. We are grateful for the work of Attorneys Reed and Gibson and know that it will have value for legal employers and beyond.

CHAPTER HIGHLIGHTS

- Our clients are best served, and it is more profitable for firms, when we provide diverse and inclusive representation. The research shows this, and clients are increasingly demanding it.

- Providing the best representation for clients, along with the personal gains individuals receive from working and interacting with people of different backgrounds and cultures, benefits an organization's bottom line and are compelling reasons for developing and sustaining a diverse legal workforce.
- Millennials and Gen Z individuals are increasingly making a diverse and inclusive workforce a priority when evaluating and selecting an employer. Employers are at a competitive disadvantage if they do not have a workforce culture that encompasses these values.
- Manifestations of implicit bias can prevent recruiting, hiring and retaining a diverse workforce, but there are specific strategies for interruption.
- Employers must acknowledge implicit bias and commit to long-term evidence-based strategies for change.
- Changing the current DEI (Diversity, Equity, and Inclusion) landscape requires changing cultural norms, which can best be achieved through implementing strategic, well-crafted training on DEI, implicit bias, and cultural humility and competency.

CHAPTER CONTENTS

Introduction

1. Calls to Increase Diversity and Inclusion
    A. Shockingly Low Numbers
    B. Responding to the Numbers
    C. Setting the Stage for Change, Recognizing Implicit Bias
    D. Practical Reasons to Increase Diversity
2. Acknowledging Bias and Promising DEI Practices
3. Best Practices for Diverse Recruiting
    A. Be intentional and deliberate with the hiring pipeline.
    B. Collaborate with predominately minority law schools.
    C. Collaborate with minority and female bar associations and participate in minority job fairs.
4. Best Practices for Increasing Diverse Hires
    A. Use objective hiring standards—and stick with them.
    B. Use blind resume reviews.
    C. Use a standardized interview process.
    D. Use job-related problem-solving tests.
    E. Engage a diverse interview panel.
    F. Separate and then aggregate evaluators' scoring.

G. Re-evaluate predictors of future job success.
5. Best Practices for Retaining and Developing Diverse Attorneys
   A. Make the organizational culture more inclusive and equitable.
   B. Use specific DEI implementation strategies.
6. Avoiding Reverse Discrimination Liability When Implementing Initiatives to Increase Diversity, Equity, and Inclusion

Conclusion

Introduction

While the authors acknowledge that certain concepts referenced in this Chapter are not universally accepted and some literature contradicts these concepts, the perspectives and best practices discussed are grounded in the authors' collective thirty-plus years of personal and professional experience and training, in addition to dozens of candid interviews with minority and non-minority attorney colleagues.

You don't look like a lawyer, is a mantra commonly directed to minorities in the legal profession, and it highlights one of the primary challenges underlying the push to increase minority representation in the legal profession. It is a mantra that has often been directed to the authors of this Chapter. One indisputable fact, however, is that historically, lawyers have been White males. For many years, every on-screen lawyer in a long line of courtroom television and film dramas was a White male. (e.g., *12 Angry Men*, *Perry Mason*, *Matlock*, *To Kill a Mockingbird*). The Atticus Finch model, a White male in a buttoned up suit with glasses and a serious persona, has persisted as the stereotypical lawyer. Minority lawyers have existed since the 19th century, with Macon Bolling Allen believed to have become the first Black lawyer in 1844 and Charlotte E. Ray becoming the first Black female lawyer in 1872. But the decades-long portrayal of exclusively White males as lawyers has, along with other factors, instilled a level of attribution bias in the general population that causes a cognitive disconnect when one is confronted with a minority lawyer. Changing this picture will require motivated, sustained commitment from the profession.

1. Calls to Increase Diversity and Inclusion

Because of the broad societal acceptance of a stereotypical lawyer's image, minority lawyers are often denied the presumptions of intelligence and competence that their counterparts enjoy. Instead, they often have their qualifications questioned or face heightened levels of scrutiny in their work. This inequity manifests in shockingly low numbers of minorities entering and remaining in the legal profession[1] and has led to important calls and initiatives for change.

A. Shockingly Low Numbers

As the ABA summarizes: "Nearly all people of color are underrepresented in the legal profession compared with their presence in the U.S. population."[2] Eighty-six percent—a decrease from 89% ten years previously—of lawyers are non-Hispanic Whites, compared to 60% of the population. Five percent of lawyers are African-American compared to 13.4% of the population. Five percent are Hispanic compared to 18.5% of the population. Two percent are Asian compared to 5.9% of the population. Less than half a percent (.04%) of lawyers are Native American compared to 1.3% of the population. Two percent are mixed race compared to 10.2% in the population. The ABA reports that lawyers of color are 10% of law firm partners and 25% of associates.[3]

At about 37%, the number of women practicing law, albeit growing, remains disproportionate to the number of women in the population. This is the case even though women law students outnumber men law students.[4] Women are disproportionately represented in law firms where they "make up only 25 percent of firm governance roles, 22 percent of firm-wide managing partners, 20 percent of office-level managing partners, and 22 percent of practice group leaders."[5] The recent Law360 *Glass Ceiling Report* found that, for the firms surveyed, women were 37.7% of all attorneys, 48.5% of associates, 46.6% of nonpartners, 33% of nonequity partners, and 23.3% of equity partners; women of color were reported at 9% of attorneys, 4% of partners, and about 3% of equity partners. Less than one-third of state judges in the country are women, and only about 20% are people of color.[6] In the federal judiciary, 27% of sitting judges are women, and only 6.7% are percent women of color.[7]

B. Responding to the Numbers et al.

In an era where the sociopolitical climate is one of noticeable and, in some settings, palpable social and racial unrest, it is impossible for employers to ignore the importance of recruiting, retaining, developing, and, in appropriate circumstances, promoting a diverse workforce. This is particularly true in the legal profession as "the communities served by lawyers, the practice contexts in which they work and the issues that they face are increasingly diverse, complex, transnational, and global in character."[8]

Diversifying a profession where diversity has been historically absent requires a long-term commitment to dismantling the cultural norms and belief systems that caused the diversity chasm. It will require those who have contributed to widening and sustaining the diversity gap to acknowledge, accept, and appreciate its importance and to acknowledge the biases that caused them to advance non-progressive practices. Simply hiring more minorities and women may increase an organization's immediate diversity numbers (sometimes called representational diversity), but if those minorities are placed in workplaces where the culture and norms are not inclusive and equitable, that is, where their workplaces are unfamiliar, unwelcoming, and often hypercritical, the end result is a revolving door of otherwise qualified minority lawyers and meaningless numbers.[9]

The need to diversify the legal profession is continually highlighted in calls for action and bar resolutions. For example, in 2016, 24 general counsel, including the general counsel of American Express, PepsiCo, eBay, and McDonalds, joined in a letter encouraging chief legal officers of Fortune 1000 companies to support American Bar Resolution 113 to Help Promote Diversity in the Legal Profession. Their letter highlighted the continued lack of diversity in the legal profession and called on legal service providers to "expand and create opportunities at all levels of responsibility for diverse attorneys."[10]

In 2019, when this initiative in support of American Bar Resolution 113 was not manifesting tangible results, 170 general counsel revisited the issue and penned another open letter to law firms, indicating a clear message—improve on diversity or lose our business.[11] In that letter, the GCs emphasized the expectation that retained law firms "reflect the diversity of the legal community and the companies and the customers [they] serve," while applauding "those firms that have worked hard to hire, retain, and promote to partnership this year outstanding and highly accomplished lawyers who are diverse in race, color, age, gender, gender orientation, national origin, religion, and without regard to disabilities," and highlighting that "a diverse workplace is evidence that you have created an environment where all employees feel they belong and are accepted." For firms failing to progress in this regard, the GCs expressed disappointment that "many law firms continue to promote partner classes that in no way reflect the demographic composition of entering associate classes," with those partner classes remaining "largely male and largely white." While recognizing that these partners deserve their success, the GCs particularly observed that "[w]e also know that there are women, people of color, and members of the LGBTQI+ community and others who are no doubt equally deserving, *but are not equally rewarded*," and called into question whether such firms' "partners value diversity enough to put into place programs to develop, promote, and retain talented and diverse attorneys." The GCs admonished those firms with lackluster diversity track records against "commit[ing] your firm to diversity during the recruiting process or [hiring] a diversity and inclusion officer and expect[ing] that person can effect change without the full commitment of each member of the firm." Recognizing that this issue persists, the GCs expressly committed to "direct our substantial outside counsel spend to those law firms that manifest results with respect to diversity and inclusion, in addition to providing the highest degree of quality representation."[12]

Some corporate clients have been even more precise. For example, in 2019, Intel announced that starting in 2021 it would no longer "retain or use outside law firms in the U.S. that are average or below average on diversity," which Intel defined as the firms' U.S. equity partners being at least 21% women and at least 10% underrepresented minorities (which, for this purpose, we define as equity partners whose race is other than full White/Caucasian, and partners who have self-identified as LBGTQ+, disabled or as veterans). In announcing this requirement Intel's GC reflected on Intel's long commitment to diversity and the slow progress:

> despite these improvements, for the legal profession overall, progress has been frustratingly slow – especially when it comes to retention and promotion. According to most surveys, at large U.S. law firms, only about 20% of full equity partners are women, and only about 8 or 9% are underrepresented minorities. Indeed, the data suggest that the largest 200 firms in the country as a group will not reach 50% women and 33% racial and ethnic minorities in their equity partner ranks – which would mirror the composition of recent law school graduating classes – for at least another 50 years.[13]

Previous calls to action have not resulted in much progress in real numbers. Other organizations—including companies that hire outside counsel—are tying diversification efforts to compensation. For example, some employers have tied executive bonuses to a metric measuring the leaders' effort to advance and advocate for the organization's diversity initiatives.[14] The creation of such a metric not only ensures that leadership will be financially motivated to successfully implement such initiatives, but it embeds a commitment to diversity within the organization's other core values and missions. This approach is not without criticism, however, as some have raised concerns that while such metrics promote diversity, an unintended consequence is the inadvertent relegation of such initiatives to hiring and promotion quotas. Although misguided, the criticism highlights the importance of implementing diversity policies focusing on the expansion of the hiring pool, rather than numerical targets.

C. Setting the Stage for Change, Recognizing Implicit Bias

Responding to the call for diversity from the GCs and achieving diversity and inclusion is neither simple nor quick, but it is necessary. As with every other aspect of the process to eliminate the harmful effects of implicit bias in the legal community, accepting the existence of such biases is critical to implementing necessary changes in outreach, interview and hiring processes and beyond. But, as a general matter, we have not acknowledged the basic premise, rather many leaders of the profession are disproportionately satisfied with their current policies.[15] As an example, the percentage of White men holding the opinion that it is important to increase diversity is staggeringly low compared to minority and White women—27% compared to 87% and 61%, respectively. The following quote captures the importance of turning this around so that decision-makers appreciate and accept the importance of diversity and anti-bias-driven initiatives in developing an effective plan:

> [C]hanges recommended to address race can cause tension if they are not accompanied by a persuasive justification. Partners may feel they are being subtly accused of being racist" and diverse associates may feel self-conscious that their presence is triggering resentment or pity. Policies that focus on recruitment of underrepresented groups... are better accepted among both beneficiaries and potential opponents of policies if the justifications are explained. In contrast, policies justified only by underrepresentation provoke resistance from majority employees who believe protected groups are being favored to their detriment. Furthermore, policies that are thoroughly explained will counter the implicit bias that minorities did not achieve their success through merit. Once it is accepted that people can have egalitarian intentions but nonetheless fall victim to practices that have harmful outcomes, the need to change practices can be addressed without triggering a defensive reaction. Educational programs for all attorneys that discuss cognitive science and the implications of implicit stereotype activation may have the benefit both of engaging participants in a less threatening discussion of bias and... may help motivate participants to do more to correct for bias in their own judgments and behaviors. For these reasons, education about the influence of implicit bias is an important first step in addressing the diversity crisis.[16]

As outlined in the next section there are best practices that law firms and corporate legal departments can employ to ensure effectiveness in the recruiting, hiring, and evaluation processes, and there are bottom-line reasons for their adoption.

D. Practical Reasons to Increase Diversity[17]

Our clients are best served, and it is more profitable for firms, when we provide diverse and inclusive representation. The research shows this, and clients are increasingly demanding it. The McKinsey Global Survey and many similar studies consistently show that diversity within an organization increases innovation and improves financial performance.[18] For instance, a 2018 report by McKinsey & Co. found that organizations in the top quartile for gender diversity and ethnic and cultural diversity on their executive teams were 33% more likely to experience above-average profitability than companies in the bottom quartile.[19] Moreover, these same survey results indicate that individuals from all demographics take an organization's inclusiveness into account when making career decisions and that they desire their organizations to do more to foster inclusion and diversity. The McKinsey survey reported that 38% of respondents, despite demographics, said that they declined or decided not to pursue a job because of a perceived lack of inclusion at an organization. This percentage of respondents increased to 45% among respondents who identified as minorities and increased to 50% among respondents who identified as LGBTQI+.[20] Notably, this survey was conducted before the pandemic and before the social justice movement ignited by George Floyd's death. One can only imagine that, in a post-pandemic and more socially conscious world, measurable diversity statistics within an organization are even more important to maintain morale, competitiveness, and profitability. Organizations that compete for top talent should heed these survey results as yet another indicator that diversity, inclusion, and equity matter.

As the research suggests, and as our lived experiences attest, there is value inherent in ensuring that all members of underrepresented groups get equal opportunities based on merit in a manner reflective of the population the organization serves. Diversity in law firms and legal departments, in particular, necessarily results in strengthening the representation provided to their clients and maximizing efficiency in that representation of a globally diverse population. At some point, someone in every age, race, gender, and ethnic demographic will require legal representation. Those potential clients have experiences and perspectives that should be represented to the greatest extent possible. This is extremely difficult without diverse voices. Having a diverse legal team permits an organization to stay in tune with various clients' shifting needs and provide representation tailored to the needs of the client.[21]

2. Acknowledging Bias and Promising DEI Practices

Recognizing the importance of addressing bias better prepares employers in the legal profession to develop plans that begin at the recruiting and hiring phases and extend into a successful, inclusive, and equitable employment relationship. Interrupting bias requires that we "acknowledge and remember that everyone has bias."[22] A critical first step is actively deciding to do so, and actively deciding to do what is necessary to achieve that goal.

Individual and institutional initiatives are needed. This includes leaders and decision-makers acknowledging their own implicit biases and committing to their interruption individually and systemically.[23] Attorneys who want to take individual steps to learn about their potential unconscious biases can use assessment tools such as the Harvard Implicit Association Test ("IAT"). The Project Implicit site at Harvard offers individuals the opportunity to assess their unconscious biases on a range of characteristics, attitudes, and stereotypes including race, gender, weight, and age. One caveat: the notion that a hiring manager, recruiter, or other decision-maker could harbor implicit biases often triggers a defensive response that can prevent an individual from learning from self-assessment and can render organizations unable to effectively address bias and its effect on the workforce. Well-crafted DEI, implicit bias, and cultural humility and competency training can overcome this.

To reiterate, active decision-making and intentionality is necessary given the ever-looming threat of implicit bias and the covert role it can play in sabotaging diversity efforts. In affirmatively deciding to work toward diversifying a workforce, law firms, corporations, and other legal organizations must consider the biases that could exist in their workplaces and develop an appropriate plan. Ideally, once an organization has done the work of identifying potential biases and their impact, a more effective recruiting process can begin to increase the likelihood of hiring minority lawyers by increasing the number of diverse candidates being considered for hire.

The following section covers these best practices: being intentional and deliberate with the hiring pipeline, collaborating with minority and female bar associations, collaborating with minority law schools, participating in minority job fairs, and maintaining a diverse preliminary interview committee. Later sections follow along with the hiring and retention aspects of DEI.

3. Best Practices for Diverse Recruiting

A. Be intentional and deliberate with the hiring pipeline.

To achieve and maintain diversity requires a long view over an extended time horizon. Success demands that this work is *not business as usual*. We need to understand factors that limit the pipeline to the profession and to plan for our outreach to be unbiased, early, and often. That is, intentionality is not limited to introspection and the understanding that a recruiter will need to interrupt natural tendencies in order to achieve the diversity desired. Intentionality also requires creating opportunities, recruiting from a pool of diverse applicants, seeking applicants from diverse sources, and creating programs encouraging minority candidates to enter the legal profession, and/or providing fellowship opportunities to minority law students early in their legal education.[24]

Increasing the pool of minority candidates is vital; it mitigates the effect of affinity bias—the natural tendency to gravitate to those who are similar to those who look like us or share our culture, likes, beliefs or values—in the hiring process.[25] For example, consider a White male who enjoys baseball. He is reviewing two law clerk candidates; one candidate is a White male who played baseball in high school and the other is a Black female with no sports background. Affinity bias may cause the decision-maker to implicitly have a more favorable opinion of the White male candidate. Because interacting with those different from ourselves is more difficult than interacting with those who are like us, building diversity requires that we interrupt our implicit associations in these situations and choose consciously to resist falling into the stereotype of the familiar. This requires those making recruiting and hiring decisions to appreciate that it is normal to have implicit biases, such as affinity bias, and to seek to have a more objective lens.[26] If the person responsible for hiring cannot accept that certain biases are inherent in being human, the decision-maker will likely be unable to make a conscious choice to recruit and evaluate candidates fairly and equitably. As the next section explores, a variety of strategies can help achieve objectivity, starting with the pipeline and extending to the hiring process and beyond.

B. Collaborate with predominately minority law schools.

It is a worthwhile endeavor to seek partnerships and collaboration with predominantly minority law schools. Here, there are not only large numbers of potential minority candidates, but an organization can avail itself of many of the resources available in such spaces that provide insight into the concerns and perspectives of minority students. An organization applying what has been learned through such resources would have the advantage of first-hand perspective to build into its overall diversity recruiting and retention efforts. The law schools include North Carolina Central University in Durham North Carolina; Howard University School of Law in Washington, DC; Thurgood Marshall School of Law at Texas Southern University in Houston, Texas; David A Clarke School of Law in Washington, D.C.; Southern University Law Center in Baton Rouge, Louisiana; and Florida A & M University School of Law in Orlando, Florida.[27] Leading Hispanic Serving Institutions include parts of the University of California and California State systems, Texas Tech, Central Florida, and the University of Arizona.[28]

C. Collaborate with minority and female bar associations and participate in minority job fairs.

Organizations seeking to diversify their legal workforce should not limit their efforts to collaborating with diverse law schools, but should also partner with other minority organizations focusing on the legal profession. For example, organizations should collaborate with bar associations, such as the local chapters of the National Association of Women Attorneys or the National Bar Association and other minority bar associations or other groups. Such bar associations are commonly called affinity bar associations, highlighting the human tendency to prefer those similar to ourselves. Affinity bar associations have different missions, but share a common theme of seeking to advocate for and protect the interests and needs of their members and serve traditionally underrepresented groups in the legal profession. Given that such bar associations seek, specifically, to serve the underrepresented groups that law firms and corporations desire to recruit, the members of such bar associations will likely have a treasure trove of resources and perspectives not readily available to the general public. The bar association's members would also serve as a pipeline of minority candidates. Depending on the organizations' areas of interest, they might even consider reaching out to student associations in allied fields, for example, a firm specializing in intellectual property might find potential in minority student engineering associations—just one example, and obviously something that requires a long view.

In addition, organizations should participate in job fairs specifically designed to place minority lawyers and students with employers.[29] Often, minority-focused organizations such as the National Bar Association and the Black Law Students Association will host local, regional, or national job fairs to introduce qualified minority candidates to law firms and corporations seeking to diversify their workforces. The Southeastern Minority Job Fair is an example of a "legal interview program which brings together employers from all over the country and diverse students from more than 50 law schools."[30]

4. Best Practices for Increasing Diverse Hires[31]

As discussed above, those of us who are self-aware realize that we all have implicit biases that affect our decision-making, including hiring decisions. None of us are immune from implicit bias, and this plays out in employment decisions, including the way we review and respond to candidates. A recent study published in *Administrative Science Quarterly* called *Whitened Resumes: Race and Self-Presentation in the Labor Market* summarized data from numerous previous studies: "Resumes containing minority racial cues, such as a distinctively African American or Asian name, lead to 30—50% fewer callbacks from employers than do otherwise equivalent resumes without such cues. Minority job seekers might try to avoid discrimination by omitting or strategically presenting race-related information in their job application."[32] Researchers in this study also looked at other kinds of whitening—changing first names (Lei Zhang to Luke Zhang), changing or skipping experience (belonging to a Taiwanese Cultural Society), or changing both name and experience. The more whitened the resume, the more likely a call back. The researchers also studied whether those employers who included pro-diversity language in their job announcements (for example, stating that diversity is central to the organization's culture) were less likely to show this bias and concluded that "we do not find evidence that employers using pro-diversity language in their job postings discriminate less against unwhitened resumes."[33] Despite studies like this, many interviewers and decision-makers still deny that their biases influence the way they review and hire job candidates, which makes it crucial for internal interviewing teams to address bias long before the interview process begins.

A. Use objective hiring standards—and stick with them.

One effective method to increase diverse hiring is to establish and define objective hiring standards at the outset. Employers should create well-drafted job descriptions that clearly define the skills, experience, knowledge, and behaviors expected of the candidates. These standards should be in writing and govern the application and interview process. There should be a commitment to the standards in advance to avoid the tendency to alter priorities to capture someone who is seen as a "better fit."[34] If these standards are set forth properly, they can mitigate subjective and inarticulable ideas of who may be a "good fit" for a position, which is often based on implicit bias.[35] How a candidate fits into your corporate culture is important, but it should not be considered in the candidate review process, which should be completely objective.

B. Use blind resume reviews.

As the study on whitened resumes discussed previously suggests, it may be helpful to avoid certain cues (such as those suggesting race, gender, age, and religion) that might elicit an early implicitly negative response. This approach is sometimes described as blinding or dimming resume review,[36] and candidates can be viewed more objectively if you remove these indicators.[37]

The best way to make the initial candidate review process objective is to evaluate candidates on skill, experience, and cognitive aptitude alone. However, most resumes reveal the demographics of the candidate, which may allow a decision-maker to unconsciously make presumptions about the candidate before ever meeting her. For instance, a candidate's name and the languages spoken often reveals ethnicity. An address can lead to assumptions about socio-economic background. A graduation year can reveal a candidate's age. Upon reviewing one of our own resumes, we noticed that there were multiple indicators of race, including references to graduating from a historically Black university (Tennessee State University), being in a Black fraternity (Alpha Phi Alpha Fraternity Inc.), and leading predominantly African American organizations. To enable blind resume reviews, an organization could designate someone (who will not participate on the interview panel) to process resumes and remove information that can lead to bias. While there will likely still be a face-to-face interview that reveals these demographics, an organization can eliminate some biases at earlier phases of the process.

C. Use a standardized interview process.[38]

Where interviews are standardized, all candidates are asked the same questions in the same order. This minimizes the manifestation of implicit bias in the questions and emphasizes performance-based factors. Harvard Business School's recruiting team suggests that employers:

> [c]raft a list of questions that are aligned directly with what will define success in this role and remove any that are superfluous or could exacerbate bias. Also, ensure that multiple people within your company either sit in on the interview or conduct their own standard individual interviews so that candidate success is evaluated with different perspectives.[39]

This approach keeps an interview on track and avoids reliance on personalized connections and interviewer/candidate idiosyncrasies such as shared sports favorites or hometown connections.[40] It also avoids biased approaches such as asking minority candidates probing questions about where they grew up to confirm a belief that minorities grow up in impoverished and broken homes, or asking female candidates questions about their life goals to assess the likelihood of their having children while employed. These kinds of questions effectively divest minority candidates of an equal opportunity to engage in a manner permitting them to highlight their skills and qualifications.

D. Use job-related problem-solving tests.

Another effective method to reduce bias in the interview process is to ask all candidates to provide a solution to a problem your organization may face (or a hypothetical problem) and then to review each candidate's work side-by-side without bias influencing the review.[41] One law firm, Schiff Hardin, reports using a writing exercise that the candidates complete at the firm on call back interviews. Each candidate gets a personalized letter describing a discrete, brief client problem crafted to be answered in the time given and without needing to know specifics about the subject. In developing this approach, the firm notes that the "exercise does not resemble any law school assignment that we know about and therefore does not favor candidates who have performed well in legal writing class." As Schiff attorneys describe the approach, they are looking to measure "analytical and communication abilities that all lawyers must have: how to read and digest a legal issue and explain it to a lay person who is experiencing a problem." In evaluating the work (which is blinded), they focus "both on the tone of the work—especially the candidate's ability to convey empathy and relate to the writer—as well as the substantive content and writing style."[42]

In blinding their review, the Schiff attorneys recognized possible issues with confirmation bias, a problem to be watchful for with this suggested approach—as well as with many other issues. Confirmation bias occurs when we focus on information that confirms what we otherwise believe to be true and disregard other information. The depth of impact of confirmation bias in legal settings was highlighted in a study by Nextions where researchers and law firm partners collectively drafted a research memo from a fictional litigation associate.[43] The memo, intentionally seeded with 22 errors, was distributed to 60 law firm partners, half of whom were told the writer was Black and half of whom were told the writer was White. When the results were revealed, the memo believed to be drafted by a Black associate averaged a 3.2 out of 5.0 rating, while the identical memo, believed to be drafted by a White associate, averaged a 4.1 out of 5.0 rating. Additionally, the qualitative comments were more positive and forgiving for the memo believed to be drafted by the White associate. The fictional White associate received comments such as "generally good writer, but needs to work on... ;," "has potential," and "good analytical skills," while the fictional Black associate received comments such as, "needs lots of work," "can't believe he went to NYU," and "average at best." A key takeaway from the study was that availability bias—the tendency to make judgments based on readily available or "top of mind" information, such as an assumption that the lawyer or judge referenced in a given scenario is a man or White—[44] affects a person's ability to objectively assess legal writing, and these preconceived notions translate into confirmation bias.[45]

E. Engage a diverse interview panel.

As the Harvard researchers quoted in the previous section recommend, it is important to have diverse interview panels both to take advantage of a diversity of expertise and perspective and to ensure that every candidate has an equal opportunity to meaningfully engage with interviewers.[46] Because interviewers bring their personal experiences and backgrounds into the interview process, an interview committee should consist of persons with diverse experiences and backgrounds. For a candidate, there is no worse feeling than participating in an interview and feeling little in common with anyone on the interview panel. Research conducted by psychologists in the early 1970s shows how this plays out. The researchers found that in scripted mock job interviews, where "interviewees" were trained to respond alike, White job "interviewers" placed chairs an average of four inches further from Black candidates, spent 25% less time with them, and had more speech errors when talking to them—even though they had the same set of scripted questions for Black and White candidates. Not surprisingly, Black candidates so treated, performed less well.[47] This kind of divide makes it difficult for an interviewer and interviewee to connect and causes the age-old adage that a candidate *just isn't a good fit* to rear its ugly head.

A diverse panel also serves to equalize input from various perspectives and participants. When conducting a group interview, one person may be more assertive than others on the panel and his voice can drown out others and introduce bias. If evaluators share similar backgrounds or similar biases, it is likely their biases will either confirm each other or one's bias will affect the other's evaluation of the employee.

The concerns raised by nondiverse panels are not corrected by simply placing women and people of color on interview panels. The panels must be assembled thoughtfully, with each member having a voice and appreciating the value of diverse opinions. When done properly, anecdotal evidence shows that diverse interview panels increase diversity in hiring. For example, several years ago, Intel, a major U.S. technology company, required that its interview panel for new hires include at least two women and members of underrepresented minorities. The company saw the diversity of new hires increase dramatically. In 2016, 45.1% of new hires were women or people of color, up from 31.9% in 2014, and the company attributes this increase, largely, to diverse hiring panels.[48] This is a trend companies apparently find effective, as seven of the 2017 Best Companies for Multicultural Women require diverse interview panels for all new hires.[49]

We also recommend that a member of the panel be a Human Resources professional and that all interviewers receive training in this area. There is well-documented research showing that training around implicit bias can increase diverse hires.[50] It would also benefit interviewers to work on what is commonly seen as the leading strategy to recognize and interrupt implicit bias, increasing their diverse contact.[51] They can educate themselves about minority populations by reviewing various resources—books, articles, etc.—regarding these communities; and, at the appropriate time, they should seek opportunities to interact with minority individuals. One way of doing this is to heed the suggestion above to collaborate with predominantly minority bar associations and law schools. Taking proactive steps to educate leadership should enable those with hiring power to better understand the global population and diverse perspectives and should enable them to recognize and address biases in a legal organization's processes.

F. Separate and then aggregate evaluators' scoring.

Holding evaluators and interviewers accountable interrupts implicit bias and can contribute to more diverse, fair hires.[52] One way to do this when assessing candidates is to focus on scoring methods and require each interviewer to score each answer for each candidate right after the answer is given[53] and to submit her written assessments before the group discussion about the candidate. This allows the organization to compare scores "horizontally" for each question and then aggregate them. Researchers have shown that these kinds of structured and comparative evaluations

> not only help us calibrate across candidates but also decrease the reflex to rely on stereotypes to guide our impressions....we have shown that biases that lead us to expect women to be better at stereotypically female jobs, such as nursing, and men at stereotypically male jobs, such as engineering, tend to kick in when we focus on and vertically evaluate one candidate at a

time. In contrast, people are less likely to rely on whether a candidate "looks the part" when evaluating several candidates simultaneously and comparing them systematically.[54]

After the scoring occurs, the panelists should discuss their results; this helps to neutralize the stronger voices on the panel. Then, the candidates above a threshold score should advance to the next level of the interview process. In sum, without thoughtful and intentional pre-planning and structured interviews, post-interview decisions are often permeated by implicit bias along the way, putting final decisions at risk of being based on qualities unrelated to future job performance.

G. Re-evaluate predictors of future job success.

While there are some job performance predictors that apply across various jobs and industries, most key predictors of job performance will vary from one position to another.[55] A predictor for a successful courtroom litigator may be different from one for a successful business transactions lawyer. Every job has a unique set of skills necessary to be successful, and the key is to track which indicators actually predict future job success, instead of simply assuming certain factors do, especially where these assumptions may have a disproportionately negative impact on minorities.

To avoid these negative impacts on minorities, organizations may want to re-evaluate adequate predictors of future job success. For instance, candidates' grade point averages and the institutions of higher learning from which they graduated have long been heavily weighted in the hiring process. Admittedly, these are important factors to consider, but when was the last time someone tracked the nexus between these factors and job success?[56] Other factors, like prior work experience and work-life balance, may equally or even more accurately reflect important characteristics like work ethic or time management skills.

A study from Georgetown University's Center on Education and the Workforce illustrates the value of reconsidering factors that an employer chooses to weight. The Georgetown researchers found that close to 70% of all college students work while in school, but low-income working Black and Hispanic students are more negatively impacted.[57] As a result, these low-income students actually work more than their counterparts, which creates a socioeconomic-caused GPA inequity, assuming more hours studying correlates to a higher GPA. Therefore, setting a rigid minimum GPA requirement may disproportionately exclude minority candidates early in the hiring process. Placing undue emphasis on GPA also ignores the reality that some students choose easier classes to boost their GPA, while more ambitious students challenge themselves by choosing classes with a more difficult subject—possibly resulting in a lower overall GPA. But, which student is more attractive to an organization?

The same principle applies to the premium put on an Ivy League or elite college education. We often hear, *We only hire the top 10% of the top 10*. To fail to re-evaluate this will leave many employers with a mathematical impossibility. The historical focus of law firms and corporations recruiting from Ivy League and other top ranked law schools works against building diversity because minorities are historically underrepresented in such schools.[58] In 2019, of the top 25 law schools, U.S. News only reported eight with minority populations exceeding 30%, (with the definition of minority broadly including those who identify as Black, Hispanic, American Indian, Pacific Islander, Asian, or mixed heritage). The eight schools included were: Columbia, ranked 4th, 32.9% minority population; UCLA, ranked 15th, 32.9% minority population; University of Chicago, ranked 4th (tie), 36.6% minority population; Stanford, ranked 2nd, 37.7% minority population; Cornell, ranked 13th, 37.8% minority population; USC, ranked 18th, 38.3% minority population; Yale, ranked 1st, 40% minority population; and UC Berkeley, ranked 9th, 41% minority population.[59]

As with these statuses, focusing hiring only on students who participated on law journals limits the applicant pool to predominantly White, male applicants. The law reviews themselves have recognized the underlying problem. Realizing the need to increase the diversity of the journal's membership, Harvard Law Review implemented affirmative action practices, taking race, gender, and other demographic characteristics into account during their selection process.[60] Indeed, for the first time, last year the nation's top law journals were all led by women.[61] More typically though, while selections are reportedly anonymous, minority students have historically made up a very small percentage of members of law reviews across the nation.[62] Women—particularly women of color—were rarely elected to editorial positions.[63] The law review qualification requirements of a rigorous "write-on" competition that includes legal research and writing as well as a high GPA have often operated to limit the success of many first-generation students who do not have the necessary mentorship or background to apply or compete in the selection process.

The dearth of minority law students overall, coupled with the limited number of high-ranked law schools touting competitive numbers of minority students, illustrates the need for law firms and corporations to expand their recruiting to law schools, particularly Historically Black Colleges and Universities, where they will find much higher populations of minority students in the law school and on its journals. As of 2019, U.S. News listed the following as law schools with the most diverse population of law students: Howard University, 97.5% minority population; Florida A&M University, 71.6% minority population; University of Hawaii—Manoa (Richardson), 68.2% minority population; University of the District of Columbia (Clarke), 67.4% minority population; and North Carolina Central University, 66.8% minority population.[64] Greater recruitment from larger pools of minority students significantly increases the likelihood that an organization will have a more diverse pool of candidates, and as a result, a greater number of minority hires.

5. Best Practices for Retaining and Developing Diverse Attorneys[65]

Overcoming organizational bias does not end with the hire of minority lawyers, law clerks, and interns. Overcoming such bias requires that minority lawyers be brought into the pipeline, hired, and retained. The primary reason law firms and corporations experience high rates of turnover among minority employees is the existence of a culture of implicit and covert bias and exclusion.

Minority lawyers are often placed in circumstances and environments where they feel alone, being the only minority or woman in the room, sharing few, if any, commonalities with those whom they are expected to work and socialize. The experience has often been described as isolating, hurting the mental health of many such employees.

The real-life impact of such biases was captured in a study conducted by the Center for Work Life Law at the University of California, Hastings College of Law on behalf of the Minority Corporate Counsel Association (MCCA) and the American Bar Association Commission on Women in the Profession. The study revealed that:

- 63% of women of color report a perception that they have to work much harder than their counterparts to receive the same recognition;
- minority men and White women report a perception of having to work harder and prove themselves more often to establish competence at a rate 25% higher than White men, while minority women report this perception at a rate 35% higher than White men;
- 67% of minority women report disproportionately high standards for them compared to their colleagues, while over 50% of minority men and White women report disproportionately high standards as to them and their work (consistent with the confirmation bias writing study results, discussed above);
- only 50% of minority women reported equal access to high-level work, while 81% of White males reported access to high-level work; and
- 75% of White men reported fair opportunities for promotion, compared to 52% of minority women.[66]

In environments where these large majorities report negative experiences—likely arising from implicit biases and from failing to recognize and remedy these issues—will have high turnover and attrition rates among minority employees and will not achieve a meaningfully diverse workforce. The good news is that there are best practices for overcoming implicit biases so as to address these concerns and inhibit equitable inclusion, retention, development, and promotion. To take advantage of these approaches, employers should consciously assess the prevalence of bias in their respective organizations through encouraging self-reflection; incentivizing implicit bias testing; offering diversity, inclusion and cultural competence training to employees and leadership at all levels; and consciously and intentionally seeking feedback from minority employees. From there, organizations should implement plans and programs tailored to the needs identified in their workplace bias assessments. The plans and programs should focus on both consciously interrupting in the workplace and on dismantling the norms from which bias originates within the workforce itself.

A. Make the organizational culture more inclusive and equitable.

Best practices for sustaining a diverse workforce are grounded in the canon of Diversity, Equity, and Inclusion—DEI. The conceptual grounding is important as are the practical implementation strategies. This section clarifies distinctions and core principles and then focuses on effective tools and fruitful investments that can aid an organization's culture with increasing perceptions of equity and inclusion.

i. Understand diversity, equity, and inclusion.

Increasing representational diversity is merely the starting point.[67] To avoid high turnover and a resultant waste of resources invested in increasing diversity, organizations must simultaneously focus on equity and inclusion to retain and develop minority talent and reap a return on their investment. The differences between diversity, equity, and inclusion have become blurred because it is common to refer to any work in this space with the acronym "DEI." However, a clear understanding of the distinctions among these terms is beneficial to ensure we are operating under the same framework.

Diversity focuses on creating a workforce that contains an appreciable, valuable mix of backgrounds, ethnicities, experiences, socio-economic status, geographic environment, and gender. Increasing diversity in a workforce means adding to the number of underrepresented demographics. **Inclusion** pertains to employees' perceptions of having uniform access to opportunities and resources and having the opportunity to meaningfully contribute to the organization's success. Inclusion also involves looking at an employee's individual needs and ensuring those needs are met, supported, and respected. An inclusive work environment enables employees to feel welcomed at work regardless of whatever differences they have from their co-workers and to feel that their differences are valued. Some minority employees feel compelled to assimilate to an organization's culture, but in a truly inclusive environment—one that can reap the advantages that accrue to a diverse organization—employees' authentic selves are acknowledged and celebrated.[68]

ii. Lead from the top.

Employees' sense of inclusion is influenced by their experiences with the organization, the organization's leaders, and their co-workers. One of the most important principles in organizational management is ensuring that employees know that the organization's commitment to DEI comes from the "C Suite."[69] It is crucial that an organization's leaders exhibit inclusive behavior. This not only includes a strong proclamation of the company's commitment, but also demands that the organization leaders be seen to have committed themselves to educating themselves on DEI. This can be done by leaders attending the organization's training and staying abreast of the latest research in this area. Organization leaders can also demonstrate their commitment by participating in affinity groups (that should be inclusive of all demographics) or allies programs that support minority groups.

Enlightened employees adopt the philosophy that *if an issue is important to my boss, it's vital to me.* It is equally important for the organization's leadership to clearly set out the competitive and business justification for DEI, in addition to the moral justification. Understanding that diversity impacts the bottom line of the organization, and also feeling a personal benefit helps employees throughout the ranks buy in to the initiative and work toward its success. While it would certainly be nice for every employee to be internally motivated to value DEI on moral grounds alone, the reality is that some employees need more direct incentives.

Overall, an organization's top executives should demonstrate that DEI is a top priority, not just with words, but more importantly with resources. An organization's priorities are reflected in its investments. So, if an organization is serious about its commitment to DEI, it will invest dollars in surveys, recruiting and marketing, training, policy changes, mentorship and sponsorship programs, affinity groups, financial incentives for achieving DEI goals, etc.

To these ends, diagnosing the problem is an initial step. Conducting annual detailed employee-experience surveys and focus groups helps an organization identify and understand the kinds of implicit bias and perceived unfairness that may be problematic.[70] The survey should contain questions that will help the organization to both understand the current climate and track improvement on inclusion and equity over time. The survey should be sent not only to current employees, but also to former employees because people who experienced bias may have changed jobs. For current and former employees, the survey should solicit the instances of implicit bias and other negative experiences they faced during their employment, remedial measures they suggest, and how they feel these instances affected their respective careers. Once survey results are collected, leaders should use the information to guide next steps.[71]

iii. Align the culture.

Many organizations devote attention and expend great resources to hire minority candidates and increase diversity, but they make the crucial mistake of limiting their efforts to representational diversity in hiring. Then, these organizations are baffled as to why there is such a high rate of turnover among their minority employees. These organizations would be wise to re-examine their organizational culture—practices, policies, and behavior that exemplify their underlying beliefs, core values, and mode of operation—to see what may be impeding retention and development of their minority employees.[72] Simply put, organizational culture is how things get done; it's the prevailing code of unwritten policies and values.[73] Wide-ranging global research shows that organizations with clear and aligned cultures have significantly more engaged employees among all demographics, not just minority employees.[74] Aligning the organization's goals for diversity with its culture, even if this means working to change cultures, is critical.

Aligning organizational culture with organizational DEI goals requires attention at both individual and institutional levels. Typically, an organization's leadership dictates the culture of the workplace through policies, mission and vision statements, and organizational priorities.[75] These paradigms establish the foundation for the organization's culture, but the cultural backgrounds of the employees and management also affect the organization's decision-making, which in turn can shift its cultural dynamics.

Given the many influences at play and the difficulty of changing cultural norms, an intentional and strategic approach is needed. It's important to recognize that trying to significantly change an organization's culture to be more inclusive to people who differ from the majority or the status quo may not always be welcomed with open arms.[76] Such changes disrupt routines and habits the organization has intentionally or unintentionally developed over time, and it can be hard for employees to immediately adapt. Helping employees adjust to this positive change means informing them of the changes that are going to happen, explaining why the change is beneficial, and encouraging and acknowledging feedback.

B. Use specific implementation strategies.

i. Offer customized employee training to address identified bias.[77]

After surveys and other data have been collected and analyzed, the organization can implement customized employee training to target the specific types of bias identified. For instance, if the survey reflects historical affinity bias that negatively affects underrepresented minority groups, training should be devised to specifically help decision-makers recognize this type of bias and equip them with tools to combat it. The training should establish a safe space for employees to discuss their experiences of implicit bias and unfairness that harmed or demotivated them. The training should allow time for all attendees to explore these issues and brainstorm practical solutions. Merely airing grievances will not solve the problem. Non-profit organizations, like the Center for Excellence in Decision-Making, are making great strides in this type of training.

ii. Have minority leaders in the organization.

The adage that *you can show me better than you can tell me* rings especially true in organizational culture. The presence of minorities in leadership positions in an organization, along with the organization's focus on inclusive leadership, makes a lofty concept a tangible reality employees and candidates can see. Optics—optics based in substance—are important when demonstrating that the stated commitment to diversity is real.

The 2020 McKinsey survey reviewing barriers to inclusion tested 26 organizational practices and employee experiences to determine which factors are strongly linked with an individual's sense of inclusion. The survey results indicate that when respondents see that leaders at their organizations are diverse, they are 1.5 times more likely than peers from organizations without diverse leaders to feel very included.[78] And, when there are existing minority leaders in the organization, a snowball effect occurs, and it becomes exponentially easier to attract and retain other minority employees.

iii. Offer an anonymous complaint channel.

Another good tool to address implicit bias in an organization's culture is to provide an anonymous complaint channel.[79] Some employees may not want to publicly escalate complaints of bias, especially the more subtle types of implicit bias. This anonymous complaint channel will allow these employees to be heard and allow the organization to better understand how their employees are perceiving their employment experiences. In addition to the employee survey, it also can be a valuable source of information to customize the organization's training agenda.

iv. Intentionally build diverse business units.

Organizations can also set targeted goals to build more representative teams. Beginning with recruitment, organizations can set tangible and incremental goals to make specific business units more representative of the communities they serve. Ideally, these goals should work toward making an organization's business units resemble the local labor force by increasing the number of underrepresented employees within each unit. Two frameworks organizations can use as models for increasing underrepresented groups in their workforce are the Rooney Rule and the Mansfield Rule. The Rooney Rule was named for Pittsburgh Steelers owner Dan Rooney, who chaired the league's diversity committee. The Rooney Rule was adopted by the National Football League and requires teams to interview at least one minority candidate for each vacant coaching and general manager position.[80] The Mansfield Rule, which originated in the legal profession, examines whether law firms are active in their consideration of minority candidates for at least 30% of open leadership roles.[81] Organizations can use these models to develop inclusive recruitment and hiring without running afoul of anti-discrimination laws.

Similar goals should also be set in the promotion process. An organization can set goals to develop minority talent and prepare underrepresented groups to be competitive for promotional opportunities. Business units can track the candidates from underrepresented groups for each leadership opening and report on the advancement of these employees. Organizations should track progress toward these goals like they do for other important business objectives. And, management incentives, such as bonuses or company equity, can be tied to efforts to achieve these goals. Formalized and strategic succession planning can also help increase the number of leaders from underrepresented groups.

v. Provide for meaningful mentor and sponsor opportunities.

All employees benefit from strong and effective mentor and sponsor programs. This is especially the case for minority employees who may be first-generation lawyers (or other professionals) or who may not have a built-in support system. While both mentorship and sponsorship are valuable, we distinguish between them.

Mentors serve as a sounding board for ideas about navigating the workplace, the mentee's career, and personal advice; and the mentor provides valuable guidance on these issues. Mentors use listening skills, empathy, and experience to help mentees think through some of the challenges they face. Mentor opportunities increase retention and aid in development by pairing employees with dedicated mentors and sponsors. According to a study by Heidrick & Struggles, over three in four respondents said their most impactful mentoring relationship was important to their career development.[82] The study also revealed that organizations with effective mentoring programs are viewed as more desirable places to work, and they retain employees at a higher rate. The Heidrick & Struggles study found that women and minorities were most likely to say their mentoring relationship was "extremely important."[83]

Sponsorship is a relatively recent idea first raised by Sylvia Ann Hewlett, author, economist, and Columbia University professor, in her 2013 book *Forget a Mentor, Find a Sponsor*.[84] Sponsorship assumes a level of familiarity with an employee such that the sponsor knows the employee's skill set, value, potential, and contributions and thus can effectively and honestly advocate for him or her. A sponsor wields influence and can advocate for and aid an employee's advancement opportunities. One important function of a sponsor is to provide substantive access to senior-level leaders within the organization. Sponsors actively open doors and create opportunities for visibility to maximize an employee's career growth and potential. Professor Hewlett's non-profit think tank found that 70% of men and 68% of women with sponsors felt more satisfied with their career advancement, compared to 57% of men and 57% of women without sponsors. Even more compelling is that minority employees with sponsors were 65% more satisfied than non-sponsored minority employees.[85]

A sponsorship program to help retain and develop minority employees entails pairing existing leaders with minority employees who have exhibited leadership potential; sponsors take co-ownership of the employee's career development. When employees feel that members of management have made special efforts to create professional advancement opportunities for them, they are more likely to feel a strong sense of inclusion. The McKinsey survey reported that employees with at least one sponsor were 1.6 times more likely than others to feel very included.[86]

There is debate about whether formal or informal programs are most effective; and, indeed because of the nature of sponsorships, they rarely evolve naturally and thus must be formed intentionally. While both can be beneficial and both can have deficiencies, a formal program can be tied to tangible goals and measurable results, which is why we think formal programs are preferrable. However, whichever approach is used, it is even more important for organizations to create a culture where these programs are valued and prioritized. Leadership must devote time, effort, and creativity to establishing these programs so that meaningful pairings can be made and they are not simply check-the-box type exercises. To prepare for successful programs, everyone involved should be trained on how to build productive relationships.

Many organizations with good intentions pair employees with mentors and sponsors who are within the same demographic group, but by no means is this the sole formula for success. In fact, Terrence Reed, one Chapter author, suggests leaning toward the opposite approach. From his personal experience, he can attest that his most effective mentors and sponsors did not share many of his demographics, as they were older Caucasian females of a different faith.

vi. Support employee network and affinity groups.

Another powerful tool to improve organizational culture is to support and fund employee network and affinity groups.[87] These groups are an instrumental asset to an organization's DEI strategy because they are tools for championing employees and making them feel included. An active affinity group contributes to an organization's success through candidate recruitment and employee retention, training, networking, career development, and mentoring. Membership in these groups helps form an inclusive environment and foster retention by creating a supportive work environment. Through programming, affinity groups also help employees understand and appreciate the culture of other employees with differing demographics. Many such groups are also active in the community and serve as the face of the organization within that target community, which enhances the organization's brand and outreach.

There are numerous best practices that organizations and their affinity groups should undertake for these groups to thrive and provide members and the organization maximum benefit. First and foremost, the organization's leadership should assume responsibility for the progress and success of these groups, provide a clear and powerful message of support, and assume active roles within them. For instance, the organization's website should highlight its affinity groups and their contributions to the organization and community-at-large.

It's critical that affinity groups and related activities be endorsed and funded by executive leadership. Annual funding can be tied to the groups' past performance and approved annual business plan, which should be aligned with business objectives and workforce contributions and address the group's roles in activities such as recruiting, mentoring, and community outreach. Measurable metrics of success, such as a calendar of activities and programs during a designated time frame, undergird success. Even where budgetary resources are limited, affinity groups can partner with business units for additional in-kind or financial support, while playing an integral role in setting and achieving shared DEI goals. For example, an organization's public relations department can assist with an affinity group's community outreach efforts and expenses related thereto.

vii. Rid your organization of microaggressions and use microaffirmations.

Another vital way to improve organizational culture is to recognize and rid it of deleterious microaggressions, also called microinequities.[88] The first step to eliminating microaggressions is defining and recognizing them. Microaggressions are everyday intentional or unintentional verbal and nonverbal slights, snubs, or insults rooted in bias. They communicate hostile, derogatory, or negative messages to individuals based upon their marginalized demographic. Often the microaggression and its impact is not known to the perpetrator. Common examples of microaggressions include:

- Refusing to try to pronounce an employee's name by claiming it is too difficult, suggesting that the employee is *other* and the correct pronunciation of his name is not worth the effort.
- Telling a woman she's bossy or shrill, demeaning her leadership skills.

- Telling an African American or Native American man he is "so articulate," implying you didn't expect him to be.
- Mistaking one employee for another employee from the same underrepresented group, signaling that individuals in the group look alike and you do not respect them enough to differentiate each employee.
- Scheduling important deadlines on a minority group's religious or cultural holiday, expressing the prioritization of American-dominant holidays.
- Using the term "gay" to describe an undesirable characteristic, implying that being homosexual is a negative trait.
- Asking a person with non-Anglo Saxon features where they are from, assuming they were not born in the United States.
- Projecting stereotypes onto employees because they belong to a particular demographic, implying that the demographic is a monolithic group.

Many minority employees report experiencing microaggressions like these that taint their work experience, even to the point of leaving the organization. The McKinsey Global Survey reported that minorities experience more microaggressions at work than non-minority respondents.[89] For example, respondents in each demographic minority category (women, racial and ethnic minorities, and LGBTQI+) experienced exclusion from work-related social events and heard derogatory comments or jokes about people like them. In every category surveyed—gender, gender identity, minority status, and sexual orientation—over eight in ten respondents reported these indignities. Other research findings reveal that consistent exposure to microaggressions can lead to increased levels of trauma among employees.

One method of neutralizing microaggressions is to utilize microaffirmations to counteract the unconscious slights that create a toxic culture. MIT organizational behavior expert Mary Rowe defines microaffirmations broadly as "small acts, which are often ephemeral and hard-to-see, events that are public and private, often unconscious but very effective, which occur whenever people wish to help others to succeed."[90] Microaffirmations may inspire others to engage in such positive behavior, which would help transform the organizational culture into a more supportive and inclusive environment. Examples of microaffirmations include:

- Inviting members of an underrepresented demographic to join your lunch group.
- Inviting members of an underrepresented demographic to a business networking event.
- Including members of an underrepresented demographic on work committees and projects.

- Actively listening when an employee is speaking and asking thoughtful questions.
- Giving public credit to acknowledge an employee's efforts and contributions.
- Standing up for employees when they are being unfairly demeaned.

The best way to prevent the reoccurrence of microaggressions is for employees to listen to each other and respond respectfully.

Another method of addressing microaggressions is through implicit bias training. Again, the customized employee training and anonymous complaint channels discussed previously should indicate whether microaggressions are a systemic problem permeating the organizational culture that needs focus. This training should help employees recognize microaggressions, coach targets of microaggressions to advocate for themselves and other targets, and train others to intervene. The training should also assist the organization with creating an atmosphere that encourages open and meaningful dialogue. Organizations should also periodically review policies, marketing, and practices to ensure macro-level microaggressions are not tainting the culture. These are more prevalent on a systemic or organizational level, as opposed to individual employees committing them. Examples include only featuring employees of a certain demographic on an organization's website; or displaying artwork or statues that may offend a particular demographic or invoke feelings of inferiority.

viii. Overcoming Implicit Bias in the Employee Evaluation Process

There are several strategies for minimizing implicit biases to ensure fairness in evaluating minority lawyers. These include mindfulness, perspective-taking, slowing down, and individuation. Borrowing from our sister profession, the American Academy of Family Physicians summarizes: **Mindfulness** requires the evaluator to take a moment to ensure that she is not under pressure when assessing an employee, as one "is more likely to give in" to unconscious biases when under stress. **Perspective-taking** causes an evaluator to "consider experiences from the point of view of the person being stereotyped" before assessing her performance. **Slowing down**, as the name indicates, requires an evaluator to "pause and reflect to reduce reflexive actions," and to "consider positive examples of people from [the] stereotyped group," before making assessments. **Individuation** is the evaluation of employees "based on their personal characteristics rather than those affiliated with" the stereotyped group.[91]

Another practical strategy evaluators should consider was coined "flip it to test it" by Kristen Pressner in 2017. Admitting to her unconscious bias toward women leaders,[92] Pressner urges evaluators to consciously assess how they would evaluate an employee who falls into a class for which the evaluator has no bias. Alternatively, the evaluator could consciously assess how she would evaluate a person who represents the class of persons most frequently hired. As an example of this technique in practice, evaluators assessing a minority woman as angry should consider whether they would similarly assess a White male for the same behaviors.

Strategies such as these can mitigate and actively address bias in the evaluation process and thus level the playing field in the promotion and advancement process. They can also significantly increase the likelihood that an organization will fairly and equitably sustain and grow diversity in its workforce.

6. Avoiding Reverse Discrimination Liability When Implementing Initiatives to Increase Diversity, Equity, and Inclusion

Organizations can adopt policies aimed at increasing DEI in the workplace without running afoul of anti-discrimination laws. In particular, organizations can strive for diverse slates of qualified candidates when recruiting and making hiring and promotion decisions. Specifically, these initiatives should be lawful:

- Increasing respect for diversity in the workplace.
- Requiring mandatory training on DEI issues.
- Promulgating a commitment to hire, develop, and promote qualified minority candidates.
- Recruiting a more diverse applicant pool.
- Hiring recruiters to target underrepresented populations.
- Advertising on predominately minority platforms (e.g., Historically Black Colleges and Universities, Hispanic Serving Institutions, or predominantly minority bar associations).
- Developing employees from underrepresented demographics.
- Participating in minority job fairs.
- Supporting and funding affinity groups that are inclusive to all employees.
- Collecting data to identify underrepresented groups within a workforce.
- Tracking information to evaluate the success of DEI initiatives.

However, organizations may face claims of unlawful discrimination if initiatives result in discrete employment action that tangibly benefits one individual in a protected class to the detriment of another individual in a different protected class. Tangible benefits can include hiring, promotional selections, and termination. And, organizations will have difficulty defending minority-conscious employment decisions like these on the grounds of "business necessity." It is therefore important to carefully curate a more inclusive environment without discriminating against others.

In addition, organizations should be careful and thoughtful when rewarding members of management and leadership for attaining the organization's diversity goals. To avoid liability, organizations must ensure that selection decisions are merit-based and that successful candidates, including minorities, are qualified. In this context, questions often arise when a minority candidate or employee is selected over an equally qualified non-minority candidate. Will the law protect the organization under the premise that consideration of diversity is a "plus?" Organizations have a legal argument, supported by caselaw, that considering minority status in this situation is permissible. For example, in the college admissions context, the Supreme Court held that the Equal Protection clause did not prohibit a law school admissions program from considering race and ethnicity as a "plus" factor for admission because it affected the school's diversity.[93] Similarly, in the employment context, the Supreme Court held that the employer appropriately considered, as one factor, the sex of the female employee in promoting her over a similarly qualified male employee, under a voluntary affirmative action plan.[94]

Conclusion

The reasons to diversify the legal profession are well known to all of us. They are wide and deep. The efforts to diversify the legal profession are also well known, but, despite their importance, have shown little sustained success. If we believe, as we do, that the key decision-makers are acting in good faith, then we need to find the explanation for the intransigence of the image of the successful White male lawyer somewhere besides intentionality. We find that explanation, at least in part, in the growing science on implicit bias and its unintended impact on our decisions. Acknowledging this bias is a first step toward change, and, following that acknowledgment with the strategic, evidence-based approaches outlined in this Chapter can bring us to realize that change.

So, You'd Like to Know More

- GCs for Law Firm Diversity, An Open Letter to Law Firm Partners.
- Diversity Lab, Mansfield Rule 4.0.
- Paul Gompers & Silpa Kovvali, The Other Diversity Dividend, Harv. Bus. Rev. July–Aug. 2018.
- Tsedale M. Melaku, Why Women and People of Color in Law Still Hear "You Don't Look Like a Lawyer," Harv. Bus. Rev., Aug. 2019.
- McKinsey & Company, Diversity Wins: How Inclusion Matters (2020).
- Am. Bar Assoc., You Can't Change What You Can't See (2018).

- McKinsey Survey, Understanding Organizational Barriers to a More Inclusive Workplace, June 23, 2020.
- Eight Tactics to Identify and Reduce Your Implicit Biases, American Academy of Family Physicians FPM Journal Quick Tips Blog, https://www.aafp.org/journals/fpm/blogs/inpractice/entry/implicit_bias.html.
- Minority Corporate Counsel Association, Hiring-Firing-and-Inspiring-Outside-Counsel (2018).

About the Authors

Terrence O. Reed is the Managing Director of Employment Litigation for Federal Express Corporation and has been litigating since 2000. In addition to employment litigation, Terrence specializes in class action litigation. Terrence was a faculty member of the 2019 International Association of Defense Counsel's Trial Academy, conducted on Stanford Law School's campus, and serves as an adjunct professor at the University of Memphis School of Law teaching Fair Employment Practices. He is the past president of the non-profit organzation, The Center for Excellence in Decision-Making, which provides training in the area of implicit bias. He is a frequent presenter on diversity, equity, and inclusion issues. He earned his Juris Doctor from the University of Memphis School of Law, and his undergraduate degree from Tennessee State University, graduating *summa cum laude*.

Tannera G. Gibson, in 2017, became the first African-American female partner with the law firm, Burch Porter & Johnson, PLLC, in the firm's then 113 year history. A member of the firm's employment law, healthcare liability, and commercial litigation groups, Ms. Gibson represents large corporations, emerging businesses, individuals, and municipal entities as lead counsel in federal and state litigation. Ms. Gibson also provides advice, counsel, and risk evaluation to a number of private businesses and municipal entities. She received a B.S. in Computer Science from the University of Memphis prior to graduating from the University Of Memphis Cecil C. Humphreys School of Law in 2008. Ms. Gibson has extensive trial experience and significant experience in conducting investigations and presiding over administrative matters. She is currently serving as the first African-American female President of the Memphis Bar Association in the association's 147 year history and as Chair of the Tennessee Bar Association's Litigation Section Executive Council.

Endnotes

1. Am. Bar Ass'n, ABA National Lawyer Population Survey 10 Year Trend in Lawyer Demographics (2021).

2. ABA Profile Of The Legal Profession (2020). See also Am. Bar Ass'n, Statistics, https://www.americanbar.org/groups/legal_education I resources/statistics/.

3. ABA Profile Of The Legal Profession 37 (2022) (noting that the percentage of lawyers of color varies tremendously based on location; for example, at 35% Miami has the highest percentage of partners of color, and, at 3%, Indianapolis has the lowest).

4. *See id.* at 32, 58; *see also* Statista, *Share of Lawyers in the United States in 2020, By Gender*, www.statista.com/statistics/1086790/share-lawyers-united-states-gender; U.S. Census, *Quick Facts United States*, https://www.census.gov/quickfacts/fact/table/US/SEX 255219 (showing that women comprise 50.8% of the U.S. population); ABA, *Various Statistics on ABA Approved Law Schools*, https://www.americanbar.org/groups/legal_education/resources/statistics/.

5. Hank Greenberg, *Diversifying the Legal Profession: A Moral Imperative* (2019), https://archive.nysba.org. *See also, e.g.*, Debra Cassens Weiss, *Female Lawyers Still Underrepresented, Especially in Partnership Ranks; Which Law Firms Do Best?*, ABA J. (Sept. 16, 2021).

6. Jacqueline Bell, *Law360's Glass Ceiling Report: What You Need to Know* (September 13, 2021) (observing that, based on a survey of 270 firms: "Law firms are facing renewed calls to step up their efforts on equity and inclusion. But when it comes to closing the gender gap, law firms still have a long way to go, our annual survey shows.").

7. Nat'l Ass'n of Women Judges, *2019 US State Court Women Judges*, https://www.nawj.org/statistics/2019-us-state-court-women-judges; Danielle Root, *Women Judges in the Federal Judiciary*, Ctr for Am. Progress (Oct. 17, 2019).

8. Trevor C. W. Farrow, *Ethical Lawyering in a Global Community* (2013); *Comparative Research in Law & Political Economy. Research Paper No. 9/2013,* https://digitalcommons.osgoode.yorku.ca/clpe/258.

9. Luis J. Diaz & Patrick C. Dunican, Jr., *Ending the Revolving Door Syndrome in Law*, 41 Seton Hall L. Rev. 947 (2011); https://www.americanbar.org/news/abanews/aba-news-archives/2018/09/new-study-finds-gender-and-racial-bias-endemic-in-legal-professi1.

10. *Id.*

11. GCs for Law Firm Diversity, *An Open Letter to Law Firm Partners*, https://drive.google.com/file/d/1EfzrIJ_nxOpaZTSAdVu_ercVGCbLEZpU/view.

12. *See* Christine Simmons, *170 GCs Pen Open Letter to Law Firms: Improve on Diversity or Lose Our Business*, Am. Lawyer, January 27, 2019, www.law.com/americanlawyer/2019/01/27/170-gcs-pen-open-letter-to-law-firms-improve-on-diversity-or-lose-our-business/.

13. Steven Rodgers, *The Intel Rule: Action to Improve Diversity in the Legal Profession*, Intel Newsroom, Nov. 21, 2019, https://newsroom.intel.com/editorials/intel-rule-action-improve-diversity-legal-profession/#gs.vcwtny; *see also* https://www.law360.com/articles/1222606/intel-unveils-diversity-demands-for-law-firms-it-hires.

14. *See Minority Corporate Counsel Association (MCCA),* https://www.mcca.com/wp-content/uploads/2018/10/Hiring-Firing-and-Inspiring-Outside-Counsel-Materials.pdf.

15. Diversity Lab, *Mansfield Rule 4.0*, https://www.diversitylab.com/mansfield-rule-4-0/.

16. Nicole E. Negowetti, *Implicit Bias And The Legal Profession's "Diversity Crisis": A Call For Self-Reflection,* 15 Nev. L.J. 930, 954–55 (2015).

17. Dev Stahlkopf, *Why Diversity Matters in the Selection and Engagement of Outside Counsel: An In-House Counsel's Perspective*, ABA, May 6, 2020, https://www.americanbar.org/groups/litigation/publications/litigation_journal/2019-20/spring/why-diversity-matters-the-selection-and-engagement-outside-counsel-inhouse-counsels-perspective/.

18. *See* McKinsey & Company, Delivering through Diversity (2018), www.McKinsey.com/business-functions/organizations/our-insights/delivering-through-diversity McKinsey

& Company, Diversity Wins: How Inclusion Matters (2020); Paul Gompers & Silpa Kovvali, *The Other Diversity Dividend*, Harv. Bus. Rev. July–Aug. 2018.

19. *Id.*

20. *Id.*

21. Sheryl Lyons, *The Benefits Of Creating A Diverse Workforce*, Forbes, Sept. 9, 2019. https://www.forbes.com/sites/forbescoachescouncil/2019/09/09/the-benefits-of-creating-a-diverse-workforce/?sh=773b5367140b.

22. Paula T. Edgar, *Understanding and Addressing Unconscious Bias in the Legal Profession*, The American Law Institute Continuing Legal Education, VCCJ0925 ALI-CLE 1 (2018); *see also generally* Anthony G. Greenwald & Mazarin R. Banaji, *Implicit Social Cognition: Attitudes, Self-esteem, and Stereotypes*, 102 Psychol. Rev. 4, 5, 8 (1995); Komal Gulati, *Here's Why Having a Brain Means You Have Bias*, NeuroLeadership Institute (July 22, 2020), https://neuroleadership.com/your-brain-at-work/unconscious-bias-in-brain.

23. Shannon Thyme Klinger & Teresa T. Bonder, *Understanding the Diversity Baseline*, SPARTNER § 39:4 (2021) stating "These aspects of diversity are not susceptible to the type of analysis and discourse about 'hard facts' to which practicing lawyers are accustomed and with which they are most comfortable. Implementing a robust D&I program, then, requires that legal organizations undergo awareness education and training, critical self-examination, and attitudinal changes."

24. As an example, Schwabe Williamson & Wyatt in the Pacific Northwest and Drew Eckl & Farnham in Atlanta have employed efforts such as creating a diversity fellowship program for 1L students and incorporated a practice of recruiting from Historically Black Colleges and Universities. Meredith Hobbs, *As Midsize Firms Recruit More Diverse Associates, Retention Remains an Issue*, LAW.COM, Jan. 07, 2021, https://www.law.com/mid-market-report/2021/01/07/as-midsize-firms-recruit-more-diverse-associates-retention-remains-an-issue/?slreturn=20210414141601.

25. *See generally* Pascal Molenberghs & Winnifred R. Louis, *Insights from fMRI Studies into Ingroup Bias*, 9 Frontiers in Psychol. (2018); Anthony G. Greenwald & Thomas F. Pettigrew, *With Malice Toward None and Charity for Some: Ingroup Favoritism Enables Discrimination*, 69 The American Psychologist 669 (2014).

26. Kimberly Giles, *Why You Mistakenly Hire People Just Like You*, Forbes, May 1, 2018, https://www.forbes.com/sites/forbescoachescouncil/2018/05/01/why-you-mistakenly-hire-people-just-like-you/?sh=56b028db3827.

27. *See Fast Facts: Historically Black Colleges and Universities*, NCES, https://nces.ed.gov/fastfacts/display.asp?id=667; Historically Black Colleges and Universities, U.S. News & World Report (2021), https://www.usnews.com/best-colleges/rankings/hbcu.

28. *2022 Best Hispanic-Serving Institutions in America*, Niche, https://www.niche.com/colleges/search/best-hispanic-serving-institutions/; *see also Colleges with the Highest Percentage of Native American or Alaskan Native Students*, https://www.collegexpress.com/lists/list/colleges-with-the-highest-percentage-of-native-american-or-alaskan-native-students/373/.

29. *Crisis at the Bar: the Need for Diversity in the Legal Profession*, Chicago Bar Association, 15-SEP CBA Rec. 36 (2001).

30. Southeastern Minority Job Fair, https://semjf.org/

31. Ruchika Tulshyan, *How to Reduce Personal Bias When Hiring*, Harv. Bus. Rev., June 28, 2019, https://hbr.org/2019/06/how-to-reduce-personal-bias-when-hiring; *see also generally* Kamna Singh Balhara, P. Logan Weygandt, Michael R. Ehmann & Linda Regan, *Navigating Bias*

on Interview Day: Strategies for Charting an Inclusive and Equitable Course, 13 J. GRAD. MED. EDUC. 466 (2021).

32. Sonia K. Kang, et al., *Whitened Résumés: Race and Self-Presentation in the Labor Market*, 61 ADM. SCI. Q. 469, 470 (2016), https://journals.sagepub.com/doi/10.1177/0001839216639577.

33. *Id.; see also, e.g.,* Marianne Bertrand & Sendhil Mullainathan, *Are Emily and Greg More Employable than Lakisha and Jamal?*, 94 AM. ECON. REV. 991 (2004).

34. *See* Eric Luis Uhlmann & Geoffrey L. Cohen, *Constructed Criteria: Redefining Merit to Justify Discrimination*, 16 PSYCHOL. SCI. 474 (2005).

35. *See generally, e.g.,* Joan C. Williams, Marina Multhaup & Sky Mihaylo, *Why Companies Should Add Class to Their Diversity Discussions*, HARV. BUS. REV., Sept. 5, 2018; Lauren R. Rivera & Andras Tilcsik, Class Advantage, Commitment Penalty: *The Gendered Effect of Social Class Signals in an Elite Labor Market*, 81 AM. SOC. REV. 1097 (2016).

36. *See* Dina Gerdeman, *Minorities Who 'Whiten' Job Resumes Get More Interviews*, HARV. BUS. SCHOOL RECRUITING, July 20, 2020, www.hbs.edu/recruiting/insights-and-advice/blog/post/minorities-who-whiten-job-resumes-get-more-interviews; *see generally* Jerry Kang, *What Judges Can Do about Implicit Bias*, 57 CT. REV. 78 (2021).

37. *See generally* Claudia Goldin & Cecilia Rouse, *Orchestrating Impartiality: The Impact of "Blind" Auditions on Female Musicians*, 90 AM. ECON. REV. 715 (2000).

38. Becca Carnahan & Christopher Moore, *Actively Addressing Unconscious Bias in Recruiting*, HARV. BUS. REV., July 7, 2020, https://www.hbs.edu/recruiting/blog/post/actively-addressing-unconscious-bias-in-recruiting

39. Becca Carnahan & Christopher Moore, *Actively Addressing Unconscious Bias in Recruiting*, HARV. BUS. REV., July 7, 2020.

40. Lisa A. Brown, *An Innovative Approach to Hiring Lawyers: One Firm's New Program Reflects Its Firm Values and Eliminates Implicit Bias in Metrics, Diversity, and the Law*, AMERICAN BAR FOUNDATION PAPERS AND PROCEEDINGS OF A CONFERENCE OF THE RESEARCH GROUP ON LEGAL DIVERSITY, May 5–6, 2016, http://www.americanbarfoundation.org/uploads/cms/documents/abf_metrics_diversity_and_law_volume_8_30_18.pdf.

41. Rachel Feintzeig, *The Boss Doesn't Want Your Resume*, WALL ST. J., Jan. 5, 2016, https://www.wsj.com/articles/the-boss-doesnt-want-your-resume-1452025908n-trend-blind-hiring.

42. Lisa A. Brown, *An Innovative Approach to Hiring Lawyers: One Firm's New Program Reflects Its Firm Values and Eliminates Implicit Bias in Metrics, Diversity, and the Law*, AMERICAN BAR FOUNDATION PAPERS AND PROCEEDINGS OF A CONFERENCE OF THE RESEARCH GROUP ON LEGAL DIVERSITY, May 5–6, 2016.

43. ARIN N. REEVES, WRITTEN IN BLACK & WHITE EXPLORING CONFIRMATION BIAS IN RACIALIZED PERCEPTIONS OF WRITING SKILLS (2014), https://www.ncada.org/resources/CLE/WW17/Materials/Wegner%20_%20Wilson--Confirmation%20Bias%20in%20Writing.pdf

44. Emma Bienias et al., *Implicit Bias in the Legal Profession*, Intellectual Property Owners Association, https://ipo.org/wp-content/uploads/2017/11/Implicit-Bias-White-Paper-2.pdf.

45. *Id.*

46. *See* Ben White, *3 Benefits to Making Diversity a Priority in Interview Panels*, TITUS TALENT STRATEGIES, www.titustalent.com/insights/3-benefits-to-making-diversity-a-priority-in-interview-panels; *see also* ABIGAIL J. STEWART & VIRGINIA VALIAN, AN INCLUSIVE ACADEMY (2018).

47. Carl O. Word, Mark P. Zanna & Joel Cooper, *The Nonverbal Mediation of Self-fulfilling Prophecies in Interracial Interaction*, 10 J. EXPERIMENTAL SOC. PSYCHOL. 109, 119 (1974); *see also* Ioana M. Latu & Marianne Schmid Mast, *Male Interviewers' Nonverbal Dominance Predicts Lower Evaluations of Female Applicants in Simulated Job Interviews*, 15 J. PERSONNEL PSYCHOL. 116, 121, 122 (2016).

48. *See* Katherine Reynolds Lewis, *Diverse Interview Panels May Be a Key to Workplace Diversity*, WORKING MOTHER, June-July 2017, www.workingmother.com/diverse-interview-panels-may-be-key-to-workplace-diversity.

49. *Id.; see also Making Intel More Diverse*, HBR IDEACAST/EPISODE 567, https://hbr.org/podcast/2017/03/making-intel-more-diverse.

50. Patricia G. Devine et al., *A Gender Bias-Breaking Intervention Led to Increased Hiring of Female Faculty in STEM Departments*, 73 J. EXPERIMENTAL SOC. PSYCHOL. 211, 213–4 (2017).

51. *See, e.g.*, Nilanjana Dasgupta & Shaki Asgari, *Seeing Is Believing: Exposure to Counterstereotypic Women Leaders and Its Effect on the Malleability of Automatic Gender Stereotypes*, 40 J. EXPERIMENTAL. SOC. PSYCHOL. 642 (2004); Nicole E. Negowetti, *Implicit Bias and the Legal Profession's "Diversity Crisis": A Call for Self-Reflection*, 15 NEV L. J930, 952 (2015) ("Intergroup contact reduces people's anxiety about each other, promotes empathy, and encourages friendships, all of which result in more positive attitudes toward each other."). https://scholars.law.unlv.edu/cgi/viewcontent.cgi?article=1600&context=nlj.

52. *See generally e.g.*, Greg Morris, *Research and Measurement in* DIVERSITY PRIMER 226 (2009); Jennifer S. Lerner & E. Philip Tetlock, *Accounting for the Effects of Accountability*, 125 PSYCHOL. BULL. 255 (1992).

53. *See* Iris Bohnet, *How to Take the Bias Out of Interviews*, HARV. BUS. REV., April 18, 2016, www.hbr.org/2016/04/how-to-take-the-bias-out-of-interviews.

54. *Id; see also* Iris Bohnet, Alexandra van Geen & Max Bazerman, When Performance Trumps Gender Bias: Joint vs. Separate Evaluation 62 Management Science (2015).

55. *See* James Sudakow, *4 Ways To Predict A Candidate's Job Success (That Work Much Better Than A Traditional Job Interview)*, INC. NEWSLETTER, https://www.inc.com/james-sudakow/4-ways-to-predict-a-candidates-job-success-that-wo.html.

56. *See generally* MARJORIE M. SHULTZ & SHELDON ZEDECK, IDENTIFICATION, DEVELOPMENT, AND VALIDATION OF PREDICTORS FOR SUCCESSFUL LAWYERING (Sept. 2008), www.law.berkeley.edu/files/LSACREPORTfinal-12.pdf; William D. Henderson, *Solving the Legal Diversity Problem*, in METRICS, DIVERSITY, AND THE LAW: PAPERS AND PROCEEDINGS OF A CONFERENCE OF THE RESEARCH GROUP ON LEGAL DIVERSITY, May 5–6, 2016, http://www.americanbarfoundation.org/uploads/cms/documents/abf_metrics_diversity_and_law_volume_8_30_18.pdf.

57. Anthony P. Carnevale, Nicole Smith, Michelle Melton & Eric W. Price, *Learning While Earning: The New Normal*, GEORGETOWN UNIVERSITY CENTER ON EDUCATION AND THE WORKFORCE 55, cew.georgetown.edu/workinglearners.

58. *E.g.*, Overall, in 2019, only 7.8% of law students identified as Black, while 13.4% of the overall U.S. population identifies as Black. Gabriel Kuris, *What Underrepresented Law School Applicants Should Know*, U.S. NEWS & WORLD REPORT, June 8, 2020, https://www.usnews.com/education/blogs/law-admissions-lowdown/articles/what-underrepresented-law-school-applicants-should-know; https://www.census.gov/quickfacts/fact/table/US/PST045219.

59. Ilana Kowarski, *46 Racially and Ethnically Diverse Law Schools*, U.S. NEWS & WORLD REPORT, Sept. 1, 2021, https://www.usnews.com/education/best-graduate-schools/top-law-schools/slideshows/law-schools-with-the-highest-percentage-of-racial-or-ethnic-minorities.

60. Juliet E. Isselbacher, *Lawsuit Alleging Harvard Law Review Discriminates in Member Selection Process Dismissed*, THE HARV. CRIMSON, August 11, 2019, https://www.thecrimson.com/article/2019/8/11/fasorp-suit-dismissed/.

61. Anne E. Marinow, *For the First Time, Flagship Law Journals at Top U.S. Law Schools are Led by Women*, WASH. POST, Feb. 7, 2020, https://www.washingtonpost.com/local/legal-issues/for-the-first-time-flagship-law-journals-at-top-us-law-schools-are-all-led-by-women/2020/02/07/b4d3bc64-4836-11ea-bc78-8a18f7afcee7_story.html.

62. Frederick Ramos, *Affirmative Action on Law Reviews: An Empirical Study of Its Status and Effect*, 22 U. MICH. J.L. REFORM 179, 179, 198 (1988) ("In its first seventy-three years of existence, the Virginia Law Review never had a black member.").

63. Adriane Kayoko Peralta, *The Underrepresentation of Women of Color in Law Review Leadership Positions*, 25 BERKELEY LA RAZA L.J. 69, 73 (2015).

64. Ilana Kowarski, *46 Racially and Ethnically Diverse Law Schools*, U.S. NEWS & WORLD REPORT, Sept. 1, 2021, https://www.usnews.com/education/best-graduate-schools/top-law-schools/slideshows/law-schools-with-the-highest-percentage-of-racial-or-ethnic-minorities?slide=48.

65. Kathy Gurchiek, *Try These Strategies to Reduce Implicit Bias in Your Workplace*, SHRM, April 20, 2020, https://www.shrm.org/resourcesandtools/hr-topics/behavioral-competencies/global-and-cultural-effectiveness/pages/try-these-strategies-to-reduce-implicit-bias-in-your-workplace.aspx.

66. *New Study Finds Gender and Racial Bias Endemic in Legal Profession*, ABA NEWS, Sept. 06, 2018, https://www.americanbar.org/news/abanews/aba-news-archives/2018/09/new-study-finds-gender-and-racial-bias-endemic-in-legal-professi1/; AM. BAR ASSOC. YOU CAN'T CHANGE WHAT YOU CAN'T SEE (2018).

67. *See, e.g.,* Frank Dobbin & Alexandra Kalev, *Why Diversity Programs Fail*, HARV. BUS. REV. (2016).

68. *See generally* Mary B. Young & Michelle Kan, *Do Ask, Do Tell Encouraging Employees with Disabilities to Self-Identify*, http://pages.conference-board.org/rs/conferenceboardusa/images/TCB_1569_15_Do%20Ask%20Do%20Tell.pdf

69. *See* Stefanie K. Johnson, *What 11 CEOs Have Learned About Championing Diversity*, HARV. BUS. REV., Aug. 29, 2017, www.hbr.org/2017/08/what-11-ceos-have-learned-about-championing-diversity.

70. *See* Anne Maltese, *Diversity and Inclusion Survey Questions To Improve D&I at Work*, QUANTUM WORKPLACE, October 29, 2020, www.quantumworkplace.com/future-0f-work/diversity-and-inclusion-survey-questions.

71. *Id.*

72. *See generally* Amarette Filut, Anna Kaatz & Molly Carnes, *The Impact of Unconscious Bias on Women's Career Advancement*, THE SASKAWA PEACE FOUNDATION EXPERT REVIEWS SERIES ON ADVANCING WOMEN'S EMPOWERMENT (2017).

73. *Organizational Culture*, SHRM, https://www.shrm/ResourcesandTools/.ages/Organization-Culture.aspx.

74. *See* Michael Couch, *It's More Than the Numbers: Organizational Culture and Diversity, Equity and Inclusion*, Forbes, April 18, 2021 (citing global research by Dennison Consulting with 90 large organizations supporting this emphasis on core values, empowerment and capability and clear DEI vision as employee motivators).

75. *See Understanding and Developing Organizational Culture*, SHRM, www.shrm.org/resourcesandtools/tools-and samples/toolkits/pages/understandinganddevelopingorganizationalculture.aspx (member resource).

76. *See* David Rock & Heidi Grant Halvorson, *Is Your Company's Diversity Training Making You More Biased?*, 88 strategy+business (2017).

77. *See* Edward H. Chang, Katherine L. Milkman, Laura J. Zarrow, Kasandra Brabaw, Dena M. Gromet, Reb Rebele, Cade Massey, Angela L. Duckworth & Adam Grant, *Does Diversity Training Work the Way It's Supposed To?*, Harv. Bus Rev., July 9, 2019.

78. *See* McKinsey Survey, *Understanding Organizational Barriers to a More Inclusive Workplace*, June 23, 2020, https://www.mckinsey.com/business-functions/organization/our-insights/understanding-organizational-barriers-to-a-more-inclusive-workplace.

79. *See* Osasumwen Arigbe, *Diversity, Inclusion, and Anonymous Feedback,* inkrement (2021), www.inkrement.io/blog/diversity-inclusion-and-anonymous-feedback/.

80. *See* Michael Middlehurst-Schwartz, *NFL Expands Rooney Rule Requirements on Interviews, Per Report*, USA TODAY, May 18, 2020, www.usatoday.com/story/nfl/2020/05/18/nfl-rooney-rule-diversity-hiring-interview-requirements/5216528002/.

81. Diversity Lab, *Mansfield Rule 4.0,* https://www.diversitylab.com/mansfield-rule-4-0/.

82. *See* Ave Rio, *Mentoring Matters, Especially for Women and Minorities*, Feb. 8, 2018 (citing executive search firm Heidrick & Struggles report, Cynthia Emrich, Mark Livingston & David Pruner, *Creating a Culture of Mentorship* (2017), https://imdiversity.com/diversity-news/mentoring-matters-especially-for-women-and-minorities/).

83. *Id.*

84. *See* Dan Schawbel, *Sylvia Ann Hewlett: Find a Sponsor Instead of a Mentor*, Forbes, Sept. 10, 2013, www.Sylviaannhewlett.com/find-a-sponsor.html.

85. *See Id.*

86. McKinsey Survey, *Understanding Organizational Barriers to a More Inclusive Workplace*, June 23, 2020, https://www.mckinsey.com/business-functions/organization/our-insights/understanding-organizational-barriers-to-a-more-inclusive-workplace.

87. *See* Daniel Bortz, *Benefits of Having Affinity Groups at Work*, Monster, www.businessinsider.com/reasons-why-you-should-start-employee-affinity-group-at-work-2020-9.

88. *See* Artika R. Tyner, *Unconscious Bias, Implicit Bias, and Microaggressions: What Can We Do about Them?,* ABA Solo Small Firm and General Practice Division, Aug. 26, 2019, www.americanbar.org/groups/gpsolo/publications/gp_solo/2019/july-august/unconscious-bias-implicit-bias-microaggressions-what-can-we-do-about-them/.

89. *See* McKinsey Survey, Understanding Organizational Barriers to a More Inclusive Workplace, June 23, 2020, www.mckinsey.com/business-functions/organization/our-insights/understanding-organizational-barriers-to-a-more-inclusive-workplace.

90. *See* Mary Rowe, *Micro-affirmations & Micro-inequities*, 1 J. Internat'l Ombudsman Ass'n 1 (2008), www.researchgate.net/publication/265450386_Micro-affirmations_Micro-inequities.

91. *Eight Tactics to Identify and Reduce Your Implicit Biases*, American Academy of Family Physicians FPM Journal Quick Tips Blog, https://www.aafp.org/journals/fpm/blogs/inpractice/entry/implicit_bias.html.

92. *See Kristen Pressner*, TedxBasel, www.tedxbasel.com/txb-blog/2016/11/4/tedxbasel-talks-15-kristen-pressner.

93. *See* Grutter v. Bollinger, 539 U.S. 306 (2003).

94. *See* Johnson v. Transp. Agency, 480 U.S. 616 (1987).

EIGHTEEN

From Rosie the Riveter to Health Equity

The Kaiser Permanente EID Journey

Mark Zemelman, Kaiser Permanente
Dr. Ronald L. Copeland, M.D., F.A.C.S., Kaiser Permanente
Professor Sarah E. Redfield, University of New Hampshire

A Note from the Editors: In this Chapter, we interview two leaders in EID (Equity, Inclusion, and Diversity) at Kaiser Permanente (KP or Kaiser): Dr. Ronald Copeland, Senior Vice President and Chief Equity, Inclusion and Diversity Officer, and Mark Zemelman, Senior Vice President and General Counsel for Kaiser Foundation Health Plan, Inc. and Kaiser Foundation Hospitals.* We first met Mark Zemelman in working with him on a conference focused on bringing together diverse experts to discuss interruption of implicit bias. Mark in turn introduced us to Ron Copeland, who heads up Kaiser's equity initiatives. While that conference has been delayed due to Covid-19, the relationship with Mark and Ron has grown and endured as we have learned more from them about their corporate work to these ends.

    Kaiser Permanente is the nation's largest nonprofit integrated health system and a leader with respect to implementing equity, inclusion, and diversity throughout its workforce and management team. Most major corporations in the United States are directly or indirectly tied to the mass consumer market. That consumer market is multi-ethnic and multi-cultural. So too as the United States has moved towards "majority minority," most corporations have found that they need to attract diverse

---

    * At its core, the Kaiser Permanente Medical Care Program (Kaiser Permanente) consists of three closely cooperating entities in each of its markets: Kaiser Foundation Health Plan, Inc. or one of its subsidiary Health Plans; Kaiser Foundation Hospitals, which owns hospitals or contracts for hospital services; and one of the Permanente Medical Groups.

talent, and they have found that retention of diverse talent requires a pathway for diverse personnel into management. For these reasons, and because companies with diverse management have proven to be more successful in the competitive marketplace, corporations have engaged Equity, Inclusion, and Diversity (EID) professionals and developed ongoing EID programs. As we all know, there is no one "recipe" for EID programs in corporations or other institutions; each is necessarily different. Kaiser doesn't claim to have achieved perfection, but it has a longer track record of sustained effort and success than most other corporations. As we have learned more about them, our respect for their initiatives has continued to grow. Much of Kaiser's work and thinking is generalizable, and we all have much to learn from them. We are personally and professionally grateful for this opportunity to do so.

Participants

Dr. Ronald Copeland

Dr. Ronald Copeland, M.D., F.A.C.S., is Senior Vice President and Chief Equity, Inclusion and Diversity Officer for Kaiser Foundation Health Plan, Inc. and Kaiser Foundation Hospitals.

Mark Zemelman

Mark Zemelman is Senior Vice President and General Counsel, Kaiser Foundation Health Plan, Inc. and Kaiser Foundation Hospitals.

Sarah E. Redfield

Professor Redfield conducted the interview. We have supplemented the interview with some specific graphics and detailed descriptors.

***

Sarah: I know that Kaiser Permanente has a long history of conscious engagement with diversity and inclusion. Indeed, I understand that the Rosie the Riveter National Park is located at Kaiser's former Richmond shipyards because many "Rosies" worked at the shipyards. Did the shipyard workers get healthcare?

Mark: Kaiser Permanente has a rich history of pioneering efforts to increase diversity and equity in both employment and the delivery of healthcare. As an integrated healthcare system (i.e., a health system that includes both the delivery of healthcare services and the financial mechanism by which people obtain the services), Kaiser

Permanente was formed during World War II at the Kaiser Shipyards in Richmond, California, and Vancouver, Washington. Henry J. Kaiser's shipyards were notable not only for being the most productive, but also for hiring many women and African Americans. The 30,000 Black workers in the Kaiser Shipyards received fully equal treatment in the new healthcare system that was established to care for the workers and their families.

At this time in American history, many hospitals refused to provide services to African Americans, and those that were willing to serve them generally established segregated in-patient facilities (i.e., separate rooms and often separate wards). The Kaiser hospitals and medical offices were rare in that they were desegrated to the room level. This decision arose from the socially-progressive views of Henry J. Kaiser himself, who, probably more than any of the great industrialists of the mid-20th century, was inclined to look at such questions from the standpoint of the worker or patient. The following quote illustrates Kaiser's approach:

> [Henry] was asked, "Should we [] separate our patients? After all, we only have two beds in each place, and so it would be easy to manage it." He scratched his bald head, so I was told, and he said, "You know, if I were a black man, and you were going to put me along with everybody like me on the right side of the hall, and you had gold carpets there, and there was that miserable tile that I told you not to put in on the left side of the hall where the whites were placed, I still wouldn't believe that you treated me equally."

Sarah: That certainly puts a spin on rejecting "separate but equal." And certainly prescient.

Mark: The physician who ran the hospital and clinical operations during the war, Dr. Sidney Garfield, shared the same progressive social beliefs. During the war, Dr. Garfield hired Dr. Beatrice Lei, one of the first (if not the first) Chinese American women to be hired as a physician in a major U.S. medical group. Following the war, at the request of West Coast unions, Henry Kaiser and Dr. Garfield decided to open the Kaiser medical care system to the public (not just to Kaiser workers and families). This new health plan followed the same philosophy of inclusion, as shown by the following quote from Avram Yadidia, a health care economist who helped set up Kaiser Permanente after WWII.

> I recall one day, probably in 1946, when the chief of police of Oakland, along with his top staff, came to visit the hospital to see what we were doing, with the view that maybe some of them would like to join the health plan.... [T]he police chief said to me, "You know, when we walked through, I saw that you had some Negroes and whites in the same room. I don't think we like that."...
> I responded, "Do you know this plan started that way, with blacks and whites

in the shipyards, and that's the way it goes. They worked together, and they were sick together." He said, 'I don't think my men would like it.'"... As I recall, my response was, "Those who don't like it shouldn't join the plan."

Sarah: I assume this history plays out today at Kaiser Permanente.

Ron: The modern Equity, Inclusion and Diversity effort at Kaiser Permanente began in 1987 with a KP-sponsored study group called the "KP Minority and Promotions Task Force," which produced a report called the "Workforce 2000 Report". This led to the formation of national and local "Diversity Councils" and, in 1991, the Board of Directors' adoption of a National Diversity Agenda focused on diversity and representation. This agenda has since evolved over time, bringing in the elements of inclusion in 2012 and most recently equity in 2018. Kaiser Permanente now has an EID strategic framework that is guiding our work, priorities, and areas of focus.

Over these years, the focus of our EID work can be viewed as having two components: a medical care component directed to improving care through the use of EID tools, and a corporate component directed to improving equity, inclusion and diversity within the workforce and through the interaction of KP and the communities we serve.

Sarah: Can you describe the medical care component?

Ron: As already described, our medical component was based on our integrated model and our commitment to diversity and desegregation related to health care. As per the diagram below, we've been on a learning journey. The graphic below shows Kaiser Permanente's long journey from culturally responsive care to disparities, social needs and social determinants of health and in 2020, we acknowledged, formally and explicitly, that social injustice and all forms of oppression and racism are also determinants of health.

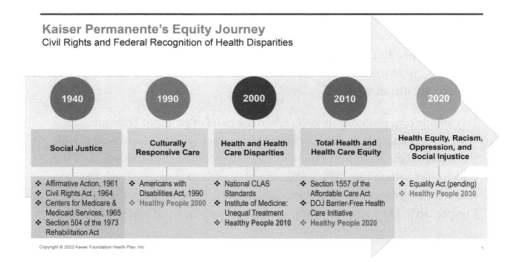

As we progressed through the diagram above, Kaiser Permanente's focus on culturally responsive care was prevalent through its Institute for Culturally Competent Care, which promoted initiatives to improve our ability to deliver care in a manner that is most effective for specific populations based on their cultural norms. From 1999–2012, Kaiser Permanente had established facilities that specialized in developing programs to serve specific populations which we refer to as "Centers of Excellence for Culturally Responsive Care." These centers fulfilled our mission by documenting their learnings whereby any market and/or health system could benefit from the work. In the same way that effective population care requires attention to age-related factors, effective population care requires attention to factors that are specific to gender, race, ethnicity, and other social determinants. We have since integrated culturally responsive care into our day-to-day operations. A few examples of our Centers of Excellence in Culturally Responsive Care are: Kaiser Foundation Rehabilitation Center; National Center for Transgender Equality; Black and African American Sickle Cell Center; and Clinica de Salud.

Sarah: Can you provide a bit more detail on how healthcare data associated with race and ethnicity has driven healthcare programs?

Ron: Kaiser Permanente studies proved that the healthcare outcomes for non-English speaking populations are improved when primary care physicians speak the same language as the patient. As a result, Kaiser Permanente has undertaken a number of initiatives to align patients with primary care physicians who speak the same language, or, where that option is unavailable, establish real-time translation services. Kaiser Permanente believes providing culturally responsive, equitable care throughout an entire member's journey is also critical to one's overall health; thus KP also provides services such as multi-language outreach, call center staff fluent in more than 140 languages, and medical facilities uniquely focused on the needs of specific communities. The result has been a measurable increase in health in non-English speaking populations.

First launched in 1990, Healthy People 2020 laid out the U.S. Department of Health and Human Services' roadmap for improving the health of Americans by the turn of the century. In addition, the Institute of Medicine's report on unequal treatment helped pave the way for Kaiser Permanente to bring light to the fact that we do have health disparities and we need to do something about it.

Kaiser Permanente uses data and analytics as one way to address health disparities. Through an effort led by our National EID and Quality departments, our outcomes reporting has brought greater visibility into health disparities and their impact on our members. Comprehensive plans to address and reduce disparities are often derived through insights from this reporting. We analyze how we can maximize the utilization of our electronic health record system and are beginning to compare various aspects of demographic data to enhance our analytical insights, expanding disparity analysis beyond race/ethnicity to look at social determinants of health and other factors.

A number of programs have been developed to address these health equity gaps, most notably a program to address blood pressure control in the Black/African American population, and a program to address colon cancer in the Latino population.

There are numerous barriers to achieving equitable health outcomes, such as inadequate transportation, lack of health care coverage and affordability, cultural and language discordance with providers, trust issues, and discrimination/bias. In our efforts to improve blood pressure control for our Black/African American patients, we took time to understand which of these preventable and/or unjust barriers were at work by engaging in culturally humble conversations, respecting every voice, and meeting our patients in their own communities. We then gained important insights that informed evidence-based care protocols in collaboration with patients and trusted community advocates (family, faith-based community, barber shops/salons, etc.). These adaptations, as well as insuring that our care teams were adhering to effective medication, diet, and trust building behaviors, led to significant and sustained improvements in blood pressure control and narrowing of disparity gaps. This approach has been formalized and integrated across our care system and has led to impressive results when applied to other populations as well. Success is informed more by what we co-design with our patients, than to them!

As we continue our journey to providing equitable care, we have found that research is a significant tool in helping to close those gaps. The Kaiser Permanente Research Bank is a long-term research effort that helps scientists understand how peoples' health is affected by their genes, behaviors, and the environment. Major research programs in this area include but are not limited to: Social Determinants of Health; Vaccines & Infectious Diseases; Cardiovascular Health & Metabolic Conditions; Cancer; Chronic Illness Management; Infectious Diseases; Behavioral Health and Aging (e.g., Mental Health, alcohol and drugs, chronic pain); Women's and Children's Health.

Sarah: This is all part of the planning and strategy referenced in the chart you provided?

Ron: Referring back to the diagram, as a result of focusing on the pursuit of health equity and addressing the barriers provided by systemic oppression/racism and social injustice, Kaiser Permanente implemented several initiatives to address social determinants as a barrier to total health. A few examples include:

Thrive Local, launched in 2019, is a transformative social health network that will help millions address social needs, including food, housing, and transportation.

This comprehensive online and searchable social services resource directory network was created to integrate social factors into Kaiser Permanente's care delivery. Thrive Local is in the process of being rolled out to Kaiser Permanente members and a growing network of health care and social service providers working together across its service areas. In 2020, Kaiser Permanente shared more than 26,000 community resources with its members and launched 18 community networks.

Economic opportunity is also foundational to healthy communities; it supports housing stability and food security, as well as physical, mental, and social health. We know that support for under-resourced business owners of color can change the trajectory for individuals, families, and entire communities.

Kaiser Permanente invests in programs that create equitable economic opportunity for underrepresented communities and work to dismantle racist systems that create barriers to success. We promote these shifts to help close the racial wealth gap. Accordingly, we are using our purchasing power to build healthy, equitable, and sustainable economies. An example is our commitment to the Billion Dollar Roundtable and related supplier diversity efforts to spend $2 billion per year on individuals of color-, women-, LGBTQ+, veterans-, veterans with disabilities-, and individuals-with-disabilities-owned enterprises.

Sarah: There is obviously a great deal of important EID work going on at Kaiser. In addition to all this, you took the step of directly expanding the pipeline to the medical profession.

Ron: Yes. To address the under-representation of minorities in medicine and to help transform medical education for the next generation of physicians and leaders, Kaiser Permanente opened the Kaiser Permanente Bernard J. Tyson School of Medicine in 2020, where we are committed to teaching future physicians about the social and environmental factors that affect the health of patients and populations that are under-resourced, underserved, and culturally diverse. Students learn in an environment that reflects the changing demographics of America and the multifaceted health care issues facing society, with the opportunity to learn from the physicians and care teams in Kaiser Permanente's integrated health care system. By re-imagining how physicians are trained, the school aims to create outstanding physicians who will be skilled advocates for their patients and communities and drive change in the health care profession. In addition, we know that economic challenges can prevent members of underrepresented populations from becoming physicians, so the first five graduating classes at the School of Medicine are tuition-free.

The school's values highlight the intersection of health equity and the elimination of disparities, and it will develop the next generation of courageous leaders who challenge the status quo with inquiry and innovation. We want our graduates to be intentional disruptors for equity and social justice for all the people we serve.

Some of the highlights of the school's values are: achieving health equity for all and the elimination of health disparities wherever they exist; advocating for change in medical education, the profession, and the healthcare system; promoting inclusiveness and diversity in medical education and the health professions.

Sarah: Is this medical component of EID coordinated with the corporate EID program? Or to ask the question more broadly: How has Kaiser Permanente institutionalized EID so that there is ongoing development of policy and programs in both its medical and corporate aspects?

Ron: We brought together the medical and business sides of the EID work in 1991 through the formation of the National Diversity Council, a council of health plan, hospital, and physician leaders that focus on furthering EID at Kaiser Permanente. Operationally, Kaiser Permanente established a National Equity, Inclusion and Diversity (NEID) Office in 1997. This office is led by the Senior Vice President and Chief Equity, Inclusion and Diversity Officer [currently, Dr. Copeland] and has a substantial staff and budget. Additionally, NEID is closely connected to market and functional leaders across the enterprise to ensure Kaiser Permanente's EID strategy is executed. This includes EID leads and champions, as well as employees who serve on our business resource groups which are a critical part of our diversity infrastructure and a key source of cultural expertise and diversity advocacy.

By having both physician and business leadership on the National Diversity Council, the Council was able to drive activities that instill EID into the heart of our organization's operations. For example, in 2004, Kaiser Permanente became the first national health care organization (other than the Veterans Administration) to implement an electronic medical records (EMR) system across the entire organization. At the recommendation of the National Diversity Council, KP leadership decided to modify the purchased software to permit the collection of demographic information on race, ethnicity and language preference data into individual electronic medical records. As a result, KP has developed what may be the largest medical database in the nation with such demographic information. The database often is used for research on medical diagnosis and treatment differences among populations. Recognizing that these efforts must be sponsored at the most senior levels of the organization, the work of the National Diversity Council has now evolved into the Executive Equity Inclusion and Diversity Council (members include senior leaders from KP's health plan, hospital and medical group entities). Fast forward to today, physician and health plan collaboration and partnership in the EID space remains strong and steady, with our most recent achievement being the creation of KP's equity commitments rolled out in 2020 and is also being integrated into our formal business strategy.

Sarah: In American industry, diversity at the operational level doesn't mean that there is diversity at the top. Has Kaiser Permanente also been a leader in EID at the most senior levels?

Ron: Each of the CEOs since the beginning of the Program have been champions of diversity and inclusion, and the KFHP/KFH Boards of Directors has sought to achieve diversity for decades. As a result, Kaiser Permanente has been a leader in the nation in placing minorities and women in leadership. Kaiser Permanente's Board in 2020 consisted of 40% women and 40% people of color. With respect to the CEOs of Kaiser Foundation Health Plan, Inc., all have been men, but the current and prior CEOs were both African American.

Just like many other organizations, we are on a journey to equity and have several initiatives in play to increase diversity among all levels at KP.

Sarah: The time and depth of KP's commitment to the EID mission is clearly evident in what you've said. One of the things that I find with organizations is that they tend to get the diversity part, at least in terms of numbers, and they tend to at least be beginning on the inclusion part, but they seem less able to engage with equity. This must be something you've thought about. How do you think this kind of focus is best achieved?

Ron: Fully incorporating EID into an organization is a multiyear proposition; and, given the sensitivities, it requires a great deal of planning and thought to have it roll out in a manner that builds a stronger and more effective culture and has appropriate buy-in.

Our strategic priorities are reflected in our strategic framework and apply an equity, inclusion and diversity lens across three interdependent areas that collectively advance equity. These three areas are: Workplace, Care Delivery, and Community. Our approach includes the following:

Workplace: Achieve diversity at every level with a fully engaged and high-performing workforce in equitable and inclusive environments

- Workforce Equity: we build sustainable, effective practices throughout the employee lifecycle to achieve the best workforce performance and equity at all levels and partner with external vendors on benchmarking.
- Inclusive Environments: we enable a high-performing, inclusive culture that drives collaboration, engagement, belonging, and continuous learning.

Care delivery: Achieve equitable health outcomes by providing inclusive care and eliminating avoidable and unjust disparities

- Health Equity: We institutionalize practices that allow us to continuously identify and eliminate inequities that prevent the best possible health outcomes for all populations. Equity is also now a standard dimension of how we define quality improvement and will be a critical part of how we're defining quality outcomes moving forward. We will examine our outcomes and other quality metrics by various social determinants so we can intervene when necessary to address health care and health inequities.

- Inclusive Care: Through continuous learning and skill development, we advance scalable cultural competence, agility, empathy, respect, and humility as key attributes to working within equitable systems.

Community: Enhance health equity in the community and Kaiser Permanente's measurable impact on economic and social inclusion (which includes collaboration with National Supplier Diversity)

- Total Health: We are committed to helping people be healthier in all aspects of their lives and to building stronger, healthier communities.
- Economic and Social Inclusion: We ensure that the money we spend helps create jobs and increases the economic and social vitality of our communities.

Those priorities are then turned into goals, then data is used to evaluate process and outcome improvements and leaders are held accountable for results.

Sarah: Could you provide a bit more detail on a few of these?

Ron: Belong@KP is a key initiative under the workforce equity agenda that is worth highlighting. It is a multiyear, action-focused awareness and behavior change program to foster inclusion, combat bias and racism, and incorporate social justice into everything that we do. The program has two parts to it, first focusing on anti-bias and the second focusing on anti-racism core principles.

Throughout Kaiser Permanente's 75-plus years, we have consistently and intentionally taken a stand for equity, inclusion and diversity, which are inextricably linked to our mission and serve as a foundation upon which our enterprise has been built. We are committed to lead unapologetically with purpose, conviction and a sense of urgency. The times demand it and the people we are privileged to serve deserve it.

Sarah: Dr. Copeland, I want to thank you for providing an overview of Kaiser Permanente's EID strategy and operation. I would now like to turn to Mark Zemelman, the General Counsel for Kaiser Permanente's National Legal Office.

Mark, your Legal Department has been particularly active in advocating for EID both at Kaiser Permanente and in the legal industry, correct?

Mark: Robert Erickson was General Counsel from roughly 1968 to 1993, and he was a pioneer in the diversity movement. He was the executive that initiated the annual Diversity Conference at KP in 1977. He made a point of bringing diverse lawyers and executives into the company, both at the line level and at the management level. Of course, he could not have accomplished much without the support of the CEOs, and Kaiser Permanente has always had the benefit of having CEOs who are strong believers in the importance of EID from the perspectives of population health, business success, and social progress.

Sarah: In your view, why is EID important to a legal department? Is it just the right thing to do from a social perspective?

Mark: It is much more than that. First, there is simply the practical reality that Kaiser Permanente, like most large organizations, serves a consumer base that is increasingly diverse. (Indeed, the base of our membership is in California, which is majority minority.) Moreover, our employee base is highly diverse. And the government agencies are diverse. If our Legal Department is not diverse, then it doesn't adequately represent the realities and values of our organization or the people we serve.

Second, we are a far better department due to the diversity of our staff. A key attribute of great lawyers is the ability to engage with, and to be convincing with, everyone. One is not born with this skill; it is learned through experiences with many different types of people. An even more important attribute is the ability to engage in difficult, emotionally charged conversations in a thoughtful and objective manner. What is the most difficult and emotionally charged issue in America? Race. A well-run EID program puts the issue of race on the table. In the KP Legal Department we have many intentional conversations on the subject. This helps develop great legal professionals. If you can have thoughtful and objective conversations about race, then you can pretty much handle any highly charged issue.

Third, our leadership in the EID space has helped us in our hiring process. As corporations begin to understand the importance of having a diverse bench of lawyers on their team, law firms pull out all the stops to attract and hire them, making it more difficult for us to recruit. We have been able to draw diverse lawyers from other organizations (particularly law firms) by building a reputation for being a place where legal professionals from underrepresented groups can flourish. Our commitment to EID is demonstrated in the end-to-end hiring process, from the intentionality of our recruitment, to structured interview panels and rankings, and including discussions about the EID vision and strategy.

Finally, I have become convinced over the years that failure often comes from "group think," that is, following conventional wisdom. A legal department with an effective EID program is one that inherently minimizes "group think."

Sarah: Yes, group think is an interesting concept. Psychologist Irvin Janis is thought to have coined the term in his study on the Bay of Pigs, where President Kennedy is said to have asked: "How could we have been so stupid?" Given the intellectual talent advising the President, Janis rejected stupidity as a reason, finding instead that decisions made under conditions of stress tend to go with the leader; we want to belong, and it is difficult to take a hard line against others in such circumstances. It isn't discussed much today, but perhaps it should be.

Mark: If I can recommend one article for you to read regarding the value of EID in a professional environment, it is Rock, et al.: *Diverse Teams Feel Less Comfortable--And That's Why They Perform Better* in the Harvard Business Review (Sept. 22, 2016). The point of the article is that diverse institutions typically have greater business success than their competitors because there is a constructive tension that arises in a diverse office that disrupts group think.

Sarah: Given this context, walk me through the steps that your department has taken to build a diverse legal team.

Mark: It starts with the hiring process. When I became a manager, I used a number of recruiting firms to conduct the hiring for my team. They kept coming back with panels of candidates that typically were all White, telling me that it was impossible to find lawyers from underrepresented groups in this or that specialty. In the mid-2000s, I worked with the California Minority Counsel Program to identify legal recruiting firms owned and operated by lawyers from underrepresented groups. We found three, and I tried all of them out. My favorite was a small recruiting firm owned and operated by Merle Vaughn. She did not know the healthcare area, but quickly learned it; and she was able to locate highly qualified and diverse candidates. Eventually, she joined Major, Hagen & Africa, the largest legal recruiter in the nation; and this made her even more effective. When I became General Counsel, I moved all of our recruiting to her.

What has been particularly interesting to me is that, in switching the recruiting to Merle, the overall quality of our candidate pools has increased, regardless of diversity. I don't fully understand the reason for this, but I suspect that the search for diverse candidates—particularly in a heavily White field such as health law—compels the recruiter to dig deeper, i.e., make a more extensive search.

At this point, our lawyer staff is majority women and about one-third members of underrepresented groups. The paraprofessional staff and administrative staff is even more diverse. It also is the best Legal Department that Kaiser Permanente has ever had. For the reasons I've talked about, I think there is a connection between the excellence of the department and its diversity.

Sarah: From these numbers, it certainly seems that your approach to outreach and hiring is successful. A lot of firms talk about EID, and to me they seem most often to be talking about the numbers or what is sometimes called representational diversity. I think though we all know that numbers alone, while important, will not be sufficient. Given your diverse base, tell us more about how you assure an inclusive and equitable environment.

Mark: The most important step was to establish and support a formal EID Committee within the Legal department. Under the leadership of one of our African American lawyers, Tamara Mason Morgan, the Committee has established six streams of work, each with a leader or co-leaders; and it is continuously producing programs and initiatives that move our Department along the EID path. The leadership of the Department (what we call the Practice Management Group, i.e., the VPs who respectively lead each of our substantive sections of legal professionals) supports the EID Committee by aligning a portion of our compensation with the EID Committee's objectives, by participating in the EID Committee, by helping the Committee members find the time to participate in Committee activities (although, admittedly, it is a lot of extra work for some) and by financial support.

Let me detail the EID Committee's work. The Committee has a mission statement that is broad and ambitious: "To embrace, promote, and serve as a catalyst for diversity, equity and inclusion through our department's policies and practices, and our work at Kaiser Permanente, in the health care and legal professions, and in the communities we serve." The point is that the consciousness of equity and inclusion should permeate all of our activities as legal professionals and members of the Kaiser Permanente organization.

The EID Committee encourages participation by all segments of the department, i.e., the administrative assistants as well as the lawyers, paralegals, and claims examiners. In fact, the Committee has proven to be a mechanism by which people in administrative positions can exercise creativity and leadership in the department, which greatly increases their job satisfaction. In a law department, where there is a clear hierarchy in the allocation and performance of work, it is easy to forget that most of the members of the department—the administrative assistants as much as the attorneys —have many other skill sets and characteristics that they bring to the department. When, for example, an administrative assistant gets the opportunity to organize and lead an initiative (for example, a seminar where members of the department talk about how their families came to live in the United States), that assistant takes a leadership role in a meaningful event for the department that stays in our memories. It fills out the picture that we have of that assistant, permits them to develop and demonstrate leadership skills, makes them more of a recognized personality and force in the department, and chips away at unconscious biases in a more direct way than any canned training. Yes, it takes some time away from regular assistant duties, but I believe that the time is more than compensated by the commitment and enthusiasm that it creates in each individual for our department.

Sarah: The EID Committee has a lot going on. How do you assure their work remains central and relevant?

Mark: The EID Committee constantly stays relevant to the Legal Department because it formulates a portion of our Annual Incentive Plan (AIP) goals and puts together the programs that implement the goals. For many years now, we have had three goals that are tied to incentive pay and that directly contribute to greater equity and diversity in our profession, organization, and communities. These are the "community benefit" goal; a supplier diversity goal for law firms certified as minority and women-owned business enterprises (MWOBE); and a supplier diversity goal for majority-owned firms.

The "community benefit" goal is our version of a similar goal that most Kaiser Permanente executives have. Initially, the goal simply required a minimum number of hours of work for a wide variety of community organizations. Over the years, we have narrowed the focus of the activities, asking the members of our department to work with community organizations that are aligned with our healthcare or diversity goals, and, more importantly, organizing our own events in the community. A good example is an event that I participated in: Working with a local community organization to help construct a community garden in a low-income housing project. While the project involved relatively little time, it exposed our lawyers and other professionals to the living conditions of a large number of people who live meagerly in an otherwise well-off community. More recently, we have encouraged volunteerism focused on civic engagement (voter education) and outreach to students in underserved communities.

I'm particularly proud of the supplier diversity goal for MWOBE firms. The large majority-owned firms in the United States have, with only a few exceptions, resisted taking a leadership role in diversifying the legal profession and controlling costs. Our department has, since the late 1990s, sought to identify MWOBE firms to whom we could send business, but, about six years ago, in response to the lack of diversity leadership in the large firms, we established an AIP goal to send at least 20% of our new matters (matters that require outside counsel) each year to minority and women-owned firms, with more money being tied to increasing that percentage. Tying money to this goal was a game-changer. For a couple of years, we hit 30%. On average, we have achieved more than 20% per year. This has had a great and favorable impact for certain MWOBE firms, and it has lowered our costs because the MWOBE firms generally are smaller and less expensive than the large majority firms. Often, the responsiveness and service quality of these firms exceeds the big firms as well: They work very hard to keep a big client like Kaiser Permanente.

Our greatest problem with this program is that some of our best MWOBE firms have been purchased by majority firms, no doubt in part because of the business we provide them. That has raised the interesting question of whether we should shift new work away from these former MWOBE lawyers who are now part of a majority firm, and start fresh with new MWOBE firms. We are trying to strike a balance and have not yet articulated a clear approach to the issue.

The third AIP goal—supplier diversity for majority firms–has focused on assuring that the legal teams assigned to Kaiser Permanente matters reflect the diversity of the KP membership and communities we serve. At first, it was hard to track this at a level of detail that could assure us that lawyers from underrepresented groups were not just tokens on our teams. In the past year, however, we have implemented software that enables us to quickly see what kind of work all of the lawyers on our teams are doing, the hours spent, the billing rates, and to slice and dice the data to ensure that mindful staffing—matching talent to tasks with an eye towards equity and career advancement—is a key driver.

Sarah: Does some of your work extend beyond KP?

Mark: We also engage the majority firms directly regarding their broader efforts (i.e., beyond just KP work) to create diversity in their equity partnership ranks. Optimally, these engagements take a win-win approach, although sometimes we also need to make clear that we will stop sending work if a firm does not improve. Let me give you an example of a win-win approach. The health law field has many women in it, but few lawyers of color. I've encouraged the health law partners in certain firms to reach across to their litigation and employment law practices to draw some of their lawyers of color, saying that we (i.e., Kaiser Permanente's Legal Department) will test them and, if they perform well, continue to provide them with work. This means more business for the firm and assures us with long-term representation by a diverse outside legal team. I hope that this kind of approach leads to a "pipeline to partnership" for attorneys of color in the healthcare space.

Sarah: To make this even more tangible, what is your EID team's strategy for this year?

Mark: Our EID Program's infrastructure is intentionally designed to challenge unconscious bias and to provide leadership and collaboration opportunities for members of our department, regardless of their standing in the department or their "day job." To that end, a quarter of the EID Executive Council are paralegals or non-lawyer administrators who staff seven teams: Career Progression & Development, Centralized Functions, Community Benefit, Education & Training, Impact Spending, Kulture & People and Pipeline & Pathways. Each of these teams is tasked with specific goals and objectives that breathe life into our mission. We design these goals to meet a three part strategy that we call: Engage, Equip, and Ignite which we describe as follows.

- ENGAGE: We will continue to **engage** with one another and learn how *to be better*–better colleagues, better lawyers, better leaders, better citizens. We do this through the development of initiatives that fortify our department as a psychologically safe space grounded in empathy, cultural agility, and respect.

- EQUIP: We will **equip** ourselves *to make better decisions*; to scrutinize the way things are done and identify and interrupt patterns and practices that exclude segments of society and have discriminatory impact, and practice inclusive behaviors. We do this by providing tools to normalize inclusive practices and create and sustain equitable experiences for our workforce.
- IGNITE: We will **ignite** ourselves *to do better*; to move beyond the KP walls and take these tools and learnings to our communities and the legal profession to make a meaningful impact within our spheres of influence. We do this by designing and offering opportunities for impactful ways to achieve equity and inclusion in our communities and the legal profession.

Sarah: I am interested in the seven teams that you mentioned. Can you give us more detail regarding the work of each team?

Mark: The following is a high-level description of the priorities of each team:

CENTRALIZED FUNCTIONS TEAM: This team is responsible for maintaining the visibility of the Legal Department's EID work both within and outside the department; building an EID competency pathway to guide the department's development of EID programs and measuring its progress; developing new programs; and maintaining connections with other EID programs at KP.

CAREER PROGRESSION AND DEVELOPMENT. This group runs three programs:

- New lawyer mentoring program: Each new lawyer in the department receives a mentor to guide their introduction to Kaiser Permanente's structure, clients, and legal practices. To emphasize the EID aspect of the mentorship relationship, the program is entitled "Authentic Reliance on Colleagues" or "ARC." This is in recognition that the titles of mentor and mentee are not determinative; the ARC program drives inclusion and belonging in a functional way.
- Professional Networking & Development Initiative: This program identifies and promotes external leadership development activities with legal specialty organizations and associations.
- Workforce equity: This group supports the Legal Department's leadership in developing best practices in hiring, selection, and development of legal professionals in the department.

COMMUNITY BENEFIT: This team identifies and develops programs in which legal professionals participate to meet their Community Benefit incentive pay goals. This year, each legal professional must select or create a CB activity which aligns with one of four "paths": Civic engagement, Community engagement, Pro Bono services, and Education/Youth.

- Enrichment and Development: This team develops and hosts EID trainings and forums for purposes of education. Where possible, Continuing Education credit is arranged for these trainings. Topics are wide-ranging and have included AI and Coding Bias, Defining Society's Heroes, and Accountability and Integrity in Law Enforcement.

- Impact Spending: This team is responsible for supporting the Legal Department in its achievement of the incentive goals related to outside law firms. This includes identifying MWOBE firms and diverse attorneys within majority firms to whom work may be sent; analyzing outside counsel spending trends related to diversity; using the data to drive our initiatives, such as incorporating mindful staffing, redistributing work and restructuring the KP teams; and working with outside organizations, such as the Move the Needle Fund, that focus on the strategic career development of diverse attorneys.

KULTURE AND PEOPLE: This team focuses on inclusion and belonging through various short-term programs in which Legal Department members share personal experiences. For example, C.U.R.E. Chats (Connect Unwind Refresh Enrich) serve as virtual water cooler gatherings on topics as disparate as self-care, hobbies, elder care, parenting, and the cumulative impact of trauma on the African American community; a book club (six books per year by authors from underrepresented groups); and the rollout of an organization-wide Inclusion program called Belong@KP.

PIPELINE AND PATHWAYS. This team has three programs:

- Law school externships: Over the last decade, we have established an externship program with several Northern California law schools. We are pleased to have expanded the program to additional law schools, including our first virtual externship in 2020 with the HBCU, Southern University Law Center.

- Law school 1L summer fellowships: Partnering with two law firms and in conjunction with both LCLD (the Leadership Council on Legal Diversity) and Move the Needle, our Legal Department hosts two diverse 1L summer fellowships designed to expand the reach of majority law firms to students from schools they might not otherwise consider and to utilize a more holistic screening and selection process to ferret out unconscious bias.

- Legal career panels: Groups of legal professionals meet with high school, college, and law school students to share their professional journeys and provide career advice.

Sarah: I'm curious as to how a structured operation like yours responds to a crisis. How did your department respond to the George Floyd murder?

Mark: I think it's important to note that the George Floyd murder and its aftermath came about at a unique time in our country's history–the early months of a global pandemic–and that his murder was by no means the first or even one of the first assaults on the spirit of the African American community and their allies. People were already in a state of frustration, fear, and disillusionment. Members of the Legal Department had begun working remotely for the first time and were feeling disconnected. What helped us, in retrospect, was that for years we had been working on unconscious bias–defining it, accepting that it exists in all of us, talking about it, searching for and developing tools to remediate it.

In 2014 all members of the Department took the Harvard Implicit Bias Association Test (IAT) and participated in a mandatory unconscious bias training program taught by a lawyer who runs unconscious bias trainings for judges who have exhibited such bias. Our program consisted of small seminars, each four hours long. The participants for each seminar were intentionally selected so that there would be a mixture of people from different job classifications, economic, social, and ethnic backgrounds. The primary focus of the seminars was the science of unconscious bias, i.e., training the group on the neurobiology of unconscious bias, and making it clear that everyone (regardless of race, gender, or ethnicity) has unconscious bias. We have doubled down on that initial training with regular refresher sessions, sometimes with well-known scholars in the field and sometimes with consultants who have focused on using the newly found understanding of unconscious bias to build cultural agility.

Additionally, we instituted what we call "CURES Chats" soon after the pandemic shutdown. These were regularly scheduled open discussions, once per week, convened for the purpose of talking about issues (other than legal issues). The Chats were moderated by various members of the EID Committee, but loosely structured so that spontaneous feelings could arise and be discussed. The moderator in each instance was prepared to start the discussion with some experience or feeling of his or her own in order to get the discussion moving. The moderators also were prepared to address conflicting perspectives: It was made clear throughout the Chats that they were an opportunity to express feelings without being judged.

With the scientific grounding provided by the unconscious bias training, and the experience of open dialogues through the CURES Chats, the department was ready to receive the programs that were created in the immediate aftermath of the Floyd murder.

Sarah: What were those?

Mark: The George Floyd murder led to a set of EID Committee responses and programs that truly were transformational. While the frequency and intensity of the response were driven by the emotional response to the barbaric murder, I think that the structure, order and content of the programs transcend that moment in time and serve as an example of what a department or organization can do to address both conscious and unconscious bias.

The first program was a 21-day program of readings, videos, and discussions about structural racism. (The program, modified by a law firm, was broadly distributed through the U.S. legal community by the American Bar Association.) It involved roughly 30 minutes of reading and/or viewing each evening and an hour group discussion ("reflection circle") about the prior day's readings/videos. While the 21-day exercise was optional, a high percentage of the department's lawyers and administrative staff attended the discussions. In fact, there was so much interest that our EID Program provided additional content and extended the program by 30 days. It was a lot of time, but, in the wake of the Floyd murder, the intensity of the program seemed appropriate and in some ways cathartic.

I should note that, privately, a few lawyers approached me with concerns about some of the points of view being expressed and the potential of lawsuits. My evaluation was that the risks of lawsuits were much less than the risks of damage to the cohesiveness of our highly diverse department if we did not have these open sessions. But we did respond to the concern by inviting an outside speaker to host a candid conversation about the difficulties that surround these types of conversations. In the end, there were no lawsuits.

The second program---the most powerful---was conceptualized and carried out by the EID Committee. To demonstrate that unconscious bias permeates all of history and culture, and is not just a Black experience, the EID Committee developed a "Race, Ethnicity & Immigration Series." The series began with a grounding in American immigration history, providing curated resources for those interested in a deeper dive. It was followed by six hour-long events at which four or five members of the Legal Department discussed their families' stories (often with photographs) of how they came to the United States. The impact was both revelatory and dramatic. It turned out, for example, that several of the current members of our department had spent a substantial portion of their childhood in refugee camps in Asia, with extended families sharing one-room shacks, unsure of where they would end up.

The program, which took place as the Black Lives Matter movement was sweeping the country, had the effect of emotionally connecting almost all members of the department to the importance of remedying unconscious bias and discrimination.

With this base, the EID Committee then implemented a series of seminars on current issues, including workshops on how to get voters to turn out on propositions related to equity. The seminars addressed subjects, such as law enforcement accountability, on which members of the Legal Department had strong and conflicting views. While these discussions were at times uncomfortable, the moderators did an excellent job of assuring that all viewpoints were represented and treated with respect. As I mentioned earlier, great lawyering is characterized by the ability to listen to and thoughtfully discuss difficult issues. My observation was that these seminars were beneficial not just for their topical content but were a step for many individuals in their growth as legal professionals.

We are doing this interview more than a year after George Floyd's murder. The workshops that the EID Committee developed in the aftermath of that murder are continuing, and they are assured in their continuation by the Committee's development of standing subcommittees charged with training and development. As a department, we took advantage of an important moment in the nation's history, using it both to improve our awareness and interaction at that moment, and to build ongoing programs to better ourselves and our department in the future.

Sarah: I'm sure it is obvious to our readers now that asking you and Dr. Copeland to be a part of the book was a deliberate choice. Before we close, I wonder if you could speak just for a minute about the particular role of the General Counsel in this work.

Mark: In one sense it is no different than any other department head or leader in any organization. The job is to build an effective department and company through, among other things, constructing diverse teams that can serve a diverse population, and addressing the unconscious biases and tensions that impair our effectiveness and enjoyment of work.

That said, there is a special role that lawyers and other legal professionals play in this context. Most people are afraid of, and avoid, conflict and conflictual feelings. Lawyers should be expert in conflict resolution, and I would hope that lawyers and other legal professionals can help guide other departments, and the company itself, through the difficult discussions and actions that are necessary to address unconscious bias and the problems that arise from it.

As legal professionals, we also, of course, have a role in protecting the organization. Given that the promotion of EID is important to companies (and society), this role should not take the form of shutting down difficult discussions and controversial actions. Rather, the role should be to make sure that they are carried out in a way that is constructive and appropriate given the purposes of the organization. We learn how to do this not only by reading cases and understanding current legal boundaries, but by deeply investing ourselves in understanding the realities and feelings underlying the issues so that we can be thoughtful partners in crafting programs.

About the Authors

Ronald L. Copeland, M.D., F.A.C.S., is senior vice president of National Equity, Inclusion, and Diversity strategy and policy and chief equity, inclusion, and diversity officer for Kaiser Permanente. Through multiple collaborations, he leads Kaiser Permanente's program-wide efforts to ensure our strategic vision for equity, inclusion, and diversity is successfully implemented to drive strategic business and mission outcomes, empower communities we serve, and result in all Kaiser Permanente members achieving health and health care outcomes that are high quality, equitable, and increasingly more affordable.

Dr. Copeland is a member of Kaiser Permanente's Executive Equity, Inclusion, and Diversity Council, a group composed of the Chairman/CEO and other C-level leaders who oversee executive accountability for embedding the equity, inclusion, and diversity strategy throughout the organization. A recently retired board-certified general surgeon, Dr. Copeland joined Kaiser Permanente in 1988 after a six-year honorable tour of duty in the United States Air Force Medical Corps. Dr. Copeland served as president and executive medical director of the Ohio Permanente Medical Group prior to assuming his current role in 2012. The Rochester, N.Y., native earned his bachelor's degree from Dartmouth College and his medical degree from University of Cincinnati Medical College. He completed his residency in general surgery at State University of New York Upstate Medical Center in Syracuse. He also attended the Advanced Management Program at Harvard Business School. Dr. Copeland is a board member of Kaiser Permanente School of Medicine, the National Organization on Disability and the Center for Healthcare Innovation; an advisory board member for the Centre for Global Inclusion; and a member and the chair of the Institute for Health Care Improvement's equity advisory group.

Mark Zemelman was the General Counsel of Kaiser Foundation Health Plan, Inc., from 2010 to 2021. He graduated with honors from Hastings College of Law in 1983, practicing at Orrick, Herrington & Sutcliff and McCutchen Doyle Brown & Enerson before joining the Kaiser legal department in 1991.

NINETEEN

Confronting the Hurricane

The Honorable Kevin S. Burke, Hennepin County, MN*

A Note from the Editors: Judge Burke is an expert extraordinaire on matters of procedural justice, a theme that runs through many chapters of this book and its predecessor. We are grateful to have him back to share his wisdom on the related topics of implicit bias and procedural justice. Judge Burke sets this Chapter in an important context—eroding trust in our courts and the need to rebuild that trust for the very survival of our legal system. And he offers us a metaphor: Hurricane Bias. If we don't accept the existence of implicit bias and its negative manifestations, we can well expect the damage to be the equivalent of a disastrous hurricane, and, simply and starkly put, as a society we cannot afford that. Judge Burke's long and well-respected work in this field shines through here; we've learned additional perspective and approaches and trust our readers will as well.

CHAPTER HIGHLIGHTS

- There is danger from natural disasters and serious danger from those disasters we create ourselves. Bias is such a disaster. Both can be deadly.

CHAPTER CONTENTS

Introduction
1. Recognizing There Is Bias
2. Progress in Reducing Bias

---

* Special thanks to Natalie Cote, a University of St. Thomas law student who helped with this Chapter.

3. The Dimensions of the Problem Facing Courts
4. Significant Forces Impeding Effective Action to Combat Bias
5. Preparing for Hurricane Bias: The Parable of Two Wolves
6. Dealing with Hurricane Bias with Procedural Fairness
7. Is There a Storm in the Courthouses?

Conclusion

Introduction

Each year our nation has seen the horror that hurricanes cause. In 2005, Hurricane Katrina caused over 1,800 deaths and $161 billion in damage.[1] As a result of Katrina, large parts of the City of New Orleans were totally destroyed. In 2012, Hurricane Sandy inflicted nearly $70 billion in damage and killed 233 people across eight countries from the Caribbean to Canada.[2] New York state and federal courts were decimated. More recently, Hurricane Maria took the lives of 2,975 Puerto Ricans, displaced more than 200,000 individuals, and caused nearly $90 billion in damage.[3]

What happens with hurricanes is not simply the loss of life, but the ravaging and destruction of communities that frequently take years to rebuild. There is no silver lining in these natural disaster tragedies. Yes, we usually come together. Yes, the politically polarized Congress usually rises above hyper-partisanship to act swiftly to fund a response taskforce and send monetary and humanitarian aid to families affected. It is also true that when communities act in concert, even the most generational catastrophes can be overcome. Communities board up their homes and businesses in preparation for the impending disaster. Once the hurricane subsides, there is an outpouring of donations and support for the victims. People of faith open their hearts, and in a nation divided by partisanship to the extreme, there is usually little of it. The victims of the destruction are occasionally caught crying in public and many more cry in private. Everyone knows this hurt. Everyone feels at some level the pain of those people that they do not even know. *Thank God it was not our family going through that!* At some level we all know that the damage is not limited to physical destruction; it also causes destruction to the soul.

Hurricanes produce a natural tragedy. But there is another kind of hurricane we should not ignore, but too often do. This other kind of hurricane is just as destructive, but it is not a natural disaster. This hurricane is manmade: it is bias—bias against people of color, women, and a host of other groups that have been traditionally excluded by society. If courts and the legal profession do not address this manmade Category 5 hurricane, we are doomed to a fate equal to the destruction wrought by the annual natural disaster hurricane season. Indeed, like the preparations done in anticipation of a hurricane, similar community efforts should be launched to address bias and to lessen its effects in society.

Black parents of sons worry about what may happen to them. Will they be stopped by the police? Will something get out of hand? If their children end up in court, will they be treated fairly by the various players in the judicial system? Will a judge listen to them? Will a judge treat them with respect? Can they trust the judges? The hurricane in Black parents' lives persists throughout their lifetimes and will not subside after the storm passes.

Symbols show how a society thinks of itself and what values it honors. While there is much to celebrate, there is another side of our nation's history. America's dark history is still displayed in historic statues and flags flaunted in Southern cities. If you are from the South, how do you explain to your child what the Confederate soldiers and statues stood for? Although the United States recently made a lot of progress in removing Confederate statues, it has not been easy, and there are those who persist in loudly protesting that removing these statues is desecrating a noble past. Beyond symbols like these, there are other storm-like questions. How do you explain the Ku Klux Klan to a six-year-old child? Thankfully, those men in white sheets are not very visible anymore. The absence of the white sheets and the burning of crosses reduced the terror of an era when the KKK flourished. But if the attitudes reminiscent of the KKK toward race are still in the hearts and minds of some people, we have a manmade disaster just as dangerous as a hurricane.

1. Recognizing There Is Bias

There are few, if any, who do not believe there are actually hurricanes. There is also a surface-level consensus about discrimination in the lives of some Americans. But, like attitudes toward hurricanes that strike in some other state, there are many who think discrimination does not affect them or that it is not serious. Just as with hurricanes, these people don't evacuate or board up the windows with plywood. They quietly think, *It won't affect me. I can just ride the storm out.*

According to a Pew Research Center study, Americans say there is at least some discrimination against several groups in the United States, including 79% who say there is a lot of or some discrimination against Black people, 76% who say there is a lot of or some discrimination against Hispanic people, and 71% who see discrimination against Asian people. Recognizing there is a problem is the first step to recovery. But if you take a closer look at the Pew results, it's akin to being told that 21% of the people do not believe there are actually hurricanes, 24% of the people do not believe there are tornadoes, and 29% of the people deny there are wildfires. Imagine if you heard, *all those pictures of the destruction are fake hurricanes, tornadoes, and wildfires and are produced in Hollywood, so there is no reason to evacuate, board up your house or business with plywood, or take other safety precautions.* Your reaction might well be, *I am shocked there are so many crazy people in our country.* Although the percentages are not large, they are significant. When we deconstruct the hurricane/bias metaphor, these percentages illustrate that a consensus that might prompt a constructive response to racism bias or discrimination is quite fragile.

What drives perceptions about the extent and impact of bias and discrimination? There are hate crimes and blatant examples of overt racism and bias. But there are also smaller examples that contribute to the milieu of the hurt caused by bias. Micromessages are small, commonplace, typically implicit messages. A simple example might be the way I acknowledge or introduce everyone at a court meeting. I could acknowledge everyone the same way: I could address everyone by their first names or by their last names. Or I could acknowledge some one way and others not: e.g., Attorney or Mr. Williams as compared to Susie or nothing-said for the woman at the meeting, whether she's an attorney or not. This difference is a negative micromessage to the women in this example, and it is a negative micromessage about them to others observing.[4] As this example suggests, micromessages can be positive or negative. When negative they are described as *microaggressions,* communicating hostile, derogatory, or negative attitudes toward stigmatized or culturally marginalized groups. Harvard University psychiatrist Chester Pierce coined this term to describe insults and dismissals that he regularly witnessed being inflicted upon people of color.[5] The term morphed into a word used to describe the casual degradation of any socially marginalized group, including LGBT people, people living in poverty, and people who are disabled.[6]

Microaggressions are measured by how they are perceived by the recipient. The persons making the comments may be otherwise well-intentioned and unaware of the potential impact of their words.[7] If you are a victim of microaggressions, you are hurt in a way that the perpetrator is not. The perpetrator of the microaggression may well ask *What? What did I say wrong?* Or the perpetrator may cast blame, *She is really oversensitive!* Frequently the product of our implicit biases, these messages are cumulative to a point where psychologically they are equivalent to more blatant forms of harassment.[8]

While there are critics of the microaggression concept, studying microaggression is a starting point to better understand the role implicit bias plays in the justice system.[9] Courts have become more sophisticated in eliminating the kind of blatant bias that existed in the past. Racial bias and gender bias task forces helped, and in some instances, judicial misbehaviors have resulted in ethics violations.[10] But microaggressions still plague the judicial system, and much remains to be done.

2. Progress in Reducing Bias

We are a nation where many people believe in American exceptionalism. However, the nation can only achieve that exceptionalism by confronting the racial inequality and bias that has been a part of our nation's fabric for far too long. Over 50 years ago, President Lyndon B. Johnson appointed the Kerner Commission in response to the wave of riots in many U.S. cities. "White society," the Kerner Commission reported, "is deeply implicated in the ghetto. White institutions created it, white institutions maintain it, and white society condones it."[11] The nation, the Kerner Commission warned, was so divided that the United States was poised to fracture into two radically unequal societies—one Black, one White. The Kerner Commission Report concluded: "Racial prejudice has shaped our history decisively; it now threatens to affect our future. . . . This deepening racial division is not inevitable. The movement apart can be reversed. Choice is still possible. Our principal task is to define that choice and to press for a national resolution."[12]

To be blunt, it is time for an honest assessment of the role the players in the judicial system (judges, administrators, lawyers, and correctional officials) have played in contributing to where we presently are. Yes, there has been progress in many areas identified in the Kerner Commission Report. Overt racism and efforts to constrain where Americans of color live, work, or attend school have greatly diminished. But there is still a lot to do. We have not fully achieved the kind of justice system that is fair, effective, and respected. Until we do, the real American exceptionalism will not happen.

To put this in the context of our hurricanes, the reason we are so good at confronting natural disasters is because they arrive quickly and are ferocious and graphic. Almost everyone knows total denial is not a safe shelter. Maybe more of us need to be shaken by pictures of the bewildered faces of small children who cannot understand the brutal parts of our nation's racial history. Maybe more of us need to hear the agony of mothers' fear for the fate of their Black sons. Many Americans are worn out about the struggle for equality. The reason we have not made sufficient and sustained progress in reducing bias is like a failed response to a hurricane. There are people who do not respond to: *Evacuate Now! Board up your house and flee!* Like the people who are willing to risk their lives to ride out the hurricane, there are people in denial about the manmade disaster of racial bias.

3. The Dimensions of the Problem Facing Courts

In 1906, Roscoe Pound gave a speech at the American Bar Association entitled *The Causes of Popular Dissatisfaction with the Administration of Justice*.[13] Pound spoke of the many factors that contributed to dissatisfaction with the American system of justice. A century later, there have been enormous improvements in the structure of the administration of justice. We have seen technology make courts more efficient. Courts have e-filing and, as a result of the Covid-19 pandemic, many courts have become more accessible via Zoom hearings. But despite all of the technological innovations, courts have still not met the fundamental challenge of reducing popular dissatisfaction with the administration of justice.

Fewer than four in ten Americans believe they can trust other people.[14] If you don't trust the people you know like your co-workers or neighbors, why would you trust a public institution? Why would you trust people who do not look like you? That lack of trust drives a lack of trust in public institutions generally. While the lack of trust in institutions is not specifically focused on courts, lack of trust in the court system is especially problematic because of the courts' reliance on voluntary acceptance and obedience of its orders. Courts resolve conflicts ranging from parenting time in divorce settlements, to criminal law, to the great unresolved issues of our day. A belief in a court's wisdom or legitimacy is essential.

The loss of confidence in all public institutions in the United States has been significant over the past several decades. Gallup has asked about confidence in seven institutions from 1973 to the present: "organized religion, public schools, the Supreme Court, Congress, newspapers, organized labor, and big business."[15] Respondents were asked to rate their confidence as either a great deal, quite a lot, some, very little, or none. Gallup considers "a great deal" and "quite a lot" as expressions of confidence.[16] The average confidence among those seven institutions was 44% to 46% from 1973 to 1976, fell to 32% in 1991, rebounded slightly to 38% in 2001, and more recently has settled in at about 27% from 2007 to 2019.[17] While trust in local government fares better, more than three-quarters of adults say that, compared to twenty years ago, Americans are less confident in the federal government.[18]

Courts have not escaped the general dissatisfaction Americans have with the legislative and executive branches of government. The bellwether for approval of the court system is typically the United States Supreme Court. Gallup regularly asks respondents whether they "approve or disapprove of the way the Supreme Court is handling its job," and the overall numbers show a decline in approval and an increase in disapproval.[19] The Marquette University Law School conducted a study in September 2021 that found nationwide approval for the United States Supreme Court falling to 49%—down from 66% in 2020. That poll showed that 39% of people view the court as a mechanism to decide cases mainly on politics. These results are similar to Gallup's 2021 survey in which only 40% of respondents indicated approval of the Supreme Court's decisions. This represents, by two percentage points, a new low in Gallup's trend dating back to 2000.[20] Blacks and Hispanics generally have less trust in all U.S. institutions. Historically, Gallup has reported lower United States Supreme Court approval numbers for non-Whites than for Whites.[21] Recently, approval of the United States Supreme Court by women has diminished. In 2018, for the first time, a gender gap surfaced. Approval by men for the United States Supreme Court rose to 60%, and approval by women fell to 43%.[22] The Gallup's 2021 survey shows that for the last several years, a 12-point gender gap of Supreme Court approval remained at a standstill.[23]

Perhaps the United States Supreme Court's diminished favorability is affecting how the public views all federal courts, or maybe there is a general feeling that federal courts are not working well. The Gallup 2021 survey also reveals a steep decline in the percentage of Americans who express "a great deal" or "fair amount" of trust in the judicial branch of the federal government, from 67% in 2020 to 54% in 2021. The current reading is only the second sub-60% trust score for the judicial branch in Gallup's survey, along with a 53% reading from 2015.

And if all this is not enough troubling news, a survey from the Annenberg Public Policy Center of the University of Pennsylvania found that more than a third of Americans say they might be willing to abolish the Supreme Court or have Congress limit its jurisdiction if the court were to make decisions they or Congress disagreed with. The survey found that 34% of Americans might be willing to do away with the Court if it "started making a lot of rulings that most Americans disagreed with." And 38% said that when Congress disagrees with the Court's decisions, "Congress should legislate against the Supreme Court's ruling on that issue or topic." This erosion of respect for the Court and its judicial independence is certainly alarming.

While the Annenberg study focused on the United States Supreme Court's approval as a bellwether for approval of the nation's judiciary, the majority of the cases decided in this country are in state courts. It is plausible that state courts are viewed more favorably than either the United States Supreme Court or the federal courts. For years, the National Center for State Courts has commissioned a series of annual surveys to benchmark the public trust in state courts. In 2021, they found that 64% of those surveyed said they had either *some* or *a great deal of* confidence in state courts,[24] down from the 2018 high of 76%, and the lowest since they started measuring in 2012 (though higher than for other institutions and higher than federal courts, which they reported at 60% and the Supreme Court at 63%).[25] When asked if state courts provide equal justice to all, 47% responded *not well* or *not well at all*. In terms of demographics, the 2021 analysis reported that "ratings of the courts' performance reached a new low among White voters (46 percent excellent/good, 53 percent just fair/poor) but are still higher overall than among Black (35 percent excellent/good, 63 percent just fair/poor) or Latino voters (44 percent excellent/good, 55 percent just fair/poor)."[26]

Should we be concerned about polling results? Truly independent courts will not endure long if there is not at least significant public support for courts. Courts need adequate and stable funding and are unlikely to get that if there is not public support. But beyond funding, one need only to look around the world to see examples of courts, which were once respected for their important role in protecting liberty and which are now crushed by authoritarian forces with little pushback from the populace. Divisions about how people see their courts based upon their race or gender is simply not healthy. Court leaders cannot afford to be delusional about the degree to which courts are respected and trusted.

4. Significant Forces Impeding Effective Action to Combat Bias

Courts are led by judges but employ a lot of people. Some of those people are in constant contact with individuals who enter the courthouse or seek the assistance of courts. Security is emphasized in many courthouses, making the security personnel likely to be your first courthouse encounter. When you enter, you must go through a magnetometer and perhaps be searched by a security guard. If that routine security process does not appear fair or otherwise results in a microaggression from a security guard, the person may well then enter the courtroom with an edge. But entry into the courthouse is only one part of the issue. Courts have their own organizational cultures. Those court cultures are driven in part by a workforce that likely mirrors the attitudes of the country. Do judges have implicit biases? Of course.[27] Do court employees (like the security guard who committed a microaggression on someone going through the court security screening process) have implicit biases? The answer to that question is yes as well.

Court leadership to address bias issues is critical. The actions of judges and court employees are a signal not just to the public, but to all the other judges and court employees. A court's culture can be a place of serenity, committed to elimination of bias, but the culture can also be an impediment to reducing bias. Attempts to reduce bias can be stifled by entrenched cultures, systemic dysfunction, and shifts in leadership.

Is diversity in the workplace an important value for courts? Would more diversity in courts, whether among judges or judicial staff, make a difference? The premise of the importance of workforce diversity is that a diverse workforce is more likely to understand the perspectives and experience of those we serve. In July 2019, the Brennan Center for Justice published *State Supreme Court Diversity*, which detailed disparities on state courts across the country, drawing on more than sixty years of data.[28] At that time, in 22 states, no judges publicly identified as people of color, including in eleven states where people of color make up at least 20% of the population. There were no Black justices in 28 states, no Latino justices in 40, no Asian American justices in 44 states, no Native American justices in 47 states.

Courts are almost uniquely incapable of impacting their own composition. A law firm can focus hiring practices to create a firm with diverse lawyers and support personnel, but courts cannot demand much of appointing authorities and are wholly without influence when it comes to elections of judges. Diversity of the employees of a court, however, is something court leadership can impact; and there are other opportunities to promote diversity within the legal profession.

Recently, the Florida Supreme Court decided to prohibit faculty diversity quotas for continuing legal education programs. While saying that it understood the objective of a policy requiring a minimum number of diverse faculty at section-sponsored CLE (Continuing Legal Education) programs, the Court said such a policy was "out of bounds" and that "quotas based on characteristics like the ones in this policy are antithetical to basic American principles of nondiscrimination." The Florida Supreme Court found it "essential" that "the Florida Bar withhold its approval from CLE programs that are tainted by such discrimination."[29] Rigid quotas are controversial. There are those who believe that quotas for CLE panels are remedial and address long standing deficiencies of diversity. Diversity on panels can produce a more meaningful discussion. Three older White men talking about the challenges of gender discrimination simply have very little likelihood of creating an engaging discussion. But the mere mention of even loose quotas or a commitment to diversity can bring out the worst in us. Unfortunately, there are also those who oppose diversity for all the wrong reasons.

If achieving workforce diversity in courthouses is a challenge, perhaps education is a good complementary strategy to reducing bias. California, Florida, New York, Texas, and Vermont are among the states that require some form of implicit bias training for judges and lawyers.[30] Education might lead individuals to acknowledge that bias, racism, and discrimination are features of our society and are embedded within systems and institutions. Surely that is a productive start in the journey of reform. The idea that bias, racism, or discriminatory incidents are not aberrations but instead are manifestations of structural and systemic features of our society might serve as the foundation for progress.

The National Center for State Courts recently released a report entitled *The Evolving Science on Implicit Bias*.[31] The report cites two lessons regarding how courts have addressed implicit bias. First, some change strategies may slightly reduce the strength of negative implicit associations. Second, the reductions of negative implicit associations typically do not last long. It is difficult to change people's attitudes and behaviors with short-term educational interventions. But does this mean we should not seek to educate ourselves on the promising and best practices to interrupt biases?

Poorly conceived implicit bias training can unintentionally reinforce harmful stereotypes. Poorly conceived implicit bias training can also lead to complacency by artificially inflating confidence that there has been cultural change. If you are an avid gardener, you know that tending to the weeds is a regular event. The same is true of trying to achieve cultural change to eliminate racism, bias, and discrimination. *We did implicit bias training two years ago, why would we need to do anything this year?* is a lot like the gardener who says, *I picked the weeds in the spring when I planted the garden, why would I need to do it again this year?* People cannot leave their implicit biases in the trunk of their car when they arrive at work and put them back on when they head home. If we are to be effective in reducing racism, bias, and discrimination, we cannot underestimate the headwinds of the manmade hurricane that has descended upon us.

Fear is a powerful enemy of reason. Both fear and reason are essential to human survival, but the relationship between them is unbalanced. Reason may sometimes dissipate fear, but fear frequently shuts down reason. As Edmund Burke wrote twenty years before the American Revolution, "No passion so effectually robs the mind of all its powers of acting and reasoning as fear."[32] Our Founders had a healthy respect for the threat fear poses to reason. They knew that, under the right circumstance, fear can trigger the temptation to surrender freedom to a demagogue promising strength and security in return. They worried that when fear displaces reason, the result is often irrational hatred and division. As Justice Louis D. Brandeis later wrote, "Men feared witches and burnt women."[33] Fear contributes to the ferocity of the manmade hurricane of bias that we face. Not being dismissive of those fears may well be a third lesson of the evolving science of implicit bias. "White population decline does not merely trigger the threat considered in most studies of demographic change—that is, status threat," but it may also "elicit fears that the in-group will actually cease to exist."[34]

Complacency can set in when trying to achieve cultural change to reduce bias. *We completed training programs, and I thought we all agreed they were good, and we were committed to a new view of the world.* People often suppress their real desires and feelings for a variety of personal reasons in group settings. Fear of *what happens if I speak up* is a common concern. The result is that the groups appear to agree when they really do not, and bad decisions are made, and actions are taken that are contrary to everyone's desires. Some refer to this as the Abilene Paradox.[35]

Theories of social conformity suggest that human beings are often very averse to acting independently or contrary to the trend of the group. The crux of the Abilene Paradox is that groups have just as many problems managing their agreements as they do their disagreements.[36] Conversations about race, sexuality, and other aspects of bias are so scary for some people that they simply sit quietly through the training program and after work put their implicit biases back on after retrieving them from the trunk of their car.

It is too often difficult to have an honest conversation about race and bias. The key to achieving an honest conversation about race and bias is trust. As Robert Shaw said about trust and balance:

A high level of trust allows people to say what is on their minds and not feel that it will come back to hurt them. A sufficient level of trust ensures that lines of communication are open and that no one is hiding information or wasting time trying to decide the political implications of his or her views.[37]

In 1997, President Bill Clinton announced, One America, the President's Initiative on Race, or the One America Initiative.[38] The goal was to convene and encourage community dialogue throughout the country about race. The One America Advisory Board's legacy was its publication of "best practices" for racial reconciliation and dialogue, guidelines designed to help communities discuss how to address racial and ethnic divisions in productive ways.[39] The idea was that national dialogue on race will lead to positive race relations. There are no simple answers about racial and other forms of bias, but there are uncomfortable truths. Talking about race or bias in general can arouse intense emotions such as dread (for White men or straight people) and anger and frustration (for people of color or other groups who feel discriminated against). Dread, anxiety, anger, and frustration are bound to disrupt communication and healthy dialogue. Discussions about bias will reveal a variety of world views. Even if the discussion about bias is offensive to some, there are forces that impede constructive progress.

We cannot underestimate the headwinds of the manmade hurricane that has descended upon us. Change is difficult for many of us. A bad known is too often preferred over a potentially good but uncertain unknown. There are forces that impede constructive progress toward eliminating racism, bias, and discrimination. Giving up is not an option, nor can we, as with a hurricane, simply evacuate.

5. Preparing for Hurricane Bias: The Parable of Two Wolves

"A fight is going on inside me," the grandfather said to his grandson. "It is a terrible fight, and it is between two wolves. One is evil—he is anger, envy, sorrow, regret, greed, arrogance, self-pity, guilt resentment, inferiority, lies, false pride, superiority, and ego." The grandfather continued, "The other is good—he is joy, peace, love, hope, serenity, humility, kindness, benevolence, empathy, generosity, truth, compassion, and faith. The same fight is going on inside you—and inside every other person, too." The grandson thought about it for a minute and then asked his grandfather, "Which wolf will win?" The grandfather simply replied, "The one you feed." That same good wolf is in each of us. It must rise up and do something that contributes to the cultural change of how we see people who are not like us. There really cannot be a place in courthouses for those who are driven by the evil wolf. Instead, we need to feed the good wolf.

Systematic or cultural change is, in a sense, like an effective response to the Covid pandemic. We need herd immunity from the evil wolf of implicit bias. Do you want a start at introspection about the implicit bias you might have? Take the Harvard Implicit Association Test (IAT).[40] Implicit biases are based on implicit attitudes or stereotypes that operate below the radar. As a result, individuals are not necessarily aware that implicit biases may be affecting their behaviors and decisions. Indeed, research shows that even individuals who consciously strive to be fair and objective can nonetheless be influenced by implicit biases.

Social scientists use a variety of methods to measure implicit bias, but the most common is reaction time.[41] Reaction time measures are based on the reflexive system's pairing of two stimuli that are strongly associated (e.g., elderly and frail) more quickly than two stimuli that are less strongly associated (e.g., elderly and robust).[42] The Harvard IAT offers web-based reaction time tests in over fifteen areas such as weight, age, race, and religion that anyone can take.[43]

Are judges influenced by implicit biases despite their training and conscious efforts to be fair and objective? The safest answer is to concede that judges are appointed, sometimes elected but never anointed as a saint. Judges (and lawyers) are humans with all the frailty that brings with it. Neutrality is important for a judge unless it masks that the judge cares. There has historically been a view that a judge should emphasize impersonality and dispassion. Emotions have been viewed as inherently irrational, disorderly, impulsive, personal, and inconsistent with the legitimate exercise of judicial authority in the courtroom. But insight about emotion, including bias, is critical. In *State v. Hutchison* the court said, "Judges, being flesh and blood, are subject to the same emotions and human frailties as affect other members of the species."[44] And at her confirmation hearing, Justice Sotomayor said,

> What I was talking about was the obligation of judges to examine what they're feeling as they're adjudicating a case and to ensure that that's not influencing the outcome. Life experiences have to influence you. We're not robots to listen to evidence and don't have feelings. We have to recognize those feelings and put them aside. That's what my speech was saying...[45]

Research by Professors Jeff Rachlinski, Chris Guthrie, and Judge Andrew Wistrich, suggests that judges are influenced by implicit bias. Professor Rachlinski and his colleagues found a strong White preference on the IAT among White judges. In keeping with the general population findings of the Implicit Association Test, the Black judges showed no clear preference overall. The researchers also reported some evidence that implicit bias affected judges' sentencing decisions, though this finding was less clear. Most importantly, the researchers found that, "when judges are aware of a need to monitor their own responses for the influence of implicit racial biases, and are motivated to suppress that bias, they appear able to do so."[46]

6. Dealing with Hurricane Bias with Procedural Fairness

People that come to court are highly sensitive to the processes of procedural fairness. For decades, social scientists have studied procedural fairness in courts. What are the conditions that will increase the likelihood people will leave the courtroom feeling good about the process? Former Congresswoman Barbara Jordan would often say that what the people want is very simple: the people want an America as good as its promise.[47] That is precisely what the people want of courts. Fairness is a value that the American public expects and demands from judges. Fairness is also a value that people who work in a courthouse share. Judges want to achieve fairness. Court employees want to serve people fairly, and they want to be treated by judges and court leadership fairly.

With all due deference to Roscoe Pound, who claimed there were multiple causes of the American dissatisfaction with the administration of justice, the perception of unfair or unequal treatment "is the single most important source of popular dissatisfaction with the American legal system."[48] Yale law professor Tom Tyler, who is the most-cited scholar in the field, has suggested that there are four key components to achieving procedural fairness:

- *Voice*: individuals' ability to participate in the case by expressing their viewpoint before decisions about them are made;
- *Neutrality*: consistently applied legal principles, unbiased decision-makers, and transparency about how decisions are made;
- *Respect*: the treatment of individuals with dignity and explicit protection of their rights; and
- *Trust*: that authorities are benevolent, caring, and sincerely trying to help individuals—a trust garnered by listening to individuals and by explaining or justifying the decisions that address litigant needs.[49]

When judges adhere to these procedural fairness components, people are more satisfied with their court experience. When courthouse staff, who frequently interreact with the public more than judges, adhere to these procedural fairness components, it is even better. In an extensive study of the California state courts, perceptions of procedural fairness were "the strongest predictor by far" of public confidence in the state court system itself.[50] Researcher David Rottman, who led the California study, concluded that "[p]olicies that promote a sense of procedural fairness are the vehicle with the greatest potential to change how the public views the state's courts and how litigants respond to court decisions."[51]

In addition to improving satisfaction with the individual proceeding and the overall court system, there's another important effect—increased compliance with court orders.[52] Professor Tom Tyler's research (as well as the research of many other scholars) found that adherence to procedural fairness principles leads to a greater sense of the legitimacy of an authority figure, a legitimacy that leads to greater compliance.[53] Whatever the sequence, studies show a direct relationship between people's judgments about the fairness of a proceeding and "a variety of law related behaviors, including immediate decision acceptance or rejection; decision adherence over time, rule-breaking behavior, well-being and recovery, and cooperation with police, courts, and school officials."[54]

Voice is a powerful component in achieving procedural fairness. People who come to court have a powerful urge and need to express their thoughts, experiences, or even their questions. Being listened to is *symbolically* important, as it reveals that group authorities value the individuals' standing in their social group. Litigants make a correlation between the ability to speak and a judge's respectful treatment of them as individuals. From a litigant's point of view, if the judge does not respect litigants enough to hear their side or answer their questions, how can the judge arrive at a fair decision? The belief that one can go to legal authorities with a problem and receive a respectful hearing in which one's concerns are taken seriously is central to most people's definition of their rights as citizens in a democracy.

Voice is an interactive process. Messages being sent are sometimes not the same as those being received, which can result in conflict, mistrust, ambiguity, or confusion. Intimidation can inhibit voice. But even if you appropriately eliminate intimidation, achieving voice also requires good listening skills. Listening is both visible and invisible. As we listen, we make judgments. In interpersonal communication generally, studies indicate that nonverbal behaviors account for a high percentage of the meaning conveyed.[55] Many of those nonverbal behaviors are things we may not be aware of. And therein lies one of the implicit bias problems.

As we listen, we may not even be aware of the unintended messages we are sending. *She wasn't listening to me. He acted like he had already made up his mind!* If you are a judge, you can (and should) video tape yourself. You may learn you are a great interactive listener, but you may also learn that you did not appear to be listening or that you came across as having already made up your mind. And you might learn that there are differences in how you come across to those who come before you that vary with what they looked like.

Judges face real-world pressures. For many judges, volume creates pressure to move cases in assembly-line fashion—a method that obviously lacks in opportunities for the people involved in those proceedings to feel that they were listened to and treated with respect. The vast majority of cases do not go to trial. Judges cannot rely then on the safeguards attendant to trial to provide litigants and others with a feeling of respect, voice, and inclusion. People's impressions of judges and our justice system—for better or worse—are largely formed by their participation in mass-docket arraignments, probation revocations, calendar calls, and other settings that are not trials.

In this context, the National Center for State Courts (NCSC) Report on the Evolving Science of Implicit Bias (see Chapter 2) notes that there are certain situations that are more likely to elicit implicit responses. These include those situations where complex decisions need to be made quickly, or where the decision-maker cannot otherwise fully process all of the incoming information. In other words, as NCSC reports the psychological research as finding: "Decision makers who are rushed, stressed, distracted, or pressured are more likely to apply stereotypes–recalling facts in ways biased by stereotypes and making more stereotypic judgments–than decision-makers whose cognitive capacities are not similarly constrained."[56]

There are ways to lessen the effects of implicit biases. The first step is introspection. Identifying your own tendencies or putting it in the language of the parable of the grandfather speaking to his grandson: "I know the good wolf and I intend to feed that good wolf." But beyond self-awareness of your own implicit biases, some of the causes of diminished decision-making abilities include fatigue (like sleep deprivation), depleted resources (like glucose levels), mood, fluency (i.e., ease of processing information), and multitasking. Each of these has the possibility of feeding the bad wolf. Each has the potential to unleash our implicit biases upon our decision-making or our appearance. For example, fluent, easy-to-understand information appears to be more accurate than dense, hard-to-understand information, but that is not necessarily the case all the time. Mood affects the way we process information. Although it seems counterintuitive, people in a positive mood are generally more likely to engage in reflexive decisions, which raise the potential for the evil wolf to prevail. Those in a negative mood who are aware of their mood are more likely to engage in more reflective, deliberative processing. If you are in a negative mood, the good wolf may have the upper hand.

7. Is There a Storm in the Courthouses?

Many people have little contact with the court system, so it is understandable that they feel overwhelmed and lost when they are confronted with an unfamiliar legal system. This lack of knowledge about the court creates a state of ambivalence or anxiety, and in part explains the lack of trust too many courts face. The lack of depth to most news coverage about the courts, little education about the courts in school, and the misinformation of entertainment television all contribute to the challenges that courts face. *Law & Order* might be a successful television drama, but it is a poor substitute for knowing what to expect when you show up in court. The experience that people have in our court system is critically important. That experience will shape how people perceive the justice system as a whole. People who come to court share their experience with family and friends. And that is why it is imperative that steps are taken to ensure that these courts enhance public trust in the justice system.

In our era of diminishing trust in institutions, trust is earned, not given. If there ever was an era that people just trusted the judiciary to do the right thing, it is an era long since passed.[57] Just as trust can be earned, it can be dissipated. There is a certain majesty to some courthouses. The building is magnificent, almost like being in a museum or on a movie set. But there are other courthouses that are frankly pretty shabby, or a multi-use room used by the City Council as well. In some courtrooms the benches are perched high, and everyone is told to rise when the judge enters the room.[58] Judges usually wear robes.[59] All of this contributes to intimidation, and there is a cost of overdone intimidation,[60] which suppresses a willingness to talk or ask questions.[61] Honest misunderstandings about what a judge expects a person to do could easily be corrected, and that does not happen if people are afraid to ask questions. Intimidation is not a prerequisite for dignified court proceedings.[62]

Intimidation may create false impressions or false positives. The judge sternly asks *Sir, do you understand my order? Yes, your honor!* replies the person, even though the person is completely bewildered. The people may have questions about what is expected of them, but intimidation drives them to just want a way out of the courthouse. Asking a judge why he or she ruled a certain way, even in a very polite manner, does not happen often. If litigants understand why the decision was made, they may not like the result, but they are more likely to comply with the order.[63] This atmosphere of intimidation makes people vulnerable to microaggressions when what is really important is that they leave the courthouse feeling like they were listened to and treated with respect.

If you shop at a high-quality store and you stand looking lost, there is a very good chance that some employee will approach you and ask, *May I help you?* Although you might leave without buying anything, you feel good about the place. Unfortunately, if you come to many courthouses early in the morning and stand looking lost, the security guard will kick you out. Moreover, judges and court leaders often don't know what their courthouse experience is like for the average citizen. Perhaps courts need silent shoppers.

Justice Mary Russell, when she was the Chief Justice of Missouri, decided to be her own courthouse silent shopper. Dressed in t-shirt and capris she went unannounced to courthouses and had the opportunity to talk with all types of visitors to the courts. No one recognized that she was the Chief Justice of the State. She called it "undercover judge." And this is what she learned: "As I sat shoulder to shoulder with people in the hallways, I could feel their anxiety, their worry and their apprehension as they waited their turn to appear in front of the judge. For most, it was their first time in any courtroom, and they did not know what to expect."

Silent shoppers need not be an undercover judge (or Chief Justice). Dr Laurinda Porter conducted observations of the Hennepin County Minnesota District Court. Dr. Porter noted that "almost all the judges (she) observed used nonverbal behaviors...that are considered to be ineffective and in need of improvement. About one-third of the judges used these ineffective behaviors frequently." Some of these behaviors on the bench included the more obvious concerns such as a failure to make eye contact, focusing on a cup of coffee, and the use of a sarcastic, neutral, or exasperated tone of voice. She also noted actual displays of negative emotions, such as anger or disgust, and sighing audibly.[64]

Conclusion

In this period of turbulence where trust in institutions is fractured and there are profound differences about how to deal with bias, the most difficult topics must be honestly discussed. It is not an easy era to be a leader, and a natural tendency is not to welcome dissent or embrace conflict. Dissenters can be obstructionists and a pain to deal with, but dissenters who provide a different perspective need to be heard. Court leaders need to listen to unfamiliar voices and set a tone for candor and risk taking. Now, more than ever, tone is important in the courthouse.

The lack of trust in courts as an institution and the biases that courts exhibit will not be reversed simply by focusing on judges, albeit they are critical. The experience in a court is many times driven not just by the judge but by a lot of people. As a person walked through security, did they experience microaggressions from the security guard? When they went to the clerk's counter to find their assigned courtroom, what was that experience like? To prepare for Hurricane Bias, courts need an entire workforce that is prepared to effect cultural change. Panic, fear, and low morale are not conducive for creative change.

Motivating court employees and judges starts with court leaders motivating themselves. If court leaders are stressed out, everyone else is also. If court leaders are afraid to take on the challenge of reducing and then eliminating bias everyone else will be afraid too. But if court leaders are obviously enthusiastic and committed to make a culture change everyone (OK nearly everyone) will be enthusiastic too. Enthusiasm is contagious. It can start at the top with the attitude of court leaders; regrettably, it can end there too. Change to address bias starts within the soul and then works outward. You can change, and then the next time you hear someone say they can ride out a natural hurricane or the manmade Hurricane Bias, tell them how dangerous that is.

So, You'd Like to Know More

- Tom Tyler, Why People Obey the Law (1990).
- Center For Court Innovation, To Be Fair: Conversations About Procedural Justice (Emily La Gratta ed.), https://www.courtinnovation.org/sites/default/files/documents/To_Be_Fair.pdf.
- Hon. Kevin S. Burke, It Is All About the People Who Work in the Courthouse, Trends in State Courts (2011).
- Hon. Kevin S. Burke, Innovative Courts Encourage Dissent, Trends in State Courts (2015).
- Roger A. Hanson & Brian J. Ostrom, Understanding and Diagnosing Court Culture, https://www.ncsc.org/__data/assets/pdf_file/0017/15461/understanding_court_culture.pdf.

About the Author

Kevin Burke is a Senior Judge in Minnesota and founding member of Procedural Fairness for Judges and Courts. He teaches at the University of Minnesota Law School and the University of St. Thomas Law School. His website is JudgeBurke.com.

Endnotes

1. Kathryn Reid, *2005 Hurricane Katrina: Facts, FAQs, and How to Help*, WORLD VISION (Nov. 25, 2019).

2. Esther Fleming, *What Locations Did Hurricane Sandy Affect?*, SIDMARTINBIO (Sept. 16, 2020); Michalis Diakakis, *Hurricane Sandy Mortality in the Caribbean and Continental North America*, 24 DISASTER PREVENTION & MANAGEMENT 132 (2015).

3. *See, e.g.*, Sarah Lynch Baldwin & David Begnaud, *Hurricane Maria Caused an Estimated 2,975 Deaths in Puerto Rico, New Study Finds*, CBS NEWS, Aug. 28, 2018, https://www.cbsnews.com/news/hurricane-maria-death-toll-puerto-rico-2975-killed-by-storm-study-finds/.

4. Mary Rowe, *The Saturn's Rings Phenomenon*, 50 HARV. MED. ALUMNI BULL. 14 (1975).

5. Tori DeAngelis, *Unmasking 'Racial Micro Aggressions;' Some Racism Is So Subtle That Neither Victim Nor Perpetrator May Entirely Understand What Is Going On—Which May Be Especially Toxic for People of Color*, 40 MONITOR ON PSYCHOL. 42 (2009), https://www.apa.org/monitor/2009/02/microaggression.

6. *Id.*

7. *See, e.g.,* Lilia M. Cortina, Vicki J. Magley, Kerri Nelson & Dana Kabat-Farr, *Researching Rudeness: The Past, Present, and Future of the Science of Incivility*, 20 J. OCCUPATIONAL HEALTH PSYCHOL. 299 (2017).

8. Bernice B. Donald & Sarah E. Redfield, *Arcing Toward Justice: Can Understanding Implicit Bias Help Change the Path of Criminal Justice?*, 34 CRIM. JUST. No. 2 (2019); *see also, e.g.,* Ian Cheney, Sharon Shattuck & Manette Pottle, *Picture A Scientist*, TRIBECA FILM FESTIVAL (2020).

9. Scott O. Lilienfeld, *Microaggression: Strong Claims, Inadequate Evidence*, 12 PERSPECTIVES ON PSYCHOL. SCI. 138 (2017).

10. Specific ethics rules address issues of fairness, such as Model Rule 2.2, which explicitly instructs judges to "perform all duties of judicial office fairly and impartially." Rule 2.3 (A) calls for judges to perform these duties "without bias" and Rule 2.3 (B) reads: "A judge shall not, in the performance of judicial duties, by words or conduct manifest bias or prejudice, or engage in harassment, including but not limited to bias, prejudice, or harassment based upon race, sex, gender, religion, national origin, ethnicity, disability, age, sexual orientation, marital status, socioeconomic status, or political affiliation, and shall not permit court staff, court officials, or others subject to the judge's direction and control to do so." Judges are also required to hold attorneys in proceedings accountable for conduct that manifests bias.

11. REPORT OF THE NATIONAL ADVISORY COMMISSION ON CIVIL DISORDERS (KERNER REPORT) (1968), http://www.eisenhowerfoundation.org/docs/kerner.pdf.

12. *Id; see also* Kevin S. Burke, *The Kerner Commission: 50 Years Later, What Has—and Has Not—Changed?*, MINNPOST, Mar. 20, 2018.

13. Roscoe Pound, *The Causes of Popular Dissatisfaction with the Administration of Justice*, ABA (1906), https://law.jrank.org/pages/11783/Causes-Popular-Dissatisfaction-with-Administration-Justice.html#:~:text=Roscoe%20Pound%2C%201906%20ROSCOE%20POUND%20presented%20"The%20Causes,and%20a%20preview%20of%20his%20theory%20of%20law.

14. *See* Lee Rainie, Scott Keeter & Andrew Perrin, *Trust and Distrust in America*, PEW RES. CTR. (July 22, 2019), https://www.pewresearch.org/politics/2019/07/22/trust-and-distrust-in-america/.

15. GALLUP, CONFIDENCE IN INSTITUTIONS, https://news.Gallup.com/poll/1597/confidence-institutions.aspx (hereinafter Gallup, Confidence) (showing annual data through 2020); Lydia Saad, *Military, Small Business, Police Still Stir Most Confidence* (June 28, 2018), https://news.Gallup.com/poll/236243/military-small-business-police-stir-confidence.aspx. [hereinafter Saad, *Military*].

16. *Id.* (Saad, *Military*).

17. GALLUP, CONFIDENCE, https://news.Gallup.com/poll/1597/confidence-institutions.aspx.

18. *Trust and Distrust*, PEW RES. CTR., https://www.people-press.org/2019/07/22/trust-and-distrust-in-america/.

19. GALLUP, SUPREME COURT, https://news.Gallup.com/poll/4732/supreme-court.aspx.

20. Jeffrey M. Jones, *Approval of U.S. Supreme Court Down to 40%, a New Low*, GALLUP, Sept, 23, 2021, https://news.gallup.com/poll/354908/approval-supreme-court-down-new-low.aspx.

21. GALLUP, SUPREME COURT, In July 2016, disapproval led approval 52% to 42%, and in June 2005, disapproval led approval 48% to 42%. *Id.*

22. *Id.*

23. *See* Justin McCarthy, *Women's Approval of SCOTUS Matches 13-Year Low Point*, GALLUP, https://news.gallup.com/poll/243266/women-approval-scotus-matches-year-low-point.aspx.

24. *State of the State Courts 2021 Poll*, https://www.ncsc.org/topics/court-community/public-trust-and-confidence/resource-guide/state-of-the-state-courts.

25. *Id.*

26. GBAO, *2021 State of the State Courts—National Survey Analysis*, available through link at https://www.ncsc.org/topics/court-community/public-trust-and-confidence/resource-guide/state-of-the-state-courts.

27. Jeffrey J. Rachlinski, Sheri Lynn Johnson, Andrew J. Wistrich & Chris Guthrie, *Does Unconscious Racial Bias Affect Trial Judges?*, 84 NOTRE DAME L. REV. 1195 (2009).

28. ALICIA BANNON & LAILA ROBBINS, BRENNAN CENTER FOR JUSTICE, STATE SUPREME COURT DIVERSITY (2019) https://www.brennancenter.org/our-work/research-reports/state-supreme-court-diversity.

29. Amanda Robert, *Florida Supreme Court's Order Blocking Diversity Quotas for CLE Instructors Could Impact ABA Programs*, ABA JOURNAL (2021), https://www.abajournal.com/news/article/florida-supreme-courts-order-may-also-impact-aba-programs.

30. Melissa H. Stanzione, *ABA Groups Urges Implicit Bias Training for Judges, Lawyers*, BLOOMBERG LAW (2020), https://news.bloomberglaw.com/us-law-week/proposal-seeks-implicit-bias-training-for-judges-lawyers.

31. JENNIFER K. ELEK & ANDREA L. MILLER, NATIONAL CENTER FOR STATE COURTS THE EVOLVING SCIENCE ON IMPLICIT BIAS: AN UPDATED RESOURCE FOR THE STATE COURT COMMUNITY (2021), https://ncsc.contentdm.oclc.org/digital/collection/accessfair/id/911. See Chapter 2 in this book.

32. EDMUND BURKE, ON THE SUBLIME AND BEAUTIFUL (1757).

33. Whitney v. Cal., 274 U.S. 357, 376 (1927).

34. Hui Bai & Christopher Federico, *White and Minority Demographic Shifts, Intergroup Threat, and Right-wing Extremism*. PSYARXI (Oct. 2020).

35. Jerry B. Harvey, *The Abilene Paradox: The Management of Agreement*, 3 ORG. DYNAMICS (1974).

36. *Id.*

37. ROBERT BRUCE SHAW, TRUST IN THE BALANCE: BUILDING SUCCESSFUL ORGANIZATIONS ON RESULTS, INTEGRITY, AND CONCERN (1997).

38. https://clintonwhitehouse2.archives.gov/Initiatives/OneAmerica/PIR.pdf (figure out how to cite this)

39. *Id.*

40. *IAT*, https://implicit.harvard.edu/implicit/takeatest.html.

41. Patricia G. Devine, *Stereotypes and Prejudice: Their Automatic and Controlled Components*, 56 J. PERSONALITY & SOC. PSYCHOL. 5 (1989).

42. *Id.*

43. *About Us*, PROJECT IMPLICIT, http://www.projectimplicit.net/about.html.

44. State v. Hutchinson, 271 A.2d 641, 644 (1970).

45. Transcript of the Sotomayor Confirmation Hearings, OPENING STATEMENT BY JUDGE SONIA SOTOMAYOR BEFORE THE SENATE JUDICIARY COMMITTEE, July 13, 2009 (as prepared for delivery), sotomoyor_transcript.pdf (epic.org).

46. Chris Guthrie, Jeffrey J. Rachlinski & Andrew Wistrich, *Inside the Judicial Mind*, 86 CORNELL L. REV. 777 (2001).

47. *Barbara Jordan Quotes on the Constitution,* https://everydaypower.com/barbara-jordan-quotes/.

48. Jason Sunshine & Tom R. Tyler, *The Role of Procedural Justice and Legitimacy in Shaping Public Support for Policing*, 37 LAW & SOC'Y REV. 513, 517 (2003).

49. Tom R. Tyler & Justin Sevier, *How Do the Courts Create Popular Legitimacy? The Role of Establishing Truth, Punishing Justly, and/or Acting Through Just Procedures*, 77 ALB. L. REV. 1094, 1105–07 (2013/2014); Tom R. Tyler, *Procedural Justice and the Courts*, 44 CT. REV. 28, 30–31 (2008).

50. DAVID B. ROTTMAN, TRUST AND CONFIDENCE IN THE CALIFORNIA COURTS: A SURVEY OF THE PUBLIC AND ATTORNEYS 6, 24 (2005), http://www.courts.ca.gov/5275.htm.

51. *Id.* at 24; *see also* David B. Rottman, *Procedural Fairness as a Court Reform Agenda*, 44 CT. REV. 32 (2008).

52. *See, e.g.*, TOM R. TYLER, WHY PEOPLE OBEY THE LAW 8, 172 (1990); Tom R. Tyler, *Legitimacy and Legitimation*, 57 ANN. REV. PSYCHOL. 375 (2006); Tom R. Tyler, *Procedural Justice, Legitimacy, and the Effective Rule of Law*, 30 CRIME & JUST. 283, 286 (2003); Kevin J. Burke, *Just What Made Drug Courts Successful?*, 36 N.E.J. CRIM. & CIV. CONFINEMENT 39, 56–58 (2010); DEBORAH A. ECKBERG & MARCY R. PODKOPACZ, FAMILY COURT FAIRNESS STUDY 3, 29, 32–33, 34–35, 38 (Fourth Judicial Dist. [Minn.] Research Division 2004), http://www.mncourts.gov/Documents/4/Public/Research/Family_Court_Fairness_Report_Final_(2004).pdf.

53. *Tyler & Sevier*, 77 ALB. L. REV. at 1101–02.

54. *Id.* at 1102–05.

55. *See generally* R.E. Riggio & H.R. Riggio, *Face and Body in Motion, in* ENCYCLOPEDIA OF BODY IMAGE AND HUMAN APPEARANCE (Thomas F. Cash ed., 2012).

56. *See* NCSC, STRATEGIES TO REDUCE THE INFLUENCE OF IMPLICIT BIAS 4; *see also* Galen Bodenhausen & Meryl Lichtenstein, *Social Stereotypes and Information-processing: The Impact of Task Complexity*, 52 J. PERSONALITY & SOC. PSYCHOL. 871 (1987); Daniel D. Gilbert & J. Gregory Hixon, *The Trouble of Thinking: Activation and Application of Stereotypic Beliefs*, 60 J. PERSONALITY & SOC. PSYCHOL. 509 (1991).

57. *See* Susan M. Olson & David A. Huth, *Explaining Public Attitudes Toward Local Courts*, 20 JUST. SYS. J. 41, 42–43 (1998).

58. *See Trauma-Informed Courts*, OFF. FOR VICTIMS OF CRIME TRAINING & TECH. ASSISTANCE CTR., OFF. OF JUST. PROGRAMS, https://www.ovcttac.gov/taskforceguide/eguide/6-the-role-of-courts/63-trauma-informed-courts/.

59. *See, e.g.*, TEX. MUN. CTS. ASS'N, SO, NOW YOU'RE A JUDGE!, http://www.tmcec.com/public/files/File/Judges/So%20now%20youre%20a%20judge.pdf (last visited Jan. 15, 2021) (giving municipal court judges the option to wear robes).

60. *See generally* PA. COMM'N ON CRIME & DELINQ., FREE TO TELL THE TRUTH - PREVENTING AND COMBATING INTIMIDATION IN COURT: A BENCH BOOK FOR PENNSYLVANIA JUDGES (Jan. 2011), https://crimegunintelcenters.org/wp-content/uploads/2017/11/FreetoTelltheTruthPreventingandCombatingIntimidationinCourt_PA2011.pdf.

61. *See, e.g.*, Cynthia Gray, *Reaching Out or Overreaching: Judicial Ethics and Self-Represented Litigants*, 27 J. NAT'L ASS'N ADMIN. L. JUD., no. 1, 2007 at 97, 112–16 (describing negative effects that intemperate judges have had on *pro se* litigants).

62. *See* OFFICE OF JUSTICE PROGRAMS, OFFICE FOR VICTIMS OF CRIME TRAINING & TECHNICAL ASSISTANCE CENTER, TRAUMA-INFORMED COURTS, https://www.ovcttac.gov/taskforceguide/eguide/6-the-role-of-courts/63-trauma-informed-courts/.

63. *See* Tom R. Tyler & Yuen J. Huo, Trust in the Law: Encouraging Public Cooperation with the Police and the Courts, 43–45 (2002); Leon Jaworski, *Judicial Intimidation: A Threat to the Advocate's Independence*, 1 Litig. 11, 13 (1975).

64. Laurinda Porter, Report on Observations of Fourth Judicial District Judges in March and April 2001 4 (Hennepin Co., Minn., June 2001).

TWENTY

Roundtable Conversation: Reflections on Implicit Bias, Silence, and Invisibility

Patty Ferguson-Bohnee, Pointe-au-Chien, Faculty Director Indian Legal Program, Sandra Day O'Connor College of Law at Arizona State University

Mary Smith, Cherokee, Vice Chair, VENG Group; Chair and Founder, Caroline and Ora Smith Foundation

Professor Sarah E. Redfield, University of New Hampshire

A Note from the Editors: Our primary goal for the first *Enhancing Justice* book was to increase awareness of implicit bias and its negative manifestations. For this book, our primary goal was to address the question of what next. Once we are aware of implicit bias, what strategies can be used to interrupt that bias? We also had a second goal, to broaden the very diversity of the book itself—to have more diverse authors, to hear more voices. In this, we particularly wanted to assure a space for Native voices, so often silenced, to be heard. We are honored to be supported in this by the voices of Patty Ferguson-Bohnee (Pointe-au-Chien) and Mary Smith (Cherokee) in this Chapter and Jack Fiander's (Yakama) Chapter, *Should Justice Really Be Blind? Can We Really Stay Silent? Implicit Bias in the Courtroom.* We have ourselves learned much from working with them. For just one example, we've included as an Appendix, Chief Standing Bear's 1879 speech, which strikes us in its language as perhaps a perfect parallel to our current language defining an ingroup, perspective taking, and the use of privilege—all topics relevant to interrupting implicit bias.

From our research and our own lived experiences, we know the many ways that explicit and implicit bias play out to exclude and limit others—the very antithesis of the sought-after inclusion in Diversity, Equity, and Inclusion (DEI). We know that this exclusion is perceived by the human brain in the same way as physical pain. In this Chapter, we confront exclusion in its starkest form: invisibility. It is sobering. We asked Professor Ferguson-Bohnee and Attorney Smith for strategies to use now that we are more aware. They suggested we learn more, be more conscious of whom we are including and whom we are excluding—be aware of falling into stereotypes and into confirmation bias. They also suggested we further support Native students along a pathway to the profession and visit a reservation to understand their heritage and their presence in the modern world. We have already benefited from hearing these Native leaders, and we invite and urge our readers to join us in taking up their suggestions.

Sarah Redfield: My name is Sarah Redfield. I'm a Professor of Law at the University of New Hampshire. I am participating in this interview from my home in Maine.

I acknowledge that the land we occupy is territory of the Maliseet, Micmac, Penobscot, and Passamaquoddy, known collectively as the Wabanaki, People of the Dawnland. Maine remains the home of over 8,000 members of these tribes who enhance the life and fabric our State.

I'd like to welcome both of you and ask you to start by introducing yourselves and giving just a bit of your own past experience with the concept of implicit bias. That said, I know in our current milieu it is hard to speak about implicit bias without speaking about explicit bias, so please introduce yourselves however you feel most appropriate to our topic overall.

Patty Ferguson-Bohnee: My name is Patty Ferguson-Bohnee. I am Pointe-au-Chien from Louisiana. I teach at the Sandra Day O'Connor College of Law at Arizona State University in Phoenix. I run the law school's Indian Legal Clinic and am the Faculty Director of the Indian Legal Program.

I am participating from the ancestral lands of the Akimel O'odham and further acknowledge that Arizona is home to 22 Tribal Nations covering 27% of the land base.

As I think about our topic, the first thing I realize first that growing up in Louisiana, invisibility was a major part of my life from very early on. When I started school, it was the first year that the elementary schools in my area integrated. Louisianans saw people as either Black or White, and they didn't often recognize Indians. This was supported by a legal structure that focused on race. I remember the teachers taking head counts. They would say, "Okay, all White girls raise your hands; all White boys raise your hands; all Black girls raise your hands; all Black boys, raise your hands." And I never raised my hand. The teacher would get so upset because the count was off: *Somebody is not raising their hand.* The other students would say, *Patty's here, and she's not raising her hand.* But the school didn't have a spot on the teacher's tally for anything other than Black and White and so they had to report the count was off. But my siblings and I would never raise our hands.

Sarah Redfield: That's a pretty clear, early example of not being seen or valued for who you are.

Patty Ferguson-Bohnee: Yes. I also remember one time the science teacher was talking about Louisiana and how there used to be tribes, but they're all gone now. My sister raised her hand and said, *Well, I'm Native American, I'm from Pointe-au-Chien*, to which the teacher simply replied that he didn't know there were any Indians in Louisiana. So it was just part of the fabric of the school that we were excluded.

Sarah Redfield: And you and your sister were children. We know implicit biases start being seen at a very young age. But these examples are more than that. These are the grown-ups, the leaders in your school, who don't know you exist in your state. Might I ask if things improved as you continued on in your education and work?

Patty Ferguson-Bohnee: My experiences with the American Bar Association (ABA), especially my early experiences, are good examples to answer this. I remember when I first started attending ABA meetings. One of the first meetings I attended was with other minority attorneys, and they were presenting the findings from a report about minority lawyers. I noticed that there was no mention about Native Americans in that report. When I asked why Native Americans were excluded, the response was that they are not statistically significant.

Sarah Redfield: Well, it's not much different from the teachers in Louisiana, an underlying message that you don't exist, aren't worth counting, or don't count for enough.

Patty Ferguson-Bohnee: I was actually very upset at the time. Mary was President-elect of NNABA (National Native American Bar Association) at that point, and she focused her presidential term on developing and producing a study about Native American attorneys.

Sarah Redfield: I'm hoping we will talk about that study and its impact a bit more later in our conversation. At this point, can you talk about the impact of being labeled "not statistically significant"? Is it the same as not being important?

Patty Ferguson-Bohnee: Yes, or worse, not being there at all, not present in the legal landscape. This impacts Native attorneys, Native people who are working in the law, and our tribes as a whole. I think it's because we're not visible that law schools don't necessarily think about us with regard to recruiting students, that employers don't think about us with regard to hiring. We are not really a focus for the job market, and that impacts our ability to become judges and achieve other professional success. This has real word consequences—it impacts students, the profession, and the Native American community as a whole.

Sarah Redfield: Mary, do you want to comment on Patty's remarks? Or take us in some other direction?

Mary Smith: I'm Mary Smith. I am Vice Chair of the VENG Group where I consult on legal and regulatory issues. I am also Founder, Chair, and CEO of the Caroline and Ora Smith Foundation, named after my mother and grandmother, respectively. The foundation supports and trains Native American girls and women in the science, technology, engineering, and mathematics (STEM) fields. I am participating from the Chicago suburbs.

Chicago is located on and near the traditional home and meeting place for many Tribal Nations. We acknowledge and honor the Three Fires Confederacy—Potawatomi, Odawa, and Ojibwe Nations. Tribes who have historical relationships with the lands in greater Chicago and Northern Illinois through trade, travel, and habitation also include the Peoria, Kaskaskia, Miami, Ho-Chunk, Sac & Fox, Mascouten, and Menominee, as well as other tribes whose names have been lost as a result of genocide and ethnocide in European colonialism and United States expansion. We honor the many other Indigenous peoples who call this place home—past, present, and future. Not only do we honor the history and traditions of Native Americans but also acknowledge the diverse and vibrant indigenous community of approximately 75,000 who currently reside in Chicago and its surrounding area.

I agree with Patty. I don't know how many times, not just in written studies but even when you're watching the news or you're reading newspapers—they talk about all the groups, they'll say African American, Latinx, Asians. And then I'll wait to hear Native Americans, but I don't hear us mentioned.

Sarah Redfield: And do you then hear that the Native American population is not statistically significant or that they tried to find a Native American to include but they just couldn't find anyone?

Mary Smith: Yes. I hear that a lot. I note that the Native American population is actually one of the fastest growing populations in the country.

Sarah Redfield: Can you give us an example of this kind of situation?

Mary Smith: Yes. I guess each group experiences discrimination and the manifestations of implicit bias in different ways. Situations are different for different populations. But I can give a couple of recent examples. We're taping this interview in November, which is National Native American Heritage Month, so I'm sure Patty, like me, has gotten a lot of requests for speaking engagements.

One thing that's been happening lately is the effort to offer land acknowledgments to acknowledge the indigenous lands on which we're all sitting. While there is some controversy about this, I try to look at it in a positive way as an indication that people are at least making an acknowledgement of our histories, even if there's not action behind it. I hope we can build off this and press for action as well as acknowledgement.

Just a couple of weeks ago, I got a draft for a land acknowledgement that was going to be used for a Chicago program. Luckily, it was sent to me before it was issued. Chicago is on the lands of the Three Fires Confederacy (the Ojibwe, Odawa, and Potawatomi Nations). The proposed acknowledgement included text about how Jean Baptiste Point du Sable, a Black man who married a Native American woman, settled and developed what became Chicago. I was a bit outraged because I didn't understand why acknowledging du Sable did anything to acknowledge the Indigenous communities. As I told the drafter of the announcement, I could see that because du Sable was not White, in one sense you wouldn't consider it White supremacy that he sold land in Chicago. But he still represented European traditions, not Indigenous ways. That's a second point about this episode and the whole idea of du Sable being the first non-White developer. The land didn't need to be developed, there was a thriving Indigenous community here long before the Europeans came. And a third point is that the proposed acknowledgement failed to speak at all to the very vibrant community of about 75,000 Native Americans in Chicago now.

On this last point, seeing Native Americans only in the past is another aspect of invisibility. People like the drafters of the acknowledgment seem to think that Native Americans are a people of the past and fail to recognize that they are here now.

Sarah Redfield: I just want to be sure I understand your point with this story. Instead of acknowledging Chicago's Three Fire Confederacy, the acknowledgement was for a Black settler, making him the visible figure. Could you also talk about Patty's reference to the study you did for the Native American Bar?

Mary Smith: Yes, we did do the study for the National Native American Bar Association when I was president. On one of the first pages there's a quote I love from Chief Joseph of the Nez Perce tribe: "It does not take many words to speak the truth." Indeed. The overarching sentiment of the Native American attorneys we studied in the NNABA study was that they felt invisible. They could be sitting alongside other attorneys in a law firm or law school or bar meeting. They're there if you choose to take a look at them, but I think it's easy for people to ignore them.

Sarah Redfield: Are you saying that we make an explicit choice to say, *I'm not going to include Mary or Patty* or are you saying that our quick implicit response is not to connect you to the work we are doing?

Mary Smith: I think it is the latter. It's part of being invisible. I have one other anecdote that really encapsulates this as well. I was working on a project for a political campaign. What works to engage Native Americans politically, as you can imagine, is different than what might engage other groups. I think one difference is that Native Americans are more attuned to visuals than some other groups. There were four or five different versions of a poster the project wanted to use;

each had a different image on it, and each had verbiage about Native voices being heard. Myself and my colleague, who were the only Native Americans working on this project, both were very clear which poster we thought would be most successful. Our recommendation went up the hierarchy in the organization, where an Asian woman, a Black man, and a White guy all decided that a different poster would be the best. The irony was that the whole point of the poster was that Native voices should be heard (but not ours).

Sarah Redfield: This is such a telling anecdote. You have both talked powerfully about the idea of invisibility and about the label "not statistically significant." We all know from our lived experiences and also from the overwhelming research on this point, how powerful labels are. They have power not only in translating us to the outside world but also in translating what the outside world thinks of us to us, what Claude Steele and other researchers call a stereotype threat. That idea makes these stories troubling in even more ways. They certainly run contrary to our goals for meaningful DEI and contrary to the current thinking and wisdom about the importance of people being able to be authentic in their work experiences.

I'm wondering if you could talk a bit about how you see these ideas playing out in terms of the pipeline to the professions and how this kind of invisibility and messaging might impact young people who might want to enter that pipeline or even others who may be considering leaving it.

Patty Ferguson-Bohnee: I've been thinking about some of the things that Mary said about being basically relegated to the past and how this invisibility really impacts the present—because people don't think about Native Americans in the present. If people don't think about us in the present, it's hard to address issues impacting us in the present.

In schools, where all the children are learning and forming their ideas, we do not generally teach about Native Americans as being part of the modern-day society. With regard to the legal profession, Native Americans entry into in the legal profession started much later than our sister bars of color. It wasn't until the late 1970s that Native Americans were really gaining entry to the profession, so young Native Americans who might be interested in law don't have many role models. Mary was able to uncover a lot of information around these issues, which I think she can talk about. For now, let me say that it's hard for young Native students to see themselves as attorneys or judges. As a young Native person, I did not even meet a lawyer until I was in high school in a mock trial competition. In fact, the opposite is often the case, where young Native Americans do meet or see a lawyer, it's often in a negative situation. The law has been used to force the removal of Native Americans from their homelands also, and to take children from their homes to boarding schools. Forced removal operates through legal infrastructure. Then there are issues that may impact families, which are often through the court system, and which often have negative results. There hasn't been a lot of discussion about how the law can positively impact Native people.

Sarah Redfield: I love this mock-trial story It's a great illustration of how intervention along the educational pipeline can have positive impact. Could you tell us the details?

Patty Ferguson-Bohnee: Yes, I agree. I'm from a small town, and none of the kids I went to school with had parents who are lawyers. I participated in a mock trial competition in high school where we beat the area magnet schools. We went to the State competition, and I thought *I can do this, you know.*

This was obviously a great experience for me and helped build my confidence. But, speaking more generally, there hasn't been a lot of investment to show Native youth what those opportunities are. There are some efforts; ASU has a pathway to law program where we try to do some outreach to reservation students and Native students. We are trying to offer a different entry to the pipeline than the more negative one that catches Native students in the entry to the juvenile justice system. I know that you worked a lot on that, Sarah, with the school to prison pipeline. We both know that that's where we see a significantly disproportionate number of students of color and Native children.

Sarah Redfield: Yes, the school to prison pipeline is disproportionately populated. There are far more Native youth there than there are in the general population. And I think it's important to emphasize for our readers that the research documents that this is *not* because they are more poorly behaved. Some of the research suggests the explanation, at least in part, is in implicit biases and low expectations held by educators.

Patty Ferguson-Bohnee: Yes. The whole idea of the school to prison pipeline is not likely to generate any positive experiences. I think that we have to figure out how to address that school to prison pipeline and then also show Native people that there are other opportunities.

Sarah Redfield: We also see the same issues in other areas beyond education.

Patty Ferguson-Bohnee: Yes, invisibility impacts us in all areas—access to resources, legal rights, land rights, the justice system, opening the door to go to law school, healthcare, infrastructure, environment, voting: everything. Invisibility is part of a systemic pattern that has undermined Native American inclusion in modern-day society. I was watching a TV show this weekend where the main character is supposed to be a Native American but is played by a Chinese American. This was something recently filmed, so even though it's modern, and even though there are definitely Native actresses, it's okay in the producer's view for non-Natives to play these parts.

Sarah Redfield: So it's an interesting example, isn't it, of how we make choices. Perhaps the producers set out saying, I'm not hiring a Native woman for this. But more likely not. If pushed, they probably would say they couldn't find someone Native. It sounds remarkably like other hiring examples. We all know this; we all favor our own cultural groups, do good for our ingroups, not necessarily meaning to do bad for people who are in the outgroup, but that's the result. Maybe in this case, it was also an example of not needing to be authentic and not doing the perhaps-harder pipeline work to hire diversely and inclusively.

Patty Ferguson-Bohnee: My guess is that the people who made the decision aren't concerned with how this impacts Native people. I also think there's just been a long history of excluding Native Americans from opportunities. This means people always think that they can dress up or pass as a Native and that there aren't likely to be any repercussions for it, where there might be for another race or another group.

Sarah Redfield: There are other issues around passing as a Native, times when people try to take advantage.

Patty Ferguson-Bohnee: Yes. This is another issue that Mary worked on, what we call box checking. We know that many individuals check the box indicating that they are Native to get into law school. But the number who check that they are Native American on law school applications doesn't match the number of Natives graduating or going into the profession. Until recently there hasn't been any repercussion for that. But now the Native bar is asking schools to adopt policies against it.

Sarah Redfield: This seems both ironic and egregious.

Patty Ferguson-Bohnee: It is really harmful. On the one hand, schools can look at the numbers of boxes checked and applaud themselves on their diversity. At the same time, it misrepresents what it is to be a Native attorney. It's so easy for people to just check that box when they have no real affiliation with the tribe, but it's something different to be a tribal person. And you don't become that person by checking the box. So that's why we are engaged in a big push for tribal affiliation, because it's a political affiliation, because tribes are political entities.

Sarah Redfield: Mary, Patty's been talking about work you've been doing. Do you want to add something to this piece of the conversation?

Mary Smith: Patty raised a good point when she started with the story of a non-Native person playing a Native American in a film. In the media or in movies, we're kind of lagging behind. No one would even try to cast someone in blackface to be Black in a movie, but somehow this respect is not extended to Native actors. It's still okay today to present yourself as Native American if you're not Native American. This is similar to the point I was making with my land acknowledgement example. We would not think it's acceptable to feature Asian Americans in a Black history month proclamation, but we do think it's acceptable to highlight a Black settler in an acknowledgement intended to recognize the Indigenous peoples ties to the lands.

Sarah Redfield: As I'm listening to you talk about the importance of visibility and authentic visibility in the modern world, I'm remembering a small exercise that I tried. Mahzarin Banaji, one of the researchers who developed the Implicit Association Test, suggests creating a diverse screensaver as a strategy for interrupting implicit bias. The idea is to show yourself different images of people that don't look exactly like you. I set out to do this for myself, googling to find images of Native Americans to put in my implicit bias-interrupting screensaver. It turned out to be very difficult and a lesson in its own right. I think it comes back to what Patty said earlier about being in the past. I could find many images of Chiefs and of battles but very few modern pictures. I didn't find the Native American computer scientists. Mary, I know you work with supporting Native American women in STEM—I didn't find the images of Native American researchers. You won't be surprised to know that I did find an image of a terrific law professor who to this day appears on my screensaver!

Patty Ferguson-Bohnee: Glad to be there, Sarah!

Mary Smith: I want to reflect a bit further on how influenced we are by media. If that media reflection is predominantly in the past, I think it's hard for the society to understand the present and change this idea of invisibility. The past perpetuates its image too well. If you were to ask anybody to name a famous Native American, I'd bet the answer is Sitting Bull or names like his; I'd actually bet no one who was born in the 20th century would make the list.

Sarah Redfield: This is serious in both directions, for the Native Americans whose prominence is not recognized and for the rest of us who just don't see them. As you said before, if you've never known a lawyer or a judge, it's hard to picture yourself in the profession. To me it's a little bit reminiscent of the many women scientists who actually did the work and saw men get the credit. We know very few of their names, we don't recognize their pictures.

There is also another side to this labeling and visibility. It's when the labels perpetuate an offensive history or image. I think most of us are familiar with this either from the national headlines or, like me, from team names or mascots at schools right near where I live. Would you talk about how the changing of these sports images has played an important part in addressing some of the concerns we've been talking about?

Mary Smith: I think it's part of the same things we've been exploring already, that Native Americans are not seen as real present-day, vibrant people, that they're somehow of the past, and they're cartoonish or caricatures. What we've seen in some of these cases—and I think most famously with the Washington football team—is that there were years of advocating for them to change the name and all that time harm was being done.

Those kind of sports names and mascots do real harm to Native people, particularly Native youth. And despite the studies, despite all the advocacy, the only reason the name or the mascot got changed is because sponsors pulled their funding; until money talked, it wasn't done. I think there are still three major professional sports teams in the United States with offensive names or mascots. I think it's going to take some further corporate help to get to zero.

Sarah Redfield: Could you talk a bit more about the harms here?

Patty Ferguson-Bohnee: Just adding on to what Mary has said, because major sports teams have misused names and mascots for so long, people engage in behaviors that really are offensive. I went to Stanford as an undergrad, and while I was there one of the newspapers and the alumni association were trying to bring the Indian back as a mascot. As part of this effort, when some of the alumni would come to campus, they would wear headdresses, and make war whoops—really ridiculous and offensive things. They would never think to do anything to try to honor the Ohlone who were ancestral to that land. It goes back to this acceptance of allowing negative stereotypes that perpetuate more negative stereotypes. This inevitably encourages bullying and does psychological harm to Native students. Some of this continues and sustains itself because we have such a lack of accurate history about Native Americans in the U.S. public education system that then can be perpetuated by these stereotypes, so that's very unfortunate.

Sarah Redfield: You've raised a lot of issues for us to consider. I'd like to focus in on those near to our own professions. We three are all lawyers, and many of the folks who will be reading this book will be lawyers. And so, we all know—we learned this in law school if we didn't know before we got there—the incredible power of language. In many ways, that's what you're both talking about, the power of language to be used to label or to make invisible or to silence. Or, in the alternative, to do good, to support a modern positive image. So what is it we can do? In the context of being lawyers, what is it we can do to help change that reality?

Mary Smith: I think we have to start at an early age. All three of us have worked on pipeline issues, and we know that if you want to change the trajectory, and you're starting at college or even high school, you're probably starting too late. It's a matter of showing the Native kids that they can be whatever they want—if they want to be a doctor, if they want to be a scientist, if they want to be a lawyer. I think that a lot of Native children don't see that for themselves and then it impacts what they study.

The other point here, as Patty mentioned, is that a lot of Native history is not taught, or to the extent it is taught, it's taught in simplistic and often incorrect ways. You know, all cowboys are good and Indians are bad. It's not really a nuanced history. We're taping this the day after Thanksgiving. There's the traditional Thanksgiving story that I think most of us were taught as kids and most kids are still taught. It's not the real story, but, unfortunately, it's still what's taught.

Sarah Redfield: I'd just take a minute here to mention a new book for young people on this—*If You Lived During the Plimoth Thanksgiving*. It's written by Chris Newell, a Wabanaki leader and educator whom I know from his work as the first Native director of Maine's Abbe Museum. The book is being promoted as one for elementary school readers, but I think we can all benefit from its careful research and writing that provides an often undiscussed perspective on Thanksgiving.

Patty Ferguson-Bohnee: This kind of perspective is so important. Stories are important. It also goes well beyond that, especially within our legal system. We see systemic racism against Native people to rid the U.S. of its Indian problem: explicit legal policies that were meant to terminate, exclude, or assimilate Native people, to get rid of Native peoples' culture, to take children away from their families and heritage. We know these policy decisions were made, and I think we have to consciously recognize the role of the law in their implementation. We know the history of colonialism and the doctrine of discovery. But we don't pay much attention to hundreds of years of treaties between tribal nations and the colonial powers and then the United States. We have done little to really address all the problems that have resulted from these policies and their language, including the related court decisions calling Native Americans savage or inferior.

Sarah Redfield: I'm wondering what you say to those people who may say *Oh, that's so long ago, that wasn't us, it doesn't have to do with us today?*

Patty Ferguson-Bohnee: I disagree. Those legal policies have long term impacts, and you can see their results to this day in the lack of infrastructure and disproportionate access to healthcare, water, and electricity in certain places. For example, the Supreme Court used paternalistic language to create the concept of the guardianship and the trust responsibility. Almost one hundred years later, once Native Americans were declared United States citizens, this guardian/ward relationship was used to prevent Natives from voting. States and counties used the guardianship language to conclude that Native Americans "lacked the mental competency requirements as wards of the government" and were incapable of managing their own affairs. Similarly, in the early 2000s, there was an effort to prevent Native Americans from serving on state commissions because they live on reservations and therefore are not fully part of the state's body politic. There is a lot of ignorance with regards to Native people.

Sarah Redfield: Could you reflect a little further on the power of public language, particularly in court opinions? These writings carry with them additional and enduring authority. Jack Fiander talks about this in his Chapter, where he discusses the *Towessnute* opinion in Washington. There the state Supreme Court recently overruled a 1920 decision that was tremendously demeaning to Native Americans. I'm interested in what you think about that approach, going to courts and asking for these very negative decisions or negative language and negative decisions to be overruled.

Patty Ferguson-Bohnee: At least once overruled a case cannot be cited again as precedent. As you suggest, addressing language is important. I think that was an important step for the Washington Supreme Court and the court system to address that. Recognizing that the earlier opinion was wrong and that there's a harm to allowing it to remain can play a role in moving forward with Indigenous or tribal people from those areas. They are part of some sort of healing with past wrongs.

Sarah Redfield: As I'm listening to you both talk about the importance of being visible and present in the present day, I'm thinking about the Native women who are missing and murdered. Could you could talk a bit about that issue and how it relates to the other points we've been discussing?

Mary Smith: There is an epidemic of missing Indigenous women. It's a kind of implicit bias or confirmation bias that starts at the point when someone is reported missing and law enforcement responds by saying, *Oh well, she was known to run away*, and just dismisses the concern. The investigation doesn't start out full throttle and then—because of the policies Patty was discussing earlier and because of decisions that were made decades or even hundreds of years ago—the investigation is poorly set up or not set up at all. The approach is further complicated by jurisdiction in Indian country, which, particularly for criminal jurisdiction, has been called a jurisdictional maze, and it really is. Because in many cases tribes cannot prosecute felonies, it's left to the U.S. attorney's office to do so. Missing and murdered Indigenous women are not a priority, and the cases never even get prosecuted. There are other complicating factors. When a crime occurs in Indian Country, determining the location of the crime, the victim, and perpetrator all impact who has jurisdiction. For example, tribes typically do not have jurisdiction over nonmembers or White people. Many indigenous women are in relationships with non-Native people, so you basically have these lawless enclaves within the United States, where people can commit murder literally with impunity.

Sarah Redfield: So, there are places or possible perpetrators where there is no jurisdiction to proceed?

Mary Smith: Sometimes trying to decide who actually has jurisdiction can be overwhelming. Last year, during National Native American Heritage Month, we presented a live performance of a play called Sliver of a Full Moon. It's the story over several years of survivors, advocates, tribal leaders, and legislatures trying to get the Violence Against Women Act reauthorized. There's one scene in the play that you would think is just concocted for theatrical purposes, but it actually is a real portrayal of a situation where a crime is committed and there's literally no jurisdiction for anyone to respond. There is state law enforcement, there's tribal law enforcement, there is federal law enforcement, and they take out their tape measures to see where the crime occurred and who has jurisdiction.

We live in a system that was set up like that, and it allows a lot of injustice, particularly for Indigenous women.

Sarah Redfield: There are, of course, many other examples of a system that is oblivious to Native American communities or set up in ways that allow and perpetuate injustices for these communities. Patty, I know you have been visiting and staying with your family in Louisiana in an area heavily damaged by the most recent of our terrible hurricanes. I'm listening to Mary, and I'm thinking about some of what you have reported about how FEMA isn't really helping. There seems to be an extraordinary failure of government to recognize that Pointe-au-Chien live there and a disproportionate failure of our government to provide support. Could you just talk about this kind of experience as it relates to some of the other themes of this conversation?

Patty Ferguson-Bohnee: August 29 was the 16th anniversary of Hurricane Katrina. It was also when Hurricane Ida landed in our community. It was a second landing of Hurricane Ida. I knew it was going towards my community, and I could see that it was going to land in our community, and it did land in our community. But if you just went by the news coverage, you wouldn't know this. It's another example of our invisibility. There was no discussion anywhere, the news or on The Weather Channel anywhere, of Ida landing in our community. Even if you google it today, it's hard to find. Of course, I was watching the coverage at the time intensely. I did see one commentator point to the map and say the second landing was here but didn't say our name. When I looked at NOAA's (National Oceanic and Atmospheric Administration) mapping and reporting right after the storm, they had no pictures of our community or the Indigenous community next to us, even though the hurricane wreaked destruction straight through us. And of course, it's not just the news that didn't notice us; this invisibility has a cascading effect. Only 10% of our homes are habitable. We didn't get electricity or water back for over a month after Ida. State and federal resources have been absent; FEMA has been absent. We, along with the other tribes on the Gulf Coast, are not federally recognized. Disaster response is set up in three levels: federal response, state response, and then the local, which is the parish level response. We weren't a priority for any of those, and our people suffer the effects of these response failures.

Sarah Redfield: We've moved from invisible and not statistically significant, I'd say, to sometimes barely visible but still significantly unserved or disproportionately represented in negative ways. The two of you both have a visible presence in your communities and organizations, locally and nationally. I know Mary from our involvement with the ABA. In fact, Mary, you're running for president of the ABA, and if elected you will be the first Native American to head this prestigious organization.[*] Running has proven you to be very visible. I've known Patty from our work as well, much of it focused on law schools and on the school to prison pipeline research and intervention. ASU is the leading Indian law institution in the country. Again, a visible and important role. Despite your visibility, we have obviously not succeeded in addressing the systemic racism in our institutions or in achieving diversity, equity, and inclusion. I'm hoping each of you could give advice to our mutual communities and beyond.

Mary Smith: Well, we've talked a lot about experiences of really negative implicit bias and discrimination and, frankly, just horrendous acts that have happened and are still happening to Native Americans. But one thing that has not come out during this conversation that I think is very important to emphasize—and I think most Native people would say this—is that we are very resilient. Despite everything that has happened, and continues to happen, we are still here. We are still here despite, as Patty described, both the explicitly and implicitly biased experiences we have had. These are actions that massacre us; these are the scourges of diseases—we even see them today with Covid. Still, we are here, and we are one of the fastest-growing populations in the country. So I guess the advice I would give to people is to just try to listen and learn and ensure that Native communities are not forgotten, that Native people are treated as equal, that they are included and have a seat at the table. Bad decisions have happened in the past and continue to happen now. I believe that a lot of those decisions were made by other people making decisions on behalf of Native people, not Native people making decisions for themselves and being in charge of their own self-determination.

Sarah Redfield: That's a powerful closing, Mary. The story you told earlier about the poster is a tiny, tiny ironic illustration of this. My guess is that the poster the others chose didn't work out all that well.

Patty Ferguson-Bohnee: Right, and I think that I would just add that we know from the research that a lot of the negative impacts on Natives today, a lot of that is caused by the lack of knowledge among other decision-makers about Native people in modern-day society. This means efforts to make education curricula and programs more inclusive so important.

More specifically, I think also providing more support for Native kids for undergrad and the pathway to law school would be valuable. Our Native kids still have lower LSAT scores than other communities, we still have Native students who are

---

[*] Mary Smith is president-elect of the ABA, slated to take office in 2023.

first generation college. Accessing scholarships and funds to go to school and offering summer associate positions are needed.

To just put this in a bit of perspective. When I was an undergrad, one of my classmates was from the Navajo reservation. She studied by a kerosene lamp. We still have Native students in this country who don't have electricity or who have to take a bus for two hours to get to school; these factors really limit what they can be doing compared to their peers. We do know that if Native students are supported, once they get to school they are highly likely to succeed. This is true all along the pipeline, including law school. To use my own pathway as an example—when I went to law school, it was difficult. Because my dad had passed away, I couldn't qualify for private loans. Because my uncles were all fishermen, they couldn't qualify either. My little brother gave me some money for my rent, which helped me make it through.

Sarah Redfield: And I and all of us who work with you are grateful to him, and to you and your family for the ways you enrich our work. Could you expand on the pipeline idea and talk briefly about the specifics of a Native-relevant curriculum in law school?

Patty Ferguson-Bohnee: Native American issues transcend all areas of law. Even basic things like teaching that there are three sovereigns in a constitutional law class can help to increase recognition of, respect for, and an understanding of tribal governments. This is not just important for Native students but also for others who might practice in this area. Enhancing competence is good for the justice system, potential clients, and the ability to deliver legal services. There is likely to be malpractice if attorneys in some states, for example, where one of the 574 federally recognized tribes live, are not familiar with Indian law and the difference between federal Indian law and tribal law.

Sarah Redfield: On that point, one more question for you as an academic: How do you advise people to approach research regarding Native issues? As backdrop for this, I'd like to specifically recognize the importance of the groundbreaking work by Mary and the NNABA studying Native attorneys and the profession. It's not by chance that their report was called *The Pursuit of Inclusion*. I'd also acknowledge that there have been two more recent studies of the profession that have not included Native voices.

Patty Ferguson-Bohnee: Yes. If you're working on a study or doing an analysis, just think about who you know and who you don't know. Don't just rely on your ingroup. Ask yourself if you have sought out Native voices so that they are not just a footnote or less. It is important to ensure that we include Native people in studies and statistics and materials that will influence policy.

Sarah Redfield: I want to give each of you a chance to comment on anything that we haven't covered that you would like our readers to think about.

Mary Smith: My closing comments would be to advise people to try to learn more, whether it's reading or discussion groups or some other outreach to Native colleagues. I always suggest that folks read the Marshall Trilogy or the more recent Supreme Court cases. Or mentor a Native student or Native law student.

Sarah Redfield: I think you are both saying to seek out contact, be curious, educate yourself, ask questions. And perhaps we should add, think critically about information you hear or could gather. I can't thank you enough, each of you. I'm honored to count you as friends and colleagues and grateful for you taking the time to share your experience and knowledge with us.

So, You'd Like to Know More

Maybe you are a history buff?

- Read some of the famous Cherokee cases written by the first Justice Marshall that laid the groundwork for U.S. Indian law. The Marshall Trilogy:
    - Johnson v. M'Intosh, 21 U.S. (8 Wheat.) 543 (1823)
    - Cherokee Nation v. Georgia, 30 U.S. (5 Pet.) 1 (1831)
    - Worcester v. Georgia, 1 U.S. (1 Dall.) 515 (1832)
- Or, perhaps read another famous Indian law case, *United States ex rel. Standing Bear v. Crook*, 25 F. Cas. 695 (C.C.Neb. 1879). Seventy-five years before the Supreme Court would decide *Brown v. Board of Education*, this civil rights case was decided. The court had agreed to let a Ponca chief named Standing Bear speak. The Chief said: "This hand is not the color of yours, but if I pierce it, I shall feel pain. If you pierce your hand, you also feel pain. The blood that will flow from mine will be of the same color as yours. I am a man. The same God made us both." (See Appendix.)

Books we recommend:

- Dee Brown, Bury My Heart at Wounded Knee: An Indian History of the American West (1970).
- Roxanne Dunbar-Ortiz, An Indigenous Peoples' History of the United States (1977).
- Tony Horwitz, A Voyage Long and Strange: On the Trail of Vikings, Conquistadors, Lost Colonists, and Other Adventurers in Early America (2008).

- Tommy Orange, There There (2018) (New York Times bestselling novel).
- David Grann, Killers of the Flower Moon (2017).

Other materials

- The Pursuit of Inclusion: An In-Depth Exploration of the Experiences and Perspectives of Native American Attorneys in the Legal Profession (2015).
- Native American Institute, Guide to Land Acknowledgements, https://nai.msu.edu/about/guide-to-land-acknowledgements.
- State v. Towessnute, 197 Wash. 2d 574, 486 P.3d 111 (2020) (included with Chapter 6).

So, You'd Like to Do More

- Mentor a Native American law student. Or, better yet, mentor a Native American high school student.
- Visit a reservation. And, no, simply visiting the casino does not count!
- Support efforts to eliminate Native American team names and mascots.

About the Panelists

Patty Ferguson-Bohnee is a clinical professor of law, the faculty director of the Indian Legal Program, and the director of the Indian Legal Clinic at ASU. She has substantial experience in Indian law, election law and voting rights, and status clarification of tribes. Professor Ferguson-Bohnee has testified before the United States Senate Committee on Indian Affairs and the Louisiana State Legislature regarding tribal recognition and has successfully assisted four Louisiana tribes in obtaining state recognition. She has also advocated for the rights of unrecognized tribes in response to environmental disasters. Professor Ferguson-Bohnee has assisted in complex voting rights litigation on behalf of tribes, and she has testified before Congress on voting rights issues.

Before joining ASU, Professor Ferguson-Bohnee clerked for Judge Betty Binns Fletcher of the United States Court of Appeals for the Ninth Circuit and was an associate in the Indian Law and Tribal Relations Practice Group at Sacks Tierney P.A. in Scottsdale. As a Fulbright Scholar to France, she researched French colonial relations with Louisiana Indians in the 17th and 18th centuries.

Professor Ferguson-Bohnee, a member of the Pointe-au-Chien Indian tribe, serves as the Native Vote Election Protection Coordinator for the State of Arizona. She is a co-founder of the Native American Bar Association of Arizona and a former president of the National Native American Bar Association. She earned her J.D. from Columbia University School of Law and her B.A. from Stanford University.

Mary Smith, an enrolled member of the Cherokee Nation, is one of the most high-profile Native Americans in the country. Mary Smith is an independent board member and former CEO of a $6 billion national healthcare organization, the Indian Health Service. Mary currently serves on the board of PTC Therapeutics, Inc. (NASDAQ: PTCT), a global biopharmaceutical company focused on the development and commercialization of medicines that provide benefits to patients with rare disorders. She also serves on the board of HAI Group, a leading member-owned property-casualty insurance company for the affordable housing industry. She is also Vice Chair of the VENG Group, a national consulting firm. Earlier in her career Mary served as an attorney at Skadden, Arps, Slate, Meagher & Flom LLP, as a senior in-house counsel at Tyco International (a Fortune 200 company), and in government, both as Associate Counsel to the President in the White House and as a trial attorney at the U.S. Department of Justice.

In her bar association activities, Mary is the immediate past National Secretary of the American Bar Association and a former president of the National Native American Bar Association. She was the first Native American to serve as a commissioner on the ABA's Commission on Women in the Profession, and she has received the ABA Spirit of Excellence award for her trailblazing work on diversity and inclusion. She is also the founder and president of the only national organization that promotes Native American girls in STEM, the Caroline and Ora Smith Foundation.

Professor Redfield's bio is included with Chapter 1.

Appendix

All quoted from https://library.timelesstruths.org/texts/Stories_Worth_Rereading/Standing_Bears_Speech/

Standing Bear arose. Half facing the audience, he held out his right hand, and stood motionless so long that the stillness of death which had settled down on the audience, became almost unbearable. At last, looking up at the judge, he said:

> That hand is not the color of yours, but if I prick it, the blood will flow, and I shall feel pain. The blood is of the same color as yours. God made me, and I am a man. I never committed any crime. If I had, I would not stand here to make a defense. I would suffer the punishment and make no complaint.

Still standing half facing the audience, he looked past the judge, out of the window, as if gazing upon something far in the distance, and continued:

> I seem to be standing on a high bank of a great river, with my wife and little girl at my side. I cannot cross the river, and impassable cliffs arise behind me. I hear the noise of great waters; I look, and see a flood coming. The waters rise to our feet, and then to our knees. My little girl stretches her hands toward me and says, 'Save me.' I stand where no member of my race ever stood before. There is no tradition to guide me. The chiefs who preceded me knew nothing of the circumstances that surround me. I hear only my little girl say, 'Save me.' In despair I look toward the cliffs behind me, and I seem to see a dim trail that may lead to a way of life. But no Indian ever passed over that trail. It looks to be impassable. I make the attempt.
>
> I take my child by the hand, and my wife follows after me. Our hands and our feet are torn by the sharp rocks, and our trail is marked by our blood. At last I see a rift in the rocks. A little way beyond there are green prairies. The swift-running water, the Niobrara, pours down between the green hills. There are the graves of my fathers. There again we will pitch our teepee and build our fires. I see the light of the world and of liberty just ahead.

The old chief became silent again, and, after an appreciable pause, he turned toward the judge with such a look of pathos and suffering on his face that none who saw it will forget it, and said:

> But in the center of the path there stands a man. Behind him I see soldiers in number like the leaves of the trees. If that man gives me the permission, I may pass on to life and liberty. If he refuses, I must go back and sink beneath the flood.

Then, in a lower tone, "You are that man."

TWENTY-ONE

Children and the Law

Bias and the Juvenile Justice System

The Honorable Rhonda Hunter, 303rd Family District Court, Dallas, TX

A Note from the Editors: We have long admired Judge Hunter's work at the American Bar Association and in her home state of Texas and beyond. We respect and have learned from her lifelong work to achieve diversity, inclusion, and equity and her commitment to juvenile justice in our legal system. Judge Hunter recognizes the many critical junctures and decision points along the school to prison pipeline where discretion and implicit bias can influence outcomes in ways we might not intend. She offers suggestions for change from her own diverse experience. Her historical and personal perspectives help us to understand the issues more deeply. We are grateful for her work and her willingness to join us here to extend the reach and expertise of this book.

CHAPTER HIGHLIGHTS

- The trajectory of a child's entry into the juvenile legal system is formed by decision-making by teachers regarding who remains in the classroom, disciplinary actions of principals regarding referral to law enforcement or suspension or expulsion, police interaction with youth in neighborhoods, and security forces and police in the schools.

- Students are inequitably and disproportionately treated in the juvenile legal system, and early decisions can have lifelong collateral consequences.

- It is well-documented that decisions in the juvenile legal system are impacted by implicit biases. Virtually all decision-makers can benefit from becoming aware of their biases and following a more deliberate and thoughtful path for critical decisions. Examples of strategies are provided.

CHAPTER CONTENTS

Introduction

1. Historical Context
2. The Supreme Court Speaks to Juvenile Due Process et al.
   A. *In Re Gault* (1967), Juvenile Due Process Rights
   B. *Kent v. United States* (1966), Juveniles' Rights Before Transfer to Adult Court
   C. *Roper v. Simmons* (2005) and *Graham v. Florida* (2010), Life Without Parole and Death Sentence for Minor as Cruel and Unusual Punishment
3. Collateral Consequences and Adultification of Youth of Color
4. The Impact of Discretionary Decision-Making
5. Promising Approaches for Addressing Implicit Bias in Decision-Making

Conclusion

Introduction

Charlie, an 11-year-old African American child, has already spent a portion of his school day avoiding his teacher's threat of sending him to the principal's office for disrupting the class. He has now missed his bus and finds himself in the position of having to walk home. His mother is working, and he knows she cannot pick him up, just as he knows that if she finds out that he missed the bus he will be in big trouble. Beacuse he's walking home, he wants to stop to get a soda at the corner store. There's a sign on the door that says no more than four students can be in the store at any one time. Charlie knows that if he goes in, he will be followed as he walks around the store looking at candy and chips until he pays for his items and leaves the premises. Charlie knows that when he leaves the store and continues his walk home, women of other races will cross the street as they see him approaching with a small bag in his hand. As much as he wants to get home, he knows that running down the street in this neighborhood could result in a passerby calling the police. His mother has told him that if he encounters the police that he should place his hands where they can be seen and not talk back to the officer. Charlie watches his step, carrying the key to the apartment where he stays on a chain around his neck. Really, every step along the journey is made easier if he is entirely alone, if he avoids encountering another person along the way.

Now, imagine if this child were Anglo in an Anglo neighborhood. Imagine if the child were an African American female. Imagine this child as Hispanic, openly gay, or on the autism spectrum. Who are these children perceived to be in the situations that have been described? How would Charlie's experience be different were he not an African American male? Why would this seemingly normal experience of events in a school day place this child at risk of becoming a participant in the legal system? What effect do these experiences have on the psychological makeup of a child each day as he grows older? What stressors can we predict that this child will experience? How did we get to the point where a child's experience could be so different merely because of his race, ethnicity, gender, ability, or sexual orientation? What can we do, if anything, to change the trajectory that these experiences will have on this child's future?

Children are introduced to the juvenile legal system in a variety of ways. School officials, medical personnel, and police are the reporters most likely to introduce a child to the American judicial system. Once there, children are most often found in either the juvenile justice courts or the child dependency or child protection courts. Children who overlap both systems are identified as "cross-over" youth. These children all experience trauma by virtue of their mere presence in the system. The juvenile justice and the child protection systems contain a disproportionate number of children of color and especially of African Americans compared to their numbers in the population as a whole. How did we get to this point? Did bias play a role, or are there other reasons that African American youth are more likely to be in positions that introduce these children to the law?

1. Historical Context

The criminalization of activities of youth in America has a long and storied history. The first juvenile court was opened in Chicago in 1899.[1] Early juvenile courts were based on the belief that children were less culpable and more amenable to rehabilitation than adults.[2] Reformers of this period focused on the environmental causes of delinquency, deemphasizing the specific misconduct of the child in favor of evaluating the broader needs—social, physical and educational—of the family.[3] Philanthropists and reformers identified as *Child Savers* blamed parents for their children's delinquent behavior and saw state intervention in the form of *parens patriae*—where the state serves as the surrogate parent to the child when the parents do not meet their obligations—as a solution.[4] The "Rehabilitative Ideal" of this era had three basic tenets: "first, children are capable of rehabilitation; second, all that rehabilitation requires is the proper intervention; and third, the appropriate goal of rehabilitation was for 'all Americans to become middle class Americans.'"[5]

Consistent with these principles, from 1899 through the 1920s, children were removed from their parents' care and placed in reform schools for their own protection. But not all children. During this time, upper middle class urban Whites tried to reform poorer Whites.[6] African American children had a different experience with the justice system and did not benefit from ideas about lessened culpability and the rehabilitation philosophy reserved for White children.[7] As law professor Robin Walker Sterling describes it:

> The confluence of desperate labor needs, the reassertion of the racist social norms that survived the abolition of slavery, and the legal and economic vulnerability of newly-freed slaves meant blacks involved in the criminal justice system suffered severe penalties for relatively minor crimes and brutality for serious offenses. Convict leasing, a system of forced labor in which white business owners paid local sheriffs for each black person the sheriff arrested and delivered, quickly emerged to fill the labor void left by the abolition of slavery.[8]

Black children were swept up for relatively minor violations into the convict labor market, described by some as worse than slavery.[9] One study by W.E.B. DuBois analyzed the 1890 census and showed that more than 18% of all Black prisoners were juveniles.[10] Once convict leasing came to an end, Jim Crow—the system of laws designed to keep Blacks as second-class citizens—emerged. These systems led to the disproportionate overrepresentation in the number of Black children in the juvenile court system and their underrepresentation in rehabilitative agencies and services.[11]

After World War I, courts were focused less on the presumption of innocence or the presence and advice that an attorney could provide for a child and more on "saving" the child through punitive incarceration. In many jurisdictions the criminal rules of evidence and procedure did not apply.[12] Procedural informality became the norm in dealing with children in court—non-adversarial and civil, instead of "rigid, technical, harsh," and criminal. Not surprisingly, criticism arose that the juvenile legal system was widely discretionary in assessing issues related to guilt and punishment and that children were not equally afforded protections that a legal system should provide. The perception of juvenile court as a largely informal, non-evidentiary proceeding became pervasive over the course of the next decades. By this time, Black youth had displaced poor White immigrants as the youth population disproportionately involved in juvenile court proceedings.[13]

It is against this backdrop of history that we view the present-day juvenile legal system.

2. The Supreme Court Speaks to Juvenile Due Process et al.

By the mid-1960s, an increase in juvenile crime and an increase in social disorder, often caused by racial unrest, led politicians to call for "law and order" and "get tough" measures.[14] At the same time, other societal factors were coming together to support the move from rehabilitative to punitive approaches: the media continued to stoke fear about the threat from juvenile offenders, particularly youth of color; disillusionment set in about rehabilitation; and victims' rights campaigns increased. Not surprisingly, informalities in handling juvenile court proceedings and the effect such informalities were having on children in the system came to the attention of the U. S. Supreme Court.

A. *In Re Gault* (1967), Juvenile Due Process Rights

Amid the change in focus from rehabilitation to punishment came the 1967 Supreme Court decision in *In re Gault*.[15] Gerald Gault was fifteen years old when he and a friend were arrested. Gault was accused of making a lewd phone call to a neighbor. At the time of his arrest, Gault had been on probation for being present when another youth stole a woman's purse. Gault's parents were not notified of the arrest. When Gerald did not come home from school, his mother sent his brother to locate him. Gault's mother eventually located her child at the detention home and was told that a hearing was set the next day. No recording was made of that hearing. A petition was filed but never received by Gault's parents, and neither of the first two hearings was recorded. No one was sworn in prior to testifying at the early hearings, and conflicting reports were made regarding statements made by Gault. The complaining witness did not appear at the hearings or at trial. At the trial, the probation report was not given to the parents. An adult charged with the same crime would have received no more than two months in jail and a $50 fine. Gault was sentenced to juvenile detention for six years until he reached the age of 21.[16] A writ of *habeas corpus* was denied by the Superior Court and the Supreme Court of Arizona, and the United States Supreme Court agreed to determine whether juvenile criminal defendants had certain rights to due process.

The United States Supreme Court held in *Gault* that juveniles are entitled to the same procedural due process protections under the Fourteenth Amendment as adults. According to the Supreme Court, notice of the charges to both parents and the child sufficient to prepare an adequate defense is required, and, where delinquency could result in incarceration, notice of the right to be represented by counsel and to be appointed counsel if indigent are also required. The Court held that children are subject to the privilege against self-incrimination and that, without a valid confession, a finding of delinquency and commitment to an institution cannot be sustained in the absence of sworn testimony and the opportunity to cross-examine.¹⁷ Although there are legitimate reasons for treating youth differently, the Court ruled that youth are entitled to procedural due process when facing adjudication and incarceration.

B. *Kent v. United States* (1966), Juveniles' Rights Before Transfer to Adult Court

Transfer or waiver proceedings determine whether a child will be prosecuted in juvenile court or in adult court. Transfer refers to those jurisdictions in which a case involving a youth begins in juvenile court and is transferred to an adult court. Waiver refers to a juvenile court that waives its juvenile jurisdiction in favor of proceeding with the youth's case in adult court. In many jurisdictions, transferred children are housed with adults. Transfer from juvenile to adult court has also subjected many youth to severe sentencing options, including the death penalty.¹⁸

The Supreme Court considered the issue of due process in juvenile court transfer proceedings in *Kent v. United States*.¹⁹ Sixteen-year-old Morris Kent was accused of housebreaking, robbery, and rape. Acting under the authority of the District of Columbia's Juvenile Court Act, the Juvenile Court waived its jurisdiction and transferred the case to adult criminal court.²⁰ Kent was indicted by a grand jury of the United States District Court for the District of Columbia for eight counts alleging instances of housebreaking, robbery, and rape. There was no hearing on the waiver decision, and no findings of fact were made. The Supreme Court found that "as a condition to a valid waiver order, the youth was entitled to a hearing, including access by his counsel to the social records and probation reports or similar reports which presumably are considered by the court, and the youth was entitled to a statement of reasons for the Juvenile Court's decision."²¹ The Court concluded a child is entitled to counsel and an opportunity for a meaningful, albeit informal, hearing prior to entry of a waiver order:²²

> The right to representation by counsel is not a formality. It is not a grudging gesture to a ritualistic requirement. It is of the essence of justice. Appointment of counsel without affording an opportunity for hearing on a "critically important" decision is tantamount to denial of counsel. There is no justification for the failure of the Juvenile Court to rule on the motion for hearing filed by petitioner's counsel, and it was error to fail to grant a hearing.²³

Despite the Supreme Court's rulings regarding due process procedures, *Kent* endorsed the process of transferring youths to be prosecuted as adults, a process which exists to this day. All states have established a minimum and an upper age of jurisdiction for children whose cases may be transferred to adult court, and almost all have provisions where juvenile court judges have discretion to waive jurisdiction and refer the cases to adult court.²⁴

Transfer laws in general have changed over time. Responding to an increase in juvenile crime in the 1980s and 1990s, laws allowing for transfer of youth to adult court or direct filing in adult court of a youth's juvenile cases expanded dramatically. Nearly every state extended the scope of transfer to adult criminal court, including lowering the age requirements for transfer.[25] This happened as an image of a new generation of juvenile "super-predators" emerged who, according to academics, sociologists, and criminologists, would kill, maim, and steal without remorse. This image was ultimately perpetuated by politicians both Black and White. Princeton Professor John DiIulio projected that "as many as half of these juvenile super-predators could be young black males" and that "the demographic bulge of the next [ten] years will unleash an army of young male predatory street criminals who will make even the leaders of the Bloods and Crips...look tame by comparison."[26] The view that youth of color were deserving of harsher treatment was intensified by this perpetuation of the myth of the "superpredator" described as "a new breed of brutal youth commonly viewed as youth of color," who were going to terrorize the country.[27] This view still haunts youth justice today.

Since 1999, some states have made it harder for youth to be tried as adults. Four states have added reverse waiver provisions to send cases initiated in adult court back to juvenile court, and seven states have blended sentencing provisions to allow adult courts to impose juvenile dispositions.[28] Still, despite the rollbacks, in 2018, the likelihood of a youth's case in juvenile court being waived to adult court in cases involving a person offense (as opposed to a property offense) for Black youth was still more than double the likelihood for White youth, and the likelihood for Hispanic youth to be waived to adult court was 1.4 times the likelihood for White youth.[29]

C. *Roper v. Simmons* (2005) and *Graham v. Florida* (2010), Life Without Parole and Death Sentence for Minor as Cruel and Unusual Punishment

Critics suggested that while *Gault* and other Supreme Court opinions extended constitutional protections to juveniles, they failed to pay sufficient attention to the science about adolescent brain development and to the capacity youth might (or might not) have for exercising their rights such as the privilege against self-incrimination.[30]

Courts began considering adolescent brain development in dealing with youth sentencing for youth who remain in the juvenile legal system as well as those youth who are transferred to the adult system. In 2005, the United States Supreme Court, in *Roper v. Simmons,* considered the death penalty imposed by Missouri on a youth named Christopher Simmons who was tried for murder. Simmons was seventeen at the time of the crime and tried as an adult when he was eighteen. The aggravating factors raised during sentencing included that the crime was committed for money, to avoid arrest, and with "depravity of mind and was outrageously and wantonly vile, horrible, and inhuman." Simmons was sentenced to death. After conviction and imposition of sentence, Simmons retained new counsel who argued in part that Simmons was very immature, impulsive, and "susceptible to being manipulated or influenced" and that these and other mitigating factors from his background should have been considered in the sentencing proceedings.[31] In the Supreme Court, Simmons's age was the central issue in deciding whether the sentence violated the Eighth and Fourteenth Amendments. The Court considered adolescent brain development in ruling that sentencing a minor to death constituted cruel and unusual punishment: "It is proper that we acknowledge the overwhelming weight of international opinion against the juvenile death penalty, resting in large part on the understanding that the instability and emotional imbalance of young people may often be a factor in the crime."[32]

Similarly, in 2010, the United States Supreme Court, in *Graham v. Florida*, ruled that sentencing a youth to life without the possibility of parole, in a non-homicide case, was unconstitutional.[33] The Court stated:

> developments in psychology and brain science continue to show fundamental differences between juvenile and adult minds. For example, parts of the brain involved in behavior control continue to mature through late adolescence. Juveniles are more capable of change than are adults, and their actions are less likely to be evidence of "irretrievably depraved character" than are the actions of adults. It remains true that "[f]rom a moral standpoint it would be misguided to equate the failings of a minor with those of an adult, for a greater possibility exists that a minor's character deficiencies will be reformed."[34]

That these Supreme Court opinions acknowledge the science of adolescent brain development is significant. This has not stopped the generally pervasive perceptions regarding the adultification of youth of color, however, which have in turn perpetuated disparity and disproportionality in sentencing.

3. Collateral Consequences and Adultification of Youth of Color

There now exist many court decisions acknowledging that youth should be treated differently from adults. The United States Supreme Court has acknowledged the brain science confirming that adolescents think significantly different from mature adults. While children in most societies are considered to be endowed with characteristics such as innocence and the need for protection, not all children are perceived in the same way. When youth are perceived as older, decisions about those youth could lead to introduction into the youth legal system. Decision points in the juvenile court process emerge prior to any court intervention or action. Decision-making by teachers regarding who remains in the classroom, disciplinary actions by principals regarding referral to law enforcement and suspension or expulsion, police interaction with youth in neighborhoods, and security forces and police in the schools, all affect the trajectory of a child's entry into the juvenile legal system.

Placing a youth in the juvenile legal system has significant collateral consequences for that child. Misbehavior in class could lead to expulsion from school. Or behavior at school can result in a school security officer referring a case to a juvenile court. Once on this path, a child's education can be limited or moved to an alternative education program. Or a later referral to juvenile detention and a finding of delinquency may affect a family's ability to live in certain housing or certain neighborhoods. Youth who have juvenile criminal records may have difficulty getting into college, securing a job, or advancing to the military because of the seemingly simple barriers in questions about whether they have been convicted of a crime. Any and all of these collateral consequences of involvement in the juvenile legal system create barriers to future success after rehabilitation. Considering these consequences, decision-makers should be aware that each decision moving a youth through the juvenile justice process may lead to negative societal outcomes.

The difficulty of these consequences is compounded by "adultification" where a child is perceived as being older than the child's age and subject to standards that older children would be subjected to. In these cases, behaviors that would be considered immature or youthful transgressions for some children call for more severe punishment and consequences than for others of the same age. As education and psychology professor Dr. Jamilia Blake summarizes: "Adultification contributes to a false narrative that Black youths' transgressions are intentional and malicious, instead of the result of immature decision-making—a key characteristic of childhood." This has led to children of color "not being afforded the opportunity to make mistakes and to learn, grow, and benefit from correction for youthful missteps to the same degree as white children of the same age."[35]

Other researchers have reached similar conclusions. Dr. Phillip Atiba Goff and his colleagues have found "converging evidence that youth of color, particularly Black and Native American boys, are seen as older and less innocent and that they prompt a less essential conception of childhood than do their White same-age peers."[36] In a study of university students from a large public university, researchers found that from ages 0–9, children were seen as equally innocent regardless of race. As children got older, however, the perceived innocence of children of color, particularly boys, was the equivalent of older children of different races. Black children age 10–13 were perceived as the equivalent of a non-Black child age 14–17. A Black child age 14–17 was perceived as the equivalent of a non-Black adult age 18–21.[37] Perceptions of Black youth as older relative to peers of other races can mean that these youth lose the protections afforded by assumed childhood innocence well before they become adults, with the average age overestimation for Black boys exceeding four-and-a-half years. This means that in some cases, Black children may be viewed as adults when they are just 13 years old.[38]

The issue is no less prevalent for Black girls. A study from Georgetown University Law Center on Poverty and Equality reported that when compared to their White age peers, Black girls are seen to need less nurturing, protection, support, or comfort; they are perceived to be more independent and more knowledgeable on adult topics and sex.[39] Given these views, it is hardly surprising that teachers, law enforcement officials, and even parents see these girls' behavior as less innocent and more adult like, more disruptive and malicious than other children's perceived age-appropriate behaviors. Nor is it surprising that girls of color are more likely to be punished and punished more severely.[40] Nationally, at the school level, Black girls are suspended from school more than five times as often as White girls, and Black girls are 2.7 times more likely to be referred to the juvenile justice system than their White peers.[41] The research shows that "these differences in rates of suspensions are a result of policies and adult perceptions and biases—not a result of differences in behavior. In other words, Black and Native girls are not more likely to misbehave, but they are more likely to be disciplined."[42] Once referred to the juvenile legal system, research shows that prosecutions show similar results. On average, prosecutors dismiss three out of every ten cases for Black girls but seven out of ten for White girls.[43] Similarly, diversion is less often offered to Black girls; and these girls are punished more severely and are far more likely to be put in custody in state facilities than their White peers.[44] These facts highlight the importance of educating decision-makers about the effect that their decisions may be having on creating disproportionality in the juvenile legal system.

4. The Impact of Discretionary Decision-Making

I have served in several of the roles that involve discretionary decision-making in juvenile legal cases. This experience has given me insight on when these decision points most often occur and where our own experience, education, and socialization can affect decision-making in both implicit and explicit ways. Other chapters of this book provide definitions of implicit and explicit bias. I note here the critical distinction between our quick, implicit responses and our more careful decisions. I particularly draw attention to a point I often hear Professor Redfield make—it's hard for lawyers to accept that not all of our legal decisions reflect our thinking carefully and rationally *like a lawyer*.[45] It is this incongruence that, at least in part, explains the disproportionalities we see in the juvenile legal system. I also note that implicit bias is more likely to occur in situations that are ambiguous or where the decision involves the exercise of discretion.⁴⁶ And it is exactly these situations that we find in juvenile legal systems across the country.

Multiple people exercise discretion along every juncture of the juvenile legal system, and many of their decisions contribute to criminalization of childhood behavior and a road from school to prison—often termed the school to prison pipeline.⁴⁷ Prosecutors play a pivotal role. When I served as chief of the juvenile district attorneys, I regularly was called on to make these kinds of discretionary decisions. For example, I had the authority to decide whether cases would be filed as juvenile or whether requests to transfer to adult court would be made. I developed an approach to them that could limit my implicit biases coming to the fore: The team making the recommendation would meet with me to discuss the decision to file. In those meetings, although the prosecutors would know many of the details regarding the youth, I required that they provide only the facts and law that would bear on the decision-making process, without regard to race and sometimes without regard to gender.

Of course, it is not just prosecutors who exercise this kind of discretion in making decisions about young people in the juvenile legal system. Probation officers also have wide discretion at both the front and back end of juvenile court proceedings. During intake they determine whether a youth qualifies for immediate diversion and, if not qualifying for diversion, whether a child will remain in custody and whether the case will be sent to the prosecutor for filing. Probation officers often make decisions on whom to divert, and they continue to influence other decision-makers throughout the legal process. Probation officers also make detention recommendations, many of which are readily accepted by many courts and often have great sway over the judge at disposition.⁴⁸

Judges, too, play a key role and exercise wide discretion in a variety of settings throughout a child's journey in the juvenile legal system. Studies with judges from across the country have found that implicit racial biases are widespread and that such biases could influence their judgment and decision-making.⁴⁹ This should not come as a surprise, as we all have biases that affect our decision-making. The good news here is that the research also shows that when attention is called to the fact that judges are being influenced in a way not intended by the judge, then judges can interrupt bias in decision-making.⁵⁰

5. Promising Approaches for Addressing Implicit Bias in Decision-Making

Like others, judges who have taken the Harvard Implicit Association Test [IAT] have found differences in their expressed or outward beliefs and their results on the IAT. At the same time, research has shown that those who are motivated to reduce the negative effects their biases may cause can do so.[51] Jerry Kang, a researcher and author on this subject, suggests that "motivation to be fair means that we are striving to achieve our personal values, consistent with our genuine ethical commitments."[52] My experience as a litigator and as a judge suggests that this is indeed the essence of what motivates judges. Research continues to emerge as to promising practices to these ends. Many are discussed in other Chapters in this book. From my own experience, I recommend these:[53]

- **Blinding**. My experience as a prosecutor suggested the value of this, and it has value for judges as well. Of course, removing information from the judge in some legal settings could be difficult, expensive, or even counterproductive.[54] For example, some decisions on parole, punishment, or child custody may require an appreciation of a youth's biography.[55] My suggestion here is to consider the decision as a whole and to consider blinding in part or for a limited time.

- **Checklists**. I find that it is easy to assume that I'm treating similar decisions similarly. But I've also found that having a short benchcard-type rubric or checklist can help to consciously focus on each relevant piece I need to consider. I know that these kinds of checklists can sometimes promise more than they deliver. Consider, for a large-scale example, that while federal sentencing guidelines were designed to create a range of punishment for similar offenses, with the goal of similarity in punishment for similar offenses, in practice they led to a different sentencing structure for crack cocaine as opposed to powder cocaine and affected certain categories of people, poorer people, differently, leading to harsher sentences for defendants convicted of offenses involving crack cocaine. Even so, I think a personal reminder to stay clear of our own blindspots can be helpful.

- **Training**. I've learned much about implicit bias and its manifestations and interruptions from training. Training allows us to understand and recognize that our associations, upbringing, group involvement, environment, media, and social media contacts all play a part in how we view others. Training also allows us to recognize that information we absorb this way may limit our ability to see and decide fairly. Well-constructed training gives us space to consider our individual and institutional situations and to construct approaches and to hear other participants' approaches to craft something that will work for us. I find that sustained training can offer support for understanding the issues and addressing them creatively. Trainings on bias require more than a one-hour introduction. Trainings involve giving the participants an opportunity to assess which methods may work for their individual situations. As a Judge, I keep sticky notes on my computer with reminders to "stare not blink" and "no snap judgments." Training allows us to understand why and how techniques make us better at decision-making.

- **Keeping count**. Judges interested in interrupting bias in their rulings can conduct an audit of their decisions. This can be a self-generated tally or a simple request to a trusted staff person to keep count of how people are addressed. Or this can be a more extensive review conducted with one's clerk or a neighboring university.

  Judges have many discretionary decision points, particularly in the juvenile legal system. Collecting data at key points in the discretionary decision process of a single decision-maker, as well as looking at data over a period of time for a single decision-maker or from multiple decision-makers in a region, may reveal patterns where introduction of bias interruption methods would be beneficial. "If you know that your exercise of discretion, which historically has been invisible, will now suddenly become more visible through individual and institutional counting practices, you will start taking greater care [in decision-making]."[56]

- **Slowing down**. Of course, this is easier said than done, but nearly all of us can benefit from slowing down when making decisions.[57] Research is clear that reminding ourselves to stop and deliberate (or even stop for lunch) instead of jumping or rushing to conclusions can reduce unwanted biases.[58] As judges, we are taught to rule immediately. In contrast, methods such as writing out our thoughts, putting them aside, and coming back to them after careful thought can lead to more deliberate decision-making.

Each of us will have our own needs and ways, but I'm confident that incorporating these types of practices can go a long way toward improve decision-making in the juvenile legal system.

Conclusion

Reducing the disproportionality of the numbers of youth and the outcomes of youth of color in the system is not merely a worthy goal but one desperately needed to improve justice for youth. Let's return to the 11-year-old that started out this Chapter. What can we expect the trajectory of Charlie's life to be, based on what we have learned and reviewed? Introduced into the juvenile legal system, what can he expect? Arguably, the most devastating impact of introduction to the legal system is the lifelong stigma that comes as a result of starting with a minor offense and progressing to the point where there is no diversion from the system. The collateral damage of a minor conviction could be more damaging than a sentence imposed by a judge. For example, in the early 1980s, the effect of minor drug convictions was to prosecute and to intimidate Black men and to stigmatize those young men with arrest and conviction records.[59] Even if the majority of such men avoided jail time, they still had to report their arrests and convictions on employment, housing, and school applications. A criminal record would often render Black men effectively unemployable, creating a downward spiral of criminality.[60] In a system that has a history of over-reliance on incarceration and a lack of consideration of a youth's strengths, accountability, and development, can Charlie beat the odds? Yes, change is possible. Recognizing and reducing bias at each point of entry and egress to and from the juvenile legal system can change the trajectory of a youth's life. We have the tools and understanding of brain science to make this so; we need to sustain our motivation to these ends.

So, You'd Like to Know More

- James Bell, Repairing the Breach: A Brief History of Youth of Color in the Justice System, The W. Haywood Burns Institute for Youth Justice Fairness & Equity (2016).
- Jerry Kang, What Judges Can Do about Implicit Bias, 57 Ct. Rev. 78 (2021).
- Rebecca Epstein, Jamilia J. Blake & Thalia González, Georgetown Law Center on Poverty and Equality, Girlhood Interrupted: The Erasure of Black Girls' Childhood Law Center on Poverty and Inequality (2017).

About the Author

Rhonda F. Hunter serves as judge of the 303rd Family District Court of Dallas County, Texas. She is the former Chief of the Juvenile Division of the Dallas County District Attorney's Office, is Chair of the State Bar of Texas Child Protection Law Section and former President of the Dallas Bar Association. She has practiced juvenile and child welfare law since 1986.

Endnotes

1. Tamar R. Birkhead, *Delinquent by Reason of Poverty*, 38 WASH. U. J.L. & POL'Y 53, 63 (2012); *see also* Quinn Myer, *How Chicago Women Created The World's First Juvenile Justice System* (NPR Station WBEZ broadcast May 13, 2019), https://www.npr.org/local/309/2019/05/13/722351881/how-chicago-women-created-the-world-s-first-juvenile-justice-system.

2. *See* In re Gault, 387 U.S. 1, 22 (1967).

3. Birkhead, 38 Wash. U. J.L. & Pol'y at 64.

4. *Id.* (citing *Black's Law Dictionary*).

5. Robin W. Sterling, *"Children Are Different": Implicit Bias, Rehabilitation, and the "New" Juvenile Jurisprudence*, 46 LOY. L.A. L. REV. 1019, 1047 (2013). [Sterling].

6. *Id.* at 1049.

7. *Id.* at 1048.

8. *Id.* at 1049.

9. JAMES BELL, W. HAYWOOD BURNS INSTITUTE FOR YOUTH JUSTICE FAIRNESS & EQUITY, REPAIRING THE BREACH: A BRIEF HISTORY OF YOUTH OF COLOR IN THE JUSTICE SYSTEM, 6–7 (2016).

10. JAMES BELL & LAURA JOHN RIDOLFI, W. HAYWOOD BURNS INSTITUTE FOR YOUTH JUSTICE FAIRNESS & EQUITY, ADORATION OF THE QUESTION: REFLECTIONS ON THE FAILURE TO REDUCE RACIAL & ETHNIC DISPARITIES IN THE JUVENILE JUSTICE SYSTEM (2008).

11. Sterling, 46 LOY. L.A. L. REV. at 1050.

12. *Id.* at 1048.

13. Kristen Hennings, *Criminalizing Normal Adolescent Behavior in Communities of Color*, 98 CORNELL L. REV. 383, 406 (2013). [Hennings]

14. Barry C. Feld, *The Transformation of the Juvenile Court, Part II: Race and the "Crack Down" on Youth Crime*, 84 MINN. L. REV. 327, 340, 345–46 (1999).

15. In Re Gault, 387 U.S. 1 (1967).

16. *Id.*

17. *Id.*

18. Hennings, 98 CORNELL L. REV. 383 at 407 (citing GEOFF K. WARD, THE BLACK CHILD-SAVERS: RACIAL DEMOCRACY & JUVENILE JUSTICE 116–20 (2012)).

19. Kent v. United States, 383 U.S. 541 (1966).

20. *Id.* at 546.

21. *Id.* at 556–57.

22. *Id.* at 561.

23. *Id.* at 561–62.

24. SARAH HOCKENBERRY U.S. DEPT. OF JUSTICE, DELINQUENCY CASES WAIVED TO CRIMINAL COURT, 2018, JUVENILE JUSTICE STATISTICS, NATIONAL REPORT SERIES, Jan. 2021, at 1, https://ojjdp.ojp.gov/publications/delinquency-cases-waived-2018.pdf.

25. *Id.*

26. Sterling, 46 LOY. L.A. L. REV. at 1057–58 (citing John J. Dilulio, Jr., *My Black Crime Problem, and Ours*, CITY JOURNAL 1 (1996)).

27. National Juvenile Justice Network, Why Implicit Bias Matters for Youth Justice, Implicit Bias Snapshot, Sept. 2017, http://www.njjn.org/our-work/implicit-bias-snapshot.

28. *Id.* at 3.

29. *Id.*

30. Birkhead, 38 Wash. U. J.L. & Pol'y at 93.

31. Roper v. Simmons, 543 U.S. 551, 558–59 (2005).

32. *Id.* at 578.

33. Graham v. Florida, 560 U.S. 48, 74 (2010).

34. *Id.* at 68 (internal citations omitted).

35. Rebecca Epstein, Jamilia J. Blake & Thalia González, Georgetown Law Center on Poverty and Equality, Girlhood Interrupted: The Erasure of Black Girls' Childhood 1 (2017), https://genderjusticeandopportunity.georgetown.edu/wp-content/uploads/2020/06/girlhood-interrupted.pdf [Epstein, Girlhood]; Jamilia Blake et al., *Unmasking the Inequitable Discipline Experiences of Urban Black Girls: Implications for Urban Education Stakeholders*, 43 Urb. Rev. 90 (2011).

36. Phillip Atiba Goff & Matthew Christian Jackson, *The Essence of Innocence: Consequences of Dehumanizing Black Children*, 106 J. Personality & Soc. Psychol. 526, 526 (2014).

37. *See id.* at 529–30.

38. *See id.* at 532.

39. Epstein, Girlhood at 1.

40. A. Rochaun Meadows-Fernandez, *Why Won't Society Let Black Girls be Children*, N.Y. Times Parenting, April 7, 2020, https://thedailyconversation70059941.wordpress.com/2020/04/17/why-wont-society-let-black-girls-be-children-by-by-a-rochaun-meadows-fernandez/.

41. *See Research Confirms that Black Girls Feel the Sting of Adultification Bias Identified In Earlier Georgetown Law Study*, Georgetown Law (May 15, 2019), https://www.law.georgetown.edu/news/research-confirms-that-black-girls-feel-the-sting-of-adultification-bias-identified-in-earlier-georgetown-law-study/.

42. Kayla Patrick, Adaku Onyeka-Crawford & Nancy Duchesneau, *"... and They Cared": How to Create Better, Safer Learning Environments for Girls of Color*, Education Trust & Nat'l Women's Law Center 22 n.15 (2020); *see also* Shoshana N. Jarvis & Jason A. Okonofua, *School Deferred: When Bias Affects School Leaders*, Social Psychol. & Personality Sci. (2019); Injun Lai, *A Better Understanding of School Suspensions: Bias, Policy Impact, and Student Experiences* (Sept. 2018) (Ph.D. dissertation, Northwestern University 2018), *available at* https://arch.library.northwestern.edu/concern/generic_works/tx31qh880; U.S. Dep't of Justice & U.S. Dep't of Educ., Dear Colleague Letter on Nondiscriminatory Administration of School Discipline 3 (Jan. 8, 2014) (Rescinded), https://www2.ed.gov/about/offices/list/ocr/letters/colleague-201401-title-vi.html.

43. Kim Taylor Thompson, *Girl Talk—Examining Racial & Gender Justice in Juvenile Justice*, 6 Nev. L. J. 1137 (2006).

44. Epstein, Girlhood at 12.

45. Jerry Kang, *Implicit Bias in the Courts*, 59 U.C.L.A. L. Rev. 1124, 1129 (2012).

46. *See* Calvin K. Lai & Mahzarin R. Banaji, *The Psychology of Implicit Intergroup Bias and the Prospect of Change*, Harvard Univ. 10–11 (2018), http://www.people.fas.harvard.edu/

banaji/research/publications/articles/2017_Lai.pdf; Bernice B. Donald & Sarah E. Redfield, *Implicit Bias: Should the Legal Community Be Bothered?*, 2 PLI CURRENT 615 (2018); *see also* Jerry Kang, *What Judges Can Do about Implicit Bias*, 57 Ct. Rev. 78, 85–86 (2021).

47. *See generally* NATIONAL JUVENILE JUSTICE NETWORK, IMPLICIT BIAS: WHY IT MATTERS FOR YOUTH JUSTICE, September 2017.

48. Birkhead, 38 WASH. U. J.L. & POL'Y at 93.

49. Jeffery J. Rachlinski, Sheri Lynn Johnson, Andrew J. Wistrich & Chris Guthrie, *Does Racial Bias Affect Trial Judges?*, 84 NOTRE DAME L. REV 1195 (2009).[Rachlinski, *Trial Judges*].

50. Andrew J. Wistrich & Jeffrey J. Rachlinski, *Implicit Bias in Judicial Decision Making in* ENHANCING JUSTICE: REDUCING BIAS (Sarah E. Redfield ed. 2017).

51. Kang, *What Judges Can Do* at 78.

52. *Id.*

53. *See generally, e.g.,* Rhonda Hunter, Judge, 303rd Family District Court of Dallas County, Texas & Sarah E. Redfield, Professor, University of New Hampshire, Training Toward Intentional Equity, Practising Law Institute (San Francisco, CA, November 8, 2021).

54. Kang, *What Judges Can Do* at 83.

55. *Id.* at 84.

56. *Id.* at 89.

57. *Id.* at 85.

58. *See, e.g.,* Shai Danziger, Jonathan Levav, Liora Avnaim-Pesso & Daniel Kahneman, *Extraneous Factors in Judicial Decisions*, 108 PNAS 6889, Fig. 1 (2011).

59. *See* JAMES FORMAN, JR., LOCKING UP OUR OWN: CRIME AND PUNISHMENT IN BLACK AMERICA 24 (2017).

60. *Id.* (quoting former Superior Court Judge, Charles Halleck).

TWENTY-TWO

Implicit Bias and People with Mental Disabilities

Taking Stock of the Criminal Justice System

Elizabeth Kelley, Esq., Criminal Defense Lawyer
Nick Dubin, PsyD

A Note from the Editors: There are some chapters of this book where we felt fairly competent or experienced. Admittedly not as experienced as our expert authors, but knowledgeable. As we watched this Chapter develop and had the chance to see and better understand the work of our Criminal Justice Section friend and colleague, Elizabeth Kelley, and her (now our) colleague, Nick Dubin, we understood how much we had to learn about bias and ableism. The need for more awareness and discussion of these issues is obvious and urgent in the context of criminal justice and beyond. We greatly appreciate the contribution and work of Attorney Kelley and Mr. Dubin and look forward to continuing to learning from and with them.

CHAPTER HIGHLIGHTS

- Implicit bias against individuals with mental disabilities deserves more research and recognition in the criminal justice system.
- Ableism causes implicit bias on the part of those in the criminal justice system against those with mental disabilities, which requires training in de-escalation and mental health issues to combat this unconscious bias.
- Cognitive reframing even a single variable can help reduce implicit bias against those with disabilities.

- The criminal justice system is adversarial, and both sides tend to use sanist language to achieve their aims. Members of the legal profession should resist the temptation to do so when it is possible.
- Barriers against the enforcement of the Americans with Disabilities Act (ADA) need to be re-examined to ensure protections are working at every stage, from arrest to post-conviction.
- Judges, prosecutors, defense lawyers, police, correctional officers, and other criminal justice professionals, need to closely examine their own implicit biases toward individuals with mental disabilities.

CHAPTER CONTENTS

Introduction

1. Types of Prejudices Against Persons with Disabilities
    A. Ableism
    B. Essentialism
    C. Sanism
    D. Intersectionality
2. Interventions or Strategies for Participants in the Criminal Justice System
    A. Training
    B. Using Bias-Free Language
    C. Re-examining Barriers and Assumptions
3. Participant-Relevant Approaches to Implicit Bias
    A. Judges
    B. Prosecutors
    C. Criminal Defense Lawyers
    D. Jail and Prison Officials
    E. Police and Other Law Enforcement

Conclusion

Introduction

We are told over and over again in our society not to judge a book by its cover, not to assume what is inside before we have had a chance to read it. Yet humans size up and make assumptions about other humans based upon what they look like many times a day. We prejudge complicated breathing beings in ways we are told never to judge inanimate objects.[1]

This quote from Isabele Wilkerson's groundbreaking, award-winning book *Caste*, perfectly captures the concept of implicit bias, and in particular, implicit bias against people with disabilities. We know from our lived experience and from the research that this bias exists. In one recent study, researchers found that prejudice against individuals who are developmentally disabled—autism and Down syndrome being the most common—was predominantly hostile. The prejudice reflected dehumanization and correlated with the beliefs that the developmentally disabled may harm others, are dependent on others, and should be kept separate from others.[2]

The criminal justice system is no exception to bias; studies show that implicit bias against those with disabilities is prevalent. One study found that preference for people without disability was among the strongest implicit and explicit biases: 76% of participants exhibited an implicit preference for people without disabilities, in comparison to nine percent for people with disabilities. Particularly disturbing, participants who themselves had disabilities still showed a preference for people without disabilities.[3]

The significance of this implicit bias is underscored by the fact that approximately half the people in our jails and prisons have some form of mental disability; and half the use of force incidents with police involve individuals with disabilities.[4] Indeed, to see a vivid illustration of this implicit bias across society, we need look no further than the local governmental response establishing protocols for treating and allocating treatment for those with Covid-19 in the Spring of 2020. People with both physical and mental disabilities reported disparate treatment when it came to access to facilities and care during the pandemic. These reports were especially disheartening as we celebrated the thirtieth anniversary of the enactment of the Americans with Disabilities Act (ADA). Various groups such as the American Bar Association (ABA), The Arc, and disability rights groups voiced outrage and filed lawsuits.[5] Meanwhile, wardens and courts denied compassionate release to incarcerated individuals with disabilities while the pandemic raged, infecting many who were unable to escape enclosed and shared spaces. The Marshall Project reported that wardens in the Federal Bureau of Prisons denied practically every request made to them before these motions were sent to judges in federal courts across the country. Many of these physically ill and disabled people died while incarcerated.[6]

We often judge people with mental disabilities based on how they act or look. Law enforcement may see a person in the middle of a psychotic episode and assume he or she is a danger to themselves or to others. They arrest or make the decision to shoot. But what about people with mental disabilities who don't "act disabled" or "look disabled?" Indeed, there are many mental disabilities which are called "invisible disabilities" because there are no obvious visible outward manifestations or because of the individual's seeming ability to function. For example, when jurors see a defendant who fails to make eye contact, they may assume he or she has something to hide, when in fact that person may be on the autism spectrum, and eye contact may be excruciatingly difficult. So too, an autistic defendant who does not look the judge in the eye or twiddles his thumbs or her pencil during a plea colloquy or at sentencing can appear unremorseful. We *do* prejudge (the root of prejudice), often reaching erroneous conclusions, sometimes creating devastating, if not deadly, consequences.

Implicit bias against people with mental disabilities in the criminal justice system is an area that deserves greater research and initiatives, and, more fundamentally, greater awareness and basic knowledge. This Chapter serves as a starting point by exploring key concepts of ableism, essentialism, sanism, and intersectionality. The Chapter then discusses some general strategies to raise awareness of implicit bias against those with disabilities in the criminal justice system and some specific strategies for judges, prosecutors, criminal defense lawyers, jail/prison personnel, and law enforcement.

But first, a note about terminology. While the term "functional diversity" is gaining acceptance in some circles, it is not widely used. In this Chapter, we use the term "mental disabilities" as a global term to include issues such as bipolar disorder, schizophrenia, and depression, as well as intellectual/developmental disabilities such as autism spectrum disorder (ASD) and Fetal Alcohol Spectrum Disorder. In doing so we note that we are not entirely comfortable with this term. For example, it seems inaccurate to describe as disabled those on the autism spectrum who are high-functioning and indeed, brilliant in many ways; what they truly have are communication and social deficits.[7] What is important, however, is to understand and make clear that mental illnesses are not intellectual/developmental disabilities, and vice versa, and at the same time, to acknowledge that many individuals have co-occurring disorders.

1. Types of Prejudices Against Persons with Disabilities

A. Ableism

Broadly speaking, ableism is the intentional or unintentional discrimination or oppression of individuals with disabilities. The term itself dates to the 1990s, but the concept goes back centuries to times when it was believed that people with mental illness were possessed by the devil or evil spirits.[8] This definition applies to people with both physical and mental disabilities, and, for purposes of our discussion, applies to people with both mental illness as well as intellectual/developmental disabilities.

Bias is a personal preference, tendency, or inclination, toward or against something or someone, especially as related to another. Discrimination, on the other hand, means "to distinguish by discerning or exposing differences, and to recognize or identify as separate and distinct."[9] Intentional discrimination is easy to spot where it involves derogatory and discriminatory remarks against another person based on their appearance or conduct. The law provides some recourse, making intentional discrimination illegal in many settings. Unintentional discrimination is less obvious. For example, the ADA requires that all buildings including courthouses, jails, and prisons be handicap accessible. No architect or building manager would intentionally deprive people of these accommodations, but failure to accommodate, due to neglect or lack of knowledge, is one example of unintentional discrimination.

Unfortunately, children with mental disabilities learn at an early age how ableist the world can be. A disproportionately high number of children in schools who "act out" are suspended, referred to law enforcement, or subjected to school-related arrests. They are disproportionately restrained or placed in seclusion or even taken into custody.[10] By the time many of these children reach middle school and high school, their same-aged peers have "moved on" from friendships involving simple play dates in elementary school to more complex group interactions. School cliques tend to exclude those who are different. If the teachers and school security onsite police can be ableist in criminalizing disability, then their peers are certainly not immune to ableism—the peers know what is considered cool and want to remain in the "cool crowd" due to peer pressure. A lot of autistic teenagers struggle to find and keep friends. Some stumble into the wrong crowd of people willing to take advantage of their gullibility or naivety, leading to encounters with the criminal justice system.

The purpose of recounting these struggles is simply to emphasize that those children with mental disabilities and other developmental differences eventually grow up to be adults. Society at large often thinks of developmental disabilities as "childhood disorders," but these are lifetime struggles, and this important realization requires us to shed our ableism when working with the adult population. It is easier to be ableist to adults than it is to children, even though there are plenty of examples where children are criminalized for their mental disabilities. Think of how much worse it is for adults traversing through the criminal justice system. Moreover, our implicit biases of mentally disabled people are formed in childhood, and are often difficult to shed because these beliefs are unconscious in nature. These biases then influence our perception of others, sometimes with deadly consequences.

There are other tragic examples of ableism at work. Law enforcement expects those being approached, questioned, pursued, or in custody to behave by a certain set of norms. They expect mild-mannered courtesy. Anything that looks outside of this norm is viewed as suspicious behavior. But for an individual with a mental disability, being approached by the police can be overstimulating and lead to an unregulated emotional response on the part of the suspect. The case of Linden Cameron, a thirteen-year-old boy on the autism spectrum, illustrates these ableist norms. Linden's mother called the police because he was suffering from an anxiety attack. She told the police he was unarmed. Instead of trying to de-escalate the situation, the police ordered Linden to get on the ground, and when he started running, they shot him. He sustained injuries to his shoulder, ankles, intestines, and bladder. Someone like Linden may be intimidated by uniforms, unable to understand commands, not like to be touched, and instinctively flee.[11] Another example is the death of Daniel Prude, a man with a history of serious mental illness who had cycled in and out of jails and psychiatric facilities. Mr. Prude was stopped by the police while he was naked in the freezing cold. Mr. Prude was in the midst of a psychotic break. Police placed a spit hood over his head, handcuffed him, and shot him.[12]

In these kinds of encounters, law enforcement does not set out to be consciously discriminatory. Instead, the response is a combination of a lack of training and a lack of knowledge in dealing with individuals with mental disabilities, especially in what law enforcement perceives to be exigent situations. Thus, the implicit responses officers have must be reprogrammed and reframed during police training in order to prevent such tragic events from happening again.

Ableism happens more frequently in situations where individuals have "invisible disabilities" as opposed to those who are clearly intellectually impaired, or other individuals having a marked break with reality (psychosis), which would be apparent to the casual observer. In their conceptual analysis of autistic masking, Professor Amy Pearson and her colleague Kiernan Rose explain that individuals with invisible disabilities frequently, often unconsciously, use "masking behaviors" to try to appear as neurotypical as possible in order to avoid stigma and get by in the world. Their behavior can be exacerbated by areas of strength that cover up areas of weaknesses. For example, many individuals on the autism spectrum present with extremely uneven levels of development across many areas of functionality throughout their lives. They can use their cognitive abilities as a way to blend in mechanically rather than intuitively. As they attempt to blend in, they do so by mimicking—sometimes clumsily—neurotypical behavior rather than possessing a true sense of social skills or understanding. The effort required by these inhibiting behaviors often take an enormous amount of energy from the individual doing the masking.[13]

A paradox ensues from this behavior in the criminal justice system. For example, in a setting where an individual is being interrogated by law enforcement, masking would render autism as more of an "invisible disability" for as long as the person is able to mask, effectively increasing the ableist beliefs on the part of those intervening. The false thinking would be that if a person looks neurotypical and acts neurotypical, they must really have a "light" case of autism, or none at all. In the interrogation setting, the result for an individual on the spectrum trying to overrepresent their social abilities could be their false confession.[14] In an encounter with patrol officers, law enforcement may be dismissive of one's autism, seeing it as an excuse to evade a criminal charge. In relationships with defense attorneys, the ableism might result in the attorney overlooking mitigating factors otherwise favorable to their client. From a prosecutor's and a judge's perspective, the individual may seem more culpable than they actually are.

From an ableist viewpoint, all of the above examples reinforce the point that the person should have been "able" to know better because of the disabled person's learned ability to mask. They should know, for example, why their behavior was against the law at the time of their offense due to their masking capabilities, which represent them as close to normal as possible. But as the stress and pressure mounts in criminal justice encounters with autistic individuals, eventually an autistic person's ability to mask abates. Yet by then, it can often be too late. While it is hard to differentiate a mental health episode from an individual on the spectrum who is no longer able to keep the mask on, increased training in criminal justice could help.

B. Essentialism

Essentialism is another cognitive process, both explicit and implicit, where people arrive at conclusions about individuals with disabilities. Essentialism refers to the way people perceive natural categories, fundamental attributes, and the underlying essence of a given thing, which is essential to its nature—perceived to be unchangeable and applying to groups of the same name.[15] For example, avocados have pits, mammals are warm-blooded, symphonies have tubas.

Although these are simple examples, this kind of assignment of essential characteristics—characteristics that were seen as unchangeable and defective in the days of institutionalization—to those with mental disabilities has led to some of the most insidious explicit bias, dehumanization, and prejudice imaginable. People were likened to inanimate objects incapable of change and assumed to possess the same characteristics as every other person in their group or category using primitive social constructs. Some individuals with criminal records still are subject to this kind of essentialist explicit bias. Essentialism leads to stereotypical thinking and attitudes toward groups of people, such as a registered sex offender who is shunned by neighbors.

Looking at essentialism in criminal cases, we see that defense attorneys' good intentions have sometimes backfired. Take psychopathy, for example. Some defense attorneys have introduced MRIs at sentencing as a mitigating factor showing that the actions of the person were beyond their control. However, prosecutors use that same information and argue that the person is predisposed to violence and deserves a harsher sentence. Prosecutors would be playing on the essentialist tendencies of people through an implicit bias that human beings have toward those with a perceived unchangeable nature. In contrast, some research indicates judges are able to overcome their implicit bias in this regard. In a study with 181 state judges who were given explanations of a disability and its impact on behavior in hypothetical cases, most of them gave shorter sentences than judges without explanations. Researchers believe evidence of a disability might produce a net aggravating factor for juries and a net mitigating factor for judges at sentencing.[16]

C. Sanism

The term "sanism" was first used by New York attorney and physician, Morton Birnbaum in an article published by the ABA Journal in 1960 titled *The Right to Treatment*. In this groundbreaking piece, Birnbaum argued that if a mentally ill patient were confined against their will, they had a legal right to proper treatment. Birnbaum defined sanism as "irrational thinking, feeling and behavior patterns of response by an individual or by a society to the irrational behavior (and too often even the rational behavior) of a mentally ill individual." Birnbaum continued that "It is morally reprehensible because it is an unnecessary and disabling burden that is added by our prejudiced society to the very real affliction of severe mental illness."[17]

Professor Michael Perlin defines sanism more pungently as " an irrational prejudice against people with mental illness, [that] is of the same quality and character as other irrational prejudices such as racism, sexism, homophobia, and ethnic bigotry that cause (and are reflected in) prevailing social attitudes." It "infects both our jurisprudence and our lawyering practices [and] is largely invisible and largely socially acceptable." Perlin concludes that sanism is based "predominantly upon stereotype, myth, superstition, and deindividuation and is sustained and perpetuated by our use of alleged 'ordinary common sense' and heuristic reasoning in irrational responses to events in both everyday life and the legal process."[18] Focusing on the legal system, he gives examples of sanism, particularly in the context of adoption, civil commitment, forced medication, and the insanity defense. Professor Perlin also warns against sanism hidden beneath good intentions. The previous story of Daniel Prude is an example of sanism, as well as of ableism.

Paradoxically, while sanist decisions are frequently justified as being therapeutically based, sanism often results in antitherapeutic outcomes. This happens in a wide array of circumstances: for example, those charged with minor felonies found to be insane who are committed to maximum-security facilities for many years longer than the maximum sentence they would have received if found guilty; those who are indefinitely committed after being found incompetent to stand trial; and those who are forcibly medicated over their own objection even where there is a strong likelihood that neurological side effects may result.[19]

The criminal justice system has some serious sanist tendencies. It utilizes both archaic and demeaning language to describe the point of demarcation between a "sane" and "insane" person, which is still the benchmark terminology today used for criminal responsibility. It measures insanity by mental illness or "defect"—defect being a word we often think about when returning a product that doesn't work, not the description of a human being. Competing expert witnesses on both sides become the conflicting authors of the stories of defendants with mental health struggles or developmental disabilities, not those individuals themselves, who are merely a specimen for observation and description to the court.

Sanism puts defense lawyers who are in opposition to the concept somewhat at odds with their roles as advocates. Good lawyers will try not to exacerbate irrational prejudices but still have to convey why their client with a disability did what they did and is not a risk to the community. Defense lawyers may need to ask themselves how they adjust to represent their clients in an adversarial system that weaponizes sanist language against them while not giving up their integrity of a zealous representation in the process.

D. Intersectionality

The term "intersectionality" was first coined by Columbia law professor Kimberlé Crenshaw in 1989.[20] It describes how overlapping identities contribute to discrimination and oppression. In other words, multiple identities, usually of marginalized groups, raise the odds of becoming ensnared in the criminal justice system. We regularly see the impact of intersectionality, particularly, disability plus other factors such as race and socioeconomic level, in the criminal justice system.

In a chapter in the ABA's *State of Criminal Justice: 2020* titled *Advancing Equity for People in the Criminal Justice System Who Have Mental Illnesses*, social justice advocate Deanna Adams notes that people of color are frequently misdiagnosed, underdiagnosed, or incorrectly not referred for a mental health evaluation despite exhibiting behavior indicative of a mental illness. Black people, in particular, are 44% less likely to be referred for a mental health evaluation than non-Black people.

This misdiagnosis and disproportionality is often due to implicit and explicit assumptions of criminal justice decision-makers who are responsible for making mental health evaluation referrals. For example, as Adams explains, mental health referrals and evaluations may be influenced by biases, misunderstandings of socioeconomic or cultural differences, and other implicit or explicit assumptions, such as that people of color or people of certain races are inherently criminal. To illustrate this point, people of color who are exhibiting behaviors indicative of mental illnesses are more likely to be seen as being "suspicious" or "criminal" rather than as having a mental health need.[21] Adams describes how screening tools are biased against people of color from low-income backgrounds. For example, screening questions ask if a person is taking medication or has ever been treated for a mental illness. But the significance of this questions is that within correctional settings, people of color with mental health issues are least likely to be given medication and treatment. They are also more likely to be subjected to an involuntary hospitalization, which can adversely impact their other responsibilities such as job and family rather than community-based alternatives.[22]

Use of force against people with mental disabilities is another area where intersectionality is at play, especially where there is a layer of race. For example, in September of 2020, West Sacramento Police shot and killed 88-year-old Robert Coleman, who was Black and in a mental health crisis. Coleman's family had called 911 to report that he had left home, had a gun, and was in crisis. The last point seems to have been lost as police found Coleman and fired at him some 23 times.[23] Coleman was Black, and "over the life course, about 1 in every 1,000 Black men can expect to be killed by police."[24] Coleman was also disabled, and researchers report that the majority of those killed by police have disabilities, including an estimated 27% with mental disability.[25]

Although men of color who are the victims of police-involved shootings are properly mourned and serve as catalysts for reform, there is a growing recognition that women of color—and women of color with disabilities or mental disabilities—are also victims of police shootings.[26] Cases where women of color with disabilities or mental illness are victimized by the police do not get the same attention as men. While many know George Floyd, Sandra Bland, whose death in prison was ruled a suicide, does not share the same name recognition in the media or society in general.[27] This is the inspiration behind the rapidly-growing movement of "Say Her Name," founded by Professor Crenshaw.[28]

Since the 1980s, members of law enforcement across the country have undergone a variety of different programs to assist with dealing with people with mental disabilities including Crisis Intervention Team (CIT) training. This 40-hour training teaches law enforcement how to recognize mental disabilities and de-escalate encounters. However, this is not a panacea, as evident by the number of law enforcement involved fatalities, even in departments where there has been CIT training.[29] It is imperative that individuals with mental disabilities themselves participate in, and help to implement, effective training strategies, as they are best-equipped to advocate their firsthand experiences and share the perspective of the disabled individual.

2. Interventions or Strategies for Participants in the Criminal Justice System

The criminal justice system would be more equitable if all players embraced the following strategies generally and specifically in dealing with persons with disability: (1) add a component dealing with mental disabilities to Implicit Bias Training; (2) incorporate people first language and other bias-free language in its policies, procedures and decisions; and (3) audit all facets of the criminal justice system for assumptions and barriers against people with mental disabilities just as they would assumptions and barriers against people with physical disabilities.

A. Training

Thankfully, more and more organizations and workplaces are sponsoring Implicit Bias Training for their members and employees. However, it is crucial that in addition to raising awareness about implicit bias based on race, gender, age, and sexual orientation, these trainings include a component about the unique concerns of people with mental disabilities.[30]

B. Using Bias-Free Language

Probably no other profession understands the power of words better than the legal profession. Criminal justice professionals should realize the profound impact their words have on the people involved in its proceedings and on the perception of fairness. The danger lies in our unintentional use of offensive terms, statements, and questions. Admittedly our awareness is continually evolving, and the courts are cognizant of this. For instance, in *Hall v. Florida*, 572 U.S. 701 (2014), Freddie Hall argued that he should not be executed because of his mental disability. In deciding that the Florida definition of disability was too rigid (an IQ of 70, while Hall's IQ was 71), Justice Anthony Kennedy opened his opinion with an impactful statement that the Court would use the term "intellectual disability" instead of "mental retardation."[31] Although *Hall* was decided in 2014, many people, including legal professionals, still use the outmoded language, including shortened, more offensive versions of it. After all, we still use the greatly offensive term "mental defect" as a standard for someone who is planning on preparing an insanity defense. Some attorneys, perhaps in an effort to humanize their clients, call them by their first names. But in regards to clients with mental disabilities, particularly those with intellectual or developmental disabilities, this could telegraph implicit bias.

Another way to reduce bias is to use "people first" language, which is now fairly widespread. We now say that someone is "a person with a mental illness" or "a person with bipolar disorder" rather than saying someone is "mentally ill." Often, in personal encounters, it is wise to ask people what they want to be called and how they are most comfortable being described where a description is needed.

C. Re-examining Barriers and Assumptions

At bottom, the criminal justice system should examine its policies and trainings so as to reduce the assumptions and barriers against people with mental disabilities, the same way it would on behalf of people with physical disabilities or other marginalized groups or statuses.

The ADA defines disability as "A) a physical or mental impairment that substantially limits one or more major life activities of such individual; (B) a record of such an impairment; or (C) being regarded as having such an impairment..."[32] The statute clearly applies to people with mental disabilities, but this aspect is often not enforced.

From the moment of the initial encounter with law enforcement, through interrogation, court proceedings, probation, and incarceration, the accused should be able to fully access and participate in the criminal justice process.[33] For example, is there any doubt among readers of this book that Part II of the ADA (which prohibits excluding qualified individuals from "the benefits of the services, programs, or activities of a public entity, or be subjected to discrimination by any such entity"),[34] is rarely honored in the incarcerated setting? Prisoners with disabilities who have sensory issues are rarely given accommodations like ear plugs or sunglasses because it would be considered contraband. Individuals on the autism spectrum who are grouped by bunks in dormitory-like settings would find no privacy other than in solitary confinement. A mentally ill individual would have to detox off certain drugs cold turkey instead of being weaned off properly, leading to probable decompensation.

These situations are in part due to a lack of common definition and understanding. For example, no single, agreed-upon screening tool exists for individuals with autism or intellectual impairments upon intake in county jails. If individuals with autism or developmental disabilities show up at a county jail, they can be conflated with individuals with other mental illnesses or even mistaken for being intoxicated or under the influence of drugs. A screening tool could, at least, hint at the fact that the person may have a developmental disability, which would then require further analysis. These are all issues that have yet to be addressed in any meaningful way.

The advice in this section is applicable to all of us. In addition, some group-specific interventions follow to interrupt and mitigate implicit bias against people with mental disabilities.

3. Participant-Relevant Approaches to Implicit Bias

A. Judges

Judges should be keenly aware that mental disabilities are often invisible. They should also be aware that many individuals with mental disabilities, in order to avoid stigma or bullying, may mask or cover their disabilities. Moreover, every person manifests a different constellation of characteristics, and every person is capable of change. Knowledge of someone's disability has varying impacts.[35] All of these factors means that judges need to take time to learn the subtleties of different types of mental disabilities.

Sentencing provides an example. The defense expert opines that based upon psychological testing the accused has an intellectual disability. The presentence report states that the accused has a job at a bank and graduated from high school. Besides this, he "looks normal" and seems well-mannered (apart from his criminal charge). This scenario can be interpreted in more than one way, and judges should understand that these accomplishments do not contradict the presence of an intellectual disability. The defendant is not the president of the bank; he is a janitor. His duties are fairly rote, and he only was able to learn them after intensive work with a job coach. And although he graduated from high school, it was before the days of IEPs (Individualized Education Program), and social promotion was the custom in his hometown. Beneath his "normal" look is a very low IQ, and his good manners are the result of decades of wanting to please others. Therefore, judges should look beyond the initial appearance of those before them and perhaps even ask a series of questions to determine whether the person has a hidden disability.

Of course, judges are not trained mental health professionals. They rely on caselaw, statutes, and guidelines in determining sentencing. Two recent California studies focused on autism are insightful on this topic. To determine the attitudes of judges toward autistic individuals who come before them at sentencing, the qualitative studies reviewed data over a course of years.[36] Not surprisingly, judges had varying attitudes and biases. Many viewed autism as a mitigating factor, but some viewed it as an aggravating factor. The study revealed an implicit bias that autistic people have no impulse control and are stubborn; this perceived lack of impulse control led one judge to conclude autistic people are more dangerous if they cannot control their actions. Such explicit or implicit attitudes that autistic people are stubborn could have negative implications when it comes to a judge's perception that treatment would not help the individual rebuild his or her life. Just as we would never send a deaf person into an important meeting without a sign language interpreter, we should not send an individual with a social disability into a presentence interview where the probation officer is using neurotypical standards of behavior to judge remorsefulness. We strongly recommend the client's lawyer be present at such a meeting.

A growing population in the criminal justice system is comprised of older defendants who may manifest dementia. This is certainly an invisible disability, one that might be particularly difficult to accept in what were previously high-functioning, law-abiding individuals. For dementia as well as others with disabilities not readily visible on the surface, we should not assume that because someone doesn't appear to fit a stereotype or preconceived notion of what it means to have a cognitive impairment, that it is not present—and that it may constitute an impediment to functioning including complying with the terms of the court, probation, or perhaps jail or prison. In sum, when presiding over cases involving people with mental disabilities, to use Isabel Wilkerson's words, judges should resist the temptation to "prejudge complicated breathing beings in ways we are told never to judge inanimate objects."

Consider, too, that many nursing homes do not allow elderly residents to live there if they have been convicted of any kind of sex offense. Such was the case for 82-year-old Leonard Bailey of Florida, who hit his head in a fall and could no longer remember to take his medicine.[37] No nursing home would take him in. Who can take care of such a person if that individual has no family or friends in old age? Are we to put them out to pasture and in a complete state of helplessness because of a behavior of which they did not have any volitional control over at the time they committed the offense?

B. Prosecutors

Many people contend that prosecutors are the most powerful players in the criminal justice system, and with good reason. They have the ability to charge, and the power to indict is the power to destroy. The threat of mandatory sentencing can be a persuasive weapon in forcing a plea. They are often the gatekeepers for various diversionary programs, including mental health and other specialty courts. And they are often a powerful force in preventing the exoneration of the wrongly convicted.

Prosecutors should avoid the reflexive response of "he knew exactly what he was doing" when encountering an accused who raises a mental disability as mitigation, or presents an insanity defense. For example, a successful executive may have bipolar disorder, and during a manic episode, have killed someone. Or, a seemingly brilliant computer analyst with Autism Spectrum Disorder (ASD) may have been lured by an undercover police officer posing as an underage female. An often-fallacious argument made by those quick to assign guilt based on implicit bias is that they have met many autistic people, or people with bipolar or with Obsessive Compulsive Disorder (OCD), and those people would never do what the defendant is accused of doing. A common variant on this theme may go something along the lines of: *My mother is autistic, and she would never do that.* Or, *My brother is bipolar, and, even in a manic phase, he knows right from wrong.* Or even, *I am autistic, and I would never do that.*

The kind of thinking illustrated by these remarks is ableist and is classic stereotyping. It assumes that all neurodiverse people manifest their symptoms in exactly the same way in all situations and, thus, everybody in the same category should be held to the same standards. Not all diabetics go into diabetic comas, just as not all individuals with congestive heart failure have the exact same progression. Intuitively, this argument makes no sense on its face, but people still routinely use it. Let's go back to the seemingly brilliant computer analyst with Autism Spectrum Disorder. Is it possible to be brilliant in some areas and mind-blind in other areas? Our implicit bias and ableist assumptions would emphatically say such a discrepancy is not possible in human behavior. If one is a genius-level computer analyst, they cannot have factors that would clearly tell them something obvious to most people is against the law. This "ordinary common sense" attitude is the consensus reality of most prosecutors. Yet consider that a 2017 study by Klin *et al.* found that in a sample of children and adolescents with an average or above average IQ and a mean chronological age of 12.4 years, their mean interpersonal social age was 3.2 years.[38] This fact would have serious implications for the prosecutions of juveniles and adults on the autism spectrum. Also consider that measurements like the Vineland Adaptive Behavior Scales actually decrease with age for autistic people, meaning decompensation is likely for these individuals over the course of a lifespan.[39] Among other things, adaptive functioning involves daily living skills in social domains which rely heavily on interpersonal communication, being able to take the perspective of another person (known as "theory of mind") and emotional regulation. Therefore, it is possible to be intellectually brilliant but at the same time, unaware of social taboos which could actually involve inadvertent law breaking. Prosecutors must be aware of this counterintuitive fact in helping to guide them toward an appropriate adjudication for this population. Moreover, the growing use of neuroimaging is providing visual proof mental disabilities such as dementia and traumatic brain injury, and prosecutors should be open to that proof.

Prosecutors should also be cautious about accusing a defendant of malingering. Granted, a defendant may not have raised the issue of a mental disability before. That could be for a variety of reasons, including defense counsel's failure to recognize the need for an evaluation or to raise the fact that the client may not have had the resources to obtain a diagnosis prior to entering the criminal justice system. One way to guard against malingering would be for a forensic psychologist to use tests with malingering scales built in, such as the MMPI-2. Prosecutors also should keep in mind that to malinger a developmental disability would be extremely difficult for even the most brilliant psychopath. If those who know the defendant historically, such as parents, extended family, former bosses, therapists or former educators can help to verify that developmental milestones were not met and the defendant's file is backed up with data, it can alleviate the concern of malingering for prosecutors even if no current diagnosis existed prior to the arrest. Nonetheless, it might be a good opportunity to secure the help the defendant needs in order not to re-offend, to keep the community safe, and for the prosecutor to fulfill his or her ethical duty to achieve justice.

C. Criminal Defense Lawyers

As with other segments of society, criminal defense lawyers (present company included) are also susceptible to all sorts of implicit bias, including ableist and sanist assumptions. In the spirit of Isabele Wilkerson's quote, we size up and make assumptions quickly, and then impose our own standards about how a "normal" client should behave. The following anecdote about an initial client meeting by Public Defender Alison Mathis about a young man on the autism spectrum is a good example. It illustrates that even a compassionate, dedicated, smart criminal defense lawyer like her can get off on the wrong foot with a client:

> When a client I'll call Dino and his mom came into my office for the first time, I did everything wrong. Dino was accused of a moderately serious assault against a convenience store owner, and he already had a significant juvenile record of which I was aware. The new offense was captured on video, and there were not really any legal issues to wrangle. This was his first adult offense. Sheepishly, his mother pushed him into my office nearly an hour late for our first appointment. "He was sleeping," she said quietly. "I didn't want to wake him up." I looked over at the clock on my desk. It was 1:45 p.m. I was irritated and showed it. I like my clients to take at least some interest in their own cases, and I disliked that his mother was so tentative that she "didn't want to wake him up" for an appointment in the mid-afternoon. "Sleeping? Isn't this case the most important thing in your life right now? More than that, aren't you supposed to be in school?" I asked. Silence. Dino didn't look up at me. His mom squirmed after a few seconds of me trying to make eye contact with him. "He... dropped out two years ago" she said. "Oh," I said, a little pointedly, "then do you have a job?" More silence. Dino drummed on the side of his chair with his fingers and looked out the window. "No, he's... not working right now." "Oh? What do you do? What do you want to do?" Silence. More drumming.
>
> "Hmmm..." I said, "Well, this isn't great. What are we going to tell the prosecutor and the judge? What are we going to tell them about you that makes them not want to send you to jail?" Silence. More drumming.
>
> At no point in the conversation did Dino or his mother tell me that he had been diagnosed with ASD. What I was reading as "bored, disrespectful, flippant teenager" was actually ASD.[40]

The second type of implicit bias we can fall prey to is that of being paternalistic toward our clients with mental disabilities, that is, presuming that we know best. One way we do this is the tendency to diminish the client with an intellectual/developmental disability, by, for instance, addressing only the parent in a meeting and talking about the client as if he or she were not in the room. And there are many other ways. We are not referring here to instances where our clients are clearly incompetent. Nor are we wading into the debate about standards for civil commitment. Rather, we are talking about our tendency to discount much of what they say because of their disability. When we do this, we may well miss important information. Hidden in their delusions, for example, may be a legitimate alibi or other defense.

What can be done? What strategies can we use to combat our own implicit bias as lawyers? For starters, we may need to get creative with how we communicate with our clients—or rather, be flexible in terms of how they communicate with us. If their preferred method of communication is visual, it might be appropriate to allow them to draw visual representations of what their recollection is, instead of asking them to verbally respond to a series of rapid-fire questions. We might have to illustrate our ideas to them through flow charts or visual depictions, rather than a verbal stream of information. Sometimes using a verbal command such as, "knock once for no, knock two times for yes" can simplify communication and may be appropriate when trying to elicit information from clients. Other times, it may simply just be giving them the space they need while they are overwhelmed until they are less overwhelmed and more comfortable communicating. Finally, like many clients, individuals with mental disabilities may simply take time to develop a sense of trust with their attorneys, and this may not happen at the first meeting.

There is, once again, a delicate balance that needs to be met between not being paternalistic and also appropriately relying on family members for help, more than we would in other cases. Many defense lawyers have made the observation, accurately so, that parents and guardians are much more participatory in the defense of their loved ones involving mental disabilities than the family member of the average client. This is to be expected and not resisted, so long as the client consents. If a client does not consent, the defense attorney's hands are tied. But we cannot emphasize enough the importance of historical accuracy in defending these individuals which may not always be possible to get directly from the client due to their communication challenges.

Make no mistake. We have a difficult task: to advocate for a client with a mental disability within a system not created for them, a system which often punishes them for manifesting the symptoms of their disability, and a system which treats the public health issue of lack of resources for people with mental disabilities as a criminal justice issue.

D. Jail and Prison Officials

When it comes to recommending strategies to end implicit bias in jails and prisons, we freely acknowledge that this calls for a wholesale change in philosophy and that effecting change in this environment may be particularly difficult. To begin, we need to look at the fundamental purpose of our jails and prisons in the first quarter of the 21st Century. Jails are primarily holding facilities for people awaiting the disposition of their case or serving sentences less than twelve months. They were never intended for long-term care, let alone treatment. They are managed by police and sheriffs, and, other than a few part or full-time medical staff, are run by people who didn't sign up to be social workers or medical personnel. In contrast, prisons are intended for people serving sentences of at least a year. And despite some well-intentioned efforts, the primary purpose of prison is to punish, not to rehabilitate, and certainly not to treat. Like jail staff, prison staff did not sign up to take care of people with mental disabilities, although approximately half the inmates have some sort of mental issue.

Both jails and prisons were designed according to ableists assumptions, that is, that all inmates must behave in a certain manner and conform to a strict set of rules. There is no tolerance for those who are incapable of doing so. A person can't follow the rules if they don't understand them. Many prison rules are "unwritten" and expected to be known or understood without any explicit, direct instruction. This presents a problem for many individuals on the autism spectrum, who need rules spelled out in a very clear and formal way. At the same time, any perceived behavioral infractions result in punishment, including the most inhumane practice of putting a suicidal inmate in solitary confinement, sometimes for years. Research shows that autistic people are less likely to encounter empathy from correctional staff due to their behavioral differences, likely due to implicit bias and exacerbating the problem of solitary confinement for this population.[41]

Only when we understand that correctional facilities are inherently not therapeutic environments will we begin to send those with mental disabilities to places where they can be treated and responded to according to their unique needs. We seem to understand this when it comes to, for example, crimes such as possession of methamphetamine, which can carry up to a 10-year prison sentence but where users often get probation. Yet, because many of the crimes committed by the developmentally disabled can be of a sexual nature, like stalking or voyeurism, such an extreme departure from the guidelines is quite rare. These types of crimes have mandatory minimums or plea agreements where probation is not an option, leaving these individuals to most likely to mentally decompensate in a prison setting. Might implicit bias be part of the reason why the default response is punitive and not restorative or therapeutic in these types of cases? After all, autism is not associated whatsoever with psychopathy[42] and autistic people are likely to complete their probationary periods without a violation.[43]

In her compelling book, *Waiting for an Echo: The Madness of American Incarceration*,[44] Dr. Christine Montross details how Norway completely rethought and reimagined its philosophy of sentencing. Norway used to be like the United States, that is, it harshly punished for long periods of time, and still had a high recidivism rate. Then, it decided to upend that model. Now, their prisons are relatively humane: Inmates have rooms, and are given keys to their own rooms; staff is respectful of inmates; and sentences are short. In particular, inmates with mental disabilities are given medication and treatment with the recognition that they will be re-entering society upon release. The result: recidivism is low.

E. Police and Other Law Enforcement

Just as meaningful and significant change in our jails and prisons will only come through a change in philosophy about the purpose of incarceration, so too, change in law enforcement's behavior toward those with mental disabilities will only come through a change in how we see their roles.

This Chapter has already discussed the practices of police and other law enforcement, how ableism and sanism influence their actions, and how the phenomenon of intersectionality renders some individuals particularly vulnerable. This country is engaged in a dialogue about police reform, and the recent acts of violence against people with disabilities like Linden Cameron and Daniel Prude should inform that dialogue.

But, if we are going to acknowledge the impact of mental disability system-wide, we should also acknowledge that law enforcement itself is also vulnerable to the burden of disability, that is, to the cumulative impact of work-related trauma on their conduct. We should acknowledge that law enforcement sees some dreadful sights. Simply because one officer is able to carry on in the face of danger and after witnessing a horrific event or events does not mean that another officer in immune to this.[45] The movement toward a trauma-informed criminal justice system should include law enforcement.

Conclusion

The issue of implicit bias against people with mental disabilities in the criminal justice system is one worthy of further study, discussion, and analysis. We hope that this Chapter will provoke all this and that this brief introduction to the terms of ableism, essentialism, sanism, and intersectionality will serve as a foundation. We also hope that our colleagues will adopt the strategies and interventions suggested and share their experiences in doing so.

So, You'd Like to Know More

- Implicit Bias, www.americanbar.org/resources/implicit-bias.
- Legal Reform for the Intellectually and Developmentally Disabled, www.lridd.org.
- Treatment and Advocacy, www.treatmentadvocacycenter.org.
- Nick Dubin, Autism Spectrum Disorder, Developmental Disabilities, and the Criminal Justice System: Breaking the Cycle (2021).
- David M. Perry & Lawrence Carter-Long, The Ruderman White Paper on Media Coverage of Law Enforcement Use of Force and Disability: A Media Study (2013–2015) and Overview (2016).
- Disability Language and Style, National Center on Disability and Journalism, Resources Guide, https://ncdj.org/resources.

About the Authors

Elizabeth Kelley is a criminal defense lawyer with a nationwide practice focusing on representing people with mental disabilities. She is the editor of *Representing People with Mental Disabilities: A Practical Guide for Criminal Defense Lawyers* (Elizabeth Kelley ed., 2019); *Representing People with Autism Spectrum Disorders: A Practical Guide for Criminal Defense Lawyers* (Elizabeth Kelley ed. 2020); and *Representing People with Dementia: A Practical Guide for Criminal Defense Lawyers* (2022), all published by the ABA. She chairs The Arc's National Center for Criminal Justice and Disability and serves on the ABA's Criminal Justice Section Council, Editorial Board of *Criminal Justice Magazine*, and Commission on Disability Rights.

Nick Dubin was diagnosed with Asperger's Syndrome (now Autism Spectrum Disorder) in 2004. He holds a Bachelor's Degree in Communications from Oakland University, a Master's Degree in Learning Disabilities from the University of Detroit Mercy, and a Specialist Degree in Psychology and Psy.D. from the Michigan School of Professional Psychology. He has authored many books on autism spectrum disorders including *Asperger Syndrome and Anxiety*, published by Jessica Kingsley Publishers. He also has personal experience of the criminal justice system.

Endnotes

1. Isabel Wilkerson, Caste: The Origins of Our Discontents 223 (2020).

2. Developmental disabilities are "chronic mental and/or physical impairments that begin before the age of 22 and cause severe limitations in several domains." Laura R. Parker, Margo J. Monteith & Susan C. South, *Dehumanization, Prejudice, and Social Policy Beliefs Concerning People with Developmental Disabilities*, 23 Group Processes & Intergroup Relations 262, 262, 264, 280 (2020).

3. Brian A. Nosek et al., *Pervasiveness and Correlates of Implicit Attitudes and Stereotypes*, 18 Eur. Rev. Soc. Psychol. 36, 54 (2007).

4. David M. Perry & Lawrence Carter-Long, The Ruderman White Paper on Media Coverage of Law Enforcement Use of Force And Disability: A Media Study (2013–2015), https://rudermanfoundation.org/wp-content/uploads/2017/08/MediaStudy-PoliceDisability_final-final.pdf; Overview (2016).

5. Elizabeth Pendo, *Covid-19 and Disability-Based Discrimination in Health Care*, Am. Bar Ass'n (May 22, 2020), https://www.americanbar.org/groups/diversity/disabilityrights/resources/covid19-disability-discrimination/; HHS-OCR Complaints Re Covid-19 Medical Discrimination. The Arc (Mar. 23, 2020), https://thearc.org/resource/hhs-ocr-complaint-of-disability-rights-washington-self-advocates-in-leadership-the-arc-of-the-united-states-and-ivanova-smith/.

6. Keri Blakinger & Joseph Neff, *1,000 Prisoners Sought Compassionate Release During Covid-19. The Bureau of Prisons Approved 36*, The Marshall Project (June 11, 2021), https://www.themarshallproject.org/2021/06/11/31-000-prisoners-sought-compassionate-release-during-covid-19-the-bureau-of-prisons-approved-36; *see also* Katie Park, Keri Blakinger & Claudia Lauer, *A Half-Million People Got Covid-19 in Prison. Are Officials Ready for the Next Pandemic?*, The Marshall Project, June 30, 2021, https://www.themarshallproject.org/2021/06/30/a-half-million-people-got-covid-19-in-prison-are-officials-ready-for-the-next-pandemic.

7. Sam Farmer, *Criminal Injustice Toward Autistic Individuals and the Regrettable Necessity of Labeling Autism a Disability*, The Hill (Sept. 23, 2020), https://thehill.com/changing-america/opinion/517820-criminal-injustice-towards-autistic-individuals-and-the-regrettable (an excellent piece describing how the term "disability" is misplaced when referring to some people with autism spectrum disorder as well as the media's inaccurate portrayal of people with ASD being prone to violence).

8. *Ableism*, Nat'l Conf. Cmty. & Just., http://nccj.org/ableism (last visited July 28, 2021).

9. *Discriminate*, Merriam-Webster Dictionary, https://www.merriam-webster.com/dictionary/discriminate#etymology.

10. *See, e.g.*, C.J. Ciaramella, *North Carolina Mother Sues School Resource Officer Who Handcuffed and Pinned Her 7-Year-Old Autistic Son*, Reason (Oct. 16, 2020), https:\\reason.com/2020/10/16/north-carolina-mother-sues-school-resource-officer-who- handcuffed-and-pinned-her-7-year-old-autistic-son; *see generally* U.S. Dept. Ed., Off. Civ. Rts., Civ. Rts. Data Collection 2015–2016 (2018).

11. Kenya Evelyn, *Police Shoot 13-Year-Old Boy with Autism Several Times After Mother Calls for Help*, The Guardian, Sept. 8, 2020, https://www.theguardian.com/us-news/2020/sep/08/linden-cameron-police-shooting-boy-autism-utah.

12. Edgar Sandoval, *Daniel Prude Was in 'Mental Distress.' Police Treated Him Like a Suspect.*, N.Y. TIMES, Oct 9. 2020, https://www.nytimes.com/2020/10/09/nyregion/daniel-prude-rochester-police-mental-health.html.

13. Amy Pearson & Kieran Rose, *A Conceptual Analysis of Autistic Masking: Understanding the Narrative of Stigma and the Illusion of Choice*, 3 AUTISM IN ADULTHOOD 5260 (2021); *see generally* Kenji Yoshino, *Covering*, 111 YALE L.J. 769 (2002).

14. Samson J. Schatz, *Interrogated with Intellectual Disabilities: The Risks of False Confession*, 70 STAN. L. REV. 6430 (2018).

15. John Pyun, *When Neurogenetics Hurts: Examining the Use of Neuroscience and Genetic Evidence in Sentencing Decisions through Implicit Bias*, 103 CALIF. L. REV. 1019 (2015).

16. *Id.*

17. Morton Birnbaum, *The Right to Treatment: Some Comments on its Development*, in MED., MORAL, & LEGAL ISSUES IN HEALTH CARE 97, 106–07 (Frank Ayd ed., 1974).

18. Michael L. Perlin, *Sanism and the Law*, 15 VIRTUAL MENTOR, AM. MED. ASS'N J. ETHICS 878, 878 (2013).

19. *Id.* at 880.

20. Kimberlé Crenshaw, *Demarginalizing the Intersection of Race and Sex: A Black Feminist Critique of Antidiscrimination Doctrine, Feminist Theory and Antiracist Politics*, U. CHI. L. F. 139 (1989).

21. Deanna M. Adams, *Advancing Equity for People in the Criminal Justice System Who Have Mental Illnesses*, in THE STATE CRIM. JUST. 182 (Mark E. Wojcik ed., 2020).

22. *Id.*

23. Maria Grijalva, *Guest Commentary: Mental Health Crisis Leads to Shooting Death of 88-Year-Old Robert Coleman by WS Police*, DAVIS VANGUARD, Sept. 28, 2020, https://www.davisvanguard.org/2020/09/guest-commentary-mental-health-crisis-leads-to-shooting-death-of-88-year-old-robert-coleman-by-ws-police/.

24. Frank Edwards, Hedwig Lee & Michael Esposito, *Risk of Being Killed by Police Use of Force in the United States by Age, Race–Ethnicity, and Sex*, 116 PNAS 16793 (2019).

25. David M. Perry & Lawrence Carter-Long, THE RUDERMAN WHITE PAPER ON MEDIA COVERAGE OF LAW ENFORCEMENT USE OF FORCE AND DISABILITY: A MEDIA STUDY (2013–2015), https://rudermanfoundation.org/wp-content/uploads/2017/08/MediaStudy-Police Disability_final-final.pdf; OVERVIEW (2016).

26. *See* Frank Edwards, Hedwig Lee & Michael Esposito, *Risk of Being Killed by Police Use of Force in the United States by Age, Race–Ethnicity, and Sex*, 116 PNAS 16793 (2019); *see also e.g.*, Matt Stevens & Joseph Goldstein, *New York City Agrees to Pay $2 Million to Family of Mentally Ill Woman Killed by Police*, N.Y. TIMES, Dec. 13, 2018, www.nytimes.com/2018/12/13/nyregion/deborah-danner-settlement.html; David Montgomery, *Her Name Was Miriam Carey*, WASH. POST, Nov. 26, 2014, http://www.washingtonpost.com/sf/style/2014/11/26/how-miriam-careys-u-turn-at-a-white-house-checkpoint-led-to-her-death/.

27. *See generally* THE RUDERMAN WHITE PAPER ON MEDIA COVERAGE OF LAW ENFORCEMENT USE OF FORCE AND DISABILITY: A MEDIA STUDY (2013–2015) and OVERVIEW (2016).

28. Alisha Haridasani Gupta, *Since 2015: 48 Black Women Killed by the Police. And Only 2 Charges*. N.Y. TIMES, Sept. 24, 2020, https://www.nytimes.com/2020/09/24/us/breonna-taylor-grand-jury-black-women.html.

29. Eric Westervelt, *Mental Health and Police Violence: How Crisis Intervention Teams Are Failing*, NPR (Sept. 18, 2020), https://www.npr.org/2020/09/18/913229469/mental-health-and-police-violence-how-crisis-intervention-teams-are-failing.

30. *See, e.g., Implicit Bias Guide: Implicit Biases & People with Disabilities*, AM. BAR ASS'N. COMM'N. DISABILITY RTS, https://www.americanbar.org/groups/diversity/disabilityrights/resources/implicit_bias/.

31. Hall v. Florida, 572 U.S. 701 (2014).

32. 42 U.S.C. § 12102.

33. According to Professor Robert Dinnerstein of American University School of Law: "There is a split in authority on whether Title II of the ADA... applies to arrests. The 9th Circuit said so in *Sheehan v. City of SF* [San Francisco], a case that went up to the Supreme Court (but which the Court did not decide on this issue because the city and county of SF conceded the point after filing their petition for certiorari), but the 11th Circuit disagrees (based on a so-called 'armed and dangerous' exception to coverage)." Email from Dinnerstein to authors, Oct. 7, 2020.

34. 42 U.S.C. § 12132.

35. *See, e.g.,* Katie Maras, Imogen Marshall & Chloe Sands, *Mock Juror Perceptions of Credibility and Culpability in an Autistic Defendant*, 49 J. AUTISM & DEVELOPMENTAL DISORDERS 996 (2019).

36. Colleen M. Berryessa, *Judiciary Views on Criminal Behaviour and Intention of Offenders with High-functioning Autism*, 5 J. INTELLECTUAL DISABILITIES & OFFENDING BEHAVIOR 97 (2014); Colleen M. Berryessa, *Brief Report: Judicial Attitudes Regarding the Sentencing of Offenders with High Functioning Autism*, 46 J. AUTISM & DEVELOPMENTAL DISORDERS 2770 (2016).

37. Meryl Kornfield, *Housing Elderly Sex Offenders*, ASSOC. PRESS, May 2, 2019, https://apnews.com/article/723104c28c824f56a49d4eaa47e158c6.

38. Ami Klin et al., *Social and Communication Abilities and Disabilities in Higher Functioning Individuals with Autism Spectrum Disorders: The Vineland and the ADOS*, 37 J. AUTISM & DEVELOPMENTAL DISORDERS 748 (2007).

39. Leann E. Smith, Jan S. Greenberg & Marsha R. Mailick, *Adults with Autism: Outcomes, Family Effects, and the Multi-Family Group Psychoeducation Model*, 14 CURRENT PSYCHIATRY REPORTS 732 (2012).

40. Allison Jackson Mathis, *Creative Mitigation, in* REPRESENTING PEOPLE WITH AUTISM SPECTRUM DISORDERS: A PRACTICAL GUIDE FOR CRIM. DEF. LAWS 122 (Elizabeth Kelley ed. 2020).

41. Randy Shively, *Treating Offenders with Mental Retardation and Developmental Disabilities*, 66 CORRECTIONS TODAY 84 (2004).

42. Diana Loureiro et al., *Higher Autistic Traits Among Criminals, But No Link to Psychopathy: Findings from a High-Security Prison in Portugal*, 48 J. AUTISM & DEVELOPMENTAL DISORDERS 3010 (2018).

43. David Allen et al., *Offending Behavior in Adults with Asperger Syndrome*, 48 J. AUTISM & DEVELOPMENTAL DISORDERS 748 (2008).

44. CHRISTINE MONTROSS, WAITING FOR AN ECHO: THE MADNESS OF AMERICAN INCARCERATION (2020).

45. *Most Police Officers Never Seek Mental Health Care, Despite Apparent Need*, HEALIO, Oct. 16, 2020, https://www.healio.com/news/psychiatry/20201016/most-police-officers-never-seek-mental-health-care-despite-apparent-need.

TWENTY-THREE

Educational Disparity, the Great Unequalizer

How Racial and Learning Disability Biases Thwart Equity in Education

The Honorable Julian Mann, III, Chief Administrative Law Judge, NC (Ret.)
The Honorable Stacey Bice Bawtinhimer,[*] Administrative Law Judge, NC

A Note from the Editors: As lawyers, we know full well the value and power of words—spoken words, written words, words we listen to, words we read. As you approach this Chapter, we ask you to stop for a minute and reflect on your own experiences learning to read. Reflect too on the importance of reading to education and of education to your life and work. Put yourself in the shoes of someone who learns to read differently and who may be stigmatized because of that.

    The issue of implicit bias in education is one with which we are both familiar from our prior work, including work on interrupting the school to prison pipeline. The knowledge to be gained from this Chapter enriches and broadens our experience. Focusing on the intersection of groups that often call out implicit bias—disability and race and ethnicity—the authors recognize what we see in other arenas, that is, that intersections are more troubling than the sum of their parts. By choosing to focus more particularly on students with dyslexia, Judges Mann and Bawtinhimer offer us an important lens to see the issues. Additionally, this Chapter's attention to special education law expands our understanding of implicit bias as it plays out in decisions in schools and administrative proceedings. The authors here have long,

---

    [*] Special recognition is owed to Amy Mull, a 3L at the University of North Carolina Chapel Hill Law School for her invaluable research assistance through the multiple drafts and revisions of this Chapter. Thanks also to Daniel Leake, II, a 3L at Campbell University Law School for his research early in the development of the Chapter

broad, and deep history and experience in this area of law and practice, and their analysis is thoughtful, eye-opening, and wise. Their specific suggestions, if adopted, could change the experience of many of our young people. Interestingly, they are much like strategies in other chapters, for example, when they advocate removing discretion in evaluation decisions. They end with an irony that has stuck with us as a call to action (no spoilers, read on).

CHAPTER HIGHLIGHTS

- The ability to read is the foundation for educational success, and the inability to read is disproportionately based on race, ethnicity, socioeconomic status, and learning disability.
- We focus on the intersecting biases against students based on their learning disabilities (particularly dyslexia) and their race/ethnicity to demonstrate the impact of implicit bias on the way students are taught to read.
- For students with learning disabilities, "difficulties in learning... cannot be attributed to poor intelligence, poor motivation, or inadequate teaching." (National Commission)
- Researchers looking at the comparative data observe that while teachers may well care very much about their students, they nevertheless may make implicitly biased decisions that do not support student achievement.
- Strategies that emphasize proper procedures and support can change results.

CHAPTER CONTENTS

Introduction

1. Historical Perspective on Race, Disability, and Educational Disparities
    A. Race and education disparities became deeply rooted during slavery and the Jim Crow era.
    B. The separate but equal doctrine was eliminated, but education disparities persist.
2. Current Civil Rights Legislation Concerning Educating Students with Disabilities

3. Perspective from the School to Prison Pipeline
   A. Comparative Reading Scores
   B. Disproportionate Graduation Rates
   C. Disproportionality in Students with Disabilities
4. Literacy Skills & Lifelong Achievement
   A. The Need for Early Literacy Skills Foundation
   B. Dyslexia and Problems with Early Identification
   C. Considering Dyslexia in the Context of the IDEA Mandate
5. Implicit Bias and the Disconnect Between Educational Aspirations and Achievement
   A. Expectations
   B. The So-Called Uncaring Parent
   C. Stereotype Threat
   D. Race
6. The Detrimental Impact of Teacher Bias and Racial Disparity in Public School Teachers
   A. Teachers don't know what they don't know.
   B. Communication must be improved between teacher and students.
   C. The eligibility process must be objective.

Conclusions and Recommendations
   A. Identify dyslexia early and use proven teaching methods.
   B. Remove subjective race-based eligibility decisions.
   C. Support school funding reform.

Postscript: The irony is we know how to teach kids to read.

Introduction

Impoverished as a child, Horace Mann began his early education in a one-room schoolhouse where school was held for a mere ten weeks out of a year. But, even in that limited time, his teachers ingrained into him a love of learning that propelled him in later life far beyond his early educational opportunities. For Mann, reading was the key that opened the doors to learning, and learning opened the doors to college. Mann thrived in formal education, and he launched a successful career in law and state and federal politics. Although Mann worked tirelessly on many reforms, accessible public education always remained at the forefront for him. Mann believed that education "is a great equalizer,"[1] that "education is preventative" while "[o]ther reforms are remedial."[2] This Chapter discusses how biases can interrupt the delivery of equitable learning opportunities in public education—specifically how implicit racial bias and its associated unconscious negative perceptions reduce the power of education to be the great societal equalizer Mann envisioned.[3] In this Chapter we narrow our focus to the significance of Mann's paradigm that reading ability is the path to an individual's educational and career trajectory. Within that focus we use as our primary example dyslexia, a reading learning disability. In using this example, we anchor our discussion in the context of both learning to read and the manifestations of the failure to so learn. Children of color, especially those in need of special education services for dyslexia, are the ones who are most vulnerable. In other words, inadequate support for these children, coupled with implicit biases, feeds the school to prison pipeline (the "pipeline"), derailing life-saving educational opportunity.[4] The Chapter also points to a path forward: by earlier identification of dyslexia and the use of objective data, the devastating effects of implicit bias can be mitigated and education can take its intended place as the great equalizer.

1. Historical Perspective on Race, Disability, and Educational Disparities

A. Race and education disparities became deeply rooted during slavery and the Jim Crow era.

Race and educational disparities are deeply rooted in America's history of slavery and the Jim Crow era. Most antebellum states in the South, by statute, made it illegal to teach an African American child to read or write, although it was not illegal to write numbers because that was helpful to slaveowners.[5] Promoting literacy, it was thought, would bring opportunities for slaves to forge passes and free papers, to access and spread abolitionist literature, and, as applied to the Bible, to encourage visions of freedom.[6] Ironically, as these laws suggest, even then people knew that freedom flowed from knowledge and literacy.

Consider Fredrick McGhee, born a slave in Mississippi in 1861 and orphaned at age 13.[7] His self-educated father unlawfully taught him to read as a child.[8] McGhee, not unlike Horace Mann, but facing greater obstacles because of his race, pursued formal education—remarkably receiving his law degree.[9] In 1889, he moved to Minnesota, becoming the state's first African American practicing attorney; he was widely respected as a dynamic, skilled orator.[10] Committed to removing racial barriers to education and other opportunities, in 1891 McGhee brought suit challenging separate-but-equal laws in Tennessee.[11] Although McGhee found himself unable to afford this long-distance legal battle, he offered a legal approach that would eventually end segregation.[12] McGhee continued his civil rights efforts, and in 1905, he and W.E.B. Du Bois co-founded the Niagara Movement, a predecessor to the NAACP.[13]

For a short period after the Civil War, *de jure* desegregation prevailed; but as Reconstruction ended in the mid-1870s, a host of local and state laws were enacted restricting African American rights and imposing various forms of segregation.[14] With *Plessy v. Ferguson*, the U.S. Supreme Court enshrined such restrictions as constitutional.[15] In *Plessy* an almost-unanimous United States Supreme Court (all but one of the seven concurring justices were from states north of the Mason-Dixon Line) decided that a Louisiana law prohibiting African Americans from sitting in all-White railway cars was constitutional as long as passengers had separate but equal cars. The lone dissenter was Justice John Marshall Harlan, a former slaveowner from Kentucky. Harlan famously wrote, "Our Constitution is color-blind, and neither knows nor tolerates classes among citizens." After *Plessy*, separate-but-equal became the law of the land, and segregation in public schools was institutionalized.

B. The separate but equal doctrine was eliminated, but education disparities persist.

The United States Supreme Court finally reversed *Plessy* in its *Brown* decision in 1954.[16] While the Supreme Court recognized that the Constitution was colorblind, it deemed that educational opportunities were not, and could not remain segregated. Guided by Justice Harlan's dissent in *Plessy* and the brilliant arguments of Thurgood Marshall, a unanimous United States Supreme Court in *Brown v. Board of Education* abandoned the separate-but-equal doctrine. Instead, equal educational opportunities were to be available for all students regardless of race.[17]

In *Brown*, the Supreme Court recognized a universal truth that "it is doubtful that any child may reasonably be expected to succeed in life if he is denied the opportunity of an education."[18] When considering public education, the Court looked at its "full development and present place in American life throughout the Nation,"[19] finding that then and now "education is perhaps the most important function of state and local governments."[20]

Despite the *Brown* mandate for equal opportunity many children's opportunities remained unequal. This inequality was often race-based, but there were other reasons as well. For example, consider the life of Judy Heumann, a disabled student, who became paralyzed after contracting polio as a young child.[21] About the same time as *Brown* was decided, Heumann was denied the right to attend public school because she could not walk.[22] With her mother's continued advocacy on her behalf, Heumann was finally admitted to public high school.[23] During college, Heumann staged protests demanding ramps for access to classrooms. Discrimination followed her after college graduation. She was denied her teaching license because officials feared she could not evacuate the school building in case of a fire.[24] Heumann successfully sued the New York City school system and became the first teacher in the state to use a wheelchair.[25] Heumann became a leading disability rights activist, advocating for equal educational access.[26]

2. Current Civil Rights Legislation Concerning Educating Students with Disabilities

Current civil rights legislation concerning educating students with disabilities remains inadequate. Centuries of U.S. history and African American anthropology undeniably confirm that the connection between race and educational disparities is longstanding in American society. But only in more recent times have students with disabilities been added into this unfortunate calculus. Millions of children were not receiving any appropriate educational services. Some children were being excluded entirely from the public school system.[27] Others had undiagnosed disabilities that clearly prevented them from having a successful educational experience.[28] More generally, there was a lack of adequate resources within the public school system to provide remedies to restore a successful educational experience.[29] As a consequence, families, by necessity, had to find resources outside the public school system.[30]

In the wake of cases challenging the exclusion of students with disabilities from public schools, and in the face of unrelenting advocacy against this exclusion,[31] lawmakers enacted Section 504(a) of the Rehabilitation Act of 1973,[32] with the stated goal of "[a]chieving equality of opportunity, full inclusion, and integration" in society, employment, and education.[33] In 1975, Congress enacted the Individuals with Disabilities Education Act [IDEA], which mandated a free public education for all children with disabilities and required states to ensure that all students with disabilities receive a free and appropriate public education.[34] IDEA governs preschool, elementary, and secondary education of students with disabilities. Like Section 504, the goal was to close the achievement gap between students with disabilities and their nondisabled peers.[35] Both the IDEA and Section 504 have Child Find requirements[36] so that all children with disabilities who are in need of accommodation or special education and related services are identified, evaluated, and assisted.[37]

With the enactment of the 1973 and 1975 legislation, it was assumed that significant progress would be made to equalize public education for the disabled, but progress was far from assured or immediate. Congress itself recognized the failures. In the 2004 IDEA reauthorization, based upon over 30 years of research and experience, Congress found that "low expectations" and the "insufficient focus on applying replicable research on proven methods and teaching and learning" impeded the IDEA's successful implementation.[38]

Even though educators are mandated to "find" children with disabilities, the data suggest that the failure to do so continues, particularly in districts that are poor and low-performing.[39] The high percentage of incarcerated youth with disabilities certainly supports this view that children in need of services are not being "found." If the schoolhouse is to become the great equalizer, then students with all capacities must have equal access to the classroom, passing freely through the front door to the classroom. Objective data must drive the decision to correctly identify all students in need of services but particularly minority students who still have limited access to the instruction needed to succeed in school."[40] Although many improvements have been made under Section 504 and IDEA creating accessible education, as recently as 2018 the National Council on Disability cited "the disproportionate segregation of students with certain disabilities (e.g., autism and intellectual disabilities), and the disproportionate segregation of students of color by both race and disability."[41]

McGhee and Heumann are examples of those who faced and overcame exclusion based on explicit racial and disability discrimination. They fought for their education, and, through education, they were able to attain impressive achievements and advocate so others would have better opportunities in the face of these biases. Yet their work and Congress' efforts remained insufficient. In the 1990s, researchers called our attention to another kind of barrier faced by students with disabilities. Like discrimination and segregation in past decades, we now understand that implicit biases—biases that operate on an implicit or unconscious level, typically without intentionality—impede educational opportunities and a path forward for students of color and with disabilities in the new Jim Crow era.[42]

3. Perpsective from the School to Prison Pipeline

In February 2016, the American Bar Association (ABA) released the ABA Preliminary Report on the School To Prison Pipeline (the ABA Report).[43] This project began in 2014 when the ABA Coalition on Racial and Ethnical Justice focused on the continuing failures of the education system to teach children with disabilities, particularly students of color. The ABA reported that these failures have contributed to harsher discipline, lower achievement, greater referral to law enforcement, disproportionate school dropouts, and eventually to disproportionately high representation in juvenile justice facilities and prisons.[44] This pattern is commonly referred to as the school to prison pipeline. The ABA Report characterizes this failure as one of "our nation's most formidable challenges," one which originates from "low expectations and engagement, poor or lacking school relationships, low academic achievement, incorrect referral or categorization in special education, and overly harsh discipline including suspension, expulsion, referral to law enforcement, arrest, and treatment in the juvenile justice system."[45]

The U.S. Department of Education's National Center for Educational Statistics (NCES) collects data on American students' knowledge in various subject areas annually. It compiles this data in the National Assessment of Education Progress (NAEP), commonly referred to as the Nation's Report Card.[46] Since 1969, the NAEP has monitored the academic performance of 9-, 13-, and 17-year-old students in long-term trend assessments of reading and mathematics achievement.[47] Beginning in 1990, the NAEP began tracking student performance in grades 4, 8, and 12.[48] This data is gathered to provide the underlying information necessary to close achievement gaps, "a goal of both national and state education policy."[49] The NAEP data has many components, but especially relevant to our discussion are (A) comparative gaps in reading scores and reading deficits at various levels; (B) disproportionate graduation rates of Black and Hispanic students in comparison to White students; and (C) disproportionate identification of Black and Hispanic students as students with disabilities in comparison to White students.[50]

A. Comparative Reading Scores

Historically, Black and Hispanic students show the largest gaps in reading ability. As of 2017, the gap between average reading scores of Hispanic and White students in 4th, 8th, and 12th grades is 20 points (down from a 27-point difference in 1992). The reading score gap between Black and White students in the same grades decreased only modestly from 32 to 30 points over this same period.[51] Between 1992 and 2017, progress towards decreasing the gap between Black and White students in grades 4th and 8th reading levels flatlined and the gap widened for the 12th grade.[52]

Disparities in reading ability begin early in a student's education, and most gaps identified in preschoolers persist.[53] These gaps in reading scores are imperative to consider in light of several studies of incarcerated youths and adults which document that a child's failure to read well is a principal predictor of future incarceration.[54] Consistent with this indicator, 70% of all incarcerated adults cannot read at a 4th grade level.[55] On the other hand, using remediation to correct illiteracy or poor reading abilities for adult inmates is most effective at reducing recidivism.[56] It seems self-evident that helping children to read well can have a significant preventative value.

B. Disproportionate Graduation Rates

From 1972 through 2018, the dropout rates of Black and Hispanic students in grades 10 through 12 continued to be almost double those of White students. In 1972, the percentages of student dropouts were: 5.3% of White, 9.6% of Black and 11.2% of Hispanic students.[57] In 2018, the dropout rates declined for all races; however, the difference in the dropout rate between Black and Hispanic compared with White students was still almost double—3.6% of White, 6.8% of Black, and 6.1% of Hispanic.[58]

C. Disproportionality in Students with Disabilities

Adding to the gaps and disproportionality in reading and dropout rates between students of color and their White peers, students with disabilities fare even worse. In general, significant research shows that African American and Hispanic students are disproportionally identified as disabled under Section 504[59] and the IDEA,[60] and they are then more often segregated instead of integrated in the regular education classroom.

Table 3: Number of Students with Disabilities by Race in the Total Special Education Population and Percent Educated at Least 80 Percent of the Time in General Education

	2005–2006[1]		2015–2016[2]	
	Total # Students with Disabilities (SWD)	% Included 80% or More (%)	# Students with Disabilities (SWD)	% Included 80% or More (%)
American/Alaskan Native	91,814	52.9	85,690	64.1
Asian/Pacific Islander	133,271	52.2	140,382	56.5
Native Hawaiian/Pacific Isl.			23,420	55.3
Black	1,245,304	43.9	1,107,606	58.0
Hispanic	1,089171	47.1	1,531,699	61.0
White	3,551,269	59.1	2,966,782	65.5
Two or more races			195,147	64.1
All Disabilities	6,110,829	**53.6**	6,050,725	**62.7**

[1] U.S. Department of Education, 29th Report to Congress, 2010 Table 2.2, pp. 210–219.
[2] *Source:* U.S. Department of Education, ED*Facts* Data Warehouse (EDW), "IDEA Part B Child Count and Educational Environments Collection," 2015–2016, http://www2.ed.gov/programs/osepidea/618-data/index.html. Data extracted as of July 14, 2016, from file specifications 002 and 089.

In other words, classifying African American and Hispanic students as disabled in need of special education "masks segregation and allows their continued segregation under a seemingly natural and justifiable label."[61]

Speaking more specifically in terms of the reading gap, students with disabilities are an average of 3.3 years behind students without disabilities.[62] Students with diagnosed learning disabilities were an average of 4 years behind students without disabilities.⁶³ The challenges persist in this category through high school and result in high dropout rates for students with disabilities. In the 2017–18 school year, the dropout rate of students served under the IDEA was 16.0%.⁶⁴ The issues remain as these youth move on to incarcerated settings. According to a 2017 report by the U.S. Department of Education's Office of Special Education and Rehabilitative Services Blog:

> the percentage of incarcerated youth with disabilities typically range from 30 percent to 60 percent, with some estimates as high as 85 percent. This means that in a class of 15 students, anywhere from 5 to 13 of those students are likely to have a disability, most commonly specific learning disabilities (SLD), emotional or behavioral disorders (EBD), intellectual disability (ID), or attention deficit hyperactivity disorders (ADHD).⁶⁵

4. Literacy Skills & Lifelong Achievement

*A student who is not a modestly skilled reader by the end of third grade is quite unlikely to graduate from high school.*⁶⁶

*Schools far too often fail to acknowledge, much less identify, students who are dyslexic.*⁶⁷

***

Without an early foundation of strong literacy skills, students' chance of successful school outcomes are in jeopardy.⁶⁸ This makes the problems involved with identification of students with dyslexia, a common reading learning disability, particularly concerning.⁶⁹

A. The Need for Early Literacy Skills Foundation

What happens to a child between the ages of one and five may determine what happens to that child for the rest of his or her life. Incredibly, 90% of brain development occurs by the age of five, with more than one million neural pathways forming every second.⁷⁰ Since reading relates to many other academic and societal skills, early literacy development is crucial.⁷¹ This is especially true as "[d]ifferences in reading skills begin early and endure."⁷² For example, only 50% of Hispanic and 57% of Black children recognize the letters of the alphabet when they enter kindergarten, compared to 71% of White children.⁷³ These early gaps continue and tend to worsen over time.[74] Students who do not read proficiently by third grade are four times more likely to drop out of high school than proficient readers. Factors such as poverty exacerbate the problem.[75] For example, students who have lived in poverty and lack reading proficiency are six times more likely to drop out than their peers: "For [B]lack and [Hispanic] students, the combined effect of poverty and poor third grade reading skills makes the rate eight times greater."[76] What makes this data so sobering is that the failure to acquire even a modest reading skill by the age of eight portends a significant likelihood of a failure to graduate from high school **ten years later**.[77] This failure also signals that the student may be heading to juvenile detention, welfare, and/or adult incarceration eight years later.[78]

The data demonstrates that our educational system too often fails to identify students with reading disabilities and to teach them to learn this most basic skill in a timely way. The data raises troubling questions: (1) Why has this student's inadequate reading ability not been identified and remedied and what can teachers do to correct this? (2) What academically has been going on with this student for ten long years? and (3) What happens to the at-risk student when implicit bias combines with other interfering causes to place these students at even greater risk of failure?

B. Dyslexia and Problems with Early Identification

Dyslexia is one of the most common types of learning disability, if not *the* most common, "affecting 80% to 90% of all individuals identified as learning disabled."[79] Although already considered a common learning disability, dyslexia is likely to be even far more prevalent than currently realized. Data from sample surveys indicates that 20% of children are dyslexic, yet only about 4% of children are identified as dyslexic.[80] Even the 20% estimate may be too low given the NAEP's data on reading ability by Grade 4 and given that dyslexia may be under-identified in Black and Hispanic children.[81]

Signs of dyslexia are apparent in early childhood and can include a delay in speaking, difficulty with pronunciation, and inability to detect rhyming words.[82] Differences in brain function and structure are present with those with dyslexia using different neural systems to read.[83] Consistent with this underlying difference in brain structure, dyslexia is a lifelong condition, not a passing developmental phase.[84]

As with other learning disabilities, dyslexia is not a reflection of a student's intellect or drive. Rather, dyslexia is "characterized by an unexpected difficulty in reading by people who possess the intelligence, motivation, and schooling necessary to read."[85] For students without dyslexia, IQ and reading are linked and typically track each other. For dyslexic readers, reading and intelligence are not linked; they develop more independently so that a child can have a very high IQ and, *unexpectedly*, a low reading level.[86] Consistent with this dichotomy, people with dyslexia do not typically have difficulty with comprehension, reasoning, vocabulary, or syntax, but they do have difficulty decoding the printed word.[87] For example, "a woman may know the precise meaning of the spoken word 'eligibility'; however, until she can decode and identify the printed word on the page, she will not be able to use her knowledge of the meaning of the word and it will appear that she does not know the word's meaning."[88] To correct for this, students with dyslexia must use more effort to achieve the same results in reading. For instance, research has shown that "dyslexic people use 4.6 times as much of the brain to do the same language task as non-dyslexics."[89]

The important point here is that with correct diagnoses, assistance, and advocacy, all children with dyslexia can successfully learn to read. Noted authority and special education attorney, Peter Wright, made the following observation about dyslexia in his own childhood educational experience: "I can tell you about the frustrations of reversing letters... and being labeled 'dumb,' 'immature,' 'emotionally disturbed,' and 'lazy'... until my label was changed to 'strephosymbolia' (dyslexia) when I was in the third grade." Expressing his gratitude to his reading tutor and his counselor at a camp for dyslexic children, Wright continued: "Without their help, I might be able to give you the personal experiences of a probationer or a convict, not the experiences of a dyslexic probation officer. Until I received help from them, I was headed for a life of illiteracy and unhappiness."[90]

As Wright's experience suggests, dyslexia often remains unidentified for White students and more so for students of color. Even when identification occurs, it's often in third grade or later—likely too late for meaningful remediation.[91] Testifying before Congress, neuroscientist Dr. Sally Shaywitz summed up our failure to provide appropriate remediation as a failure to act to address dyslexia: "remarkably in America... we have not a knowledge gap but an action gap."[92] This leaves our children, as Wright suggests, in a reality where their self-confidence and expectations are low and where they lose interest in reading, often resulting in depression and behavioral problems.[93] Dyslexic minority children have additional hurdles to overcome where bias against those with learning disabilities intersects with implicit racial bias:

> As the African American saying goes, "You have to work twice as hard to be considered half as good." If you are dyslexic, as well as black, that needs to be multiplied a lot more.... It does not take much imagination to see how [B]lack children, who do not know that they are dyslexic, might respond to how they are treated. Race and dyslexia may be compounded, but the pupils are conscious of one and not of the other.... Teachers and advocates must realize that dyslexic Black and Hispanic children are subject to simultaneous oppression and as a consequence of this we cannot simply prioritize one aspect of... oppression to the exclusion of others.[94]

Educators must realize that dyslexia knows no racial boundaries. Part of the challenge of early identification is to overcome race and disability based implicit bias and to help educators understand that low reading ability is neither a reflection of a child's behavior or "laziness" nor a deficiency on the parent's part in trying to assist their child to learn to read.

C. Considering Dyslexia in the Context of the IDEA Mandate

As previously discussed, the purpose of IDEA is to provide children with disabilities a free appropriate education designed to meet their unique needs and prepare them for further education, employment, and independent living.[95] The purpose of Section 504 is "to empower individuals with disabilities to maximize employment, economic self-sufficiency, independence, and inclusion and integration into society...."[96] Both the IDEA and Section 504 are civil rights statutes that protect individuals from discrimination. Both seek to secure a disabled student's access to education, though eligibility and protections differ. Section 504 does not include a guarantee that a child will receive an education that provides educational benefit,[97] but IDEA does, and we focus on this to set the context for IDEA treatment of a dyslexic student. The ability to read is fundamental to all learning. Students learn to read by third grade; then read to learn. Identified reading disabled students under the IDEA must be provided timely appropriate reading instruction and placement in the general curriculum.

The appropriateness of a student's educational program under the IDEA is determined on a case-by-case basis, in light of the individualized consideration of the unique needs of the child.[98] The U.S. Supreme Court in *Endrew F. ex rel. Joseph F. v. Douglas Cty. Sch. Dist. RE-1* clarified that to "meet its substantive obligation under the IDEA, a school must offer an Individualized Education Program (IEP) reasonably calculated to make progress appropriate in light of the child's circumstances," and "every child should have the chance to meet challenging objectives" and be offered an educational program that is "appropriately ambitious."[99]

While the goals envisioned by Congress and the Supreme Court are laudable, the reality is bleak for African American and Hispanic students with disabilities. Ideally, identification of the need for special services, and particularly the need for separation from the regular classroom, should be race and gender neutral but the statistics support the opposite conclusion.[100] Based on the NCEA statistics from 2000–01 through 2017–18, African American children ages 3 to 21 years old have been disproportionally served under the IDEA.[101] In the 2017–18 school year, Black and Hispanic students were 29% (Black 16.0%; Hispanic 13.0%) of the total students served under IDEA while White students comprised only 14.1% of the total.[102]

Recent statistics (2018–19) show that there were 7,134,248 eligible students with disabilities under the IDEA.[103] The predominant areas of disability are shown in the following table.[104]

	TOTAL, 3 TO 21 YEARS OLD							
Type of disability	Total	White	Black	Hispanic	Asian	Pacific Islander	American Indian/ Alaska Native	Two or more races
	NUMBER OF CHILDREN SERVED							
Select	7,134,248	3,443,646	1,251,037	1,844,011	192,916	20,639	90,489	291,670
Autism	761,625	375,783	112,230	184,118	47,749	2,005	5,737	34,035
Developmental delay	478,637	244,159	84,153	99,437	16,235	1,660	9,779	23,249
Emotional disturbance	358,028	182,143	83,356	63,344	3,764	792	4,716	19,873
Intellectual disability	439,046	180,671	112,719	112,967	11,565	1,511	5,508	14,116
Other health impairment	1,048,689	577,551	190,869	203,647	15,863	2,427	10,939	47,404
Specific learning disability	2,367,868	1,014,119	448,349	740,034	37,000	8,168	34,790	85,476
Speech or language impairment	1,378,490	715,738	173,658	367,308	47,248	2,852	15,153	56,568

This pattern of identification, perhaps even misidentification, due to race, presents a complicated picture. In general terms, for example, students of color are overrepresented in the categories of Intellectual Disability and Emotional Disturbance; White children are overrepresented in the Autism category.[105] There are also instances of race-related under-identification; for example, some research shows that Black four-year-olds are disproportionately underrepresented in early intervention programs. The latter is particularly concerning when considering learning disabilities like dyslexia.[106]

How a student is categorized affects the resources that will be available and affects the end results of a child's educational experience. The data is troubling because, with the exception of the Speech/Language Impairment category, children in the other categories have the lowest graduation rates.[107] At 46.2%, children with intellectual disability (ID) have the highest percentage of dropouts and alternative certificates. Children classified as having Emotional Disturbance have the second highest at 38.5%; Other

Health Impaired ("OHI") is third at 23.3%; and Specific Learning Disabled ("SLD") children fourth at 21.2%.[108] In the 2017–18 school year, the percentage of 14–21-year-old White, African American, and Hispanic students served under the IDEA who exited school with a regular high school diploma were respectively 76.6%, 65.8%, and 70.7%.[109] The dropout rates combined with the percentage of students who received an alternative certificate are 21.9% White, 32.8% Black, and 27.6% Hispanic.[110]

The numbers of young people receiving special education services in school are reflected in the juvenile justice system. While jurisdictions vary, there is "wide agreement that disabled youth are overrepresented in the juvenile justice system."[111] It is estimated that between 30–70% of youth in the juvenile justice system have a learning disability and this is the most common disability.[112] Estimates of the percentage of incarcerated youth offenders with learning disabilities range from 28–50%, even though disabled youth make up only 4–9% of the adolescent population.[113] These percentages are consistent with the adult prison population: 30–50% of adult prisoners have a learning disability whereas only 6% of the overall adult population has one.[114]

5. Implicit Bias and the Disconnect Between Educational Aspirations and Achievement

No one rises to low expectations.[115]

When these low expectations based on race or ethnicity combine with special education, the children who are in the nexus of both groups are likely to be doubly harmed.[116]

***

The underlying point is that the essential skills needed to achieve student aspirations require effective reading and writing, and the foundation for this skill development begins at a young age. This is especially true for lower socioeconomic status students with dyslexia, many of whom are students of color and many of whom cannot learn to read without specialized instruction. Implicit bias contributes to our failure to assure these basic skills for students with disabilities generally, and for students with dyslexia particularly, in a variety of ways ranging from low expectations to biased perceptions of parents and biased against students with disabilities.

Both general and special education teachers can be biased towards students with disabilities. Some believe that special needs students are deliberately not trying hard enough, that they should not be given accommodations unavailable to their nondisabled peers, and that some behaviors associated with their disabilities are willful.[117] The extent to which a teacher may engage in such false or stereotypic thinking about the ability of a student will have lasting impact on the pattern of that child's education and beyond.[118]

A. Expectations

Even the most dedicated and well-meaning teachers hold stereotypes and beliefs that affect their students,[119] and their view and "treatment of students has tremendous influence on their educational and emotional development, and also impacts how students are labeled, and thus able to access educational resources."[120] Since the 1960s, researchers have known that teacher expectations affect student performance regardless of gender or race.[121] White teachers default to the expectation that all students, those who are White and those who are not, should follow "codes" or implicit rules that embody the values, culture, and norms of middle-class Whites. White teachers may thus easily also default implicitly to the conclusion that students who deviate from these rules are not intelligent.[122]

Many educators also implicitly hold lower expectations for racial minorities and students of lower SES status.[123] It is a truism perhaps to observe that, as one educator has, "Many teachers make assumptions about a child who comes from poverty or from 'that part of town.' They may believe that the students are not 'up to the task' or 'will never catch up,' and immediately start limiting this student's potential."[124]

B. The So-Called Uncaring Parent

Implicit bias is also reflected in the stereotype of the uncaring parent. Many educators accept the prevailing narrative that low-income parents of color aren't good enough or don't love their kids enough.[125] This stereotype transfers responsibility for poor performance from student to parent—and away from the school. Equally troubling, this stereotype tends to alienates parents, who are the most powerful agents of change for their children.[126] Even though research demonstrates that in fact Black and Hispanic students' and their families' educational aspirations have continued to rise over time, the stereotype remains.[127]

C. Stereotype Threat

Implicit biases also turn inward for students, a reality sometimes labeled stereotype threat.[128] Students will detect biases in society and among their teachers and peers and will disengage from class and perform poorly (in keeping with that stereotype).[129] As Peter Wright's experience suggests, many dyslexic students also view themselves as less intelligent because of their challenges in reading, which in turn affects their ambitions and self-confidence.[130]

D. Race

While dyslexia is colorblind, the eligibility process is not. The race and sex of every student being referred is known by every member of the team which comprises the parents, teaching staff, and for special education eligibility school administrators.[131] Most teachers and administrators in elementary and secondary education continue to be White.[132] Of the total public elementary and secondary schools teacher population, 76.5% of the teachers are female and 79.3% of them are White.[133] Only 6.7% are Black and 9.3% Hispanic.[134] By comparison, their students are 51% non-White.[135] We were unable to identify the percentage of teachers with disabilities in the public schools.

If asked explicitly about race and disability discrimination, few teachers or school administrators would openly admit to being biased against dyslexic students or students of color. But the data suggests otherwise.[136] Put another way: Why are Black and Hispanic disabled students still disproportionally unable to read and graduate from high school? The explanation is a combination of factors particularly including insufficiently high expectations, insufficient teacher preparation, and insufficient focus on applying replicable research on proven methods of teaching and learning for children with disabilities.[137] But White children presumably subject to this same educational paradigm are still graduating. Does this mean our teachers are racist? We think not. Rather, presumptively, implicit bias must play some part in the eligibility process.

6. The Detrimental Impact of Teacher Bias and Racial Disparity in Public School Teachers

The impact of implicit bias for dyslexic students is seen in the way educators perceive their students and the way they communicate with and about them. Detrimental impacts also flow from the way teachers themselves have been educated—about implicit bias and about the appropriate reading methodologies for dyslexic students.

A. Teachers don't know what they don't know.

As discussed previously, being a proficient reader by the third grade helps a child achieve successful school outcomes and escape the prospects of the school to prison pipeline and economic stagnation.[138] To be able to teach a child to be a proficient reader demands corresponding teacher competency in the appropriate reading methodology. The appropriate methodology, a multi-sensory systematic reading program that focuses on phonemic awareness, has been known and recommended for decades for the remediation of dyslexia.[139] But teachers are not taught this methodology in their teacher training programs, and, without sufficient training, they will be simply unable to identify and remediate a student with dyslexia.[140]

B. Communication must be improved between teacher and students.

Many of the biases and deficits previously discussed can be offset through effective communication, communication with parents, with other students, and with dyslexic students directly.

Consider for example how a student's peers can promote implicit bias towards a student with dyslexia with explicit statements such as other students during class that a "student with dyslexia is retarded or dumb and does not belong in the class...."[141] Such misconceptions fuel implicit bias, undermine a student's self-esteem,[142] and forecast educational failure. Teachers can and should intervene and set a different tone, one that signals that dyslexic students are intelligent and capable.

Being seen as capable boosts a student's sense of self-affirmation and can facilitate long-term academic success, including college attendance.[143] As psychologists and educators report: "Self-affirmation is the process by which people try to reaffirm a sense of moral and adaptive adequacy, or self-integrity, when it comes under threat, sometimes by bolstering it in another domain...such as a teacher's positive feedback or a student's positive relationship."[144] Teachers who adopt the "wise feedback" intervention method[145] can contribute to a dyslexic student's self-affirmation by assuring the student that the teacher has high expectations and knows the student can reach them. For example, one study showed that 72% of students whose paper had a handwritten note that expressed high expectations revised their papers compared to 17% of students who did not.[146] The greatest increase occurred among Black students.[147]

C. The eligibility process must be objective.

Implicit bias fuels the teacher's assumptions and decisions about a student's academic capabilities. While the achievement gap between Black and Hispanic versus White students is at least partially explained by a differential opportunity to learn, it is also the case that "there are high-performing black students who are being overlooked by education professionals because of presumptions made about their academic capabilities—presumptions that are *not* connected to the students' actual performance in mathematics."[148] For example, working with the Early Childhood

Longitudinal Study: Kindergarten Cohort (Kindergarten–8th grade), researchers considered students' mathematics test performances, their teachers' ratings of their performance, and their background characteristics (e.g., racial group). Students with low test scores were unlikely to be placed in 8th grade algebra regardless of their race. However, even Black students with *high* test scores were unlikely to be placed in 8th grade algebra.[149]

Researchers looking at the comparative data observe that "[w]hile teachers may care deeply about their students, the unfortunate reality is that at times they make decisions that undermine student achievement, perhaps due to involuntary and unrecognized bias."[150] The recommendation that performance data should be the primary driver for student placement seems self-evident.[151] To this end, some researchers advocate the use of the "less is more" approach, which relies less on teachers' impressions of student achievement or student group identity and more on actual, individual academic performance.[152]

Conclusions and Recommendations

A. Identify dyslexia early and use proven teaching methods.

The achievement gap between students with dyslexia and typical readers is evident as early as first grade and persists as children continue their education. Thus, early identification of dyslexia is critical to close this achievement gap.[153] Early identification may be accomplished by screening all children for dyslexia during kindergarten or first grade, instead of just those showing certain tendencies.[154] Once a child has been identified as dyslexic, schools must be intentional in how they structure and resource intense and high-quality reading instruction.[155] It's essential that schools and parents work together in a "system of constant, seamless communication" in support of dyslexic students[156]—including communication with the child, who needs to know that she is intelligent and can become a strong reader as well. Unsurprisingly, studies have shown that highly skilled teachers have had better results than inexperienced teachers in helping dyslexic children achieve better reading progress.[157] Computers, while a useful tool to assist dyslexic children, are "not a substitute for a good teacher."[158]

Early identification and assistance for dyslexia can save enormous time and costs later, while having a huge impact on the students' success and future outcomes.

> A child with dyslexia who is not identified early may require as much as 150 to 300 hours of intensive instruction.... if she is going to begin to close the reading gap between herself and her peers. The longer identification and effective reading instruction are delayed, the longer the child will require to catch up.[159]

B. Remove subjective race-based eligibility decisions.

Teachers must be trained to become aware of their own implicit biases.[160] The "less is more" approach rightly advocates that teacher's discretionary subjective judgment must be removed from the formula of determining the individual student's ability and potential. The IDEA includes specific requirements for evaluations, reevaluations, eligibility, IEPs, and educational placements.[161] These evaluations must be selected and administered so as not to be discriminatory on a racial or cultural basis.[162] Assuming that the evaluations are properly selected and used, an objective review should result in an accurate eligibility determination.

C. Support school funding reform.

While this large topic is beyond the scope of this Chapter, we note that increased school funding and funding for students needing accommodation and special education should be revisited across the board. In the context of this Chapter, an option would be to target funding for effective reading remediation programs in all schools using scientifically-based instruction and trained and qualified teachers. To address dyslexia, the goal of increased aid must be the elimination of student reading deficits before the third grade. Otherwise, failure to achieve a successful reading program will simply fund the Pipeline.

Postscript: The irony is we know how to teach kids to read.

While a review of reading methodology is beyond the scope of this Chapter, we do note for readers who are interested in this particular aspect that "for over [40] years there has been scientific knowledge about how to prevent failure of at-risk students."[163] The proven method is Direct Instruction (DI), which is an evidence-based, "explicit, carefully sequenced and scripted model of instruction."[164] DI is based on two core principles: (1) all students can learn when taught correctly, regardless of history and background; and (2) all teachers can be successful, given effective materials and presentation techniques.[165] Data shows DI outperforms all the other models. DI was first with Blacks, first with non-English speakers, first with Native Americans, first with Whites, first in rural areas and urban areas, first with high performers, and first with the lowest disadvantaged children.[166] "The third graders who went through DI programs also had the highest self-esteem. The reason was that they had a lot of evidence to show that they were smart kids."[167]

About the Authors

The Honorable Julian Mann, III, served eight terms as North Carolina's Chief Administrative Law Judge and Director of the Office of Administrative Hearings. Five Chief Justices appointed Judge Mann to this office, and he is now retired. Prior to serving in this capacity, Judge Mann was engaged in the private practice of law, primarily representing the professional licensing boards for Architects and Veterinarians. For thirty years he served continuously as adjunct faculty in three different departments at North Carolina State University. Judge Mann was selected by the nominating committee to serve as Vice Chair of the ABA Judicial Division in 2021–22. He received his B.S. (1969) from the University of North Carolina, M.P.A. (1971) from North Carolina State University, J.D. (1974) from Samford University, and Certificate in Public Leadership, JFK School of Government, Harvard University (2021).

The Honorable Stacey Bice Bawtinhimer is an Administrative Law Judge with NC-OAH who manages the special education cases in that Tribunal. She holds a B.A. degree in Human Relations from the College of William and Mary and a J.D. from Georgia State College of Law. Prior to being appointed as a judge, for twenty-five (25) years Ms. Bawtinhimer represented disabled students and their families throughout North Carolina. She has taught special education law and made presentations on special education law for many state and national organizations.

So, You'd Like to Know More

- Angela Koo, Correctional Education Can Make a Greater Impact on Recidivism by Supporting Adult Inmates with Learning Disabilities, 105 J. Crim. L. & Criminology 233 (2015).
- Asher Hoyles & Martin Hoyles, Race and Dyslexia, 13 Race Ethnicity and Educ. 209 (2010).
- Sarah E. Redfield & Jason N. Nance, Reversing the School to Prison Pipeline, 47 U. Mem. L. Rev. 1 (2016).

Endnotes

1. Dana Goldstein, The Teacher Wars: A History of America's Most Embattled Profession (2015).

2. Susan Ritchie, *Horace Mann*, Dictionary of Unitarian & Universalist Biography (Nov. 11, 2000); *Horace Mann Biography*, Biography.com (June 20, 2020).

3. We focus in this Chapter on racial bias and disproportionality but acknowledge that there are relationships between race and other factors, particularly socioeconomic status (SES), which relationships may well influence or confound educational outcomes. *See generally, e.g.*, The Interplay Between Race/ Ethnicity, Socioeconomic Status and Social and Emotional Skills, ACT Research Report 2 (2020) (concluding "The interactions of race/ethnicity and socioeconomic status (SES) in predicting social and emotional (SE) skills was examined for 81,950 6th–8th graders. At low levels of SES, White students tended to have the lower SE scores. However, as SES increased, they tended to have higher scores relative to minority groups. Across SES levels, Asian students showed higher Academic Discipline and Self-Regulation scores. The SES and SE skill relationship was less pronounced for underserved minority groups.").

4. *See generally* Sarah E. Redfield & Jason N. Nance, *Reversing the School to Prison Pipeline*, 47 U. Mem. L. Rev. 1 (2016) [hereinafter "Redfield & Nance"].

5. North Carolina was typical and enacted such a statute in the legislative session of 1830-31. *See* Act Passed by the General Assembly of the State of North Carolina at the Session of 1830—1831 (Raleigh: 1831).

6. Frenise A. Logan, *The Legal Status of Public School Education for Negroes in North Carolina, 1877-1894*, 32 N.C. Hist. Rev. 346-57 (1955), http://www.jstor.org/stable/23516256. North Carolina became the first state to offer publicly funded universal White education.

7. TBT Originals, *Fredrick McGhee, The Post-Emancipation Generation's Attorney*, PBS (Oct. 9, 2019), https://www.youtube.com/watch?time_continue=3&v=8oqLLKCC22c&feature=emb_logo; *Fredrick McGhee, Minnesota's First Black Lawyer*, African American Registry; *see also* Paul D. Nelson, Fredrick L. McGhee: A Life on the Color Line, 1861–1912 (Minn. Hist. Soc'y Press 2002).

8. *Id.* (TBT Originals).

9. *Id.*

10. *Id.*

11. *Id.*

12. *Id.* (quoting Paul D. Nelson).

13. *Id.*

14. *See The African American Odyssey: A Quest for Full Citizenship — Reconstruction and Its Aftermath*, Library of Congress, https://loc.gov/exhibits/african-american-odyssey/reconstruction.html.

15. Plessy v. Ferguson, 163 U.S. 537 (1896); *Jim Crow and Plessy v. Ferguson*, PBS, http://www.pbs.org/tpt/slavery-by-another-name/themes/jim-crow/.

16. Brown v. Board of Education, 347 U.S. 492, 493 (1954).

17. *Id.*

18. *Id.*

19. *Id.* at 492.

20. *Id.* at 493.

21. Diana Pastora Carson, *Judy Heumann,* Ability Mag., https://abilitymagazine.com/judy-heumann/. Among her other accomplishments, Heumann went on to co-found the World Institute on Disability, serve as Assistant Secretary in the Office of Special Education and Rehabilitative Services in the Clinton administration, be the World Bank Group's first Advisor on Disability and Development, and serve as Special Advisor on International Disability Rights for the State Department in the Obama administration. *See also* Judy Heumann, Being Heumann: An Unrepentant Memoir of a Disability Rights (2020).

22. *Id.* (Carson).

23. *Id.*

24. *Id.*

25. Heumann v. Board of Educ., 320 F. Supp. 623 (1970).

26. Deborah Leiderman, *The Activist Star of 'Crip Camp' Looks Back at a Life on the Barricades*, N.Y. Times, March 25, 2020, https://www.nytimes.com/2020/03/25/movies/crip-camp-judy-heumann.html.

27. Individuals With Disabilities Education Act (IDEA), 20 U.S.C. § 1400(c)(2)(B) (2004). The IDEA was reauthorized in 1990, 1997, and 2004. *See* Education of the Handicapped Act Amendments of 1990, Pub. L. No. 101-476, 104 Stat. 1103 (1990); Individuals with Disabilities Education Act Amendments of 1997, Pub. L. No. 105-17, 111 Stat. 37 (1997); Individuals with Disabilities Education Improvement Act of 2004, Pub. L. No. 108-446, 118 Stat. 2647 (2004).

28. § 1400(c)(2)(C).

29. § 1400(c)(2)(D).

30. *Id.* The ABA Report, Redfield & Nance, 47 U. Mem. L. Rev. 1 (citing Claudia Rowe, *Race Dramatically Skews Discipline, Even in Elementary School*, Seattle Times, June 23, 2015, http://www.seattletimes.com/education-lab/race-dramatically-skews-discipline-even-in-elementary-school/).

31. In 1972, students with disabilities challenged their exclusion from public school on equal protection grounds in *PARC v. Commonwealth of Pennsylvania*, 343 F. Supp. 279 (E.D. Pa. 1972) and *Mills v. Board of Education of the District of Columbia*, 348 F. Supp. 866 (D.D.C. 1972). Both courts held that local laws excluding children with disabilities from public schools violated the Constitution.

32. 29 U.S.C. § 701(b)(1) (2020).

33. *Id.*

34. Education for all Handicapped Children Act of 1975, Pub. L. No. 94-142; Individuals With Disabilities Education Improvement Act of 2004 (IDEA), 20 U.S.C. § 1400 *et seq.* (2020).

35. 20 U.S.C. § 1400 *et seq.; see also* regulations at 34 C.F.R. pt. 300.

36. *See* IDEA, 20 USC § 1412 (a)(3); 34 C.F.R. § 300.111.

37. 34 C.F.R. § 104.32(a).

38. 20 U.S.C. §§ 1400(c)(4)-(5).

39. Crystal Grant, *Special Education by Zip Code: Creating Equitable Child Find Policies*, 52 Loy. U. Chi. L.J. 127, 128 (2020) ("In many school districts, the current "child find" policies and practices leave the most vulnerable children with disabilities, from poor and low-performing school districts, without the Individuals with Disabilities Education Act's intended protections and supports.")

40. *Is Progress Being Made Toward Closing the Achievement Gap in Special Education?* UT PERMIAN BASIN, Asher Hoyles & Martin Hoyles, *Race and Dyslexia*, 13 RACE ETHNICITY & EDUC. 209, 223 (2010).

41. *IDEA Series: The Segregation of Students with Disabilities*, NAT'L COUNCIL ON DISABILITY 1, 49 (Feb. 7, 2018) https://ncd.gov/sites/default/files/NCD_Segregation-SWD_508.pdf.

42. *See generally* MICHELLE ALEXANDER, THE NEW JIM CROW (2010).

43. ABA Report, Redfield & Nance, 47 U. MEM. L. REV. at 1.

44. *Id.* at 11.

45. *Id.* at 13. The ABA Report noted that 22% of White and 20% of Asian/Pacific Islander fourth graders were below grade level in reading. In comparison, 53% of American Indian students, 51% of African American students, and 49% of Hispanic students were below grade level in reading in the fourth grade.

46. NAT'L CTR. FOR EDUC. STAT., https://nces.ed.gov/. The National Center for Education Statistics (NCES) is the part of the U.S. Department of Education's Institute of Education Sciences that collects, analyzes, and publishes statistics on education and public school district finance information in the United States. THE NATION'S REPORT CARD, https://www.nationsreportcard.gov/.

47. U.S. DEP'T OF EDUCATION, INSTITUTE OF EDUCATION SCIENCES, NCES, NAT'L ASSESSMENT OF EDUCATIONAL PROGRESS (NAEP), THE NATION'S 2019 REPORT CARD, 1, 2, https://www.nationsreportcard.gov/mathematics/supportive_files/2019_infographic.pdf [hereinafter The Nation's 2019 Report Card].

48. *Id.* NCES provides an interactive map for literacy and numeracy skills with data from the county level: https://nces.ed.gov/surveys/piaac/skillsmap/.

49. THE NATION'S 2019 REPORT CARD at 3.

50. U.S. DEP'T OF EDUCATION, NCES, NAEP, 1992, 1994, 1998, 2000, 2002, 2003, 2005, 2007, 2009, 2011, 2013, 2015, 2017, and 2019 Reading Assessments, retrieved October 30, 2019, from the Main NAEP Data Explorer, https://nces.ed.gov/nationsreportcard/naepdata/. (This table was prepared in October 2019.)

51. *Id.*

52. *Id.* Digest 2019, Table 221.10. *Average NAEP reading scale score, by sex, race/ethnicity, and grade: Selected years, 1992 through 2019.*

53. ABA Report, Redfield & Nance, 47 U. MEM. L. REV. at 25.

54. *Literacy Statistics*, BEGIN TO READ, https://www.begintoread.com/research/literacystatistics.html. *Compare* Irwin S. Kirsch et al., *Adult Literacy in America: A First Look at the Results of the National Adult Literacy Survey*, EDUC. TESTING SVC. (Sept. 1993), https://files.eric.ed.gov/fulltext/ED358375.pdf *with* NCES, *National Assessment of Adult Literacy Fact Sheets, Prison Component*, https://nces.ed.gov/naal/fct_prison.asp.

55. *Id.*

56. Angela Koo, *Correctional Education Can Make a Greater Impact on Recidivism by Supporting Adult Inmates with Learning Disabilities*, 105 J. CRIM. L. & CRIMINOLOGY 233, 237 (2015).

57. U.S. Dep't of Commerce, Census Bureau, Current Population Survey (CPS), 1972 through 2018. Digest 2019, Table 219.55. (This table was prepared in October 2019.) Among 15–24-year-olds enrolled in grades 10 through 12, percentage who dropped (event drop-out rate), by sex and race/ethnicity: 1972 through 2018.

58. *Id.*

59. In 2016, of the 50,452,567 students with disabilities, 12.6% were served under IDEA and only 2.3% of students were served solely under Section 504. U.S. Dep't of Education, 2015–16 Office for Civil Rights, Civil Rights Data Collection, http://ocrdata.ed.gov. Data notes are available at https://ocrdata.ed.gov/Downloads/Data-Notes-2015-16-CRDC.pdf.

60. IDEA, 20 U.S.C. § 1400(c)(12)(E) (finding of disproportionality by Congress).

61. Liat Ben-Moshe & Sandy Magaña, *An Introduction to Race, Gender, and Disability: Intersectionality, Disability Studies, and Families of Color*, 2 Women, Gender, and Families of Color, 105–14 (2014).

62. Allison F. Gilmour, Douglas Fuchs and Joseph H. Wehby, Are Students with Disabilities Accessing the Curriculum? A Meta-analysis of the Reading Achievement Gap between Students with and without Disabilities, Exceptional Children 1, 16 (April 2019).

63. *Id.* at 17.

64. *Id.*

65. *Supporting Youth with Disabilities in Juvenile Corrections*, Office of Special Education and Rehabilitative Services Blog, U.S. Dep't of Education, https://sites.ed.gov/osers/2017/05/supporting-youth-with-disabilities-in-juvenile-corrections/.

66. Preventing Reading Difficulties in Young Children 21 (Catherine E. Snow, M. Susan Burns & Peg Griffin eds., 1998).

67. *The Science of Dyslexia: Hearing Before the Comm. On Science, Space, and Technology*, 113th Cong. 21 (2014) (statement of Dr. Sally Shaywitz).

68. Rollins Ctr. for Language and Literacy, https://www.atlantaspeechschool.org/professional-development/rollins-center/.

69. *The Importance of Early Detection of Dyslexia*, UT-Permian Basin, https://online.utpb.edu/about-us/articles/education/the-importance-of-early-detection-of-dyslexia/

70. *Why Early Childhood Literacy Is So Important*, The Carol Pufahl Literacy Found. http://www.cpliteracyfoundation.org.

71. The ABA Report, Redfield & Nance, 47 U. Mem. L. Rev. at 25.

72. *Id.*

73. *Id.*

74. *See* Amy Rathbun, Jerry West & Elvira Germino-Hausken, U.S. Dep't of Educ., From Kindergarten Through Third Grade: Children's Beginning School Experience 16 fig. 5 (2004), http://nces.ed.gov/pubs2004/2004007.pdf.

75. *See, e.g.*, The Latino Family Literacy Project, Issues of Poverty in Reading and Language Development https://www.latinoliteracy.com/issues-of-poverty-in-reading-and-languagedevelopment/#::text=lt%20is%20undeniable%20that%20poverty,the%20various%2Ostages%20of%20development.

76. *Third Grade Reading Skills & Drop Outs*, The Annie E. Casey Found., https://www.aecf.org/blog/poverty-puts-struggling-readers-in-double-jeopardy-minorities-most-at-risk/.

77. Donald J. Hernandez, *Double Jeopardy: How Third-Grade Reading Skills and Poverty Influence High School Graduation*, ERIC Number: ED518818 {2011).

78. Governor's Early Literacy Foundation, *Early Literacy Connection to Incarceration* https://governorsfoundation.org/gelf-articles/early-literacy-connection-to-incarceration/.

79. The Science of Dyslexia: Hearing Before the Comm. On Science, Space, and Technology, 113th Cong. 23 (2014) (statement of Dr. Sally Shaywitz).

80. *Id.* at 29–30.

81. *Id.* at 29.

82. *Id.* at 112–14.

83. *Id.* at 81.

84. *Id.; see also* Angela Koo, *Correctional Education*, 105 J. Crim. L. & Criminology 233.

85. *What is a Learning Disability?* ADA.GOV (May 27, 1998), https://www.ada.gov/learnfac.htm.

86. The Science of Dyslexia: Hearing Before the Comm. on Science, Space, and Technology, 113th Cong. 25 (2014) (Dr. Sally Shaywitz, emphasis original).

87. *What is a Learning Disability?* ADA.GOV (May 27, 1998).

88. *Id.*

89. Asher Hoyles & Martin Hoyles, *Race and Dyslexia*, 13 Race Ethnicity & Educ. 209, 223 (2010).

90. Peter D. Wright, *Reading Problems and Juvenile Delinquency*, Wrightslaw (2007), https://www.wrightslaw.com/info/jj.deling.read.probs.htm.

91. For just one recent example of a dyslexic child's experience from preschool through fourth grade, *see* Falmouth Sch. Dep't v. Doe, Docket No. 2:20-cv-00214-GZS, 2021 U.S. Dist. LEXIS 186907 (D. Me. Sept. 29, 2021) (upholding hearing officer decision in favor of parents' reimbursement for tuition and evaluation).

92. The Science of Dyslexia: Hearing Before the Comm. On Science, Space, and Technology, 113th Cong. 23 (2014) (statement of Dr. Sally Shaywitz, Audrey G. Ratner Professor in Learning Development, Yale Univ. School of Medicine and Co-Director, Yale Ctr. for Dyslexia and Creativity, Yale Univ.).

93. Sally Shaywitz & Jonathan Shaywitz, Overcoming Dyslexia 30 (2d ed. 2020); *see generally* Emily M. Livingston, Linda S. Siegel & Urs Ribary, *Developmental Dyslexia: Emotional Impact and Consequences*, 23 Australian J. Learning Difficulties (2018).

94. Hoyles & Hoyles, 13 Race Ethnicity & Educ. at 223.

95. 20 U.S.C. § 1400(d).

96. 29 U.S.C. § 701(b)(1).

97. Peter W.D. Wright & Pamela D. Wright, IDEA 2004 (Harbor House Law Press, Inc. 2006) 132.

98. *See* Bd. of Educ. v. Rowley, 458 U.S. 176 (1982).

99. Endrew F. ex rel. Joseph F. v. Douglas Cnty. Sch. Dist. RE-1, 137 S. Ct. 988, 999, 1000 (2017); see also M.C. v. Antelope Valley Union High Sch. Dist., 858 F.3d 1189, 1200 (9th Cir. 2017) (finding that in *Endrew F.* the Supreme Court "provided a more precise standard for evaluating whether a school district has complied substantively with the IDEA").

100. *See* Sarah E. Redfield & Theresa Kraft, *What Color is Special Education?*, 41 J.L. & Educ. 129 (2012).

101. Individuals with Disabilities Education Act (IDEA) database, Office of Special Education Programs, U.S. Dep't of Education (retrieved December 21, 2018), https://www2.ed.gov/programs/osepidea/618-data/state-level-data-files/index.html#bcc. *State Nonfiscal Survey of Public Elementary and Secondary Education, 2000–01 through 2017–18,* and *National Elementary and Secondary Enrollment Projection Model, 1972 through 2028,* Common Core of Data, NCES. The current data does not delineate between race/ethnicity/sex for graduation rates; data is available about the number of White/Black/Hispanic students served in the various eligibility categories for that school year and prior years.

102. *Id.*

103. *See* Table 204.50. Children 3 to 21 years old served under Individuals with Disabilities Education Act (IDEA), Part B, by age group and sex, race/ethnicity, and type of disability: 2018–19, Digest of Education Statistics, NCES, https://nces.ed.gov/programs/digest/d19/tables/dt19_204.50.asp.

104. *Id.*

105. *See* Kristen Harper, *5 Things to Know About Racial and Ethnic Disparities in Special Education*, CHILD TRENDS (2017).

106. *Id.*

107. Graduation under the IDEA is defined as a student having obtained a "regular" high school diploma, not an alternative certificate. 34 C.F.R. § 300.102(a)(3)(i); 20 U.S.C. § 1412(a)(1)(B)-(C).

108. *See* Digest of Education Statistics 2019, Table 219.90 in U.S. Department of Education, Office of Special Education Programs, Individuals with Disabilities Education Act (IDEA) Section 618 Data Products: State Level Data Files. Retrieved February 20, 2020, from http://www2.ed.gov/programs/osepidea/618-data/state-level-data-files/index.html. (This table was prepared Feb. 2020.)

109. *Id.*

110. *Id.*

111. The ABA Report, Redfield & Nance, 47 U. MEM. L. REV. at 46.

112. *See* Angela Koo, *Correctional Education Can Make a Greater Impact on Recidivism by Supporting Adult Inmates with Learning Disabilities*, 105 J. CRIM. L. & CRIMINOLOGY 233, 237 (2015).

113. *Id.*

114. *Id.* at 254. The strongest predictor of recidivism for both Black and White adolescents is a mental health diagnosis.

115. Kevin Carey, *No One Rises to Low Expectations*, CHRON. HIGHER EDUC., Nov. 28, 2008.

116. The ABA Report, Redfield & Nance, 47 U. MEM. L. REV. 1; Sarah E. Redfield & Theresa Kraft, What Color is Special Education? 41 J.L. & EDUC. 129 (2012); Dustin Rynders, *Battling Implicit Bias in the IDEA to Advocate for African American Students with Disabilities*, 35 Touro L. Rev. 462 (2019).

117. Teresa Cooper, *It's Time to Address Teacher Bias Against Special Education Students*, THE EDUCATOR'S ROOM, May 1, 2017, https://theeducatorsroom.com/time-address-teacher-bias-special-education-students/#wpautbox_about.

118. Yasemin Copur-Gencturk *et al.*, *Teachers' Bias Against the Mathematical Ability of Female, Black, and Hispanic Students*, 40 EDUC. R. 30 (2019).

119. *Teacher Bias: The Elephant in the Classroom*, THE GRADE NETWORK, INC. (2019), http://www.thegradenetwork.com.

120. M. Cochran-Smith, *Knowledge, Skills, and Experiences for Teaching Culturally Diverse Learners: A Perspective for Practicing Teachers*, in CRITICAL KNOWLEDGE FOR DIVERSE TEACHERS AND LEARNERS, 27–88 (J. Irvine ed. 1997); JEANNIE OAKES, MARTIN LIPTON, LAUREN ANDERSON, & JAMY STILLMAN, TEACHING TO CHANGE THE WORLD. (5th ed. 2018); Camille Wilson Cooper, *The Detrimental Impact of Teacher Bias: Lessons Learned from the Standpoint of African American Mothers*, 29 TEACHER EDUC. Q, 101–16 (2002), https://files.eric.ed.gov/fulltext/EJ852360.pdf.

121. *Teacher Bias: The Elephant in the Classroom,* THE GRADE NETWORK, INC. (2019), http://www.thegradenetwork.com. In a 1960s experiment by Harvard Professor Robert Rosenthal and Principal Lenore Jacobson teachers were told that a test could determine which students' IQs were about to increase rapidly. Random students were labeled with this potential growth. If the teacher had been led to expect greater gains in IQ, then increasingly, those kids gained more IQ. *See* ROBERT ROSENTHAL & LENORE JACOBSON, PYGMALION IN THE CLASSROOM (1965).

122. Camille Wilson Cooper, *The Detrimental Impact of Teacher Bias: Lessons Learned from the Standpoint of African American Mothers*, 30 TEACHER EDUC. Q. 101, 104 (2003) (beginning with this observation: "It was like being a Black boy was something that was not good, and you have to feel good within yourself to succeed... And you'd be surprised how you trust your kid with a teacher, and the teacher's with him more than you are. They're with him the majority of the day, and for someone to just really lower your child's self-esteem was horrible.—A former public school mother with a son now enrolled in private school."). See also generally Jason A. Okonofua & Jennifer L. Eberhardt, *Two Strikes: Race and the Disciplining of Young Students*, 26 PSYCHOL. SCI. 617 (2015).

123. *See, e.g.,* Dustin Rynders, *Battling Implicit Bias in the IDEA to Advocate for African American Students with Disabilities*, 35 TOURO L. REV. 462 (2019); Seth Gershenson, Stephen B. Holt & Nicholas W. Papageorge, *Who Believes in Me? The Effect of Student-Teacher Demographic Match on Teacher Expectations*, 52 ECON. EDUC. REV. 209, 209 (2016).

124. Anna Quirk, *Implicit Bias and the Self-Fulfilling Prophecy Phenomenon and Their Affects on Literacy Performance in Elementary Students*, Hamline DigitalCommons@Hamline (2017); *see also generally* Walter S. Gilliam, Angela N. Maupin, Chin R. Reyes, Maria Accavitti & Frederick Shic, *Do Early Educators' Implicit Biases Regarding Sex and Race Relate to Behavior Expectations and Recommendations of Preschool Expulsions and Suspensions?* YALE RESEARCH STUDY BRIEF (2016).

125. *3rd Grade Reading Success Matters, Changing the Narratives,* THE CAMPAIGN FOR GRADE LEVEL READING, https://gradelevelreading.net/our-work/changing-the-narrative.

126. *Id.*

127. After the *Brown* decision, Black students' and their families' educational aspirations began to change. By the 1960s, many Black students aspired to attend college. Despite this rise in aspirations, these students continue to experience lower educational opportunities. For example, for those who do stay in school, Blacks and Hispanics are more likely to graduate with a lower level of math completed (e.g., Algebra II or below), and less likely to earn Advanced Placement (AP) or International Baccalaureate (IB) credits—all of which will influence postsecondary aspiration and achievement. Students may not have received the educational foundation to succeed in these courses. They may also experience less rigorous courses either because of implicit bias or because there are fewer teachers able to teach AP and IB courses in lower-income and minority schools, and higher teacher turnover in those schools may disrupt course availability. The Equality of Educational Opportunity report found that more Black than White high school students reported that they wanted to continue their education past high school. Yet the aspirations do not follow reality, as the report also found that Blacks did not enroll in college at the same rate as Whites, with total postsecondary enrollment comprising 2 % Black, 95 % White, and 3 % other non-White students. *See* James S. Coleman, Ernest Q. Campbell, Carol J. Hobson, James McPartland, Alexander M. Mood, Frederick D. Weinfeld & Robert L. York, *Equality of Educational Opportunity*, 67–68, 78, 20 OFFICE OF EDUCATION, U.S. DEP'T OF HEALTH, EDUCATION, AND WELFARE (1966).

128. *See, e.g.,* Claude M. Steele & Joshua Aronson, *Stereotype Threat and the Intellectual Test Performance of African Americans*, 69 J. PERSONALITY & SOC. PSYCHOL. 797, 808 (1995).

129. David M. Quinn, *Experimental Evidence on Teachers' Racial Bias in Student Evaluation: The Role of Grading Scales*, 42 ED. EVALUATION & POLICY ANALYSIS 375 (2020).

130. Russell A. McClain, *Helping Our Students Reach Their Full Potential: The Insidious Consequences of Ignoring Stereotype Threat*, 17 RUTGERS RACE & L. REV. 1, 13–16 (2016).

131. Parents, the student's regular and special teachers, and a school representative (usually the principal) are mandatory members of the IEP Team and sit across the table. 20 U.S.C. § 1414(d)(B)(i), (ii), (iii), (iv).

132. Thomas S. Dee, *A Teacher Like Me: Does Race, Ethnicity, or Gender Matter?*, 95 AMERICAN ECON. REV. 158 (2005).

133. "Public School Teacher Data File" and "Private School Teacher Data File," 1987–88 through 2011–12, NCES, U.S. DEP'T OF EDUCATION; Schools and Staffing Survey (SASS), "Charter School Teacher Data File," 1999–2000; and National Teacher and Principal Survey (NTPS), "Public School Teacher Data File" and "Private School Teacher Data File," 2017–18, NCES, U.S. DEP'T OF EDUCATION. (This table was prepared November 2019.)

134. *Id.*

135. A.W. Geiger, *America's Public School Teachers Are Far Less Racially and Ethnically Diverse than Their Students*, PEW RESEARCH (Aug. 27, 2018).

136. NICHOLAS P. TRIPLETT & JAMES E. FORD, CTR. FOR RACIAL EQUITY IN EDUC., THE E(RACE)ING INEQUITIES: THE STATE OF RACIAL EQUITY IN NORTH CAROLINA PUBLIC SCHOOLS 45 (2019), https://www.ednc.org/wp-content/uploads/2019/08/EducationNC_Eraceing-Inequities.pdf.

137. 20 U.S.C. § 1400(c)(5).

138. *See, e.g.,* Jason A. Okonofua & Jennifer L. Eberhardt, Two *Strikes: Race and the Disciplining of Young Students,* 26 PSYCHOL. SCI. 617, 617, 622 (2015).

139. *Multisensory Structured Language Teaching Fact Sheet*, INT'L DYSLEXIA ASSOC., https://dyslexiaida.org/multisensory-structured-language-teaching-fact-sheet/.

140. SALLY SHAYWITZ & JONATHAN SHAYWITZ, OVERCOMING DYSLEXIA 283 (2d ed. 2020).

141. *Parent and Educator Resource Guide to Section 504 in Public Elementary and Secondary Schools*, OCR (Dec. 2016).

142. *See* Camille Wilson Cooper, 30 TEACHER EDUC. Q. at 110–11.

143. J. Parker Goyer et al., *Self-affirmation Facilitates Minority Middle Schoolers' Progress Along College Trajectories,* 114 PNAS 7, 594–99 (July 18, 2017).

144. *Id.* at 7, 595.

145. *See Locked Out of the Classroom: How Implicit Bias Contributes to Disparities in School Discipline*, NAACP LEGAL DEFENSE & EDUCATIONAL FUND, INC. (2017).

146. David S. Yeager et al., *Breaking the Cycle of Mistrust: Wise Interventions to Provide Critical Feedback Across the Racial Divide*, 143 J. EXPERIMENTAL PSYCHOL. 804, 804–809 (2014), https://www.apa.org/pubs/journals/releases/xge-a0033906.pdf.

147. *Id.* at 811–12.

148. Valerie Faulkner, Patricia L. Marshall, Lee V. Stiff & Cathy L. Crossland, *Less is More: The Limitations of Judgment*, 98 PHI DELTA KAPPAN 55, 58–59 (2017).

149. *Id.* at 57.

150. *Id.* at 59. The authors cite to *Blindspot* here for the proposition that many disciplines grapple with such issues. Mahzarin Banaji & Anthony Greenwald, Blindspot: Hidden Biases of Good People (2013).

151. *Id.* (Faulkner) at 59.

152. *Id.* at 56.

153. Sally Shaywitz & Jonathan Shaywitz, Overcoming Dyslexia 281 (2d ed. 2020).

154. *Id.* Pearson Assessment offers early identification tools (including Shaywitz Dyslexia Screen), professional development, and other resources at https://www.pearsonassessments.com/professional-assessments/featured-topics/dyslexia.html.

155. The North Carolina Senate has introduced Excellent Public Schools Act of 2021, An Act To Modify The Implementation Of The North Carolina Read To Achieve Program In Order To Attain Statewide Reading Proficiency By The Third Grade, S. 387 (2021–2022). This Act requires the use of scientific, research-based intervention, remediation, and progress monitoring.

156. *Id.* at 278.

157. Sally Shaywitz & Jonathan Shaywitz, Overcoming Dyslexia 283 (2d ed. 2020).

158. *Id.*

159. *Id.* at 284.

160. *See generally Project Implicit*, Harvard Univ., https://implicit.harvard.edu/implicit/.

161. *See* 20 U.S.C. § 1414.

162. 20 U.S.C. §§ 1414(b)(2), (3)(A)(i).

163. Siegfried Engelmann, Reading First = Kids First (2005), https://www.zigsite.com/OregonsFuture.htm.

164. *Direct Instruction*, Granite St. C. (Sept. 14, 2020), https://granite.pressbooks.pub/teachingdiverselearners/chapter/direct-instruction/.

165. Lucie Renard, *The Direct Instruction Method; A Practical Guide to Effective Teaching*, BookWidgets (March 28, 2019).

166. Siegfried Engelmann, Teaching Needy Kids in our Backward System 229 (ADI Press, 2007). Chapter 5 can be downloaded at the NIFDI site, https://www.nifdi.org/. Project Follow Through is also described in a special issue of Effective School Practices (1995–96) which can be downloaded at https://www.nifdi.org/what-is-di/project-follow-through.

167. *Id.*

TWENTY-FOUR

The Logic of Poverty

Rethinking Approaches to Socioeconomic Bias in Judicial Decision-Making

The Honorable Jennie D. Latta, United States Bankruptcy Court, Western District of Tennessee

A Note from the Editors: We tend to think of implicit bias as negative and as race or ethnicity-oriented. But the word bias itself contemplates both positive and negative; and some of the early work on the topic involved measuring how quickly we made associations between flowers and insects and good and bad. We've found in our training that having the correct vocabulary for bias is useful and that broadening that vocabulary is equally valuable. In this Chapter, Judge Latta applies these concepts to address one of the most significant and enduring biases, that based on class and socioeconomic status. While this is an area not discussed often enough, as Judge Latta writes, it's critical to achieving fair and equitable results. By providing the court background in the topic, she helps us see the issue clearly. As she tells us, no truly poor people are likely to be appointed to the bench, nor are they likely to be in the ingroup for those who are. Judge Latta's suggestions for her colleagues recognize this and call for more diversity, more empathy, and more collegiality—all ideas that resonate with us and with our other authors. Her particular approaches, drawn from her own lived-experience, are thought-provoking for the bench and beyond. We are honored to count Judge Latta as a colleague, and are grateful for her insight and her work.

CHAPTER HIGHLIGHTS

- Social class, socioeconomic status, and implicit socioeconomic bias are logically and actually distinct.

- The Supreme Court has not identified the "poor" or any other socioeconomic class as a protected group for purposes of due process or equal protection analysis.
- Shared experiences and careful listening to judges of different backgrounds will lead to better judicial decision-making.
- Greater judicial diversity and collegiality is one of the best ways of countering the potential for implicit socioeconomic bias in judicial decision-making.

CHAPTER CONTENTS

Introduction

1. Social Class, Socioeconomic Status, Socioeconomic Bias—What's the Difference?
    A. Social Class
    B. Socioeconomic Status
    C. Socioeconomic Bias
2. Supreme Court Approaches to Constitutional Questions Concerning the Poor
    A. The District Court's Opinion–In re Kras
    B. The Supreme Court's Opinion–United States v. Kras
    C. The Court's Analysis of Poverty
    D. The Rest of the Story on In Forma Pauperis Bankruptcy
3. The Potential for Implicit Socioeconomic Bias in Judicial Decision-Making
4. Judicial Empathy and Judicial Diversity as Protections Against Socioeconomic Bias in Judicial Decision-Making

Introduction

In an earlier volume, *Enhancing Justice Reducing Bias,* Judge Andrew J. Wistrich and Jeffrey J. Rachlinksi wrote a chapter devoted to implicit bias in judicial decision-making.[1] They focused especially upon biases arising from race, noting the substantial gap in confidence in the judicial system between White Americans and Black Americans.[2] This observation was based in part upon the 2015 State of the State Courts survey conducted by the National Center for State Courts (NCSC).[3] Among other findings, NCSC reported that a majority of Americans felt that the poor, poor Blacks, divorced fathers, and Hispanics are treated worse than others by the courts.[4] Looking specifically at the role of judges, Wistrich and Rachlinski found that judges resemble most American adults in their responses to the Implicit Association Test for race, that is they show implicit bias for White-positive and Black-negative associations. But these associations did not affect their judgment in an explicit racial identification experiment.[5] The authors did find a different outcome when the race of fictional defendants was merely implied. Judges who harbored strong White-positive/Black-negative associations assigned more severe dispositions or sentences when primed with African-American words than when primed with race-neutral words.[6] The lesson the authors suggested should be taken from these experiments is that "thinking about race explicitly is a better approach than trying to ignore it."[7] The authors cited unpublished studies supporting the presence of implicit gender bias in the context of wrongful death and divorce cases and in criminal sentencing. Other studies have found that federal judges and state judges harbor positive implicit biases toward Whites and Christians and negative biases against Asian-Americans and Jews, "so-called privileged minorities."[8] Again, however, these unconscious biases do not seem to alter the judges' decision-making when the subject of the bias is made explicit. The authors concluded from this that although judges, like most adults, rely heavily on their intuition in their approaches to decision-making, they can be encouraged and trained to avoid unwanted influences on their judgment.[9] This was good news to me, a United States bankruptcy judge. As a bankruptcy judge, I naturally wondered whether these and perhaps other forms of unconscious associations might be influencing my decision-making.

As a result, I was intrigued by the research of Professor Michelle Benedetto Neitz, the first academic to suggest that socioeconomic status may be another source of unintended influence on the judiciary. In her 2013 article, *Socioeconomic Bias in the Judiciary,*[10] Professor Neitz explored the ways in which the privileged socioeconomic status of judges could be affecting their decisions from the bench. She suggested that the "'unselfconscious social elitism' of judges...can manifest as implicit socioeconomic bias."[11] In its simplest form, her thesis is that as the result of their high socioeconomic status, judges may unconsciously favor wealthy litigants over impoverished ones, with significant negative consequences for low income people. Professor Neitz suggested changes to the American Bar Association's Model Code of Judicial Conduct and improvement in judicial training to counter the possible invidious influence of judicial elitism.[12]

In the first section of this Chapter, I will distinguish social class, socioeconomic status, and socioeconomic bias. In the second section, I will briefly discuss the Supreme Court's approaches to constitutional questions concerning the poor. In the third section, I will turn to the possibilities for socioeconomic bias in judicial decision-making before turning in a final section to a discussion of the possibility of judicial empathy and the need to promote judicial diversity as the most effective remedies for possible socioeconomic bias.

1. Social Class, Socioeconomic Status, Socioeconomic Bias—What's the Difference?

A. Social Class

Americans, who eschew any sort of caste system, are somewhat more comfortable dividing themselves into upper, middle, and lower classes. Sociologist Dennis Gilbert, for example, divided Americans into six social classes: capitalist, upper middle, lower middle, working, working poor, and underclass or poor based upon measurements of income, education, and occupation.[13] Professor Will Barratt, of Indiana State University, argues that social class is not something that can be measured.[14] Rather, he suggests that social class is personal and cultural. Social class, especially one's social class of origin, he suggests, is not something you have but something you are, similar to your gender identity and ethnic identity.[15] Interestingly, the majority of Americans identify themselves as "middle class" no matter their income or occupation.[16]

B. Socioeconomic Status

Sociologists and other researchers tend to speak about socioeconomic status ("SES") rather than social class. SES is a collection of attributes or attainments more or less easy to measure that point to social class but are not social class. Professor Barratt suggests that the relationship between SES and social class is like that of a map to the territory itself, that is, while SES attempts to measure outward manifestations of the experience of social class, that's not the same as an individual's subjective experience of their social class.[17] Professor Barratt's work builds upon that of August D. Hollingshead of Yale University, known for his Four Factor Index to Social Status, which correlates education, occupation, sex, and marital status.[18] In describing his research, Hollingshead said:

> The new index takes into consideration the fact that social status is a multidimensional concept. It is premised upon three basic assumptions: (1) A differentiated, unequal status structure exists in our society; (2) The primary factors indicative of status are the occupation an individual engages in and the years of schooling he or she has completed; other salient factors are sex and marital status and; (3) These factors may be combined so that a researcher can quickly, reliably, and meaningfully estimate the status positions individuals and members of nuclear families occupy in our society.[19]

Hollingshead's emphasis on educational attainment and occupation are widely used as markers of socioeconomic status but they are not the only ones. Class or socioeconomic status may be thought of in terms of income, wealth, capital, education, prestige, occupation, culture, and as a system combining some or all of these.[20]

SES has been the subject of research in a number of different fields. For example, the American Psychological Association (APA) created its Task Force on Socioeconomic Status in 2005, which issued its Report on Socioeconomic Status in 2006.[21] Its report notes that social stratification can occur at societal, community, and individual levels:

> There are various theoretical and conceptual approaches to capturing critical aspects of social stratification. Studies addressing the distribution of resources at a societal level use social-level variables such as income distribution and income inequality that reflect the extent of inequality. Research on the social context of health or well-being may use community or neighborhood socioeconomic characteristics such as median income, percent unemployed, or percent with a college degree for a given community. At the individual level, most research on the effects of social stratification has used educational attainment, income (personal or household), and/or occupation as indicators of SES. Each of these captures a different dimension of social stratification and provides a partial indicator of resources available to the person.[22]

The APA Task Force Report focuses on three factors or aspects of SES—education, income, and occupation—rather than limiting its inquiry to income or poverty. Of these three factors, the report found education to be the most fundamental because higher education is associated with better economic outcomes, greater social and psychological resources, and fewer health risk behaviors.[23] The task force found that wealth is a better indicator of socioeconomic position over time than any single measure of income because wealth may reflect intergenerational transfers as well as an individual's earnings and savings. It found that the third factor, occupation, reflects more than merely the means to earn a living but also points to available access to social networks and sources of personal identity and pride. It found that lower SES jobs are more often associated with greater physical hazard, less autonomy, and monotony.[24]

SES is also widely studied in the field of public health. According to Professors Jo C. Phelan and Bruce G. Link, "There is a strong, well-established, and very robust association linking both morbidity and mortality to educational attainment, occupational standing, and income."[25] These authors show that persons who are richer in resources are much more likely to benefit from advances in medical knowledge and technology. The tremendous advances in medical knowledge and technology during the twentieth and early twenty-first centuries has led to ever-widening disparity in access to and benefit from healthcare. In the current pandemic, disparities in access to testing for Covid-19 have been widely reported[26] as has a disproportionate impact of the disease upon socioeconomically "worse off" racial minorities.[27] In an interesting move to counter this disproportionate impact, the National Academies of Sciences, Engineering, and Medicine recommended prioritization of these minorities in the receipt of anticipated vaccines.[28] The authors of a report concerning this recommendation made note of the legal limitations of race-based classifications, and therefore recommended using distribution criteria based upon geography, SES, and housing density "that would favor racial minorities de facto, but not explicitly."[29] This recommendation points to the frequent overlap between racial and ethnic classifications and SES.

Socioeconomic status has also been studied in the field of education. For example, Elizabeth Schlosser devoted her doctoral dissertation at the University of Southern Mississippi to the intersection of race, socioeconomic status, age, and race implicit bias in Mobile and Baldwin County School Systems.[30] Specifically, she was interested in how implicit bias may be impacting science teachers and thus contributing to the achievement gap between Black and White students in the sciences. Schlosser reviewed the literature demonstrating that poverty is a major cause of the achievement gap in education. Children from poorer families are less likely to receive proper nourishment and medical care than are children from families with greater resources. They are more likely to suffer from hearing loss, lead poisoning, asthma, and other health-related factors that hamper cognition and learning. She noted that children growing up in low SES conditions tend to have much smaller vocabularies than other socioeconomic groups, and that socioeconomic segregation is an important cause of educational inequality.[31]

In the field of criminal justice, Bernadette Rabuy and Daniel Kopf, writing for the Prison Policy Initiative, reported in 2015 that incarcerated persons had a median annual income in 2014 dollars of $19,185 prior to their incarceration, which was 41% less than non-incarcerated persons of similar ages.[32] The authors found this income disparity to hold true across all gender, race, and ethnicity groups. "[I]ncarcerated people," they found, "are dramatically concentrated at the lowest ends of the national income distribution."[33] When these same persons are eventually released, they must bear the burden of one of the few legally-acceptable forms of employment discrimination–criminal background–further fueling the cycle of poverty and incarceration.

Perhaps it should go without saying that socioeconomic status impacts outcomes and achievement across many fields. By definition, those with high socioeconomic status have access to greater resources than those with low socioeconomic status. Socioeconomic discrimination or bias, however, is something else altogether.

C. Socioeconomic Bias

When we speak of socioeconomic bias or implicit socioeconomic bias, we refer to utilizing social class or socioeconomic status as an unfair or improper basis for decision-making. We are considering whether, as Professor Neitz suggests, judges may unconsciously use social class or socioeconomic status as a basis for decisions. Part of the difficulty of understanding this bias, as Professor Neitz admits, is that there is no generally accepted outward manifestation of social class or socioeconomic status. Appearances can be deceiving! Even in my work in the bankruptcy court, a wide range of persons seek bankruptcy relief, from the very wealthy to the very poor, and from the highly-educated to the illiterate. Debtors must disclose their income, assets, and occupations in the schedules that are filed with their bankruptcy petitions, but even this information does not completely capture social class in the sense of personal identity discussed by Professor Barratt. Moreover, this information, which is also available to judges in a number of settings, tends to move the judge from unconscious to conscious awareness of the socioeconomic status of the litigants or defendants, and once made aware, judges generally perform fairly.

Professor Neitz focused both on the SES status of litigants appearing before a judge and on the SES of judges in general as a potential source for implicit socioeconomic bias. Judicial salaries are one key indicator of the SES of judges, but judges just as the litigants who appear before them, come from a wide range of social classes. Judicial salaries are above the average salaries of American workers but well below those of many professionals and corporate executives. Income, however, is just one indicator of socioeconomic status and, by itself, is a poor indicator of the social class of origin. Social class, as Professor Barratt suggests, is a more enduring part of personal identity. It is this inherited sense of social class that a judge carries into his or her work. This fact, I think, opens up possibilities for countering the potential for implicit socioeconomic bias in ways I will discuss below.

2. Supreme Court Approaches to Constitutional Questions Concerning the Poor

I was drawn into Professor Neitz's article because of its reliance upon the Supreme Court's decision in *United States v. Kras*, concerning the inability of a poor man to afford a bankruptcy discharge.[34] Although waiver of the fee for obtaining a bankruptcy discharge was subsequently addressed by Congress, a close reading of the thought processes of the District Court and Supreme Court in deciding *Kras* provides a framework for considering Supreme Court jurisprudence concerning the poor and the potential for socioeconomic bias in judicial decision-making.

A. The District Court's Opinion — *In re Kras*

In 1971, Robert William Kras filed a motion in the United States District Court for the Eastern District of New York seeking leave to file a petition in bankruptcy without prepaying any of the filing fees (a total of $50) that were imposed as a condition for obtaining a discharge.[35] In support of his motion, Kras filed an affidavit of facts, which, for purposes of the motion, were taken to be true. He lived in a two and one-half room apartment with his wife, his two young children, his mother, and his mother's daughter. His younger child suffered from cystic fibrosis and, at the time of the filing of the motion, was in Cumberland Medical Center. Except for some odd jobs, Kras had been unemployed since May 1959. His last steady employment had been with the Metropolitan Life Insurance Company, which fired him when some premiums he had collected were stolen from his home. He had been unable to repay Metropolitan and this prevented him from finding other employment because of the negative reference provided by Metropolitan. Kras's wife had worked until March 1970 but had stopped working when she became pregnant with their younger child. Mrs. Kras could not return to work because she was devoting all of her time to caring for their younger child. The household subsisted on a public assistance allotment of $366.00 per month, all of which Kras said was necessary to pay for rent and the necessities of life. Kras owned no assets that were not exempt from the claims of creditors. His exempt assets consisted of $50.00 worth of essential household goods and clothing.

Kras alleged that he could neither pay the filing fees with his petition nor promise to pay them in installments. He said that he wanted a discharge in bankruptcy in order to get a new start in life and to better his chances of securing employment. Kras was represented by the Legal Aid Society of New York City, which argued that the federal *in forma pauperis* statute, 28 U.S.C. § 1915(a), should be applied to bankruptcy proceedings and that the sections of the Bankruptcy Act requiring payment of fees as a condition for discharge violated the Fifth Amendment of the United States Constitution. Because of the constitutional questions, notice was provided to the Attorney General, who intervened in order to submit a brief in opposition to the motion. The motion was considered and decided by a district judge, Judge Anthony J. Travia, rather than a bankruptcy referee, because the Clerk of Court would not accept the petition for filing without further instruction.

Judge Travia rejected Kras's statutory argument because Congress specifically amended the Bankruptcy Act in 1946 to abolish *in forma pauperis* bankruptcy petitions.[36] The original Bankruptcy Act of 1898 provided for waiver of fees at the time of filing upon an affidavit of inability to pay. The Senate Report on the Bankruptcy Referee's Salary Bill acknowledged that notwithstanding the statutory requirement that the filing fee be paid upon filing or waived, many referees had adopted the practice of collecting the fees in installments after a bankruptcy petition was accepted for filing. The Senate Report suggested that this practice was more advisable than "pauper petitions." Although the assumption that consumer debtors could afford to pay $50 to file a petition in bankruptcy ($100 for a married couple) had been questioned,[37] Judge Travia felt constrained by the Senate Report to conclude that Congress was fully aware of the impact that the Bill had on bankruptcy filers. The effect of the amendment was that the bankruptcy fee might be paid in installments but ultimately had to be paid as a condition precedent to discharge This was the opinion reached in two other decisions predating Judge Travia's consideration of the issue, *In re Garland*[38] and *In re Smith*.[39]

Judge Travia thus turned to the constitutional issues raised in Kras's motion, which had also been addressed in *Garland* and *Smith*. In *Garland,* the United States Court of Appeals for First Circuit held in a unanimous decision that the requirement of paying a filing fee before receiving a discharge in bankruptcy did not amount to a denial of due process. In *Smith,* the Colorado District Court disagreed, finding that the imposition of the bankruptcy filing fee upon an indigent petitioner amounted to a denial of equal protection. Judge Travia noted that both *Garland* and *Smith* were decided before the Supreme Court issued its opinion in *Boddie v. Connecticut,*[40] which held that a Connecticut statute having the effect of denying individuals access to its divorce courts based upon their inability to pay filing fees and process costs violated the Due Process Clause of the Fourteenth Amendment. Justice Harlan, writing for the majority, said that requiring indigent persons to pay a filing fee to access the courts was tantamount to exclusion from the courts. Justice Douglas concurred in the result but would have decided the case based upon equal protection rather than procedural due process. He felt that Connecticut's fee requirement was tantamount to invidious discrimination based upon poverty (i.e., implicit socioeconomic bias). Justice Douglas wrote that states could no more deny divorces to those who were poor than to those who were Black rather than White, resident aliens rather than citizens, Catholic rather than Protestant, convicted of larceny rather than convicted of embezzlement.[41] Justice Brennan wrote a separate opinion concurring in part. He agreed that Connecticut denied procedural due process to indigent persons by denying them "access to its courts for the sole reason that they cannot pay a required fee."[42] He did not agree with the majority insofar as its decision rested on the State providing the only forum for the granting of a divorce because he could not distinguish resort to the courts to obtain a divorce from resort to the courts to vindicate any other right arising under federal or state law. In other words, he felt that the reasoning of the majority would open the courts to indigent persons for all purposes. He, too, would have rested the decision on equal protection because Connecticut did not deny a hearing to everyone seeking a divorce but only to those persons who failed to pay certain fees. He noted the development in the protections of indigent persons in criminal cases under the due process and equal protection clauses. "A State," he wrote, "may not make its judicial processes available to some but deny them to others simply because they cannot pay a fee."[43]

Justice Black wrote the one dissenting opinion in *Boddie*. He would have maintained the distinction between the constitutional rights of indigent defendants in criminal cases and the rights of indigent litigants in civil cases:

> [N]either [the Due Process Clause nor the Equal Protection Clauses]... justifies judges in trying to make our Constitution fit the times, or hold laws constitutional or not on the basis of a judges' sense of fairness. The Equal Protection Clause is no more appropriate a vehicle of the 'shock the conscience' test than is the Due Process Clause.[44]

Following the issuance of the decision in *Boddie* on March 2, 1971, the Supreme Court denied *certiorari* in *In re Garland* on May 3, 1971, with three justices dissenting. The basis of Justice Black's dissent was precisely that if *Boddie* were the law, it should not be limited to divorce. Justice Douglas, also dissenting, wrote:

> Today's decisions underscore the difficulties with the *Boddie* approach. In *Boddie* the majority found marriage and its dissolution to be so fundamental as to require allowing indigents access to divorce courts without costs. When indigency is involved I do not think there is a hierarchy of interests. Marriage and its dissolution are of course fundamental. Similarly, obtaining a fresh start in life through a bankruptcy proceeding or securing adequate housing and the other procedures in these cases violate the Equal Protection Clause.[45]

Against this background, Judge Travia concluded that a proper interpretation of *Boddie* could only result in the conclusion that the application of the requirement of payment of the bankruptcy filing fee to Kras, a petitioner presumed to be indigent for purposes of the question, "violated his Fifth Amendment right of due process, including equal protection."[46] Judge Travia treated the question as one of access to the courts rather than one of entitlement to a bankruptcy discharge. Significantly, his decision was not that Kras's status as indigent could not be questioned by the trustee, nor that the requirement that he pay the bankruptcy filing fees be forever waived. His ruling was limited to the requirement that payment of the fee be made a condition precedent to obtaining a discharge because it denied the indigent access to the courts. He felt that access to the courts is a fundamental interest that cannot be abridged by the government absent a compelling interest. According to Judge Travia, the justifications put forward by the United States—its fiscal interest in preserving a self-financing bankruptcy system, and its desire to prevent frivolous bankruptcy petitions—did not rise to this level.[47]

B. The Supreme Court's Decision—*United States v. Kras*

The United States appealed the district court's decision directly to the Supreme Court, which reversed. Justice Blackmun wrote the majority opinion, agreeing that the federal *in forma pauperis* statute did not apply in bankruptcy but adopting the reasoning of the First Circuit in *Garland* on the constitutional question. The Court disagreed with the district court's reliance on *Boddie's* due process analysis because "Kras's alleged interest in the elimination of his debt burden, and in obtaining his desired new start in life, although important and so recognized by the enactment of the Bankruptcy Act, does not rise to the same constitutional level" as the Connecticut appellants' interest in dissolving their marriages.[48]

> If Kras is not discharged in bankruptcy, his position will not be materially altered in any constitutional sense. Gaining or not gaining a discharge will effect no change with respect to basic necessities. We see no fundamental interest that is gained or lost depending on the availability of a discharge in bankruptcy.[49]

Moreover, the majority was not convinced that bankruptcy was the only method available for adjustment of the debtor-creditor relationship. Kras might enter into a negotiated agreement or wait for the passage of the applicable period of limitations to obtain relief from his debts. The Court also rejected Kras's equal protection argument:

> Bankruptcy is hardly akin to free speech or marriage or to those other rights, so many of which are embedded in the First Amendment, that the Court has come to regard as fundamental and that demand the lofty requirement of a compelling governmental interest before they may be significantly regulate. Neither does it touch upon what have been said to be the suspect criteria of race, nationality, or alienage. Instead bankruptcy legislation is in the area of economics and social welfare. This being so, the applicable standard, in measuring the propriety of Congress' classification, is that of rational justification. There is no constitutional right to obtain a discharge of one's debts in bankruptcy.[50]

The Court found the structure adopted by Congress in the Bankruptcy Act to pass the rational basis test, finding that they permitted the "bankrupt" to avoid the harassment of his creditors, while protecting his future earnings and property from the claims of this existing creditors, and providing for the payment of the bankruptcy filing fee in installments over six months from these newly-liberated earnings. In the part of the opinion found particularly objectionable by the dissenting justices, the majority noted that the $50 filing fee owed by an individual debtor might be paid at the rate of $1.28 per week if the repayment period were extended to the full nine months permitted by the General Order adopted by the Court. There followed a series of statements by Justice Blackmun that brought scorn from Justice Marshall:

> This is a sum less than the payments Kras makes on his couch of negligible value in storage, and less than the price of a movie and a little more than the cost of a pack or two of cigarettes. If, as Kras alleges in his affidavit, a discharge in bankruptcy will afford him that new start he so desires, and the Metropolitan then no longer charge him with fraud and give him bad refer-

ences, and if he really needs and desires that discharge, this much available revenue should be within his able-bodied reach when the adjudication in bankruptcy has stayed collection and has brought halt to whatever harassment, if any, he may have sustained from his creditors.[51]

In a footnote, Justice Blackmun said, "We fail to see how a discharge in bankruptcy in itself will prevent the Metropolitan from issuing an unfavorable reference letter about Kras."[52] Justice Blackmun concluded that *Boddie* stopped short of announcing "an unlimited rule that an indigent at all times and at all cases has the right to relief without payment of fees" and that extension of the principle of *Boddie* to no-asset bankruptcy cases should come from Congress not the courts.[53] Chief Justice Burger wrote a separate concurring opinion emphasizing the propriety of the distinction made between the exclusivity of the State's control over divorce cases and the degree of government control over the relations between debtors and creditors. Chief Justice Burger also called attention to the ongoing work of the bankruptcy review commission, which he felt would take up the question of waiver of bankruptcy fees for indigent persons.

Justice Stewart wrote a dissenting opinion, which Justices Douglas, Brennan, and Marshall joined. They would have affirmed the decision of the district court on due process grounds—that is, on the basis that Congress could not permit some persons to obtain a discharge in bankruptcy while preventing others, in this case indigent persons, from doing so. Justice Stewart concluded: "The Court today holds that Congress may say that some of the poor are too poor even to go bankrupt. I cannot agree."[54] Justices Douglas and Brennan wrote a separate dissenting opinion. They would have decided the case on the basis that invidious discrimination against the poor is a denial of due process because it denies equal protection relying upon *Bolling v. Sharpe,* which held that segregation of students on the basis of race in the District of Columbia violates the Due Process Clause of the Fifth Amendment.[55]

Justice Marshall wrote a separate dissenting opinion as well. He agreed with Justice Stevens that the majority failed to distinguish Kras's case from *Bolling* but wrote separately to emphasize what he called the "extraordinary route" by which they did so.[56] He was particularly concerned that the majority did not accept the facts set out in Kras's unchallenged affidavit. For example, Justice Marshall said that even if Kras's statement that he was unable to pay the fees was mistaken, he could not have been mistaken in saying that he could not promise to pay the fees in installments. Without making that promise, Justice Marshall felt that Kras could not have relief from the creditor harassment that he believed was preventing him from earning what was necessary to pay the fees. Moreover, Justice Marshall did not agree with the majority's finding that it would be easy for a desperately poor person to save $1.92 each week over the course of six months:

It may be easy for some people to think that weekly savings of less than $2 are no burden. But no one who has had close contact with poor people can fail to understand how close to the margin of survival many of them are. A sudden illness, for example, may destroy whatever savings they may have accumulated, and by eliminating a sense of security may destroy the incentive to save in the future. A pack or two of cigarettes may be, for them, not a routine purchase but a luxury indulged in only rarely. The desperately poor almost never go to see a movie, which the majority seems to believe is an almost weekly activity. They have more important things to do with what little money they have—like attempting to provide some comforts for a gravely ill child, as Kras must do.[57]

Justice Marshall would have decided the case on the basis of *Boddie* as one involving the right of access to the courts and the right to be heard upon a claim of legal right, rather than simply on the question of the right to discharge in bankruptcy. Private settlements, he said, disagreeing with the majority, do not determine the validity of claims. That can only be done by a court, and Kras was denied access to that determination because of his indigency.

C. The Court's Analysis of Poverty

I included this extensive history of the various opinions in *Kras* to suggest that, not surprisingly, the treatment of the poor in our courts is a bit more complicated than the inability of privileged jurists to assess the rights and conditions of the poor.[58] Justice Marshall did assert that Justice Blackmun was a bit tone deaf, and perhaps unwilling to accept the facts of Kras's affidavit. It is possible, however, that Justice Blackmun drew different conclusions from the facts than did Justice Marshall. Footnote 9, for example, questions the logic of Kras's assertion that a discharge in bankruptcy would somehow change his former employer's mind about the recommendations they would give him. I suspect, as perhaps the majority did, that a discharge of Kras's obligation to it would have made Metropolitan even less inclined to give him a favorable recommendation. And while the comment about expenditures upon movies and cigarettes seems unfortunate because we do not know whether Kras actually included those items in his budget, the reference to a "couch of negligible value in storage" is so specific as to raise the question of whether the Court had more facts before it than made their way into the opinion, facts that the majority felt indicated poor choices on Kras's part. All of this is to say that judging necessarily involves attempts to put yourself in someone else's shoes, and judges may not always get that right. What cannot be said, however, is that the Justices failed to carefully consider the plight of the poor and whether or not the poor, as a class, should enjoy constitutional protection. What can be taken away from *United States v Kras* are principles concerning the treatment of indigency as a socioeconomic status that continue to inform judicial decision-making today. The Court did not then, and has not since, declared indigency to be a suspect class such as race, ethnicity, and national origin, or even a semi-suspect class, such as gender and illegitimacy, for purposes of equal protection analysis.[59] Congress continues to struggle with whether and how to enact laws that relieve the burdens of the poor appropriately and fairly.

D. The Rest of the Story on *In Forma Pauperis* Bankruptcy

Even Judge Travia would not have waived the required filing fees on the basis that the requirement for payment *in itself* impermissibly discriminated against an identifiable group of people. Under his ruling, Kras would have remained obligated to pay the fees after he received his discharge. Whether, when, and how the Clerk of Court could have gone about collecting them was not specified. The rest of the story of waivers of bankruptcy fees is that Congress did not amend the United States Code to provide for waiver of the bankruptcy filing fees until 2005 as part of the Bankruptcy Abuse Prevention and Consumer Protection Act.[60] Under that Act, 28 U.S.C. § 1930 was amended to add subsection (f) which provides for waiver of the filing fee in a case filed under Chapter 7 of the U.S. Bankruptcy Code, for an individual if the individual has income less than 150 percent of the income official poverty line (defined by the Office of Management and Budget) *and* is unable to pay the fee in installments.[61] Both prongs must be satisfied. One hundred fifty percent of the income official poverty line for a family of four in the contiguous forty-eight states in 2021 is $3,312.50 per month.[62] The fees required with respect to a Chapter 7 case consist of a $245 case filing fee, a $75 miscellaneous administrative fee, and a $15 trustee surcharge, for a total of $335. If a debtor's application to pay these fees in installments is denied (e.g., because the court finds that a debtor whose income is below the income poverty line nevertheless has regular income from which she might pay the filing fee in installments), the debtor may pay the filing fee in installments over a period of up to 180 days.[63] Significantly, the waiver of the bankruptcy filing fee is not available to persons who choose Chapter 13 bankruptcy—an option for persons with regular income, presumably because they should be able to pay the filing fee in installments. Through an unfortunate quirk in the current bankruptcy laws, however, persons who cannot afford a Chapter 7 bankruptcy attorney fee file petitions under Chapter 13 in order to pay their attorney's fee in installments, resulting in a delay in their receiving a discharge for up to five years.[64]

3. The Potential for Implicit Socioeconomic Bias in Judicial Decision-Making

Kras decided that the indigent do not form a suspect class for purposes of equal protection analysis. A second case relied upon by Professor Neitz to demonstrate the potential for implicit socioeconomic bias in judicial decision-making was *United*

States v. Pineda-Moreno,⁶⁵ in which Chief Judge Kozinski, and Judges Reinhardt, Wardlaw, Paez, and Berzon dissented from the denial of a motion to rehear *en banc* a decision of the Court of Appeals for the Ninth Circuit permitting police officers to surveil the activities of a suspect by attaching a GPS tracking device to the underside of his car. The panel that heard the case held that the defendant had no expectation of privacy with respect to the car parked in his driveway, which had no special features such as a gate, a "No Trespassing" sign, or any other feature to prevent someone from seeing the entire driveway or walking upon the driveway to deliver mail or packages to the front door. Chief Judge Kozinski insisted that the case should have been decided upon the basis that the driveway formed part of the curtilage entitled to the same Fourth Amendment protection as the house itself:⁶⁶

> There's been much talk about diversity on the bench, but there's one kind of diversity that doesn't exist: No truly poor people are appointed as federal judges, or as state judges for that matter. Judges, regardless of race, ethnicity or sex, are selected from the class of people who don't live in trailers or urban ghettos. The everyday problems of people who live in poverty are not close to our hearts and minds because that's not how we and our friends live. Yet poor people are entitled to privacy, even if they can't afford all the gadgets of the wealthy for ensuring it. Whatever else one may say about Pineda-Moreno, it's perfectly clear that he did not expect—and certainly did not consent—to have strangers prowl his property in the middle of the night and attach electronic tracking devices to the underside of his car. No one does.
>
> When you glide your BMW into your underground garage or behind an electric gate, you don't need to worry that somebody might attach a tracking device to it while you sleep. But the Constitution doesn't prefer the rich over the poor; the man who parks his car next to his trailer is entitled to the same privacy and peace of mind as the man whose urban fortress is guarded by the Bel Air Patrol. The panel's breezy opinion is troubling on a number of grounds, not least among them its unselfconscious cultural elitism.⁶⁷

The rest of the story in this case was that the United States Supreme Court made short work of it. The entire opinion reads as follows:

On petition for writ of *certiorari* to the United States Court of Appeals for the Ninth Circuit. Motion of petitioner for leave to proceed in forma pauperis and petition for writ of *certiorari* granted. Judgment vacated, and case remanded to the United States Court of Appeals for the Ninth Circuit for further consideration in light of *United States v. Jones*, 565 U.S. 400, 132 S. Ct. 945, 181 L. Ed. 2d 911 (2012).⁶⁸

United States v. Jones decided that the attachment of a GPS device on a vehicle and subsequent use of the device to monitor a vehicle's movement constitutes a search for purposes of the Fourth Amendment.⁶⁹ On remand, the Ninth Circuit held that the police acted within existing precedent when they placed the device and further that the evidence gained from the device was cumulative of other, sufficient evidence.[70]

Although Chief Judge Kozinski was understandably upset—and not just because of the lack of understanding that not all persons have the means to secure their driveways—the lesson that I take away from this case is that the system works. The appellate system provides some protection against the potential for socioeconomic bias in judicial decision-making, and greater diversity of backgrounds for those elected and appointed to our state and federal benches would provide more assurance that the system will continue to work. As I discuss below, a wide variety of life experiences helps judges to develop a greater understanding of the "logic of poverty." It is not necessary that all judges be poor, but it is necessary that all judges be empathic. As Professor Barratt explains, a person's (and thus, a judge's) sense of his or her own social class is an important part of their personal identity. Greater diversity in judicial backgrounds and the creation of an environment in which the sharing of diverse experiences is welcomed and encouraged among judicial colleagues will inevitably lead to better judicial understanding of persons of different SES.[71]

4. Judicial Empathy and Judicial Diversity as Protections Against Socioeconomic Bias in Judicial Decision-Making

My friend Frances Riley tells the following story that I have recounted in numerous settings:

> Many years ago, while working at a community center in a low income area of Memphis, I drove an old clunker car. The guys playing on the neighborhood basketball court used to laugh at my car and occasionally cheer when it started. Cars have never been important to me, so it was friendly banter that I needed a new car. The only time I begrudged the car was when I had to take it though the city's mandatory annual auto inspection—a dreaded event. Eventually, I succumbed and purchased a new car.
>
> I joked with my work mates that at least I no longer had to fear the auto inspection process. Shortly after my purchase, one of the basketball guys approached me and kindly offered to fix my car. I told him it didn't need fixing—it was a new car. He said, "No, I can fix it! I can fix it so it won't pass inspection." I was shocked. "Why would I want to do that?" I asked. I, after all, was relieved that I no longer had to dread the inspection experience. He was shocked at my shock. I obviously didn't know the utility of flunking inspection. It took a "meeting of the minds" for us to understand each other's position.

My middle-class view was that I could now fly through the process and not be concerned with minor obligatory repairs to my vehicle. His offer involved tweaking the new car so that it would fail the emissions test that was part of the inspection. Passing the annual inspection led to renewal of the auto tag. And renewal of the auto tag meant payment of a fee.

As I found out from him, if you failed the test, you were given a sheet of paper to display in your car's rear window. It identified that you had failed the inspection and granted you 30 days to fix the issue and return. What my viewpoint had failed to comprehend was that the 30-day extension allowed you to drive on the city streets without fear of being pulled over and ticketed for driving with expired tags. I also discovered that you (at that point) could continue to repeat this process, obtaining additional delay before the day for payment.

My friend was offering me a glimpse into "economic survival" in South Memphis. The auto inspection process was free and failing it allowed you to drive on the streets without paying the annual registration fee. What I saw as an annual required fee for car tags, my friend saw as a major and unnecessary government expense that prevented him from using his limited cash for necessary living expenses. His process allowed him continued economic survival while balancing his very limited money for essential food and shelter.

I realized that his offer was a sharing of "survival wisdom" of which I had been completely unaware and a true act of kindness to a clueless person.

Fran identifies this story as one of "survival wisdom." I tend to think of it as an example of the logic of poverty. From Fran's middle-class perspective, her basketball-playing friend's suggestion was illogical. Had she not taken the time to listen, her encounter might have reinforced a belief, either explicit or implicit, that "lower class" persons are uneducated, illogical, or unreasonable. In fact, her friend's solution to a very pressing problem in his world was brilliant, and it points out to me an alternative approach to thinking about the potential for socioeconomic bias in judicial decision-making.

One of the best protections against the possibility of socioeconomic bias in judicial decision-making is the development of judicial empathy. As Professor Neitz pointed out, judges' salaries on the whole are two or more times the average salary of the American worker. In addition, because they usually possess professional degrees, judges are more highly educated than most American workers,[72] and "judge" continues to be considered to be a high prestige occupation.[73] All of these factors point to a high socioeconomic status being attached to the position of judge. As Professor Barratt points out, however, the social class of origin is more indicative of an individual's identity than her current income, education level, and occupation. Moreover, as Judge Wistrich and Dr. Rachlinksi report, judges are actually quite good at setting aside personal negative associations when rendering a decision based upon explicit racial and gender characteristics. The goal in judicial decision-making is even-handed application of the law neither favoring nor disfavoring any socioeconomic class. This does not mean, however, that a judge's personal history and ability to understand the lives of the litigants before them are not essential to this process.

Judge Arrie W. Davis has argued, quite persuasively I think, that the personal experiences of judges do matter. In his article, *The Richness of Experience, Empathy, and the Role of a Judge: The Senate Confirmation Hearings of Judge Sonia Sotomayor*,[74] Judge Davis asserts that it is neither possible nor advisable to expect a judge to set aside her personal background and life experiences when she dons a black robe:

> In the context of judicial decision-making, empathy, which, as its core, involves the ability to understand life experiences or emotions of another person, need not mean "intuition" nor should it be perceived as injecting the "mystical" into the ordered resolution of disputes. Rather, as Professor Lynne Henderson explains, 'empathy enables the decision-maker to have an appreciation of the human beings of a given legal situation," ultimately aiding the judge both in the process of reaching a legal conclusion and in justifying that conclusion "in a way that disembodied reason simply cannot."[75]

In my own reflections on the role of the judge, I have found myself thinking that one could create a judicial kiosk loaded with the Bankruptcy Code and Rules into which one might enter the facts of his financial life and receive a standard response, but this would fall far short of the work that I think we expect from human—and humane—judges. We want judges to be human beings who, like my friend Fran, take the time to enter into the lives of those whose backgrounds are different from their own in order to understand the challenges and logic of persons from other backgrounds. This is where the judges in the majorities fell short in *Kras* and *Pineda-Moreno* according to the Justice Marshall and Chief Judge Kozinski—they could not step outside of their positions of privilege to understand the plight of the poorer persons appearing before them. Whether their analyses of the other judges were correct or not is beside the point in this context. Their dissents point to the need for judges to employ empathic listening in approaching their work.

As a final note, I would say that one of the best ways for judges to develop appreciation for the lives of persons outside their usual orbits is through the promotion of greater judicial diversity and collegiality. In my own field, significant efforts have been made to increase diversity in the selection of magistrate and bankruptcy judges.[76] Greater diversity in judicial decision-makers can only lead to greater depth in judicial decision-making.

So, You'd Like to Know More

- Will Barratt, Social Class on Campus: Theories and Manifestations (2011).
- Sudhir Alladi Venkatesh, Off the Books: The Underground Economy of the Urban Poor (2006).
- David K. Shipler, The Working Poor: Invisible in America (2004).

About the Author

The Honorable Jennie D. Latta was appointed as a bankruptcy judge for the United States Bankruptcy Court for the Western District of Tennessee in 1997. She received her J.D. degree from the Cecil C. Humphreys School of Law, University of Memphis, in 1986. In addition, she holds an M.A. in Catholic Thought and Life from Saint Meinrad School of Theology (2003) and a Ph.D. in philosophy from the University of Memphis (2014). She is an adjunct professor at the Cecil C. Humphreys School of Law where she teaches Debtor Creditor Law.

Endnotes

1. Andrew J. Wistrich & Jeffrey J. Rachlinski, *Implicit Bias in Judicial Decision Making: How It Affects Judges and What Judges Can Do About It*, in ENHANCING JUSTICE REDUCING BIAS 87 (Sarah E. Redfield, ed. 2017).

2. *Id.* at 88–89.

3. NAT'L CTR FOR STATE COURTS, *The State of the State Courts: A 2015 NCSC Public Opinion Survey* (Nov. 17, 2015), https://www.ncsc.org/topics/court-community/public-trust-and-confidence/resource-guide/2015-state-of-state-courts-survey.

4. *Id.* The 2019 State of the State Courts survey did not ask about perceptions of disparate treatment in the courts. It did find that while courts are more trusted than other government institutions in the United States, there was a decline in confidence in the Supreme Court, the federal court system, and the state court systems from the previous year. The survey nonetheless found that "many of the attributes underpinning public trust [in the courts] remain solid." NAT'L CTR FOR STATE COURTS, *The State of the State Courts: A 2019 NCSC Public Opinion Survey* (January 3, 2020), https://www.ncsc.org/topics/court-community/public-trust-and-confidence/resource-guide/2019-state-of-state-courts-survey.

5. Andrew J. Wistrich & Jeffrey J. Rachlinksi, *Implicit Bias in Judicial Decision Making: How It Affects Judges and What Judges Can Do About It*, in ENHANCING JUSTICE REDUCING BIAS 101 (Sarah E. Redfield, ed. 2017).

6. *Id.* at 102.

7. *Id.* at 103.

8. Justin D. Levinson, Mark W. Bennett & Koichi Hioki, *Judging Implicit Bias: A National Empirical Study of Judicial Stereotypes Beyond Black and White*, 69 Fla. L. Rev. 63, 63 (2017).

9. Wistrich, *Implicit Bias in Judicial Decision Making* at 104.

10. Michele Benedetto Neitz, *Socioeconomic Bias in the Judiciary*, 61 Clev. St. L. Rev. 137 (2013).

11. *Id.* at 137 (quoting Chief Judge Alex Kozinski, in United States v. Pineda-Moreno, 617 F.3d 1120, 1123 (9th Cir. 2010)).

12. *Id.* at 162–65.

13. Dennis L. Gilbert, The American Class Structure in An Age of Growing Inequality, (10th Ed. 2018).

14. Will Barratt, *SES Is Not Social Class*, Social Class on Campus Blog (May 6, 2013), http://socialclassoncampus.blogspot.com/2013/05/ses-is-not-social-class.html.

15. Will Barrett, *The Barrett Simplified Measure of Social Status (BSMS)*, Social Class on Campus Blog (June 14, 2012), http://socialclassoncampus.blogspot.com/2012/06/barratt-simplified-measure-of-social.html.

16. Pew Research Center, *Few with Family Incomes of $100K+ Embrace Level 'Upper Class'* (March 4, 2015), https://www.pewresearch.org/politics/2015/03/04/most-say-government-policies-since-recession-have-done-little-to-help-middle-class-poor/few-with-family-incomes-of-100k-embrace-the-label-upper-class-2/.

17. Will Barrett, *Introduction to Social Class*, Social Class on Campus Blog (February 17, 2008), http://socialclassoncampus.blogspot.com/2008/02/i-am-putting-together-manuscript-for.html.

18. August B. Hollingshead, *Four Factor Index of Social Status* (Working Paper, Rep. No. 8, 1975), 8 Yale J. Soc. 21 (2011).

19. Hollingshead, 8 Yale J. Soc. at 22.

20. Will Barrett, *Introduction to Social Class*, Social Class on Campus Blog (February 17, 2008), http://socialclassoncampus.blogspot.com/2008/02/i-am-putting-together-manuscript-for.html.

21. Am. Psychol. Ass'n, *Report of the APA Task Force on Socioeconomic Economic Status* (2006), https://www.apa.org/pi/ses/resources/publications/task-force-2006.pdf

22. *Id.* at 9.

23. *Id.*

24. *Id.* at 10.

25. Jo C. Phelan & Bruce G. Link, *Controlling Disease and Creating Disparities: A Fundamental Cause Perspective*, J. Gerontol. B. Psychol. Sci. Soc. Sci., 27 (Oct. 2005), available at https://pubmed.ncbi.nlm.nih.gov/16251587/.

26. *See, e.g.*, Shahmir H. Ali, Yesim Tozan, et al., Regional and socioeconomic predictors of perceived ability to access coronavirus testing in the United States: results from a nationwide Covid-19 survey, 58 Ann. Epidemiol. 7 (Mar. 7, 2021), available at https://www.ncbi.nlm.nih.gov/pmc/articles/PMC7937327/; Monika Goyal, Joelle N. Simpson, et al., *Racial and/or Ethnic and Socioeconomic Disparities of SARS-CoV02 Infection Among Children*, 146 Pediatrics, e2020009951, https://pediatrics.aappublications.org/content/146/4/e2020009951.

27. Harald Schmidt, Lawrence O. Gostin, et al, *Is it Lawful and Ethical to Prioritize Racial Minorities for Covid-19 Vaccines?* 324 J. Am. Med. Ass'n 2023 (Oct. 14, 2020), available at https://jamanetwork.com/journals/jama/fullarticle/2771874.

28. *Id.* at 2023.

29. *Id.* at 2024.

30. Elizabeth Schlosser, *Race, Socioeconomic Status, and Implicit Bias: Implications for Closing the Achievement Gap* (Dissertations, No. 1466, 2017), https://aquila.usm.edu/dissertations/1466.

31. *Id.*

32. Bernadette Rabuy & Daniel Kopf, *Prisons of Poverty: Uncovering the Pre-Incarceration Incomes of the Imprisoned*, Prison Policy Initiative (July 9, 2015), https://www.prisonpolicy.org/reports/income.html.

33. *Id.*

34. 409 U.S. 434 (1973).

35. In re Kras, 331 F. Supp. 1207, 1208 (E.D. N.Y. 1971).

36. *Kras*, 331 F. Supp. at 1210.

37. Henry W. Shaeffer, *Proceedings in Bankruptcy In Forma Pauperis*, 69 Colum. L. Rev. 1203 (1969). Subsequent articles concerning the irony that bankruptcy was until 2005 the one legal proceeding that could not be filed *in forma pauperis* include Karen Gross & Shari Rosenberg, *In Forma Pauperis In Bankruptcy: Reflecting on and Beyond United States v. Kras,* 2 Am. Bankr. Inst. L. Rev. 57 (1994); Michael C. Markham & V. Bethann Scharrer, *In Forma Pauperis: An Unnecessary Privilege in Bankruptcy,* 2 Am. Bankr. Inst. L. Rev. 73 (1994); Richard H. W. Maloy, *Should Bankruptcy Be Reserved for People Who Have Money? Or Is the Bankruptcy Court a Court of the United States?,* 7 J. Bankr. L. & Prac. 3 (1997).

38. 428 F.2d 1185 (1st Cir. 1970), *cert. denied,* 402 U.S. 954 (1971).

39. 323 F. Supp. 1082 (D. Colo. 1971).

40. 401 U.S. 371 (1971).

41. *Id.* at 385–86 (Douglas, J., concurring in result).

42. *Id.* at 386 (Brennan, J., concurring in part).

43. *Id.* at 389 (Brennan, J., concurring in part).

44. *Id.* at 394 (Black, J., dissenting).

45. *Id* at 961.

46. *Kras*, 331 F. Supp. at 1212.

47. *Kras* 331 F. Supp. at 1214–15.

48. United States v. Kras, 409 U.S. 434, 444–45 (1973).

49. *Id.* at 445.

50. *Id.* at 446.

51. *Id.* at 449.

52. *Id.* at n.9.

53. *Id.* at 450.

54. *Id.* at 457(Stevens, J., dissenting).

55. *Id.* at 45758 (Douglas, J. and Brennan, J., dissenting) (citing Bolling v. Sharpe, 347 U.S. 497, 499 (1954)).

56. U.S. v. Kras, 409 U.S. at 458 (Marshall, J., dissenting).

57. U.S. v. Kras, 409 U.S. at 460.

58. A statement with which I do not for a moment think Professor Neitz would disagree.

59. Although some have argued that they should. *See, e.g.,* Mario L. Barnes & Erwin Chermerinsky, *The Disparate Treatment of Race and Class in Constitutional Jurisprudence*, 72 LAW & CONTEMP. PROBS. 109 (2009); Cass R. Sunstein, *Why Does the American Constitution Lack Social and Economic Guarantees?*, 56 SYRACUSE L. REV. 1 (2005); Frank I. Michelman, *Forward: On Protecting the Poor Through the Fourteenth Amendment*, 83 HARV. L. REV. 7 (1969). For a thoughtful discussion of the possibility of protection for socioeconomic status under discrimination laws, see Danieli Evans Peterman, *Socioeconomic Status Discrimination*, 104 VA. L. REV. 1283 (2018).

60. Bankruptcy Abuse Prevention and Consumer Protection Act of 2005, Pub. L. No. 109–8, 119 Stat. 23.

61. *See* 11 U.S.C. § 1930(f).

62. *Bankruptcy Case Policies*, U.S. COURTS.GOV, https://www.uscourts.gov/rules-policies/judiciary-policies/bankruptcy-case-policies (last visited Jul. 29, 2021).

63. 28 U.S.C. § 1930(a); FED. R. BANKR. P. 1006(b).

64. *See, e.g.,* Pamela Foohey, Robert M. Lawless, et al., *"No Money Down" Bankruptcy*, 90 SO. CAL. L. REV. 1055 (2017); Paul Kiel, *How the Bankruptcy System is Failing Black Americans*, PROPUBLICA (September 27, 2017), https://features.propublica.org/bankruptcy-inequality/bankruptcy-failing-black-americans-debt-chapter-13/; Jean Braucher, Dov Cohen, et al., *Race, Attorney Influence, and Bankruptcy Chapter Choice*, J. EMPIRICAL LEGAL STUD. 393 (2012); A. Mechele Dickerson, *Racial Steering in Bankruptcy*, 20 AM. BANKR. L. INST. L. REV. 623 (2012). Chapter 7, or "straight bankruptcy," results in discharge within a few months of filing while Chapter 13 involves a repayment plan of up to five years and delays discharge until all payments are complete.

65. Pineda-Moreno, 617 F.3d 1120 (9th Cir. 2010) (Kozinski, C.J., dissenting).

66. *Id.* at 1121.

67. *Id.* at 1123.

68. Pineda-Moreno v. United States, 565 U.S. 1189 (2012).

69. United States v. Jones, 565 U.S. 400 (2012).

70. United States v. Pineda-Moreno, 688 F.3d 1987 (9th Cir 2012).

71. The process of building a diverse bench begins in law school. For a couple of articles that discuss socioeconomic stratification in law schools see Michael J. Higdon, *A Place in the Academy: Law Faculty Hiring and Socioeconomic Bias*, 87 ST. JOHN'S L. REV. 171 (2013); Lucille A. Jewell, *Bordieu and American Legal Education: How Law Schools Reproduce Stratification and Class Hierarchy*, 56 BUFF. L. REV. 1155 (2008).

72. America Counts Staff: *About 13.1 Percent Have Master's, Professional Degree or Doctorate*, U.S. CENSUS.GOV (February 21, 2019), https://www.census.gov/library/stories/2019/02/number-of-people-with-masters-and-phd-degrees-double-since-2000.html#:~:text=About%2013.1%20Percent%20Have%20a%20Master's%2C%20Professional%20Degree%20or%20Doctorate&text=The%20educational%20level%20of%20American,master's%2C%20professional%20and%20doctoral%20degrees.

73. Tom W. Smith & Jaesok Son, *Measuring Occupational Prestige on the 2012 General Social Survey*, GSS METHODOLOGICAL REP. 122 (October 2014), available at https://gss.norc.org/Documents/reports/methodological-reports/MR122 Occupational Prestige.pdf.

74. 40 U. BALT. L. F. 1 (2009).

75. Davis, 40 U. Balt. L. F. at 17 (citations omitted).

76. *See* Kate Berry, *Building a Diverse Bench: Selecting Magistrate and Bankruptcy Judges,* BRENNAN CTR FOR JUSTICE (2017), https://www.brennancenter.org/our-work/policy-solutions/building-diverse-bench-selecting-federal-magistrate-and-bankruptcy-judges.

TWENTY-FIVE

Sexual Orientation and Gender Identity (SOGI)

Meghan DuPuis Maurus

A Note from the Editors: This was a topic we very much wanted to include in the second book, and we are grateful to Attorney Maurus for their work on bringing these insights to us; we also thank our colleague Elizabeth Kelley for introducing us to Meghan. For this a Chapter where we had a lot to learn, and we did, and we recognize we have further to go. We urge everyone to take time to understand the terminology and significance of intersectionality, as well as the legal context for SOGI issues. And the strategy list here is excellent. That said, we note that much of what is here is similar to what you would expect to learn in well-constructed implicit bias training—e.g., the idea of focusing and focusing longer, the importance of getting a person's name and pronouns right, the concept of critical mass. We look forward to continuing to listen and to work and learn with Attorney Maurus.

CHAPTER HIGHLIGHTS

- LGBTQI+ (lesbian, gay, bisexual, transgender, queer, intersex, plus) communities have been disproportionately impacted by the legal system in ways that often are negative. This is the case in family law, criminal law, employment law, interactions with law enforcement officers, and beyond.

- Biases and the overall criminalization of LGBTQI+ persons' bodies and identities are extremely harmful. Homophobia, transphobia, or lack of knowledge about the lived experiences of LGBTQI+ all create incredibly negative experiences and outcomes for LGBTQI+ persons.

- Understanding relevant terminology is crucial, as is recognizing how the legal system often negatively affects LGBTQI+ communities.
- Ways in which legal professionals can mitigate negative effects are described so as to offer a fair and enhanced rule of law within the legal practice.

CHAPTER CONTENTS

1. It's critical to learn the terminology.
    A. Gender Identity
    B. Sexual Orientation
    C. A Note on the Use of Pronouns
2. Even where laws protect LGBTQI+ persons, society has not always caught up.
3. Legal systems can fail to protect LGBTQI+ persons or disproportionately impact them.
    A. Employment
    B. Criminal Law and Prisons
    C. Identification Laws
4. There are best practices when working with LGBTQI+ Individuals.
    A. Eight General Strategies
    B. Best Practices Specific to the Legal Profession

Conclusion

Appendix A: Terminology Continued

1. It's critical to learn the terminology.

This Chapter will refer to LGBTQI+ communities, as well as LGBTQI+ people. Over the next few pages, the very basics of terminology will be outlined to guide our conversation, and a more in-depth discussion of terms that are vital to working with LGBTQI+ individuals is offered in the Appendix.

Injustice and implicit bias do not land on each individual person within LGBTQI+ communities in the same ways. LGBTQI+ individuals are not one homogenous group or identity. The acronym LGBTQI+ encompasses a broad spectrum of gender expressions, identities, and sexual orientations (that which is *not heterosexual*). In fact, it is vital to always approach working with LGBTQI+ persons from an intersectional lens. Another acronym that is increasingly used is sexual orientation and gender identity (SOGI). SOGI encompasses the idea that we all have a sexual orientation and gender identity. It is a term that applies to everyone.

The language we use to address individuals is hugely important, and this is no less true for LGBTQI+ individuals. It is true for all of us that being treated respectfully and addressed correctly makes us feel more at ease. Imagine in a coffee shop someone calling out your order with a nickname you hate, then commenting that you left your phone at the counter saying *that man* when you identify as a woman. Whether the person intended it or not, most of us would be uncomfortable to some degree. Gender and sexual identities are some of the most fundamental aspects of our sense of self. This manifests in our names, pronouns, mannerisms. Putting someone at ease by taking care and intention to address them correctly, whether it is name pronunciation, gender pronoun, or lived name, establishes they are in a safe space. Unfortunately for many LGBTQI+ persons, governmental and legal appointments and interactions are sites where those fundamental identities are often ignored.

In conversation with law students or groups of attorneys, I always begin my presentations by establishing a common ground via a shared terminology. Terminology surrounding LGBTQI+ persons is growing and expanding at the rate of our understanding and freedom to define our own identities. Therefore, it is perfectly understandable if you don't know every term, but it is our shared responsibility to have a base to begin each interaction with respect. (I discuss how to work with LGBTQI+ persons, as well as some ideas on how to discuss terminology with them later in the Chapter.)

As mentioned above, LGBTQI+ communities are not a single fixed identity or orientation. Rather, they are a grouping of identities that are not heterosexual and cisgender that are, and were, othered and singled out for oppression and distain. The *Gender Unicorn*, an illustration created by the TransStudent Educational Resources (TSER), is a vehicle for understanding the concepts of gender identity, expression, and sexual orientation, which is how we'll use it here.

Image 1: The Gender Unicorn Graphic by TSER*

The first distinction to make is that sexual orientation and gender identity are not synonymous.

A. Gender Identity

The rainbow in the Unicorn signifies its gender identity. **Gender identity** is a characteristic that everyone possesses, informed by the internal and self-identified understanding of gender. Do you feel like a man, a woman, something else? This often corresponds, but does not need to conform, to your gender expression.

---

* Readers please note that we were not able to produce this graphic in color and thus lose the rainbow aspects of the illustration. You can see the original at TSER's trans-related infographic series, https://transstudent.org/graphics/. The creators "encourage you to share and print these graphics! (You are welcome to use these graphics in any manner (even commercially) as long as they include credit and are not altered. You do not need to contact us to request permission.)" There are other helpful graphics at the site including several on visibility and legal rights as well as a pronoun poster.

Gender expression is how people outwardly express gender identity. Examples include word choices, names, clothes, hairstyles, mannerisms, and other physical manifestations. Gender identity can be male, female, genderqueer, transgender, etc. Gender expression, on the other hand, can be masculine, feminine, androgynous, etc.

The Unicorn above (along with every human on this planet) has a gender identity, their innate sense of gender, and a gender expression, how they choose to express gender identity. Perhaps the most basic distinction is between an individual who is cisgendered and one who is not. A cisgendered person is a person whose sense of gender identity corresponds with that gender and/or sex that was assigned medically at the moment of birth, or by society. On the other hand, a non-cisgendered person is a person whose gender identity does not correspond to the gender and/or sex medically-assigned at birth or that with which they were socialized as a child. {For those readers who are new or unfamiliar to many of these terms, a skim of Appendix A before moving on with the Chapter may be beneficial.}

In TSER's Gender Unicorn, "sex assigned at birth" is defined as the medical designation of an individual's sex based on personal genitalia and gendered stereotypes regarding "sex." For example, when most of us are born, a doctor or nurse will almost automatically assert, *It's a boy/girl*! That sex marker, based on personal genitalia detected by medical professionals, is placed on the newborn's birth certificate. That is how a person's sex is assigned at birth. Many people go through life with their sex assigned at birth, their gender identity, and their gender expression all matching up to a dichotomous male or female, that is, a cisgendered person. For some, however, sex, gender identity and gender expression are beyond the binaries that were often presented as the only, or only correct, manifestations of sex and gender.

B. Sexual Orientation

As we move down TSER's Gender Unicorn, we leave gender expression and identity and move into one's sexual orientation. What is the difference? Well, everyone has both a **gender identity** and a **sexual orientation**. Important to understanding these concepts is understanding that they are related but different. **Gender identity** is one's internal sense of gender. **Sexual orientation** is who someone is attracted to. As you look back up to the Unicorn, you'll see two hearts over the Unicorn's heart to illustrate who they are physically and emotionally attracted to. {Again, for a more comprehensive discussion of terms and identities that define or explain sexual orientation, please see Appendix A.}

It is important to understand that none of these categories are rigid or unchanging. Many people may evolve or change their sexual or gender identity over time. Moreover, they are not the same. A transgender person may identify as heterosexual, lesbian, gay, bisexual or questioning. This is just a brief and non-comprehensive overview of terminology and important key concepts, which serves as a basic foundation as we discuss how to support and advocate for LGBTQI+ persons in courts.

C. A Note on Pronouns

The concept of **pronouns preferred** or **pronouns** is an example of how to ensure people feel comfortable in a particular setting. The practice consists of individuals in a social setting introducing themselves by giving their name and the pronoun they use. An example would be, *My name is Alex, and my pronoun is they/them*. Identifying pronouns this way is becoming the norm in many meeting spaces, offices, and courtrooms in the United States. Over time, many people have begun to say *pronouns* as opposed to *preferred pronouns*. The rationale is that it is not really the pronouns you prefer but rather those pronouns that best illustrate your gender identity. If a person in a meeting said preferred pronouns, would it be wrong? No. But when someone outlines for you why saying pronouns may be better, it's a moment for growth, and no one should feel shame in the learning moment. You'll notice even our Gender Unicorn has a space at the top for preferred name and pronoun. This goes to show the growth of vocabulary and concepts in just a few short years. One last point to note on pronouns is the growing use of *they* as a pronoun. There are many terms one can use to describe a gender. If you are unsure, one tactic is to simply ask, what are your pronouns? Another would be to use *they* as a gender neutral alternative until you know for certain.

In order to facilitate a good provider-client relationship, it is important not to make assumptions about the identity, beliefs, concerns, or sexual orientation of transgender and gender nonconforming individuals. If you are unsure what a person's gender identity or expression is, ask them (privately, if possible) what name and pronouns they would like you to use, and how they would like to be addressed. For instance, you can ask, *How would you like to be addressed?*; *What name would you like to be called?*; and *Which pronouns do you use?* If you are in a larger setting, you can fold the question into introductions. *Let's go around the room quickly and just say our names and pronouns. I'll start.*

Asking someone their pronouns or gender identity may take a few tries before it feels like a practice; but it is not something that should be passed over because of discomfort, as it is incredibly uncomfortable and triggering to be a person being misgendered throughout a social interaction. One way to incorporate this into your life is to ask everyone; not just when *you* think you need to do so. One other important note on this topic, which is addressed further below: As important as it is to ensure you ask appropriate questions to properly address someone, you must also ask yourself if you need to know the thing you are asking. In representing someone, it is important to ask pronouns, but do you need to know if they identify as gay? Maybe, maybe not.

2. Even where laws protect LGBTQI+ persons, society has not always caught up.

This Chapter will not cover in depth the many advances in law that LGBTQI+ persons have attained, and it is undisputed that there have been great strides for LGBTQI+ persons in the United States. In one generation, same sex marriage is legal, LGBTQI+ persons can serve in the military, and there are slowly increasing numbers of federal protections, to name a few. However, in many other categories, LGBTQI+ individuals' lived experiences fall way behind heterosexual and cis individuals, and LGBTQI+ individuals continue to suffer from misunderstanding and prejudice in society and in the law. Moreover, there are many gains still to be made for LGBTQI+ individuals in the legal arena. Legal structures and systems still fail LGBTQI+ individuals. Legal protections do not always move at the speed of societal views. And societal views do not always move at the speed of LGBTQI+ individual lives.

Data indicates that LGBTQI+ folks, particularly transgender people, still suffer disproportionately from bias violence, bullying, unemployment, poverty, and discrimination, irrespective of legal protections.[1] For example, transgender people live at elevated rates of poverty compared to society in general, and for transgender people of color, these rates are even higher. More specifically, 21–29% of trans adults live in poverty.[2] That rate increases when broken down by racial group: around 39% of Black transgender adults; 48% of Latina/o/x transgender adults; and 35% of Alaska Native, Asian, Native Americans, and Native Hawaiian or Pacific Islander trans adults.[3] The 21–29% rate is compared to 15.7% of straight cisgender people who live in poverty.[4] Similarly, according to one study, transgender people were 11% less likely to be working compared to non-transgender, or cisgender, people.[5]

While society is shifting positively, it is moving in fits and starts for many LGBTQI+ persons. Polling data suggests that as few as ten years ago only 25% of people supported trans rights. By 2019, that number had increased to 62%.[6] But even people who wish to be supportive often feel overwhelmed at how to "accommodate" LGBTQI+ persons, or they feel as though they *don't know how to act.*

Conversations around inclusion and genuine acceptance of all LGBTQI+ people are still far on the horizon for many. Left out of nearly all of these surveys are intersex individuals for example. So too, while more and more people know one or several members of LGBTQI+ communities, that does not always correspond with understanding lived experiences. There is still very much a place where LGBTQI+ persons are striving for tolerance and basic rights and equality. It is recent lived history (and in some cases not history) where LGBTQI+ individuals were considered mentally ill, socially deviant, and sexual predators. Lawmakers still propose laws that try to outlaw transgender lives. Young people continue to lose friends and blood relatives when they disclose their identities. Bullying and violence are still common.

Violence against LGBTQI+, particularly trans people of color, is an all-too-common occurrence, and, in fact, it is increasing in frequency over the past few years. According to research conducted by the Transgender Law Center, there have been 139 reported anti-trans murders in the U.S. since 2017. By November 2020, 350 transgender people had been killed in the United States.[7] Today, the U.S. ranks third in the world for trans homicides, after Brazil and Mexico.[8] In addition, over 54% of transgender people have experienced intimate partner violence in their lifetime, and 47% have been sexually assaulted.[9] Beyond the violence that disproportionately affects transgender people, stigma impedes their ability to access necessary services. Despite protections built into shelters funded through the Violence Against Women Act (VAWA), only 30% of women's shelters are willing to house *trans*women.[10] Every year, there are between 1,500 and 2,000 reported incidences of hate crimes based on sexual orientation as well.[11] To summarize, while U.S. and state laws continue to improve, and society continues to become more comfortable with LGBTQI+ people, violence, stigma, and barriers entrenched in normative systems of power create a society where LGBTQI+ individuals still disproportionately fall behind simply because of their identities.

3. Legal systems can fail to protect (or disproportionately impact) LGBTQI+ persons.

LGBTQI+ persons encounter a legal system that is still debating whether they are, or are not, entitled to equality and self-determination in the United States, and if so, what that looks like in practice. This is the case in many areas of society including education,[12] public accommodation, health care,[13] employment, and criminal law and prisons. An overview of the last two subject areas is provided in this Chapter together with a discussion of laws and policies regarding identification, which topic runs throughout.

A. Employment

The unemployment and poverty rates of the LGBTQI+ communities are disproportionately high. A 2017 survey conducted by CivicScience reported that 13% of LGBTQ people were unemployed compared to 9% of the general population.[14] The unemployment rate among transgender and non-binary workers was even higher, at 16%. A National Center for Transgender Equality survey reports that 30% of transgender people lost their jobs, were denied promotion, or were otherwise mistreated at work "due to bias" based on their gender identity or expression.[15] In addition, 77% of survey responders reported that over "three-quarters (77%) of respondents who had a job in the past year took steps to avoid mistreatment in the workplace, such as hiding or delaying their gender transition or quitting their job."[16]

In its decision in *Bostock v. Clayton County*, the U.S. Supreme Court addressed the protections to be afforded to such individuals under the Civil Rights Act of 1964.[17] In this case, Gerald Bostock had been fired by Clayton County for "conduct 'unbecoming' a county employee" after joining a gay recreational softball team; Aimee Stephens had been fired from G. & G. R. Harris Funeral Homes after she told her employer that she planned to "live and work full-time as a woman" even though she had presented as a male when she was hired;[18] and Donald Zarda was fired from his position as skydiving instructor after he told a customer he was gay and was found to have failed to provide "an enjoyable experience" for the customers.[19] Each employee sued because of their gender transition. The Court held that the Title VII prohibition against employment discrimination based on sex includes protection against discrimination based on a person's being homosexual or transgender: "The statute's message for our cases is equally simple and momentous: An individual's homosexuality or transgender status is not relevant to employment decisions. That's because it is impossible to discriminate against a person for being homosexual or transgender without discriminating against that individual based on sex."[20] As important as this opinion is, it does not extend to providing federal statutory protection against discrimination on the basis of gender identity or expression (and does not yet necessarily extend beyond the employment arena).[21] Employment issues are also exacerbated by the underlying issue of inadequate access to identity documents that match gender expression, as discussed further below.

B. Criminal Law and Prisons

LGBTQI+ are disproportionately present in and disproportionately harmed by the criminal justice system.[22] Many criminal laws are still applied in such a way as to disproportionately affect transgender people. One example is "walking while trans" laws wherein transgender women experience high rates of profiling for "being sex workers." Prisons are still one of the most gendered spaces in our contemporary society. Violence against trans persons, where they are housed, fighting to be named, and the struggle to receive gender-affirming care are never ending.

A report jointly authored by the Movement Advancement Project and the Center for American Progress documents that "pervasive stigma and discrimination, discriminatory enforcement of laws, and discriminatory policing strategies mean that LGBT people are disproportionately likely to interact with law enforcement and enter the criminal justice system."[23] For example, they face discrimination in legal proceedings. In one study, 44% of LGBTQI+ reported their negative experience in court including being treated unfairly by prosecutors and defense attorneys, being addressed by incorrect pronouns, hearing "negative comments about their gender identity or sexual orientation," receiving inadequate counsel, and facing discrimination from juries.[24] Not surprisingly, LGBTQI+ people are disproportionately overrepresented in juvenile justice, detention, and prison facilities.[25] There they are subject to "[u]nfair and inhumane treatment" in jails, prisons, and other confinement facilities," including extraordinarily high rates of victimization by prison staff and other prisoners.[26] LGBTQI+ people are more likely to be on probation and parole, particularly LGBTQI+ women,[27] and they continue to face unique and considerable challenges in the struggle to rebuild their lives after experiences with law enforcement—particularly after time spent in a correctional facility.[28]

C. Identification Laws

Another example of barriers that prevent full access to society arises in the area of identity documentation. Many people have birth certificates, state identification, social security cards, etc. that do not match their gender identity or expression. Without identification one cannot travel, register for school, access essential services, or feel comfortable in uncomfortable places such as jails, doctors' offices, or government buildings. People sometimes have so much anxiety or trauma around this issue that they will avoid accessing benefits they are entitled to because they fear prejudice at a state office where they will present as female but have an identification with a male name and gender marker. Many states do not allow trans people to update their identification documents to match their gender identity. Some allow for changing of gender markers on identifications, but only with proof of medical procedures that are not accessible to everyone. And, as always, large fees and a lot of time are required. According to a survey by the National Transgender Discrimination Survey only one-fifth (21%) of transgender people have been able to update all of their identity documents and records with their new gender, and one-third (33%) had not updated any of their IDs or records.[29]

How will proposed voter laws affect individuals with legal names that do not match a bill in a lived name? Too often, harassment has led trans people to avoid exercising their most basic rights to vote. Human Rights Campaign Foundation research shows that 49% of trans adults, and 55% of trans adults of color, said they were unable to vote in at least one election in their life because of feared or experienced discrimination at the polls.

The above examples are a brief overview of some of the ways in which LGBTQI+ persons suffer from prejudice in society and in our legal systems. It is nowhere near comprehensive. However, it serves to illustrate some of the life experiences with which LGBTQI+ persons will come into our courtrooms or law offices laden with the trauma of knowing they simply do not fit societies' categorizations.

4. There are best practices when working with LGBTQI+ individuals.

I offer here a non-exhaustive list of concepts and best practices for limiting the amount of trauma an LGBTQI+ person feels in legal and other settings and for creating a truly inclusive space for all people around gender and sexual identities.

A. Eight General Strategies

- **ONE, keep learning.** Approach the topic of other people's identities with humility and with the understanding that everyone is their own unique person. Conversations around gender and sexuality are in a few ways constant, but in many others ever-changing and evolving in often beautiful ways. If you make a mistake, genuinely apologize and learn.
- **TWO, be respectful.** Always be respectful of what you hear from your client, co-worker, or person in front of you if you are on the bench. You may not understand someone's identity, but you must respect it. Listen, be respectful, and you will go far.
- **THREE, don't assume someone's gender or sexuality.** Some people "don't appear visibly trans" or "pass." Some people seem "straight" or "gay," but looks can be deceiving. This is why it is so important to not assume. Along these lines, avoid perpetuating gender stereotypes. Many, if not most of us, perpetuate gender norms often without being aware of it. Don't assume one's gender or sexuality based on sex stereotypes.
- **FOUR, recognize that there is no "right way" to be LGBTQI+.** There is a plethora of ways in which one transitions or expresses their gender identity, whether by choice or circumstance. Again, don't assume, and unless you have some form of approval, don't compare one person's identity with another person you know.

    There is no one way to transition or express being transgender. There is no one coming out of the process. If you know one person who has a transgender identity, don't assume that's how everyone is. Listen, listen, listen. Watch for your implicit bias and your micromessaging. One particularly important set of examples here includes backhanded compliments or tips, such as:

    ○ I would never have known you were transgender;
    ○ You look so pretty; you look just like a real man/woman;
    ○ She's so gorgeous, I would have never guessed she was transgender;

- He's so hot. I'd date him even though he's transgender;
- You're so brave;
- You'd pass so much better if you wore less/more makeup, had a better wig;
- Have you considered a voice coach?
- You are such a guy's guy. I'd never imagine you were gay,
- Since you are so masculine, does that mean you are the 'man' in the relationship?

You should never say these types of things. It is offensive and transphobic, and non-LGBTQI+ people can be allies here and interrupt this kind of messaging.

- **FIVE, don't assume someone wants to talk, but don't assume they don't.** Almost every LGBTQI+ person has a story about being in public and having someone ask them incredibly personal questions about their gender or sexuality, their partners, their sex life, their coming out story, etc. Put yourself in their shoes and consider whether you are pushing for juicy details or listening to the experiences they are sharing with you. The key here is listening to what they are sharing, not what you want to know.

  Expose yourself to art, stories, friends, and just listen and learn. Talk to trans/GNC people to learn more about who they are, but don't assume that everyone wants to share their story or speak for their group. Remember, you are not entitled to information because you are curious! Don't ask people what their real name is. Don't ask people how long they've been transgender, or how they first knew. Don't ask people what type of medical procedures they have had. One exercise is to pause and ask yourself, *does it matter what their gender or sexual orientation is at this moment?*

- **SIX, listen to feedback from LGBTQI+ people.** Feedback is important to all of our growth. Genuinely listen and avoid becoming defensive just because you feel ashamed or uncomfortable. Appreciate that someone wants to help you become a better ally. Along those lines, when you see a non-cis person making a mistake take the opportunity to be an ally and help out.

- **SEVEN, intervene and take action when you hear terminology,** especially particularly harmful terminology being used against LGBTQI+ persons.

- **EIGHT, don't assume everyone is out!**

B. Best Practices Specific to the Legal Profession

i. In Your Workplace, with Your Coworkers

For LGBTQI+ persons in your workplace, either as coworkers, staff, or clients, a few simple changes go a long way to signal you are a safe space that cares about LGBTQI+ people.

- Advocate for and have a meaningful and enforceable nondiscrimination policy, which includes gender identity, gender expression, and sexual orientation. Have policies in place to ensure accountability.
- Have policies that allow for gender-affirming dress codes, names, and pronouns.
- Have trainings in your workplace.
- Display LGBTQI+ positive cues. For example, LGBTQI+ community center fliers, safe space stickers, a magazine or poster, name tags to write name and pronoun upon entering the space, gender neutral bathrooms, to name just a few.

ii. With Clients

All people have the same need for respect, effective representation, promptly returned phone calls, and understanding of what is happening to them. At the same time, it is undeniable that previous traumas or subtle but telling misunderstanding of LGBTQI+ persons identities can disproportionately affect the relationship. The following are strategies that can make these relationships and interactions more productive:

- **Being heard.** Much of this Chapter has been an information guide to understanding the concepts LGBTQI+ people must navigate in a world that doesn't always make space and actively discriminates against them. LGBTQI+ clients are clients who are engaging with you because they are having some legal issue. However, as illustrated above, they may be carrying with them years of discrimination, abuse from the legal system, and mistrust due to poor treatment. It is important to create spaces for us to feel safe and heard, as well as to create and implement laws in such a way as to avoid disproportionately harming LGBTQI+ people.
- **Being really heard.** As much as it is vital to make space for and understand LGBTQI+ persons, it is also just as important to not assume every problem is about their LGBTQI+ identities or to assume that the legal challenge facing a client is about gender or sexual identity. Don't get narrow vision. Every one of us, including LGBTQI+ people, has racial, class,

educational, religious, etc. identities that are all intersecting to create our lived reality.

- **Ask only what you need to know only when there is a real need.** When you do need to discuss a person's sexual or gender identity, preview why you need the information. There is a very lived reality of people asking inappropriate and irrelevant questions about a client's medical transition. If you need to ask, explain why; give people the ability to understand and share what is pertinent or relevant.

- **Discuss privacy policies and confidentiality.** Differentiate to whom you will disclose information about their gender and sexual identity, and who will not know.

- **Know that names are critical.** Use the client's lived name and pronoun in all correspondence, court papers, and settlement agreements. If there are legal reasons you are unable to do this, explain why and accommodate. Discuss a court strategy ahead of time with your client, hear and follow their wishes, and fight for them.

- **Know why names are critical.** In most circumstances, if you are an individual's lawyer, you are one of the only, if not the only, person who is trying to advocate and protect them from whatever ill effects they are facing in a court procedure. If you do not stand up for them, who will? Moreover, by using their name and pronoun, you are building the vital trust you need. If you are the judge, you are illustrating that the person can expect respect and fairness in front of you.

- **How to get it right.** You must ensure the name you are using is what your client wants. Sometimes a client may not know using their name is an option. For any number of reasons (they are scared to upset the judge, their family will be in court, etc.), your client may prefer to use a name and pronoun that is associated with the gender that is different from what they feel or prefer. That is ok! This is not for you to determine. It is for them. Let them know that they can always change their mind and that you can and will advocate for them. You can use the legal name in a caption or once in a document then drop a footnote indicating that you will be using gender-affirming pronouns and/or name for the reminder. Another option is to use the last name and a salutation. You can write an initial letter to let all parties know of your client's name and pronoun at the outset. I have usually found a way to use a client's name and make accommodations in legal documents. However, much of this is dependent on jurisdiction and ultimately you and your client must decide best course of action

- **Urge the others involved with your client to get it right.** It is vital you at least try to respectfully urge opposing counsel, court staff, and judicial officers to also get names and pronouns right. Your efforts may not work, but your client will know you tried. I've heard colleagues say that they don't want to advocate for names and pronouns because they don't want to upset the judges or prosecutors in a case. In this writer's experience, I've never seen it held against a client.

- **An example—names in court**. One example was a criminal case in which I represented one of two co-defendants who were both transgender women. I simply asked my client what their name was, and she responded my legal name or real name? I said both. She answered, and we were off. The other lawyer would walk into the back pens, and in a very friendly way, call out their client's legal name. Every time it just changed the energy in the room. The client knew they had a good lawyer, but using just a legal name created a distance you don't want to have with a client. In court, I entered my appearance and informed the judge that my client was transgender, they used a different first name, and I'd simply say Ms. X. The judge had absolutely no clue what I was talking about, but also just shrugged their shoulders and moved on to the next topic. Both clients got successful outcomes in that case, but the difference was palpable in client trust and quickness of resolution.

When in doubt, ask questions. Because there are so many unique legal issues concerning LGBTQI+ people, and many are still of first impression or being developed, it is always a good idea to reach out to knowledgeable people in working with these communities. If you think there is a relevant personal/private question you need to ask your client about their sexual orientation or gender identity, explain to them why the question is important prior to asking the question.

Conclusion

This Chapter outlined a basic framework on how to understand LGBTQI+ communities, and, in a non-comprehensive manner, some of the ways in which one's gender expression and/or sexual orientation can subject someone to bias of law enforcement and courts. The Chapter provides basics and ideas of simple steps that professionals at all levels can take to lessen traumatic and negative experiences and outcomes for LGBTQI+ communities.

So, You'd Like to Know More

- Walking in Two Worlds: Understanding the Two-Spirit & LGBT Community, Tribal Court Clearinghouse (2014), http://www.tribal-institute.org/2014/INCTwo-SpiritBooklet.pdf.

- Movement Advancement Project & Center for American Progress, How the Broken Criminal Justice System Fails LGBT People (2016).
- Transgender Law Center, Tips for Lawyers Working with Transgender Clients, available at https://tlcenter.app.box.com/s/ynlx2f50vl3q5d6fzu6qo9erbv79v0gc.pdf.

About the Author

Meghan DuPuis Maurus is an attorney licensed to practice in New Jersey and New York. They currently work with a bi-national project that accompanies LGBTQI+ asylum seekers in Mexico and the United States. Prior to moving to Mexico, Meghan was a public defender at the Office of the Public Defenders of Essex County and Neighborhood Defender Service of Harlem. Meghan also worked for the National Lawyers Guild, providing legal representation to people arrested as part of Occupy Wall Street and coordinating the legal support to the movement. They continued on as part of the Mass Defense Committee and have assisted with mass defense response in various locations.

Appendix: Terminology Continued—Terms that Can Express Gender Identity

Terms that express gender identity include, but are not limited to the following:

- **Transgender/Trans** describes the gender identity of people whose medically-assigned sex at birth does not correspond to personal lived experiences and self-identification. A transgender person may adopt, and might prefer to reclaim, a gender expression consistent with their gender identity but may or may not desire to permanently alter their physical characteristics to conform to their gender identity. "Transgender" is an umbrella term used to describe people whose gender identity does not correspond to the medically-assigned sex at the moment of birth and/or the stereotypes associated with that sex.

- **Transgender Men** describes persons medically designated female at birth but who identify and may or may not present themselves as male. Transgender men are usually referred to with male pronouns, such as he, him, and his.

- **Transgender Women** describes persons medically designated as male at birth but who identify as female. They may or may not present themselves feminine or femme. Transgender women utilize female pronouns, such as she, her, and hers.

- **Gender Nonconforming** describes people whose gender expression, the outward communication of gender through behavior or appearance, differs from expectations associated with the medically-assigned sex at birth.

- **Non-Binary:** Most people—including transgender people—are either male or female. But some individual's identities go beyond a gender binary and are more fitting within a spectrum beyond the categories of "man" or "woman," "male" or "female." For example, some people have a gender that blends elements of being a man and a woman, or a gender that is different from either male or female. Some people do not identify with any gender at all. Some people's gender changes over time. People whose gender is not male or female will use terms such as **non-binary** (being one of the most common) to describe themselves. Similar terms may also include **genderqueer**, **agender**, **bigender**, and more. None of these terms mean exactly the same thing—but all speak to an experience of gender that is not simply male or female and is more fitting within a spectrum.[30]

- **Androgynous** is a less frequently used term, but used to denote those who have both male and female qualities.

- **Two-Spirit** is a modern pan-Indigenous umbrella term used by some Indigenous Native North Americans to describe Native people in their communities who fulfill a traditional third gender ceremonial and social role in the community. The term two-spirit is attributed to Elder Myra Laramee, who proposed its use during the Third Annual Inter Tribal Native America, First Nations, Gay and Lesbian American Conference in 1990. The term is a translation of the Anishinaabemowin term *niizh manidoowag*, two spirits,[31] and refers to a person who identifies as having both a masculine and feminine spirit. The term is also used by some Indigenous people to describe their sexual, gender, and/or spiritual identity. Research shows that more than 150 different pre-Columbian Native American tribes acknowledged third genders in their communities and that may have been a unifying feature of various pre-colonial cultures. Historians have also documented the highly regarded role of spiritual leaders in pre-colonial West Africa, who were assigned male at birth but presented in a feminine manner; the existence of *Muxes* in Zapotec culture, in what is now South-eastern Mexico; *Bakla* in pre-colonial Philippines and *Hijra* in South Asia are similar.

- **Gender Questioning** describes persons who are questioning their gender identity and/or might be wondering whether they identify as a boy, girl, man, woman, or another gender. Gender questioning individuals might also be experimenting with different genders.

- **Cisgender** denotes or relates to a person whose sense of personal identity and gender corresponds with that assigned medically at the moment of birth as "sex."

- **Sex Assigned at Birth** is the medical designation of an individual gender identity based on personal genitalia and gendered stereotypes regarding "sex." For example, when most of us are born a doctor or nurse will almost automatically assert, *It's a boy/girl!* That sex marker, based on personal genitalia detected by medical professionals is placed on the newborns' birth certificate. That is how a person's sex is assigned at birth.

Intersex Identities

An important identity that will not get the time it deserves in this Chapter are people who are intersex. **Intersex**[32] isn't a discrete or natural category. Intersex is a socially constructed category that reflects real biological variation. Intersex is a general term used for a variety of conditions in which a person is born with a reproductive or sexual anatomy that doesn't seem to fit the typical definitions of female or male. For example, a person might be born appearing to be female on the outside but having mostly male-typical anatomy on the inside. Or a person may be born with genitals that seem to be in-between the usual male and female types—for example, a girl may be born with a noticeably large clitoris or lacking a vaginal opening, or a boy may be born with a notably small penis or with a scrotum that is divided so that it has formed more like labia. Or a person may be born with mosaic genetics, so that some of her cells have XX chromosomes and some of them have XY. Though we speak of intersex as an inborn condition, intersex anatomy doesn't always show up at birth. Sometimes a person isn't found to have intersex anatomy until she or he reaches the age of puberty, or finds himself an infertile adult, or dies of old age and is autopsied. Some people live and die with intersex anatomy without anyone (including themselves) ever knowing.[33]

Terms that Can Express Gender Expression (but not limited to)

Gender expression is the way in which one expresses a gender on any given day. It consists of clothing, hair style, accessories, activities, mannerisms, word choice, and a multitude of other ways in which one expresses a gender. Terms that speak to gender expression included but are not limited to the following:

- **Gender nonconformists** are people whose behavior does not conform to traditional expectations based on their biological gender.
- **Gender neutral** denotes a word or expression that cannot be taken to refer to one gender only.
- **Cross-dressing** is the practice of wearing clothes made for the opposite sex.

Sexual Orientation

Sexual Orientation Gender Identity (SOGI) is an acronym which is quickly growing in popularity because it encompasses the idea that we all have a sexual orientation and gender identity. It is a term that applies to everyone.

Important to understanding these concepts is to understand that they are related but different. What is the difference? Well, everyone has both a **sexual identity** and a **gender identity**. Gender identity is one's internal sense of gender. Sexual orientation is who someone is attracted to. As you look back up to the Unicorn, you'll see two hearts over the Unicorn's heart that illustrates who they are physically and emotionally attracted to. Terms that express sexual orientation include but are not limited to the following:

- **Heterosexual**: someone who is attracted to the opposite sex.
- **Homosexual**: someone who is attracted to the same sex (Lesbian, gay).
- **Bisexual**: someone who is attracted to both men, women, and multiple genders.
- **Questioning**: someone who is still exploring who they are attracted to and cannot yet determine (or doesn't know) their sexual orientation.
- **Aro/aromantic**: As the names suggest, aromantic people don't experience romantic attraction.
- **Ace/asexual**: people who don't experience sexual attraction. (Some people identify as both aromantic and asexual.)

- **Pansexual**: sexual, romantic, or emotional attraction towards people regardless of their sex... strictly men or women, and pansexuality therefore rejects the gender binary; it is considered by some to be a more inclusive term than bisexual.

One Other Important Term

- **Queer**: a very big topic, but at its most basic is an umbrella term for sexual and gender minorities who are not heterosexual or are not cisgender. To many individuals it is also a political identity more than anything else. It can be used to denote both gender identity and sexual orientation.

Endnotes

1. *See, e.g.*, Christopher Carpenter, *Transgender Americans Are More Likely to Be Unemployed and Poor*, THE CONVERSATION, June 16, 2020, https://theconversation.com/transgender-americans-are-more-likely-to-be-unemployed-and-poor-127585.

2. *Understanding the Transgender Community*, HUMAN RIGHTS CAMPAIGN, available at https://www.hrc.org/resources/understanding-the-transgender-community (last accessed on June 20, 2021).

3. *Id.*

4. M.V. Lee Badgett, Soon Kyu Choi & Bianca D.M. Wilson, *LGBT Poverty in the United States: A Study of Differences Between Sexual Orientation and Gender Identity Groups*, UCLA School of Law: Williams Institute, Oct. 2019, https://williamsinstitute.law.ucla.edu/wp-content/uploads/National-LGBT-Poverty-Oct-2019.pdf.

5. Masterpiece Cakeshop, Ltd. v. Colo. Civil Rights Comm'n, 138 S. Ct. 1719 (2018).

6. *Understanding the Transgender Community*, HUMAN RIGHTS CAMPAIGN, https://www.hrc.org/resources/understanding-the-transgender-community.

7. Jamie Wareham, *Murdered, Suffocated and Burned Alive—350 Transgender People Killed In 2020*, FORBES MAGAZINE, Nov. 11, 2020, available at https://www.forbes.com/sites/jamiewareham/2020/11/11/350-transgender-people-have-been-murdered-in-2020-transgender-day-of-remembrance-list/?sh=3f56548a65a6.

8. *The Roots of Anti-Transgender Violence*, TRANSGENDER LAW CENTER, https://transgenderlawcenter.org/regional-reports.

9. *Understanding the Transgender Community*, HUMAN Rights Campaign, https://www.hrc.org/resources/understanding-the-transgender-community.

10. *Id.*

11. *See* FBI CRIME DATA EXPLORER, https://crime-data-explorer.fr.cloud.gov/pages/explorer/crime/hate-crime. The FBI site define "hate crime" as ate crime as "a crime motivated by bias against race, color, religion, national origin, sexual orientation, gender, gender identity, or disability." FBI, https://www.justice.gov/hatecrimes/learn-about-hate-crimes/chart.

12. While a discussion of education issues facing LGBTQI+ communities and individuals is beyond the scope of this Chapter, readers may want to consider the background provided by the 2019 GLSEN School Climate survey showing the high prevalence of negative school experiences for many LGBTQI+ students. *See generally* GLSEN, https://www.glsen.org/research/2019-national-school-climate-survey. It is also important to consider that for many young people who identify as LGBTQI+ it is a battle for them to simply be at school without policing one of the most fundamental pieces of their identities. Seventeen-year-olds are in court debating whether they can be prom king. Five-year-olds are the subject of cases about what clothes they can wear to school or what name they are called. Teenagers are in court over whether they can play sports in a gender-affirming uniform or how their scores are categorized because "they are neither boys nor girls" in the crude categories we have created. In places where laws do protect young people in schools, it falls on students and parents to fight for these protections. These are the children who fight in order to thrive. There are more who simply put their head down and try to survive.

13. While a discussion of health care issues facing LGBTQI+ communities and individuals is beyond the scope of this Chapter, readers should note that the issues are many, varied, and complex. *See, e.g.,* Alvin Powell, *The Problem with LGBTQ Health Care*, HARVARD GAZETTE (March 23, 2018), https://news.harvard.edu/gazette/story/2018/03/health-care-providers-need-better-understanding-of-lgbtq-patients-harvard-forum-says/; NATIONAL ALLIANCE ON MENTAL ILLNESS (NAMI), MENTAL HEALTH AND LGBTQI COMMUNITIES: CHALLENGES, RESOURCES, COMMUNITY VOICES, https://namica.org/lgbtqi/https://publichealth.tulane.edu/blog/advocating-for-lgbtq-health-access/; TULANE SCHOOL OF PUBLIC HEALTH AND TROPICAL MEDICINE, LGBTQ AND HEALTH CARE: ADVOCATING FOR HEALTH ACCESS FOR ALL, https://publichealth.tulane.edu/blog/advocating-for-lgbtq-health-access/.

14. Rich Bellis, *LGBTQ Workers Still Face Higher Unemployment Rates,* FASTCOMPANY, Nov. 08, 2017, https://www.fastcompany.com/40493319/lgbtq-workers-still-face-higher-unemployment-rates; *see also* Julie Moreau, *LGBTQ People Face Higher Unemployment Amid Coronavirus Pandemic, Survey Finds*, NBC NEWS, May 12, 2020, available at https://www.nbcnews.com/feature/nbc-out/lgbtq-people-face-higher-unemployment-amid-coronavirus-pandemic-survey-finds-n1205296.

15. NATIONAL CENTER FOR TRANSGENDER EQUALITY, THE REPORT OF THE 2015 U.S. TRANSGENDER SURVEY (2016). The 2020 survey has been delayed.

16. *Id.*

17. Bostock v. Clayton Cnty., 140 S. Ct. 1731 (2020); 42 U.S.C. § 2000e-2(a)(1).

18. *Bostock,* 140 S. Ct. at 1738.

19. *Id.;* Zarda v. Altitude Express, 855 F.3d 76, 80 (2d Cir. 2017).

20. *Bostock,* 140 S. Ct. at 1741.

21. *See* Nina Totenberg, *Supreme Court Delivers Major Victory to LGBTQ Employees,* NPR, June 15, 2020, available at https://www.npr.org/2020/06/15/863498848/supreme-court-delivers-major-victory-to-lgbtq-employees; *see generally*, Pamela S. Katz, *Now Something for the Glass*

Half-Empty Crowd: Bostock v. Clayton County, Georgia *Explained*, 30 TUL. J.L. & SEXUALITY 53 (2021).

22. *See generally* Alexi Jones, *Visualizing the Unequal Treatment of LGBTQ People in the Criminal Justice System*, Mar. 2, 2021, https://www.prisonpolicy.org, blog/2021/03/02/lgbtq/.

23. MOVEMENT ADVANCEMENT PROJECT & CENTER FOR AMERICAN PROGRESS, BROKEN CRIMINAL JUSTICE SYSTEM DISPROPORTIONATELY TARGETS AND HARMS LGBT PEOPLE iii (2016). For similar reports on LGBTQI+ youth, people of color, transgender persons, see https ://www.lgbtmap.org/lgbt-criminal-justice.

24. *Id.* at iv-v.

25. *Id.*

26. *Id.* at v.

27. Alexi Jones, https://www.prisonpolicy.org/blog/2021/03/02/lgbtq/.

28. *Id.*

29. *National Center for Transgender Equality*, available at https://transequality.org/issues/identity-documents-privacy.

30. *Understanding Non-Binary People: How to Be Respectful and Supportive*, NATIONAL CENTER FOR TRANSGENDER EQUALITY, Oct. 5, 2018, https://transequality.org/issues/resources/understanding-non-binary-people-how-to-be-respectful-and-supportive.

31. *Walking in Two Worlds: Understanding the Two-Spirit & LGBT Community*, TRIBAL COURT CLEARINGHOUSE (2014), http://www.tribal-institute.org/2014/INCTwo-SpiritBooklet.pdf.

32. The author has included intersex identities as part of the broad umbrella of non cisgender identities that are affected by the law. However, it is beyond the scope of this Chapter to fully address this group of individuals who face numerous obstacles that fall as distinct to these folks.

33. *What Is Intersex?*, INTERSEX SOCIETY OF NORTH AMERICA, https://isna.org/faq/what_is_intersex/ (last accessed on June 20, 2021).

TWENTY-SIX

Law Enforcement and Implicit Bias

Chief Anthony Holloway
Major Patrice Hubbard
Major Markus Hughes
Supervisor Jo-Anne Swensson
    City of St. Petersburg, Florida Police Department

A Note from the Editors: Chief Holloway is a colleague and friend whom we first met through our work together at the Criminal Justice Section of the ABA. Chief Holloway and his team offer an important and well-thought out perspective on understanding procedural justice and interrupting implicit bias in policing. If we had to choose an exemplar of someone who practices what he (and we) preach, it would be the St. Pete Police Department. This police force has concerned itself with cultural competence and interrupting bias for decades. One particularly noteworthy approach is their reaching out to community partners to offer training with particular expertise, for example, Law Enforcement Officer Training in Autism Spectrum Disorders; Law Enforcement and Society: Lessons from the Holocaust; and Transgender Awareness Training. Starting with a highlight that police offers are held to an especially higher standard as they deal in stressful and intense situations (where we know implicit biases and falling into stereotypes are more likely) and offering a road map for learning and training and practice, this Chapter shows an approach that can work for both internal decisions and community settings. We have this highest respect for this police department and trust our readers will benefit from their perspectives whether for police forces or for other institutions.

CHAPTER HIGHLIGHTS

- Generally, our biases are our own and are seldom called into question. Police officers are an exception. Police officers are held to a higher standard of behavior by the public because they deal with the public daily and often during stressful and intense situations.
- It is critical to our communities that police officers learn and understand the principles of procedural justice and the impact their implicit bias has on policing.
- Community partnerships are key to addressing implicit bias in hiring and in training.

CHAPTER CONTENTS

Introduction
1. Why Do We Train Biased-Based Policing?
   A. Procedural Justice
   B. Manifestation of Implicit Bias
2. Who Receives Biased-Based Policing Training?
3. Best Practices for Implementing Biased-Based Policing Training
   A. Training
   B. Park, Walk and Talk
   C. Community Partnerships
Conclusion

Introduction

I am convinced that men hate each other because they fear each other. They fear each other because they don't know each other and they don't know each other because they don't communicate with each other, and they don't communicate with each other because they are separated from each other.

Reverend Martin Luther King, Jr.[1]

Implicit or unconscious bias steers our behavior and influences how we interact with other individuals. From an early age, we are taught what is right and what is wrong by our parents, older relatives, and our teachers. As we age, we expand our view of the world through our interactions and relationships with a wider circle of individuals including friends and people in our community. Our social-economic background and life experiences play a part in shaping our views on different cultures. What we see, hear or learn on television, social media, news media, movies, etc., contributes to this understanding. The development of bias is unavoidable and often invisible.

Generally, our biases are our own and are seldom called into question. Police officers are an exception. Police officers are held to a higher standard of behavior by the public because they deal with the public daily and often during stressful and intense situations. Police officers' interactions with the people differ from those of judges or elected officials. An officer is more likely to experience a tense encounter or a prolonged exchange with an individual as part of their daily work. A police officer does not have the luxury of control over the environment where the initial contact takes place and is routinely required to make split-second judgments or decisions regarding his or her initial interaction with a citizen.

Implicit bias and its influence on how we behave towards others are becoming more widely known. This is true within the law enforcement community. Although the main task for police is the prevention of crime and disorder, they are also expected to provide a wide array of other public services to the communities they serve. These communities are comprised of individuals of many different ethnicities, races, ages, religions, sexual orientations, etc. The public demands this.

So, like any other young adult, new officers are hired with a pre-conceived view of what they believe individuals from different cultures are supposed to be and how they are supposed to act. Upon entering the police academy, they are immersed into another new culture, that of law enforcement. A key component of their law enforcement training is officer safety.

The task, or more accurately, the challenge, faced by a law enforcement instructor is how to best help new officers identify their personal biases and see how these biases might impact future decisions they are forced to make regarding their safety and that of others once they are assigned to the street. The instructors have eight months to do this. Specific training about implicit bias enables young officers to better address any situation they may encounter and to see it through to the best possible outcome.

As an African American male in charge of a mid-sized law enforcement agency, my perspective on the topic of implicit bias in law enforcement is limited to my personal experiences. To provide a broader understanding of this subject, I have asked three individuals from within my Department to assist me in writing this Chapter, Major Patrice Hubbard, an African American female, Major Markus Hughes, an openly gay White male, and Training Supervisor Jo-Anne Swensson, a Hispanic female. I have asked them for their perspective on the role implicit bias plays in providing law enforcement services, the training that must be accomplished before new officers can be released from training, and the impact of implicit bias on the community we serve.

To understand the role of implicit bias and its importance, we will explain why training is needed, who need the movement, and the best practices learned through its implementation. As societal norms and expectations change with advancements in technology and the demand for fairness and transparency from police officers, there is a need to increase the level of understanding on the part of law enforcement officers. The St. Petersburg Police Department recognizes this and has made it a priority to train officers on how vital it is to be fair and impartial in all aspects of performing their duties. As law enforcement professionals, we understand this and have spent the better part of the last decade implementing it at all levels across our agency.

1. Why Do We Train Biased-Based Policing?

The word bias has a negative connotation and elicits feelings of anger and sadness. To many Americans, the history of bias and law enforcement has been entwined for far too long. There is a difference between having implicit bias and having a prejudice, and it is important to define these words to understand why teaching Biased-Based Policing to law enforcement officers is critical to begin unwinding the negative perception of law enforcement in some communities. Left unaddressed, implicit bias is detrimental to obtaining and maintaining community support for law enforcement and it erodes the community's trust in law enforcement officers.

Implicit bias can best be defined as, "a bias or prejudice that is present but not consciously held or recognized."[2] It can be argued that implicit bias is present in everyone, however, it is not a bias of purpose as is prejudice. Ensuring that police officers understand that everyone has an unconscious bias is important to combat the negative implications of such a bias. Societal norms have made exhibiting any type of bias a negative action. To ensure that law enforcement presents transparent services to their communities, the understanding of how procedural justice and implicit bias are connected is vital.

A. Procedural Justice

The Office of Community Oriented Policing Services (COPS), operated by the U.S. Department of Justice, published *Community-Oriented Trust and Justice Briefs: Procedural Justice* in 2016.[3] COPS defined procedural justice as, "the idea of fairness in the processes that resolve disputes and allocate resources. It is a concept that, when embraced, promotes positive organizational change and bolsters better relationships."[4] Further focus divides it into four basic principles: fairness, transparency, voice, and impartiality. Others have defined procedural justice as "citizen participation, neutrality, dignity and respect, and trustworthy motives."[5] Regardless of the semantics, procedural justice, at its core, is about fairness. National expert and Yale Law School Professor Tom Tyler draws a connection between procedural justice and implicit bias: "What is particularly striking about procedural justice judgments is that they shape the reactions even of those who are on the losing side of cases. If a person who does not receive an outcome that they think favorable or fair feels that the decision was arrived at in a fair way, they are more likely to accept it."[6]

Further examination of each principle exposes the frequent intersections with impartial bias. The first principle, fairness or neutrality, is geared towards the law enforcement officer. To ensure that the judicial process remains fair and untainted by personal bias, an officer needs to refrain from allowing their implicit bias to affect their law enforcement decisions, even if those biases are implicit. Otherwise, the officer loses the ability to remain neutral while engaging with the public. It is important for law enforcement officers to remain cognizant that their implicit bias could manifest as a confirmation bias while engaged in investigations. As summarized by Dr. Fridell, developer and lead trainer for Fair and Impartial Policing: "Confirmation bias is the tendency to search for, interpret, favor, and recall information in a way that confirms our preexisting beliefs, including our stereotypes and biases."[7] If an officer succumbs to confirmation bias and focuses solely on theories that support their biases, it is possible they will dismiss relevant witness testimony or disregard possible evidence or leads that do not fall into the narrative of their theory. When this happens, the officer's actions and decisions are no longer neutral or fair.

The second principle of procedural justice is transparency. This principle is also referred to as trustworthiness and extends beyond a law enforcement officer's actions to include the organization's accessibility to the public. When a law enforcement agency allows its policies and decisions to be transparent and available to the public, it creates and reinforces trust with the community. This trust can be destroyed if a police officer allows unconscious bias to affect their actions. As a result, doubt arises within the community, and the trust built with the law enforcement organization begins to erode. However, the transparency and openness of the agency and the criminal justice process provide a means to the public for improved understanding of the decision. The basic concept of taking the time to explain the "why" behind a decision provides the public with a conduit for straightforward understanding and an increased acceptance of the results. Conversely, when this does not take place, the public loses that trust in law enforcement and raises the question–what are they hiding? Additionally, the law enforcement officer is afforded the benefit of another opportunity to examine the situation to ensure there was no bias involved in the policing action or contact when they take the time to explain why an arrest was made or a citation was issued.

The third principle, voice, is providing an individual the opportunity to speak and share their side of a situation. This harkens back to Tyler's study of procedural justice. It is an innate human trait to want to be heard. Adults who were raised with siblings learn early in life the impact of being able to tell their side of the story, but also feel a sense of unfairness when they do not. This yearning for justice persists, especially when a citizen is confronted with an authority figure. The small act of a law enforcement officer allowing someone to have a voice during these interactions, even if the decision is unfavorable toward them, still builds upon the trust of that officer. In providing voice, it is important for law enforcement officers to be aware of attention bias. This form of implicit bias focuses on whom an individual pays attention to first, the length of time associated with the attention, and if this is affected by implicit bias. In a study from Yale University Child Study Center, researchers set out to measure the attention bias of early educators. Their subjects were provided a video of young children in various activities and were told to identify those children with emerging misbehavior. The researchers then tracked the eye movements of the educators to see whom they were focusing on first and whom they focused on the longest. The results showed that the teachers focused more on Black children than White, and more on the male children than the female. There were in fact no misbehaviors, but the educators' implicit bias was affecting their focus.[8] Allowing attention bias to influence whom officers pay attention to runs the risk of jeopardizing procedural justice. By placing the officer's attention on one person and failing to give someone else their full attention or the opportunity to tell their whole side of the story, the former person of focus may have been incorrectly singled out, and the latter citizen's voice was not heard.

The fourth principle of procedural justice is respect. An officer embodies this principle by exhibiting respect and dignity toward citizens without bias. There is a universal desire of human beings to be respected. Implicit bias could adversely affect the respect shown to the public without the officer's awareness. Does the officer show the same level of respect and dignity to a transient as they would to a well-dressed businessman? If questioned, the officer would consciously and explicitly state they treat everyone with the same respect and dignity; however, their unconscious bias could drive their behavior in a way that contradicts their conscious attitude.

Procedural justice is pivotal in maintaining the trust of the public, which in turn supports the concept of police legitimacy. Implicit bias on the part of the officer could contradict any of the four principles of procedural justice. Even the most well-intentioned officer with the best motives could be affected by their own implicit or unconscious bias in the execution of their duties. It is important for law enforcement officers to be made aware of these biases and understand how they were developed, and how those biases could ultimately affect their actions or daily decisions.

B. Manifestation of Implicit Bias

Implicit bias manifests in everyone and originates from a variety of sources. Although an unconscious bias, it is directly impacted by an individual's upbringing—from familial influences, faith-based sources, community, friendship circles, media, geographic locations, etc. The manifestation comes to fruition at a very early age. Studies have shown that children as young as four and five years old have biases. The best example of this is an experiment conducted by Drs. Kenneth and Mamie Clark in the 1940s. Their study, *Emotional Factors in Racial Identification and Preference in Negro Children*, as summarized by Dr. Fridell, presented 253 young African American children ranging from three to seven years old with four dolls—two brown dolls, with black hair, and two white dolls, with blonde hair. The children were from segregated schools in Arkansas and racially mixed schools in Massachusetts. The children were asked eight questions about the dolls and their preference for a doll. The finding showed that the majority of the children preferred the White doll and rejected the "colored" doll. The Clarks concluded that "prejudice, discrimination and segregation" damaged the self-esteem of Black children and created a feeling of inferiority. Many would argue that society has made significant strides since the 1940s, however, when this experiment was recreated in 2010 it was met with similar results.[9]

How many childhood norms affect adult biases is yet to be quantified. Some people believe that fairy tales and Disney stories may have a larger influence than other factors. Author and educator Dr. Nancy Larrick researched this in 1965 when a five-year-old African American girl asked her, "Why are they always *White* children?"[10] Education Professor Dr. Dorothy Hurley also researched this phenomenon in 2005 and noted, "It is reasonable to assert that the perceptions of all children are likely to be impacted by texts, written or visual, which evidence White privileging and a binary color symbolism that associates white with goodness and black with evil."[11] If these fairy tale stories color the perception of a human being's unconscious bias, how is this undone in those who choose to become law enforcement officers?

2. Who Receives Biased-Based Policing Training?

The mission of the St. Petersburg Police Department is to deliver professional police services, to protect and ensure the safety of the community, to enforce laws and preserve the peace, and to protect the rights of all citizens by policing with the tenets of loyalty, integrity, and honor.

(St. Petersburg Police Department 2021)

Consistent with the Department's mission, the short answer is everyone receives bias-based training. If the law enforcement profession continues to hire human beings who bring with them their own implicit bias, then training to address bias-based policing will need to take place. The diversity of people that apply to the St. Petersburg Police Department is quite varied. As such, these individuals bring with them a vast range of life experience, education, law enforcement experience, *and* biases.

To level the playing field and select the right individuals to represent the City of St. Petersburg, each aspect of the hiring process is monitored for fair-mindedness. The St. Petersburg Police Department recruits and hires candidates for the position of police officer from candidates that are already state certified in law enforcement, as well as those with no prior training or experience. The St. Petersburg Police Department is one of a small group of agencies in the Tampa Bay area that offers candidates a chance to be hired before attending the police academy. Additionally, with the opportunity to apply as a lateral entry candidate, the application pool widens to include candidates at different points in their lives and career paths. These candidates can be divided into three general categories: those with no law enforcement experience or training, out-of-state officers looking to relocate to the area, and already certified officers from other agencies within the State of Florida. Each of these groups has its strengths and limitations, and each group brings with them implicit biases that may have developed due to the individual's experiences.

As an agency that provides the opportunity to applicants to attend the police academy while earning a salary, the largest group of new hires originates from the pool of candidates that have no previous law enforcement experience. These individuals tend to be younger and are often entering law enforcement as a first career. These individuals may have just completed college or spent time in military services. The commonality is that these individuals have no law enforcement experience. Thus, this allows the agency to develop the behaviors and understanding of law enforcement that meet the mission and philosophy of the agency. The St. Petersburg Police Department has the opportunity to "mold" the candidates into the caliber of officer that is expected by the agency as well as the community it serves.

Currently, the St. Petersburg Police Department (SPPD) accepts applications for police cadets, in-state transfers, and out-of-state transfers. The recruitment effort varies across many mediums from web-based recruiting sites, in print publications, and college and career fairs. Members of the St. Petersburg Police Department regularly attend diversity recruiting initiatives around the state. These range from attending career fairs at historically Black colleges and universities in Florida to military job fairs and advertising in police publications. During the Covid-19 pandemic, the St. Petersburg Police Department did not suspend recruiting efforts nor accepting applications. The recruitment opportunities became virtual events, and more emphasis was placed on web-based site advertisement. While most of the surrounding agencies suspended acceptance of applications, SPPD had an increase of application submissions received over the prior year by over twenty percent.

A unique aspect of the St. Petersburg Police Department hiring process is the administrative interview panel. After several meetings with members of the community who requested transparency in the hiring process of police officers, Chief Holloway invited faith-based leaders and members of community organizations in the City of St. Petersburg to submit applications of interest to participate in the Department's interview panels. The applications were reviewed and vetted, and the faith-based leaders and community organization members were notified of their approval to participate.

The administrative interview panel consists of a minimum of three sworn Department members, from the rank of sergeant and above, and one community member. The panel members rotate for each monthly interview. Sworn Department members are chosen to reflect the race and gender of the interviewees; this ensures parity in hiring so members of minority communities are represented by members of their community. The Department members with training and field experience are preferred panelists because they are aware of the challenges facing the candidates at the police academy and during agency-specific training. Exemplification of the tenants of the St. Petersburg Police Department within the candidates is integral in the interview process. These tenets are important qualities in all employees of the Department, sworn and non-sworn. It is important to note that those candidates interviewed have completed the background check, polygraph interview, medical and fitness testing required by all police applicants.

After each interview, the faith-based leader or community member is encouraged to ask questions to the sworn members of the interview panel and to offer feedback and their perspective on the characteristics and traits they found to be the most important in the police candidate. The overall feedback received from the faith-based leaders and community members has been positive. For many, the experience is eye-opening and not what they expected. Others have expressed surprise at how fair the process is and the recognition and appreciation of such diversity among the interview panel. Most have enjoyed being a part of the process and have expressed a desire to return to the panel should the opportunity arise again.

3. Best Practices for Implementing Biased-Based Policing Training

A. Training

Since the early 1990s, the St. Petersburg Police Department has been providing human relations training to its employees. The training began with *Human Relations and Interpersonal Communications*, part of the Multi-Cultural Diversity Training Program developed by the Department specifically for its law enforcement officers.[12] Since then, many new opportunities have developed to embrace active partnerships with community organizations and bring awareness from and to cultural subsets within the community. These partnerships continue to grow and evolve and have developed into invaluable relationships to reduce biases. In the late 1990s, another course, taught by an outside consultant, was provided to all Department employees. What began as open discussions about human diversity, transformed into a four-hour lecture about human diversity. The crux of this class was to increase the awareness of the different cultures within the St. Petersburg community and improve relationships between the community and the Department.

Other diversity classes have been taught on various related topics, including race-based profiling, cultural aspects of terrorism, tools for tolerance, and most recently, in 2015, *Fair and Impartial Policing* developed by Dr. Lorie Fridell.[13] This course was designed for law enforcement and took what was then thought of as a radical approach by looking at implicit bias as a natural part of the human mind and how it affects an officer's ability to deliver fair and impartial policing. Dr. Fridell's social science-based course was taught to all officers of the St. Petersburg Police Department. One key objective of the course is understanding that "biases are normal, and all people, even well-intentioned people, have biases."[14] What distinguishes the course from previous, subjective, human diversity courses is not only the social science message but the high quality of the training program. The instructors were certified by Dr. Fridell to instruct this program, but more importantly, they possess a passion to teach the course. All the instructors for this course are also current members of the Department. Officers often display a dislike towards training around diversity or biases, but this mindset can often be overcome when they feel the material is presented from a peer rather than an outsider. Coupling the evidence-based material provided in the course with peer instructors that have a passion for the material greatly helps promote "buy-in" from the officers receiving the training.

Another beneficial factor in the education of St. Petersburg Police Officers in *Fair and Impartial Policing* was the support of command staff. The support of the leaders of the organization brought credence to the course and the message the course delivered. Every single member of the Department attended the training from Chief Holloway to the newest police recruit. They not only attended the course but committed the entire four hours required and participated in every aspect of the training to include group exercises and scenarios. This is pivotal to demonstrating their support of the material presented and does not go unnoticed by the rank and file. This training was enhanced further when Chief Holloway required civilian employees to also attend training and the material and scenarios were tailored to suit the particular group.

The law enforcement officer experiences provided in the *Fair and Impartial Policing* course material were relevant and timely, with scenarios that were accurate enough to allow the officers to place themselves within the context of the scenarios. The course was not intended to deliver a message of not having biases, but rather to draw attention to the multitude of biases that exist and how the biases could adversely affect an officer's behavior. With the data provided about implicit bias and examples of various biases studied by researchers, officers were better informed in what to watch for in their daily interactions with the public. The underlying message of not focusing strictly on eliminating implicit bias, but rather on delivering a controlled response, empowers the officers to self-assess as needed and truly engage in biased-free policing.

The *Fair and Impartial Policing* course was just the first step in engaging officers in identifying and evaluating their implicit biases. The course was mandatory for all sworn members of the Department and is still provided to all new officers before transitioning to the field training program. The challenge then turned to how the agency will continue to provide additional training in the subject area of diversity and implicit bias on a reoccurring basis after the initial course. This requires engaging with community stakeholders to provide new and engaging experiences for officers to continue to develop throughout their careers.

B. Park, Walk and Talk

One of the ways community engagement was improved was the introduction of the Park, Walk and Talk initiative by Chief Holloway. A part of this program allows each officer to commit a minimum of one hour per week engaging directly with the public in the areas where they work. As Chief Holloway stated to the Tampa Bay Times, "We're going to get out of our cars, we're going to start talking to our communities to find out what we can do to help reduce crime in our community, in our city."[15] This initiative falls right into the type of positive contact that is most beneficial to the officer in reducing their implicit biases. The positive contact theory referenced in *the Fair and Impartial Policing* course illustrates that more contact with people of differing backgrounds, specifically not during a time of crisis, can help to reduce implicit biases.[16] The Park, Walk and Talk initiative provides a neutral opportunity for officers and citizens to break down barriers, establish relationships, and enhance mutual trust. Casual officer and citizen encounters were routine interactions for Community Service Officers and School Resource Officers, however, the Park, Walk and Talk initiative has made these encounters a regular occurrence for all patrol officers. These conversations have given many citizens, who previously felt unheard, a voice and have helped many officers relate to others of differing backgrounds.

C. Community Partnerships

Over the course of many years, the St. Petersburg Police Department has developed partnerships with community organizations that provide cultural awareness and human relations training. The training begins within the context of agency-specific training. Coupled with the *Fair and Impartial Policing* course, newer SPPD officers also attend a day-long training on cultural awareness. Chief Holloway initiated this program to educate the newer St. Petersburg police officers of the subcultures prevalent in the St. Petersburg community and to build positive relationships with the community. Members of community organizations participate in the training as educators and as partners.

The partnerships built between the community and the St. Petersburg Police Department have developed into other specialized training opportunities. By collaborating directly with community members and organizations, the agency was afforded the ability to provide training in topics and fields that other law enforcement agencies traditionally may not have available. Working directly with the community, a partnership emerged with the SPPD training staff to develop specific courses in topics where the public expressed a great interest in training officers. By engaging with a diverse public, the St Petersburg Police Department provides courses that focus on areas that may have been underrepresented in the past. As an additional benefit of offering this new type of training, officer's implicit biases towards various groups could be reduced as well.

The St. Petersburg Police Department was the first law enforcement agency in the Tampa Bay area to develop a policy specific to interactions with the Transgender Community. It states, "It is the policy of the St. Petersburg Police Department to treat all individuals with dignity, respect, and professionalism. No person shall be discriminated against based on gender identity, sexual orientation, or any other basis prohibited by local, state, or federal laws."[17] Additionally, SPPD partnered with Metro Inclusive Health to provide a Transgender Awareness Training program. This program was developed to create an understanding and awareness within the law enforcement community that is supportive of the Transgender Community. The course is taught by a transgender individual who shares their story with the officers. The class covers the basics of pronoun usage and helps to dispel any concerns officers may have regarding searches, arrests, or other interactions with transgender individuals.[18]

The St. Petersburg Police Department partnered with The Florida Holocaust Museum and the Anti-Defamation League of Florida to share their course *Law Enforcement and Society: Lessons of the Holocaust*; this course "increases law enforcement's understanding of their role as protectors and as our first line of defense to ensure that the constitutional rights of everyone are protected."[19] More importantly, this course encourages tolerance and acceptance of diversity. The class takes place at The Florida Holocaust Museum in St. Petersburg, and the officers are invited to tour the museum afterward and ask questions to the docents and instructors. This partnership began in 2016, and all officers are encouraged to attend. It continues today with annual classes for new officers. During the Covid-19 pandemic, The Florida Holocaust Museum and the Anti-Defamation League of Florida made the course virtual and interactive and will continue to offer it accordingly until classes can resume at the museum.

In 2017, the St. Petersburg Police Department was approached by Johns Hopkins All Children's Hospital's Autism Program to assist in the development of an Autism awareness training program directly geared to law enforcement. The training program, *Law Enforcement Officer Training in Autism Spectrum Disorder*, includes a four-hour lecture-style class followed by live-action simulation training.[20] Three St. Petersburg police officers and one civilian employee were asked to assist with the development and assure the practicality of the scenarios. This partnership has proven invaluable to bringing awareness of the presenting signs of Autism, providing the officers with de-escalation techniques for interacting with individuals with Autism and their families, but more importantly, this program provides resources for the officers and the community.

One of the longest operating community partnerships for bias awareness training that has been in existence at the St. Petersburg Police Department is the Crisis Intervention Team Training program (CIT). The partnership with the mental health service providers in the county educates officers on the signs and symptoms of mental illness, teaches de-escalation techniques for communication, and establishes resources for law enforcement and those in need. This class follows The Memphis Model that is used across the nation.[21] The partnership with National Alliance on Mental Illness (NAMI) and local mental health service providers offers this specialized training to law enforcement officers on identifying when someone is experiencing a mental health crisis and the de-escalating techniques needed to reduce the need for use of physical force. Members of the mental health community, consumers and peers, participate in the instruction of the officers by sharing their stories and providing the officers with alternatives to incarceration.

Conclusion

Remembering the conflict of the inhabitants of the 19th Century and now living as part of a civilized society, it is incumbent upon us to learn, develop, and evolve. Policing is no exception. The policing model followed across the United States is facing a time where change is not only wanted but also demanded. Despite the influence of the news media and social media, it is imperative to police with an impartial lens. As a progressive police Department with over 800 sworn and civilian employees, serving a city of over 266,000 citizens, we continue to embrace the city's vision to honor our past while pursuing our future. The St. Petersburg Police Department has shown the ability to implement innovative ways to proactively address implicit bias as it pertains to hiring, training, and requiring transparency and impartiality from the officers serving our community.

So, You'd Like to Know More

- Community Oriented Policing Services (COPS), U. S. Department of Justice (2016), https://cops.usdoj.gov/.
- Susan Fiske, Are We Born Racist? New Insights from Neuroscience and Positive Psychology (2010).
- Lorie Fridell, Producing Bias-Free Policing: A Science-Based Approach (2017).
- Malcolm Gladwell, Talking to Strangers: What We Should Know About People We Don't Know (2019).

About the Authors

Chief Anthony Holloway began his law enforcement career with the Clearwater Police Department in 1985. Upon his retirement in 2007, he was selected as the Chief of Police for the City of Somerville, Massachusetts. In February 2010, he rejoined the Clearwater Police Department as Chief of Police, and in August 2014, he was selected and now serves as Chief of Police for the St. Petersburg Police Department. Chief Holloway earned his Bachelor of Arts degree (Business Management) in 1999 and master's degree (Business Administration) in 2001. He has taught law enforcement to national and international governmental, military, educational, and community organizations.

Major Patrice Hubbard has been a sworn officer with the St. Petersburg Police Department since 2003. She has served in various capacities including Field Training and Community Policing. She was also the inception Sergeant of the Career Offender Tracking and Apprehension (C.O.T.A.) Unit, Traffic Commander, Special Projects Major and she was one of the four pilot Fair and Impartial Policing instructors. She earned her bachelors degree in Management from the University of Phoenix and her master's degree in Security Studies, Homeland Security, from the Naval Postgraduate School.

Major Markus Hughes has been with the St. Petersburg Police Department for over 21 years, and has served in various assignments to include Field Training, Recruitment, Major Crimes, Special Victims Unit, Internal Affairs, Youth Resources, and with the Tampa Bay Area Human Trafficking Task Force. He is also the LGBTQ Liaison for the Department, and was one of four pilot instructors for the Fair and Impartial Policing curriculum developed by the University of South Florida. He has a bachelor's degree in Biology and Chemistry from the University of Colorado.

Supervisor Jo-Anne Swensson has been with the St. Petersburg Police Department since 2008. She earned her master's degree from the University of South Florida. She currently oversees the training curriculum for the Department, manages the professional development for all employees, and ensures state and national training standards are met. She is an advocate for officer wellness programs, manages the Department's Peer Support team and is Executive Director of the West Central Florida Critical Incident Stress Management team.

Endnotes

1. Martin Luther King, Jr., Address at Cornell College (Oct. 15, 1962).

2. *Implicit Bias*, Merriam-Webster, Inc. (Apr. 2021), https://www.merriam-webster.com/dictionary/implicit%20bias.

3. Community Oriented Policing Services (COPS), U. S. Department of Justice, Community-Oriented Trust and Justice Briefs: Procedural Justice (2016), https://cops.usdoj.gov/RIC/ric.php?page=detail&id=COPS-W0795.

4. *Id.* at 1–2.

5. Lorraine Mazerolle, Sarah Bennett, Jacqueline Davis, Elise Sargenant & Matthew Manning, *Legitimacy in Policing: A Systematic Review,* 9 Campbell Systematic Reviews I (2013).

6. Tom R. Tyler, Jonathan Jackson & Ben Bradford, *Psychology of Procedural Justice and Cooperation*, Encyclopedia of Criminology & Crim. Just. (2013), https://www.researchgate.net/publication/236004084_Psychology_of_procedural_justice_and_cooperation.

7. Lorie P. Fridell, Fair and Impartial Policing: Patrol Officers' Booster Training (2020).

8. Walter S. Gilliam, Angela N. Maupin, Chin R. Reyes, Maria Accavitti & Frederick Shic, *Do Early Educators' Implicit Biases Regarding Sex and Race Relate to Behavior Expectations and Recommendations of Preschool Expulsions and Suspensions?*, Yale Res. Stud. Brief (2016); H. Andrew Sagar & Janet W. Schofield, *Racial and Behavioral Cues in Black and White Children's Perceptions of Ambiguously Aggressive Acts*, 39 J. Personality & Social Psychol. 590 (1980) (finding that sixth grade students interpret ambiguous behaviors as "more mean and threatening when the perpetrator was black than when he was white.").

9. Lorie P. Fridell, Fair and Impartial Policing: Science Overview (2019); Kenneth B. Clark & Mamie P. Clark, *Emotional Factors in Racial Identification and Preference in Negro Children*, 19 J. Negro Educ. 241 (1950); Kiri Davis, *A Girl Like Me* (2005), https://www.youtube.com/watch?v=Mk58Fq9Qza (Harlem student documentary revisiting Dolls Study).

10. Nancy P. Larrick, *The All White World of Childrens Books*, 3 J. African Children's & Youth Literature 1 (1991–92).

11. Dorothy L. Hurley, *Seeing White: Children of Color and the Disney Fairy Tale Princess*, 74 J. Negro Educ. 221 (2005); *see also* Stephanie McCall, *How Princesses of Color Have Improved the Disney Princess Narrative*, The Artifice (2020), https://the-artifice.com/disney-princesses-of-color/.

12. St. Petersburg Police Department, Training Records (2021).

13. Lorie Fridell, Fair and Impartial Policing: Recruit Academy and Patrol Officers' Training at Tampa (2013).

14. *Id.*

15. Zachary T. Sampson, *St. Petersburg Police Begin 'Park, Walk, and Talk' Program*, Tampa Bay Times, Oct. 1, 2014.

16. *See generally* Malcom Gladwell, Talking to Strangers (April 2021).

17. St. Petersburg Police Department, Training Records (2021).

18. *Metro Inclusive Health* (2021), https://www.metrotampabay.org/.

19. St. Petersburg Police Department, Training Records (2021).

20. Johns Hopkins Medicine, *Law Enforcement Officer Training in Autism Spectrum Disorder*, Johns Hopkins All Children's Hospital (2021), https://www.hopkinsallchildrens.org/Services/Autism-Center/Autism-Training-for-First-Responders.

21. National Alliance on Mental Illness, *C.I.T.–Crisis Intervention Team*, National Alliance on Mental Illness - Pinellas County (2021), https://nami-pinellas.org/c-i-t-crisis-intervention-team/.

Index

A

ABA, 19, 24, 53, 119, 121, 123, 140, 141, 151, 177–181, 225, 245, 249, 254–256, 290, 291, 347, 388, 414, 415, 419, 420, 463, 464, 469, 480, 484, 485, 507, 512, 513, 524, 535, 536, 549, 551–553, 555, 605
Abilene Paradox, 454, 464
ableism, 16, 279, 505, 506, 508–512, 519, 520, 523–525
accessible, 4, 34, 44, 67, 313, 450, 509, 532, 535, 592
accountable, 27, 94, 238, 299, 303, 313–315, 399, 432, 463
adolescents, 33, 54, 56, 57, 275, 494, 519, 555
affinity, 163, 282, 302, 393, 394, 405
algorithm, 63
allyship, 294, 301, 322
ambiguity, 208, 458
amygdala, 187, 206, 380
antiracist, 179, 180, 344, 368, 526
artificial intelligence, 101–103, 106, 108, 109, 111–120, 122–124, 439
attitudes, 29, 31–33, 35, 37, 45, 54–56, 59, 61, 63, 71, 87, 142, 181, 192, 196, 204, 206, 208, 211, 217, 258, 262, 267, 268, 270, 274, 275, 288–290, 297, 310, 312, 322, 340, 371, 392, 416, 418, 447, 448, 452, 453, 456, 465, 511, 512, 517, 525, 527
attribution, 208, 289, 366, 387
autism, 508–511, 517–519, 522, 523, 525–527

B

backlash, 56, 60, 70, 253, 336, 345, 361
bail, 142, 152, 153, 164, 183, 185, 223, 226, 238
bankruptcy, 7, 14, 23, 57, 216, 559–561, 565–572, 576, 577, 579–581
Batson, 16, 77, 78, 81–85, 92, 93, 95–97, 188, 207, 219, 220
Biden, 52, 67, 72, 76, 197, 210, 265, 357
BIPOC, 294, 296–312, 314–320

C

Chauvin, 233, 253, 289
children, 55, 59, 122, 130, 198, 441, 495–497, 500, 502, 509, 539, 540, 546, 553, 611
cisgender, 589
confirmation bias, 4, 18, 163, 280, 282, 289, 338, 345, 366, 397, 398, 402, 417, 468, 478, 609
COVID-19, 8, 21, 27, 53, 224, 233, 235, 253, 259, 268, 271, 273, 289, 291, 340, 346, 365, 392, 440, 450, 456, 480, 507, 525, 564, 578, 603, 612, 617
counterstereotypic, 62, 291, 418
courthouse, 5, 9, 14–19, 60, 77, 89, 92, 101–103, 112, 125–127, 132, 133, 152, 166, 181, 186, 190, 206–208, 222, 223, 248, 256, 283, 359, 387, 400, 452, 456, 457, 461, 467
cultural competence, 169, 180, 181, 316, 378, 403, 432, 605

D

debiasing, 63, 263
debtor, 569, 572, 577
DEI, 4, 6, 7, 17, 24, 139, 293–295, 297–300, 303, 304, 310, 313, 314, 317–319, 386, 387, 392, 393, 403–405, 408, 409, 412, 420, 467, 472
delinquency, 159, 205, 210, 489, 491, 495, 501, 554
demographic, 13, 94, 108, 111, 118, 259, 270, 330, 333, 360, 389, 392, 401, 408–411, 427, 430, 454, 464, 493, 556
depression, 19, 508, 540
disabilities, 16, 389, 419, 429, 505–511, 513–519, 521–527, 530, 531, 534–545, 549, 551–556
discretion, 13, 20, 21, 34, 39, 40, 80, 81, 89, 90, 97, 98, 126, 129, 139, 146, 147, 152, 179, 208, 226, 227, 274, 350, 358, 362, 487, 492, 496, 497, 499, 530
doll, 611
dyslexia, 529–532, 538–543, 545–549, 552–554, 557, 558

E

empathy, 39, 59, 161, 166, 167, 169, 239, 240, 275, 285, 287, 291, 369, 397, 407, 418, 432, 437, 455, 522, 559–562, 574–576
evaluation, 7, 20, 37, 40, 56, 59, 60, 66, 110, 111, 118, 123, 161, 164, 173, 191, 194, 206, 226, 246, 270, 277, 325–328, 340, 354, 359, 366, 367, 369, 391, 398, 411, 412, 414, 418, 441, 513, 519, 530, 554, 557
exclusion, 81, 83–85, 92, 96, 131, 241, 281, 285, 329, 402, 410, 467, 534, 535, 540, 551, 567
explicit bias, 5, 6, 13, 19, 23, 28, 29, 69, 78, 141, 142, 155, 156, 162, 163, 196, 224, 232, 234, 235, 247, 264, 298, 313, 350, 468, 496, 511
extremism, 69–71, 73–76, 295, 321, 370, 464

F

fragility, 179, 294, 298, 307–310, 317, 321, 323, 340, 368

G

Gallup, 274, 450, 451, 463, 464
gay, 73, 212, 410, 489, 583, 588, 591, 593, 594, 599, 601, 607
GCs, 389, 390, 413, 415
GIGO, 101, 102, 105, 106, 119
groupthink, 4, 147, 148, 304, 323, 364, 372, 381

H

habit, 43–45, 64, 66, 200, 227
harassment, 27, 220, 225, 250, 256, 266, 276, 342, 343, 346, 359, 362, 379, 448, 463, 569, 570, 592
healthcare, 5, 27, 49, 56, 73, 259, 414, 424, 425, 427, 430, 434, 436, 437, 443, 473, 477, 484, 563, 564
heterosexual, 585, 587, 589, 601, 602
hindsight, 57, 146, 351
Hirabayashi, 130, 131, 138
homophobia, 71, 512, 583
homosexual, 410, 591, 601

I

IAT, 79, 149, 191, 196, 221, 222, 238, 241, 256, 258, 261–265, 269, 271, 272, 275, 276, 281, 385, 392, 440, 456, 464, 497
IEPs, 517, 548
inclusion, 3–6, 15, 17, 18, 24, 46, 47, 50, 65, 112, 139, 148, 156, 172, 177, 178, 181, 207, 221, 222, 259, 260, 263, 285, 286, 289, 291, 292, 294, 295, 297–299, 303–305, 322, 324, 348, 349, 351, 353–356, 359–361, 370, 372–374, 376–379, 381–383, 386, 387, 389–392, 403, 404, 406, 408, 412–416, 419, 420, 423–426, 430–432, 435, 438, 439, 443, 458, 467, 473, 480, 481, 483, 484, 487, 534, 541, 589
Indigenous, 17, 294, 470, 471, 474, 478, 479, 482, 599
indigent, 110, 185, 204, 239, 491, 567, 568, 570, 572
individuation, 183–185, 189, 193, 198, 205, 313, 411
ingroup, 39, 60, 94, 163, 209, 282, 289, 290, 302, 474
Intel, 389, 390, 399, 415, 418

intentions, 31, 44, 50, 56, 59, 64, 67, 260, 312, 314, 324, 332, 338–340, 342, 391, 408, 511, 512
intersectional, 8, 17, 220, 334, 345, 362, 506, 508, 513, 514, 523, 524, 553, 583
intersex, 583, 589, 600, 604
invisibility, 17, 467, 468, 471–473, 475, 479

J
January 6th, 70, 72–74
judiciary, 13, 26, 27, 57, 76, 131–134, 138, 232, 234, 237, 241, 243, 244, 247–252, 257, 258, 260, 261, 263, 264, 267, 268, 273, 276, 277, 291, 358, 388, 415, 451, 460, 464, 527, 561, 578
jury, 9, 14, 15, 30, 43, 77, 79, 81, 83–85, 87–92, 96, 97, 117, 132, 145, 178, 185, 187, 191–195, 198, 199, 201–204, 208, 210, 212, 220, 241, 249, 251, 252, 256, 280, 287, 378, 508, 512, 592
juvenile, 122, 140, 159, 209, 212, 223, 248, 252, 253, 274, 473, 487–497, 499–503, 520, 536, 539, 543, 553, 554, 592

K
Kaiser Permanente, 12, 17, 423–438, 443
KKK, 71, 74, 447
Korematsu, 130, 131, 138, 236

L
lesbian, 212, 583, 588, 599, 601
literacy, 531, 532, 538, 552, 553, 556
litigation, 5, 19, 24, 78, 108, 116, 119, 124, 177, 188, 190, 241, 245, 277, 279, 284–287, 290–292, 385, 398, 414, 415, 437, 483

M
machismo, 201, 202, 212
manifestations, 4, 24, 25, 160, 183, 196, 209, 257, 280, 283, 293, 359, 385, 386, 445, 453, 467, 470, 498, 508, 532, 562, 577, 587
Mansfield rule, 407, 413, 415, 420
Marines, 350–352, 360, 362, 364, 369, 371, 374–377, 379–383
mascots, 11, 475, 476, 483

media, 4, 9–12, 15, 29, 32, 35, 38, 112, 129, 162, 180, 184, 187, 196–198, 205, 208–210, 239, 243, 254, 265, 314, 315, 374, 376, 377, 379, 474, 475, 491, 498, 514, 524–526, 607, 611, 617
mental disability, 16, 507, 510, 514, 515, 518, 519, 521, 523
mentor, 287, 407, 420, 438, 482, 483, 526
meritocracy, 340, 355
microaggression, 31, 167, 409, 448, 452, 462, 463
militia, 70–73, 76, 128
motivation, 20, 43, 63, 193, 271, 309, 498, 500, 530, 539

N
NAACP, 179, 255, 533, 557
Navy, 348, 350, 360, 368, 374, 376, 377, 379, 381, 382
neuroscientist, 50, 540
neurotypical, 510, 511, 517
newspapers, 53, 65, 76, 119, 209, 376, 415, 450, 470, 476
nonconscious bias, 17, 27–29, 54, 56, 63, 77, 78, 81, 82, 84, 86–88, 90–93, 96, 163, 180, 207, 208, 252, 254, 274, 275, 280–282, 323, 345, 347, 349–351, 353, 355, 356, 358, 359, 361, 363, 372–375, 378–381, 411, 416, 417, 419, 420, 437, 439–442, 464, 505, 606, 608–611
nonprofits, 5, 294, 297, 298, 302, 305, 310, 313, 314, 322, 323
nonverbal, 55, 57, 167, 409, 418, 458, 461

O
Obama, 23, 61, 70, 71, 140, 337, 339, 346, 348, 351, 361, 551
OCR, 502, 557
outgroup, 39, 60, 94, 163, 209, 282, 289, 290, 302, 474

P
peremptory, 16, 81–86, 96, 97, 191, 220
pipeline, 19, 24, 55, 323, 386, 393–395, 402, 429, 437, 439, 472–474, 476, 480, 481, 487, 497, 529, 531, 532, 535, 536, 545, 546, 548–550

poverty, 14, 17, 52, 65, 170, 180, 181, 199, 253, 295, 448, 496, 500–502, 539, 544, 553, 559, 560, 563, 564, 567, 571–575, 579, 589, 590, 602
pretrial, 52, 67, 183–186, 188, 190–192, 202, 204, 209, 219, 241
probation, 105, 109, 110, 185, 206, 245, 459, 491, 492, 497, 516–518, 522, 540, 592
profile, 70, 84, 120, 295, 591, 614
pronouns, 305, 306, 583–585, 588, 592, 595–599

Q
queer, 583, 602
quotas, 290, 390, 453, 464

R
recidivism, 103, 105, 110, 111, 119, 120, 523, 536, 549, 552, 555
recommendation, 320, 357, 368, 430, 472, 497, 547, 564, 571
recruitment, 50, 153, 172, 177, 188, 297, 298, 304, 317, 318, 391, 401, 406–408, 433, 612, 619
regulation, 53, 63, 135, 284, 519
representational diversity, 19, 297–301, 303, 313, 315, 388, 403, 405, 434
resumes, 395, 396, 417
Rittenhouse, 10, 11
Rooney rule, 314, 324, 407, 420

S
salience, 20, 85, 188, 207, 270, 272, 338, 562
sanism, 17, 506, 508, 512, 513, 523, 524, 526
schemas, 30, 127, 184, 193, 198–200, 325–327, 332, 333, 335–342
segregation, 217, 235, 370, 533, 535, 537, 552, 564, 570, 611
SES, 544, 550, 562–565, 574, 578
sexism, 56, 58, 81, 82, 151, 156, 162, 296, 512
slavery, 55, 235, 236, 267, 490, 530, 532
socioeconomic bias, 5, 6, 17, 224, 559–562, 565, 567, 572, 574, 575, 578, 580

sponsorship, 404, 407, 408
STEM, 64, 66
stereotype, 10, 29, 37, 58, 61, 63, 64, 79, 94, 137, 189, 195, 200, 208, 312, 332, 366, 371, 391, 393, 472, 512, 518, 531, 544, 557
stigma, 500, 510, 517, 526, 590, 591
Stroop, 58, 91
subconscious, 82, 86, 193, 288
subjective, 30, 40, 94, 188, 235, 396, 531, 547, 548, 562, 614
subliminal, 55, 64
supremacist, 73–75, 295, 297, 299, 300, 302–306, 308, 309, 312, 315, 318–320, 322, 323, 471
suspensions, 496, 502, 556, 619
systemic, 26–28, 35, 37, 38, 45, 46, 52, 55, 56, 58, 133, 163, 205–209, 243, 246, 259, 264, 296, 299, 411, 428, 452, 453, 473, 477, 480

T
terrorism, 73, 74, 370, 381, 383
Towessnute, 126, 133–138, 219, 477, 478, 483
trainings, 18, 24, 47, 143, 157, 168, 257, 267, 364, 609
transgender, 306, 427, 583, 587–594, 597–599, 602–604, 605, 616
trauma, 166, 410, 439, 489, 523, 592, 593

U
unaware, 29, 75, 167, 202, 244, 263, 302, 335, 353, 448, 519, 575
unbiased, 106, 123, 161, 238, 245, 281, 339, 393, 457
unconscious, 247, 268, 312, 352, 396, 510, 561, 565
underrepresentation, 172, 263, 283, 322, 373, 388, 390–392, 394, 399, 401, 403, 405–407, 410, 412, 415, 418, 429, 433, 434, 437, 439, 542, 616
unintentional, 6, 32, 35, 69, 83, 189, 233, 300, 349, 350, 354–359, 361–369, 371, 381, 382, 409, 508, 509, 515

V
venire, 14–16, 78, 86, 191, 192

victim, 8, 75, 114, 150, 159–163, 165–167, 169–177, 179, 181, 182, 197, 209, 212, 319, 446, 465, 491, 514, 592, 619
voir dire, 14, 82, 85, 87, 93, 95, 97, 183–186, 188, 191, 192, 204, 207, 358, 359, 378
voter, 436, 592

Y
youth, 492, 495, 536